Battleground Berlin

Yale University Press   NEW HAVEN & LONDON

DAVID E. MURPHY, SERGEI A. KONDRASHEV, AND GEORGE BAILEY

Battleground BERLIN

CIA VS. KGB IN THE COLD WAR

Published with assistance from the Historical Research Foundation.

Designed by James J. Johnson and set in Stempel Garamond types by à la page, New Haven,
Connecticut. Printed in the United States of America by R. R. Donnelley and Sons,
Harrisonburg, Virginia.

Library of Congress Cataloging-in-Publication Data

Murphy, David E., 1921–
    Battleground Berlin : CIA vs. KGB in the Cold War / David E.
Murphy, Sergei A. Kondrashev, and George Bailey.
        p. cm.
    Includes bibliographical references (p.   ) and index.
    ISBN 0-300-07233-3 (alk. paper)

    1. United States—Foreign relations—Soviet Union. 2. Soviet
Union—Foreign relations—United States. 3. Berlin (Germany)—
Strategic aspects. 4. Espionage, American—Germany—Berlin.
5. Espionage, Soviet—Germany—Berlin. 6. Soviet Union. Komitet
gosudarstvennoĭ bezopasnosti. 7. United States. Central
Intelligence Agency. 8. Berlin (Germany)—Politics and
government—1945–1990. 9. Cold War. I. Kondrashev, Sergei A.
II. Bailey, George, 1919–   . III. Title.
E183.8.S65M86   1997
327.73047—dc21   97-16829

A catalogue record for this book is available from the British Library.

The paper in this book meets the guidelines for permanence and durability of the Committee on
Production Guidelines for Book Longevity of the Council on Library Resources.

10 9 8 7 6 5 4 3 2 1

Battleground Berlin's Western authors—David Murphy, former chief of CIA's Berlin Operations Base and later chief of the Soviet bloc division, and George Bailey, an American writer on Russo-German affairs living in Munich—visited Moscow in April 1993 to discuss the book project with the Russian Foreign Intelligence Service (SVR). After enjoying a Russian Orthodox Easter, the two were picked up on Monday by Gen. Yuri Kobaladze, head of SVR's public affairs bureau. Kobaladze warmly greeted Murphy, who had long been an adversary of SVR's Soviet predecessors. "Well, Mr. Murphy," he boomed, "how did you like spending the weekend in Moscow without surveillance?"

Contents

Illustrations follow pages 134 and 262.

Preface

This is the story of two intelligence services caught up in the struggle for Berlin and Germany during the Cold War. One, the Soviet KGB, was a highly proficient internal security and foreign intelligence service forged in the Russian Revolution, the purges of the Stalin era, and the war with Nazi Germany. But its many successes were seldom appreciated by a leadership blinded by its own misconceptions and ideology.

CIA was a newcomer. It evolved from the wartime Office of Strategic Services (OSS) as America's first peacetime, civilian intelligence service, and it combined operations and independent analysis for the first time in a single agency. In its optimism mixed with naïveté and a fierce determination to get things done, it reflected in many ways the American character—it did a great deal of its growing up in Berlin between war's end and the rise of the Wall.

The authors encountered several conceptual and technical difficulties while researching and writing this book. The collaboration of three writers can be a recipe for disaster even when they share the same backgrounds and beliefs. The team assembled for this effort did not. It consisted of David E. Murphy, chief of CIA's Berlin Base during crucial parts of the Cold War period, retired Lt. Gen. Sergei Aleksandrovich Kondrashev, one of the KGB's leading German experts, and George Bailey, former director of Radio Liberty, who is now living in Munich and writing on Russo-German affairs. Bailey often was caught between these former intelligence officers from opposing sides of the Cold War. Not only were Murphy and Kondrashev the products of dissimilar careers and personal lives, but they also brought to this project divergent experiences, attitudes, and convictions acquired over several decades. Each could understand the other's basic positions, but often not the nuances and habits of usage of that position. Even terminology intervened. What Bailey and Murphy called East Berlin or the Soviet sector was "Democratic Berlin" to Kondrashev. Equally important, each had different and often contradictory expectations for the book's content, emphasis, and conclusions. Further, each author's ability to justify his findings varied according to archival practices in each service, access to archives, and the availability and willingness of service veterans to be interviewed.

Nonetheless, this very unusual collaboration makes a unique contribution to Cold War intelligence literature. During and after the Cold War, readers of nonfiction on intelligence were deluged with books on the subject. Many of these were produced by defectors—former KGB officers living in the West—either alone or in collaboration with Western authors. (An example of this genre is *KGB: The Inside Story*, the magnum opus by Christopher Andrew and Oleg Gordievsky.) From the side of Soviet and Russian intelligence, the memoirs of Kim Philby and George Blake were written when both men were in the Soviet Union. These works were followed by carefully edited books that were published by former senior KGB officers with the approval of the Russian Intelligence Service (SVR).

The collaboration with Kondrashev, who is on good terms with his former service and resides in Moscow, fits none of these patterns. In fact, it is the first time in post–Cold War history that former CIA and KGB officers have produced a joint account of their experiences. The collaboration reflects the different societies within which CIA and the KGB operated, differences that naturally affected the project's development. But the most difficult task was to find consensus on what the book should be about.

At first, Bailey and Murphy saw *Battleground Berlin* as the story of the CIA and KGB elements in Berlin from war's end to the erection of the Wall. By combining archival material and personal reminiscences from both services, they would have traced the origins and growth of the CIA and KGB Berlin units within the bureaucracies of both countries and described operations as documented by those who actually participated in them: in short, they envisioned an insider's view of the CIA-KGB rivalry in Berlin as these services responded to critical Cold War events like the Berlin blockade. Accordingly, the book would portray each side's organizational structure, personnel, and operations. Bailey and Murphy knew that although a great deal has been written in the West about CIA's role in the Cold War, very little is known publicly about how KGB went about its business in Berlin. By combining useful SVR archival material with background that Murphy could obtain on the CIA side, they expected to provide a reasonably balanced view of the period.

Kondrashev, on the other hand, wished to focus on KGB's collection of political intelligence to support Soviet postwar goals for Germany. Nevertheless, he was always willing to resolve disagreements about the direction or specifics of the book. The result is an approach that we hope combines the best of these two visions for *Battleground Berlin*. Our fruitful exchanges are apparent in discussions of such important issues as the Berlin blockade and the effects of the Korean War on Germany's role in the defense of Europe.

Kondrashev had no problem obtaining access to the several archives administrated by SVR. But some specific documents could not be located. Kondrashev found that many intelligence reports on Berlin were never disseminated because it would have been politically risky to do so. He asserted that it was not uncommon for KGB officials to have suppressed information that might have contradicted established policy or the party line. On balance, however, an extraordinary amount of new, pertinent information was found. The archival material took two forms: eighty-seven photocopies of original documents and about 250 file extracts. The preponderance of extracts is explained by the difficulty of securing approval to remove documents from the files—they are literally sewn into the folders—and the time required for SVR to declassify the copied documents. Access to archival matter by researchers will be decided by the SVR Public Affairs and Press Bureau.

Kondrashev's material was reviewed against unclassified publications, against Murphy's recollections and those of his CIA colleagues, and finally against relevant CIA files. These files covered the origins, structure, operations, and personalities of the CIA operations base in Berlin, beginning with its founding by Allen Dulles in summer 1945. In order to be given archival access, Murphy had to undergo a security reinvestigation and submit to polygraph testing. All CIA documents cited in the book were reviewed for security considerations and have been declassified by CIA's Historical Review Group. Copies of the documents will be made available to requesters.

A book like *Battleground Berlin,* reflecting the insights of Soviet and American intelligence officers who actually participated in many of these events, can probably never be written again—we are all well into our seventies as this book goes to press. Our goal has therefore been ambitious: to provide never-before-seen documentary evidence of what each side knew during the crises, and to give readers a sense of what it was like to face off with an intelligence foe in Cold War Berlin. The result, we trust, is a singular contribution to the literature of the postwar struggle between East and West.

Acknowledgments

David Murphy would like to express his appreciation for the encouragement and support received from David Gries, former director of the CIA Center for the Study of Intelligence, his successor Brian Latell, and John Pereira and James Hanrahan of the Center's Historical Review Group; former CIA Historian Kenneth McDonald and his successor, Kay Oliver, and members of the History Staff; Bill McNair, DDO Information Review Officer and his marvelous assistants; and John Hedley, chairperson of CIA's Publications Review Board. Special thanks are due Paul Redmond, ADDO for counterintelligence, for his help during the research phase of this book; to David Hunt, former special assistant to the DCI for counterintelligence; and to Jeanne Vertefeuille of the Counterintelligence Center, who took time from her other pressing duties to review key chapters. The CIA Publications Review Board has posed no security objections to publication of *Battleground Berlin*, but its review does not constitute an official release of information, confirmation of accuracy, or an endorsement of the authors' views.

Murphy is also grateful to the many retired CIA colleagues, too numerous to name individually, who shared their experiences with him and without whose contributions and advice this book could never have been undertaken. This was particularly true of his successor in Berlin, William Graver, who until his death in December 1996 gave freely of his time to read and comment on the manuscript. Finally, Murphy owes a special debt of gratitude to his wife, Star, for her loving support and the untold hours she spent on this seemingly never-ending project.

Sergei Aleksandrovich Kondrashev wishes to express his gratitude to Maj. Gen. Yuri Kobaladze, chief of the SVR Press Bureau, for his support and assistance. Thanks also to senior Press Bureau consultant Col. Vladimir Nikolaevich Karpov for his help in the declassification process. Kondrashev is greatly indebted to Maj. Gen. Aleksandr Belozerov, chief of SVR Archives, for advice and help in his research, and to senior colonels Vyacheslav Mazurov and Dmitri Vorobyev for the time that they spent searching for documents and preparing them for declassification. All the authors join Kondrashev in thanking his wife, Rosa, for her kindness and hospitality.

George Bailey owes a special debt to the members of the Ullstein Archive of the Axel Springer Verlag, especially Eva Trapp, for their assistance. Also, thanks must go to Mstislav "Slava" Trushnovich and Yevgeny Redlich of the Popular Labor Alliance of Russian Solidarists (NTS) for their cooperation, especially in providing information about the kidnapping and murder of Slava's father, A. R. Trushnovich, in Berlin in April 1954, and to Klaus Schuetz, former lord mayor of Berlin, for his wonderfully candid interview. Equally deserving of thanks is Henrik Bonde-Henriksen, the Danish journalist and rescuer of Otto John, for his tireless cooperation, and Heinz Felfe, whose courtesy in responding to a complex series of questions was exemplary. Special thanks to his wife, Beate, for her active support in researching German source material, and for her understanding and good humor.

All the authors agree that without the interest, support, and enthusiasm of Jonathan Brent, executive editor of Yale University Press and creative force behind the Annals of Communism series, *Battleground Berlin* would never have been completed. Our thanks also to Yale University Press editors Julie Carlson, for her extraordinary contribution, and Dan Heaton, for his constructive patience. We are likewise grateful for the understanding shown by our literary agent, Peter Matson, in working with three authors with totally different backgrounds.

Communications with and support in Moscow were a vital aspect of this effort. Special thanks are due our friends Serge Karpovich and Gennady Inozemtsev and his family for their abundant hospitality. Also to Daniel J. Mulvenna, for both his wise counsel and his indispensable help in keeping the ends of this enterprise tied together.

Key Players

The Americans

Donovan, William Joseph. Head of OSS during World War II. Established liaison with NKGB in December 1943.

Dulles, Allen. First OSS chief in Berlin. Director of CIA, 1953–61.

Durand, Dana. BOB chief during its transition to CIA administration and during the Berlin blockade.

Graver, William. Replaced David Murphy as BOB chief in August 1961.

Harvey, William King. BOB chief, December 1952–July 1959. Masterminded the Berlin tunnel operation.

Hecksher, Henry. Instrumental in BOB X-2 (counterintelligence) operations, 1945. Deputy chief of BOB, 1949–53.

Helms, Richard. Replaced Allen Dulles in Berlin during fall 1945, reorganized BOB. Returned to Washington to head Foreign Division M. Director of CIA, 1966–73.

Kisevalter, George. CIA case officer who handled the Popov case, 1953–58.

Murphy, David. Deputy chief of BOB and head of BOB Soviet operations, 1954–59. Chief of BOB, 1959–61.

Rowlett, Frank. Directed Berlin tunnel operations from CIA Washington headquarters as chief of CIA Staff D.

Sichel, Peter. First postwar head of BOB intelligence. Deputy chief of BOB, 1946–49. BOB chief, 1949–52. Returned in 1952 to CIA headquarters, Washington, to become chief of operations, East European division.

Stewart, Gordon. Chief of OSO station in Heidelberg (later in Karlsruhe). Deputy chief, CIA German Mission. Chief of foreign intelligence staff at CIA Washington headquarters during Berlin tunnel operation.

Truscott, Lucian K., II. Arrived in Frankfurt in 1951 as CIA senior representative and chief of the German Mission. Responsible for operations of OPC (CIA's first covert action component) and office of special operations (OSO).

Wisner, Frank. Chief of secret intelligence for OSS Germany in 1945. Head of CIA's OPC in 1948. Became deputy director of plans when OSO and OPC were combined in 1951.

The British

Blake, George (a.k.a. Diomid). KGB source in SIS, the British intelligence service. Told the Soviets about the Berlin tunnel.

Burgess, Guy. KGB source in the British Foreign Office during the Berlin blockade.

Maclean, Donald. KGB source in the British Foreign Office during the Berlin blockade and Korean War.

Philby, Kim. NKGB source in SIS during World War II, when he reported on Otto John to both the British and the Soviets.

The East Germans

Linke, Karl. Chief of military intelligence, 1956–58. Target of BOB defection operation.

Mielke, Erich. Minister of state security, 1957–89.

Wolf, Markus. Chief of foreign intelligence.

Wollweber, Ernst. Chief of state security after the June 1953 riots.

Zaisser, Wilhelm. Minister of state security, 1950–53.

The West Germans

Felfe, Heinz. KGB agent who led the Soviet counterintelligence unit of BND, the West German intelligence service.

Gehlen, Reinhard. Chief of wartime German intelligence on the Russian front who created the postwar, US-supported Gehlen Organization, which became BND.

John, Otto. Wartime German resistance figure and British agent who was appointed first chief of BFV, the West German counterintelligence service, and was later targeted for recruitment by KGB.

The Soviets

Abakumov, Victor Semyonovich. Wartime chief of Smersh, Soviet military counterintelligence. MGB minister, 1946–51.

Agayants, Ivan Ivanovich. Chief of Department D (active measures) during the campaign against "espionage swamp" West Berlin.

Fadeikin, Ivan Anisimovich. Acting chief of Karlshorst apparat during June 1953 riots.

Fedotov, Pyotr Vasilievich. Chief of MGB foreign intelligence. Deputy chair of Committee of Information (KI).

Goleniewski, Michal (a.k.a. Sniper). KGB agent and deputy chief of Polish military counterintelligence. Revealed to BOB the identities of Blake, Felfe, and other KGB agents.

Ilichev, Ivan Ivanovich. Appointed chief resident of KI Berlin, April 1950.

Kaverznev, Mikhail Kirilovich. MGB chief at Karlshorst, 1952–53. Removed by Beria after Stalin's death.

Kobulov, Bogdan Zakharovich. Beria crony and chief of Directorate of Soviet Property in Germany (USIG). Supervised Wismut, a Soviet uranium mining and processing facility in East Germany. During Beria interregnum became deputy chief MVD for foreign intelligence.

Kondrashev, Sergei Aleksandrovich. Blake's case officer in London, 1953–55. Headed KGB German department and active measures service.

Korotkov, Aleksandr Mikhailovich. Deputy NKGB resident in prewar Berlin, where he ran key members of "Red Orchestra," a Soviet agent network. First postwar foreign intelligence resident in East Berlin. Chief of Karlshorst apparat from 1957 until his death in 1961.

Kovalchuk, Nikolai Ivanovich. MGB representative in Germany, 1947–49.

Kuchin, Vsevelod Vitoldovich (a.k.a. Vladimir Karpov). Directed KGB operation to recruit Otto John.

Malinin, Leonid Alekseevich (a.k.a. Georgiev). KI resident in Berlin, 1947–48. Removed and tried for contacts with BOB.

Nalivaiko, Boris Yakovlevich. Deputy KI resident in Berlin. Targeted in a BOB recruitment operation during 1947–48 that climaxed in the Gartenbau Cafe incident. Later chief of illegals operations, Karlshorst apparat.

Orlov, Igor Grigorievich (a.k.a. Alexander "Sasha" Kopazky). Served as BOB principal agent in Soviet operations. Now believed to have been a double agent for KGB.

Pitovranov, Yevgeny Petrovich. Veteran KGB officer who reorganized Karlshorst apparat after 1953 riots and remained until 1957.

Popov, Pyotr Semyonovich. CIA source in GRU during mid-1950s. Transferred in 1957 to the illegals section of GRU, Soviet military intelligence, in Karlshorst. Provided CIA with copious military intelligence and counterintelligence. Arrested by KGB and executed, June 1960.

Semyonov, Vladimir Semyonovich. Postwar political adviser to the commander of Soviet forces in Germany. High commissioner in East Berlin during June 1953 riots.

Serov, Ivan Aleksandrovich. Under cover as Zhukov's deputy for civil affairs, veteran Chekist Serov was Stalin's secret policeman in postwar Berlin. Serov laid the foundation for the Soviet and East German security structure that dominated East Germany until 1989.

Shelepin, Aleksandr Nikolaevich. KGB chairman from 1958 until after the construction of the Berlin Wall. A controversial figure whose feud with Karlshorst apparat chief Korotkov weakened the apparat during the Berlin crisis of 1958–61.

Sokolovsky, Vasily Danilovich. Replaced Zhukov as chief of the Soviet Military Administration in Germany. As chief of staff of the Soviet Army, Sokolovsky was sent to East Berlin in June 1953 to quell riots and establish order.

Tishchenko, Yakov Fyodorovich (a.k.a. Vasily Petrovich Roshchin, Razin). Veteran foreign intelligence officer who replaced Malinin as KI resident at Karlshorst during the Berlin blockade.

Zhukov, Georgy Konstantinovich. Chief of Soviet forces and military government in postwar Germany. Zhukov's popularity as a war hero incurred Stalin's wrath, but he was restored to key positions after Stalin's death. A report by Popov on a Zhukov visit to East Germany in 1957 led to Popov's arrest by KGB.

Zvezdenkov, Valentin Vladimirovich. KGB major general and veteran counterintelligence officer responsible for investigation of Popov in both Karlshorst and Moscow.

Abbreviations

ADSO	Assistant Director for Special Operations (CIG and CIA)
Bfv	Counterintelligence service (FRG)
BND	Foreign intelligence service (FRG)
BOB	Berlin Operations Base (USA)
CDU	Christian Democratic Union of Germany
Cheka	All-Russian Extraordinary Commission for Combating Counterrevolution and Sabotage (Soviet security service, 1917–22)
CIA	Central Intelligence Agency (USA)
CIC	US Army Counterintelligence Corps
CIG	Central Intelligence Group (USA)
Comintern	Communist International
CPSU	Communist Party of the Soviet Union
CPUSA	Communist Party of the USA
DCI	Director of Central Intelligence (CIG and CIA)
DDCI	Deputy Director of Central Intelligence (CIG and CIA)
DDO	Deputy Director for Operations (CIA)
DDP	Deputy Director for Plans (CIA)
FBI	Federal Bureau of Investigation (USA)
FRG	Federal Republic of Germany
GCHQ	General Communications Headquarters (UK)
GDR	German Democratic Republic

GKO	State Defense Committee (USSR)
GPU	State Political Directorate (Soviet security service incorporated in NKVD, 1922–23)
GRU	Chief Intelligence Directorate, Soviet General Staff
GSFG	Group of Soviet Forces, Germany
GSOFG	Group of Soviet Occupation Forces, Germany
Gulag	Labor camps directorate (USSR)
GUSIMZ	Chief Directorate of Soviet Property Abroad
HVA	Main Administration of Foreign Intelligence (GDR)
KGB	Committee of State Security (Soviet state security service, established 1954)
KI	Committee of Information (Soviet foreign intelligence agency initially combining foreign directorates of MGB and GRU, 1947–51)
KPD	Communist Party of Germany
LDP	Liberal Democratic Party of Germany
Mfs	Ministry of State Security (GDR)
MGB	Ministry of State Security, 1946–54 (USSR)
MID	Ministry of Foreign Affairs (USSR)
MVD	Ministry of Internal Affairs (USSR)
NATO	North Atlantic Treaty Organization
NIE	National Intelligence Estimate (CIA)
NKGB	People's Commissariat for State Security (Soviet security service, 1941, 1943–46, predecessor of MGB)
NKVD	People's Commissariat for Internal Affairs (USSR, predecessor of MVD)
NSA	National Security Agency (USA)
NTS	Popular Labor Alliance of Russian Solidarists (anti-Soviet émigrés organization)
OGPU	Unified State Political Directorate (Soviet security service, 1923–24)
OMGUS	Office of Military Government (USA)
OO	Special departments of military counterintelligence (USSR)
OPC	Office of Policy Coordination (CIA)
ORE	Office of Reports and Estimates (CIA)
OSO	Office of Special Operations (CIG and CIA)
OSS	Office of Strategic Services (USA)
RU	Intelligence directorate (GSFG)
SBONR	Union of the Struggle for the Liberation of the Peoples of Russia
SED	Socialist Unity Party of Germany
SI	Secret intelligence branch (OSS)

SIS	Secret Intelligence Service (UK)
SMA	Soviet Military Administration, East Germany
Smersh	"Death to spies" (Soviet military counterintelligence, 1943–46)
SPD	Social Democratic Party of Germany
SSU	Strategic Services Unit, War Department (USA)
UKR GSFG	Directorate of Counterintelligence (GSFG)
UPS	Government Communications Directorate (KGB)
USFET	US Forces, European Theater
USIG	Directorate of Soviet Property in Germany
WEU	Western European Union
X-2	Counterintelligence branch (OSS/SSU)

Behind the Lines in the Cold War

Rarely does a book demand some comment from its publisher, but *Battleground Berlin* is such a work. Its origins lie in the vast complexities of the Cold War; the story it tells has never been told before; its point of view is unique in the annals of espionage literature in this century.

For schoolchildren today, the Cold War will be only another topic in history class, along with the Roman Empire and the American Revolution. Twenty years from now, it will be little more than an echo of a past to which few will have direct access any longer. The daily angst experienced by those living in the decades after World War II will seem incomprehensible to those born in the wake of the dissolution of the Soviet empire—a demise almost biblical in its suddenness, like the miraculous destruction of Sennacherib's army during the reign of Hezekiah.

But to those who feared a new world war in 1948 as the Americans airlifted food and supplies into West Berlin, circumventing the Soviet blockade; who anxiously followed the invasion of South Korea in 1950 and wondered whether divided Germany might be the next war zone; who were astounded at the sensational penetration of American, British, and French governments by Soviet intelligence services; who waited fearfully to see whether nuclear war would be averted over Berlin in 1961 and Cuba a year later; and who by the 1990s had come to suspect the very premises (legal, ethical, political) on which our own intelligence services now appeared to construe themselves—to all of those people, *Battleground Berlin* will come as a revelation.

Many books have dealt with the Berlin blockade, the Korean War, the affair of Colonel Popov, the famed tunnel project of 1954 that was betrayed by the British spy George Blake, and finally the construction of the Berlin Wall, but no book before this one has been able to tell these stories, and many more, from the perspective of *both* American and Soviet intelligence. For the first time it is possible to see how the two sides fit together, how they played against, interpreted, and misinterpreted each other. We are able now to see the choreography of move and countermove.

Further, it has never before been possible to put the two sides together with actual documents from both KGB and CIA archives, and with the whole story told by two of the actual participants: David Murphy, former chief of CIA Berlin Base, and Sergei A. Kondrashev, a retired lieutenant general of KGB and former chief of the German Section of KGB.

The picture that emerges from this joint project of recollection and reconstruction is not simply a string of intriguing anecdotes of individual spy operations. The story is immense—and the genesis of the huge bureaucratic and political machinery that drove so much Cold War espionage activity (discussed in the early chapters) provides an essential backdrop for the events to follow. The main protagonists here are not individuals, but two enormous systems confronting each other with all their bureaucratic, technological, and political might. The conflict is not contained in a particular mission—the success or failure of the tunnel operation, for instance, or the penetration of East German military intelligence by Frau K. in 1959. Rather, the conflict is between two ways of thinking and organizing the world. The weapons used in this conflict are not made of steel; they're made of information. The denouement of this immense conflict, involving thousands of protagonists on both sides, was the construction of the Berlin Wall in 1961, but the larger resolution did not occur until 1989, when the Wall came crashing down.

What we see in the course of this book is a picture of two systems in action. The American intelligence system at the end of World War II had few professional or administrative resources. It was largely an ad hoc affair—poorly funded, poorly staffed, and without a secure future.

By contrast, in 1945 the Soviet intelligence service was a highly professional bureaucracy with a history going back to the 1917 Revolution.

Soviet intelligence had access to the highest reaches of the American, British, and French governments. It was able, for instance, to obtain the minutes of a meeting of the British Government Cabinet on 10 September 1948 and transmit those minutes to Stalin by early October. The Soviets scored coup after coup in the field of intelligence gathering, yet they were never able concretely to understand the Americans or the Germans. They had no sense of what the Americans would actually *do* when confronted by the Berlin blockade. Yet the Americans, with far fewer resources—and with fewer spectacular successes—were able accurately to assess the Soviet willingness to wage war over the blockade, and it was largely this analysis that, according to the authors of this book, made the airlift a success.

What protected the West during this crucial period was not guns, tanks, planes, or bombs; it was knowledge. The great story of this book is how information becomes knowledge and how this knowledge gets transmuted into political policy.

It could be said that the Soviet people were betrayed by their leaders. Why? Because ideological commitments and all-consuming interest in protecting power were always paramount to those leaders—stifling their ability to see things, to use Matthew Arnold's homely phrase, "as in themselves they really are." Although they possessed often superior information and much more of it, the Soviets could not put it sufficiently to their larger advantage. They won battle after battle but lost the war. Rarely did Stalin receive information that he might not like. Rarely was the social or political reality of the West portrayed to Soviet leaders for what it was. Most often Soviet leaders would be told what they wished to hear and would see what their ideology told them they must. When Gorbachev attempted to reverse this, the system fell apart.

How this essential difference in point of view between East and West influenced the structure of the two largest intelligence services in the world and from there came to help shape the history of the second half of the twentieth century is the story of *Battleground Berlin.*

JONATHAN BRENT, *Editorial Director*
Yale University Press

PART I

The Sides Line Up

1

CIA's Berlin Base:
A Question of Knowledge

O n Christmas Eve 1943, Gen. William Donovan, head of America's first central intelligence organization, the Office of Strategic Services (OSS), arrived in Moscow. He had just completed an exhausting trip to China, and he was determined to establish a liaison relationship with the Soviet foreign intelligence service similar to the one that already existed between the Soviets and the British. To the astonishment of US Embassy Moscow personnel, Donovan was whisked right to the office of Soviet Foreign Minister Vyacheslav Molotov on the day after he arrived. There he explained his plans for Bulgarian operations. Although Molotov seemed displeased at OSS's plans for the Balkans, which could have interfered with Soviet objectives in the area, he nonetheless quickly arranged for Donovan to meet with representatives of Soviet foreign intelligence.[1]

Two days later, Donovan was introduced to Commissar of State Security Pavel Fitin, head of the foreign intelligence directorate of the People's Commissariat for State Security (NKGB). Fitin in turn introduced "Col. Aleksandr P. Osipov, head of the section conducting subversive activities in German-occupied areas." Colonel Osipov interpreted for Fitin, speaking American-accented English. Imagine Donovan's reaction had he known that "Colonel Osipov" was in fact Gaik Ovakimian—known to FBI as the "wily Armenian"—who had

3

been arrested in 1941 on charges of espionage but released after the German invasion of the Soviet Union and who was now deputy chief under Fitin responsible for Anglo-American operations.[2] Although the story of this meeting has been told many times, "Colonel Osipov's" true identity and function are fully revealed here for the first time.[3]

Donovan's shock would have been even greater if he had realized that Ovakimian was overseeing the extensive penetrations of oss that had begun as soon as the American service was formed in July 1941, as Roosevelt's Office of the Coordinator of Information (coi). nkgb had several well-placed agents in oss—known to Soviet intelligence by the code name Izba (the hut)—among them Duncan Chaplin Lee, code-named Koch, who was assistant general counsel and one of Donovan's personal assistants.[4]

Given that the Soviets were already well informed about internal oss plans and programs, it is not surprising that Donovan could so quickly secure an agreement to exchange intelligence information and establish liaison missions in Moscow and Washington. In the end, the idea of an nkgb liaison mission in Washington was blocked by J. Edgar Hoover, the fbi director, on grounds that it might compromise American security.

In spite of this setback, liaison between oss and nkgb continued through the us Military Mission in Moscow. nkgb was in the catbird seat. Its agents in oss could obtain information, including documents from the State and War Departments, that oss did not want revealed. nkgb was thus able to provide Josef Stalin, Vyacheslav Molotov, and Lavrenty Pavlovich Beria with a rich diet of oss information from both officials and agents— information that in many cases was supplemented by commentary from other sources. Information from oss Bern, where Allen Dulles had excellent sources in the German resistance, was particularly prized.[5]

This liaison between oss and nkgb continued fitfully until just after the end of the war, by which time oss had entered Germany and Allen Dulles was ensconced in Berlin. When the leader of a German ss agent network in southeastern Europe was captured in Austria, along with his radio center, oss proposed that it and nkgb collaborate in liquidating the operation. oss recommended that Fitin and Dulles meet in Berlin to discuss the proposition.[6]

Fitin stalled on the Berlin meeting and asked "what other leading German intelligence officers [had] been captured by the American military," and who among them had proposed "work against the Soviet Union." At this point the us Joint Chiefs of Staff directed oss to drop

совершенно секретно

81

НКГБ СССР сообщает ежедневной
разведсводки Управления Стратегических Служб США № 40
от 16 февраля 1945 г. Текст документа получен в Вашингтоне
агентурным путем.

" Кризис в Германии.

В результате недавних военных неудач немецкая администрация и
экономическая система функционируют с большим
напряжением. Советское наступление увеличило эвакуацию населения
из захваченных Красной Армией областей, усложняя политический контроль
и загружая немецкий транспорт и перенаселяя города. Потеря
важных индустриальных и сельскохозяйственных районов предвещает
серьезные затруднения недостачу военных и гражданских
продуктов снабжения. Положение усугубляется сильными
бомбардировками германских городов и, в частности, Берлина, а также
мрачным предчувствием результатов Крымской конференции и новым
наступлением союзников на двух фронтах.

Германская пропаганда до Крымской конференции заранее пыта-
лась дискредитировать любую декларацию союзников, и этим самым
свидетельствовала о увеличивающемся беспокойстве нацистов
относительно влияния этих деклараций на моральное состояние
армии и населения. Эта озабоченность нацистов указывает на их
опасение, что эффективность правительственного контроля над
населением ослабнет. Нацистские же руководители, по-видимому,
считают, что до тех пор, пока сохраняется единство командования и
эффективность правительственного контроля, ухудшение морально-
политического состояния германского населения не представляет
очень большой опасности. Превращение в настоящее время тыловых
районов в зону военных действий может временно усилить этот
контроль, но в конце концов известный распад фронта и массовая

№ 170/599

Translation of oss weekly intelligence report no. 40, 16 February 1945, "Crisis in Germany," obtained by the NKGB residency in Washington from agents in oss and distributed to the "three addresses"—Stalin, Molotov, and Beria.

the idea of collaboration. Perhaps they feared that if word got out that the United States had "betrayed" a German intelligence operation, others contemplating cooperation might shy away.[7] Accordingly, a directive went out to OSS Germany to demolish the radio center.[8]

Thus ended NKGB-OSS wartime collaboration, which from the start reflected the sublime naïveté with which OSS entered the arrangement. As the inheritors of the OSS legacy faced new challenges in Berlin and elsewhere in the postwar world, they encountered the same NKGB—a tough opponent that knew a great deal more about the American intelligence services than these services did about it.

The Soviet advantage extended beyond intelligence. The Germans capitulated on 2 May 1945 and the surrender agreements were signed on 8–9 May, but Western Allied forces were not allowed into Soviet-controlled Berlin until 4 July, when American forces ceded portions of the future Soviet zone of Germany that they had occupied during the closing days of the war. In the interim the Soviets had controlled the entire city. They and their German Communist Party (KPD) allies had taken over many of the Berlin district offices and other elements of municipal administration. They had even adapted the notorious Nazi Blockleiter system of social control by appointing block and house leaders to report to Soviet authorities.

For the OSS German Mission marking time in the American zone, the two-month delay put on hold its hope of "establishing contacts in an area which will shortly be denied to us."[9] Indeed, for Western military commanders and their intelligence officers, the Red Army's zone soon became terra incognita. The military missions that were to operate in each of the four zones had not yet begun. This absence of information on the dispositions of Red Army units was exacerbated by American innocence about the potential for Soviet-American military cooperation. When Gen. Omar Bradley first met Soviet Marshal Ivan Konev on 5 May, he gave the latter a map "showing the disposition of every US division across his group front." Marshal Konev did not reciprocate—nor, it seems, did Marshal Georgy Zhukov.[10]

Berlin Operations Base Digs In

On 4 July 1945, the first day that OSS could enter Berlin, it flew a team into the city. The plane landed at Tempelhof airfield in the American sector while the entire city was still under Soviet control. For OSS Berlin

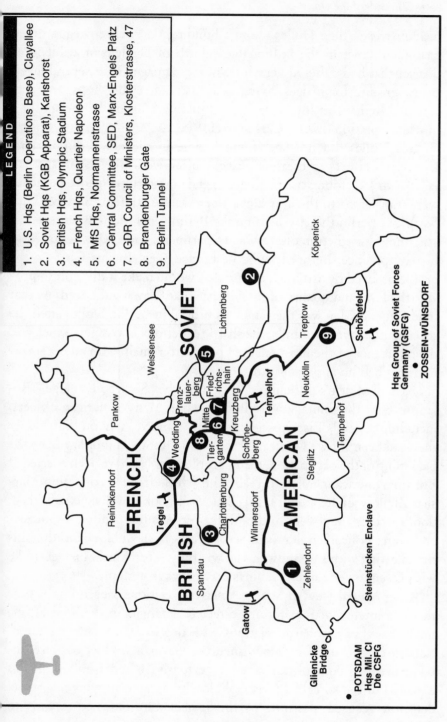

Berlin 1945–94, occupation sectors and city districts.

headquarters, Allen Dulles chose a building on Foehrenweg, a quiet, tree-lined street in the fashionable suburb of Dahlem in Zehlendorf district that had suffered very little bomb damage. With several levels below ground for offices, living quarters, and repair shops, and surrounded by its own lovely park, the building looked like the set for a movie adaptation of a Le Carré novel.[11]

But Dulles did not spend much time in the new headquarters. Donovan's efforts to create a peacetime service in the OSS image had failed. On 1 October, OSS intelligence and counterintelligence branches were transferred to the War Department as the Strategic Services Unit (SSU). OSS Berlin thereby became the Berlin Operations Base (BOB) of SSU, under jurisdiction of the War Department, and Dulles returned to his law practice. Before leaving he briefed Gen. Lucius Clay on the problems faced by SSU in Germany that would make it difficult to provide the level and quality of intelligence that Clay would need. At that time General Clay was the senior US official in Berlin. Dulles cited the severe cutback in OSS funds, the sharp reductions in OSS personnel, and the reluctance of the most talented people to remain with an organization that had no apparent future.[12]

Not all of BOB's difficulties arose from the "Soviet advantage." Relations with the military were initially cool. Many American officers, including generals Eisenhower and Clay, claimed early on that if only they had been allowed to deal directly with the Soviet military from the beginning of the occupation, many problems could have been averted.[13] But the Americans failed to realize how little freedom of action Marshal Zhukov or his deputy, Marshal Vasily Sokolovsky, actually had, dominated as they were by political overseers like Andrei Vyshinsky and secret policemen like Ivan Serov. Years later, Zhukov, recalling his first meeting with Eisenhower, said wistfully, "You know, I never spoke with Eisenhower alone; Vyshinsky was always with me."[14]

Clay's initial view of Soviet-American relations caused him to fear that OSS intelligence operations directed at targets in the Soviet zone might backfire and harm relations with the Soviets. Hence his intention, in the words of Frank Wisner, OSS Germany's chief of secret intelligence, "to control our activities extensively and firmly" and his espousal of the so-called Clay-Sokolovsky agreement whereby Soviet defectors accused of crimes by the Soviets were returned forcibly to Soviet control. But by late 1947 Clay had begun to experience a change of heart brought about by worsening relations with his Soviet

OFFICIAL DISPATCH

VIA: ____Air—Pouch—been
SPECIFY AIR OR SEA POUCH
appro   through
the HIST   * KGRAM of
the Centr.   ce Ag

DISPATCH NO.:

Date 2/16/94

CLASSIFICATION

TO   44-1

FROM :

DATE: 17 November 1947

SUBJECT: Weekly Letter, Berlin Operations Base, 15 November 1947

REF :

1. As indicated in our cable 633, the most important development affecting our position in Berlin is the apparent change in
General Clay's attitude toward intelligence. As you are only too
aware, we and other intelligence agencies have labored for the past
two years under the disadvantage of having to contend with the so-
called goldfish bowl policy. This policy was laid down at the
beginning of the occupation, and has been taken for granted by the
principal OMGUS officials (such as the Chief of Staff, Brig. Gen.
Gailey), without even venturing to suggest modifications to General
Clay. Last week, at his press conference, General Clay reaffirmed
the goldfish bowl policy, but accompanied it with two restrictions
which in effect mark the end of an era. He declared that Military
Government publicity would continue freely and openly, but that the
lid would be clamped on all items involving real security interests,
or which might prejudice diplomatic or high policy negotiations in
progress.

We are not fully informed as to the circumstances which
brought about these significant limitations. We assume that General
Clay, for many months, has been undergoing a steady disillusioning
process, insofar as concerns his relations with his Soviet opposite
numbers. The climax occurred early in October at the moment when
General Clay returned to the States. His protest against the bitter
public criticism of American policy and motives, delivered in Berlin
by Colonel Tyulpanov, was rejected by Marshall Sokolovsky with only
the barest trace of official courtesy. No doubt this sting was
sharpened by what Clay was told in Washington, though we have no
reason to believe that the recent Newsweek account of a dressing down
by Royal and Marshall was other than conjecture.

Not sent forward because subject covered here.

Weekly letter, Berlin Operations Base, 17 November 1947, describing
what the letter terms an apparent reevaluation by Gen. Lucius D. Clay of
relations with his Soviet counterpart and of his attitude toward US intelligence operations.

counterparts and by his growing appreciation of intelligence information provided by BOB.[15]

Geography added to the problems of OSS Berlin. Theoretically, con-
quered Germany was to be run from Berlin, but this never really happened. Each occupying power was supreme in its own zone and could
veto actions by individual Allied powers. The Americans, isolated in
their sector many miles from the headquarters of US Forces, European
Theater, in Frankfurt, found it difficult to maintain the fiction that
Berlin was the center of the occupation. Indeed, with Dulles's departure, the notion of Berlin as German Mission headquarters could no
longer be sustained.

The Soviets, meanwhile, made Berlin operations a high priority and
gave them all the local organizational support they needed. The Soviet
Military Administration for Germany (SMA), the Group of Soviet Occupation Forces, and the headquarters of Soviet intelligence and counterintelligence services were all located in East Berlin or the Berlin
suburbs.

The officers who remained in Berlin after Dulles's departure realized that if BOB could not overcome its difficulties there was little future for them as intelligence officers. Adding to the problems of severe
personnel shortages and inadequate funds was some involvement in
extensive black market operations. Such activities were by no means
confined to OSS; they existed on a remarkable scale throughout the
American military.

It fell to Dulles's successor and a future CIA director, Richard Helms,
to tackle these problems and begin to reorganize BOB. With the help of
Capt. Peter Sichel, whom Helms brought to Berlin to head the intelligence branch, a base structure emerged consisting of two branches that
still bore the OSS labels SI (secret intelligence) and X-2 (counterintelligence). This organizational scheme, which included reports officers, remained intact for many years.

Helms left Berlin for Washington before Christmas 1945. He was
replaced by Dana Durand, who, with Sichel as his deputy, shepherded
BOB through the transition from the Strategic Services Unit (SSU) to the
Central Intelligence Group (CIG) and finally, on 18 September 1947, to
the Central Intelligence Agency (CIA). During this period, Durand's
main concern was BOB's survival as a base of intelligence operations. To
achieve this he had to balance conflicting concepts of what his base

should become and how it should function. ssu headquarters, Washington, thought that bob should become part of a long-term covert organization that would concentrate on collecting strategic, national-level intelligence. But us occupation authorities wanted current information on the Soviet zone. The dilemma was resolved in favor of having bob respond to local, current requirements.[16]

Durand remained at bob until 1949, by which time it had become a fixture of the Berlin intelligence scene. During his tenure the base struggled to overcome significant difficulties in its intelligence and counterintelligence programs and encountered hosts of problems with cover and in its relations with the military. Nevertheless, bob survived to come of age during the Berlin blockade. Durand's reporting on this period, released for this book by the cia Historical Review Program, has been invaluable.[17]

What Was BOB's Intelligence Mission?

In late summer 1945, bob did not have an overall intelligence mission. What little reporting there was dealt with such matters as background checks on Germans deemed worthy of serving in a future German government, the activities of new trade union organizations, actions by local German officials, and occasional acts of violence by die-hard Nazis. Indeed, there was doubt whether bob would ever have an intelligence mission. Initially some believed that oss should not plan to collect intelligence outside the American zone. Reluctance to intrude on other Allies' territory was never a problem for the Soviets.[18]

The issue of whether to expand intelligence operations beyond the American perimeter was resolved for oss by the Soviets themselves. As Soviet controls tightened along the zonal demarcation lines, the American military government lacked even the most basic information needed to judge the economic and political situation in East Germany. Pressure to acquire this information prompted bob to increase its reporting on such Soviet zone issues as transportation, the food supply, land reform, public opinion, and industrial conditions, including Soviet actions to dismantle and remove whole factories and other equipment to the Soviet Union. Many of these reports relied on interviews with refugees, but increasingly the Berlin unit developed agent sources capable of providing continuing information on these topics.

Reports on the Soviet takeover of the East German railroads in late August 1945 foreshadowed the excellent coverage of this key transportation system by Berlin Base—coverage that continued through the Berlin blockade. BOB obtained the first information on the new German Central Administration, for example. The Administration was a sort of shadow government established by the Soviets to carry out the decisions of SMA's headquarters in Karlshorst, the Soviet compound whose name became synonymous with Soviet control and intelligence in East Germany.[19] BOB provided the minutes of a 26–27 September meeting between Soviet officials and the Central Administration for Industry, during which industrial conditions in the Soviet zone were reviewed, and it also tracked shipments of dismantled industrial equipment by covering the Soviet collection point at Berlin-Lichtenberg. This type of economic reporting gave US policymakers their first warning about the nature and extent of Soviet actions concerning the economy of their zone.[20]

Political reporting by BOB came to center stage later in 1945. At the time there was little appreciation of the scope of Soviet influence on East German politics, but a series of incidents during December 1945 involving the Christian Democratic Union (CDU) focused American attention on the issue.[21] On 22 December, BOB reported on a meeting ten days earlier between CDU leaders in the Soviet zone and Marshal Zhukov in which Zhukov announced that CDU was "unrepresentative of public opinion, had a highly objectionable attitude toward land reform, and thus could not be permitted to take part in political meetings with CDU leaders in the American and British zones." This intelligence was followed five days later by a BOB report on the crisis in the CDU leadership that described in detail Soviet pressure on CDU—specifically, "the method and central planning used to precipitate the crisis."[22] Apparently this and subsequent intelligence reports from Berlin on the CDU crisis alarmed SSU German Mission headquarters; Peter Sichel was summoned to explain them. Some at the mission were upset by the document's criticism of the Soviets. But Sichel stood his ground, insisting that such actions, especially when taken by the top Soviet officials, must be fully reported. Eventually, Sichel told us, everyone agreed that such information was indeed essential and urged that it continue.[23] This reporting was also being read carefully by Ambassador Robert Murphy.[24]

BOB political reporting gradually moved beyond CDU to encompass successive crises caused by the Soviets' decision to merge the KPD with the German Social Democratic Party (SPD). The merger didn't proceed as the Soviets had expected. When the Western commandants, led by General Clay, refused to permit a merger in West Berlin unless SPD members agreed, more than 29,000 voted against the proposal and fewer than 3,000 voted for it. Even after the merger was finally forced on SPD members living in East Germany, the results were far from satisfactory for the Soviets. In October 1946, for example, the combined vote for the East German CDU and Liberal Democratic Party (LDP), another "bourgeois" party of the National Front, exceeded that of the new, merged Socialist Unity Party (SED). BOB reported these events in depth. Appendix 1 documents how all of this affected the Soviets. A gloomy meeting took place in December 1946 between Marshal Vasily Soko-lovsky and the leading members of the SED, chiefly Wilhelm Pieck and Walter Ulbricht, both longtime German Communists, and Otto Grote-wohl, a former SPD official who had knuckled under to join the new party. During this meeting, SED blamed its poor showing in the Octo-ber elections on Soviet policies and practices.

BOB and the Soviet Bomb

As part of its economic reporting on the Soviet zone, BOB followed early Soviet industrial dismantling activities. Initially conceived by the Soviets as a way to revive their economy, which had been ravaged by the German invasion—and reflecting Allied agreement that Germany should never again be able to wage aggressive war—the Soviet disman-tling was a disaster. In many cases, plants and equipment sent to the USSR were badly damaged and allowed to rust. The alternative, taking reparations from plants still operated by East German managers, was pursued with better results.[25]

One of the most important of the enterprises that ultimately con-cerned American intelligence efforts stemmed from Stalin's determina-tion to build the atomic bomb using East German resources, even though doing so violated Allied agreements. General Clay wrote about this period, "A Soviet corporation was formed to mine uranium ores, and stories of forced labor in this work began to reach us."[26] This cor-poration was Wismut, an enterprise for mining and processing East German uranium.

Coverage of the Soviet atomic program was a major BOB commit-ment, one never before fully described. One of BOB's earliest successes was its discovery of a group of German scientists who had been taken to the Soviet Union in 1945. The uranium mining and ore concentration facilities in East Germany naturally became key targets, but as awareness of the scope of the Soviet atomic bomb project increased, BOB began to exploit connections in other German industries vital to the Soviet program. BOB's British counterparts were active in the same areas. Both services, for example, developed sources at an I. G. Farben plant at Bitterfeld in the Soviet zone that made distilled calcium, which is used in the production of uranium 235. BOB's unique contribution was proving that Bitterfeld calcium had made its way to the Soviet atomic facility at the town of Yelektrostal near Moscow, which was already known to make uranium 235.[27]

BOB also provided crucial reporting on the production of nickel wire mesh at the Tewa plant in Neustadt. This very fine mesh was vital to the Soviet program because it was used in producing uranium 235. Because of the importance of the wire mesh to the Soviets, BOB undertook an operation to persuade key craftsmen to leave the factory and be resettled in West Germany.[28]

Gradually, many of the firms supplying Wismut and other manufacturing sites for the Soviet nuclear program were also designated Soviet Joint Stock Companies, administered by the Directorate of Soviet Property in Germany (USIG). BOB was alerted to the developing nickel wire mesh program by agent sources within the USIG complex.[29] These firms supplied Wismut with pneumatic drills and special miners' lamps, as well as matériel like refrigerated testing chambers, which were shipped directly to the USSR for use in the atomic program.[30] Items not available in the Soviet zone were ordered through West German firms. For example, the Bitterfeld plant needed vacuum pumps and a special steel to produce pure calcium metal, and it found these goods in West Germany. Luckily for the Americans, most of these items had already been placed on an export control list: when the US European Command learned of Soviet efforts to obtain them from West German firms, it stopped the shipments.[31]

BOB also learned about the Soviet atomic bomb project from the Soviets themselves. Yevgeny Petrovich Pitovranov, a senior KGB official whom we interviewed, recalled the concern within MGB over the security of Wismut shipments in early 1952, when intelligence leaks about them were reported. Information on these shipments was transmitted by enciphered messages sent over land to Novosibirsk, but from there they were sent by radio, which was easily intercepted.[32] Soviet concern for the security of the Wismut operation was heightened considerably by the defection in June 1950 of a colonel, code-named Icarus, who had been a logistics officer in Moscow and then in Wismut. Icarus had left his German mistress behind when he defected, and he became increasingly despondent and eventually returned to Soviet control. He was apparently executed, and his mistress was sent to the Gulag. Icarus's information greatly expanded US knowledge of the Soviet atomic program in East Germany, but the tightening of security that ensued frustrated BOB's operational programs. Eventually, security measures initiated by MGB, and later by KGB, made it virtually impossible to recruit agents within Wismut.[33]

Counting Tanks

BOB's economic coverage was successful, and its monitoring of Soviet nuclear interests in East Germany seemed vital and urgent. Why, then, did BOB pursue with such fervor the collection of Soviet order of battle, or disposition of military forces, in 1946? One answer is that BOB did not choose the order-of-battle initiative. It was not a carefully considered program, but rather one that a nascent department like SSU felt it had to accept to survive. Our account is based on newly declassified CIA documents.

As of January 1946 the SSU German mission was the largest remnant of OSS overseas, and BOB was its largest base. It depended entirely on the goodwill of the US Army for its logistics, cover, and the right to conduct operations in occupied Germany. The future of all US clandestine operations depended on how well the mission functioned in occupied Germany. Its position within the military hierarchy was defined by a 30 January 1946 directive that put SSU under the general staff supervision of the Theater G-2 (intelligence officer), Gen. Edwin Sibert.[34] Sibert became the European Theater intelligence officer after US forces withdrew from their forward positions in East Germany in June 1945. Now they were faced with Red Army formations along the zonal demarcation line and had no hard intelligence on the size, disposition, or strength of these forces.[35]

Sibert plunged into this enormous mission with remarkable energy and determination. Within a short time he had made the G-2 of USFET the principal intelligence coordinator of the European Theater. His office assumed control of all army intelligence and counterintelligence but encouraged ssu to continue independent operations. In return for its autonomy, bob was asked to shift major resources to military targets. Under the military intelligence collection program code-named Grail, the Soviet Army's order of battle was given the highest priority.[36]

Grail was a throwback to wartime operations, when time-sensitive, tactical coverage of the opposing enemy was critical. This sort of in-depth coverage was possible only through the use of tough, unsentimental head agents whose motivations to undermine the Soviets often included material interests and personal scores to settle—many of the German agents had fought the Soviet Army on the Eastern Front. These head agents contacted old acquaintances and friends in East German towns adjacent to Soviet garrisons, airfields, and training sites. The locally recruited agents in turn found others to help them collect intelligence. For the most part, the local agents simply watched the Soviet installations; occasionally they took still photos with handheld cameras. Reports were either brought to Berlin by couriers or picked up by the head agents.

More than 250 agents were involved in this effort. Many were arrested, but they were quickly replaced and the operations continued. The Soviets uncovered this activity in various ways, including by infiltrating individual networks. They would investigate the networks and then "roll up the chain" through arrests as soon as all members were identified. Soviet counterintelligence leaders seldom tried to "double" or play back these agents against the West, probably because of their low level within bob. Those arrested were tried and sentenced to the Gulag.[37]

Tradecraft, or the practice of security in agent handling, was largely ignored by the Grail officers. Head agents came to know local agents, who in turn could easily identify many of their subagents. Contact meetings were held in homes in the American sector that were still intact and could be requisitioned by the us Army. It was not uncommon for several of these agents to stay overnight at such safe houses, where they learned the identities of their fellows. Christmas parties were held to boost morale, but they also broadened the exposure of agents' identities. Dick Cutler, bob counterintelligence chief until August 1946, recalls being asked to move into a safe house that on occasion held as many as twenty-five of the chain agents. It was apparently hoped that the presence of an X-2 officer would improve security discipline. This did not happen.[38] The pressure to produce continuous reporting on Soviet order of battle made it difficult to introduce standard security practices. Traditionally, a case officer handled a limited number of trained and briefed agents. He maintained contact with them through occasional, carefully planned meetings or impersonal communications involving couriers and dead drops—whereby material is hidden in a prearranged location for pickup by another agent or courier. But such time-consuming tradecraft methods would have kept BOB from meeting the demand for information.

While it lasted, this activity enjoyed enormous success and was approved not only by military customers in Frankfurt and Washington but also by higher-ups at SSU and CIG. The agents provided an incredible amount of detail on airfields, barracks, troop movements, ammunition dumps, training areas, fortifications, and troop maneuvers in the Soviet zone. All reports from these agents were given to leaders in Washington. As the BOB chief at the time, Dana Durand, pointed out, "It is easy to criticize this free and easy period, but at the time everyone—our customers, Heidelberg, Washington—was immensely pleased and kept on demanding more. There was immense gratification at being able to pinpoint a target anywhere in the Russian zone and dispatch an agent to cover it at almost a moment's notice."[39]

The bubble burst in fall 1946, when the Soviet security services began arresting entire chains of agents, thus ending the military intelligence program. It also cured BOB of any desire to use the chain approach against other targets and taught a hard lesson to the case officers involved in the program. But those who paid the price were the agents themselves. Several years elapsed before their full story became known. In 1955, when the Soviets released German prisoners as a goodwill gesture during the establishment of diplomatic relations between the USSR and the Federal Republic, many of BOB's former agents were debriefed on their experiences.[40]

One head agent, a former Wehrmacht staff officer, had been recruited in February 1946 for the BOB program. He in turn had recruited twenty or so subagents who had actually performed the collection tasks. He had taken their reports to a safe house in West Berlin, where he had stayed overnight and typed reports for the American case officer.[41] In summer 1946 this head agent was approached by a Soviet security officer who had ostensibly recruited him as an informant in his home town to report on anti-Soviet dissidence. The head agent had continued his order-of-battle collection activities for BOB until March 1947, when he was arrested by the Soviets and interrogated. When confronted with accusations that he had spent nights at the safe house and had attended a Christmas party at which photographs were taken, the head agent confessed. He was tried and sentenced to twenty-five years of hard labor.[42]

In May 1949, this agent followed the traditional route to the Gulag along with other East Germans sentenced by Soviet courts. They were not released until October 1955. From this and similar cases, it appears that the Soviets were well informed of BOB's operations and that MGB's ostensible recruitment of the head agent as an informant was merely a way of controlling the situation until it was ready to roll up the entire net in March 1947.[43]

X-2 Berlin Plays Double or Nothing

Although BOB's reporting on economic, political, and scientific issues continued to expand and gain acceptance among US officials in Berlin and Washington, its counterintelligence branch seemed out of touch with the new postwar reality. It began operating in Berlin as it had against the German intelligence services during the war, but without its trump card—ULTRA, the remarkable signals intelligence source developed by the British that had helped the Allies so much during the war. With the end of hostilities, X-2's favored position within SSU changed abruptly. The Soviet services were a new challenge for X-2. Few X-2 officers in Germany were familiar with the Soviet intelligence and security services, which were much tougher and more tightly disciplined than any of the wartime German intelligence services had been. Significantly, no one in BOB's X-2 or SI branches could speak Russian.[44]

The SI side of OSS Germany seemed poised to lead the intelligence effort in Berlin. During the war it had had outstanding leaders, with Dulles as head of the mission, Frank Wisner as chief of SI, and Richard Helms, another SI officer, already tabbed to succeed Dulles in Berlin.[45] Certainly BOB operations would have profited had the intelligence and counterintelligence branches worked together. But the layout of BOB's headquarters, with its different underground and above-ground levels, further divided the competitive branches of BOB. Each branch happily pursued its own program of operations quite independently of the other.[46] Isolated and shorn of its former special status, the Berlin X-2 branch was reduced in 1945 to a staff of five, headed by Lt. Richard W. Cutler. It was hardly capable of coping with the growing Soviet counterintelligence activity in the city, given that the Soviets had exercised total control over Berlin since its capture on 2 May. Soviet arrests of persons they wanted had begun citywide before the Western Allies entered Berlin. By July these arrests were largely confined to the Soviet sector, but the Soviets later kidnapped people in West Berlin, including many who opposed Soviet policies. The kidnappings continued even after uniformed Soviet officers were caught in the act and handed over to the Soviet komendatura.

Visible evidence of Soviet counterintelligence and security operations was paralleled by an increasing number of reports that East Berliners and East Germans were being recruited by the Soviets to spy on Allied installations. Some of these reports came from individuals on the Supreme Headquarters Allied Expeditionary Force's automatic arrest lists who, when confronted, claimed that the Soviets had recruited them to work against the Americans. Other recruits confessed their Soviet intelligence affiliation rather than carry out their espionage assignments. As a result, by early fall 1945 Berlin X-2 had a number of double-agent operations in progress. The ostensible purpose of these operations was to obtain information on the Soviet intelligence service sponsoring—"running"—each agent. Eventually, BOB hoped to bring about the recruitment or defection of the Soviet officer to whom the agent reported. But OSS operatives were kept from pursuing many of these opportunities because they were forbidden from recruiting former members of the SS or Gestapo. (The Soviet services were never so constrained: the Soviets believed that not all such individuals were hard-core Nazis and that some could be turned into productive agents.) OSS treated the German Military Intelligence Service (Abwehr) as an exception and vigorously pursued leads to former members of this organization, which had been forcibly absorbed by the SS.

The cases arising from doubling these ex-German intelligence officers against their Soviet case officers continued for several years. In fact, the double-agent approach to recruiting Soviet intelligence personnel and developing information on their units remained a staple of BOB counterintelligence operations for some time. (Some case studies are contained in appendix 2.) But it did not result in the recruitment of any Soviet case officers. In 1948 base chief Durand noted a growing disillusionment with these double-agent operations. Classical counterespionage goals were not realized because Soviet targets evaded American traps. BOB discovered the hard way that Soviet case officers were skilled "in all the tricks of agent handling: neutral meeting points, aliases, red herrings, keeping the agent in blinders so far as concerns the location of headquarters and identity of other agents or staff personnel."[47]

BOB also came to realize that the superior studies of the Soviet intelligence organization received from the British were not the product of double-agent operations but came rather from a special category of Soviet defectors: displaced persons who had been sent to Germany as laborers during the war and then were picked up by NKGB as interpreters at war's end. These individuals were particularly susceptible to Allied blandishments because they had had an opportunity to compare life in Germany with that in the USSR and because their situation with the Soviet occupation forces was a precarious one. They were not trusted by the Soviets but were tolerated for their knowledge of German. The story of attempts to recruit one such person through one of BOB's original double-agent cases appears in appendix 2.

Defectors were an obviously valuable source of information on Soviet intelligence. Durand, in his review of double-agent operations, cited a British experience in Berlin: eight months of painstaking effort with a double-agent case had produced a mere half-page of order of battle on the Soviet intelligence organization, but intensive interrogation of a few defectors who had been low-level interpreters had yielded large amounts of organizational and personality information.[48]

BOB could not take full advantage of defectors until 1947, when the base was assigned its first Russian speaker, George Belic.[49] Belic had entered CIG in 1947. After participating in the debriefings of Soviet defector Anatoly Mikhailovich Granovsky, Belic was assigned to Berlin and placed under cover in the Special Liaison Section of the provost marshal's office.[50] Here he could meet Soviets officially but also could hear firsthand about the many Soviet military who had scrapes with American military police. He was in a great place for spotting potential recruits or defectors.

Nevertheless, all operations involving the recruitment or defection of Soviet soldiers had to reckon with the Clay-Sokolovsky agreement to return to Soviet control all defectors labeled by the Soviets as deserters or criminals. Thus, whether to accept a defector always meant balancing the potential value of the individual against the possible difficulties of getting him or her out of Berlin and resettled after the

MEMORANDUM FOR THE DIRECTOR, CENTRAL INTELLIGENCE

        After considerable exploratory effort, George Belic, a
staff member of our Berlin station, ▇▇▇▇▇▇▇▇▇▇▇▇▇▇ arranged to have himself and Major
General Leonid A. Malinin, Deputy to Marshal Sokolovsky, invited
to a dinner given on 9 December 1947 by a member of the OMGUS
Press Section. After dinner Belic and Malinin separated from
the other guests and talked from 1930 hours to 0300 hours --
Malinin consumed three water-glasses of vodka and five water-
glasses of undiluted American whiskey in the course of the conversation. The freedom with which Malinin discussed various political topics of significant interest, ranging from the current
Soviet name-calling propaganda campaign to the general strike in
France and the approaching devaluation of the ruble, encouraged
Belic to arrange another dinner-party at which Malinin suggested
he would be pleased to have Ambassador Murphy present.

        On 16 January 1948 Ambassador Murphy, at the suggestion
of Mr. Durand, Chief of our Berlin station, gave a dinner-party
attended by General Malinin, Belic (interpreting), Mr. Durand,
and two members of the Polad staff. Malinin made the following
statements in the course of the evening's discussions:

        a. He depreciated attempts to settle outstanding
international issues at London-type conferences,
agreeing with Ambassador Murphy that the publicity
attending such conferences was prejudicial to understanding. He strongly urged a meeting of Truman and
Stalin to delineate "spheres of interest" stating that
he appreciated U.S. public opinion would resent the
choice of a meeting place within the Soviet orbit but
that he was sure the Politburo would veto Stalin's
travel to the Western hemisphere in view of his age and
the delicate state of his health. He stated the
Politburo might sanction a meeting at Stockholm.

        b. He agreed with Ambassador Murphy that the current
propaganda warfare has reached a dangerous pass and should
be called off. He believed that basic differences
are ideological and unlikely to lead to war, but that
the ideological conflict may last "for centuries".

033

Memorandum, undated, for the director, Central Intelligence, regarding Soviet Gen. Leonid A. Malinin, who, unbeknownst to Berlin Base, was the KI
resident in East Berlin.

TOP SECRET

Page 2 - 8 October 1946 - Director, SSU.

It would be keenly appreciated if you could obtain for us
guidance as to how we should proceed in our approach to this problem
general and to the situation in Berlin specifically.

TOP SECRET ~~OP/CMP~~   FSRo-485-a

Richard Helms
Richard Helms

WAR DEPARTMENT   ~~R 8au8xy~~ "CIG-A-~~2T.06~~"

OFFICE OF THE ASSISTANT SECRETARY OF WAR

STRATEGIC SERVICES UNIT

25th & E STREETS, N.W.
WASHINGTON 25, D.C.

8 October 1946

TO: Director, SSU

VIA: Acting Chief, FSRO

FROM: Acting Chief, FBM

      Attached hereto is a memorandum from Mr. Sichel in Berlin, with a
covering memorandum from Mr. Stewart in Heidelberg.

      These memoranda raise certain significant points which might well
merit the attention of CIG officials.

      It is not my aim to institute a special plea for Berlin. My thought
rather is that the problem on the relationship between personnel and targets
in Berlin is typical of the situation existing throughout our field organization. Unless we can get a clearer definition of our responsibilities in
the intelligence field, as well as the specific targets which we are to
cover, we will be constantly in the position of doing what we can with the
personnel at hand rather than staffing our detachments with the necessary personnel to do the job which it is felt essential to do in a specific area.

      In this connection, I would like to draw your attention to Attach-
ment 2 in FSRO-485. The targets here outlined are on the face of it of
interest to various departments of the United States Government. They include Grail targets which were specifically assigned to us by General Vanden-
burg. Also included are targets bearing on the reparations problem in Germany,
a high priority consideration in connection with the writing of the Peace
Treaty on Germany. The political objectives are basic in an appreciation of
Soviet intentions with regard to Germany and Central Europe. Scientific
information is a constant high priority.

      Also, in Attachment 2 is indicated the degree of coverage on the
various targets. In the opinion of the Berlin men themselves, they are
giving only partial and, what they call, "inadequate" coverage on the highest
priority objectives. Nevertheless, it is fair to say that most of the intelligence received on these targets by the United States Government comes from SSU.
The State Department and the War Department have few if any facilities for
covering in detail political, economic, military, and scientific information
in the Russian Zone of Germany and the Polish-administered area of Germany.

TOP SECRET

Memorandum, 8 October 1946, from Richard Helms, acting chief, Foreign
Branch M, to Col. William W. Quinn, director, ssu, discussing the relation
between available personnel and intelligence responsibilities assigned to
Berlin Base.

debriefings. Clay eventually relaxed his attitude, but until then BOB and other American intelligence units were reluctant to take chances.[51]

One source, code-named Buick, was recruited by BOB's counterintelligence branch on a lead from a civilian employee of the US Military Government in Berlin. A Soviet official stationed in Karlshorst, who had extensive background in internal counterintelligence in the USSR and in Germany after the war, had let it be known that he had information of interest to American intelligence. Because Belic had arrived only recently and was the first BOB officer to acquire effective cover, it was deemed unwise to expose him. Instead, a newly arrived member of the counterespionage branch at Mission headquarters in Heidelberg who spoke German and Russian was sent to Berlin to get the case started. Through the American civilian he met the Soviet, who agreed to remain in place in Karlshorst and provide documents from SMA archives through his mistress. Eventually the case was taken over by Belic. It remained active until the agent was resettled in the West in 1948.[52]

A more fascinating case was BOB's contact Maj. Gen. of State Security Leonid Alekseevich Malinin. Strictly speaking, it was not even a "counterintelligence" case because BOB had no idea that it was in touch with the chief of Soviet foreign intelligence in East Berlin. This case, described in detail in appendix 3, demonstrates that more than two years after war's end BOB still had a hazy vision of who was who in Soviet intelligence in East Berlin and the Soviet zone.

Whatever BOB gained from its operations against the Soviet intelligence services during the first year after the occupation, it learned relatively little about their organization, structure, and personnel. That the base even tried to operate is a tribute to the determination and faith of those who stayed on after the "glory days" of the victory over Germany. But in retrospect it is astonishing that the US government failed to establish an effective American intelligence operation in Berlin, one capable of recruiting long-term intelligence assets from among the thousands of disaffected Soviet personnel stationed there.

2

KGB Karlshorst:
How It All Began

Standing on a dark street corner in East Berlin in the damp chill of the evening, the Soviet captain fingered the note he had stuffed in his pocket. He was about to meet his contact for help in defecting to the West. No real soldier, he had recently arrived in Germany from Leningrad as a member of a team of specialists hastily assembled to oversee production in East German factories of badly needed parts for Leningrad's growing electronics industry. He had always been fascinated by the West, and he loved American jazz. When word of his new assignment came through, he made no secret of his joy. Just before leaving Leningrad, he talked about it to a friend, a fellow engineer who had recently been demobilized after serving with the Red Army in Germany. Cautiously, the friend told him that he knew of a German who could really show him Berlin. The captain made contact with the German and fell in love with West Berlin's bright lights. His new German friend claimed to know someone who could put him in touch with people who could help him stay in the West.

Now the meeting was about to take place. Despite his anxiety, he couldn't help smiling as he thought of the new life that awaited him in the West. A dark sedan pulled up, and after a moment's hesitation, the captain ducked into the plush interior. In the car, as the silent driver sped them away from the gloom that had become synonymous with

East Berlin during the past two and a half years, the captain finally turned to his German contact and accepted a cigarette. This simple and familiar act suddenly made him feel more important than frightened. As they pulled up to the imposing villa, his hosts, addressing him in what must have been American English, shook his hand warmly. Looking around him and taking in their uniforms, the captain felt further reassured.

Once inside, the captain settled into a velvet couch, lit a second cigarette, and responded to the Americans' suggestion that he tell them about himself. This he began to do with great gusto (one of the officers translated his remarks into English), but as he went on he noticed that his hosts seemed dissatisfied. Finally, one broke in and exclaimed—in unaccented Russian—"All right, enough. Tell us about your contacts with American intelligence in Leningrad!"

The captain had never been an American spy. He was the victim of Pavlovsky's Trap, a scheme to smoke out the many American and British agents who, Stalin was convinced, had been operating on Soviet territory during the war years and beyond. Counterintelligence had dossiers containing such accusations on hundreds of Soviet citizens— our "captain" is a composite of many such suspects. The operation was devised by Col. Ivan Grigorievich Pavlovsky of the British department of NKGB's counterintelligence directorate during the war years. Pavlovsky had a real talent for complicated operational gambits. The scheme was based on techniques commonly used by the directorate within the Soviet Union: a suspect is led to believe that he is in contact with a foreign intelligence officer, when in reality this "officer" is a state security officer or agent. If the suspect revealed anti-Soviet attitudes and admitted "recruitment," then arrest—and the Gulag—followed.[1]

Pavlovsky's Trap began with a Soviet agent approaching the suspect and suggesting that if he were truly fed up with Soviet life, a trip to Berlin could be arranged. Once in East Berlin, the suspect was put in touch with a second person, usually a German agent of MGB Germany (Soviet security), who offered to lead him to an American installation in West Berlin. At this point the "American" team took over, and the suspect found himself in a luxuriously furnished estate, surrounded by people in American uniforms, all speaking English (with varying proficiency). The team was given the use of Castle Dammsmuehle at Muehlenbeck, Kreis Oranienburg, just north of the point where the old French sector joined the Soviet sector—and miles away from the

American sector. Soviet citizens arriving at the castle presumably had little awareness of postwar political geography.[2]

During an interview with an "American" officer, it was hoped that the suspect, relieved at being in the presence of American intelligence officers, would express joy at finally reestablishing contact. But of the twenty-five to thirty-five cases of which coauthor Sergei Kondrashev knew, only a few suspects were found to have had any contact with an Allied intelligence service. The operation was consequently abandoned in 1948 or 1949.[3]

The sheer complexity of this trap, and the image of Stalin's suspicious mind that it conjures up, illustrates the contrast between the SSU Berlin Base and the Soviet state security presence in East Germany. American policymakers were only beginning to realize that the occupation of Germany would be much more complicated than envisaged in the Potsdam agreements, and SSU was not yet sure what its role would be. The Soviets' policy toward the occupation was simple: achieve maximum influence over postwar Germany or, failing that, retain undisputed control over their own zone. Soviet intelligence and security services were there to make sure that this policy was implemented.

The positions of the two leading players in postwar Berlin, Soviet and American, could not have been more different. OSS had never been sure of its future in Berlin. It had struggled with scarce funding from Washington, personnel shortages, little knowledge of Soviet reality and the Russian language, and contentious relationships with its American military counterparts. None of these problems had affected the Soviet services to the same degree. After all, the Soviet state security and intelligence services that converged on Karlshorst had existed since the Russian Revolution and were an integral part of Soviet society. But the American service did have one advantage, even if it did not become apparent for many years: the inability of Stalin and his successors to accept and act on intelligence contrary to their preconceptions. Perhaps the most frightening aspect of the Cold War in Berlin was how poorly informed the Soviet leaders were, even after receiving mountains of secret information from their foreign intelligence service, much of it from the offices of Western leaders themselves. Few Soviet intelligence officers dared deliver unpleasant messages to Stalin or Khrushchev lest they spend the rest of their days in the Gulag. This attitude and the consequent lack of Soviet understanding of the American perspective led both sides to the brink of war more than once.

The Beginnings of Soviet Intelligence

Some have said that if the West had really understood Stalin and the methods he used to run his country, the Cold War could have been avoided. With victory over Germany in 1945, Stalin's standing with the Russian people, exhausted from the war and hoping for better things, had never been higher. Still, he persisted in efforts to increase his power at home and expand it abroad. The bureaucracy in Moscow that controlled Soviet intelligence and counterintelligence services in Germany during early 1945 was in turn under the control of this infamous dictator, who had long regarded them as his primary instruments of control and repression. To those serving in these organizations, the image of Stalin as the "boss" *(khoziain)* inspired awe and terror. Most of the otherwise inexplicable changes made in key positions in these services could be traced to Stalin's practice of controlling ambitious state security chiefs by inserting his own often mediocre men in the chain of command. This practice, and the rivalries it engendered, stirred animosities in Germany at war's end and afterward, as bitter rivals fought for supremacy and Stalin's favor. Even after his death and the de-Stalinization of the Soviet Union, traces of his style remained.[4]

Soviet intelligence operations began with the Bolshevik seizure of power in Russia in October 1917. Feliks Edmundovich Dzerzhinsky, a Polish revolutionary who had joined forces with the Bolsheviks, created Cheka, the Russian acronym for the All-Russian Extraordinary Commission for Combating Counterrevolution and Sabotage. Cheka's foreign intelligence department was formed on 12 December 1920.[5] Cheka underwent several name changes during the 1920s, but throughout the history of Soviet intelligence and counterintelligence, the term Chekist has continued to describe members of the service.

In 1934 Stalin created a new People's Commissariat for Internal Affairs—NKVD was its Russian acronym—which was responsible for both state security and public order. Under its brutal first chief, G. G. Yagoda, this institution began Stalin's purges during the 1930s and gave the initials NKVD an aura of fear that remained long after the agency had disappeared.

In 1936 Stalin replaced Yagoda with Nikolai I. Yezhov, an even more zealous purger. Yezhov's subsequent dismissal in December 1938 provided Stalin with a convenient scapegoat on whom to blame the terrifying purges of the 1930s.[6] After Yezhov's departure, the purge machinery was turned against many in NKVD who had been too "zealous" in their pursuit of Stalin's enemies. These purges also affected the foreign intelligence components. The Shanghai and Tokyo residencies were gutted, and some, like the London residency, were forced to close down. As we shall see, this was not the last time that political infighting between Soviet leaders crippled the foreign intelligence service at a critical time.

In 1938 the notorious Lavrenty Beria became head of NKVD. He brought with him a number of cronies from the Caucasus. In early 1941 Stalin experimented with an arrangement whereby counterintelligence and foreign intelligence, the key state security directorates, became a separate entity, NKGB (People's Commissariat for State Security). After the German invasion in June 1941, these directorates were pulled back into NKVD again under Beria. Despite his paranoia, Stalin seemed willing to risk restoring Beria to his former position, realizing that a firm hand was needed to consolidate and coordinate the forces of internal affairs and state security if they were to cope with this unprecedented threat to his personal power. The struggle with Germany dominated Soviet security and foreign intelligence objectives until the end of World War II.

Soviet Intelligence During the War

In his classified memoirs, never before published, Pavel Fitin, chief of the foreign intelligence directorate, describes a Central Committee decision reflecting the scope of the German problem.[7] Because the directorate's efforts to create and sustain operational groups behind enemy lines had increased in scale and demanded ever more attention, the Central Committee decided to divide that directorate into two separate directorates, the First and the Fourth. The First, the foreign intelligence directorate, was to collect intelligence against Germany and its allies, as well as information about the policies of the United States and England toward the Soviet Union and Germany and about the policies of other capitalist countries not participating in the war. The directorate was also responsible for the conduct of technical intelligence and counterintelligence abroad.

The Fourth Directorate, known as the diversionary intelligence directorate (*diversionno-razvedyvatel'noe upravlenie*), organized and directed operational groups working with the partisans behind German

lines. According to Fitin, one of his deputies, Pavel Anatolievich Sudoplatov, was named chief of this directorate.[8] The intelligence directorate, whose main task was directing its stations abroad, assisted the
Fourth Directorate. There was, in fact, a continual exchange of personnel between the First and Fourth Directorates.[9]

In April 1943, when the tide of battle turned in Stalin's favor, Soviet
counterintelligence and intelligence services were reorganized again,
this time into a configuration that lasted until the immediate postwar
period. The Chief Directorate for State Security regained its independence as NKGB on 14 April 1943 and placed the counterintelligence components of state security and its foreign intelligence directorate again
under the single management of its former chief and a Beria loyalist,
Vsevelod Merkulov. Beria remained head of NKVD and a member of the
State Defense Committee. It was Beria's NKVD and its thousands of special troop units that undertook the massive deportations of various Soviet ethnic groups from their homelands.[10] Assisting Beria in these
operations were Ivan Serov and Bogdan Kobulov, both of whom played
important roles in postwar Germany.

At the same time, military counterintelligence was reframed within
the Soviet bureaucracy. This organization was responsible for detecting
German agents in the Red Army and for ensuring the political reliability of all personnel, from generals to the lowest private. Its special departments *(osobye otdely)* throughout the forces—along with its chief,
Viktor Semyonovich Abakumov—were removed from NKVD's Chief
Directorate of State Security and incorporated in a new organization,
the Third Chief Directorate of Counterintelligence, or Smersh (Death
to spies), under the People's Commissariat for Defense (NKO). This
reorganization made it easier to coordinate counterintelligence operations with military planning. But most members of military counterintelligence saw little change in their responsibilities, personnel, or
relationships with the troops to which they were assigned. For example, Abakumov, the new chief of Smersh and former head of military
counterintelligence in state security, actually retained the same office
at NKGB's Lubianka headquarters despite his transfer to the defense
commissariat.[11]

Stalin's reasons for this reorganization arose from the potential
threat to his power as the popularity of his generals soared and thousands of Red Army soldiers entering enemy territory saw for themselves
the relative affluence there and returned home to spread the news.[12] On

the other hand, Stalin also realized that Red Army operations would increasingly be conducted on hostile territory—the Western Ukraine, Poland, the Balkans, and Germany itself. For this he needed military counterintelligence departments capable of keeping Soviet troops in line while neutralizing and eliminating anti-Soviet opposition.[13]

Each Red Army front had its own Smersh directorate, which controlled the directorates and special departments in the armies and divisions of the front. As the Red Army advanced through Poland and into Germany, the Smersh directorates of the First and Second Belorussian fronts helped most to create the Soviet state security units that would operate in Berlin and throughout the Soviet zone.[14]

The Transition to Postwar Operations

The individual chosen to oversee the conversion of these units to peacetime operations in Germany was Col. Gen. Ivan Aleksandrovich Serov. Fresh from Poland, where he called himself General Ivanov, Serov had been responsible for directing the operational groups that had paved the way for the establishment of a Communist-dominated government in that country. To the outside world, Serov was the deputy for civil affairs to Marshal Zhukov, chief of the Soviet Military Administration, but his extensive background in state security hints at other goals. His real title was personal representative of the People's Commissar of Internal Affairs (USSR NKVD) with the Group of Soviet Occupation Forces, Germany (Upolnomochnnyi NKVD v Germanii).[15] Serov thus supervised SMA's internal affairs directorate, which dealt with police functions, firefighting, prisons, and guard forces. On 27 July 1945, for example, Serov established special NKVD prison camps (Spetslager NKVD) for Nazis and those opposing the SED regime in East Germany.[16] Directorates of internal affairs were also created within each provincial SMA and its district-level departments. Serov used directorates at all levels to create new German public security and judiciary organizations.

But Serov's top priority at war's end was to create a nonmilitary counterintelligence group that could deal with residual Nazi elements and with future opposition to the Soviet occupation. Soviet counterintelligence, like its American counterpart, was concerned by reports of an active Nazi underground. Moreover, the Soviets feared that this underground was already working closely with "reactionary circles in England and the United States in creating an anti-Soviet front."[17]

With this much power in his hands as the occupation got under way, Serov became a key player within the USSR's police state hierarchy, one who maintained his position by responding with alacrity to Stalin's slightest whim. In addition to keeping tabs on Marshal Zhukov, Serov protected Stalin's alcoholic son, who was serving with the Soviet air forces in Germany. But as Serov moved to convert some Smersh units to a new state security role, he made enemies in Moscow.

Berlin's security was paramount, so Serov detached Smersh officers of the First Belorussian Front to form the Berlin Operational Sector (Berlinsky Opersektor). The first postwar chief of the sector was Maj. Gen. Aleksei Matveevich Sidnev, a protégé of Serov's. His official title was head of public safety or internal affairs in SMA.[18] Sidnev's career and ultimate fate reveal how high-level power struggles were played out in the Soviet hierarchy. He was relieved of his Berlin post in 1947 and named minister of state security of the Tartar Autonomous Republic. Later he was arrested for alleged involvement in large-scale black-market activities while in Berlin. The Sidnev case may have played a role in the intense rivalry between Serov and Minister of State Security Abakumov as both men competed for Stalin's approbation and for a dominant position in East Germany. It was to gain favor with Stalin and to denigrate Serov that Abakumov sent a copy of the Sidnev interrogation protocol to Stalin.[19]

In addition to the Berlin opersektor, NKGB operational sectors were created in each of the provincial *(Land)* capitals to conduct counterintelligence operations. Personnel for these sectors were taken from other Smersh directorates and from state security counterintelligence organs within the USSR. In Berlin operational groups were established in each of the city districts. Normally associated with the Soviet military komendaturas or with NKVD directorates or departments in provincial and district centers, their counterintelligence responsibilities reflected Soviet security concerns for Germany in the immediate postwar period.

For Serov, Red Army security in the hectic atmosphere of the occupation was also a major concern. He assigned other elements of Smersh of the First Belorussian Front to form the headquarters of the military counterintelligence directorate of Soviet Occupation Forces, Germany (UKR GSOFG), in Potsdam. This headquarters remained in Potsdam until the Soviets withdrew their last military forces from Germany in summer 1994. The organizer and first chief of the Potsdam directorate was Lt. Gen. Aleksandr Anatolievich Vadis, who had been the chief of Smersh of the First Belorussian Front. SVR archives reveal that Vadis had an instinct for making the most of politically sensitive issues that might advance his career. He made Stalin happy, for example, by producing a captured German document blaming the British for the abortive July 1944 Warsaw uprising by the Polish underground and claimed credit for discovering the hidden diaries of Joseph Goebbels, the infamous Nazi propaganda minister.[20]

UKR GSOFG in Potsdam was responsible for the political reliability and security of members of the forces. It recruited and supervised informants among Soviet personnel and German citizens in the GSOFG garrisons or living nearby. The UKR also investigated cases of espionage by Western intelligence services against the occupation forces. These agents were ferreted out, detained, and, where possible, turned into double agents for the Soviets. A Chekist spirit permeated the headquarters of UKR GSOFG. An elderly veteran, working in the agent records section, shouted proudly to all who would listen: "I used to be a cleaning woman for Feliks Dzerzhinsky."[21]

This Chekist atmosphere was not confined to the new military counterintelligence. It also permeated the new NKGB operational sectors and groups that began to operate throughout the Soviet zone. After all, most of the senior cadres of Smersh had served earlier either in special departments or in other elements of state security. In addition, from 1943 to 1946 thousands of new Smersh officers went through state-security training schools where they learned the Chekist trade and spirit.[22] But to most Soviets, and to the Western Allies and East German citizens as well, all of these groups were known as NKVD.[23]

Soviet Foreign Intelligence Returns to Germany

Because the first Soviet priority was to establish control in the Soviet zone, Serov was preoccupied with the work of the newly created NKGB operational sectors and groups. Nevertheless, the foreign intelligence directorate of NKGB was anxious to get started in Germany. But it had to begin at the bottom to establish a new presence in the country. The Soviet foreign intelligence residency in Berlin had closed down with the outbreak of war in June 1941. For the first time, based on material from SVR archives, we can follow the methodical manner in which the new NKGB foreign intelligence residency in East Berlin was created. Its birth stands in sharp contrast to that of OSS Berlin.

On 16 April 1945, as a preliminary step to creating the new residency, Stalin approved a plan to attach political advisers to the headquarters of each of the fronts then engaged in combat operations on foreign soil.[24] With these political advisers were operational groups consisting of three NKGB operations officers, a code clerk, and a radio operator.

As the fronts advanced into Germany, these groups were expected to keep Moscow informed of conditions in the country, including the mood of the population and the economic situation. They also reported on the activities of British and American representatives in areas under joint control and prepared for intelligence operations in the West after the defeat of Germany.[25] Beginning in June 1945, the groups assigned to the First and Second Belorussian fronts and the First Ukrainian front were consolidated to form a combined residency subordinate to the First (foreign intelligence) Directorate of NKGB in Moscow. By August the residency in Karlshorst was up and running. Its first resident was Aleksandr Mikhailovich Korotkov, an experienced intelligence officer who had been deputy resident in Berlin in 1941.[26]

Korotkov served in the First Directorate during the war, making frequent operational trips abroad (Afghanistan in 1943, Poland and Romania in 1944). In addition, he often visited the front in connection with double-agent operations involving German radio operators under Soviet control. He had extensive operational background and familiarity with the German scene, and his selection as the first postwar Soviet foreign intelligence resident in Berlin was a wise choice.[27]

With the establishment of the Soviet Military Administration under Zhukov in Karlshorst, resident Korotkov was designated the deputy political adviser and his residency was covered within the directorate of the Political Adviser Arkady Aleksandrovich Sobolev.[28] According to the classified memoirs of Boris Yakovlevich Nalivaiko, a member of the residency, by the end of 1945 the residency consisted of only six operations officers, with two more arriving in January 1946. Indeed, it had been determined that NKGB's First Directorate residency in Karlshorst could not cope unassisted with intelligence requirements from Moscow on West Berlin and the Western zones of occupation. Consequently, departments for intelligence collection were created in each of the MGB operational sectors and groups.[29]

The residency had already been in contact with a number of agents, most of whom worked in district offices in Berlin and in provincial governments. In addition to keeping Moscow informed on local conditions, the residency was directed to recruit agents in the "bourgeois" parties like the Christian Democrats, which had been formed in the Soviet zone in 1945.

The Soviet intelligence situation at this time was perhaps confusing even to the Soviets themselves (we know it was to BOB). Its various organizations were scattered all over East Berlin and the Berlin suburbs. The smallest of the organizations, also located in Karlshorst, was Korotkov's foreign intelligence residency. Coordinating this multipronged monstrosity must have been difficult. The GSOFG military counterintelligence directorate and its subordinate units throughout the garrisons of the occupation forces were still theoretically subordinate to the Third Chief Directorate of NKO. The new NKGB counterintelligence operational sectors and groups reported to the NKGB counterintelligence directorate, whereas the NKGB foreign intelligence directorate was responsible to Korotkov and his people in Karlshorst. Still, the basic structure lasted, with modifications, for several years.

MGB Turns Up the Pressure in Germany

In March 1946 the Soviet government abandoned the revolutionary formula of "people's commissariats," and NKGB became the Ministry of State Security (MGB).[30] In June 1946, Viktor Abakumov, who since 1943 had headed military counterintelligence in the Commissariat for Defense, became minister, replacing Vsevelod Merkulov.

According to Pavel Sudoplatov, Stalin decided to appoint Abakumov because he did not trust Merkulov's ties to Beria.[31] Historical treatment of Beria's apparent loss of control "over the MGB-MVD empire" and the removal of several of his closest associates from posts in the state security structure supports this view. Abakumov also seemed a logical choice because of his outstanding work in military counterintelligence during the war and because of his unwavering allegiance to Stalin. But there was another important factor in this assignment, largely ignored in some quarters and important in the German context as reported in CIA archives.

With the creation on 20 August 1945 of the Special Committee under the State Defense Committee (GKO), which Beria chaired, the USSR embarked on a race to develop an atomic bomb. As David Holloway emphasized in his *Stalin and the Bomb,* "It was not an aberrant

CENTRAL INTELLIGENCE GROUP
INTELLIGENCE REPORT

128694

COUNTRY Germany (Russian Zone)	**DATE:**
SUBJECT SMA Priority List for Industrial Production	**INFO.** 27 September 1947
approved for release through	**DIST.** 18 November 1947
the HISTORICAL REVIEW PROGRAM of	**PAGES** 2
the Central Intelligence Agency.	**SUPPLEMENT** SO-9244
ORIGIN Germany, Berlin	

Date 2/16/94

94-7

EVALUATION OF SOURCE

A	B	C	D	E	F		1	2	3	4	5	6
COMPLETELY RELIABLE	USUALLY RELIABLE	FAIRLY RELIABLE	NOT USUALLY RELIABLE	NOT RELIABLE	CANNOT BE JUDGED		CONFIRMED OTHER SOUR.	PROBABLY TRUE	POSSIBLY TRUE	DOUBTFUL	PROBABLY FALSE	CANNOT BE JUDGED

EVALUATION OF CONTENT

DISTRIBUTION

STATE	WAR	NAVY	JUSTICE	R & E	C & D						
# X	# X	X #			X	A A F					

SOURCE

1. During a meeting of the executive council of the SMA (Karlshorst), I. V. Kurbashov, G. G. Alexandrov, and G. K. Blagovestov, the men responsible for the industrial output, complained that delivery dates were not being observed. Major-General Kvashnin ordered, therefore, that the Soviet AGs be investigated to determine who are the persons responsible for the delay, and that steps be taken immediately to remedy the situation. It was pointed out that the B.M.W.   in Eisenach, the Horch plant in Zwickau, and the Audi factory (formerly Auto Union) in Zwickau, which are working exclusively on reparations orders, were the worst offenders, i.e., that their deliveries were at present almost 25% behind schedule. Although it was alleged that the slow-down in the work program is due to political differences among the workers and to sabotage on the part of some technicians and foremen, the actual reason is a shortage of raw materials and dissatisfaction among the workers who have not received the special allocations they had been promised. Several men accused of sabotage have already been arrested in the Audi plant. Similar conditions exist in the Zeiss plant in Jena, i.e., orders for bomb sights and optical measuring instruments have been only about 60% filled.

2. During this meeting, a priority list for current production orders was submitted by Colonel Ruchkin of the reparations section; it contained twelve main groups, of which five were to take precedence.

   Washington Comment: The priority list mentioned above is given in detail in   of which this report should be considered a part. Both reports should be read in connection with

3. Colonel Ruchkin reiterated that all reparations orders, of whatever nature, are to take precedence over any other orders. He also made it clear that all factories, including private and socialized plants, are bound to follow strictly the above-mentioned priority classification.

4. Export orders, Colonel Ruchkin stated, are second in importance, and must be started as soon as reparations orders have been filled, in accordance

Central Intelligence Group information report, 18 November 1947, regarding the Soviet Military Administration (SMA) priority list for industrial production. The report originated in Berlin.

or eccentric act . . . to put [Beria] in charge of the atomic project, but an indication of the project's central importance for the Soviet leadership." On 23 January 1946, Stalin, Beria, and Molotov met with Igor Vasilievich Kurchatov, scientific director of the atomic project, who was told "to build the bomb quickly and not to count the cost."[32] The Soviets had acquired information about the American atomic bomb, and they had many brilliant nuclear physicists working on the project, but by this time it had become apparent that Soviet engineering and industrial capabilities lagged in many crucial areas. One remedy was more intensive exploitation of prisoners—whether as construction laborers or research scientists in the many prison laboratories.

Another approach was to ensure that East German and other East European industrial enterprises, many of which had been transformed into Soviet-owned companies, were fully exploited. For this task, Beria appointed Merkulov as head of the Chief Directorate of Soviet Property Abroad (Glavnoe upravlenie sovetskogo imushchestva zagranitsei—GUSIMZ), a "joint venture" organization that concealed Soviet influence over enterprises in Soviet-controlled areas. Other Beria favorites were sent to manage Soviet industrial properties in technically advanced bloc countries. This strategy explains why Bogdan Kobulov was sent to oversee Soviet property in East Germany—including Wismut, the uranium mining and processing facility.[33] Stalin's well-documented obsession with the atomic bomb suggests that its acquisition was his main motivation during this period. And it was understood that Beria would select associates whom he—and perhaps he alone—trusted.

But the primary threat faced by the Soviets in the immediate postwar period in Germany was growing public dissent. MGB units there came under intense pressure from Moscow to control the population. To cope with this pressure, changes were made in MGB's operational structure. This reorganization was initiated by Serov and was continued by his successor in the state security role, Lt. Gen. Nikolai Ivanovich Kovalchuk. During the war, Kovalchuk had been the chief of Smersh of the Fourth Ukrainian Front.

Serov's departure from Germany in late 1947 ended the arrangement, in place since the war's end, whereby a single senior officer was responsible for both internal affairs and state security activities in Germany. Thus Kovalchuk was appointed MGB's representative in Germany, with responsibility for all MGB operations in the Soviet zone. There was of course continued confusion on this score, and many

<u>СОВЕРШЕННО-СЕКРЕТНО.</u>
Экз.___

РАССЕКРЕЧЕНО *
Служба внешней разведки РФ   10

МИНИСТЕРСТВО ГОСУДАРСТВЕННОЙ БЕЗОПАСНОСТИ
СОЮЗА С. С. Р.

товарищу АБАКУМОВУ В.С.

ДОКЛАДНАЯ ЗАПИСКА.

По поступившим в Оперативный Сектор города
БЕРЛИНА, агентурным материалам, видно,что за последнее время военнослужащими оккупационных армий союзников
в БЕРЛИНЕ и особенно американцами среди немцев усилен-
но распространяются слухи о неизбежности войны между
СССР с одной стороны, АМЕРИКОЙ и АНГЛИЕЙ с другой, в свя-
зи с чем АНГЛО-АМЕРИКАНСКИЕ войска якобы должны в бли-
жайшее время покинуть БЕРЛИН.

Так источник "_____" сообщил, что 3 июня
1947 года _____
_____ квартиру посетил знакомый английский подполков-
ник, от которого ему стало известно, что он приехал
в БЕРЛИН по специальному заданию штаба АНГЛИЙСКИХ оккупационных войск в ГЕРМАНИИ, с целью вывоза из БЕРЛИНА на
ЗАПАД тяжелой артиллерии, так как англичане остались ра-
зочарованными после МОСКОВСКОЙ конференции и не надеются

Report, 7 June 1947, from Lt. Gen. Nikolai Kovalchuk to Minister of
State Security Viktor Abakumov, regarding conflicting reports obtained
by MGB Berlin on the inevitability of war between the USSR and the West
and rumors of the withdrawal of Anglo-American troops from Berlin.

accounts of the period still referred to NKVD or MVD (Soviet internal affairs) operations when in fact they were the province of MGB.

Under the reorganization, each MGB sector headquarters had a First Department charged with collecting intelligence in West Berlin and West Germany. The scope of this task ranged from obtaining order of battle on American, British, and French forces to acquiring political, economic, and technical information on civilian enterprises. By giving MGB this responsibility, the roles of these counterintelligence units began to overlap with those taken on by the Karlshorst residency of the First Foreign Intelligence Directorate. Competition between the departments continued to cause problems after the creation of the Committee of Information (KI) in 1947.[34]

In an organization scheme mirroring that of MGB in the USSR, Second Departments of MGB operational sectors in East Germany were responsible for counterintelligence directed at Western intelligence organizations, including offensive operations against intelligence installations and personnel in West Berlin and West Germany. The Third Departments established and ran informant networks in East German administrations, political parties, trade unions, churches, and cultural organizations. Extinguishing German opposition to the regime was MGB's top priority. During the late 1940s and early 1950s, MGB was a visible and greatly feared reminder of Soviet power across East Germany.[35]

Kovalchuk's reports to Abakumov, never before released, reflect MGB priorities during this period. In a review of activities during the first half of December 1946, Kovalchuk noted that of 487 persons arrested, 55 were Soviet citizens. Of the 432 Germans, 37 were arrested for espionage, and 191 were individuals with previous membership in the Nazi party, Gestapo, SS, or other proscribed organizations from the Hitler period. No reason was given for the arrest of the more than two hundred other Germans in the report.[36] They must have been involved with political opposition, because ordinary criminal activity would have been dealt with by the People's Police or by MVD. For a detailed picture of MGB at work in Germany, see appendix 4.

MGB Loses Foreign Intelligence

By 1947 the competition for intelligence in Germany between MGB's foreign intelligence residency and the First Departments of its counterintelligence sectors had become a problem. During 1946 the foreign intelligence residency in East Berlin had intensified its efforts to reestablish contact with prewar sources and was still searching for documents pertaining to the Nazi intelligence and counterintelligence services. According to SVR archives, information obtained by the residency revealed much about the policies and actions of the Western occupation forces, and about the activities of the Allies in Berlin.[37] Korotkov, the foreign intelligence resident in Karlshorst who was operating under the guise of deputy political adviser, left Berlin in 1946 for Moscow and took over operations involving illegals—Soviet agents documented as foreign residents and sent abroad. He was replaced by Gen. Leonid Malinin, whose links with BOB are described in appendix 3.

It was at this point that a new player joined the game, one that was to initiate major changes in how the Soviet intelligence system was organized. The Committee of Information, or KI, was formed under the USSR Council of Ministers on 30 September 1947. Some maintain that Stalin created KI in response to the American creation of CIA two weeks earlier (though given the parlous position of CIA within the US government at the time, Stalin would have been either unusually gullible or remarkably prescient had this been his motivation). In fact, there was more to his decision. Events in spring 1947 had made the Foreign Ministry a powerful Soviet office, compared with its status during the war, when the military had been dominant. The Council of Foreign Ministers, which had been created by the Potsdam Conference in 1945 and which included representatives from each of the four occupying nations, had frequent meetings whose location rotated among the capital cities of the four powers. At each of these sessions, the stakes were high as the split between East and West deepened, principally over the issue of Germany's future. Although the MGB First Directorate had highly placed agents with access to Allied negotiating positions, such information was not always made available to Soviet negotiators in time to make a difference. As the pace of negotiations picked up, Molotov became ever more demanding, insisting on immediate receipt of reports from such sources.[38] Given the reluctance of all secret intelligence services to reveal their sources or risk losing control over them, particularly those at the level of Donald Maclean or Guy Burgess in the British Foreign Office, it seems likely that an important part of Stalin's and Molotov's motivation in establishing KI was to exert direct control over the entire Soviet foreign intelligence system. Thus, both MGB and the

Chief Intelligence Directorate (GRU) of the General Staff of the Soviet Army were transferred to KI.

Initially, KI was made an independent entity subordinate to the Council of Ministers, and it was given full responsibility for all political, military, economic, and scientific-technical intelligence collection abroad as well as for counterintelligence. KI, unlike CIA, was never an openly acknowledged state organization—its existence was never publicly recognized. (Even when KI was transferred to the Foreign Ministry in 1949, its secret and autonomous status was preserved within the ministry.)[39] This is the first time that information from the decrees establishing KI has been made available.

Objections to KI within MGB were muted, perhaps because a number of senior positions were given the rank equivalent to that of minister, and twenty-five or more lesser jobs were upgraded to deputy minister. All ministers and deputy ministers had government cars with chauffeurs and could use the special government telephone service known as Kremlevka. Also, the KI decree made each ambassador the "chief resident" *(glavny rezident)* in his region and subordinated him "directly to the Committee of Information." This suggested that KI officers sent to embassies abroad would receive better cover assignments—a welcome improvement given the previous fumblings of the MGB in this regard.[40]

The various elements of KI moved to new headquarters in the former Comintern buildings near the Agricultural Exhibit in Moscow. But friction between former MGB officers and military personnel, who were overwhelmed in number and authority by members of MGB's foreign intelligence directorate, began even before the 30 September 1947 decree was formally issued. By mid-1948 Minister of Defense Nikolai Aleksandrovich Bulganin began lobbying for the return of his intelligence resources to the ministry.[41] The general staff maintained, too, that it could not rely solely on tactical intelligence elements and needed to reclaim its strategic intelligence component. By April 1949, therefore, this aspect of the KI experiment had been returned to the military. According to the official history, because "the specific character of intelligence work in the military field was not sufficiently taken into consideration in the structure of KI, . . . in January 1949, by a joint decision of the Central Committee and the government, military intelligence was removed from the functions of the Committee and again given to the Ministry of Defense." This stilted wording simply meant that the subordination of the defense ministry to MGB foreign intelligence officers had created cutthroat rivalry between the two agencies. The Ministry of Defense wanted its intelligence force back, unfettered by Chekist competition.[42]

The KI departments that remained were almost exclusively the domain of MGB foreign intelligence. In February 1949, KI was moved from its position subordinate to the Soviet Council of Ministers and placed under the Ministry of Foreign Affairs (Komitet informatsii pri MID SSSR), "with a view to better utilization of the information possibilities of the Committee of Information in the area of political intelligence, and also the subordination of political intelligence to the overall foreign policy tasks of the USSR and the current work of the Foreign Ministry (MID)." The decree limited KI to political, economic, and scientific-technical intelligence operations.[43]

The official histories do not touch on the key personalities involved or on their roles. Because KI was a secret organization within the Soviet government, there were no public announcements of assignments. Although Molotov became the first chairman of KI as foreign minister, in March 1949 he fell "out of favor with Stalin" and was succeeded in both posts by Andrei Vyshinsky, the infamous show trial prosecutor. Our review of eighty KI and MGB reports from the period 1949–52, released for the first time by SVR archives, offers a curious footnote to the story of Molotov's "downfall." Although it is true that Molotov was dropped as foreign minister and that his wife, Pauline, was exiled, he remained the "second addressee" after Stalin on all KI communications to the Politburo from March 1949 until the demise of KI in 1951. He was still the second addressee on reports from MGB as late as September 1952. During this period, the rankings of Vyshinsky and Deputy Foreign Minister Andrei Gromyko on the distribution lists varied from eighth to tenth. Given the care with which KI and MGB ranked the addressees in their dissemination lists, it seems that Molotov remained a player until Stalin turned on him at the Nineteenth Party Congress.

Vyshinsky was KI chairman for only three months. More a figure-head than a leader, he complained that "in this sensitive business I have no competence."[44] Deputy Foreign Minister Valerian Zorin served longest, but for all practical purposes KI was run by its deputy chairman, Pyotr Vasilievich Fedotov, as a virtual continuation of the foreign intelligence directorate of state security. Fedotov, who had been chief

of the MGB foreign intelligence directorate before moving to KI, was succeeded as deputy chairman in 1949 by Sergei Romanovich Savchenko.
By late 1951, in another aftershock from the arrest of Abakumov, the
former foreign intelligence directorate of state security had been removed from KI and reintegrated into MGB as the First Chief Directorate.
Consequently, the new minister of state security, Semyon Denisovich
Ignatiev, began to sign reports sent to Stalin and the Politburo.[45]

Significantly, KI initiatives in the early 1950s focused on American
targets. In February 1950, and again in September of that year (the Korean War had begun in June), KI declared intelligence work against the
United States to be "one of the most important tasks of the central apparatus and all residencies of KI in capitalist countries." In March 1951
the United States was designated by KI as the "main adversary." Intelligence work against America was not a "short-term measure but represented the very basic content of all our work for a long period of
time." Many of these decisions continued to affect the work of state security's foreign intelligence long after KI had disappeared.[46]

At the beginning of 1951, KI also zeroed in on collecting scientific
and technical information. It analyzed scientific-technical intelligence
operations and made decisions that laid the foundation for obtaining
secret documents, as well as actual models of weapons, from "the leading scientific and technical sectors of the capitalist countries." Important intelligence about nuclear weapons had been obtained earlier, but
KI's work during this period catalyzed the rapid growth of scientific-
technical operations by KGB residencies abroad in the 1960s, 1970s, and
beyond.[47]

Although KI officials failed to merge state security and military intelligence into a single entity, KI's most vexing difficulties arose from its
relations with MGB counterintelligence components in Moscow and
abroad. The initial decree establishing KI made it responsible for "the
conduct of counterintelligence work abroad." This meant that MGB
units traditionally associated with foreign counterintelligence went to
KI, along with those that pursued political and scientific-technical intelligence. These departments ensured the security of Soviet citizens
serving officially abroad, monitored the activities of Soviet émigrés residing outside the USSR, and worked with emerging security services of
the "people's democracies." All of these departments and MGB foreign
counterintelligence had worked closely together; their absorption by KI
created serious problems, particularly in residencies abroad.[48]

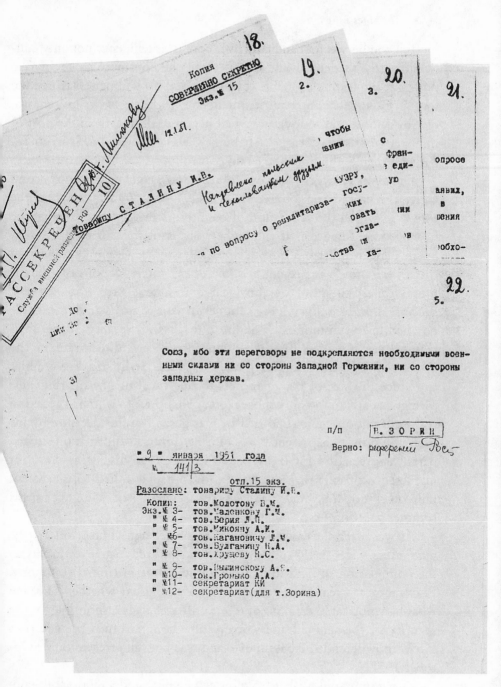

18.

Копия
СОВЕРШЕННО СЕКРЕТНО
Экз. № 15

19.

20.

21.

Товарищу Милюкову

12.1.51.

СТАЛИНУ И.В.

Направлено польским
и чехословацким друзьям

по вопросу о ремилитариза-

чтобы

с фран-
единую

УЗРУ,
госу-
ких
овать
гла-
ства и
ха-

опросе

явил,

в
нения

обхо-

22.

Союз, ибо эти переговоры не подкрепляются необходимыми военными силами ни со стороны Западной Германии, ни со стороны западных держав.

п/п   В. ЗОРИН
Верно: референт

" 9 " января 1951 года
№ 141/3

отп.15 экз.
Разослано: товарищу Сталину И.В.
Копии:
Экз.№ 3-   тов.Молотову В.М.
" № 4-   тов.Маленкову Г.М.
" № 5-   тов.Берия Л.П.
" № 6-   тов.Микояну А.И.
" № 7-   тов.Кагановичу Л.М.
" № 8-   тов.Булганину Н.А.
"   тов.Хрущеву Н.С.
" № 9-   тов.Вышинскому А.Я.
" №10-   тов.Громыко А.А.
" №11-   секретариат КИ
" №12-   секретариат(для т.Зорина)

Report, 30 January 1951, from Valerian Zorin, deputy foreign minister and head of KI after its transfer to the Foreign Ministry, to Stalin, regarding the remilitarization of West Germany. KI German specialist Samuil Meirerovich Kvastel, one of the few Jews in foreign intelligence, notes that the report was sent to the "Polish and Czech friends."

Tension between KI and MGB over counterintelligence not only contributed to KI's demise but also affected the continual jockeying for power at the top. A probable reason for Stalin's willingness to reunite foreign intelligence and counterintelligence within MGB was his removal of Abakumov, whose loyalty he had begun to doubt, from the post of minister of state security.[49] Abakumov was replaced by Semyon Ignatiev, a man Stalin knew he could control.

The case of Yevgeny Petrovich Pitovranov, chief of the MGB Second Chief Directorate for counterintelligence, is a textbook example of the extent to which the separation of counterintelligence and intelligence had become a concern at the highest levels of the Soviet leadership. Stalin played direct but also devious roles in the case.[50] It transpired that Pitovranov was present at some of the interrogations of Abakumov. Until this point, Pitovranov's career in state security had been very successful. Indeed, during the summer of Abakumov's arrest, Pitovranov had been summoned by Stalin to discuss the quality of the agent networks maintained by the counterintelligence directorate in the USSR.[51] After listening to Pitovranov's response, Stalin had directed him to reduce the size of the agent nets to one-third or one-quarter their former size, retaining only those secret collaborators who had access to real information. Stalin said that he was guided in this decision by his prerevolutionary experience in acquiring political information. In apparent appreciation for Pitovranov's frankness in discussing counterintelligence problems, he was the only outsider called to the Kursk railroad station a few days later to say farewell when Stalin left for his summer vacation.[52]

As was often the case with Stalin, this brief sign of favor offered no guarantees. Later in 1951, Pitovranov was required to give testimony to the commission investigating Abakumov. After his initial testimony, Pitovranov was called in again by Beria and asked whether he knew what had motivated Abakumov—who, after all, was responsible for the security of the senior leaders, many of whom had died prematurely. Pitovranov defended Abakumov—and was himself arrested on 29 October 1951.[53]

Pitovranov told us that from his cell he prepared a report for Stalin in which he made specific recommendations for improving state security, referring to the meeting at which they had discussed the problems of the service. He noted that jealousy and competition between

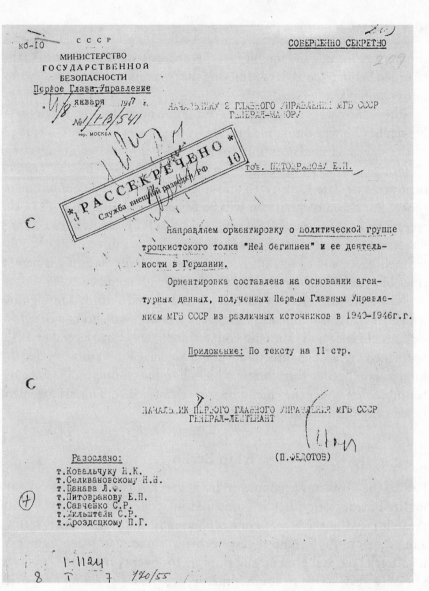

СССР

МИНИСТЕРСТВО
ГОСУДАРСТВЕННОЙ
БЕЗОПАСНОСТИ

Первое Главн. Управление

« 1/8 » января 1947 г.

№ 1-В/541

гор. МОСКВА

СОВЕРШЕННО СЕКРЕТНО

209

РАССЕКРЕЧЕНО
Служба внешней разведки РФ 10

НАЧАЛЬНИКУ 2 ГЛАВНОГО УПРАВЛЕНИЯ МГБ СССР
ГЕНЕРАЛ-МАЙОРУ

тов. ПИТОВРАНОВУ Е.П.

Направляем ориентировку о политической группе троцкистского толка "Ней бегиннен" и ее деятельности в Германии.

Ориентировка составлена на основании агентурных данных, полученных Первым Главным Управлением МГБ СССР из различных источников в 1940-1946г.г.

Приложение: По тексту на II стр.

НАЧАЛЬНИК ПЕРВОГО ГЛАВНОГО УПРАВЛЕНИЯ МГБ СССР
ГЕНЕРАЛ-ЛЕЙТЕНАНТ

(П.ФЕДОТОВ)

Разослано:
т.Ковальчуку Н.К.
т.Селивановскому Н.Н.
т.Цанава Л.Ф.
т.Питовранову Е.П.
т.Савченко С.Р.
т.Мильштейн С.Р.
т.Дроздецкому П.Г.

1-1124

8   Т   7   170/55

Letter, 8 January 1947, from Lt. Gen. Pyotr Fedotov, chief, MGB's First Chief Directorate (foreign intelligence), to Maj. Gen. Yevgeny Pitovranov, chief, MGB's Second Chief Directorate (internal counterintelligence), transmitting a study on the political organization New Beginnings, linked to OSS and believed to be still active in Germany in 1946.

counterintelligence and intelligence were interfering with the work, and he urged Stalin to consider reunifying the two services. After much ado, Pitovranov was released.

Pitovranov was recovering at a rest home near Moscow when on 10 November he was summoned to Moscow to meet Stalin and members of the newly elected Central Committee. Stalin said at the meeting: "There is consideration being given to radically improving the work of the organs of state security, to unifying intelligence and counterintelligence. For this a commission will be formed, including in it all of the secretaries of the Central Committee and also Pitovranov. Create a chief directorate of state security in which there will be a directorate of counterintelligence and an intelligence directorate. Vasily Ryasnoy is named chief of counterintelligence, and Pitovranov, of intelligence."[54]

Not content merely to have abolished KI and returned foreign intelligence to MGB, Stalin also felt that it was necessary to combine foreign intelligence and domestic counterintelligence. In December 1952, he formed a new chief directorate of intelligence. Pitovranov headed the foreign intelligence directorate, which, like the counterintelligence directorate, fell under the chief directorate's authority. This arrangement lasted only until Stalin's death.[55]

KI in Berlin

Few of the problems encountered by KI and its residencies abroad during its bureaucratic lifetime compared in scope and complexity with those it faced in the Soviet zone of Germany. MGB operational sectors and groups in Berlin, and the five provinces under MGB deputy minister Kovalchuk, had been up and running for over two years. They were not only very active in counterintelligence, issues affecting the Soviet colony, and émigré affairs, but they also continued to collect intelligence on West Germany even after KI's creation. (For more about MGB's activities in East Germany, see appendix 4.)

When KI assumed control of the MGB foreign intelligence residency in East Berlin, then headed by General Malinin, the tenuous relations between the residency and MGB only worsened. It had always been difficult for the foreign intelligence and counterintelligence groups to coordinate their operations, even when they were both under the MGB. But when KI took over, the situation got so bad that MGB counterintelligence operatives actually tried to recruit members of the KI residency as informers.[56]

Through its contacts with Malinin, BOB had inadvertently added to KI's problems in Berlin. In April 1947, Yakov Fyodorovich Tishchenko, known as Razin, was told that he would replace Malinin as Karlshorst resident, but the assignment was delayed because of the shift of the MGB foreign intelligence directorate to KI.[57] When Razin finally arrived in early 1948, just as the blockade crisis began, it was as head of a greatly enlarged residency that included military intelligence. The KI residency's main task was to conduct intelligence operations in West Berlin and West Germany. But not long after Razin's arrival, military intelligence personnel were taken out of the KI residency, as were émigré operations. Meanwhile, the first departments of the MGB operational sectors continued to collect intelligence, claiming that their "intelligence operations were carried out for counterintelligence purposes." As a result, duplication in MGB and KI operations continued.[58]

Despite this inauspicious beginning, the KI residency under Razin had excellent official cover, which provided an element of security for its operations that BOB never matched. Razin's own cover position was that of deputy to Political Adviser Semyonov, and cover for operations personnel of the residency was provided by other directorates. The deputy resident, Boris Nalivaiko, for instance, was listed as chief of the visa section. The residency also took advantage of the activities of the directorates to further its work against targets in West Berlin and West Germany.[59]

According to Razin, the residency enjoyed considerable success. He specifically praised Nalivaiko for having achieved excellent results. One coup recalled by Razin was the acquisition of the official operational diaries of Col. Gen. Franz Halder, chief of the German General Staff. The diaries, with Halder's handwritten corrections on each page, covered operations on all fronts during the war.[60]

But once the blockade was in full swing, the residency was obviously involved in more than acquiring wartime trophies. Another official KGB source states that in 1948 its agents had infiltrated the major West German political parties and had penetrated Allied military administrations. A number of valuable recruitments were made in émigré organizations in West Germany, and the quantity of agents rose significantly to include government officials, financiers, politicians, and

Копия
СОВЕРШЕННО СЕКРЕТНО
Экз. № 7

РАССЕКРЕЧЕНО
Справка внешней разведки РФ

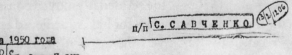

* Направлено сообщение
польским и чехословацким друзьям (декабрь 1950 г.)

    Комитет Информации располагает следующими сведениями о планах создания разведывательной службы в Западной Германии.

    На англо-американских совещаниях по вопросу о ремилитаризации Западной Германии, происходивших в Висбадене и Бад-Наугейме в середине августа с.г., было принято решение о создании при будущей западногерманской армии разведывательной и контрразведывательной службы. В задачи этой службы должно входить получение не только военной, но и политической информации о Германской демократической республике, СССР и странах народной демократии.

    Западногерманскую разведывательную службу предполагается создать на базе слияния так называемого "Оперативного бюро" (созданный недавно боннским правительством разведывательный орган) и разведывательной организации генерал-майора ГЕЛЕНА (бывший начальник подотдела "Иностранные армии - восток" главного командования германской армии), состоящей из бывших сотрудников немецкой разведки.

    Руководителем разведывательной службы намечен полковник Фридрих ГЕЙНЦ (бывший командир разведывательного полка "Бранденбург", последнее время был руководителем "ведомства по охране конституции" в земле Северный Рейн-Вестфалия).

                  п/п С. САВЧЕНКО

" 31 " августа 1950 года
    № 3130/с
         Отп. 7 экз.
Разослано: тов. Вышинскому А.Я.
         тов. Абакумову В.С.
Экз. № 2 - тов. Захарову М.В.
   " № 4 - секретариат КИ

KI report, 31 August 1950, to Vyshinsky at the Foreign Ministry, with copies to MGB chief Abakumov and GRU chief Matvei Zakharov, regarding the creation of a West German intelligence service.

important journalists, all of whom probably contributed to the KI reporting that we obtained from SVR archives on the blockade.[61]

In 1950, Razin was recalled to Moscow. His replacement in Berlin was Lt. Gen. Ivan Ivanovich Ilichev, the former chief of military intelligence and a deputy head of KI. It may be that his assignment came about when military intelligence returned to the Defense Ministry in spring 1949 and Ilichev found himself without a job.[62] In any case, the Ilichev assignment resulted in a major expansion of KI Germany. The cover arrangements for this expanded effort were superb and made it even more difficult for BOB's counterintelligence branch to develop an accurate picture of Soviet intelligence in East Berlin. We learn of it now for the first time.

On 19 April 1950 three separate foreign intelligence residencies were created, each under different cover: one in the diplomatic mission, another in the Soviet element of the Allied Control Council, and the third in Bogdan Kobulov's Directorate of Soviet Joint Stock Companies in Germany (USIG). These residencies were all under the direction of General Ilichev, whose own cover was counselor to the Soviet Control Commission; his covert assignment was representative in Germany of the Collegium of KI, or "chief resident."[63] The heads of two of the individual residencies were officers who would figure prominently in KI and KGB in later years: Vasily Romanovich Sitnikov and Yelisei Tikhonovich Sinitsyn (a.k.a. Yeliseev).[64]

The third residency under USIG cover also deserves mention.[65] USIG, as we have seen, was a primary target of BOB's scientific-technical operations aimed at the Soviet nuclear weapons program. In addition to running Wismut, the uranium facility, and other enterprises in East Germany, it canvassed West Germany and Europe for industrial components not available in the USSR. This cover, willingly provided by Bogdan Kobulov, permitted the third residency to piggyback on these activities in order to spot and recruit Western industrialists and engineers. Although it had no clue that the Soviet officers involved were affiliated with KI, BOB realized they were Soviet intelligence and followed their activities closely.[66]

After KI was abolished on 1 November 1951 and MGB regained control of foreign intelligence in January 1952, the three Berlin residencies were dissolved. Their personnel were transferred to the MGB apparat in Karlshorst, where they became Department B-1. This department assumed responsibility for all foreign intelligence operations in Germany.[67] The time was right for this change. The growing discord between KI and MGB had not only hindered Soviet intelligence gathering on the Berlin blockade and the effects of the Korean War on Germany, it had also stirred up trouble with the East German party and government that could not be kept "within the family" of Soviet intelligence services.

3

The Berlin Blockade Challenges
Western Ingenuity and Perseverance

"I always regarded the blockade as a miscalculation by the Russians. They wanted to see how far they could go, and they went too far."
—PETER SICHEL, deputy chief of BOB

As the East Germans became more resentful of Soviet occupation policies, and as disagreements between the former Allies intensified, sporadic Soviet harassment of land vehicles and airplanes entering West Berlin evolved into a blockade and sparked fear of war. Although the Soviets called the blockade a response to Western actions on currency reform, it soon became a test of Western determination to remain in Berlin. The feeling among Western leaders that Czechoslovakia had been lost as a free nation and that they were being strong-armed in Berlin made them determined to create a West German state that would be part of a European defense and would sustain close emotional, economic, and juridical ties with West Berlin. Intelligence played a key role in determining each side's position throughout this crisis. Although BOB's reports on Soviet and East German military capabilities and intentions allayed Western fears of war, extensive Soviet intelligence on Western resolve to remain in Berlin did not deter Stalin until a massive airlift of food and supplies into West Berlin, never foreseen or reported by KI, caused him to lift the blockade. The intelligence aspects of the blockade as seen from both sides have never before been revealed.

The Soviets Prepare for a Showdown

The year 1947 ended as had 1945, with SMA moving openly to remove leaders of the Soviet zone Christian Democratic Party (CDU). When Marshal Zhukov undermined the CDU leaders in December 1945, news of his action, reported by BOB, warned of Soviet intentions that many found difficult to believe but impossible to ignore. To many American officials in Berlin, the Soviets' willingness to demonstrate openly their intolerance of political opposition suggested that they were preparing to oust the Western Allies from Berlin. The press in the Soviet zone had already begun questioning the need for four-power occupation of Berlin, and the American embassy in Moscow predicted a "noisy campaign to scare us out."[1] It turned out to be more than noise. On 22 December 1947, CIA reported that "there was a possibility of steps being taken in Berlin by the Soviet authorities to force the other occupying powers to remove [their forces] from Berlin."[2]

General Clay and Currency Reform

General Clay, who since the surrender had argued that openness and persuasion could effectively counter Soviet policies in East Germany and East Berlin, had been among those American leaders converted by the compelling evidence of Soviet intentions. His new resolve came just in time to buttress his idea that currency reform was essential. By 1947 General Clay had become convinced that further economic recovery in the Western zones would be impossible as long as people no longer had confidence in the existing, worthless currency. Action on reform was needed, preferably in all of Germany, but if this proved impossible, then in the Western zones alone, and over Soviet objections. The Soviets saw that Clay's plans posed a direct challenge, and they realized that currency reform in West Germany would not only make the split between the Soviet and Western zones irrevocable but also bring into much sharper contrast the differences between their respective economies.

The Soviets learned early of Clay's currency proposal, but many of their reports to Stalin seemed designed only to soothe the dictator, who was convinced that the Americans would abandon Berlin under pressure. On 31 December 1947, for example, the Berlin KI residency passed along to Stalin a report from "well-informed Americans" that "the Berlin question causes the Americans much concern. They recognize that the

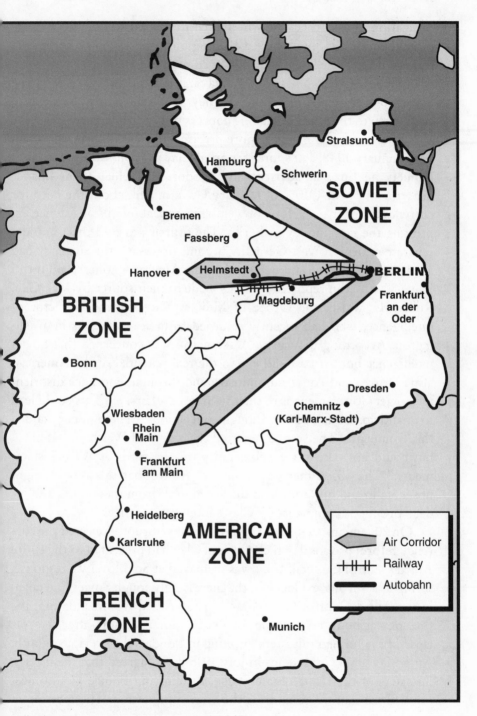

Allied transportation routes to West Berlin.

realization of a currency reform limited to the Western zones will deprive them of the possibility of holding on to Berlin, even within the framework of the present four-power administration. At the same time, all of the anti-Communist propaganda carried on by them illegally in the Soviet zone originates in Berlin. . . . They want to hold on to Berlin at all costs, even to the point of making concessions to the Russians."[3]

Other reports were even more precise and should have registered. On 5 January 1948, a KI source reported Clay's conversations with Jack Bennett, his financial adviser, and Theodore Ball, chief of the finance department of the Office of Military Government, about the need for currency reform on a four-power basis and about US insistence on printing the new money in Berlin. The source was told that should a separate reform in West Germany become necessary, the currency had already been printed and delivered to the American zone.[4] And on 15 January, KI Berlin reported remarks made to their source by Maj. Gen. Robert L. Walsh, the Office of Military Government's director of intelligence, who had recently returned from consultations in Washington. According to Walsh, "Washington was concerned that Soviet intelligence not turn a blind eye to the real potential of the American armed forces and American industry and through ignorance disorient the Soviet Government as to the true state of affairs. . . . This could lead to unanticipated and poorly thought-out actions." The residency added this comment: "The source reported the words of Walsh verbatim . . . but could not take any responsibility for the truth of Walsh's statements." This disclaimer was common. Aware that this report might upset Stalin and his cronies, KI distanced itself from these frank and indeed prophetic comments by Clay's intelligence officer.[5]

On 20 January 1948, Marshal Sokolovsky abruptly rejected the currency reform proposal, which General Clay had presented to the entire Allied Control Council. Clay was dismayed at Sokolovsky's response, seeing it as further evidence of the increasingly tough Soviet line taken in the Allied Control Council and in the Allied Kommandatura, the four-power body responsible for Berlin administration, after the collapse of the foreign ministers' meeting in London the previous month. At the Potsdam Conference in July 1945 it was agreed that the foreign ministers of the United States, USSR, Britain, and France would meet every three months to address the German question. The meeting in London in December 1947 was to be the last attempt to resolve some of the obstructions to Allied cooperation on Germany. The attempt failed.

Clay sent an alarmist cable to Washington on 5 March predicting that war "may come with dramatic suddenness." The cable was surprising because it was not based on intelligence reports that the Soviets were preparing for war. Indeed, it was not until 12 March that BOB chief Dana Durand and his deputy Peter Sichel first heard of Clay's cable. Their response was to repeat their estimate of December 1947 that the Soviets would not use armed force to achieve political goals in Germany. On 16 March, CIA came through with further assurance for President Truman: there was "no reliable evidence that the USSR intends to resort to military action within the next sixty days."[6]

The Stage Is Set for a Blockade

In retrospect, it is easy to see that the Soviets set out to make the most of the crisis of 1948–49 by furthering their goal of eliminating the Western presence in Berlin, and that when they did not succeed, they settled for improving their grip on East Germany. But the situation did not seem so simple at the time. Many factors and seemingly unrelated events elsewhere determined the outcome. January and February 1948 were relatively quiet, despite some Soviet interference with US and British military trains and the usual wrangling in the Allied Control Council and Kommandatura. Suddenly, in late February, events in Prague cast a shadow that extended to Berlin. Although the Czech decision not to participate in the Marshall Plan the previous summer had been disturbing, the uneasy coalition that had governed that country since the war seemed to be holding. It ended brutally when the leader of the Czech Communist Party, Klement Gottwald, aided by the workers' militia, forced President Eduard Benes to resign. Although Western leaders should certainly have recognized the fragility of the Czech coalition, the extent of covert Soviet influence within the Benes government and the determination of Gottwald to achieve total power shocked the West. The Communist takeover in Prague created an atmosphere of fear in Europe. It certainly contributed to the Clay "crisis" cable.

By March, Soviet interference with Western movement to and from Berlin by road and rail had begun in earnest. Next the Soviets demanded the closure of the American first-aid station on the Berlin-Helmstedt highway and the withdrawal of US Army Signal Corps teams responsible for maintaining long-distance cables running through the Soviet zone to the American zone.[7] On 20 March the Soviets walked out of the Allied Control Council. By month's end, the Soviets had threatened to halt Allied military trains unless passengers and baggage were checked by Soviet personnel. Some have thought that these actions were part of a large-scale Soviet campaign to oust the Allies from Berlin.[8] But BOB remained firm in its view that "the Russians were seeking political rather than military objectives." The March crisis ended on the last day of the month, when an American train reached Helmstedt without having been stopped or inspected by the Soviets. But the problems that were to lead to a complete blockade were still unresolved.

On 6 April tension reached a new high when a harassing Soviet fighter collided with a British passenger plane, causing it to crash and killing all on board. On 15 May KI reported a conversation with General Clay by "an American close to the general." Reportedly Clay said that "the Americans would remain in Berlin until he received a direct order to leave the city." Clay said he feared that the next step by the Russians in their campaign to force the Allies from Berlin would be the complete closure of the air corridors. In this case, Clay would be "forced to organize fighter protection for American transport aircraft. ... If the Russians wanted to prevent flights of American aircraft through the corridors, they would have to fire on the American machines."

The British and French took a somewhat different position. Clay was reported to say in the same conversation that "the French were 'fed up' with the worsening situation" and that things were not "much easier" with the British. Sir Brian Robertson, the British military governor, for example, had "orders from London not to exacerbate relations with the Russians." The British government had tied Robertson's hands following the air catastrophe on 6 April: after making an energetic oral protest to Sokolovsky, Robertson had been instructed by London to send "a much weaker letter." KI, which received a copy of this report, added this covering note: "The information is believed reliable. The SMA leadership has been advised."[9]

The Blockade Begins

When the Western Allies introduced the new currency, the West Mark, in their occupation zones on 20 June, the Soviets cut off electrical power to the Western sectors of Berlin, closed road and rail connections to the city, and stopped barge traffic. Food and fuel deliveries from the Soviet zone, on which West Berlin relied, ceased. By the end of June, a complete blockade had begun. On 1 July the Soviets walked out of the Kommandatura.

Askold Vsevolodovich Lebedev, a member of the SMA secretariat at the time, recalls the onset of the blockade as seen from Karlshorst. In his view, the arguments over currency were secondary to the Soviet decision to force the Allies to leave Berlin. People on Sokolovsky's staff rejoiced when the blockade began, believing that the Allies would be forced to leave the entire city to the Soviets. The Soviets gave little thought to whether the blockade could fail. Most took it for granted that with without food and fuel from East Germany, the Western powers had no choice but to withdraw.[10] But the Americans had a card up their sleeves: soon after the blockade began, an airlift was launched to supply the people of West Berlin with food and other necessities of daily living. This gutsy move startled the Soviets and buoyed the West Berliners, who recognized in this act American resolve to stay and support their city during the crisis.

BOB Rises to the Challenge

How did the blockade affect BOB? Just before the borders were closed, analysts in CIA's Office of Reports and Estimates (ORE) were concerned that "the Soviets have both tightened their 'security' measures and manifested greater intransigence in all city affairs. As a result, the general usefulness of Berlin as a center of intelligence has been impaired."[11] But on 30 June 1948, after the blockade had begun, a progress report by the Office of Special Operations (OSO), the element in CIA Headquarters that directed field operations, was much more reassuring: "Economic coverage of the Russian zone of Germany . . . continued during the month in the same volume and quality as heretofore. . . . Despite tightened security, our operations are still succeeding in penetrating the principal agencies of the Russian zone."[12]

One might assume that heightened Soviet security, along with restrictions of movement between West Germany and Berlin, inhibited BOB's agent operations. Actually, the opposite was true. Movement within Berlin itself was never completely halted, despite Soviet attempts to interrupt it. Further, the blockade angered many East Berliners, some of whom decided to cooperate with Western intelligence for the first time.

A good example of BOB's continuing coverage of economic issues was the account of a conference on 28 June 1948 in Karlshorst attended by Marshal Sokolovsky, Col. Sergei Tiulpanov, and members of the East German Industrial Committee. This report helped explain Soviet insistence later that interzonal trade must be resumed as a condition of lifting the blockade, and it demonstrated how surprised the Soviets were by the airlift. Sokolovsky opened the meeting by asking the German industrialists about the effect of the blockade if West German imports became unavailable. The Germans replied that sugar refineries would suffer if Western steel piping were not delivered, canneries would be at a standstill without many of their Western raw materials, the Baltic fishing fleet would encounter problems if spare parts were not available, and heavy industry, including the steel mills, would be crippled without imports.

This recital surprised the Russians, who had had no idea how dependent East German industries were on the West. Sokolovsky reportedly said that three options were possible: "1. Start a war. 2. Lift travel restrictions on Berlin. 3. Leave Berlin entirely to the West, giving them a rail line." Tiulpanov rejected war but said that Russians would lose face if travel restrictions were lifted. He opined that the West, having to feed West Berlin, "would have more on their hands than they had bargained for," although he added that the West might subsist by extensively importing "concentrated foods." Clearly, as of 28 June 1948, no one in Karlshorst had envisaged anything like an airlift.[13]

As the Berlin crisis intensified, BOB reported on SED's plans to form "action committees in factories" and to be ready to conduct strikes and demonstrations in the Western sectors in order "to give the impression that the presence of the Western Allies in Berlin is made impossible by the will of the population rather than by Soviet compulsion."[14] This strategy was reminiscent of that used in the Prague putsch, where party-controlled factory committees and militia played an important role in the takeover by the Czech Communist Party. These same BOB reports described attempts to jam the American-controlled police radio system in West Berlin, which was "essential in case of disorders and rioting." The US Air Force, apprised of the situation, supplied a transmitter strong enough to broadcast over this interference.[15]

As the blockade continued BOB provided continuous reporting on Soviet efforts to eliminate the last vestiges of a unified city administration and police force. For example, when the Soviets left the Kommandatura on 1 July 1948, it was agreed that all sides "would continue to respect quadripartite agreements." But on 14 July the Soviets ordered Police President Paul Markgraf to dismiss three senior police officials, an act that was supposed to require four-power concurrence. This split the Berlin police administration and led to the establishment of a West Berlin police force with a new chief.[16] Although Markgraf was permitted to remain in office for a while after the split, he was not considered politically reliable by either the Soviets or SED. During the next year the Soviets replaced several senior East Berlin police officials like Markgraf with more ideologically suitable candidates from the Soviet zone police.[17]

A BOB report at the end of 1948 foreshadowed the coming of the 1961 Berlin Wall. On 10 December 1948 the director of CIA sent President Truman a memorandum analyzing the recent Soviet action of recognizing "an East Berlin government." Analysts predicted that the "USSR may now impose a more stringent blockade of the western sectors of Berlin. The USSR can cite the recent 'illegal' elections in the western sectors, or the possible introduction of the western mark as the sole legal currency as an excuse to throw a cordon around the western area."[18] On the same day, BOB reported that on 28 December the Soviets planned to barricade Soviet-sector streets leading into the Western sectors, leaving open only selected, controlled thoroughfares. But police officials realized that it was "impossible to hermetically seal the sector boundaries," even with the projected increase in sector border patrols. Efforts to control passengers carrying packages on subway and elevated railroads were frustrated by resistance from passengers and by the reluctance of railroad personnel to cooperate. And finally, the East Berlin police had to contend with the thousands of West Berliners who still worked in the Soviet sector.[19] It took the Soviets and SED more than twelve years to create the cordon mentioned in the memo to Truman.

BOB also reported that the police in the Soviet sector were being trained for various contingencies. One possibility was the transfer of all authority in the Soviet zone and greater Berlin to a German government, which would be followed by the withdrawal of Soviet armed forces. It was expected that the Allies would follow suit, at least in Berlin. The East Berlin police would ensure that the Western sectors recognized the authority of the Soviet zone government throughout all sectors of Germany.[20] In its treatment of the troop withdrawal option, the press in East Berlin gave favorable attention to the "Korean action" in which the Soviets had withdrawn, followed by the Americans.

22

CLASSIFICATION   SECRET

CENTRAL INTELLIGENCE AGENCY   REPORT NO.

INFORMATION REPORT

CD NO.

COUNTRY : Germany (Russian Zone)   DATE DISTR. 30 December 1948

SUBJECT Soviet Measures to Further Tighten the   NO. OF PAGES 2
Sector Blockade in Berlin

PLACE
ACQUIRED Germany, Berlin   NO. OF ENCLS.
(LISTED BELOW).

43721

DATE OF INFO. 10-28 December 1948   SUPPLEMENT TO
REPORT NO.

GRADING OF SOURCE						COLLECTOR'S PRELIMINARY GRADING OF CONTENT					
COMPLETELY RELIABLE	USUALLY RELIABLE	FAIRLY RELIABLE	NOT USUALLY RELIABLE	NOT RELIABLE	CANNOT BE JUDGED	CONFIRMED BY OTHER SOURCES	PROBABLY TRUE	POSSIBLY TRUE	DOUBTFUL	PROBABLY FALSE	CANNOT BE JUDGED
A.	B. X	C.	D.	E.	F.	1.	2. X	3.			

THIS DOCUMENT CONTAINS INFORMATION AFFECTING THE NATIONAL DEFENSE OF THE UNITED STATES WITHIN THE MEANING OF THE ESPIONAGE ACT SO U. S. C., 31 AND 32, AS AMENDED. ITS TRANSMISSION OR THE REVELATION OF ITS CONTENTS IN ANY MANNER TO AN UNAUTHORIZED PERSON IS PROHIBITED BY LAW. REPRODUCTION OF THIS FORM IS PROHIBITED.

THIS IS UNEVALUATED INFORMATION

SOURCE

1. The head of the Kriminal Direktion of the East Berlin Police stated on
28 December 1948 that the complete sealing of Soviet Sector streets leading
into the western sectors is to be carried out soon. With the exception
of a few main thoroughfares, the streets will be closed with wooden barriers.
Traffic through the streets remaining open will be closely checked by foot
patrols. Vehicles attempting to pass from the Soviet Sector to the western
sectors without a proper police permit are to be summarily confiscated.
(Source Comment: Police officials are aware that it is impossible to hermetically
seal the sector boundaries. It is assumed that the Soviets want to show
their strength by the control of motor traffic and add further discomforts
to life in Berlin.

2. The following measures are being taken to increase sector boundary controls:

    a. Paul Markgraf stated at a meeting of his staff on 10 December 1948 that
    the auxiliary police (Wachpolizei) would be absorbed into the uniformed
    police (Schutzpolizei).
    b. The duties of the auxiliary police are to be taken over by civilian guards.
    c. On 21 December according to the Markgraf Kriminal Direktion, the sector
    boundary patrols were increased by 1000 men. Police dogs were to be used.
    d. According to a less reliable sub-source, 2000 Land Saxony paramilitary police
    garrisoned in Berlin-Friedrichshagen are to be absorbed into the Soviet
    Sector police on 28 December.

    (Field Comment: There are 1300 auxiliary police in the Soviet Sector. If the
    above figures are correct, this means that the uniformed police of the Soviet
    Sector have been strengthened by 3300.)

3. Increased control of U-Bahn and S-Bahn passengers at the sector boundaries
began on 26 December. Police are under instructions to confiscate all packages
larger than brief cases. There is no legal basis for such confiscation.
Markgraf was instructed by the Central Komendatura to issue a police proclama-
tion justifying the action. The police met with scattered resistance from
outraged passengers. Railroad personnel showed passive resistance and in
many cases, gave passengers warning or concealed parcels. As a result
police assigned to this duty are being strengthened.

Document No.
NO CHANGE in Class. ☐
☒ DECLASSIFIED
Class. CHANGED TO: TS S C
Auth: DDA REG. 77/1763
Date: By:

WARNING NOTICE: THIS DISTRIBUTION LISTING MUST BE
EXCISED BEFORE PUBLIC RELEASE OF THIS DOCUMENT

CLASSIFICATION   SECRET

DISTRIBUTION

ARMY	X	AIR	X	FBI					

BY CABLE

CIA information report, 30 December 1948, regarding Soviet measures
to further tighten the sector blockade in Berlin.

The second Soviet option, to be implemented if the Allies refused to withdraw, involved fomenting large-scale riots and disorders in West Berlin by forces under the clandestine leadership of SED. These disorders would be used to justify intervention by the East Berlin police, which in turn would result in the Western sectors' being incorporated into the Soviet zone. To this end the Berlin police would be reinforced by politically reliable policemen from elsewhere in East Germany.[21]

Two BOB reports from SED sources during early 1949 described the Soviets' and SED's apparent resignation to lifting the blockade. This meant that SED would need to make a transition to working illegally in West Berlin. The Soviets and SED expected a rapid decline in SED membership and the possible outlawing of the party. In anticipation, "all supplies, equipment, files, and other party property [in the Western sectors] that can be spared" were moved to storage points in the Soviet sector. Personnel deemed capable of performing work in illegal circumstances had been selected, and clandestine communication facilities had been set up. Among the tasks of this group would be infiltration of "bourgeois parties" and mass organizations.[22] Meanwhile, in the Soviet zone, SED was trying to purge its membership of politically unreliable and indifferent members, and to change the character of the party from that of a mass organization to that of a smaller, tightly disciplined group of activists who could transform East Germany according to the Soviet plan.[23]

At the same time, BOB's reports that neither the Soviet military nor East German police paramilitary units appeared to be preparing for the initiation of full-scale hostilities helped to dispel talk of imminent war. Coverage of the Russian liaison section of the East German police ensured that BOB would hear of any orders to make major movements in armored or motorized formations. As the case officer for one of the sources involved put it, "You don't move tanks without controlling the streets first." Even more important was information on the Soviet order of battle and troop movements, which BOB received during the blockade from a Soviet major then stationed in Dresden. The major, who had been wounded during the Soviet capture of Berlin, was nursed back to health by a German nurse who later became his mistress. Occasionally the woman, who lived in West Berlin, met him and brought back his reports. He provided information on the status of Soviet forces, their morale, and their equipment. He also identified which troop movements in and around Berlin were intended solely as scare tactics.[24]

The potential threat to West Berlin's security was thought to come not only from the Soviet military, but also from Soviet sector and Soviet zone paramilitary police, who had been deployed in West Berlin to "restore order." BOB was the first to report on plans to create these units, which would one day form the cadre of the East German People's Army.[25] They were initiated in 1948, and by early 1949 four units had been organized in East Berlin. But they were lightly armed; their heaviest weapons were machine guns. Further, they lacked conviction, discipline, and training. This was particularly true of the two units formed in Saxony. The soldiers had been recruited from among factory laborers, who were thought to be politically more reliable than Berliners. But when they were brought to Berlin to help control the city elections on 5 December 1948 (the Soviets had outlawed elections in their sector), many left their posts.[26] It was doubtful that these paramilitary units could be relied on to confront the Allied military in West Berlin.[27]

Those who served in BOB during 1948–49 remember that morale was never higher. As the blockade wore on, there was talk within the American community of evacuating some or all dependents. This did not affect BOB, where wives worked at all manner of jobs and added to the sense of a common effort. And BOB's contributions during the blockade were outstanding. Gordon Stewart, who headed the German mission in Heidelberg, felt that senior policymakers in Germany and Washington relied heavily on BOB's reports. He specifically recalled Tom Polgar's analysis, which had emphasized that there was virtually no indication that the Soviets intended to take military action against the West.[28]

KI Reporting: Often Misleading, Potentially Dangerous

"[Americans will] remain in Berlin and make maximum use of air transport to supply the civilian population."
—US Secretary of State George Marshall, 30 June 1948

"The American mood has changed from warlike to dejected. The many American aircraft arriving in Berlin are taking out documents and other property of the American administration."
—Berlin KI resident report to Marshal Sokolovsky, 3 July 1948

KI reporting during the Berlin blockade was often startlingly misleading.[29] No better example can be found of how Cold War reporting from well-placed Soviet sources was filtered and revised until a report was fashioned that was sure to appease Stalin. But although Stalin's approval may have temporarily secured the career paths of those KI officers who told him good news, the misleading reports endangered everyone in Berlin. The reports prolonged the blockade by underestimating both Western resolve and how apprehension in the West caused by the blockade led to efforts to enlist West Germany in European defense. The Soviets portrayed West German rearmament instead as an offensive move by the Allies.

On 3 August, the chief of the MGB Berlin operational sector, Maj. Gen. Aleksei Moiseevich Vul, sent a summary of conditions in Berlin to the MGB chief in Germany, Lt. Gen. Nikolai Ivanovich Kovalchuk.[30] After blaming the split in the city administration and police on the machinations of the Anglo-Americans, Vul claimed that the airlift was not providing sufficient food for the Western sectors. Vul also noted that whereas SMA expected more than two million people to take advantage of Soviet offers of food assistance, because of the SPD's "furious propaganda campaign" only nineteen thousand did so.[31] He also described Allied plans to increase the number of aircraft assigned to the airlift.[32] Vul understated the case. To increase the frequency of flights, the Allies, assisted by seventeen thousand West Berliners (half of them women), built a new airfield from scratch in the French sector in just three months. On Easter Sunday 1949, the airlift set a record of 1,398 flights—12,941 tons of goods—in one day.[33]

Meanwhile, KI was delivering its own reports to Moscow after the imposition of the blockade and during the protracted negotiations that finally ended it. The sources of these reports ranged from agents with access to "American circles" in Berlin or Frankfurt am Main to solid documentary material such as official French and British communications. The French and British sources were by far the best. The sources in "American circles" are not named, but one has the impression that the information was obtained in some cases from American officials who held left-wing views and who disagreed with US occupation policies. For example, the Berlin residency source "Brat" (Russian for brother) relayed a conversation he had had with Leo Bauer in early January 1948.[34] In the KI report, Bauer described a discussion with an employee of the Office of Military Government's Information Control Division about the failure of US anti-Communist propaganda and the plans to create a West German state. According to Bauer, his friend did not know "whether he would remain in Berlin, or be fired in a routine 'purge.'" He did not want to return to the United States, however, because "he had a politically 'tarnished' reputation [left-wing political views] and there he would be without work."[35] Because both Bauer and his friend had been in Hesse at the end of the war, it is likely that they held similar views. It would have been relatively simple for the KI residency in Berlin to exploit such individuals.[36]

On 3 July 1948, a report prepared by the Berlin KI resident himself was received in Moscow. It apparently consolidated several reports from a source in the American military administration who had not been fully tested. The source claimed that "until July, the conviction was widespread among leading American circles that Washington would concur in Clay's proposal to use force against the Russians. . . . Various members of the staff began to plan for a breakthrough by tanks from Helmstedt to Berlin, opening a corridor of two kilometers in width, ensuring movement along this corridor under the protection of American troops. Clay rejected these plans as fantasies because the tanks might not make it to Berlin after the breakthrough, and there would be no corridor."[37]

Meanwhile, the Americans and British continued to consolidate their zones in West Germany as a new territory, "Bizonia." KI received a report on 14 July 1948 of a July meeting of the American and British deputy military governors and German representatives, including Ludwig Erhard, the future West German economics minister, at the I. G. Farben building in Frankfurt. The report emphasized the desire of the West German representatives to expand trade with the Soviet zone under the aegis of the new bizonal government as soon as the blockade was lifted so that the Communist Party in West Germany could not exploit this issue either as a propaganda weapon or as a device to improve the party's finances. (The greater the volume of interzonal trade, the easier it would be for the East Germans and Communist sympathizers in West Germany to siphon a percentage of interzonal trade profits into KPD coffers.)[38]

On 6 August, KI Berlin circulated an agent report relating to the forthcoming Kremlin meetings on Berlin.[39] Entitled "A Change in American Policies on the Berlin Questions," the report claimed that "among prominent members of the American administration in Berlin, it is believed that the Western powers must give in to the Soviet Union. . . . The Americans are ready to give the Soviet administration full control over the financial and economic life of greater Berlin . . . retaining only a liaison office and a small garrison." Oddly enough, the report continued with this statement: "In the Moscow negotiations, the Americans are pursuing the goal of staying in Berlin under whatever pretext and will not permit a conference on all German questions." The report ended with the comment that "Americans in Berlin are of the opinion that General Clay is not suited to the new conditions required for the peaceful resolution of the Berlin question."[40] Ironically, by the time this report from "American circles" was received by Moscow on 6 August it had little intelligence value. The preliminary discussions in Moscow with Foreign Minister Molotov and the 3 August meeting with Stalin were over.[41]

Following the meeting with Stalin the Berlin matter was referred back to the four military governors, but it was clear from Allied Control Council meetings that the four could not agree on these issues. By 7 September their negotiations had broken down, and the blockade continued. Western leaders began to discuss the next step, and Foreign Minister Ernest Bevin addressed the British cabinet about the issue on 10 September. By early October the minutes of this meeting had been relayed to Stalin by KI in a major achievement by Soviet intelligence. The minutes should have convinced Stalin that pressuring West Berlin would never stop the Western Allies from creating a West German state. This KI report and those presented below, which have been made available for the first time, demonstrate the high quality of KI's British sources during this crucial period.[42]

On 12 September 1948 a telegram on the subject of a West German state was sent by Bevin to the British ambassador in Washington. A copy of the telegram was obtained by KI and disseminated. The source of the document was not given, but it was probably Donald Maclean, a Soviet agent who held a senior position in the British embassy in Washington until late summer 1948. An extract of this document, the original paragraph 6, was included in the archival material: "For me it would be completely impossible to bind the Government of His Majesty to an obligation of this kind which could mean war, on the basis of a simple disagreement between military governors. A definite opinion exists that the United States is trying to order us about, and that has given rise here to deep discontent. The cabinet will not agree to this, nor will the parliament. I cannot propose an obligation of this kind to the parliament. . . . If the Government of the United States pressures me on this question, as in the past, then circumstances may arise in which I will be obliged to make a public declaration on this issue."[43]

This statement was interpreted by Soviet intelligence officers as an obvious example of the difficult relations between the leaders of the United States and Britain: the British seemed to resent American pressure tactics. But it is difficult to reconcile this view of Bevin (who was obviously irritated by the seemingly irrelevant detail of some of the military governors' discussions) with the leading role Bevin played in ensuring Western solidarity throughout the blockade. Bevin believed that "abandonment of Berlin would have serious, if not disastrous consequences in western Germany and in western Europe."[44]

We now know that two messages sent by Foreign Minister Bevin on 21 and 23 September 1948 describing a meeting in Paris of the Western foreign ministers also found their way into KI hands. These telegrams reviewed the foreign ministers' proposals for sending a note to the Soviets following the breakdown of the military governors' negotiations. KI even managed to acquire Bevin's dictated notes on the meetings.[45] In any event, the note from the Western Allies was ignored by the Soviets, who merely restated their position. At a 26 September meeting in Paris, the Western foreign ministers decided to take the Berlin issue to the United Nations.

Although much of KI's material on negotiations that were under way was well documented, contributions by Berlin KI were not always welcomed by Moscow. A KI Berlin dispatch dated 2 October 1948 reported on speculation by American officials in Berlin about how the U.N. Security Council might deal with the Berlin question. The same source reported that the Americans expected and even looked forward to an attempt by the Soviets or the East Berlin SED to provoke them militarily as proof that "the Russians threatened peace." Some Americans expected war by spring 1949, and most Berlin residents did, too. At the bottom of the report was this disclaimer: "The material is an agent's report; the leadership of SMA was not informed of it, and it was not used within the department."[46]

Advance Soviet knowledge of these Western discussions, and the realization that the British and French were losing enthusiasm for supporting West Berlin because of domestic economic problems, probably gave Stalin and Molotov a considerable edge in negotiations with Western Allies. But there were moments during the 1948–49 crisis that were far more dramatic and decisive, like the Americans' decision in June

1948 not to test the Soviet blockade militarily. If KI had been able to come up with well-documented information on this American decision, it would have achieved a major intelligence coup.[47] There has been much speculation that Donald Maclean should have been able to inform the Soviets that the West was not prepared to force the blockade by ground action, thus guiding Stalin's subsequent actions in the Berlin crisis. No SVR archival material could be found to support this view.

The Soviets Revise Their Reports for Stalin

The report of the 22 September British cabinet meeting demonstrates again how difficult it was for the Soviet leadership to accept and act on intelligence they did not like. After Bevin emphasized that if "we do not now take a firm position, then our situation in Europe will be hopeless," he opined that the Soviet Union was dragging out the negotiations until winter, when supplying West Berlin would be more difficult. He then quoted statistics on the airlift from Secretary of State Marshall's briefing to the ministers, noting that larger aircraft (C-54's) were to be used but repeating Marshall's caution that "in the event of a surprise Soviet attack, the loss of a large part of the US airlift capacity would be inevitable."[48] It is interesting that this report went only to Molotov and Deputy Foreign Minister Valerian Zorin and not Stalin. Considering the large number of inconsequential reports that KI sent to Stalin, it is notable that it failed to send him this one, which was certain to irritate the irascible leader.

The reference to the airlift in the Bevin messages raises an interesting question concerning KI reporting on the blockade. Despite the decisive importance of the airlift, we found almost no reference to it other than the report cited above and the August 1948 report by MGB Berlin. Purely technical estimates of airlift capacity and of supply requirements of the garrisons and the population would have been the province of military intelligence, not KI. Nonetheless, we have no evidence that KI even directed its residencies and agent networks to cover the issue.[49] Askold Lebedev, the former SMA secretariat officer, insists that the scope of the airlift took the Soviets entirely by surprise. As winter 1948–49 drew near and flying weather worsened, the Soviets grew hopeful that the Allies would be forced to stop the airlift, but it continued. Indeed, it seemed to Sokolovsky's staff officers that the "aircraft deliberately flew low over Karlshorst to impress them. One would appear overhead,

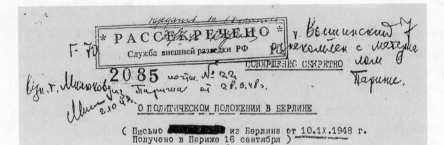

2085 почта № 22

СОВЕРШЕННО СЕКРЕТНО

Вх. т. Молотову из Парижа от 28.9.48 г.

О ПОЛИТИЧЕСКОМ ПОЛОЖЕНИИ В БЕРЛИНЕ

(Письмо ▮▮▮▮▮▮ из Берлина от 10.IX.1948 г.
Получено в Париже 16 сентября)

Одновременно с возобновлением берлинских четырехсторонних переговоров , которые протекают почти в абсолютной тайне, в бывшей столице Рейха развернулись два маневра: один со стороны берлинцев, другой со стороны русских.

У меня создалось впечатление , что большинство берлинского населения сильно настроено против русских и желает от всего сердца, чтобы в Берлине остались западные оккупанты. Последние, по крайней мере в настоящий момент , являются уже не врагами, а действительными союзниками, помощью которых берлинцы хотят воспользоваться.

Испытав два месяца тому назад настоящий страх, берлинское население западных секторов кажется сейчас от этого полностью оправилось. Утешенные рядом заявлений КЛЕЯ и посылкой самолетов с продовольствием, которые постоянно видны в небе, берлинское население увидело в возобновлении четырехсторонней деятельности в помещении межсоюзнического Контрольного Совета лишь признак начала капитуляции русских и доказательств того, что во всяком случае англо-американцы и французы не покинут Берлин. Население говорит о возможном снятии блокады, желая этого, однако не видя в этой необходимой меры, которую стоило бы провести любой ценой. Оно не считает также, что лишь восточная марка должна иметь хождение в Берлине. Западная марка продолжает повышаться в цене, причем

166б

KI translation of a 10 September 1948 report, "The Political Situation in Berlin," transmitted by a French official there and received in Paris on 16 September by an unidentified agency of the French government, probably the Foreign Ministry. The document was obtained by the KI residency in Paris and sent to KI Moscow on 28 September. The document bears the notation "Comrade Vyshinsky familiarized himself with this material in Paris." Soviet deputy foreign minister Andrei Vyshinsky was in Paris for the meeting of the UN General Assembly.

another would disappear over the horizon, and a third emerge, one after another without interruption, like a conveyor belt!"[50] Georgy Alekseevich Korotia, an MGB counterintelligence officer in Karlshorst at the time, asserted that the "entire concept of the blockade as a means of forcing the Western Allies from Berlin was an empty undertaking, and this is why the airlift was never taken into consideration." He added that "the blockade brought no benefit to the Soviet side, only damage, but it did arouse the German population against us." He concluded by saying that no one in Karlshorst was asked about the decision to mount the blockade. "We were never even warned, but presented with a fait accompli."[51]

As the intense period of negotiations began in August and September, KI received an interesting report from Paris entitled "The Political Situation in Berlin." The letter was received from the Paris residency and probably originated with a French diplomat in Berlin. In the upper right-hand corner of the report is the notation: "Comrade Vyshinsky familiarized himself with this material in Paris." Andrei Vyshinsky, who was in Paris for United Nations meetings, had been shown the report there.

The report was a dispassionate analysis of the effect of the blockade on the Berlin population and the direction of Soviet policies. At the outset the author made it clear that residents of Berlin were strongly opposed to the Russians and wanted the Western occupiers to stay. As for the Soviets, "they cannot tolerate an administration in the center of their zone that is hostile to them, which, with its freedom of the press and speech, is an unfortunate example for the entire Soviet zone population that cannot be prevented from having contact with Berlin." But Berlin was seen by the Soviets as a capital from which they could influence West Germany. That is why, the author believed, the Soviets hoped to do away with the present city government and assembly, thus avoiding the elections set for November. By replacing them with a "democratic bloc" the Soviets were betting that a future "People's Congress" would adopt a constitution drawn up by a People's Council that was to meet on 15 September with representatives from all of Germany. The outcome would be a government to rival a West German government. "At this point," the writer concluded, "the Soviets might . . . offer concessions whereby both German governments could then create a unified government that would of course have Berlin as its capital."[52] These plans did not work out, and the Soviets had to be content with controlling only their half of Berlin. But much of this French official's description of long-range Soviet planning was close to the mark, particularly his predictions concerning the attention that the Soviets would give the People's Council and congress, both of which became highly visible during the next few years.

The West Seeks to Rearm West Germany

In spite of the success of the airlift, the military implications of the blockade greatly increased concern in Washington and West European capitals over the imbalances of forces on either side in Germany and the absence of any coordinated defense plans in the event of general war in Europe. The Western European Union (WEU) established a committee of WEU defense ministers, and on 5 October 1948 Field Marshal Sir Bernard Montgomery became its permanent military chairman.[53] On 8 November, Montgomery held a meeting at Melle, West Germany, with the military governors of the three Western occupation zones to get their views on what should be done if hostilities erupted. The key problems facing Western defense planners were developing plans, finding forces that might be available in the period up to three months after mobilization, and equipping such forces given the difficult economic situation in Western Europe.[54]

The Soviets, sensitive to any hint of Western plans to rearm Germany, followed these events closely. In November 1948, KI Moscow received a report on this military governors' meeting. Gen. Clarence R. Huebner, commander of US ground forces, is mentioned as attending, but not General Clay. The decisions reportedly reached at this meeting were to

1. Create military forces in Germany;
2. Immediately arm supplemental forces from among displaced persons consisting of Polish, Ukrainian, Czech, and Baltic contingents; and
3. Supply both of these forces, as well as the French army of occupation, with American arms.[55]

The report then described these units and how they would be armed. The troops in question were used primarily to guard the occupation forces' installations in West Germany, and they were not taken seriously by most Allied military personnel (it was thought that if a real

Soviet offensive occurred, these units "would plunder the Post Exchange [military store] and head for Paris"). Even so, this KI report probably increased Soviet concern over a military buildup in West Germany. But other KI reports on Montgomery's trip indicated that the provincial prime ministers in the British zone opposed plans to create paramilitary groups and reintroduce military service. One KI report emphasized these politicians' reluctance to see such plans take shape without fully discussing them at a conference of West German provincial leaders.[56]

A German KI source, probably one of those connected with Communist Party circles, added to Soviet concerns over German rearmament when he reported that US Secretary of the Army Kenneth Royall, during a visit to Italy in December 1948, had urged the Italians to participate in arming the Western European Union. Royall pursued this course even though experts warned him that Italian participation would not be effective unless West Germany helped to defend Europe—and there was great public opposition to German rearmament both in Germany and Western Europe. Royall's urgings surprised the British, who thought that they had agreed to move slowly on the rearmament question and that General Clay had concurred.[57] Other KI reporting on this issue came from a source in Austria who described the formation of two military staffs, one in Königstein under Gen. Franz Halder and another in Oberursel under Gen. Heinz Guderian.[58]

These KI reports of Western plans to create additional forces in their zones were paralleled by reports of impending war. One such bizarre dispatch was received from KI in Berlin on 13 November. The source—"a German who by his own admission was a courier between a German intelligence group in Berlin and an Anglo-American intelligence center in West Germany"—wrote, "Before the elections in the United States, Anglo-American military circles in Germany were of the agreed opinion that military operations by the Western powers against the Soviet Union must begin by March 1949." The source went on to describe plans for a sudden attack by Anglo-American armored forces, which would attempt to reach the Oder. At the same time, "Berlin would be quickly evacuated. The few American, British, and French troops would be withdrawn by air, taking with them a few leading German political figures." But according to the report, the Americans believed that the Soviet forces could simultaneously liquidate the Anglo-American offensive and occupy West Germany up to the Rhine. "The Soviet attack would be so rapid, moreover, that only a small part of the German population would be able to escape across the Rhine." The source tied these "plans" to the outcome of the American elections but also claimed that military operations in Germany were "only a part of the Anglo-American plans for war." The last page of the report bore this notation: "1. The material was received from an agent source; 2. The leadership of SMA was not informed; and 3. It was not used in the directorate."[59] One can see why this fantasy was never distributed.

The Stalemate Continues

The winter wore on. US employment and industrial production reached new highs, and the Berlin airlift continued to deliver record payloads despite the miserable weather. A KI report from London to Stalin and the Politburo provided information on discussions over the weekend of 13–14 November between Prime Minister Clement Attlee, Foreign Minister Ernest Bevin, Undersecretary for Foreign Affairs Hector McNeil, and members of the Foreign Office, where it was agreed that President Truman, Attlee, and French Foreign Minister Robert Schuman would not meet with Stalin, and that the Berlin question would again be placed on the agenda of the U.N. Security Council. The report quoted McNeil as saying that the entire Berlin problem was a "tactical incident in the strategic struggle for all of Germany."[60]

Not to be outdone by the London KI residency, KI Paris reported on the views of the deputy French political adviser François Seydoux on the 5 December elections in the Western sectors of Berlin. The "results . . . are a huge success for the Western powers, surpassing all expectations." The outcome would, however, "complicate the situation in Berlin." Seydoux was referring here to the victory of the Social Democrats, who were totally opposed to SED and the Soviet Military Administration. Seydoux also questioned whether "in view of the success of the airlift, the blockade does not in the final analysis present more of an embarrassment for the USSR than an advantage." Seydoux noted that without coal from the Ruhrgebiet, Germany's large mining and industrial area on the Rhine River, the "Soviet zone would be in a calamitous situation, and this cannot continue for any length of time without increasing the impression of economic success in West Germany."[61]

Stalin seems to have agreed with Seydoux. On 27 January, Joseph Kingsbury Smith, European general manager of the International News

Service, submitted four questions to Stalin. This was common among foreign news organizations; questions were sometimes answered, sometimes not. Of the four questions, only one dealt with Berlin, and it was carefully phrased: "Would the USSR be willing to remove restrictions on traffic to Berlin if the United States, Britain, and France agreed not to establish a separate Western German state [before] a Council of Ministers meeting to discuss the German problem as a whole?" Stalin's assent came swiftly on 30 January. He made no mention of the currency issue that had ostensibly caused the blockade.[62]

Considering the low-key manner in which President Truman and Secretary of State Dean Acheson dealt with Stalin's response to Kingsbury Smith's question on Berlin, it is difficult to understand KI's fixation on the event. Even recognizing the utter dominance exercised by Stalin in foreign policy matters, and that KI must have been advised to query its residencies for reactions, their reporting on the issue seems overdone. By the time these reports were released, the US ambassador to the United Nations, Philip Jessup, had made his 15 February approach to Soviet Ambassador Yakov Malik—an act that brought the Berlin question before the United Nations.

Currency Finally Becomes a Real Issue

Given the Soviet contention that the introduction of the West Mark had produced the blockade, Stalin's failure to mention currency in his response to Kingsbury Smith was significant. In fact, the currency problem was heating up. The Soviets had declared East German currency valid in West Berlin, so both currencies were circulating there. On 2 March, KI received a report from its Berlin residency on the currency issue. A source close to Friedrich Haas, director of the Finance Office of the West Berlin city administration, stated that a decision to make the West Mark the sole legal tender in West Berlin would probably not occur before the middle of April. Haas had reportedly described the views of "American officials" who were concerned that "this action would make it more difficult to supply the population, but more important would constitute a break in the last links between America and Russia. A final attempt to avoid this would be possible if the East Mark could be introduced under four-power control and the blockade lifted."[63] Haas was wrong. By the time this report was received, officials had already decided to make the West Mark the only means of payment in West Berlin. This report reflects the tendency of many KI officers to report what Moscow liked to hear.

The Soviets ended the blockade just before the foreign ministers' meeting in Paris on 23 May was to consider "questions relating to Germany, and problems arising out of the situation in Berlin, including also the question of currency in Berlin."[64] The question of currency became concrete when West Berlin railroad workers, who were receiving pay in both East and West marks, went on strike over how much of their pay would be in each currency. A KI Berlin source reported that there would not have been a strike if the American commandant had not insisted on it. The goal of the strike, which reportedly had President Truman's approval, was "to force the Russians to recognize the legality of the West Mark." To this end the Americans supplied the strikers with food and other necessities. This report was forwarded to the Soviet delegation at the foreign ministers' conference, then in session in Paris.[65]

The strike ended on 28 June when the Soviet zone railroad administration agreed to pay workers 60 percent of their salaries in West Marks. But during the strike the question was also raised about who was responsible for maintaining order on large tracts of railroad property in West Berlin. The Soviets insisted that because their railroad administration owned the property, they had authority over the West Berlin police on this land. This issue posed serious problems for many years.

West Berliners Seek to Join West Germany
After the Blockade

No sooner had the blockade ended on 12 May 1949 when, as Seydoux had predicted, the Western Allies had to contend with West Berlin's desire to enter the new Federal Republic of Germany as a twelfth state (*Land*). The constitution of the new state, with its capital at Bonn on the Rhine, was enacted on 23 May 1949. On 15 September, Konrad Adenauer was to become chancellor. On 9 June, KI disseminated a report based on an official communication of 7 June between the French foreign ministry and Seydoux. In the memo Seydoux explained that a serious difference existed between British and French views on the place of Berlin within Germany and Europe itself. Seydoux believed that the British envisaged Berlin as a forward bastion against Communism in Europe, and that its loss would have serious consequences for West Germany.[66]

French concern over Berlin's relationship with the Federal Republic continued through 1949. A KI Berlin dispatch of 17 October described a session between French High Commissioner André François-Poncet and Berlin's governing mayor Ernst Reuter in which François-Poncet announced that he would continue to oppose the proposal to make West Berlin a West German state even though the Americans and British backed Reuter's wholehearted support of the idea.[67] The last salvo on this question in 1949 came by telegram from the Paris KI residency on 1 November. According to KI's report, the French commandant of Berlin, Gen. Jean Ganeval, was "struck by the persistence with which his American and British colleagues at their 15 October 1949 meeting stood by their thesis whereby the Western sectors of Berlin should be united with West Germany as a twelfth Land." The same KI Paris cable noted that François-Poncet would attempt to see West German Chancellor Adenauer before the next meeting of the High Commission in order to persuade him to stand by his disinclination to join Berlin to West Germany.[68]

West Berlin's status vis-à-vis West Germany remained a thorny problem for many years. On 21 October 1949, however, the Allies, including France, accepted, with certain technical reservations, that West Berlin would be "treated as part of the German Federal Republic."[69] These KI reports reveal that to a considerable extent, Moscow's impression that the Allies would abandon the "twelfth Land" concept came from KI's French sources. It demonstrates, as do other communications from official French sources noted in this chapter, that KI had access to messages exchanged between French offices in Berlin and those in Bonn and Paris. Given France's history of intransigence on many issues affecting not only the Allied presence in Berlin but also the entire question of the postwar treatment of Germany, it would have been interesting to examine KI reporting from the same French sources on some of these other critical subjects had it been available. At the same time, the window that this unprecedented KI reporting gives us on Allied squabbling over Berlin's relation with the FRG illustrates why Stalin might have had reason to hope that he might still come out ahead.

Soviet Concern over West Germany's Rearmament Grows

As of December 1949, KI intensified its reporting on evidence of German "remilitarization." The Western Allies believed that it was their

Совершенно секретно

Н/т № 22647 от 1.11.49.

из Парижа

Получено почтой № 35 от 10.11.49, м.б. № 2492; справка проведена. 29.11.49

СПРАВКА

Использовано в записке о Берлине в ... и в сообщении в 7 адресов. 24.11.49

—————————————

Генерал ГАНЕВАЛЬ был поражен той жесткостью-энергией, с которой ... английский и американский коллеги отстаивали 15 октября, свою точку зрения ... о присоединении западных секторов Берлина к Западной Германии в качестве двенадцатой земли. Они заявили, что Берлин является ... основным плацдармом борьбы против коммунизма и, следовательно, ... необходимо оказать политическую, экономическую и финансовую подде... ку.

ФРАНСУА-ПОНСЭ отмечает значительное сближение точек зрения ... гийского и американского правительства по этому вопросу. Он ... вает опасение, как бы АДЕНАУЭР не стал объектом давления со ... англо-американцев.

ФРАНСУА-ПОНСЭ сообщает, что он постарается повидать АДЕНАУЭРА перед следующим совещанием Верховной союзнической комиссии, чтобы убедить его сохранить свою позицию, заключающуюся в нежелании при... единить Берлин к Западной Германии.

Примечание: Источник заслуживает доверия. Посол информирова...

Резолюция:

④

Encoded telegram, 1 November 1949, from the Paris KI residency, reporting the views of Berlin Commandant Jean Ganeval and André François-Poncet of the French Foreign Ministry regarding West Berlin's possible incorporation in the FRG as a twelfth Land. The sources of the information are described as reliable, and the Soviet ambassador in Paris was informed. KI German specialist Samuil Meirerovich Kvastel notes that the telegram was used in a report on Berlin that was sent to "seven addresses."

military imbalance with the Soviets, particularly in ground forces, that had led to Soviet miscalculation with regard to the blockade. According to the West, this imbalance had convinced the USSR that the West would never challenge Soviet actions in closing the highway and rail links to Berlin. As a result, the West felt compelled to consider ways to augment its defenses. The Soviets, on the other hand, believed that the Allies had decided to rearm their zones of Germany long before and that the blockade was merely a convenient pretext.

A 20 December report from the KI Berlin residency painted a bleak picture of Western rearmament. Despite the convictions of many West Germans (including the new president of the Federal Republic of Germany, Theodor Heuss) that Germany should not participate in military programs, the "United States was determined to raise a West German army of twenty-five divisions. If a four-power foreign ministers' meeting in early 1950 did not result in approving a peace treaty for Germany, then the West, led by the United States, would sign a separate treaty with West Germany, form a West German army, and bring West Germany into NATO."[70]

As mentioned earlier, not all intelligence on the blockade was disseminated by KI Moscow, either because a given report was unbelievable, the source was unreliable, or both. Moscow KI buried a 22 September 1948 Berlin residency report from "English circles in Berlin," for example. It described a propaganda campaign against the Soviet Union that had the slogan: "Negotiations with the Soviets are useless. Only one way out of the situation remains: preparing for war." According to the report, SPD—in anticipation of an attempt by Soviet occupation authorities to try leading party members as warmongers—called for the registration of all SED members in preparation for a "day of reckoning." The Berlin residency added the comments: "The information deserves attention. The leadership of SMA will be informed." A "resolution" at KI Moscow level, however, states that "by order of Comrade Ivan Tugarinov, the report will not be sent to customers. This material is possibly disinformation."[71]

Looking back on the overall performance of the CIA and KI during the Berlin blockade, KI obviously had an impressive array of sources who acquired documentary intelligence from high levels of the British and French governments. But even though solid information on Allied attitudes toward Berlin was available to Stalin by September 1948, the information was incomplete and often delayed. In particular, because KI did not report on how successful the airlift was, Stalin felt encouraged to wait for winter to weaken both the airlift and the population's morale before deciding to back off. Intelligence provided by KI Berlin did not help to dispel Stalin's misconceptions. Its generally good sources could not compare with those of the London and Paris residencies: as a result, KI Berlin relied much more on hearsay and apparently could provide no documentary evidence from the West.

Information obtained by CIA's Berlin Operations Base had a significant and immediate effect on US decisions about West Berlin and West Germany. BOB's reports went straight to the field commander, General Clay, whose attitudes had a direct influence on those decisions. BOB's reporting on security and military issues went to the heart of Clay's concerns: Was there any evidence that the Soviets or the newly created East German forces were preparing for an armed confrontation?

One of the first results of Western fears about the blockade was the signing of the North Atlantic Treaty in Washington on 4 April 1949, while the blockade was still in force. The meager conventional military force represented by this first version of NATO bore little resemblance to the specter of Western militarism reported by KI in the months following the blockade's imposition. This nascent NATO force was unlikely to deter Moscow, but it represented an important first step in Western resolve. Its explosive growth over the next years, strangely enough, had more to do with Moscow than with the Western democracies.

4

The Korean War: Pretext or Premise for Rearming West Germany?

After the blockade, the apparent return to normal relations among the four powers made it difficult for the West to improve the defense of Western Europe. Opposition to rearming West Germany remained strong even though the Western Allies realized that without German participation the USSR would win a military confrontation in Europe. The Korean War dramatically changed these attitudes. The invasion of South Korea by the North Korean People's Army in June 1950 was instinctively seen by many in Europe as a prelude to a similar assault in Germany by the Soviets or the growing East German paramilitary forces. The West reacted forcefully to expand NATO and to enlist West Germany in the common European defense. But Stalin knew little about why the West was gearing up to defend itself against possible armed conflict with the Soviet Union. KI reporting hitherto unavailable to historians concentrated on evidence of German "remilitarization" but omitted any reference to the Korean conflict. Post–Cold War historical studies of the Korean War, seeking to understand the rationale for the North's invasion, have emphasized the relationships between Stalin, Mao Tse-tung, and Kim Il Sung. Little attention has been paid to Stalin's failure to calculate the effect of the invasion on Western Europe and the United States. This massive miscalculation laid the foundation for the strategic confrontation that dominated the Cold War until its end.[1]

The Soviets Welcome News of Economic Hardship in the West

Drawing on its excellent sources in the French government, KI learned much about the situation in West Berlin after the blockade was over and the new West Mark was introduced. KI's concentration on economic questions and its regular dissemination of such reports to Moscow reflected Stalin's personal concern about the problems of the world economy and specifically of the German economy. But his interest was still rooted in the "crude economic determinism underlying Bolshevik imperialism" in which even the most experienced Soviet diplomats either believed or pretended to believe. Thus much of KI reporting on the normal tensions between Western nations on commercial matters tended to exaggerate these "contradictions" and reinforce the views of Stalin and his advisers.[2]

Soviets were particularly concerned about the Ruhr district (Ruhrgebiet), the industrial and mining area that had been so vital to German armament production in both world wars. On 22 October 1949, the Berlin KI residency reported on various issues affecting the Ruhr in which American investments appeared to be threatening local initiative. The Americans preferred that the electrification of a railroad in the Ruhr, for example, be done by private firms rather than the state. This and other examples of the influence of American capitalism reportedly prompted several West German and European firms to work against the expansion of American influence in Europe. The report, thought to be based on reliable sources, ends with the outlandish prediction that when the Marshall Plan ended in 1953, there would be an economic crisis in the United States.[3]

On 29 August 1949 the Berlin residency submitted a four-page report on the difficult economic situation in West Germany as the new Federal Republic began to function. Noting that significant portions of West German industry were operating at less than capacity, the pessimistic analysis of West Germany's situation in summer 1949 appears to have been written by a single source, although the views expressed probably reflected information available in overt publications.[4] Moscow received additional evidence of the economic problems facing West

Berlin in a 20 October 1949 Berlin KI residency report describing discussions between Norman Collison, the coordinator for Germany of the Economic Cooperation Administration, and Paul Hoffman, the coordinator for Europe. Collison reportedly "called attention to the difficult economic situation in the Western sectors of Berlin and expressed the opinion that to save Berlin, it would be essential to make available resources systematically and in sufficient quantity from the European recovery fund." When Hoffman objected, Collison argued that the "Russians, in pursuit of their plan to unite all of Berlin with the East, would again resort to blockade in the winter of 1949–50." But this time an airlift could not sustain the population, and "if the Russians, in these circumstances, again offer the Berliners food and fuel, the majority would accept the offer this time." This report must have cheered Stalin, who knew that food shortages in the USSR and problems on East German farms would prevent any long-term Soviet effort to feed West Berlin. The report was cabled to Moscow by the residency and was widely read in Soviet circles.[5]

On 23 October 1949, KI circulated a report describing a drop in industrial production and an increase in unemployment in West Berlin—problems that allegedly had begun with the introduction of the West Mark and had worsened in the months that followed. A covering memo asserted that these problems had resulted from decisions by West Berlin authorities to obstruct restoration of "normal economic relations between the Western sectors and the Soviet Occupation Zone, specifically the purchase of raw materials." The report added that "the Berlin section of the Economic Council of Bizonia said that 'in the current political situation, purchases in the Eastern zone would be tantamount to uniting Berlin to that zone.'" According to the report, another cause of unemployment was the gradual shutdown of plants in West Berlin and the transfer of some components to West Germany. The report concluded that "the inevitable result of the splitting policies of the Western powers and their German protégés is, evidently, the subordination of the economy of the Western sectors of Berlin to the interests of American monopoly."[6]

This negative view of West Berlin's economic situation was reinforced by a report on unemployment in the Western sectors. Disseminated by KI on 12 December, the summary was based on the monthly reports for July through October of the Berlin section of the Bizonia Economic Council. In a covering memo, Deputy Foreign Minister

Valerian Zorin lamented that the "serious economic situation has hastened the process of proletarization of the population and the destruction of mechanics and handicraftsmen." In the last paragraph of his memo he noted that the substance of the report had been presented to Stalin and the Politburo.[7] Stalin also received a report that the Siemens company was interested in obtaining Marshall Plan credits and in renewing its relationships with former subsidiaries abroad.[8]

KI Reports Highlight Discord Among the Western Allies

The Soviets were eager for any evidence of dissension among the Western powers with regard to Germany. A coded telegram from the Paris KI residency, for example, conveys French commandant Jean Ganeval's dismay over American and British interest in making West Berlin the twelfth Land of West Germany and quotes French High Commissioner André François-Poncet as intending to speak to Adenauer about the matter.[9] The Americans and British also had their differences. According to a dispatch to KI Berlin from KI Moscow, "the English fully support the Americans in the question of a rebirth of German imperialism for their struggle against the USSR, but at the same time they fear that the reconstruction of German industry will mean a dangerous competitor for English industry and that their export possibilities will be sharply curtailed." Moscow continued to pressure KI Berlin for information that could help the Soviets create conflict among the competing capitalist powers.

When the foreign ministers of the United States, Britain, and France met in Paris on 9–10 November 1949 to discuss Germany, KI provided Stalin and the Politburo with the complete minutes—an excellent example of KI collection capabilities. The six-page covering memorandum provided a KI analysis of the conference. Although the "German question" had been placed on the agenda as a British initiative, KI reported, US Secretary of State Dean Acheson had dominated the discussion. Acheson "insisted on the adoption of the most far-reaching decisions, aimed at the restoration of the political and military-economic potential of Germany." According to KI analysts, "Bevin supported Acheson on all principal questions, although he expressed himself somewhat more cautiously. French Minister of Foreign Affairs Robert Schuman tried to resist the American pressure . . . but in the closing discussions on all principal questions he yielded to the American point of view."[10]

KI was always alert to attempts to restore the "military-economic potential of Germany." A 29 August 1949 dispatch from the Berlin residency entitled "On the Question of the Conferences of the General Staffs of the Western Powers in Frankfurt am Main" appeared to combine the decidedly pro-Soviet and anti-American views of several sources. This report, probably from German Communist Party (KPD) sources in West Germany, was read by the most influential Soviet decisionmakers. It stated that the West German Council of States (Laenderrat) opposed any plans to enlist West Germany in Western defense plans unless it was consulted. Many sources felt that the reason for the Americans' feverish haste to involve West Germany was their concern that the USSR would soon have the atomic bomb. The report concluded that Germans resisted rearmament because of memories of savage Allied bombings during the war. The authors believed that continued resistance would depend on whether the "proletariat and its party could prevent Western Germany from being transformed into a stronghold of fascism and anti-Communism."[11]

From the tenor of KI reporting on Western economic problems and disagreements among the Western Allies during this period, Stalin must have thought that he had a good chance of improving the Soviet position in Germany. As 1950 began, food rationing had just ended in the Federal Republic, but economic problems remained. Allied disagreements on their relations with the West German state were uppermost in the minds of most; Korean politics meant nothing to most Europeans. On 21 March, Adenauer suggested the economic union of France and Germany, and in May, French foreign minister Schuman proposed that the French and German coal and steel industries be merged under joint authority.

Aware that France would remain a key player in deciding West Germany's place in postwar Europe, KI pushed hard for information on the views of major French officials on Germany. In mid-June a KI source reported a conversation with Jean Monnet, the French plan commissioner general, in which Monnet commented that "American 'atomic diplomacy' was to blame for the worsening of the German situation" but that it was still not too late to "return to four-power control over Germany." Monnet continued: "If it is not possible to come to an agreement with the Russians, then it will be necessary for France to accept Adenauer's proposal for Franco-German economic union despite the 'terrible risks.'" Monnet underlined that "in no degree can the security of France be secured by the Atlantic pact, because the Americans have only two divisions [in Europe]. As for American arms, France should accept them, but quietly, not because the Russians will be afraid, but because to propagandize it plays into the hands of the French Communists."[12]

The alleged statement by Monnet that the United States had only two divisions in Europe was inaccurate, but it did reflect the imbalance of power between the fledgling NATO alliance and Soviet forces. In 1949–50, "the Soviet Union had present in Eastern Europe some thirty divisions. Facing them were three and a half American and two and a half British divisions scattered throughout Germany, performing occupation and police duty. The entire French establishment in Europe consisted of less than half a dozen ill-armed divisions. The Benelux countries [Belgium, the Netherlands, and Luxembourg] could, perhaps, assemble as many more."[13] It seemed unlikely that the countries of the West, even with newly allocated funds from the US Congress, could do much to improve the balance of forces. The only possible way to match the Soviet military was to rearm West Germany. But when the Joint Chiefs of Staff expressed the view on 5 May 1950 that "the appropriate and early arming of Germany is of fundamental importance to the defense of Western Europe against the USSR," there seemed to be no rush to support this position in the US government.[14]

North Korea Invades South Korea

The invasion of South Korea by the North Korean People's Army on 25 June 1950 came as a shock to politicians and military professionals on both sides of the Atlantic. There has been much debate since 1950 over the causes of the Korean War and about why the United States reacted so strongly after having proclaimed that Korea was beyond its defensive perimeter. Recent scholars have reviewed Soviet actions leading up to the attack and have concluded that Kim Il Sung was the instigator. Apparently, Kim had persuaded Stalin to provide him with the support needed to invade the South after Stalin had been persuaded by comments from American statesmen "that the United States would not intervene." For his part, Stalin was thought to have been influenced by the fact that Mao had approved Kim's proposal.[15] But whether the invasion was the result of Kim Il Sung's initiative or Stalin's passivity, it could never have been undertaken without Soviet sanction, given the enormous logistical problems involved.[16] The effect of the invasion on the United States and its European allies, and its implications for the German question, were far-reaching indeed, ultimately influencing American Cold War policies in Europe.

Even Dean Acheson, the author of the 12 January 1950 speech placing Korea beyond the US defensive perimeter, declared that the North Korean attack was "an open, undisguised challenge to our internationally accepted position as the protector of South Korea."[17] In Europe reaction to the invasion was even sharper.[18] No responsible statesman in the Western alliance had expected the Soviets to challenge postwar arrangements with armed confrontation. That this challenge had been delivered in South Korea by indigenous forces trained, armed, and equipped by the Soviet Army seemed to suggest a similar possibility in Germany—even though, as Eisenhower pointed out, "the use of East German troops on the Korean model would come very close to declaring open, all-out, war. This is because . . . [Soviet] troops are in actual occupation of East Germany and in actual control of the area."[19]

Could the East German forces have really invaded West Germany in 1950 on their own? Probably not. As we pointed out in our discussion of the blockade, creation of an East German force comparable to the North Korean People's Army would have still taken several years. The Soviets had begun developing a North Korean military capability in early 1946 under the guise of a Security Officers Training Schools Bureau within the Department of Internal Affairs. Leaders of the North Korean Army were recruited from Koreans who had served with the Chinese Communist Forces and from Soviet citizens of Korean ancestry who had been forcibly removed from Soviet eastern border areas in the 1930s and resettled in Central Asia. Many of these people and their descendants had served in the Soviet Army during World War II and spoke both Korean and Russian. Their presence complemented the efforts of full-time Soviet advisers and part-time instructors on loan from occupation units. Unlike the Chinese Communist forces in Manchuria who had had to make do with captured Japanese weapons given to them by the Soviets, the Korean units received Soviet equipment from the outset.[20]

Because of the effective cover of the "training schools," it was difficult for Western intelligence organizations to estimate the order of battle. But by mid-1947, the West knew of two rifle divisions and of at least one—and probably two—independent mixed brigades that were to serve as cadres for additional divisions. Soviet officers continued to supervise training at all levels; for example, they oversaw staff procedures and gave instructions during combined arms operations. By late 1947, the training-school fig leaf had worn thin, and more and more deserters encountered by Western agents referred to their units as part of the People's Army. It was not until February 1948, however, that this army appeared formally in that guise, resplendent in new, Soviet-style uniforms.[21] Tanks began arriving in early 1948, and through 1948–49 the force that was to attack in June 1950 took shape. At that time the People's Army had at least eight rifle divisions and one armored brigade equipped with Soviet T-34 tanks.[22]

The Soviets Create an East German Paramilitary Force

We know now that there was no possibility of an East German paramilitary force undertaking on its own any military operation comparable to that initiated by the North Koreans, even against the small, surrounded target of West Berlin. At the time, though, the parallels between the two postwar Soviet occupation regimes alarmed the Western Allies. When the Allied High Commissioners spoke with Adenauer shortly after the North Korean attack, the West German chancellor expressed hope that "some provisions [were being] made to ensure stability in the event of a Volkspolizei attack."[23]

The Volkspolizei to which Adenauer referred were the so-called Alert Police (Bereitschaftspolizei) under the East German Central Administration of Internal Affairs (Deutsche Verwaltung des Innern), which had been created in the Soviet zone in 1948. Initially, morale in these units was low, and as we have seen, they were never ready to take as active a role in West Berlin during the blockade as some sources had predicted. But in 1949 morale improved when these units were brought together in the Administration for Schooling, a cover name for the paramilitary section of the Central Administration for Internal Affairs. This cover designation was similar to that used for the North Korean People's Army. In spite of the numerous reports by Western intelligence services of Soviet arms deliveries to these units and Soviet involvement in military field exercises, by late 1949 the Western Allies had agreed that the military value of the Alert Police—or Barracked People's Police (Kasernierte Volkspolizei), as they came to be called—was "still insignificant and its political reliability untested."[24]

By the end of 1951, the foreign intelligence component of KI had reverted to the USSR Ministry of State Security (MGB). MGB reporting, which, like that of KI, has never before been made available to Western scholars, asserts that it was not until 1952 that the Barracked People's Police actually began to receive Soviet arms in significant quantities. Apparently, there was concern in Moscow that the troops might resist Soviet weapon shipments, and MGB was called upon to report on their mood because "this might determine to a significant degree the possibilities for military cooperation in defending the interests of the GDR and the Soviet Union." Consequently a report on this subject was sent to Stalin and the Politburo on 24 June 1952. According to this report, "the overwhelming majority of the Barracked Police Reserves [Rezervno-Kazarmennaia Politsiia] reacted positively to the receipt of Soviet arms. In many units, the improvement in discipline and attention to duty was noticeable." Many were persuaded to extend their service after the Soviet weapons arrived. But at the same time the report noted that many elements of the population reacted negatively to GDR measures to "strengthen the armed forces of the police." There was little public enthusiasm for the idea and considerable opposition.[25]

Unfortunately, the extent of actual Soviet arms deliveries to the East German paramilitary forces was not well documented, and the persistence of antimilitary sentiment in the GDR was not reflected in Western reports. For example, a CIA Office of Reports and Estimates (ORE) memorandum sent to the president on 21 August 1950 noted that "until recently, all bereitschaften equipment . . . was issued from captured German stocks. In March 1950, however, Soviet equipment, including tanks, was issued amid great secrecy." Furthermore, this report contended that low morale in those police units that had been thought to be militantly against any commitment outside of East Germany might have been lifted by the success of the North Koreans. In any case, in September 1950, CIA's ORE predicted that these paramilitary forces would "constitute a potential threat to West Germany and a more immediate threat to West Berlin."[26] Adenauer discussed repeatedly with US officials the possibility of a Volkspolizei attack during summer 1950, when Germans, watching American forces in Korea retreat to the Pusan perimeter, became uncomfortably aware of their own vulnerability.

The advance of North Korean troops into South Korea in July 1950 was rapid and dramatic. Whether the fear it inspired in Western capitals over the possibility of armed attack of West Germany was justified is not important. The concern was real, and it immediately reintroduced the question of West Germany's role in the defense of Europe. Headlines in the West German and West Berlin press—"War Breaks Out in Korea; North Korean Communists Invade the South"—grew more ominous as the North Korean People's Army moved south against weak resistance.[27] Dispatches from the East German wire service describing the attack by the South Korean "puppet regime" against the North Korean People's Republic—an effort guided by American "imperialists"—only irritated West Berliners, who had become adept at decoding Communist terminology.

Dean Acheson, who as late as 5 June 1950 had announced that the us policy of German demilitarization would continue, admitted that his "conversion to German participation in European defense was quick." The idea that Germany's place in the defense of Europe could evolve over time was shattered by the situation in Korea.[28] After the North Korean invasion, the United States added $28 billion to its defense budget, the American draft quota was increased, and the number of us Army divisions was expanded to eighteen, four of which were to be sent to Europe in 1951.[29]

KI Reporting Sidesteps Korea

The ki reports we do have reflect continuing Soviet concern over Allied attempts to encourage other nations to accept an independent West Germany, as well as a high state of anxiety over "German remilitarization." But there is no mention of the Korean conflict, nor any speculation about what may have caused the Western Allies' sudden push to rearm Germany. For example, ki reported on what were described as a "series of secret meetings in mid-August in Wiesbaden and Bad Nauheim of American and British representatives from West Germany." Reportedly, a decision was made during these discussions "on the necessity of creating a West German army of 200,000 by the end of 1950 under the guise of a 'federal police.'" It was also decided that "the appointment of German generals to positions of command in this army would be undertaken only upon the recommendations of the Americans." After this decision was adopted, "us High Commissioner John McCloy invited Adenauer to call on him for a discussion of the details of the declaration prepared by Adenauer on remilitarization. In this fashion, the text of Adenauer's official declaration of 18 August was co-ordinated in advance with the Americans."[30]

As we know from one of his reports, McCloy agreed with Adenauer that by 1951 the East German paramilitary police would be sufficiently well trained to pose a serious threat. To counter this challenge, the chancellor proposed training and arming a force of 150,000 volunteers. Whereas McCloy's information on the East German police did not differ greatly from that cited by Adenauer, he doubted the accuracy of Adenauer's "judgment that the Soviets feel they could, by use of Volkspolizei in a Korean-type attack, avoid an all-out war."[31] In McCloy's report of the conversations with Adenauer there are several other references to the Korean conflict and its relevance to the issue of Western security. These comments never made it into the KI summary report.

The absence in SVR archival material of KI reporting on the reactions of the West to the North Korean invasion of the South is remarkable considering that two key Soviet sources, Guy Burgess and Donald Maclean, were in the British Foreign Office when the attack occurred. In fact, as Yuri Modin pointed out in *Mes camarades de Cambridge,* these two agents were both "more active than ever" as of 25 June 1950.[32] The negative implications of the Korean War for Soviet policy in Germany were simply not discussed in official circles in Moscow. No one would have dared because everyone knew full well it was Stalin who had made the crucial decision to allow the North Koreans to invade. Any conversations among Soviets about the enormity of Stalin's miscalculation of the effect on Germany and Europe of the North Korean invasion were whispered, not spoken.[33]

With United Nations troops in Korea again on the defensive as Chinese forces entered the war, KI reported that on "6 November 1950, on the eve of the debate on general political questions in the Bundestag, McCloy received Adenauer and representatives of the Social Democratic Party. . . . During this conversation, McCloy declared that if the Bundestag expresses itself against remilitarization, the delivery of 'Marshall Plan' goods to West Germany will be halted." At the same time, McCloy stated that "with the implementation of remilitarization, 40 to 60 percent of additional resources from the 'Marshall Plan' will be made available to those sectors of West German industry that will manufacture military products." A second part of the same KI report is noteworthy for its unexplained—and obviously unnoticed—mention of "the events in Korea." Based on the source's private conversations with

American officials in Bonn, it discusses McCloy's plans for "emergency measures . . . in the event of a worsening of the situation in Germany in connection with the events in Korea." The plan reportedly envisaged, among other things, evacuating civilian employees to the left bank of the Rhine.[34] This report was not disseminated by KI Moscow until 4 January 1951. By comparison, the US State Department notes that although McCloy lunched with Adenauer on 6 November 1950, the discussion with SPD leader Schumacher took place later that day and separately. The only mention of Korea occurred when Adenauer "expressed concern lest new developments in Korea"—undoubtedly the entry of the Chinese into the conflict—"might delay the arrival of additional US forces."[35]

Here again, there is no SVR archival evidence of reporting from Maclean or Burgess at this critical juncture. When British prime minister Clement Attlee visited Washington in early December 1950 to voice his concern that the Americans were preparing to use the atomic bomb to check the Chinese, Modin claims that Maclean provided Moscow with a complete account of the results of the visit, including the commitment by Attlee and Foreign Minister Bevin to German rearmament. It seems unlikely that Maclean, who deplored what he felt to be the aggressive nature of US foreign policy, would not have reported on the German aspect of the Truman-Attlee meetings. If such reports existed, and were preserved, they were not made available by SVR or could not be declassified.[36]

Unification, Anyone? The Soviets and SED Try Another Approach

On 1 December 1950, GDR minister-president Otto Grotewohl addressed a letter to the West German government calling for all-German talks on "all-German elections." According to a CIA National Intelligence Estimate dated 27 December, this action was part of a broader Soviet effort to "hinder and delay the progress of German rearmament, and to utilize the conflicts which the problem arouses in Western Europe to gain some ground toward its ultimate objective of a unified Germany under Soviet control." Simply put, the Grotewohl letter was designed to encourage East and West Germans to initiate unification.[37]

Stalin's ploy was considered by the Western Allies. In a "secret session" of the High Commissioners' Council held in Berlin on 7 December 1950, those present anxiously "agreed that since Chinese successes in Korea, there was a general disposition among certain elements in West Germany to examine the Grotewohl letter most carefully rather than turn it down."[38] Similar appeals were heard throughout 1951. But overall these nervous rumblings did not slow the movement toward full West German membership in the European community. The Western Allies had finally recognized the pattern behind Soviet offers to exacerbate differences among the four powers. It seemed, as us high commissioner McCloy said, that "whenever new progress in the integration of Western Germany with the free world was in sight, . . . the more conciliatory the Communist terms for reunification."[39]

Continued Western Rearmament: A Soviet View

The North Koreans and their Chinese Communist allies captured Seoul, the South Korean capital, as 1951 began. The city was retaken by United Nations forces on 14 March, and their opponents began withdrawing to positions north of the thirty-eighth parallel, the former border. On 23 June, the Soviet delegate to the United Nations, Yakov Malik, proposed a cease fire. Truce talks began on 10 July. The front was stabilized, although fighting continued.

The momentum toward West German involvement in European defense and in economic partnership with its West European neighbors, which had been accelerated by the Korean conflict, continued. During this period, KI did an excellent job of informing the Soviets of developments in West Germany, except that it still ignored the role of the Korean conflict in stimulating these actions. KI also provided accurate reporting on Western reactions to Soviet and East German diplomatic and trade initiatives, which the Soviets had undertaken to wedge apart the Western Allies on the pace and exact nature of West Germany's contribution to European defenses.

Soviet goals in Germany appear to have remained the same. A CIA estimate drafted on 1 February 1951 explained that the Soviet Union's "ultimate aim" was to extend its control over all of Germany. Among its interim objectives were to "undermine the German Federal Republic, forestall its rearmament, and prevent its political, economic, and military association with the Western Powers." As for East Germany, the Soviets would "continue to strengthen Communist control within the GDR, exploit its economic potential, develop its military potential and forces, and further integrate the GDR into the Soviet orbit." Moscow would continue to use Berlin as a pressure point and planned eventually "to eliminate" the Western powers from the city so that it could be the undivided capital, first of the GDR, and then of a unified Germany.[40]

Further, the report estimated that the Soviets would try to frustrate West German rearmament "by methods short of military action." But if they saw these tactics were not working and believed that West Germany would become associated with a militarily strong Western coalition, the USSR "would regard the emergence of such a new European power situation as a barrier to its European ambitions and possibly as a threat to the security of the Soviet orbit . . . and would probably resort to military action at the time and place most advantageous to it." The Soviets, according to the CIA estimate, might risk starting another world war in order to challenge the Western Allies in Germany. Alternatively, Moscow could use the time before Western rearmament reached "dimensions considered dangerous by the Kremlin" for improving its military position and for "continuing its attempts to undermine the progress being made by the Western Powers."[41]

It is chilling to realize that during this period, when world peace was so threatened, exaggerations and stereotypes about the West in KI reporting compounded the confusion caused by Stalin's preference not to hear about South Korea. An early January report quoting former West German general Franz Halder, for example, was distributed by KI to Soviet, Czech, and Polish decisionmakers. In it, Halder explained that a plan for the West German army called for the creation of West German armed forces with a strength of from 100,000 to 150,000, which were to become part of "united European armed forces." In a private conversation the previous November, Halder had reportedly stated that "the remilitarization of West Germany would not be limited to a few divisions. In the future, these divisions would provide the framework for a mass West German army." Halder elaborated by stating that "he did not think US policy expected a Soviet attack on Western Europe, but rather was itself systematically preparing for an aggressive war."

Actually, KI Moscow did take issue with "clearly doubtful" reports from Halder's "German friends," who "exaggerated the tempo of remilitarization and characterized the policies of the western powers on this question inaccurately." In fact, KI thought it possible that for some reason Halder had "deliberately made statements of this kind to the informant, although it was also possible that the informant himself was not telling the truth [*iavliaetsia dezinformatorom*]."⁴² Here we have a unique view of the inner workings of KI as its officers wrestled with the problem of reports dissemination in a highly charged political atmosphere.

Other KI reporting on German "remilitarization" during this period appeared to conform to Soviet preconceptions of relations between the Western powers and the Adenauer government. The positions of the various players are highly distorted or even described in crude caricatures: in these scenarios, the Americans, strongly supported by the British, continued to insist on West German remilitarization over the protests of the West German people. France was thought to have resisted but in time to have proposed that any West German forces be included in a European Army under the so-called Pleven Plan. At the same time, Adenauer was depicted as a crafty politician who saw in rearmament an opportunity for the Federal Republic to achieve independence on favorable terms.

The tone and substance of these KI reports, which were distributed to Stalin and the Politburo, patently reflected the attitudes of ideologically motivated sources. Even those individuals whose cooperation was based on more venal considerations tended to report what their case officers had called for. In either case, this reporting was tempered adroitly by the case officers, who were well versed in such usages of the system. By the time the final report was prepared in the KI's Information Directorate, it had acquired the appropriate stylistic polish.

Another example of KI spin doctoring is the reporting on General Eisenhower's stopover in Frankfurt, West Germany, during his first visit to NATO facilities in January 1951.⁴³ Eisenhower spent the morning of 22 January visiting military headquarters in the American zone. After conferring with the Western high commissioners during the afternoon, he had a "brief opportunity" to meet "leading German figures" later, at a reception hosted by John McCloy. According to State Department reporting, Eisenhower's major emphasis at the reception and in a public statement made before his departure was to acknowledge the difference between the "regular German soldier and officer and Hitler," a symbolic gesture intended to soothe wounded feelings left over from the war.⁴⁴

A KI report, obtained from "Bonn governmental and military circles" and disseminated to Stalin and the Politburo on 7–8 February, cast the reception in a different light. The report was based on Adenauer's account given later at a "meeting of the Bonn government" and referred to "negotiations" between Eisenhower and Adenauer. It seems the information reflected the spin Adenauer wished to put upon the affair: he wished to portray the Germans as asking for and receiving equal status in the European defense plan. For example, when Eisenhower reportedly asked Adenauer what was needed to overcome reluctance on the part of West Germans to "participate in the 'defense' of Western Europe," Adenauer is said to have responded, "For this, West Germany must be accorded full sovereignty in political and military questions." When Eisenhower declared that "German forces must be commanded by reliable people," Adenauer pointed to Adolf Heusinger and Hans Speidel, his military advisers, as having been opposed to Hitler. Acknowledging his error in 1945 in considering all Germans to be Nazis, Eisenhower reportedly added that he had been convinced by his visit that the defense of Western Europe would not be possible without the participation of West Germany. The report concluded with Adenauer's comment that the deputy chairman of the Social Democratic Party had also been present during the negotiations with Eisenhower and had "defended the same political line as Adenauer himself."[45] Given Eisenhower's relatively brief exposure to German leaders at the reception, it appears that the lengthy exchanges reported by KI were somewhat amplified. Moreover, Adenauer's efforts to demonstrate the importance of Germany among the European Allies seem to have been translated by the KI source into a somewhat premature portrayal of intimate relations between the American and West German military administrations.

Stalin must have been aware of both the difficulties encountered and the progress achieved by the West in integrating West Germany into a defense strategy for Western Europe. A 9 January KI report, for example, described Adenauer's dissatisfaction with the outcome of the meeting of the NATO Council in Brussels in December 1950. It also documented his reaction to guidance given him before the Brussels meeting by High Commissioner McCloy, who urged West Germany to accept the meeting's decisions and continue to press for rearmament.[46] These Berlin KI reports, although generally not based on original documents, did cover topics that for the most part were classified Top Secret by the US State Department, the US high commissioner in Germany, and US embassies in West European capitals. The scope of KI reporting also demonstrated that the Berlin residency was better informed about the course of these important negotiations in the Western capitals than was BOB concerning parallel activity in East Berlin and Moscow.

KI exploited its various networks in Europe to track the activities of West German chancellor Adenauer during 1951. We have here a unique picture of its use of sources within French intelligence to provide detailed coverage of Adenauer's visit to Rome in June, including his audience with the pope. Of particular interest to the French at the time was the position expressed by Adenauer and Italian prime minister Alcide de Gasperi that both countries needed to support the American policy of a "united Europe."[47] The report was not disseminated until late September, probably because the KI sources in French intelligence would have passed this information to their Soviet handlers only after the reports had been processed for dissemination within the French service concerned.

KI was also keeping Stalin informed of the position of the West German Social Democratic Party (SPD) on key aspects of West German foreign and domestic policy. Apparently, the Soviets never lost hope that a faction within SPD could be encouraged to support Soviet policies. In late July 1951, KI circulated a detailed report of talks two months earlier between the British secretary of state for foreign affairs, Herbert S. Morrison, and Kurt Schumacher and other SPD leaders. According to the report, Morrison had expressed general support for the foreign policy and domestic line taken by SPD but had warned the party's leaders that the British government was "cooperating closely with the United States in the area of strengthening 'the security of Europe' and in connection with that is interested in the remilitarization of West Germany." From the tone and content of this report, it appears likely that the source was a Social Democratic participant in the talks rather than a source in the British Foreign Office.[48]

On 11–12 August 1951, KI's Information Directorate prepared a survey of the Paris negotiations for a "European Army." The contents reinforce the view that a large part of the KI's coverage of the European defense program came from French sources. In its covering memorandum, KI explained to Stalin and the Politburo the positions of the principal participants in the conference, noting that the "basic disagreement" was between France and West Germany over the latter's demand for "political and military equality within the framework of the 'European Army.'" Although much of the information in the survey pertaining to the German side was derived from "hearsay" reporting, the description of the French position appears to have come from an aide-mémoire sent by the French Foreign Office to André François-Poncet, French high commissioner in Germany.[49]

Although details on military cooperation between West Germany and the Western Allies had top KI priority, the Soviets were concerned as well about the emergence of a more closely integrated West European economy that would include the Federal Republic. On 13 July 1951, KI disseminated to Stalin and the Politburo a Russian translation of conversations between Adenauer and François-Poncet. Adenauer described the status of the legislative action on the Schuman Plan and seemed convinced it would pass. The two also disagreed on the nature of the West German contribution to the European Army, and Adenauer dismissed the importance in West German public opinion of the neutralist movement popularly known as "without us" *(ohne uns)*. When François-Poncet doubted Adenauer's prediction that he would be able to bring SPD leader Schumacher around to supporting rearmament, "Adenauer told a story about Schumacher's having been a German trusty *(kapo)* in a concentration camp, which he claimed had been told him by an eyewitness, a former inmate." Because he feared being compromised by this, "Schumacher avoided meetings with persons who were in the same camp." For KI, this documentary material was obviously sensitive and was apparently not disseminated to East European allies, as was the reporting from Bonn sources.[50]

Did the Soviets Lay a Trap of "Peace"?

One of the diplomatic initiatives launched by the Soviets in a campaign to complicate the inclusion of West Germany in a European army was a November 1950 request to the Council of Foreign Ministers that they meet to "consider the question of fulfillment of the clauses of the Potsdam Agreement regarding the demilitarization of Germany." For domestic political reasons, of which the Soviets were well aware from KI reporting, neither France nor Great Britain could afford to reject the Soviet proposal outright even though there appeared to be little hope of achieving an acceptable outcome. An exchange of notes made it clear that their positions on the German question were far apart, but the four powers agreed to engage in "exploratory talks" to determine the usefulness of a foreign ministers' session. These talks were broken off in June 1951.

Further KI reporting about the Council of Foreign Ministers' exploratory talks again reflected the close attention paid by the Soviet leadership to any sign of differences within SPD on four-power treatment of the German question. A 5 May 1951 report gave the views on the subject of Herbert Wehner, a prominent SPD leader and the chairman of the Bundestag's committee on all-German questions. The report, which was disseminated to Stalin and the Politburo, did not reveal where or to whom Wehner made the remarks attributed to him. After philosophizing on Soviet reasons for calling for a CFM session and commenting on the Attlee-Schuman visit to Washington as a reflection of the desire of the "war-weary" British and French peoples for peace, Wehner stated that "SPD would prefer a collapse of the Council rather than a decision to neutralize Germany. The Soviet version of neutrality would bring Germany under Soviet control." Wehner concluded by saying "if the Western powers could force the Soviet Union to give up East Germany as the price for refusing to remilitarize West Germany, they would achieve great success in the Cold War."[51] Compare this statement on "neutralization" with that of SPD leader Kurt Schumacher, chairman of the SPD Executive Committee, in discussions with McCloy on the same subject. According to Schumacher, "If the Soviets did offer or accept genuine free elections on condition that Germany remain disarmed and be denied [the] right to associate with regional defense groups, I felt we would have to accept such a solution and trust to the strength of German democracy to protect itself against inevitable Communist infiltration by which the Soviets would endeavor to capture the government." These nuanced differences within the top leadership of SPD were of continuing interest to Stalin.[52]

Throughout spring and summer 1951, as the difficult negotiations over West Germany's role in European defense and its economy continued, the Soviets complemented their deceptive diplomatic initiatives with attempts to manipulate interzonal trade. The Soviet goal appeared to be to eliminate West Berlin's role as an intermediary between East and West Germany and as a transshipping point for this trade. On 24 July, KI reported an 18 June State Department directive to "occupation authorities in West Germany" to prepare for a possible resumption of the blockade.[53] On 6 July, Peter Sichel, chief of BOB, discussed the danger of a new blockade in a report forwarded to the director of CIA. After noting the problems linked to interzonal trade, Sichel referred to other Soviet actions that could be thought of as "laying groundwork for a resumption of the blockade." He noted that the southern railroad by-pass would become operational by 1 August, thereby "permitting all rail traffic at present passing through West Berlin to be routed around Berlin." Road maintenance along the Autobahn between West Berlin and Helmstedt on the border of the British zone in West Germany had been discontinued with the result that "one third of the autobahn is one lane only." Also, plans had been drawn to dig a canal bypassing West Berlin, thus eliminating one of the most effective Allied counter-measures, the "threat of interference with Soviet Zone barge traffic in the British Sector."

Sichel also explained that a successful airlift to support West Berlin would require many more planes and supplies than were required in 1948–49 (12,000 tons daily for an industrially active city as opposed to 5,000 tons in and 2,000–3,000 tons out in 1948–49 to sustain a depressed living standard). Stockpiles were down to 157 days' supply of coal and 149 days of food. Related to increased supply needs was the integration of West Berlin into the West German economy. If, for example, the electrical industry, West Berlin's largest, were cut off, both West Germany and West Berlin would suffer. Finally, West Berlin morale had deteriorated in the previous few months as the population had begun to realize "the impossibility of the political and economic situation ever improving." The "situation was aggravated by the widening rift between [West Berlin mayor Ernst] Reuter and the Federal Republic." In addition, Sichel's memo included a BOB report of an SED meeting on 6 June 1951 at which Heinrich Rau, chairman of the GDR State Planning Commission, had indicated that a decision had been made to seal West Berlin off from West Germany.[54]

Although the Soviets were well aware of East Germany's need for interzonal trade, throughout 1951 they continued to undermine this trade, cutting off West Berlin from West Germany. KI received a December 1951 report from its source in the office of West Berlin Senator Friedrich Haas, who allegedly affirmed the Soviet viewpoint with comments about the worsening political and economic situation in West Berlin. His views were somewhat distorted in their details, but they do tend to confirm the morale problems in West Berlin. Haas is quoted as saying, for example, that "Reuter and the Americans want to increase the number of American troops in Berlin, but the city can't afford it. . . . As the economy worsens, bank accounts disappear, and the outflow of capital and industrial enterprises continues." Berliners were said to believe that their city "can be held through the speeches and promises of Reuter as long as the Russians permit it, but as soon as the situation takes a serious turn, it will be impossible to hold."[55] Such KI reporting must have indicated to the Soviet leadership that its diplomatic diversions, such as the Council of Foreign Ministers meeting and attacks on the West Berlin role in interzonal trade, were successfully confusing and demoralizing the Western Allies.

With both the Federal Republic of Germany and the German Democratic Republic supporting their own versions of laws calling for "free elections" in all of Germany, on 13 November 1951 the UN General Assembly voted to refer this question to its ad hoc political committee. At the same time, KI informed Stalin and the Politburo of "the intention of the three Western powers, at the request of the FRG, to place this item on the U.N. agenda." The report was allegedly based on a "document of the government of one of the three Western countries in which is set forth the agreed position of the three Western powers on the German problem." According to this document, the "fate of the proposal will depend on the position of the Soviet Union," which will either "speak out against elections in Germany" or "be forced to agree to opening the eastern zone to impartial mediators, and reconcile itself to all of the consequences arising from [this agreement]." The document contains the prophetic sentence: "If reunification of Germany becomes inevitable, then it must be carried out by means of incorporating East Germany within the structure of West Germany with the application of the principles and institutions of the Federal Republic."[56]

Soviet determination throughout 1951 to resist German rearmament while ignoring the events in Korea that brought it about is demonstrated most vividly in an evaluation by KI Moscow deploring the "gap" in reporting on neofascist organizations. It notes that "as formerly, little material is being received from the sources of the German friends on neofascist organizations except for Bruderschaft." The reason given by KI for its interest is that "at the present time a part of these neofascist organizations is speaking out against remilitarization and for the unity of Germany." But it was not possible for KI to sort out the real positions of neofascist circles and to "make a determination as to whether their statements can to some degree be used in the interests of the popular struggle against remilitarization and for the unity of Germany."[57] The Soviets were so eager to obtain any declarations from any political quarter in West Germany critical of rapprochement with NATO that they would even make use of statements by those on the extreme right.

A KI report of 26 July described an acrimonious discussion between Adenauer and former Wehrmacht general Heinz Guderian over the direction of German rearmament. Asked by Adenauer why he would not cooperate with the Bonn government, Guderian "expressed his hostility toward those who had violated their oath [participants in the anti-Hitler putsch of 20 July 1944]" and stated that Adenauer's policies would lead to the "sacrifice of German troops." According to the same KI report, in mid-June Guderian had visited the leader of Bruderschaft in Lübeck and given him the task of going to Berlin to establish contact with Soviet organs in Guderian's name.[58]

More concrete concerns about West German rearmament can be discerned in a KI report of 2 October 1951 that reviewed the status of the German service and guard units in the American and British zones. These troops had been added to similar units composed of East European displaced persons. In addition to providing an order of battle of the German units in the American zone, the report described actions that tightened discipline and demanded tougher terms of service for units in the British zone. This was explained to Adenauer as the Allies' determination to prepare these units to carry out specific tasks, should war come. Adenauer was told that if "we Germans had responsibility for these units, we would have taken the same steps in the interest of improving their effectiveness." Although this report was more specific than most in its descriptions of growing West German military capabilities, it was sent only to Deputy Foreign Minister Gromyko and GRU chief Matvei V. Zakharov, not to the Politburo.[59]

Soviet Leaders Try a New Reunification Proposal

In fall 1951 the Soviets launched a new reunification proposal by Otto Grotewohl, the East German premier. On 9 November a report was sent to Stalin on a lecture by Douglas W. O'Neill, first secretary and political director of the Office of the British High Commissioner for Germany, evaluating Grotewohl's proposal. O'Neill reportedly opened with the statement: "The USSR has come to the conclusion that the biggest obstacle to the realization of their plans for Germany was the decision by the Western Powers to abandon hope for four-power agreement on Germany and create instead a healthy and flourishing West

Germany in the form of the Federal Republic."[60] Noting that the only Soviet response to this situation had been propaganda demanding that the four powers unite the two parts of Germany, O'Neill observed that the Grotewohl proposal was superficially much more attractive than its predecessors were. The price for unification had been reduced to two basic demands: demilitarization and the withdrawal of all occupation forces. O'Neill emphasized that this approach was appealing to many West Germans, "every second one of which had relatives in East Germany." He added that "just as the Germans were not loved when they were occupiers, we are not loved in this role either."[61]

Nonetheless, O'Neill emphasized that under the Grotewohl formula a "united Germany would be neutral, weak, defenseless, and it would be impossible to defend it. This constitutes the greatest danger." Consequently, O'Neill pointed out, "if a unified Germany means its gradual transition to the sphere of influence of the East, we could not permit the creation of a united Germany. . . . If it became necessary, we would not stop at resorting to arms to prevent the rise of such a Germany." England did not oppose German unity, O'Neill concluded, but would welcome a reunification "which would gradually restore a natural balance in Europe."[62] This was a blunt, accurate description of not only British reactions to the Grotewohl proposal but those of the US government as well.

A 4 December 1951 copy of a weekly French intelligence service bulletin on Germany obtained by MGB's Paris residency gave a French perspective on the proposal. The part of the bulletin that discussed West Berlin evidently came from a French source within SED.[63] According to the report, the majority of West Berliners were tired of their "islander" status and blamed Adenauer's Catholicism for his lack of interest in the predominantly Protestant city. The middle class felt that it suffered most from the division of the city and hoped that "Grotewohl's proposals and the rumors of confidential contacts between East and West politicians . . . will produce change." Unfortunately, "the working class is against the proposals and does not trust Grotewohl's promises." They knew that the "standard of living of a worker in West Berlin is higher than in the GDR." The business class and industrialists "are even more skeptical, having no doubts about the intentions of the GDR government (even though for business reasons they would like nothing more than to trade, even with the Communists)." At the heart of the Berlin problem, according to the SED report, was the attitude of the Soviet Control

Commission, which recognized that the "1948 Berlin Blockade was not a very shrewd measure. The spirit of the Berlin population, the success of the airlift, the American propaganda, which accused the Soviet Government of inhumanity and a desire to reduce the city to starvation, all of this brought the Berlin problem to the forefront of international attention." At the same time, "the American declaration that any Soviet attempt to take Berlin by force would be resisted with arms made Berlin a causus belli [a cause of war]."[64]

As a result, the SED report continued, a "small Berlin war" was in progress and interzonal trade had been paralyzed. "The trade agreement signed on 20 September has not been enforced because the Soviets will not lift the restrictions on trade between West Berlin and West Germany, a precondition for the renewal of trade relations." On the political side, "much embarrassment has arisen because of the uncompromising position of the Russians." In the "SED's Berlin organization, both functionaries and active members are expressing their dissatisfaction . . . and consider that the fate of the city will remain unresolved because for the Russians it is a question of prestige and the correlation of forces. They can neither retreat nor prevail."[65]

This KI and MGB reporting describes well the different perspectives that were shaping reactions to the German question during this tumultuous time. West Germany was now a self-governing state with an economy that was not only growing but also increasingly linked to that of its neighbors, especially France. Although wartime memories of the Nazi war machine had threatened to derail the effort to enroll West Germany in the defense of the West, the proposal was still very much alive. Stalin would never admit it, but he owed this precarious state of affairs to the cumulative effect on the West of the Berlin blockade and the Korean War. These events also spurred the growth of an unprecedented CIA covert operation against East Germany.

5

Cold Warriors in Berlin: A New Era in CIA Operations

I n response to the Korean War and the perceived Soviet threat in East Germany, CIA developed a major covert action capability, much of which was centered in Berlin and directed against the Soviet zone. How this operation came about and how KGB responded is an essential part of our story. In this account we are able, for the first time, to draw upon documents and witnesses from both sides. In the United States, the idea of covert action—or "covert psychological operations" as they were then called—took shape during 1947–48, initially in response to Communist-led actions in France and Italy. At first, responsibility for US covert programs was placed in a newly created special procedures group in CIA's Office of Special Operations (OSO), even though the involvement of CIA in such activity went against the better judgment of director Adm. Roscoe H. Hillenkoetter.[1] Nevertheless, pressure to expand this effort soon mounted—pressure exacerbated by squabbles between the State Department and the Pentagon over control of these activities. Neither actually wanted to carry out covert operations, but both wanted to direct them.

Curiously, a report from the KI Berlin residency in May 1948 illustrates how difficult it must have been for Moscow to comprehend the intricacies of these bureaucratic conflicts. According to KI, Hillenkoetter said that General Clay was obstructing every attempt by American intelligence to create so-called Free Russia committees by bringing together displaced persons in the US zone. As soon as word of these committees reached Clay, Hillenkoetter complained, "he orders them dissolved, thus causing the time and effort spent on organizing them to be wasted." Clay believed that if they were necessary, such committees should be organized in the United States because "they constituted a challenge to the Russians that could lead to military complications."[2]

These comments, passed on to the KI source by Clay's intelligence officer Gen. Robert Walsh, may have reflected Clay's views on the subject of émigré organizations, but they did not capture the tone of the Washington infighting. The KI report was probably related to a 17 March 1948 study by the State-Army-Navy–Air Force Coordinating Committee (SANACC) recommending "utilization of refugees from the Soviet Union in the US National Interest." The program was supported by OSS veteran Frank G. Wisner, then deputy to the Assistant Secretary of State for Occupied Areas. Whereas the Berlin KI residency report portrays Clay as standing up to pressures from DCI Hillenkoetter, Hillenkoetter himself, in his response to the SANACC report, conveys a negative view of the usefulness of refugees from the USSR in "propaganda, sabotage and anti-communist political activity."[3] The CIA reply to the SANACC study described Soviet émigré groups as "highly unstable and undependable, split by personal rivalries and ideological differences, and primarily concerned with developing a position for themselves in the Western world." There is no indication that KI ever heard or reported these views.[4]

This specific dispute aside, dissatisfaction in the State and Defense departments with Hillenkoetter's cautious approach, and OSO's preference for the methodical buildup of clandestine assets for long-term covert operations, resulted in a new National Security Council directive. Adopted on 18 June 1948, just as Soviet preparations for the Berlin blockade were nearing completion, the directive provided for a new, independent component within CIA to conduct peacetime covert operations.[5] Designated the Office of Policy Coordination (OPC), it was activated on 1 September 1948, and Frank Wisner was made chief.[6] By October, Wisner had put together a list of planned OPC projects, including media operations, support of resistance movements, economic warfare, the creation of anti-Communist front organizations, and the development of covert organizations called "stay behinds" to conduct sabotage and intelligence operations if the Soviets overran Western Europe.[7]

Transforming these plans into reality required not only the right people but also support from OSO agents and administrators. Those OSS veterans who had remained with OSO after the war had created new liaisons with foreign intelligence and security services and with the American military. They had gained recognition and respect as a serious group interested in long-term intelligence and counterintelligence activity. They had painstakingly developed their own agent assets and were beginning to realize the high human cost of operating against the Soviets, who had unmatchable experience in intimidating and controlling those tempted to oppose the regime. Initially, OPC representatives were helped by OSO field units because OSO had realized that its agents were motivated to varying degrees by anti-Communism. Indeed, OSO officers were themselves already engaged in what would later be termed "political warfare," in which intelligence production was an important by-product.

This initial cooperation began to fray during 1949 and early 1950, as field personnel began to implement the unique OPC program. To OSO, many aspects of OPC's plans were unrealistic because its leaders did not appreciate OPC's relationships with American military commands and host governments and did not understand conditions in the USSR and in areas under Soviet control. These disagreements were exacerbated by OPC's insistence on complete independence from OSO; by recruitment practices under which OPC employees were paid much more than those in OSO performing comparable tasks; and by the air of condescension adopted by many OPC officers toward their OSO counterparts. The problems were worse in the Washington headquarters, where personnel from both departments were crowded into offices in temporary buildings lining the Reflecting Pool. It was not uncommon for OSO officers to reject a candidate for employment, only to discover later that he had walked to an adjacent building and been hired by OPC for a higher position.[8]

Relations between OSO and OPC were more congenial in Germany, even as the Soviets tested Allied nerves in the Berlin blockade. The OSO station in Karlsruhe helped "Rollo" Dulin, OPC's affable and urbane field representative in Germany, lay the groundwork for the future OPC radio stations Radio Free Europe and Radio Liberty. In February 1949, Henry Sutton, who had been responsible for BOB's hectic order-of-battle collection program, joined Dulin's staff and quickly resumed contact with his old friends in BOB, using them to find German agents.[9]

Michael Josselson became the first OPC officer in Berlin in fall 1949. His primary concern was to provide the framework for the anti-Communist "front" organization, the Congress of Cultural Freedom, which held its first session in Berlin in June 1950.[10] The Berlin "old boys" network contributed still another figure to OPC Germany when Dulin was replaced as chief in Frankfurt by Lawrence de Neufville, who had been chief of X-2 Berlin in fall 1945.[11] Still, there were so few OPC staff members in Germany in early 1949 that many OSO officers were unaware of their existence.

The group did not remain hidden for long. Former CIA director Richard Helms had it right when he said, "The OSO was small while OPC was getting larger by the moment, and when the Korean War came [OPC] really exploded."[12] This view was echoed by every former OSO officer interviewed for this book. OSO had paid scant attention to the early OPC arrivals, but as new personnel began to flood into Germany in the fall and winter of 1950–51, it became impossible to remain indifferent to their presence.[13] The new arrivals, eager to assert their independence from the OSO base in Berlin-Dahlem, established an office at Tempelhof Air Base, thirty minutes' drive away. They disdained the Department of the Army cover then in use by OSO Germany, and were set up as a civilian firm under contract to the US Air Force.[14]

OPC Makes Its Mark Countering Soviet Rallies

Both the American military and the new federal government under Konrad Adenauer feared Korean-style attacks from the Soviet zone. The precariousness of West Berlin's position was highlighted by a large Free German Youth rally in Berlin in May 1950, less than a month before the North Korean invasion. The group's East German leaders had asked for permission to march through West Berlin, but intelligence reports noted that the rally, involving a planned 600,000 youths from the GDR and other countries, was a cover to "overthrow the legal West Berlin government." Western commandants made plans to resist any incursions into the Western sectors. As a result, the rally, although it was an impressive demonstration of the East German regime's ability to mobilize massive numbers of people, was confined to the Soviet sector. Soviet support and direction for this project was reflected in a Berlin KI residency's report of 19 April 1950.[15] In it, an unnamed source complained that the decision to prepare military forces to defend Berlin during the rally was made unilaterally by the United States. This action, according to the source, reflected a tougher American line on Berlin that foreshadowed a new role for the city as a springboard for offensive political operations against the Soviet Union. Actually, the Western Allies had coordinated their responses to the planned rally; West Berlin, West German, and European political and youth organizations, some sponsored by OPC, had been enlisted to help counter the rally's influence.[16]

A year later the Soviets planned another action, the World Youth Festival, to be held in East Berlin on 5–19 August 1951. The festival was expected to draw a million participants from all over the world. Western plans this time were to encourage free access to West Berlin and to create hospitality centers for visitors. On 7 July, KI presented a seven-page report to Politburo member Mikhail A. Suslov concerning Western preparations for the festival. These included plans to receive up to 200,000 visitors from the festival, some of whom might wish to remain as refugees and would require "assistance."[17] Figuring prominently in KI's description of the coordinating committee established under Hans Hirschfeld, Mayor Ernst Reuter's press relations officer, was the participation of Ernst Tillich, leader of the Fighting Group Against Inhumanity (Kampfgruppe gegen Unmenschlichkeit).

The Kampfgruppe was a principal project of OPC Berlin. US support for the group, in fact, predated OPC's arrival in the city. US Army Counterintelligence Corps had helped fund the group when Rainer Hildebrandt, its strongly anti-Communist founder, was still its leader. OPC began to subsidize the project indirectly in 1949. Direct funding began in 1950, with OPC paying about half of the group's expenses, although it exerted no real control. During Hildebrandt's absence on a US lecture tour from October 1950 to February 1951, an OPC case officer contacted Tillich, then the group's business manager, and the group began to initiate more aggressive programs within the GDR. In November 1951 Hildebrandt agreed to step down so that Tillich could assume control, but in 1952 disagreements in the Kampfgruppe leadership gave rise to Soviet and East German press attacks on the group and on Hildebrandt personally.[18] MGB Berlin also stepped up its coverage of the group. An annual report by Gen. Mikhail Kaverznev, chief of MGB Karlshorst, described the theft in April 1952 of the briefcase of a Kampfgruppe official responsible for "subversive operations in the GDR." The same official's secretary was reportedly kidnapped. On the basis of information obtained through these actions, the report claimed that sixty-four of the group's "active diversionary agents" had been arrested.[19]

OPC continued its relationship with the group through Tillich but had to stave off repeated attempts by Hildebrandt to reestablish his relationship with CIA. In March 1959, Kampfgruppe was disbanded amid a flurry of critical press articles from both East and West. The thrust of West Berlin and West German commentary was that although the group's original intention was a "noble objective"—to be a rallying point for victims of Soviet zone "terror"—the amateurish conduct of its operations had endangered the lives of East Germans, and feuding between its leaders had tarnished its reputation. The Soviet and East German press expressed doubt that the Kampfgruppe was actually being terminated; they predicted that it would reappear under another name.[20]

Why did OPC continue to support this organization despite all its problems? The answer is simple. After managing to replace the mercurial Hildebrandt with the steady Tillich, OPC Berlin had a flexible instrument for conducting a full range of covert operations against the East German regime. Operations included dropping leaflets from balloons and distributing pamphlets by hand, but the Kampfgruppe activity that most infuriated the East was the falsification of GDR documents of all kinds, even postage stamps. One of these counterfeits was a black and white portrait of SED leader Walter Ulbricht with a noose around his neck. The Ulbricht stamp was actually placed on envelopes by some West Germans and sent through the GDR postal system. The degree of resentment over this sort of attack puzzled OPC case officers. Did the overreaction reflect SED insecurity about not having a legitimate popular mandate? Perhaps, but by attributing every incident of unrest or breakdown in the economy to sabotage, East German authorities created a mystique for the Kampfgruppe that far exceeded its actual capabilities.[21]

Helpful Ideologues: Anti-Soviet Emigré Groups

A Berlin project that resisted definition as either OSO- or OPC-sponsored was BOB's relationship with the Popular Labor Alliance of Russian Solidarists (Narodno-trudovoi soiuz rossiiskikh solidaristov—NTS), an anti-Soviet Russian émigré organization. The propaganda and publication activities of this organization in West Germany were subsidized in part by OPC. NTS had a group in Berlin that used German intermediaries to contact members of the Soviet Military Administration and the Soviet Group of Occupation Forces. Their connections appeared to offer intelligence opportunities. BOB chief Peter Sichel approached the OPC German station with the idea that BOB would make an OSO slot available for an OPC case officer, who would handle the NTS Berlin operation. Through this arrangement, worked out over a sumptuous lunch in a private room at the Frankfurter Hof, NTS operations in Berlin were handled from within the OSO base.

Working with NTS was never easy. Whereas OSO was mainly interested in obtaining hard intelligence on Soviet forces, NTS was driven by its desire to overthrow the Soviet regime. Both OPC and OSO soon determined that only those Russian-speaking case officers who could appreciate the total ideological commitment of NTS people could work with them. NTS distributed leaflets by hand via East Germans and had its own short-range balloon teams. One of these teams was run by an émigré who owned an attractive bar off the Kurfuerstendamm (Berlin's equivalent of New York's Fifth Avenue) that was frequented by BOB officers. In typical Berlin style, he never acknowledged his NTS ballooning, and those in the know at BOB pretended to be unaware of his avocation. NTS agents were also involved in the more important and dangerous work of contacting Soviets in Soviet-occupied territory. NTS once provided a welcome boost to BOB operations by acquiring a telephone directory from BOB's key scientific-technical target, the Bad Weissensee offices of the Directorate for Soviet Property in Germany (USIG). Other contacts resulted in defections by Soviet military personnel.

Meanwhile, KGB was intent on frightening NTS and on inhibiting Western support of its longtime adversary. In 1954, KGB kidnapped NTS Berlin leader Aleksandr Trushnovich and attempted to assassinate the chief of NTS operations, Georgy Sergeevich Okolovich.[22] Nikolai Khokhlov, the KGB agent who defected to Okolovich rather than kill him, noted that much of the support for this and similar operations came from the KGB's Berlin unit in Berlin-Karlshorst.[23] To gain further leverage against NTS operatives, KGB brought their relatives into Karlshorst from the USSR in order to lure the agents to the East, but this tactic generally failed. The relative was usually brought to the sector border, sometimes within sight of the NTS person, and the family members would "talk" by exchanging messages. It was always BOB's hope that the relative, disaffected by the system, might elude his or her KGB shadow and come West. This never happened. But such experiences did inflame NTS agents' hatred of the Soviets.

The British, who had begun working with NTS in Berlin in late 1950, shared the responsibility for the NTS Berlin operation. As the Americans later discovered, George Blake, the KGB source in British intelligence, apparently kept KGB informed on British activities with NTS until the British dropped the project in 1955.[24] Blake knew perhaps better than anyone why the British abandoned NTS: they were concerned about not only costs but KGB penetration of the operation. No one should have been surprised at the possibility of penetration, given the scale of KGB's effort to undermine NTS. Certainly in classical counterespionage terms NTS was a poor operational risk for CIA. Although NTS leaders did their best to preserve security, the nature of their work in emigration continually exposed them to KGB agents. Further, some NTS leaders welcomed direct confrontation with their Soviet opponents, even when the latter appeared to have the upper hand. NTS agents did not despair when one of their number fell into Soviet hands; rather, they chose to believe that one more Russian patriot had penetrated the enemy's defenses.

The enormous amount of manpower that KGB devoted to counteracting NTS—and to foiling émigré operations generally—was a continual source of irritation to other elements of the First Chief Directorate. To KGB political intelligence officers, this excessive concern for NTS seemed a holdover from the postrevolutionary period, when Russian exiles were considered a serious threat to the new regime.[25]

BOB chief Sichel also thought that the NTS project had drawbacks. All operational decisions had to be reached jointly with the British Secret Intelligence Service, and convincing NTS of the need for intelligence collection could be exasperating. So BOB looked for a similar Russian émigré organization that could approach Soviet targets in East Germany but be solely under CIA control. The group chosen was the Union of the Struggle for the Liberation of the Peoples of Russia (Soiuz bor'by za osvobozhdeniia narodov Rossii—SBONR), based in Munich. One of the people whom SBONR recommended as a member of the CIA Berlin team was Igor Grigorievich Orlov, or "Sasha."

Orlov said that he was born in Kiev in 1924 but grew up and attended school in Moscow. After the German invasion in 1941 he was sent to an intelligence school in Novosibirsk that trained people for work with partisan detachments behind German lines. In October 1943 he was dropped into German-occupied eastern Poland and was captured. By April 1944 he began cooperating with a German intelligence unit in front-line operations against the Red Army. Near war's end he was transferred to the headquarters of the Vlasov Army (which was devoted to liberating Russia) and given documents in the name of Alexander Kopazky. He was captured by American forces in May 1945 and interned until April 1946. Like many ex-Soviets who had worked with the Germans in wartime, Sasha joined one of the subunits of the Gehlen Organization, a West German intelligence unit then run by the US Army. For unknown reasons he parted with his émigré friends in the postwar intelligence world and joined a private German firm.[26] He then married a German woman.

In late spring 1951, Orlov and other SBONR members of the Berlin team were escorted to Berlin by William Sloane Coffin, the CIA case officer for the SBONR project.[27] But once in Berlin, the SBONR team members did little to encourage confidence in their suitability for the Berlin assignment. The team chief, who like Orlov had been in the Vlasov Army, was at the same time chief of the SBONR "secret section" and responsible for liaison with CIA on the full range of SBONR activities. According to the case officers who worked with the chief, he had little sense of operational security yet resented all efforts to moderate his behavior. He showed no aptitude for clandestine activities—a potentially fatal shortcoming in a city as dangerous as West Berlin. The BOB case officer recalls one incident on the Kurfuerstendamm when a sackful of Russian language leaflets with supplemental instructions in German was dropped by one of the SBONR team. Several thousand leaflets spilled onto the sidewalk. The case officer and his SBONR cohorts spent several minutes scrambling to recover the lot, to the guffaws of passersby.

In contrast to his SBONR colleagues, Orlov was a model of proper behavior. He was also a snappy dresser who, despite his small stature and Russian-accented German, appealed to the young women who formed the base of his eventual operations. On 4 September 1951, BOB proposed to drop SBONR but retain Orlov as an independent agent. He was instructed to go to Munich, announce his break with SBONR, and then return to Berlin. CIA's Combined Soviet Operations Base in Munich concurred with this plan, commenting only that his departure from SBONR should be accomplished with some finesse because OPC still wished to preserve its ties with the organization for propaganda purposes. The remaining SBONR Berlin team members, including the chief, were sent back to Munich, where they were informed by Coffin that the Berlin project had ended.[28] On 10 October, CIA's Combined Operations Base reported that Orlov had been successfully polygraphed and dispatched to Berlin.[29] The OPC phase of CIA's involvement with Orlov was finished. But his continued employment as a BOB principal agent over the next several years had serious repercussions for all who became involved with Igor Orlov, alias Sasha Kopazky.

OPC Support of the Eastern Bureaus

Among other OPC activities in Berlin was contact with the Eastern bureaus of the Christian Democratic Union (CDU) and the Social Democratic Party (SPD). Both of these relationships began under the OSO base and were transferred to OPC case officers in Berlin as soon as the officers could take on additional responsibilities. The initial reason for OSO support was the need for intelligence on the Soviet zone. But because OSO exercised no control over the activities of these organizations the information obtained was limited, mostly low grade, and unsubstantiated. The transfer of contact with the eastern bureaus to OPC management and the provision of a much more generous subsidy was welcomed by both the bureaus and OPC.

The Soviets' greatest concern was the possibility that the eastern bureaus of some political parties were supporting anti-SED actions by their party affiliates in the GDR. The CDU eastern bureau was a special problem. CDU was intended to be a compliant component of the National Front, but a great many CDU members in the GDR refused to accept this role and were encouraged in the resistance by the eastern bureau operating from West Berlin. A report of 2 October 1952 reveals that MGB had learned from agent reporting and the interrogation of arrestees that CDU's eastern bureau had created an illegal CDU leadership throughout Thuringia that was endeavoring to split members from the central party leadership in East Berlin. The report also claimed that the CDU eastern bureau was engaging in espionage against Soviet troops by using party members to collect political and economic information and by encouraging the troops to help CDU members leave West Berlin as refugees.[30] These revelations led to the arrest of forty agents and associates of the "espionage-diversionist" eastern bureau of CDU, headquartered in West Berlin. Among those arrested were CDU members in Thuringia who were serving as mayors, city council members, civil servants, and teachers.³¹

Both the CDU and SPD eastern bureaus continued to figure prominently in KGB reporting on "subversive organizations" in West Berlin. According to a 1957 report from KGB, "The eastern bureau of CDU . . . has agent networks in the GDR that are recruited above all from the reactionary members of the GDR CDU. The CDU eastern bureau uses this network to collect espionage information on the activities of government agencies and political parties in the GDR."³² The same report relates the belief that SPD's eastern bureau "carries out active espionage-subversive activity against the GDR. . . . It takes a particularly active part in the distribution within the GDR of various antidemocratic literature and provocative leaflets. Just in the period from 8 March to 6 May 1957 the SPD Eastern Bureau distributed more than five and a half million leaflets in the GDR. These leaflets are spread with the help of air balloons, others by members of the agent nets. In the second half of 1957, the . . . launching [of] balloons with anti-democratic materials [has been] significantly reduced as a result of measures taken by the GDR MfS."³³ The reduction in balloon-launched leaflet distribution was probably as much due to Western restraint as to Soviet and East German "countermeasures." When President Eisenhower's special assistant for the Cold War, C. D. Jackson, requested that BOB launch "an extensive propaganda balloon attack" in Berlin in February 1954, for example, Michael Burke, deputy chief of CIA's German station, replied that he would have to discuss with the US Commandant "lifting . . . the balloon ban."³⁴

The Story of the Free Jurists

"The Investigating Committee of Free Jurists, . . . created in 1949 in West Berlin by the lawyer Horst Erdmann (who used the alias Theo Friedenau), is financed by the Americans. Officially, the Investigating Committee offers residents of the GDR free legal advice. Actually, [it] carries out widespread espionage activities against the GDR with the help of its agent net within the GDR, and engages in a systematic campaign of slander against the GDR and other countries of the socialist camp."
—A 1957 KGB listing of "subversive organizations in West Berlin"

The CIA story of the Free Jurists' Committee, never before told, offers insight into one aspect of BOB's Cold War operations.³⁵ The Free Jurists grew out of the imagination of a single BOB officer, yet the organization's

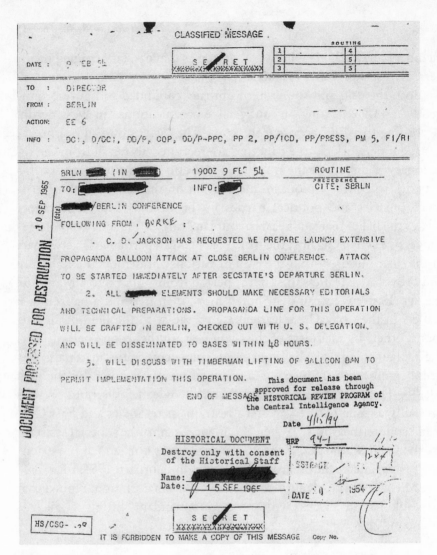

CLASSIFIED MESSAGE

SECRET

ROUTING		
1		4
2		5
3		5

DATE : 9 FEB 54

TO : DIRECTOR

FROM : BERLIN

ACTION: EE 6

INFO : DCI, D/DCI, DD/P, COP, DD/P-PPC, PP 2, PP/ICD, PP/PRESS, PM 5, FI/RI

BRLN ████ (IN ██████)   1900Z 9 FEB 54   ROUTINE

TO: ███   INFO: ███   PRECEDENCE CITE: SBRLN

████/BERLIN CONFERENCE

FOLLOWING FROM BURKE :

    C. D. JACKSON HAS REQUESTED WE PREPARE LAUNCH EXTENSIVE
PROPAGANDA BALLOON ATTACK AT CLOSE BERLIN CONFERENCE. ATTACK
TO BE STARTED IMMEDIATELY AFTER SECSTATE'S DEPARTURE BERLIN.

    2. ALL ████ ELEMENTS SHOULD MAKE NECESSARY EDITORIALS
AND TECHNICAL PREPARATIONS. PROPAGANDA LINE FOR THIS OPERATION
WILL BE DRAFTED IN BERLIN, CHECKED OUT WITH U. S. DELEGATION,
AND WILL BE DISSEMINATED TO BASES WITHIN 48 HOURS.

    3. WILL DISCUSS WITH TIMBERMAN LIFTING OF BALLOON BAN TO
PERMIT IMPLEMENTATION THIS OPERATION.

END OF MESSAGE

SECRET

HS/CSG- ██

IT IS FORBIDDEN TO MAKE A COPY OF THIS MESSAGE   Copy No.

Cable, 9 February 1954, from Berlin to director, relaying a request by presidential assistant C. D. Jackson that CIA launch propaganda balloons following the Berlin Foreign Ministers Conference.

early successes in challenging the illegal actions of the SED-controlled regime enabled it to rise to prominence among international anti-Communist organizations. The group's influence certainly accounted for the scope and ferocity of Soviet and East German efforts to blunt its effects in the GDR and abroad. This same success caused CIA to involve the organization in wholly incompatible and disastrous paramilitary activities. Indeed, the eventual destruction of the reputation of the group's leader and founder, and of the group itself, was apparent at the group's creation.

The leader of the Free Jurists' Committee, Horst Erdmann, was recruited by Henry Hecksher of OSO Berlin. Until his defection, Erdmann had resided in Belzig, in Brandenburg province, where he had served as a notary public and claimed to have practiced law. Hecksher, educated in the pre-Nazi German legal system, could see that the new SED regime emerging in the Soviet zone was increasingly indifferent to the rule of law whenever the law interfered with its efforts to eliminate opposition. By ignoring the law the Soviets and SED had incurred the enmity of many in the legal profession and had caused many ordinary East Germans to seek help in avoiding imprisonment.

As a counterintelligence officer, Hecksher realized that he and his little group in BOB could never achieve any real successes against the Soviet or East German security services by pursuing the few double-agent cases under their control. What was needed was a "force multiplier," as the military might say—an organization that could produce the level of detailed information on opposing security services, Soviet and East German, that BOB needed to target individuals or units in those services. An organization regarded by the East German population as an independent source of legal guidance would also naturally produce information on both the East German judiciary and the security system: a invaluable by-product. Hecksher went to the new OPC for funding with the understanding that he could "hand Erdmann an occasional assignment or debrief him along lines of interest to us [BOB]."[36]

Hecksher refrained from imposing intelligence requirements on the committee during its formative phase, and in the absence of an OPC case officer in Berlin, he acted as the group's fund-raiser. By summer 1950 the committee had established itself to a degree no one had thought possible. It had created in the East German legal profession a network eager to report illegal acts by the SED regime and to provide evidence that might lead to criminal indictments in a future non-Communist

Germany. The group's influence was felt throughout the GDR, and collaborators reported that members of the East German judiciary often avoided passing harsh sentences on captured members for fear of retribution.

The committee had become, in a sense, a shadow GDR justice ministry, and it was considered by West Berlin media and public opinion to be the most potent underground organization in East Germany. The Free Jurists remained focused on their primary goals: the compilation of data on illegal acts committed by GDR officials, the dissemination of information on these acts via collaborators in the GDR, and the provision of legal advice to the growing stream of daily visitors to committee offices in West Berlin. The information they acquired contained considerable detail about Soviet and East German security organizations and about other installations and localities of interest to OSO. Perhaps because it had been allowed to develop in its own way, though, the group seemed to have avoided the taint of an American intelligence connection.[37]

But a problem did emerge because of OPC officers' biases against counterintelligence operations. Inspired by the Korean War to leave civilian careers and volunteer for service with OPC, many case officers embraced their mission, often without question. Their job, in the OSS tradition, was to apply the full range of wartime methods to shake the GDR to its foundations—to create such havoc behind Soviet forces in East Germany that a Korean-style invasion would be impossible. Among these OPC officers were those who felt that introducing intelligence and counterintelligence goals and methods into the work of groups they supported was morally wrong and could corrupt them. Missing was an understanding of how their new opponents, the Soviet intelligence and security services and their East German disciples, viewed the problem. MGB automatically leveled the accusation of "espionage" against organizations like the Free Jurists, whether or not evidence existed to support the claim. This accusation served as a propaganda weapon for both internal GDR and foreign consumption. OPC officers also found it difficult to adjust to the increasingly restrictive operational security environment in East Germany. The Soviet-style police-state system had already become so constraining by 1951–52 that psychological warfare operations on the scale envisaged by OPC were nearly impossible to sustain.

The Soviets Kidnap Walter Linse, a Free Jurist

The Free Jurists' Committee had been one of many MGB targets as early as 1950, but when MGB learned in early 1952 that the committee would play a leading role in an International Congress of Jurists in West Berlin in July, their coverage intensified. Peter Deriabin, then a member of the Austro-German department of the foreign intelligence directorate of MGB, described Soviet concern and the plans to sabotage the congress in his book *The Secret World.* The high spot of the campaign to wreck the congress was originally to have been the kidnapping of Erdmann. According to Deriabin, Erdmann's departure for Sweden at the last moment forced a change of plans, and Karlshorst recommended that Walter Linse, head of the committee's economic section, be taken instead. This appealed to the Karlshorst apparat, which prepared the plan, because it viewed Linse and the economic section as the significant target: Linse's department concentrated on such matters as expropriation of property without compensation, workers' rights in nationalized industries, and labor law (which was of particular concern to MGB because it was responsible for the abysmal working conditions at the Wismut uranium mining and processing sites). The kidnapping took place on 8 July 1952.[38]

The MGB report of the kidnapping, dated 10 July, stated that "during interrogations by the GDR Mfs, Linse confirmed reports of anti-Soviet activity by this organization and the existence of its espionage networks on GDR territory." The report added that "with the agreement of the Soviet Control Commission and Comrade Ulbricht, the Mfs arrested twenty-seven of the more active agents. . . . Arrests of exposed agents continue." The final paragraph adds this interesting note: "Taking advantage of this operation, the GDR Mfs, in order to infiltrate new agents into the Free Jurists, will organize cover for them by sending them to West Berlin as 'refugees.'"[39]

The Linse kidnapping was evidently one of the highlights of MGB's year. An annual report on 18 December 1952 claimed that in "the current year, East German state security organs delivered blows in a more organized fashion against enemy formations and the agent nets of imperialist intelligence services." The Linse case was cited as an example: "Linse's kidnapping made it possible to carry out a large-scale operation to liquidate the espionage nets of the Committee in the GDR, as a result of which eighty-four agents were arrested who had been employed in responsible positions in the state apparatus of the GDR, in large factories and mills, and also in design bureaus."

The remainder of the report reflected the agony the Soviets must have felt at the scope of the Free Jurists' work:

> At the time of his arrest, a voluminous report was seized from Linse that was intended for American intelligence; it consisted of an economic review on GDR industry, trade, and planning, along with the necessary statistical data. Based on materials obtained during the preliminary and pretrial investigations, it was determined that the "Committee" had been able, through its agents in GDR enterprises, to expose more than four hundred transactions between GDR offices and West German firms that violated the American ban on trade. This resulted in the detention of about eight hundred traders involved in these deals and the interruption of receipt by GDR industry of goods and raw materials from West Germany in the amount of eight hundred million marks.[40]

These revelations in the economic sphere must have greatly angered Soviet and East German officials; they certainly explain the intensity of their attacks on the Free Jurists. In addition to the Linse abduction, on 24 July MGB took advantage of the "defection" of a secretary who had probably been MGB's spy in Linse's economic section. In the security investigation that followed Linse's kidnapping, she evidently feared exposure and disappeared. Immediately thereafter the East Germans released a letter from her accusing the committee of "criminal espionage and sabotage" on behalf of the American secret service.[41] On 26–27 July, with the congress in session, the East German media released accounts of the GDR supreme court trial of seven alleged committee agents, presided over by the notorious and greatly feared Communist judge "Red Hilde" Benjamin. The secretary who "defected" testified at the trial, which was the first of four held during the summer.[42]

According to an MGB report of 11 August 1952, "The first trial held in Berlin . . . was timed to coincide with the 25 July opening of the International Congress of so-called Free Jurists." In MGB's view, the propaganda campaign associated with the declaration by the former secretary, and the ensuing trials, "disorganized the work of the congress to a significant degree and undermined the anti-Soviet propaganda connected with it." MGB commented that "characteristically, the kidnapping of Linse itself brought no reaction from the congress."[43] The term

Товарищу МОЛОТОВУ В.М.
Товарищу МАЛЕНКОВУ Г.М.
Товарищу БЕРИЯ Л.П.
Товарищу БУЛГАНИНУ Н.А.

Согласно сообщениям Уполномоченного МГБ СССР в Германии, МГБ ГДР, после изъятия из Западного Берлина руководителя так называемого "Союза свободных юристов" ЛИНЗЕ, МГБ ГДР, после изъятия из Западного Берлина руководителя вининовской службы, арестовано всего 84 действовавших в ГДР инолинзе Вальтера, арестовано всего 27 служащих государственного учреждения, в том числе 18 работников немецких хозяйственных учреждений и предприятий.

Следствием установлено, что "Союзу свободных юристов" с помощью агентуры, приобретенной ЛИНЗЕ и его заместителем ГАТЗЕНОМ, удалось собрать для американской разведки и боннского министерства по общегерманским вопросам ряд важных сведений о местах Советской Армии и подразделениях народной полиции ГДР, о планировании и торговле в ГДР, выпущенной на предприятиях продукции, о новых изобретениях и другие секретные сведения о деятельности государственных и хозяйственных органов ГДР. С помощью агентуры "Союза свободных юристов" западно-немецким властям, в частности, удалось раскрыть и сорвать около 400 торговых сделок различных венных фирм западно-германскими торговыми фирмами, в результате чего промышленность ГДР недополучила из Западной Германии товаров и сырья на сумму 800 миллионов марок.

Арестованный директор одного из сельскохозяйственных предприятий, член ХДС, КЕЛЛЕР на следствии показал, что он, используя свои поездки по городам земли Саксония — Анхальт,

значительно понизивом том. Характерно, что самый случай похищения ЛИНЗЕ во вызвал никакой реакции со стороны конгресса, если не считать глухого замечания руководителя "Союза свободных юристов" СРЕДНИХ относительно "нарушения законности властями советской зоны, имеющего место особенно в последнее время".

По агентурным сообщениям из Западного Берлина, среди участников "Союза свободных юристов" отмечается растерянность и проявление панических настроений. Понимая также законательство среди участников жестких антисоветских влияний организаций. Руководитель одной из таких организаций, так называемого "Унтерзухунгс-Комитет", БОККАН стал появляться на улицах Западного Берлина, в сопровождении своего вооруженного шофера.

Представитель западно-германской разведки ГАНЗЕН, в Берлине РАЙС заявил, что провал "Союза свободных юристов" свидетельствует о "допокеловной" работе западно-берлинских юноновских организаций и об отсутствии у них опытных профессионалов-разведчиков, опровождают "вар-орм" Ташкт в Берлине КАЛЕР сообщил, что "Союз свободных юристов" и другие подобного типа по западноберлинскому организации теперь уже не пользуются у американцев прежним доверием.

Ввиду предложений со стороны коменданта американского сектора Берлина ЛАЙКОНА и американского верховного комиссара в Германии КАНТЕ—а по поводу секретного изъятия ЛИНЗЕ, считаем ГДР принять решение дело ЛИНЗЕ рассмотреть в закрытом судебном порядке.

С.ИГНАТЬЕВ

"11" августа 1952 года
5591/и

копия послана тов.Вышинскому

kidnapping, normally never used by the Soviets in cases of this kind, may have been intended to emphasize MGB's claim that the congress did not respond, even to an action described in the Western press as an abduction. The report also cited agent reports from West Berlin to the effect that as a result of MGB efforts, members of the Free Jurists were confused and panicked, feelings that extended to the leaders of other anti-Soviet organizations in Berlin. To illustrate the level within the Soviet government that was concerned with this case, we note that in addition to the primary recipients—Molotov, Malenkov, Beria, and Bulganin—Vyshinsky also received a copy of the report.

Contrary to MGB's spin, the Linse kidnapping did not appear to have disrupted the work of the congress. Although the FRG justice minister, Thomas Dehler, did not attend, he did send a representative, and both Mayor Ernst Reuter and the West Berlin Senator for Justice participated on opening day. In fact, the Soviets' actions gave Erdmann (alias Friedenau) a compelling premise for making a radio address to the people of the GDR. Further, the kidnapping of Linse incensed the participants, who overwhelmingly supported resolutions condemning the incident.[44] Indeed, a review of press coverage at the time demonstrates that the Linse affair greatly enhanced the image of the congress and of the Free Jurists.

As the United States (from whose sector in Berlin Linse had been kidnapped) continued to berate the Soviets, each protest and subsequent denial was made public, keeping alive the case and the cause of the Free Jurists. The final paragraph of the 11 August 1952 MGB report states: "In view of the [protests] concerning the secret removal of Linse submitted by the Commandant of the US Sector of Berlin, Maj. Gen. Lemuel Matheson, and the American High Commissioner in Germany, [John] McCloy, the GDR authorities have decided that the Linse case will be examined in closed legal proceedings."[45] Press interest in the case remained. It was reported on 11 December that the Soviets had returned a food parcel and letter sent to Linse by the new American High Commissioner, Walter J. Donnelly, disclaiming any knowledge of his whereabouts.[46]

It is not surprising that this Soviet MGB-inspired operation used an East German team for the kidnapping. Details on the team's methods in the Linse operation, and its involvement in previous abductions, were documented by the West Berlin police.[47] What is interesting in the 11 August MGB report and the 18 December summary is how any direct

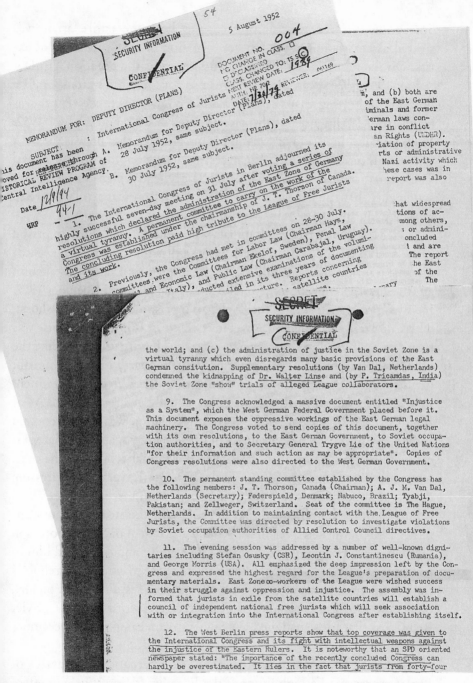

54

5 August 1952

MEMORANDUM FOR: DEPUTY DIRECTOR (PLANS)

SUBJECT: International Congress of Jurists

This document has been released through the HISTORICAL REVIEW PROGRAM of the Central Intelligence Agency.

Date 12/9/94
HRP 94-1

A. Memorandum for Deputy Director (Plans), dated 28 July 1952, same subject.

B. Memorandum for Deputy Director (Plans), dated 30 July 1952, same subject.

1. The International Congress of Jurists in Berlin adjourned its highly successful seven-day meeting on 31 July after voting a series of resolutions which declared the administration of the East Zone of Germany a virtual tyranny. A permanent committee to carry on the work of the Congress was established under the chairmanship of J. T. Thorson of Canada. The concluding resolution paid high tribute to the work of the League of Free Jurists and its work.

2. Previously, the Congress had met in committees on 28-30 July. These committees were the Committees for Labor Law (Chairman Hays, . . . and Economic Law (Chairman Ekelof, Sweden), Penal Law . . . Italy), and Public Law (Chairman Carabajal, Uruguay). . . . ducted extensive examinations of the volumi- . . . lied in its three years of documenting . . . ture. Reports concerning . . . satellite countries . . .

[right fragment:]
m, and (b) both are . . . of the East German . . . minals and former . . . erman laws con- . . . are in conflict . . . an Rights (UNDHR). . . . iation of property . . . rts or administrative . . . Nazi activity which . . . hese cases was in . . . report was also

. . . hat widespread . . . tions of ac- . . . mong others, . . . s or admini- . . . oncluded . . . l and are . . . The report . . . he East . . . of the . . . The

SECRET
SECURITY INFORMATION
CONFIDENTIAL

the world; and (c) the administration of justice in the Soviet Zone is a virtual tyranny which even disregards many basic provisions of the East German consitution. Supplementary resolutions (by Van Dal, Netherlands) condemned the kidnapping of Dr. Walter Linse and (by P. Tricamdas, India) the Soviet Zone "show" trials of alleged League collaborators.

9. The Congress acknowledged a massive document entitled "Injustice as a System", which the West German Federal Government placed before it. This document exposes the oppressive workings of the East German legal machinery. The Congress voted to send copies of this document, together with its own resolutions, to the East German Government, to Soviet occupation authorities, and to Secretary General Trygve Lie of the United Nations "for their information and such action as may be appropriate". Copies of Congress resolutions were also directed to the West German Government.

10. The permanent standing committee established by the Congress has the following members: J. T. Thorson, Canada (Chairman); A. J. M. Van Dal, Netherlands (Secretary); Federspield, Denmark; Nabuco, Brazil; Tyabji, Pakistan; and Zellweger, Switzerland. Seat of the committee is The Hague, Netherlands. In addition to maintaining contact with the League of Free Jurists, the Committee was directed by resolution to investigate violations by Soviet occupation authorities of Allied Control Council directives.

11. The evening session was addressed by a number of well-known dignitaries including Stefan Osusky (CSR), Leontin J. Constantinescu (Rumania), and George Morris (USA). All emphasized the deep impression left by the Congress and expressed the highest regard for the League's preparation of documentary materials. East Zone co-workers of the League were wished success in their struggle against oppression and injustice. The assembly was informed that jurists in exile from the satellite countries will establish a council of independent national free jurists which will seek association with or integration into the International Congress after establishing itself.

12. The West Berlin press reports show that top coverage was given to the International Congress and its fight with intellectual weapons against the injustice of the Eastern Rulers. It is noteworthy that an SPD oriented newspaper stated: "The importance of the recently concluded Congress can hardly be overestimated. It lies in the fact that jurists from forty-four

Memorandum, 5 August 1952, from John A. Bross, chief, Eastern European Division, to Frank Wisner, deputy director, plans, regarding the International Congress of Jurists. The congress was held in Berlin shortly after the kidnapping of Free Jurists official Walter Linse.

Soviet involvement was suppressed and how the entire affair was treated as an MFS initiative. But confirmation of MGB involvement exists. On the first page of the 11 August report is the notation "To Deriabin, 19 August." On the last page, also for Deriabin's attention, is a notation indicating that the information contained in the report was taken from Berlin apparat dispatches dated 20, 22, and 30 July 1952. Following his defection in 1954, Deriabin asserted that he was the desk officer in the MGB Austro-German section backstopping the Linse case. These notations on the MGB report certainly lend weight to Deriabin's statements that the genesis of the Linse operation was MGB's desire to sabotage the International Congress of Jurists.

Later testimony from individuals who encountered Linse in prison (one of whom, ironically, had been a leaflet distributor for NTS) casts additional light on the case. Following his abduction, Linse was taken to an MFS jail, where he continued to be interrogated until December 1952. He was then transferred to the Soviet MVD prison in Berlin-Karlshorst, where he was questioned by Soviet investigators. While there, Linse was treated as a "nameless" prisoner to keep his identity secret. Unlike the other prisoners, his name was never used by the guards in calling him out of his cell for interrogation. At the same time, he was given VIP treatment by his Soviet jailers, with privileges like a daily cigarette ration. As of June 1953 the "protocol" of his MVD interrogation was said to contain some 1,100 pages.[48] These accounts of Linse's interrogation by the Soviets were confirmed by General Kaverznev's final report on the case, sent to MGB head Ignatiev on 3 March 1953. But Kaverznev, expressing doubts about the wisdom of continuing to detain Linse in a Soviet jail on GDR territory, recommended that the results of the MGB Karlshorst interrogation be turned over to the Military Tribunal of Soviet Forces in Germany. This court quickly found Linse guilty and sentenced him to prison in the USSR.[49] Although the Soviets received numerous requests for information on his whereabouts, they denied responsibility. Finally, on 8 June 1960 the German Red Cross received word from the Soviet Red Cross that Linse had died in a Soviet prison camp on 15 December 1953.[50]

In retrospect, one can see that the 1952 International Congress of Jurists represented a high point in the Free Jurists' prestige and effectiveness. Certainly the Soviets paid the committee their own peculiar tribute in organizing the Linse abduction and the propaganda that followed. Within BOB, investigation of the security ramifications of the

Linse kidnapping and related incidents involved counterintelligence branch officers who were reinforced by temporary duty officers from the German mission. The committee continued to operate with CIA support, but eventually problems emerged that led to its disintegration. Some of these problems were built into the project, others arose from the continuing coverage of the organization by KGB and the East German MfS, and still others were caused by CIA itself.[51]

The Free Jurists Become a Paramilitary Group

Although the Korean conflict had degenerated into a trench war of attrition by late 1951, there was continuing concern in Washington and at NATO headquarters over a potential East-West conflict in Europe. A National Security Directive of 23 October 1951 called for developing resistance forces in areas under Soviet control, and for ensuring the availability of such forces in the event of war.[52] For OPC Germany this meant creating "stay behind" assets in East Germany—clandestine operatives who would be equipped with radios and would remain inactive unless war actually came. The preference to use agents who had both "proven motivation" and familiarity with conditions in the GDR made the Free Jurists an obvious choice.

The period 1952–53, when the proposal to involve the Free Jurists in clandestine paramilitary activities in East Germany came under consideration at Washington headquarters, was probably not the best moment for resolving an issue of this importance. CIA was undergoing a major reorganization. In January 1951, OPC and OSO had been placed under a Deputy Director for Plans (DDP), but not until August 1952 were the separate command structures dropped and these integrated services established under the DDP. The two structures were also combined in Germany, and the OPC and OSO elements in Berlin were integrated as a single unit headed by the chief of BOB. (The former OPC component was not moved from its Tempelhof offices to the new BOB offices in Dahlem until summer 1954.)[53] These changes improved the overall direction of CIA's clandestine operations, but Berlin OPC officers felt that OSO had "won." The officers missed their former independence, and their relations with a new BOB chief were tenuous.

In a 12 May 1952 memorandum to the chief, East European Division, Henry Hecksher, then at CIA's Washington headquarters, set forth his reasons for opposing the assignment of paramilitary responsibilities to the Free Jurists. Recalling his own desire in 1950 to improve the intelligence exploitation of the committee, he noted the strong opposition of the OPC station chief to any activities that would "prostitute the Free Jurists to the support of intelligence operations." Hecksher felt that the paramilitary venture, as planned, would sidetrack the organization from its primary goal of attacking legal violations in the GDR. Hecksher challenged as propaganda Horst Erdmann's claim that the Free Jurists had four thousand adherents in the Soviet zone. More important, Hecksher said, neither Erdmann nor his people had the training or temperament for the level of discipline and security required to operate a viable paramilitary network in hostile territory. Finally, Hecksher noted that linking a new paramilitary setup with the Free Jurists would invite scrutiny by the Soviet and East German security services. Why, Hecksher concluded, should we submit to this exposure such a sensitive activity as a paramilitary stay-behind operation? In his view, it would be easy for these opponents' intelligence services to shift from harassing the Free Jurists in their former role to challenging them as paramilitary forces.[54]

Hecksher's words were prophetic, yet CIA headquarters still decided to entrust the paramilitary project to the Free Jurists. Unfortunately, MGB had already been made aware of these plans by Linse. In fact, General Kaverznev devoted a good part of his 3 March 1953 final report on the case to the new secret section of the Free Jurists.[55] In late summer 1953, during security sweeps conducted in the wake of the 17 June riots, the Soviet and East German security services arrested members of the stay-behind network, along with others described as agents of the Gehlen Organization. The Gehlen involvement probably arose in part because the principal agent, a retired German naval officer of high rank who had been selected to run the paramilitary project under Erdmann, was found to be an associate of the Gehlen Organization.

In any case, the East German media accused the Free Jurists of complicity in the operation. This accusation necessitated another major counterintelligence investigation by BOB.[56] A former BOB case officer recalls that the paramilitary officers of the former OPC unit in Berlin had no conception of the lethal effectiveness of Soviet and East German counterintelligence capabilities. The networks had been organized into three-man cells that in theory were unconnected. But a postmortem by BOB revealed that nearly all members of the various cells had known the identities of everyone else. The Soviets were able to roll up the entire operation after identifying only one participant.

In spite of the negative publicity in West Germany about the Free Jurists after the breakup of the stay-behind program, the group continued to function. But its activities had the full attention of GDR security services and were attacked in the East German media. Furthermore, the head of the organization could not prove that he was a legitimate lawyer. In 1957 CIA headquarters suggested that a way be found to grant Erdmann an honorary degree. The memorandum containing this request noted, defensively, that the East German regime had never before raised this issue, even though the Free Jurists had begun work a full eight years earlier.[57] This East German reticence did not last. On 25 June 1958 a group calling itself The Association of German Democratic Lawyers held a press conference in East Berlin. They attacked the Free Jurists as a criminal organization led by a man (Erdmann, alias Friedenau) who had allegedly been a Hitler Youth leader, had falsified his place and date of birth, and had no right to the title "doctor of law."[58] On 1 July 1958, Erdmann announced his resignation, saying, "I hope it will be understood that I can no longer continue the nerve-wracking work that I have carried on for many years."

Press reactions in West Germany were mixed. *Der Spiegel* concluded that if "[Dr. Friedenau] is a former Hitler Youth leader without legal qualifications, it is hardly conceivable that he could have advanced to the position of Director of the Investigating Committee of Free Jurists."[59] The *Frankfurter Allgemeine Zeitung* sounded a note that was to be heard with increasing frequency in the Federal Republic. The article acknowledged that the Free Jurists had done much that was commendable in their attacks on "injustice as a system" in the GDR. Nevertheless, it was no longer possible for such organizations to continue under American direction without submitting to controls by authorities of the FRG. The article went on to note that as security controls had tightened, the number of Eastern visitors had dropped. In consequence, it became more difficult to maintain contact with undercover helpers in the GDR, with the result that the groups were losing touch with life as it had to be lived in East Germany and were making up for this shortcoming by including more and more items from the East German press in their information bulletins.[60]

Groups like the Free Jurists and the Kampfgruppe gegen Unmenschlichkeit were most influential during their early years, from 1948 to 1953 or 1954. During this period, when the Soviet zone was making a transition from total Soviet control to governance by an SED regime that was despised by a broad segment of the population and at best tolerated by the rest, it was still possible to move freely about the country and to visit West Berlin without hindrance or danger. In these circumstances the groups flourished, although they were frequently indifferent to the growing security threats that endangered their collaborators. The Soviets were creating an East German police state that eventually made it impossible for clandestine organizations to carry on any resistance activities in East Germany.

PART II

The Crisis Years

6

East German State Security and Intelligence Services Are Born

The largest, best equipped, and most pervasive police-state apparatus ever to function on German soil did not emerge full-blown. The Soviets had to nurture it until it became the East German Ministerium fuer Staatsicherheit (Ministry for State Security), often referred to as Stasi or MFS.[1]

In 1945–46 responsibility for security in the Soviet zone rested solely with the MGB operational sectors established immediately after the war. The informants and agents recruited by MGB for internal security coverage and for operations in the Western sectors of Berlin and in West Germany were primarily Germans, and many belonged to the newly created Socialist Unity Party (SED). MGB also relied for operational support on the German People's Police (Volkspolizei), which was responsible to the Directorate of Internal Affairs of the Soviet Military Administration (SMA). Nevertheless, the Soviets decided soon after the war to create an East German state security service patterned after the secret police of the Soviet Union. The service envisioned by the Soviets would eventually become responsible for internal security in East Germany and would develop a foreign intelligence capability.[2] How the Soviets managed this is reported here for the first time, drawing on SVR archival material.

In August 1947 SMA assigned special responsibilities to the K-5 departments—secret political police—within the East German criminal police. SMA charged them with struggling "against the criminal activity of the foes of the new democratic order."[3] In carrying out these political police duties the K-5 departments worked under the direction of MGB in East Berlin and the provinces. (Later, many members of K-5 helped to create and lead MfS.) In 1949, K-5 was placed under the Main Administration for Protection of the Economy (Hauptverwaltung zum Schutze der Volkswirtschaft) of the East German Interior Ministry, which was then headed by Erich Mielke.[4] The Soviets intended to forge an East German security service that could be the "sword and shield" of the new order in East Germany. The new organization was to include a department responsible for East Berlin and departments for operations in the Soviet zone, in addition to separate departments to cover rail and water transport. To staff this organization, 2,950 individuals were recruited, 1,535 of whom became operational staff.[5]

Personnel for these departments were selected primarily on the basis of political reliability. Some were drawn from SED, but MGB's own reserve of tested German agents was tapped as well. Persons from other political parties or organizations were deemed unacceptable for this service, testimony to the Soviet view that the "bourgeois" parties, CDU and the Liberal Democratic Party (LDP), served solely as window dressing for the new regime. By 6 October 1949, five provincial departments had begun work. The central department, responsible also for Berlin, was still being organized; the reason for this delay was probably the sensitivity and complexity of its mission in the city.

Choosing a Leader

Well aware of the political implications of the position of East German police chief, the Soviets chose that leader carefully. Concern was raised about Mielke, the leading candidate for the position. In a letter to Stalin and the Politburo, Col. Gen. Vasily Chuikov, commander of Soviet forces in Germany and chief of the Soviet Control Commission, and his political adviser Vladimir Semyonov assessed Mielke's background.[6] After relating his early membership in the German Communist Party (KPD), years in exile in the USSR, and service in the Spanish Civil War, the assessment notes that after leaving Spain, Mielke was interned in France. When the Germans invaded "Mielke allegedly escaped, but the length of his stay in the camp and the date of his escape are not known." Nothing further was heard of him until he was reportedly arrested by the Germans in 1944. After his arrest, he served in the Todt Organization, the Nazis' unit for large-scale construction projects, until war's end. In May 1945 he left the American zone, arriving in Berlin in June.

Mielke's unaccounted-for time in the West after his stay in Spain might have hurt his cause. In the Soviets' view, the greatest difficulty in creating these German state security organizations arose from the limited pool of recruits from which personnel could be selected. Beginning in May 1949, MGB officers, with the leaders of the new German units, reviewed 6,670 applications. Of the applicants, 5,898, or 88 percent, were considered unsuitable for various reasons: some had close relatives or other contacts in the Western sectors of Berlin or in West Germany; some had been prisoners of war of the United Kingdom, the United States, or France; some had served in Yugoslavia, where possible contact with the apostate Marshal Tito might raise suspicion. This insistence on the absence of Western ties or influences remained a major consideration as the service developed. Although it made recruitment difficult, over time it ensured a high level of security among the group's personnel.[7]

The Soviets found another candidate in Wilhelm Zaisser, chief of the Main Administration of Reserve Police, GDR Interior Ministry. His Communist credentials seemed impeccable. A KPD member since 1919, he was active in the Ruhr as an editor and militant trade unionist. In 1924 he attended the Comintern school in Moscow, after which he performed party work in Germany, China, and Czechoslovakia. In 1932 he became a member of the Soviet Communist Party while serving as an interpreter in the Comintern school. He served with distinction in the Spanish Civil War. After the war he returned to the USSR and became a Soviet citizen in 1940. During World War II he "served as an instructor in anti-Fascist courses in POW camps." Sent to Germany in 1947, "he showed himself to be a self-possessed, decisive individual." The report concluded, "Zaisser is the more suitable candidate for Minister of State Security. Mielke can remain as a deputy minister."[8]

It is not surprising that in 1950 the Soviet leadership would dictate to SED on an issue as important to them as the position of minister of state security. These reports in January and February provide an unusually candid view of the system at work in making such selections. The Soviet officials concerned were all well aware of Stalin's trust in the opinion of one of the SED leaders contributing to the report, Wilhelm Pieck, and if Pieck's candidate was Wilhelm Zaisser, so be it.[9] In one form or another, the "Mielke question"—the problem of whether the Soviets could fully control the administration of the East German security services—recurred several times in the years that followed.[10]

Soviet Intelligence Operations and the Party

As soon as Zaisser was in place as GDR minister of state security, another issue arose that concerned not only the relationship between MGB and the Committee of Information (KI) but also the much broader question of how far Soviet intelligence could go in exploiting members of foreign Communist parties as sources. In October 1950 the leadership of SED decided to transfer the party's intelligence networks to MfS, which was assuming new counterintelligence responsibilities in West Germany. But the networks were actually critical to KI's intelligence collection, and through them KI received a great deal of its economic, political, and military intelligence on West Germany.[11] Leading KPD members all over West Germany were involved in the nets. With the transfer of the party nets to MfS, KI would be deprived of a basic source of information. Chief KI resident Ivan Ilichev asked his MGB opposite number whether Zaisser could be persuaded to delay implementing the SED directive. He was told that reliance on the party nets in West Germany was dangerous because if a compromise occurred the connection of the West German KPD with KI could be used by the Western occupation authorities to ban KPD.

These problems were not confined to Germany. A prohibition against using party members was also instituted in Austria, where 70 percent of Austrian Communist Party members who had been MGB agents were reportedly dropped. A similar ban was instituted in other countries: Moscow ordered residencies not to contact leaders of foreign Communist parties except in situations of immediate danger. Above all, every effort was made to avoid repeating the trauma that had befallen the Soviet intelligence effort in the United States. Networks there, largely based on the exploitation of members of the US Communist Party, had been nearly destroyed after the war.[12]

Meanwhile, the development of MfS continued under the close supervision of the new Soviet MGB representative in Germany, Maj. Gen. Mikhail Kaverznev. In a February 1952 dispatch to the minister of USSR state security, Kaverznev submitted a progress report on the leadership, staffing, and activities of MfS.[13] The 1952 plan for MfS provided for a staff of 11,899, of which the operational personnel numbered 5,780. As of 20 February, however, MfS had reached only 43 percent of its authorized strength. Training departments were established in the apparatus of the MGB representative in East Berlin and in each provincial capital operational sector. There, in addition to teaching the Germans how to recruit and train agents, establish agent files, and handle agent networks, Soviet instructors worked in agent operations against the same targets for which MfS was ostensibly responsible.[14]

The Germans were not trusted to conduct independent agent operations and investigative work against Western espionage organizations and hostile groups; those were taken over by MGB. In addition, because all the German units reported to MGB's regional operational sectors, MfS's Berlin headquarters could not direct them properly.[15] As a result, the Germans lost interest and initiative.

In response to complaints from MfS officers, the Soviets made a few changes to give MfS limited and supervised authority over cases. In Kaverznev's words, this shift was made to promote "the development of creative initiative among German officials and strengthen the role of the GDR Ministry. . . . MfS, at our direction, is preparing a series of directives for intensifying the fight against espionage, diversion, terror, and underground formations."[16] In spite of the goodwill expressed in this dispatch, and the confidence Kaverznev proclaimed in the GDR state security service, he made it clear to Moscow that the Soviet instructional staff would continue to handle confidential contacts among officials of the German state security organs and that such contacts were to be developed among new recruits in the German service.

Soviet coverage of SED and of the GDR government reflect standard practice at the time. Penetration of SED had begun in Moscow much earlier, when KPD cadres had sought refuge from Hitler's Germany.[17] It is not surprising, then, that the Soviets had their own special contacts within the upper echelons of the East German SED and government. These operatives were careful to conceal their true relations with Soviet colleagues lest their role on behalf on MGB become known to Walter Ulbricht and his supporters within the SED Central Committee. Soviet sponsors considered the sources trusted friends rather than agents, but they helped prevent MGB, and later KGB, from being taken by surprise by developments in East Germany. Highly placed sources within SED, for example, informed MGB about the explosive situation there during winter 1952–53. Unfortunately, the Soviet leadership did not always act decisively on the information provided by such sources. Ulbricht eventually and with great reluctance changed course under Soviet pressure, but it was too late to forestall the riots of 17 June 1953.[18]

The situation at MFS was still far from perfect. In September 1952 Soviet instructors reviewed Stasi and found, according to Kaverznev, "serious shortcomings." Because of inadequate operational preparation and the poor quality of the German staff, penetration of enemy intelligence and hostile centers in West Germany was moving very slowly. The quality of MFS investigative work was hampered by inexperienced agents. The leadership of MFS did a poor job of assessing and training operational cadres. Even the party organization of SED had not been much help to the new organization.[19] Kaverznev also complained about the MGB advisers, recommending that better-qualified "Chekists" be assigned, especially to the MFS departments of intelligence, counterintelligence, industry, transport, and operational-technical services.[20]

In December 1952, Kaverznev brought MGB minister Sergey Ogoltsov up to date on developments within MFS.[21] Particularly impressive were MFS's operational accomplishments. During 1952 it had arrested 2,625 persons, 599 of whom were alleged spies. They also had set up active coverage of thirty-five West Berlin and West German espionage and anti-Soviet centers and of the underground organizations established by them in the GDR. They arrested 604 agents of these organizations and had attempted to abduct some of their leaders. As a result, MFS was able to conduct sixteen "show trials" of enemy spies, diversionists, and terrorists between January and November.[22]

But by March 1953 this positive evaluation, a standard feature of annual reports, had turned negative. In a 9 March report Kaverznev's deputy noted that the operations staff of MFS was unable to cope with the increasing volume of operational work because of its inadequate training, lack of experience, and weak political preparation.[23] Moreover, the need for a good East German service was growing more desperate because of "the worsening of class conflict in the GDR and the growth in the activities of imperialist intelligence and hostile underground movements." MFS seemed especially inept at finding informants among the intelligentsia, who were of special interest to the Soviets. Because of this problem, SED assigned to MFS 239 party members who had finished college. But many of these better-educated SED members had relatives in the West or were otherwise disqualified. As of 10 March only six candidates had started work.[24]

American Military Governor Lucius D. Clay, center, and British general Sir Brian Robertson, third from left, pose with ministers president of the West German Laender Bavaria, North Rhine Westphalia, Hamburg, Schleswig-Holstein, and Lower Saxony. (US Information Agency)

Dedication of the Soviet War Memorial, West Berlin, 11 November 194[
At center is Marshal Georgy Zhukov; to his left are deputies Ivan Sero[
and Vasily Sokolovsky.

ss chief William Joseph Donovan. (US Army)

avel Fitin, head of the NKGB foreign
ntelligence directorate. (SVRA)

Richard Helms, who replaced Allen Dulles in Berlin and rose to become director of Central Intelligence, 1966–73.

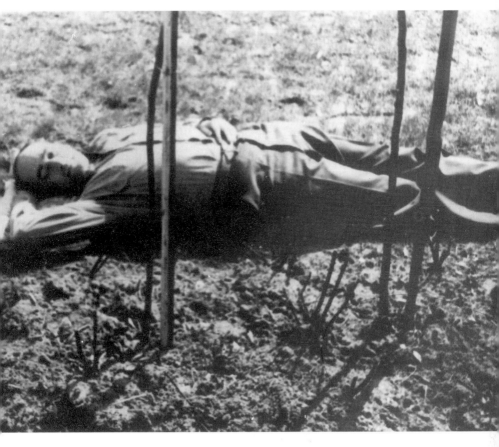

Berlin Operations Base chief Dana Durand, spring 1946.

NKVD leader Lavrenty Pavlovich Beria, left, with Georgy Malenkov, c. 1952. (David King Collection, London)

Antonius Hospital, KGB headquarters, Karlshorst, 1956.

Aleksandr Mikhailovich Korotkov, first Soviet
foreign intelligence resident in Karlshorst, 1945,
and chief KGB apparat, Karlshorst, 1957–61.

offices, Foehrenweg, Berlin-Dahlem, 1945–54.

Deputy BOB chief Peter Sichel, with cigar, confers with Henry Hecksher of Berlin X-2 in Berlin, early 1946.

BERLIN-KARLSHORST

Photograph courtesy of Christian Grabandt.

Karlshorst S-Bahn station.

or guard at the bier of Josef Stalin, March 1953: from left, Vyacheslav
tov, Kliment Voroshilov, Lavrenty Beria, Georgy Malenkov, Nikolai
anin, Nikita Khrushchev, Lazar Kaganovich, and Anastas Mikoyan.
oto)

Igor Grigorievich Orlov, "Sasha."

Yevgeny Petrovich Pitovranov, KGB chief in Karlshorst, 1953–57.

Lt. Col. Pyotr Semyonovich
v, c. 1953–60.

David Murphy, c. 1954–61.

Morale throughout the People's Police had never been lower. KGB reported that in 1952 more than one thousand members of the paramilitary maritime and air police (forerunners of the GDR Navy and Air Force) deserted to West Berlin and West Germany, along with 320 border guards. During January and February 1953 there were 492 defections from the paramilitary maritime and air police and the border guards.[25]

These defectors were described in MGB reporting as unstable young persons facing the burdens of military service and succumbing to hostile influences and propaganda. They fled to West Berlin "in search of the easy life." The political organs were thought to be extremely weak in their struggle against these hostile influences. In order to eliminate such influences on military discipline, a number of personnel were dismissed from the police at the insistence of MFS. MFS remained a disappointment to its Soviet advisers.

"Mischa" Wolf and IWF

For an intelligence service that would one day surpass its Soviet tutors in the depth and breadth of agent penetrations of the government of the Federal Republic, the beginnings of the East German foreign intelligence capability were not spectacular. Actually, its very creation may have resulted from a disagreement between the Soviet MGB in Berlin and the KI Berlin residency over the use of different sources for intelligence collection. In any case, KI was under pressure to develop an East German foreign intelligence capability, and fast. We shall describe their efforts, drawing for the first time on KI documents, and we shall also provide unique insights into BOB's coverage of this new counterintelligence target.

The Soviet directive that created the East German intelligence service emphasized that KI residencies in Berlin were still responsible for conducting their own operations against the main adversary—the United States—and for collecting information on the activities of West German governmental, political, and economic organs and scientific-technical centers, as well as on other countries.

It was clear from the outset that the principal target of this new GDR service would be the Federal Republic: the "internal political and economic situation in West Germany: . . . the activities of the Bonn government and its departments, the Bundestag, the Bundesrat; . . . the leading organs of the bourgeois and social democratic parties; scientific-technical centers and laboratories; and also churches and other public organizations." Obviously, KI did not expect its East German offspring to read newspapers for its intelligence but rather to recruit agents from among the officials and personnel of the targeted institutions. Finally, the service was directed to use its agent networks in the West German government to "shed light on the policies of the Western occupation powers."[26]

The person to be placed in charge of staffing this new intelligence service was "Comrade Akimov." Akimov was the code name of Andrei Grigorievich Graur, a senior state security foreign intelligence officer who had been considered for the position of NKVD liaison officer with OSS in Washington. Graur was directed by KI Moscow to create a cover within the Soviet Control Commission for KI representatives who would work with the new East German service. Moscow also sent Aleksandr Korotkov, a former foreign intelligence resident in Berlin and veteran German specialist, to work with Graur as a way of ensuring the cooperation of Walter Ulbricht, first secretary of SED, whom Korotkov had known for years. KI was taking no chances.

The new East German foreign intelligence service, like its Soviet counterpart, KI, was never publicly announced. It was officially but secretly known as the Foreign Political Intelligence Service (Aussenpolitische Nachrichtendienst) of the GDR, and it was led by SED Politburo member Anton Ackermann. In an added conspiratorial twist, and to provide additional cover for its employees, the service was given the designation Institute for Economic and Scientific Research (Institut fuer Wirtschaftswissenschaftliche Forschung—IWF).

The first meeting between Graur's Soviet team and its East German "friends" was held in early September 1951 in a safe house in Berlin-Bohnsdorf. Despite his experience, Graur seemed a curious choice for this assignment. He had been in Vienna in May 1951 as part of a Moscow inspection team investigating problems between the MGB and KI residencies there. One morning he had appeared at breakfast and announced to the senior team member, Deputy KI Chairman Pyotr Vasilievich Fedotov, that he had been recruited by the British Intelligence Service. Fedotov, not given to panic, asked him to explain. Graur told of having been surrounded by people in white jackets who had given him injections and then recruited him. Fedotov suspected that Graur was delusional. He went to the secure telephone, and later that day a medical evacuation aircraft arrived to take Graur back to Moscow.

Graur received intensive psychological treatment, recovered, and then left for the Berlin assignment, where he remained until November 1952. After returning again to Moscow, he had relapses and had to leave the service.[27]

The German founders joined their Soviet colleagues at this first session. Among them were the first chief, Anton Ackermann, and the future chief, Markus Wolf, then twenty-eight years old.[28] Taken to Moscow by his parents when Hitler came to power, Wolf grew up speaking native Russian, became a Soviet citizen, and during World War II worked on the Soviet-controlled German radio station *Deutsche Volksender.* After returning to Berlin in May 1945 as a Soviet officer, he moved into a luxurious apartment on Bayernallee in West Berlin, not far from the Soviet-controlled Berlin radio station *Berliner Rundfunk,* where he worked. In November 1945 Wolf was sent to Nuremberg to cover the war crimes trials, and he returned to Berlin in October 1946. Trusted by the Soviets because of this background, and fluent in both German and Russian, in October 1949 Wolf was assigned to the new GDR diplomatic mission in Moscow. There he remained until summer 1951, when he was recalled to serve in the newly created IWF.[29]

After this initial meeting in August 1951, work began in earnest on creating the new service virtually from scratch. The personnel department of the SED Central Committee took the lead in reviewing the files of party members to find those suitable for intelligence work. In November a young SED member, then employed in the foreign-exchange section of an East Berlin bank, was summoned to the Central Committee for an interview. He must have made a good impression, because shortly thereafter he was ordered to report to IWF, which only then did he discover was the GDR's new foreign intelligence service. Despite his impressive credentials and polished interview, this new intelligence officer was also reporting to BOB.[30]

Based on information from this source BOB was able to ascertain the real purpose of this mysterious IWF and to observe the methodical creation of the infrastructure needed for future intelligence operations in West Germany. BOB was the first Western intelligence unit to crack IWF. By September 1952 the source's value in supplying counterintelligence reporting and economic information was obvious. BOB urged him "to be highly selective in the material he furnishe[d] and to refrain from taking risks to obtain information not normally available to him." It was hoped that "this semi-sleeper status [might] encourage him to stay in

place."[31] An understandable hope, but the source had other ideas—
specifically, flight from East Germany. He was under family pressure
to leave, and as he realized how deadly serious an espionage operation
IWF was, he became ever more anxious. His concern increased when
Mischa Wolf took over in December 1952 and began to tighten security. The source was determined to provide every scrap of detail he
could on the new intelligence service, but toward the end of his time
with IWF he seemed near the cracking point. In time he probably would
have been uncovered, and BOB recognized the need to get him out.[32]

The service initially comprised four main departments, each with a
Soviet adviser. The first department was charged with infiltrating political parties and governmental institutions in West Berlin and West
Germany. The second was responsible for developing sources of intelligence on West German industry. The third was the information or reports department, and the fourth was the technical support unit. Over
time IWF acquired a component for collecting scientific and technical
information, as well as a counterintelligence element, also with Soviet
advisers. The job of the counterintelligence unit was to penetrate the
West Berlin police and eventually the security and intelligence services
of the Allies and the Federal Republic. The man chosen as the first
counterintelligence chief was Gustav Szinda, an old KPD adherent and
"Red Front" street brawler who had a working-class background. His
assistant at the time was Markus Wolf.[33]

Although MGB's foreign intelligence directorate took over all intelligence and counterintelligence activities in the GDR after KI's demise in
late 1951, this transition seems to have had little effect on IWF. Soviet
control of IWF had been exercised through the German department of
KI, and when this department moved back into MGB the advisory staff
in Berlin remained in place, under the aegis of MGB.

In December 1952, Wolf succeeded Ackermann as IWF chief. The
appointment surprised some, who thought Wolf too young and irre-
sponsible for the job. It was said in IWF circles that Ulbricht was
opposed to the appointment but that Wolf had the full support of
Ackermann and the Soviet advisers.[34] Responsibility for IWF remained
with the SED Politburo, although efforts were under way during this period to eliminate any direct connections between the SED Central Committee and IWF. IWF members, for example, were no longer allowed to
invoke the SED Central Committee in their efforts to persuade East German citizens to cooperate, and IWF personnel who had Central Com-

mittee credentials were issued identity documents from the GDR Ministry of State Security instead.[35]

BOB's agent reported that Stalin's death on 5 March 1953 was a severe blow to the party faithful in IWF. The women, in black mourning dress, behaved as though a member of their own families had died. The men seemed equally distraught, whether from real grief or from fear of the unknown. On 7 March, an emergency meeting of IWF personnel and Soviet advisory staff was called for 2:00 P.M. When the Soviet advisers arrived from Karlshorst, they remained closeted with Markus Wolf until nearly 4:00 P.M. before the meeting officially began. Wolf finally opened the meeting by relaying an appeal from the Soviets for any information indicating that the West was planning to take advantage of Stalin's death to mount a provocation against the USSR. Of special concern was the news that the West Berlin senate had asked the Allies to furnish military transport aircraft to fly more refugees to West Germany. The Soviets were concerned that these flights might be a clever cover for launching a military action against the GDR. Concern over the possibility of a Western invasion dominated IWF activities for several weeks after the 7 March meeting.[36]

Volcano: IWF's Baptism by Fire

It was in this precarious situation that the East German political intelligence service had its first real flap. Withdrawal of the BOB penetration agent had been scheduled for early April 1953, and on 4 April he left, along with his extended family and many documents on IWF personnel, operations, and budget. Two days later, IWF was suddenly faced with the arrest of some thirty-five agents, proudly announced by the West German government at a Bonn press conference. Although the new German Office for the Protection of the Constitution (Bundesamt fuer Verfassungsschutz—BfV) took credit for the operation, code-named Volcano (Vulkan), the material was provided by BOB.[37] In any case, the West Berlin and West German news media, from the scandal sheets to the staid *Frankfurter Allgemeine,* played the arrests and trials to the hilt. The affair hit the new East German foreign intelligence service very hard, particularly because several agents involved were connected with interzonal trade, an increasingly important issue for the GDR economy. An article in *Der Spiegel* identified SED functionary Markus Wolf for the first time as the head of IWF.[38]

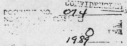
This document has been
approved for release through
the HISTORICAL REVIEW PROGRAM of
the Central Intelligence Agency.

Date 12/9/94

7/27/79

MEMORANDUM FOR: Director of Central Intelligence

HRP 94-1

SUBJECT: Roll-up of Soviet-controlled Intelligence
             Net in Western Germany

1. For the last two weeks, personnel of our German Mission have been cooperating closely with the West German Office for the Protection of the Constitution (Verfassungsschutz) in preparing the roll-up of a large net of agents in West Germany, controlled by the Soviet-controlled positive intelligence service of the East German Government. The roll-up began today and has already resulted in the arrest of at least thirty-four persons. More arrests are expected.

2. The Soviet Zone intelligence service, with the cover name Institut fuer Wirtschaftswissenschaftliche Forschung and offices in Berlin, was set up a year and a half ago for the purpose of conducting political, scientific, military, and economic espionage against Western Germany. Staffed with trusted SED men, controlled by Russian advisors, and headed for a time by Anton Ackermann, SED-stalwart, the IWF has assessed hundreds of people in East and West Germany as possible agent material and has dispatched a number of agents to Western Germany. The organization is also believed to run economic warfare and political action type operations in West Germany. Although other agencies suspected the role of the IWF, none had more than the sketchiest information on it.

3. For the past year, Berlin Operations Base has run a penetration of the IWF at a good level and collected voluminous documentary information on its aims, staffing, methods, training, and agent personnel. For security reasons, none of this data was given to other Allied or German agencies.

4. Our source in the IWF was scheduled to defect in early April 1953 and he came out safely with his immediate family and eight other relatives on 4 April. Two weeks before we had taken the German Government into our confidence and begun briefing them in detail on the IWF's operations. All necessary preparations for

Memorandum, 10 April 1953, from Richard Helms, acting deputy director, plans, to Allen Dulles, director, Central Intelligence, regarding the roll-up of a Soviet-controlled intelligence net in West Germany.

The decision to roll up IWF operatives in West Germany with great fanfare following the source's defection had not been easy. It was clear that IWF was an intelligence service in the making; most of the resident agents it had placed in West Germany were still perfecting their cover and had done little recruiting. Because the service was still learning the spy business, many of those detained in West Germany had not actively engaged in espionage and were released. Nevertheless, IWF was a serious operation, heavily oriented toward economic targets and geared to exploit the German interzonal trade system both for cover and for access to targets. Its training programs and progress reports made it clear that IWF was rapidly becoming a clandestine intelligence service in the Soviet mode.[39]

The investigation of the Volcano affair was still under way when the workers' uprising of 17 June 1953 shattered the surface calm of the East German regime. In later years KGB officers who had worked closely with IWF and its successor organization noted that Wolf was conveniently absent when the storm broke.[40] For whatever reason, IWF escaped the political and bureaucratic infighting that followed the riots and the arrest of Lavrenty Pavlovich Beria on 26 June. Beria's fall from political grace resulted in a strengthening of Ulbricht's power, the elimination of the GDR Ministry of State Security, and the dismissal of GDR State Security Minister Zaisser. In place of MfS, a Secretariat for State Security was formed, headed by Ernst Wollweber and subordinated to the Interior Ministry. The reasons for the selection of Wollweber, then GDR State Secretary for Navigation and Shipping and not an Ulbricht favorite, are not clear. The Soviets, having resigned themselves to the loss of their favorite, Zaisser, probably gave Wollweber the key post because of their previous association with him.[41]

These changes in GDR state security corresponded roughly to organizational shifts in Moscow following Stalin's death: during this time, both foreign intelligence and domestic counterintelligence were placed under the USSR Ministry of Internal Affairs. It was in this context that IWF, with Wolf still at its head, became Main Department 15 of the newly formed Secretariat for State Security. Mielke, a protégé of Ulbricht's, continued as head of counterintelligence. Relations between Mielke and Wolf, never good, worsened and eventually involved their Soviet mentors.

7

Stalin Offers Peace, but the Cold War Continues

O n the surface at least, 1952 had been the year in which Josef Stalin initiated a series of exchanges with the Western powers that appeared to offer the prospect of a united, neutral Germany.[1] The responses of the Western Allies, each of which demanded all-German free elections, were interpreted by some as a rejection of this "last chance" for reunification. Others believed that the Soviet offer was a propaganda ploy aimed primarily at delaying ratification of the Allied–West German contractual agreements and the integration of West Germany into the Western defense structure. A May 1952 CIA National Estimate viewed the proposals in this way: "The Kremlin almost certainly believes that free elections would result in a repudiation of Communism in East Germany" and "would not be satisfied that a united Germany which was not under Soviet control . . . would not eventually rearm and turn against the USSR."[2]

Some German scholars, writing in 1994 with the benefit of access to Soviet Foreign Ministry archives, have concurred that the Soviet initiative was in fact a propaganda exercise.[3] The Berlin blockade of 1948–49 and the North Korean invasion of South Korea had spurred the rearming of West Germany, and the Soviets were eager to reverse this trend by suggesting the possibility of reunification. Soviet foreign intelligence during this time focused on the need for information to support this policy.

Meanwhile, the military buildup continued as each side anticipated the worst. A January 1952 MGB Berlin residency report on a December meeting of the leaders of the Free Democratic Party (FDP) in West Berlin quotes the leaders as saying, "We must not lose time because we never know whether the Russians will attack first."[4] On 26 January the MGB residency in Berlin reported to Stalin that Adenauer intended to accelerate the remilitarization of Germany.[5]

In the same vein, on 26 March 1952 an analysis was sent to Stalin by the "small" Committee of Information (formed under the Ministry of Foreign Affairs after the dissolution of the original KI) that described preparations for creating "aggressive West German armed forces." Drawn from diplomatic channels, this report is an excellent example of information disseminated by the Small KI. In his accompanying memorandum to Stalin, Deputy Foreign Minister Valerian Zorin declared that "the democratic movement of the German people against remilitarization, and for German unity and a peace treaty, will be one of the most important factors in American calculations for carrying out their aggressive plans in Europe."[6] This emphasis on the military aspects of West German rearmament continued throughout 1952.

On 19 April, Stalin received word from MGB of Adenauer's reaction to Soviet proposals for a peace treaty with Germany. In early April, before a "narrow circle of leading personalities of the Christian Democratic Union," Adenauer had allegedly said, "We do not recognize the Potsdam Declaration and are striving for and will achieve European unity. This will create a counterweight that will exert a magnetic attraction on Eastern Europe. Russia will not start a war."[7] Another MGB report on Adenauer, dated 21 April, claimed that he had said that Soviet proposals had only one aim: "the neutralization of Germany."

In contrast to the analyses from the Small KI, on 11 May MGB provided from agent sources the full text of a fourteen-page memorandum prepared by the FRG Minister for All-German Questions, Jakob Kaiser, and the Chairman of the Bundestag Committee for All-German Questions, Herbert Wehner. The paper was circulated to members of the All-German Questions and the Foreign Affairs committees of the Bundestag. Kaiser and Wehner detected in it a hint of compromise between the USSR and the West: "If the West agrees not to incorporate Germany into the Atlantic Pact, then the Soviet Union 'might show a readiness to conduct free elections and accept a rejection of Communism in the Soviet Zone.'"[8]

The West continued to press the question of a West German role in European defense. On 26–27 May, the Western foreign ministers and the FRG signed agreements that led to the European Defense Community Treaty. This was a diplomatic formality; the real battle in the FRG over ratification of these instruments by the Bundestag was still to be won. On 22 October, MGB reported to Stalin and key members of the newly created Presidium that Adenauer still opposed a Western response to the Soviet proposal. He was confident that the Bundestag would ratify both the Allied–West German pacts and the European Defense Community Treaty and wished to delay that response until the vote occurred.[9]

One of the most significant reports by MGB on reactions to the Soviet proposals of 10 March, the Western responses, and the effect on the progress of ratification of the Allied–West German pacts and the European Defense Community Treaty was a 1 June 1952 monthly report from the French high commissioner in Bonn, André François-Poncet, to the French Foreign Ministry. The document conveyed the negative consequences of the Soviet proposals on Adenauer's ratification schedule, and his awareness that four-power negotiations would cause further delay. François-Poncet commented that Adenauer "had overestimated his influence on the parties of the coalition and underestimated the strength of the Social Democratic opposition and fluctuations in public opinion."

François-Poncet's document also revealed a shrewd appreciation of how the American presidential elections, then under way, had influenced Adenauer's behavior and timing. François-Poncet demonstrated his grasp of the German political scene with a penetrating description of the dynamics and goals of the Social Democrats in their opposition to Adenauer. He ended his report with the observation that the "FRG is making progress in every area. With each day its awareness grows that thanks to the role it is playing in international events, it can nourish hopes of power. The neutralist *ohne uns* [without us] movement that flowered two years ago is now in decline. The idea of recruiting German contingents for a European Army no longer meets resistance." Given this growing German strength and self-confidence, and the fear it aroused in the French, François-Poncet saw the inclusion of a new Germany in the European Defense Community as the best course.[10]

This was bitter medicine for an aging dictator and his henchmen. And, unlike so much of the reporting on West Germany from KI and MGB German sources in this period, it was documentary, not hearsay.

By 1952 it had become evident that the best intelligence on the position of the Western Allies on the German question and on Franco-German relations was obtained by MGB from sources in official positions in France. As early as 1948, KI reporting on the German question had included such important documentary reports from French sources that wherever these issues were discussed—in Berlin, Bonn, Paris, or other capitals—the Soviets seemed to be informed. Copies of minutes of meetings between the US, British, and French high commissioners, evidently prepared by François-Poncet, found their way to Moscow. Plans by Adenauer in 1949 to create a foreign office were reported as coming from "French intelligence sources." A detailed report of a visit to Rome and the Vatican made by Adenauer in June 1951 was taken from "agent reports of French intelligence." Portions of a KI report on negotiations for a European army were based on an aide-mémoire from the Quai d'Orsay to François-Poncet. Indeed, as KI lost its "Cambridge group" of British Foreign Office sources, including Guy Burgess and Donald Maclean, the French sources, who must have already been in place, began to fill the gap. Not until Mischa Wolf's intelligence service penetrated the FRG did KGB have a source of detailed, policy-level reporting in the West German military-political sphere comparable to its French connection.

Stalin Imposes Further Controls on East Germany

While Stalin appeared to be offering the West an olive branch of a united, neutral Germany, within the German Democratic Republic itself a process was beginning that would culminate in the 17 June 1953 riots. At the Second Congress of SED in July 1952, Walter Ulbricht announced measures to dramatically speed up the socialization of East Germany and to eliminate all remnants of the pre-Communist political, social, and economic structure. The Congress vowed to "strengthen the principles of a people's democracy in the German Democratic Republic, to protect and save the homeland and peaceful reconstruction through the creation of armed forces, and to create successfully the basis of socialism."[11]

The line taken at the July congress was a departure from earlier, more conciliatory Soviet and SED positions. But why did the Soviets choose to intensify the socialization of East Germany while offering the West peace? Intelligence reporting obtained from SVR archives does not answer this question. The MGB and KI reports we have describe only a continuing concern about the West's rejection of Soviet proposals for a united Germany.

Even as the Soviets professed interest in unification, Stalin had already decided to deepen the split between the two Germanies. In a meeting in the Kremlin on 7 April with GDR leaders Wilhelm Pieck, Walter Ulbricht, and Otto Grotewohl and high-level Soviet decision-makers, Stalin stated that "irrespective of any proposals that we can make on the German question, the Western powers will not agree with them, and will not withdraw from Germany in any case. . . . Therefore, you [the GDR] must organize your own state. The line of demarcation between West and East Germany must be seen . . . not as a simple border but a dangerous one."[12] Stalin seems to have believed that the Western Allies' insistence that reunification could not happen without free all-German elections indicated that his reunification effort had failed. But had it? MGB and KI reporting shows that the Western Allies were considering Stalin's proposals—debate on the matter was in fact delaying ratification of remilitarization treaties in both Bonn and Paris. But before these debates ended, Stalin directed Ulbricht to embark on a harsh program of forced socialization in East Germany.

It was another major miscalculation by Stalin. Western governments, of course, were following events in the GDR very closely. CIA was actively reporting on matters like the supply and distribution of foodstuffs, the establishment of new farm cooperatives, shortages of petroleum products, and measures taken to reduce "flight from the republic."[13] Curiously, we have seen no reporting from MGB sources reflecting Western concern over the effects of the Ulbricht program to sovietize East Germans. Nor have we seen reporting from MGB about the effect of the Ulbricht policies on East German morale.

Some hints about the internal situation in the GDR emerge in Soviet intelligence reports filed after Stalin's death on 5 March 1953. One was signed on 13 March by Yevgeny Petrovich Pitovranov, still head of the intelligence directorate under Stalin's last reorganization of the services. The source claims that the "large scale of this phenomenon [the refugee problem] will force the government of the GDR to take steps in the near

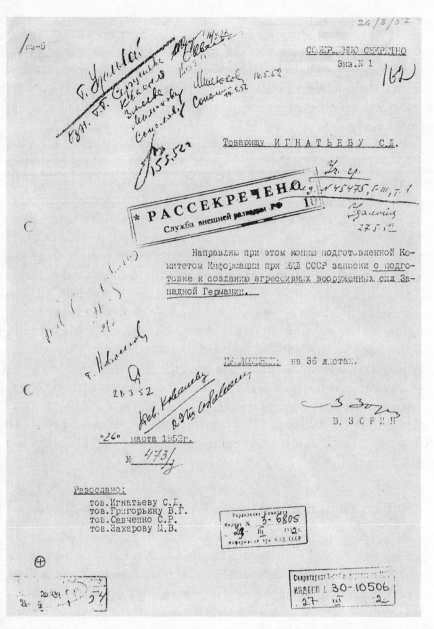

/кз-5

СОВЕРШЕННО СЕКРЕТНО
Экз. № 1

162

Товарищу ИГНАТЬЕВУ С.Д.

РАССЕКРЕЧЕНО
Служба внешней разведки РФ

Направляю при этом копию подготовленной Комитетом Информации при МИД СССР записки о подготовке к созданию агрессивных вооруженных сил Западной Германии.

ПРИЛОЖЕНИЕ: на 36 листах.

В. ЗОРИН

"26" марта 1952г.
№ 473/3

Разослано:
   тов. Игнатьеву С.Д.
   тов. Григорьяну В.Г.
   тов. Савченко С.Р.
   тов. Захарову М.В.

5-6805

30-10506

Memorandum, 26 March 1952, from Deputy Foreign Minister Zorin to MGB head Semyon Ignatiev and GRU chief Matvei Zakharov, transmitting a copy of a 1952 report prepared for Stalin by the Small KI, "Preparations for Creating Aggressive Armed Forces by West Germany."

future to cut off the outflow of the population to the West." In the past, many refugees had been pensioners or persons without specific skills, but now "in connection with the sharpening contradictions in the GDR, farmers and members of the technical intelligentsia are beginning to flee to West Berlin."[14]

A KGB counterintelligence veteran, back in Moscow in 1952 from Karlshorst, probably had it right when asked why he thought the SED regime was so unstable at that time. Without hesitation he blamed Ulbricht. "He was a Saxon, and his manner of speech aroused contradictory feelings; he did not convey the necessary authority. The way in which he copied our Soviet experiences without deviating did not help him to strengthen his position." Then, he went on to explain, there was the economy. A "resident of the GDR had only to compare the quality of goods available in the GDR to those found in West Berlin or West Germany to draw the necessary conclusions."[15] But were Ulbricht and SED fully to blame for the mistakes of 1952? It seems that when it came to informing Stalin, "tell him only what he wants to hear" was the Soviet mantra—at least this was true during the Korean War, when Stalin had no interest in being reminded of the connection between the North Korean invasion and the rearming of West Germany. Any mistakes made during the 1952 crackdown in the GDR were hard to fix given Stalin's reluctance to learn that the sovietization of East Germany had been a disaster.

Soviets Continue to Menace West Berlin Access Routes

While proceeding on their contradictory two-track approach to the German question, the Soviets and the GDR authorities continued to harass West Berliners throughout 1952. The rationale for these actions, coming as they did while the Kremlin was serving up its newest recipe for German unity, is not clear. Some of these antagonisms, particularly those pertaining to tighter border controls, were probably related to Ulbricht's program of forced socialization. Whatever the reasons, François-Poncet addressed the problem without equivocation in his 1 June monthly letter: "These measures have as their goal to isolate more and more the Western sectors of Berlin and surround them in such a way that the Russians or their agents can strangle these sectors by blockade, if they wish to take that risk."[16] In April, Soviet fighters fired on an Air France passenger aircraft in the air corridor; in May, Allied

military police were barred from travel on the Berlin-Helmstedt Autobahn; later that month telephone connections were cut between West
Berlin and both East Berlin and East Germany.

On 3 June the East Germans began occupying the so-called exclaves
along the West Berlin–East German border—parcels of territory that
had legally belonged to Greater Berlin, even though they were located
outside the city's boundaries. Perhaps most famous of these was the village of Steinstuecken, near the border of the American sector. Access to
this exclave was maintained even after the creation of the Berlin Wall in
1961, first by helicopter and later by a narrow road flanked by barriers.[17] In retaliation for these aggressive acts, the British cordoned off
Haus der Rundfunk, the building from which East Berlin radio authorities had broadcast since 1945. The pragmatic François-Poncet ap-
plauded this action: "The English, normally so phlegmatic, responded
to these measures by a blockade of the Soviet radio station in West
Berlin. The success of the step taken by the English excuses and justi-
fies it. They hit the mark."[18]

Whatever success the British may have enjoyed in public relations,
the incidents of harassment again raised concerns at CIA about the safety
of Berlin personnel. On 9 July, CIA's deputy director for plans asked for
an update on evacuation strategies. The East European division replied,
"While there is no panic or extreme fear evidenced by personnel in the
Berlin station, certain steps have nevertheless been taken within limitations to give that station some chance for successful evacuation." After
describing the plans and their link with the overall US Evacuation Plan,
the point was made that "successful evacuation of Berlin under a sudden, smashing attack is unlikely, but the Berlin Escape Plan and the
stand-by aircraft both offer some hope which has not previously been
present."[19] BOB veterans of the Berlin blockade would have smirked at
these sentiments. "Evacuation" had been and would continue to be a
concept beloved of planners, but in reality, escape for all but a few lin-
guistically gifted officers would be impossible if the Soviets were to
suddenly occupy the Western sectors.

The harassment continued throughout October. General Chuikov,
chairman of the Soviet Control Commission, demanded that the American radio broadcasting service, as well as other West Berlin media, be
shut down, and the People's Police erected more barriers between East
Germany and West Berlin. On 8 October, Soviet fighters fired on a US
medical evacuation aircraft in the Berlin-Frankfurt air corridor. The

populations of West and East Berlin were the focus of other troubling actions. West Berliners became indignant and their relatives in the East increasingly despondent when visits to cemeteries in East Berlin and adjacent areas of the GDR were forbidden on 2 November, All Souls' Day. And as Christmas approached, East German authorities delayed the delivery of gift parcels from the Federal Republic and West Berlin to GDR inhabitants.

CIA Gives Up on Coordinating US Intelligence in Berlin

At BOB, Peter Sichel, who had arrived in Berlin in 1945 with OSS and later replaced Dana Durand as base chief, returned to Washington. His departure marked the end of the postwar phase of CIA's Berlin operations. His replacement was Lester Houck, a tall, thin chain-smoker who had served in Washington since the days of OSS, primarily in the area of intelligence production. Berlin was his first overseas post.

Newcomer Houck had to address the proliferation of uncoordinated US clandestine intelligence operations. The situation had existed since the end of World War II, but until CIA was established and had evolved a bureaucracy for handling its own operational problems, there was little motivation for tackling coordination with the US military services. By 1952, though, the problem in Berlin had become acute. Lyman Kirkpatrick, the assistant director for special operations, was asked to look into it. He soon discovered that the US Army, Air Force, and Navy were engaging in clandestine intelligence collection activities in Berlin; that each of these groups had its own chain of command; and that none of the agencies would cede control of these operations to a single individual or agency in Berlin. Everyone was suffering from a shortage of personnel, yet it was impossible to prevent these agencies from duplicating each other's efforts. The situation was such a mess that Kirkpatrick thought even CIA could not make a difference. At a critical time for American interests in Germany, he recommended that "no effort be made to place a coordinator of clandestine intelligence in Berlin."[20]

8

Soviet Intelligence Falters After Stalin's Death: New Revelations About Beria's Role

With Stalin's death in March 1953, the inevitable struggle for power began: such members of the old guard as Molotov, Anastas Mikoyan, and Lazar Kaganovich were overshadowed by a new triumvirate of Georgy Malenkov, Nikita Khrushchev, and Lavrenty Beria. Each member of this uneasy partnership was eager to propose "reforms" that would give him an edge over his opponents.[1] Beria, now minister of internal affairs and a Presidium member, was no exception. Although some of his actions—like amnesty for political prisoners and his proposals for limiting Moscow's Russification programs and improving the lot of non-Russian nationalities—appealed to many, they irritated his rivals, all of whom had been involved in the excesses of the Stalinist period.

But we can now document that it was Beria's determination to reassert control over the security and intelligence apparatus that led to his downfall.[2] He recognized that without such control he could never consolidate and maintain power. But his attempt to revive his earlier hold over state security so demoralized and incapacitated these services that they were incapable of responding effectively to the worsening German crisis. The riots of June 1953 ultimately gave Beria's opponents, led by Khrushchev, the ammunition they needed to justify his ouster.

A New Face at BOB

In early January 1953, Soviet intelligence in Karlshorst had other distractions. Intercept operators monitoring the US military telephone lines between West Berlin and Frankfurt am Main in the American zone were perplexed. The Americans had evidently introduced new code names for some of their intelligence operatives. Soviet operators began to hear references to the Boy Diplomat, the Black Prince, and the Bishop, names that had never appeared in their listings.[3] Over time, the source of this lexicon must have become apparent to them. It was William King Harvey, the new chief of CIA's Berlin Operations Base.

Harvey's appointment was a departure for BOB staffing. He had never served abroad and spoke no German. A transplant in 1947 from the Federal Bureau of Investigation, where he had become deeply involved in some of the FBI's most important counterintelligence operations, Harvey had served in staff positions in the Office of Special Operations of CIG and CIA before his Berlin assignment, but he was known only to a small circle of counterintelligence specialists. To the case officers of Berlin Base he was a creature from another planet. His predecessor, Lester Houck, had been in Berlin scarcely six months when he suddenly learned that he would be replaced.

In the early fifties, Berlin had the reputation of being one of CIA's plum assignments. What had Harvey done to merit it? Only a few CIA officials knew the real reason for Harvey's Berlin assignment, and it would not become known publicly until 23 April 1956, when the Soviets announced the discovery of the Berlin Tunnel.

William Harvey: A Brief Portrait

Dispelling the caricature of W. K. Harvey as portrayed in numerous books will not be easy. His physical appearance invited ridicule—in Berlin he was known to base officers as "the pear." The alcoholism that caused him serious problems in later years was already apparent. His lifelong obsession with guns mystified even his closest associates: did it come from a desire to be seen as a "frontier legend," from a genuine liking for firearms of all types, or from a subconscious need to hold his own with the many men under his command who had been in active combat during the recent war? Perhaps his years with the FBI in New York provided an explanation—or maybe, amateur psychoanalysis aside, he just liked firearms. Harvey has been accused of being jealous of East Coast elitists, but he was in fact, proud of his Indiana origins. The image that he cultivated of a rustic Midwesterner, complete with colorfully crude speech, may have been calculated to shock his more genteel colleagues. In any case, his deliberately countrified manner offended many, and his outrageous expressions were often mocked.

Bill Harvey arrived in Frankfurt in December 1952. At this time he was divorced from his first wife and had custody of his five-year-old son, whom he had left in his own mother's care. A Women's Army Corps officer named Clara Grace Follick, known to all as C.G., was assigned to show Bill around during the holidays. C.G. had known and disliked Bill in Washington, and she had no desire to take time out of her busy social life to escort him around, but orders were orders. Two years later they were married.

In early 1953, Harvey had a lot to learn about Berlin. He moved into a magnificent house on Lepsius Strasse in the Steglitz district that had a marvelous garden with the deepest—and coldest—swimming pool imaginable. The house became a second home to base officers and their families as Bill—and later Bill and C.G.—opened its doors to all for frequent meetings, briefings, and picnics. Between running a bachelor household and settling into the Berlin Base offices in the Dahlem district, Bill began to learn that there were differences between managing BOB in the Berlin of 1953 and operating for the FBI in New York or Washington. West Berlin, though greatly transformed from the rubble pile it had been in 1945, still bore its scars as it tried to cope with demands of the new and complex Cold War. As for BOB, the wartime aura of OSS clung to it—the base continued to operate from the same site on Foehrenweg originally chosen by Allen Dulles. Peter Sichel, who had left the previous spring to become chief of operations of the East European division, was still keeping an eye on his old domain. Harvey's deputy in Berlin at the time was Henry Hecksher, who harbored few doubts about his own fitness for the job, for which he had been grooming himself since his arrival in late 1945. Except for Hecksher and the small, seasoned group working on Soviet atomic energy targets, the staff was primarily composed of very young officers recruited since the war. As it turned out, they and Harvey learned together—and because of him, many stayed on in Berlin, opting for extensions or new tours. But as 1953 began, neither Harvey nor his troops had the slightest inkling of the events that would soon engulf Moscow and East Berlin.

Stalin's Death Inspires Beria to Make Drastic Personnel Changes

It was a quiet time in Berlin, and Harvey should have had ample time to learn the ropes. Suddenly, on 5 March, Stalin died. We have seen how the news affected the small group of Soviet advisers to the new East German foreign intelligence service and the service itself. The event affected Soviet intelligence officers in Karlshorst even more deeply. But little time was spent in mourning because Beria began almost immediately to impose major changes on the state security system. He began by combining it with internal affairs in a single ministry for the first time since 1943 and by replacing with his own favorites the officers who had been appointed while he had been building Stalin's atomic bomb. Col. Gen. Bogdan Zakharovich Kobulov, formerly in charge of the atomic energy program and Soviet property in Germany, was made responsible for foreign intelligence. Another deputy was Sergei Arsenievich Goglidze, MVD chief in Khabarovsky Kray. These cronies would serve him well. But Beria foolishly retained Sergei Kruglov, whose loyalty was to Georgy Malenkov, and Ivan Serov, a Khrushchev associate from Ukrainian days, both of whom later helped to overthrow him.

Soviet intelligence reports show that just before Stalin's death the dictatorship had begun to unravel. On 23 February 1953, an important internal report on a possible bilateral agreement between the United States and the FRG on German rearmament was not even addressed to Stalin, whose name usually appeared at the top of the distribution list.[4]

Also indicative of the bureaucratic confusion of the period is an MVD report dated 13 March 1953. It was sent to Deputy Foreign Minister Y. A. Malik by Yevgeny Pitovranov, who had headed foreign intelligence since the December 1952 reorganization. Precisely when did Beria make his changes to the security services, including the transfer of Pitovranov from chief of foreign intelligence to deputy chief of counterintelligence? Some have suggested that they occurred just after Stalin's death, but the date of this report indicates that several days had elapsed. This seems odd in a bureaucracy in which portraits of deposed or deceased leaders were typically replaced before the paint was dry on the new ones.[5]

On 19 March, a report was received from French sources on an "American ultimatum to France" in connection with delays in the ratification of the "European Army" treaty. The report went only to Beria and not to the other members of the Presidium. It was signed by Vasily Riasnoy, whom Beria had retained as head of the foreign intelligence directorate despite his suspicions that Riasnoy had been a Khrushchev crony inserted into the MGB when Stalin's hold was weakening. With his reputation for inordinate stupidity, Riasnoy was referred to by his subordinates as Vasily Temny after a fifteenth-century Russian grand duke, blinded by his rivals, whose name over time came to mean ignorant or benighted.[6] The report distribution is marked "Copy No. 1 to Beria," which suggests that Beria was following German affairs closely.

New Evidence About Beria's Motives

In Berlin, Beria fired Gen. Kaverznev, chief of the Karlshorst unit; the deputy for intelligence, Col. Ivan Fadeikin, became acting MVD representative. After this point it becomes difficult to follow Beria's actions on the German question as a whole, the German department of foreign intelligence in Moscow, and the Karlshorst unit. Since the advent of glasnost—and even before—many participants in the power struggles of the time, as well as their supporters and relatives, have described the events from essentially partisan points of view. Were Beria's proposals on the nationality question, on relations with Yugoslavia, and above all on the reunification of Germany the work of a genuine reformer, or were they designed primarily to help him rise to the top after Stalin's demise? The victors' version of that struggle, particularly the Khrushchev memoirs and official documents of the period, are still the major sources for researchers looking for answers to this question. These documents provide no convincing evidence that Beria really "favored a grand bargain that would reunify Germany as a capitalist, neutral government"; selfish interests seem a more likely inspiration.[7]

Some information about the accusations leveled against Beria by his rivals to justify his arrest has already been published. But we found additional details in documents from SVR archives. In a "special folder" *(osobaia papka)* of the Bill of Indictment, it was alleged that "Beria, acting as a spy and traitor, deliberately disorganized the defense of the Caucasus by opening to the Hitlerites the passes through the main Caucasus range." The document also accused Beria of planning to transfer portions of Soviet territory to "capitalist governments." According to testimony on 23 June 1953 from Boris Ludvigov, in Beria's secretariat, Beria was prepared to return Königsberg to the Germans, the Karelian

Isthmus to the Finns, and the Kuril Islands to the Japanese.[8] These fantastical indictments are reminiscent of the standard "foreign spy" accusations made during Stalin's purges.

The strongest language in the official indictment was reserved for Beria's alleged plans and actions concerning Germany. During the "period preceding the American provocation in Berlin [the East German uprising on 17 June 1953]," Beria had proposed the "liquidation of socialist development in the GDR, the support of private capitalist elements, dissolution of the collective farms, and the transformation of the GDR into a bourgeois state, which would have meant complete capitulation before the imperialist forces." The testimony contained other damning accusations: "Beria thought that collective farms should be dissolved altogether. . . . Beria often said that collective farms in the GDR were a sham. In general, Beria regarded the development of socialism in the GDR negatively."[9]

Did Beria actually propose these dramatic changes in Germany, and if so, would he have carried them out? We may never know. It is clear that he, and indeed the Presidium as a whole, were aware of the problems plaguing the GDR. On 19 February, even before Stalin's death, MGB circulated a report from a senior French official that described the situation in the GDR as extremely serious, leading the Soviets to conclude that the GDR had lost "any attraction for citizens of West Germany."[10] On 9 March, the deputy chief of the Karlshorst advisory unit sent to Moscow a pessimistic report in which he complained that the GDR MfS was not up to the job and that control was becoming more difficult because of "worsening class conflict in the GDR."

On 6 May, Beria himself, in his capacity as minister of internal affairs, circulated a report to the senior members of the Presidium describing in stark terms the deteriorating situation in the GDR. The report began by noting the sharp increase in the refugee flow. Totals for the second half of 1952 had jumped to 78,831 from 57,234 in the first half of the year. And in the first quarter of 1953 alone, 84,034 East German citizens had fled west, of which 1,836 were members of SED and 1,781 were from the Communist youth organization.[11] From available data, Beria's report went on, "the number of refugees cannot be explained only by the hostile propaganda directed by West German organs at the population of the GDR." Rather, it is the "unwillingness of individual groups of peasants to enter the agricultural production cooperatives now being organized, the fear on the part of small and middle-level

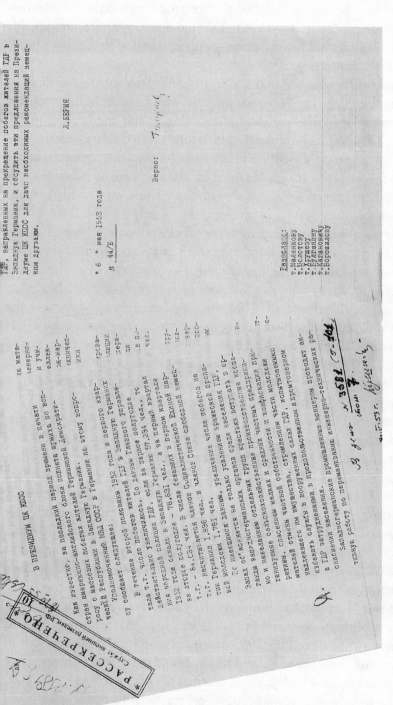

Report, 6 May 1953, from Lavrenty Beria to the Presidium of the Central Committee, CPSU (Malenkov, Molotov, Khrushchev, Bulganin, Kaganovich, and Voroshilov), regarding the flow of refugees from the GDR. In the report, Beria states, "As long as there exists the possibility of free movement of the GDR population to West Berlin, mass flight to the West is inevitable."

businessmen of the abolition of private property and the confiscation of their goods, the desire of youth to avoid military service, and the difficulties experienced in the GDR in supplying the population with foodstuffs and consumer goods."[12]

The report continues to describe problems arising from the flight of qualified people to the West, noting that "West German industrial firms are conducting active work to entice technical and engineering workers. . . . Their flight continues despite efforts taken by the Central Committee of SED to improve their material well being." Desertion from the armed forces of the GDR is "blamed on the low state of political work among them [but] desertion is also due to a failure to provide personnel with adequate food and clothing. The Central Committee of SED and the responsible state organs of the GDR do not conduct a sufficiently active fight against the demoralizing work carried out by the West German authorities; they falsely assume that as long as free circulation exists between West Berlin and the GDR, such flights are inevitable."[13]

After reciting the GDR's problems with defection and desertion, the report ends on an unrealistic but politically acceptable note. Beria asked the Soviet Control Commission to submit proposals for measures to strengthen the work of the corresponding organs of the GDR—by preventing the flight of East Germans—and to discuss these proposals at a meeting of the Presidium of the Central Committee for the Communist Party of the Soviet Union (CC CPSU) "in order to make the necessary recommendations to our German friends."[14] It is likely that this report formed part of the agenda for the Presidium meeting on 27 May, although it could scarcely have been sufficient basis for the shocking proposals that Beria allegedly made there. For in spite of its unusually frank descriptions, the report was still a pale reflection of the true state of affairs in the GDR.[15] Beria writes of 84,034 refugees as of 31 March, for example. A 1990 study based on SED data claims that by the end of April, 120,000 people had fled to the West, which suggests that the flow was increasing rapidly.[16] Was there other MVD reporting on this situation, from the apparat in Berlin or elsewhere? Ivan Fadeikin, then acting chief of the Karlshorst apparat, has insisted that reports submitted in the months before June 1953 described a political disaster about to happen. But these reports could not be found in the SVR archives. They were either missing or had never reached the proper files.[17]

MVD foreign intelligence reports on reactions to Stalin's death and to signs of movement in the Soviet position on the German question (as suggested in *Pravda* articles on 25 April and 25 May 1953) also seem to be missing. In spite of the blows suffered by the Cambridge group, the foreign intelligence directorate had demonstrated only the year before in its reporting on Stalin's reunification proposal that their French sources were fully capable of covering all aspects of the German problem. What happened?

Why Did Beria Nearly Dismantle Soviet Foreign Intelligence?

Beria's combining of state security and internal affairs in MVD has been seen logically as evidence of his desire to reimpose his hold over these agencies. As we have seen, his involvement in nuclear weapons development caused him to lose some control over the police and security forces during the last years of Stalin's life. He consequently tried to replace as many as possible MVD officers who had been selected by his rivals, so it is easy to see why his enemies made these personnel changes an important part of their case against him. Portions of his indictment pertaining to intelligence matters, never before released, reflect the specifics of such charges. For example, it is stated that "in April 1953, Beria and [Bogdan] Kobulov simultaneously recalled to Moscow all residents of the MVD in the principal capitalist states. That led to the compromise to American intelligence of Soviet intelligence networks abroad and brought about significant damage to our intelligence service because until the moment of Beria's arrest, that is, for more than two months, all of the recalled residents were in Moscow and the receipt of information from foreign agent nets was cut off."[18]

In his testimony the former deputy chief of the Second Directorate of the MVD, Sergei Romanovich Savchenko, stated that "Beria's . . . simultaneous recall of all of our residents and operational staff under the pretext of examining their work and considering measures for improving it was . . . dangerous for intelligence work. The pretext for this chosen by Beria was an enciphered telegram from one of the residents forwarding an intelligence report which was not worth his attention." According to Savchenko, the various area desks prepared for the return of the residents by drawing up extensive proposals concerning the staffing and mission of each residency in order to expedite the expected reviews. "However, neither Beria nor Kobulov ever read these proposals or spoke to the residents, as a result of which no decisions were reached on any residency. Thus, the residents and their operational people loafed around Moscow for a considerable period of time, doing nothing."[19]

The recall was not the main problem. In Savchenko's words, "It was known in mid-June that the Americans were able to determine that those members of Soviet missions abroad recalled to Moscow were in fact intelligence officers. . . . There can be no argument that Beria and Kobulov, as individuals well versed in intelligence work, could not have foreseen the effects of their actions." Even worse, "Beria and Kobulov, having learned in the middle of June that American intelligence had guessed the reason for the recall of the Soviet intelligence officers, delayed in informing the government and Central Committee. They actually concealed this information."[20]

Although the comment in the indictment concerning "American intelligence" was evidently put there for dramatic effect, Savchenko was essentially correct in his description of the Western response to the recall. Right after Stalin's death, CIA's Soviet Russia Division sent instructions to all field stations to "cable immediately any movement of Soviet personnel from their areas." As a result, CIA gradually became aware of these departures, realized that they were not routine, and noted that those involved were MVD officers, not GRU. As of September 1953 only a few had returned to their assignments. This bizarre action by Beria would have explained the dearth of reporting on foreign reactions to Stalin's death and on subsequent diplomatic moves by Beria.[21]

Beria's recall of residents from abroad resulted in a counterintelligence disaster for MVD foreign intelligence, but his actions regarding the group's presence in Germany caused him more immediate problems. Obviously, the state of the apparat in Karlshorst would have been the key to any plan Beria might have had for German reunification. We have found substantial evidence that Beria virtually dismantled both the field and headquarters elements of the German department of the service. The indictment asserted that "at the beginning of June 1953, immediately before the 17 June events in Berlin, Beria and Kobulov carried out a sevenfold reduction in the strength of the intelligence apparat of the MVD in the GDR with the result that at the moment of the hostile attack of American agent nets, Soviet intelligence organs were deprived of information concerning enemy actions and could not carry out an effective struggle against their subversive activities."[22] These circumstances were confirmed by the testimony of Savchenko and Aleksandr Mikhailovich Korotkov. Korotkov said, "The directives of Beria and the staff reductions of the apparat in the GDR on such a large scale in essence brought about a breakdown in Chekist work in Germany."[23]

Other sources have confirmed Beria's actions with regard to the staffing of the Berlin apparat. According to Peter Deriabin, for example, "Berlin was an admittedly critical area of State Security's operations," but 1,700 of its officers out of 2,800 "were transferred, recalled from Germany or dismissed from the service."[24] Vasily Ilich Bulda was in Karlshorst in spring 1953 serving as a senior counterintelligence officer. He recalls that on the eve of the 17 June events Beria ordered the immediate recall by air of the senior officers of the Karlshorst apparat, including the chiefs of departments and sections and the heads of district offices. The remainder of the staff was to follow later. On arrival in Moscow, having reported to MVD Headquarters in the Lubianka, they simply sat around until one or two o'clock in the morning waiting for instructions, tasks, or new assignments.[25] From another source we learned that among the officers recalled was Col. Pavel Nikolaevich Medvedev, who had been deputy chief of the apparat and chief adviser to MfS.[26] During the uprising these officers knew from telephone calls to their families still in Berlin that something horrible was happening on the streets, but this was all they knew until some of them were sent back to the city.

Beria asked Fadeikin to draw up new staffing arrangements for the apparat. Apparently only officers who spoke German were to be included, which meant that Bulda, who had been named by Fadeikin as his deputy, could not make the new list.[27] It is difficult to determine whether Beria's fixation on language ability was serious or was part of his strategy to shake things up in Germany. Another Karlshorst veteran, Yevgeny Viktorovich Berezin, then serving in the West German sector in the apparat, had studied Albanian years before. Asked by Beria about his knowledge of Albanian, Berezin replied: "Nearly forgotten." Beria replied: "You'll have to remember—you're going to Albania."[28] We have some idea of how difficult it must have been for the German department at Moscow Center to cope with this influx of officers from Karlshorst when we learn from the then department chief, Leonid Yemelianovich Siomonchuk, that he had been told to reduce the staff of the department from sixty-five to eighteen. No reason or justification for the order was given.[29]

Behind these actions to reduce and reshape the MVD apparat in Karlshorst and the German department in Moscow was the work of a special investigative commission appointed by Beria and headed by Amaiak Kobulov and Grigory Ivanovich Zabolotny, deputy chief of cadres responsible for foreign intelligence directorate personnel. This assignment was seen as an indication in the Cadres Department that Amaiak Kobulov, whose brother Bogdan was then Beria's first deputy and responsible for foreign intelligence, would be appointed chief in Karlshorst, one of the most important and prestigious foreign posts in MVD.

By late May events were unfolding at breakneck speed. On 25 May *Pravda* called for "four-power coordination of the German reunification issue." Following the critical 27 May Presidium meeting on Germany, Vladimir S. Semyonov was sent to East Berlin as high commissioner. The commander of the Group of Soviet Forces, Germany, Colonel General Chuikov, also left in May to assume command of the Kiev Military District. His replacement in Germany was Andrei Antonovich Grechko, who had commanded the Kiev MVD since 1945. This assignment should have been an obvious clue to Beria and his friends that danger was lurking because Grechko was close to Khrushchev from their years together facing armed anti-Soviet resistance in the western oblasts of Ukraine.[30]

The SED leadership, along with Semyonov, spent 2–4 June in Moscow receiving instructions concerning the new "line," which moderated many of the Stalinist aspects of SED economic policy adopted in July 1952. After their return to Germany, the SED Politburo met on 9 June and the "New Course" was announced in the SED party newspaper *Neues Deutschland* on 11 June. The Soviets had insisted that these policy changes be published immediately. Unfortunately, this new course did not adjust the rise in work norms (the amount an individual worker must produce), an issue that was already causing much worker resentment. Recognizing that the new party line would come as a shock to the SED faithful who would have to implement the program, SED Politburo member Rudolf Herrnstadt pleaded with Semyonov for a two-week delay. Semyonov refused, remarking that in "fourteen days you may not have a state anymore."[31] Behind the scenes in SED a power struggle was also under way in which SED Politburo members like State Security Minister Wilhelm Zaisser and Herrnstadt were maneuvering to oust Walter Ulbricht. In a 14 June editorial in *Neues Deutschland,* Herrnstadt attacked retention of the work norms. The stage was set for 17 June.[32]

9

The Events of June 1953

sked by a newspaper interviewer about the "Fascist putsch" in East Berlin on 17 June 1953, Yevgeny Pitovranov, the senior MVD officer sent to command the Karlshorst apparat after Beria's arrest, replied: "Putsch—that's an exaggeration. It was the reaction of people to the blunders of the country's leadership, an abscess that in those circumstances could not help but break open. Moreover, it was inadmissible to use tanks in such a situation."[1] Not every retired KGB officer who remembers those times would agree. But there is consensus that the strikes and demonstrations that developed in East Berlin and other GDR cities came as a complete surprise to Moscow and whatever remained of the MVD apparat in East Germany.[2] The story of the strikes and demonstrations that began on 16 June and grew larger and more violent the next day has been told countless times. Here we concentrate on the responses of the Soviet and American intelligence services to these events, using new archival material wherever possible.[3]

The Initial Strike: Kuchin's Report

At 11:45 P.M. on 16 May 1953, Vadim Vitoldovich Kuchin, MVD's German affairs specialist who had been in Karlshorst since 1945 and was assistant to acting MVD representative Col. Ivan A. Fadeikin, prepared a situation report for Deputy MVD Minister Bogdan Z. Kobulov, who was responsible for foreign intelligence. Contrary to MVD practice, Kuchin signed the report—which was unusually critical of the East German party—as both the originator and the releasing officer. It was MVD Moscow's first detailed report from the disorganized Karlshorst apparat on the developing crisis.[4] Its description of this unprecedented challenge to the East German regime must have shocked the Soviet leadership. Subsequent scholarly research drawing on materials from East German and Soviet archives (other than KGB) has produced far greater detail on the June events. These recent discoveries reveal that Kuchin's report, which appears to be based on information from agents in the East German State Security Ministry and the East German party and government, only scratched the surface. The report provides evidence of the dismal state of affairs in MVD's Karlshorst apparat when the crisis exploded.[5]

According to Kuchin, unrest began among construction workers in East Berlin as early as 11 June, with the announcement of the GDR's New Course. At one construction site a twenty-four-hour sit-down strike was called to protest the "capricious increase in production norms." On the evening of 13 June, members of a hospital construction trade union organization at Friedrichshain organized a steamer cruise, during which the plan to conduct protests against the work increases was reportedly devised.[6] Although the East Berlin SED party leaders were informed of these events, they "did not react but continued to prepare construction site foremen and party workers for the introduction of the increased norms."[7]

On the evening of 15 June construction workers at Stalinallee announced that they would go on strike if the new norms were not annulled. They sent a letter of complaint to Prime Minister Grotewohl, asking for a reply by noon the next day.[8] At a meeting of the SED Berlin City Committee that evening, the workers' intention to strike was debated. Despite the threat, the SED committee voted to preserve the increases, adopting instead a resolution to explain the plan to workers the next morning. But SED representatives who arrived at the plants were whistled down by workers. By 11:30 A.M. the workers had placed banners in the factories demanding a reduction in work norms and had headed in columns for the city center, joined by workers from other sites. Kuchin's report from the discussion in the SED City Committee, based on agent reporting, illustrated the serious nature of the workers' grievances. Although the GDR government had announced that the workers had "voluntarily" accepted a 10 percent increase in work norms, an increase of 25 percent had been added to the first by order of the SED City Committee. In addition, a pay cut of up to 35 percent was introduced for those who did not fulfill the norms.

Attempts by party activists to dissuade the demonstrators were met by threats of violence. In one case, Bruno Baum, the SED functionary responsible for the construction industry, narrowly escaped injury by speeding away in a car. The column of workers continued toward the GDR government house on Leipzigerstrasse, where they demanded to see GDR President Pieck and Prime Minister Grotewohl. When there was no response, the workers continued on to the SED Central Committee building. Two trucks equipped with loudspeakers, manned by SED propagandists, were demolished by the strikers. The activists commandeered a third truck for their own use, seriously injuring an SED member in the process.[9]

When the demonstrators reached the SED Central Committee building they again demanded to speak with Pieck, repeating slogans broadcast from the truck. At first these slogans called only for a reduction in the work norms, but gradually the demands became more political: "Down with SED," and "We demand free elections and a united Berlin." When the crowds reached the East Berlin Police Presidium, they stopped, shouting, "We, the workers of Stalinallee, call on all Berlin workers to begin a general strike at 7:00 A.M. on 17 June." According to Kuchin, the demonstrators' goal was to involve workers from all Berlin industrial enterprises. Indeed, when later in the day the GDR state radio tried to counter the plea for a general strike by broadcasting announcements that "production meetings" would start at all construction sites at the same time as the strike, the demonstrators destroyed several of the street loudspeakers. Kuchin also noted the presence of young men on bicycles "of Western manufacture" riding along the columns, carrying messages and encouraging the demonstrators. The demonstrators also stopped streetcars and motor vehicles, informing the passengers of plans for the general strike and threatening anyone who planned to report for work.[10]

As the demonstrators moved through the streets, "passersby voiced their approval, as did the residents of houses along the way." Kuchin also reported that among the demonstrators were SED members, including party officials, who declared that "they could not remain on the sidelines." Actually, according to agent reports cited by Kuchin, the leadership of the SED City Committee was uninformed concerning "their scope and true character" of the demonstrations until they ended on 16 June at 6:30 P.M.[11]

At the end of his report Kuchin added a pro forma statement that "persons from West Berlin played an active part in the organization of the demonstrations." He cited SED CC information that "leaflets . . . printed in the Reinickendorf Borough" (the French sector of West Berlin) called on workers in two East Berlin factories to strike against the norm increase and to lobby "for the return of the enterprises to their former owners." But Kuchin did not support the claim made later by Soviet and East German officials that the strike effort and demonstrations on 15 and 16 June were organized and led by West Berlin provocateurs. If the Karlshorst apparat had had any concrete information on Western involvement as of 16 June, Kuchin would certainly have included it.[12]

As it was, Kuchin pushed all of the Moscow leaders' buttons in his hastily prepared report: he documented an open challenge by workers to party-approved labor policies, illegal demonstrations and strike actions, violence against party activists, the confiscation and destruction of party property, participation in the demonstrations by SED members and functionaries, and most important, the poor judgment and passivity of the SED leadership as the crisis developed.

Another Soviet Perspective

For a second Karlshorst view of the worsening situation we have a report prepared by Colonel Fadeikin, who had become acting MVD representative after Stalin's death.[13] It has been said that "the Center regarded General [*sic*] Fadeikin, whom Beria had put in charge at Karlshorst, as completely out of his depth."[14] It is unclear whether he was overwhelmed during the crisis. But some of the tension in the air at Karlshorst on that fateful morning can be seen in the fact that Fadeikin wrote his message by hand—partly in ink, partly in pencil. It was then sent to foreign intelligence chief Sergei Romanovich Savchenko, and to the deputy chief of foreign intelligence for Europe, Aleksandr Mikhailovich Korotkov, at 12:25 P.M. on 17 June.[15]

Fadeikin reported that "throughout the night of 16–17 June, the situation in East Berlin remained tense. Hooligans destroyed several state shops. The question of a general strike has been decided. By 7:00 A.M. today, large crowds had begun to gather in various parts of the city and move toward the center. Several factories are already on strike." After citing how many workers were involved in the demonstrations, Fadeikin stated that the East German police "cannot maintain order." He noted that "since 6:00 A.M. Soviet troops have occupied all of the important installations: post and telegraph offices, bridges and railroad stations. Patrols consisting of two armored personnel carriers each have been organized near the locations of the SED Central Committee and GDR government. A regiment of East German Barracked People's Police has been deployed at the Central Committee building where the SED Politburo is still located. . . . The movement of columns toward the city center continues."[16]

Fadeikin repeated an earlier statement that "Soviet troops, tanks, and motorized infantry have been deployed in Berlin," but added that "among the strikers there is the impression that the authorities will not resort to force because Berlin is under four-power control. If military force is used, Western tanks will come to their aid."[17] After declaring that "the strikes and demonstrations are led from West Berlin" (without citing evidence to support this claim), Fadeikin again criticized the East Germans. He noted that GDR Minister of State Security Zaisser spent the entire day of 16 June meeting with the SED Politburo, thereby "placing all the work of insuring state security on his deputy [Erich] Mielke who . . . underestimated the seriousness of the developing situation and did not take the tough, punitive measures necessary to identify and arrest the instigators of and active participants in the demonstrations." Fadeikin complained that during that day "the East German police and MGB arrested only twenty-five persons, mainly ordinary demonstrators."[18]

After a promise to "take steps to increase the arrests of the organizers and activists of the strikes and demonstrations," Fadeikin repeated the widely known fact that the West German Minister of All-German Affairs, Jakob Kaiser, was to speak at a large meeting in West Berlin at 6:00 P.M. on 17 June—and editorialized that Kaiser "flew to West Berlin to lead the protest movement in East Berlin." When the report was sent at 12:25, much was happening about which Fadeikin seemed unaware, suggesting that in this crisis the MVD Karlshorst apparat was out of the loop. By now, for example, the SED Politburo had been moved into the Soviet compound in Karlshorst, and Marshal Vasily D. Sokolovsky, chief of the Soviet general staff, was already en route to Berlin from Moscow, signaling Soviet Army primacy in dealing with threats to East Germany.[19]

The Soviet Military Response

At 12:30 P.M. Soviet troops were commanded to restore order. There has been considerable debate—recall Pitovranov's comments on the inadmissibility of tank deployment—as to what role, if any, the MVD's Karlshorst apparat had in the decision to commit Soviet troops to suppressing the riots. From a 24 June report by Sokolovsky, Semyonov, and Pavel Yudin, deputy high commissioner, it is clear that the decision to employ Soviet force had been made on the evening of 16 June and, as Fadeikin noted, Soviet troops had begun their deployment in Berlin early the next day. But Kuchin's description of SED impotence could have contributed to the Moscow decision.[20]

As Soviet forces began to move against the crowds, Semyonov prepared a message for Moscow describing the situation in the streets, disruption of the movement of public transport between East and West Berlin, and the introduction of martial law.[21] According to Rudolf Herrnstadt, Semyonov also informed the SED Politburo members in Karlshorst that Soviet martial law would be invoked at 1:00 A.M. "It will all be over in a couple of minutes past 1," he predicted. He went on to report that Soviet Chief of the General Staff Marshal Sokolovsky and Marshal Leonid Aleksandrovich Govorov, chief inspector of the Soviet Ministry of Defense, were on their way.[22] The arrival of Sokolovsky at this time, as well as the very early morning deployment of Soviet units, indicates that the Group of Soviet Forces, Germany (GSFG), must have already been communicating with the Soviet general staff about the growing crisis. Sokolovsky was intimately familiar with the problems of Berlin and East Germany, having served there from 1945 to 1949. He was the perfect person to send.

At 11:30 P.M. on 17 June, Semyonov and Andrei Antonovich Grechko, GSFG commanding general and chief of the Soviet Control Commission, sent a "telephonogram" to Moscow noting that all movement by Germans through the sector borders had been forbidden. A separate message was sent by Semyonov and Sokolovsky declaring that "the disturbances in Berlin have ceased. The streets are quiet." By early morning on 18 June, East German police, supported by Soviet troops and East German paramilitary units, had closed the sector border to all vehicles and pedestrians. It was the most complete isolation of West Berlin from Soviet-controlled areas yet seen. Although public transportation had been shut down the day before and was still erratic, the city was calm.[23]

On 19 June Semyonov and Sokolovsky sent a telegram to Molotov and Bulganin describing "a very active organizational role of the American military in the disorders in Berlin." For example, arrested persons reportedly testified that "American officers personally selected and gathered residents of West Berlin in large groups and gave them instructions to organize disorders in East Berlin." If true, this account would have supported Sokolovsky's contention, voiced within minutes of his arrival in Karlshorst, that the crisis had been organized in advance by hostile forces. But from the Kuchin and Fadeikin reports described above, we know that neither the MVD apparat nor East German state security could support this claim. Although observers from both Berlin Command and the Eastern Affairs Division did visit East Berlin, personnel from CIA's Berlin Base had long been forbidden by their Washington headquarters to enter the Soviet sector.[24]

Were the Americans Involved?

The issue of direct American (particularly CIA) involvement in support of the disturbances has received much attention. Some have speculated that because Eleanor Dulles was in Berlin during this time as a State Department desk officer, Allen Dulles, her brother and the new CIA director, may also have been there, but he was not. Actually, like its Karlshorst counterpart, the CIA base in Berlin was completely surprised—as one BOB reports officer put it, "We were caught flatfooted!" Some East Berlin agents contacted their BOB case officers in West Berlin to report on the events, but as soon as the border closed, this kind of firsthand information was no longer available. The CIA German mission was equally surprised. Chief of Mission Gen. Lucian Truscott was in Nuremberg at the time with his deputy, Michael Burke, and his assistant, Thomas Polgar, discussing Czech crossborder operations with the US military. They read about the riots in the evening editions of newspapers on the train ride back to Frankfurt.[25]

One anecdote of dubious origin concerning CIA Berlin's possible involvement first appeared in 1979 and seems to have been resurrected in every historian's account of 17 June. Christian Ostermann's 1994 paper on the uprising, for example, states: "The CIA's Berlin station chief, Harry Hecksher, cabled Washington seeking permission to supply the rioters with arms in the face of overwhelming Soviet firepower, but was instructed to limit support to 'sympathy and asylum but no arms.'"[26]

This dramatic exchange never happened. In the first place, Bill Harvey was base chief at the time, not Henry Hecksher, and Harvey was in Berlin throughout this period. Second, there is no record that an operational cable of this sort was ever sent from Berlin, and no officers then stationed in Berlin or at German mission headquarters recall it. Polgar, Truscott's assistant, stated flatly that if Hecksher (or Harvey) had sent such a message, Truscott would have fired him immediately. Gordon Stewart, Truscott's deputy, recalls the day well because he was acting mission chief when Truscott, Burke, and Polgar were in Nuremberg. Had there been such a message he would certainly remember it. Peter Sichel, former Berlin base chief and as of 17 June 1953 chief of operations of the East European division, also denies that there was ever such a message.[27]

There was, of course, a great deal of handwringing within CIA over Western impotence during the uprisings. On 18 June, Deputy Director of Plans Frank Wisner sent John Bross, his Eastern European division chief, a memorandum after participating in a "high-level consideration of the developments of the last 48 hours in Germany" and of American propaganda tactics to be adopted. Wisner noted, "We seem to have hit pretty close to the right line in our own effort of yesterday and last night," adding that CIA "should do nothing at this time to incite East Germans to further actions which will jeopardize their lives." Wisner emphasized the unreliability of the East German security forces and the fact that "the Russians had to come in with their own troops." In this memorandum, which certainly reflected Wisner's own frustrations, there is no reference to a Berlin Base proposal to arm the rioters, nor do such references occur in any of the postmortems.[28]

The Soviet Foreign Intelligence Service Reacts

On Saturday, 20 June, Ulbricht met with Semyonov, Yudin, and Sokolovsky in Karlshorst to discuss the need for improving the arms and deployment of the paramilitary police and for having SED leadership fan out to the factories to deal with the dissatisfaction. Once more,

Sokolovsky referred to the lack of warning, saying, "The German comrades were probably somewhat shocked by the suddenness of the whole thing."[29] This sentiment is confirmed by Kuchin's and Fadeikin's reports.

Even though the Soviet Army seemed in charge at the height of the crisis, MVD Moscow could still react. Beria sent to Berlin a special group headed by Deputy Minister Sergei Goglidze. The group also included foreign intelligence directorate veteran Pyotr Vasilievich Fedotov. On 20 June, Goglidze, Fedotov, and Fadeikin, still acting chief of the Karlshorst apparat, advised Beria of actions taken to carry out his instructions. The nature of these actions demonstrates how Soviet intelligence responded, albeit belatedly, to this extraordinary challenge to vital Soviet interests in East Germany.[30]

MVD intended to use both its foreign intelligence elements and those of the military counterintelligence directorate to reinforce the East German security forces, much as their counterparts in the Soviet Army were doing. According to the report, thirty-eight operational-investigative groups were created from military counterintelligence personnel of the GSFG and the Karlshorst apparat. Other investigative and operational groups, consisting of sixty officers each, were created within the apparat itself. Their tasks were to "uncover the organizers, ringleaders, and instigators of the revolt."[31]

Beria called for the investigation of "cases of those arrestees participating in the revolt from among residents of West Berlin sent to the East sector of Berlin by foreign intelligence and West German subversive organizations." In addition, the investigative group would be "oriented to uncover the circumstances of the revolt, and the issues which could be exploited by reactionary forces for provoking the broad masses into antigovernment speeches."[32]

The last sentence of Beria's instructions displays a certain ambivalence. Although the report hews to the line that the disturbances were planned and carried out by the Western Allies, the officers were urged to look into local conditions that could have enabled the "provocateurs" to have succeeded so dramatically.[33] Nonetheless, the writers of this report had not lost their professional touch. "During the screening and interrogation process" their investigative units were ordered "in appropriate situations to recruit participants in the revolt to help uncover the organizers of these anti-government demonstrations."[34]

The second part of the report dealt with organizational problems and personnel assignments connected with the disturbances and the demoralization of GDR police and security forces. To assist the security forces, a special group of forty-three operational personnel was made available from the Karlshorst apparat under the "command of Capt. Vasily Morgachev, an assistant to the [MVD] Representative, and Colonel [Yevgeny Ignatievich] Kravtsov, chief of a department in the USSR MVD." The group's mission was to help the Berlin elements of the GDR Mfs organize "screening, interrogations and agent-operational work." About 120 similar operational groups, made up of MVD personnel, were organized to support GDR Mfs directorates in other districts.[35]

The message also described the work of the MVD's independent agents in Germany. Both the Karlshorst apparat and military counterintelligence in Potsdam were given the job "of mobilizing all agent resources to clarify the circumstances that caused the events and to uncover the organizing centers in both West Germany and the GDR." Steps were taken to establish contact with "available agent networks in West Berlin and West Germany to uncover the future plans of West Berlin and West German reactionary circles and those of foreign intelligence organs."[36]

A further indication that in this emergency Beria had to delay his plans to revamp the MVD and its East German units can be seen in the staffing of an operational group established under the leadership of Lt. Gen. Amaiak Kobulov "to ensure that this important work was carried out properly." It consisted of German operations specialist Kuchin and Col. Andrei Yefimovich Kovalev, a leading German affairs analyst from Moscow Center.[37]

In conclusion the report stated that a meeting would be held that day, 20 June, with the leadership of the GDR Mfs to work out measures "for strengthening GDR Mfs organs, reinforcing the frontier guards, and ensuring reliable guarding of Mfs installations and GDR prisons." On Monday, 22 June, the report was forwarded to Deputy Minister Bogdan Zakharovich Kobulov under a "resolution" signed by Korotkov and Savchenko—the same senior foreign intelligence officers who later testified against Beria.[38]

Amid the chaos in Karlshorst, someone must have been tending to business in MVD's foreign intelligence directorate, because a request was evidently sent from Moscow Center to residencies abroad asking for information that would "explain the real reasons . . . for the popular demonstrations in Berlin." The 28 June response from the Paris residency, the only one we have, admitted an inability to respond to the

Encoded telegram, 28 June 1953, from Paris MVD residency to Moscow Center, reporting that "we have not been successful in clarifying the true reasons underlying the popular disturbances in Berlin."

question—a lapse uncharacteristic of the Paris residency, which normally supplied excellent material on German questions.[39] Because the request for information was probably sent soon after 17 June, Beria and his group would still have been in charge of MVD.

Although the Paris residency could not respond to Moscow with authority, one of its sources was able to debrief a French journalist who was in Berlin on the fateful day and claimed to have visited East Berlin with Arno Scholtz, editor of the West Berlin SPD newspaper *Der Telegraf.* This journalist's account, as cabled by the residency, probably provided what Moscow wanted to hear: "It seems almost certain that interference of representatives and agents of the German Social Democratic Party (SPD) transformed at least partially the demands of the construction workers of Stalinallee into a political demonstration. . . . A plan of action was worked out long ago by this [SPD] apparatus. Only the date for implementing this plan was not determined; it would depend on the course of events. . . . 16 June developed as the denouement of these events, yet the SPD leadership had not determined it in advance. . . . The Social Democrats of the former capital, not waiting for orders from their chairman, began to implement the directives worked out earlier for such a case."[40]

Beria Is Blamed

The report from Paris was the last document among those obtained from SVR archives on the situation in East Germany before Beria's arrest. Other elements of the Soviet establishment on both sides of the power struggle between Beria and Khrushchev were evidently competing to have their views of the situation heard. In a 24 June memorandum to Khrushchev, Dmitry Shepilov, then editor of *Pravda,* forwarded a copy of the eyewitness account of the 16–17 June events by "P. Naumov," *Pravda*'s man in East Berlin. Naumov's account is a factual, reasonably accurate reflection of the events. He describes the appearance of Soviet troops early on the morning of 17 June, for example, and the crowds' hostility. He notes the frequent appearances near the demonstrations of motor vehicles with West Berlin and American license plates. The implication here is that vehicles with West Berlin or Allied military registration were assisting the rioters. In fact, Allied personnel had every right to be in East Berlin. Only West Berlin civilian vehicles were then subject to Volkspolizei checks. Naumov also emphasized that not only workers participated; many citizens who might have been expected to support the regime, including SED members, also took part. He was scornful of SED's cowardice and its inability to understand the mood of the masses. His final paragraph seems somewhat at odds with his descriptive passages and appears to have been added at the last minute: "There is no doubt that the entire operation was painstakingly prepared ... in advance and was directed from one center." This view, written on 22 June, accords with the line that was to dominate subsequent treatment of the events and that was to be used against Beria.[41]

Sokolovsky and Semyonov apparently had no inkling of the plans to arrest Beria. The recommendations of their report of 24 June reflected their determination to continue the New Course, improve the situation in the GDR, and strengthen reform forces within the SED Central Committee.[42]

Two days later, Beria was arrested at a Presidium meeting. Amy Knight, in her detailed account of the day's events in *Beria: Stalin's First Lieutenant,* offers several conflicting versions. The official records of the Presidium meeting are "missing," so we are left with the various accounts of the victorious participants in the plot to eliminate Beria.[43] Whatever the truth about 26 June, it appears that Beria was taken by surprise. Others seemed equally uninformed. On 29 June 1953, for example, Ivan Tugarinov, chief of the so-called Small KI, sent to Beria's deputy for foreign intelligence, "Comrade Kobulov, B. Z.," a copy of an eighteen-page memorandum on "The Position of the Western Powers on the German Question" prepared by his group. Based primarily on overt material, the report ended, "The information outlined above shows that serious differences exist between the United States and England on the issue of whether they should enter into negotiations in the near future with the USSR on the German question. These differences were apparently one of the basic reasons for the postponement of the Bermuda Conference."[44] This information suggested that the apparent flexibility being displayed in Moscow on the German question was indeed having an effect on the Western Allies. Beria would have been interested in this memorandum, but he obviously never received it. The same is true of Kobulov, who was arrested on the same day Beria was taken.

In the indictment and later in their explanation of Beria's ouster and arrest at the July 1953 CC CPSU Plenum, Beria's opponents maintained that all of his actions with regard to MVD had stemmed from his espionage role on behalf of "German and English intelligence." This chestnut aside, and even acknowledging Beria's compulsion to settle scores with those in the security service who had been close to the previous security leaders, how are we to explain his virtual decapitation of the foreign intelligence service's residencies abroad at this crucial time? Beria must have been anxious, if not desperate, to obtain foreign reactions to the signals he was sending, particularly on the German question. His actions, therefore, appear totally irrational—unless he, like others in Moscow, had no inkling of the forthcoming 17 June events. He may have assumed that he would have time to make the changes he desired in the service and in the German component. Yevgeny Berezin, one of the Karlshorst senior officers recalled to Moscow, remembers remarks made by Beria to his group: "There is a new situation in Germany, one that requires a new approach. We must assign people to Germany of a higher intellectual level, and this is the reason for reducing the numbers in Germany, particularly in the provinces."

Meanwhile, back in Karlshorst, it was necessary to deal with Beria's friends, Goglidze and Amaiak Kobulov, who were presumably busy cleaning up after the 17 June riots. According to Sudoplatov in *Secret Tasks*, they were arrested by General Grechko and returned to Moscow under guard. A CIA report states that their arrest was actually arranged by having Semyonov summon them on business. When the two had not rejoined the special team, two of the members, Fedotov and Kovalev, learned from a reluctant Semyonov that they had been recalled to Moscow. Later, Fedotov allegedly learned that the arrest had been carried out by Marshal Sokolovsky on 27 June, and that Goglidze and Kobulov had been bound and placed aboard a plane to Moscow.[45]

On 30 June, Fedotov and acting MVD representative Fadeikin reported in a telephonogram to Moscow Center that as of 29–30 June all was quiet in East Berlin and East Germany. The remainder of the report consists of quotations by Germans from all walks of life who had been invited to comment on the current situation and the causes of the disturbances. Some of the statements attributed to GDR citizens were harshly critical of the SED and GDR regime. The quotation was commonly used by state security officers, even at the level of Fedotov and

Копия
Совершенно секретно

Принято по "ВЧ"
из Берлина

102

М В Д   С С С Р

Докладываем о положении в Берлине и на территории
ГДР по состоянию на 30 июня с.г.

I. В течение 29 июня и дня 30 июня в Берлине и на территории ГДР было спокойно. Предприятия, транспорт и учреждения работали нормально.

На фабриках, заводах и в сельских общинах продолжают проходить собрания, одобряющие мероприятия, проводимые правительством, и осуждающие действия провокаторов.

Поступают сведения, что население ГДР явственно ощущает улучшения в области продовольственного снабжения.

Рабочий калийной шахты Глинцау Эрфуртского округа [...] Фридрих заявил: "Решения правительства стали заметны. В магазины поступают свежие овощи, фрукты, масло и другие продукты".

Жительница г.Бессонов [...]ранденбургского округа домохозяйка МАРТИРИХ заявила: "Я довольна решениями правительства [...] об увеличении количества товаров, продаваемых населению. [...] удивляюсь, откуда сразу достали такое большое количество товаров. Неужели нельзя было направить их в магазины рань[...] Если бы правительство сделало это своевременно, то не бы[...] бы никаких выступлений".

Житель г.Ростов адвокат АРТИНГ, выступая на собрании

V Ch (secure telephone) message, 30 June 1953, from acting MVD Berlin chief Ivan Fadeikin and senior foreign intelligence official Pyotr Fedotov to MVD USSR on the situation in Berlin and the GDR following the 17 June riots.

Fadeikin, when they wished to convey unpleasant news to the center without assuming responsibility for the statements.[46]

It was not until after a secret plenum of the CPSU Central Committee was held on 2–7 July that the arrest of Beria and his friends was announced.[47] Along with other Soviet bloc leaders, Ulbricht and Grotewohl were briefed in Moscow on the results of the plenum by Malenkov, Molotov, and Khrushchev, and they returned to inform SED leaders on 9 July. A *Pravda* article with the news appeared the next day.[48] These events were followed quickly in the GDR by the expulsion of Security Minister Zaisser and Rudolf Herrnstadt from the SED Politburo. Obviously, Herrnstadt had not realized that the Soviets would opt to stick with Ulbricht, who for all of his faults was someone they could rely on to do the messy work of putting the GDR back together again.[49]

After the Beria arrest had been made public, a meeting was held in the Second Chief Directorate (for foreign intelligence) by the new MVD minister Sergei Kruglov to announce the appointment of Aleksandr Semyonovich Paniushkin as the new directorate chief and deputy minister. Paniushkin had been Soviet ambassador in Washington from 1947 to 1952 and had served as chief KI resident during that period. In early August, Paniushkin called a meeting of department chiefs and party secretaries of the directorate and asked them how they would restructure their departments. He based the need for change on the "grounds that during his tenure as minister, Beria disrupted the work of the directorate, unnecessarily discharged a large number of employees, and put through a completely faulty reorganization of the directorate."[50]

The American Food-Package Program

Yevgeny Pitovranov emerged unscathed from the Beria drama. By 1 August he was in place as head of the Karlshorst apparat and caught up in plans to rebuild both his apparat and the shattered East German state security service. But before he got far in this work he was called on to cope with a new "provocation," the American food-package program. Launched on 10 July by an exchange of letters between President Eisenhower and Chancellor Adenauer, the program was incredibly successful: "By mid-August, 75 percent of the East Berlin population had received food packages." SED at first seemed unconcerned, but as the program's influence grew, the party realized the "extent to which the food program exacerbated tensions within the GDR."[51]

On 7 August, Kruglov advised Molotov of Pitovranov's attempts to cut off "the subversive activity by hostile elements exploiting the American 'food aid' campaign." The MVD apparat, too, saw that "the American food program posed a serious threat to security and stability in the GDR." After directing East German state security to coordinate efforts to disrupt the program, MVD urged that testimony from arrestees be exploited by SED media outlets "to expose the 'true' character of the American 'aid.'" At the same time, all elements of the East German security system were directed to concentrate on investigating and "repressing" people organizing mass excursions to Berlin to collect food packages. To avert more riots, the Soviets urged GDR leaders to strengthen security forces at government buildings, radio stations, and power plants. The MVD apparat was told to increase its operations against hostile underground elements, using not only East German security organs but also the resources of the apparat and its regional operational groups. Even the MVD counterintelligence departments of the Group of Soviet Forces, Germany, became involved: they were ordered to improve counterintelligence within the East German paramilitary forces.[52]

The food aid program did prolong a state of unrest and uncertainty in the GDR, but Soviet determination to maintain control over East Germany never wavered. Moreover, at least one American agency had misgivings about the long-term effects of the program. BOB lobbied the East European division of CIA to protest the distribution of food. The division did so, noting in a memorandum to the director of Central Intelligence that the program might invite Communist complaints about the use of "food as Cold War propaganda." And because the interzonal borders were much more difficult to cross, the East European division observed, those wishing to obtain parcels would gravitate to distribution points along the Berlin sector boundaries. The Russians would then "be furnished with a pretext for sealing the sector border. . . . This would greatly hamper our operations both in Berlin and East Germany." But the program had strong support within the National Security Council and the Psychological Warfare Strategy Board, so this protest had no effect. Nevertheless, the specter of a complete crackdown on movement between East and West Berlin haunted BOB operators.[53]

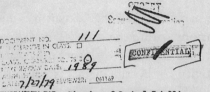

DOCUMENT NO. 111
CHANGE IN CLASS. □

Date 12/7/94
HRP 94-1

MEMORANDUM FOR: Director of Central Intelligence

SUBJECT : Proposal for establishment of food depots along
zonal boundaries

1. The Working Committee of the PSB prepared a draft reply to the
Soviet note of July 11, 1953, in which it was proposed that the United
States set up depots along the interzonal boundary at which East Germans
could pick up food packages. This draft was not used because of the
objections of Ambassador Bohlen. The State Department then proposed to
U. S. High Commissioner Conant on 10 August that the offer to establish
food depots be incorporated in a note to Soviet High Commissioner Semenov
and that if this offer were rejected "as we presume it would be . . .
scattered food depots / would be established / along the frontiers to
which East Germans would be invited to come and collect packages". The
U. S. High Commissioner has not yet commented on this proposal.

2. It is our understanding that, at the PSB meeting on 12 August,
the State Department will propose that action be taken to set up the
food depots immediately, unless Mr. Conant in the meanwhile expresses
very strong opposition. EE Division feels that a favorable decision on
this proposal would be contrary to the best interests of the United States.
If the proposal were carried out, it would evoke not only the usual
Communist denunciations but also lend further substance to the statements
of some West Europeans that we are using food as cold war propaganda. We
will thus dissipate much of the good will which we have acquired since
June 16. Furthermore, as the interzonal borders are much more difficult
to cross than the Berlin Sector boundaries, we incur the risk of Soviet
countermoves resulting in bloodshed or repressive measures against the
Soviet Zone population. The Russians would thus be provided with a
pretext for sealing the Sector border as well as the Zonal boundary.
This would, of course, greatly hamper our operations both in Berlin and
East Germany.

3. While the need for food does exist, it is not so great that an
East Zone citizen would put his life in jeopardy to obtain a five pound
package. Those who did attempt to cross the boundary would do so in the
conviction that they were somehow being protected by us. The would not
believe that we would invite them to cross the sterilized belt between
the zones unless we were ready to accept full responsibility for their
action. The Soviets, aware that we were not prepared to accept such
responsibility, could turn this situation into a politico-psychological
victory. We would be accused, and stand convicted, of irresponsibility --
particularly if any violence or bloodshed should result from our invitation.

Memorandum, 11 August 1953, from John A. Bross, chief, Eastern European Division, to Allen Dulles, director, Central Intelligence, regarding proposal for establishment of food depots along zonal boundaries.
The memorandum advises against the proposal on the grounds that the
action would risk "sealing of the [Berlin] Sector border."

After describing the breakup by the West Berlin police of an SED-organized demonstration against American "provocations," Kruglov suggested prohibiting the sale of railroad tickets to Berlin as a way to reduce the number of GDR residents traveling to Berlin to obtain parcels. The number of travelers—previously twenty thousand to forty thousand per week—dropped immediately to eight thousand. But MVD had to contend with protests: 150 women at Hennigsdorf near Potsdam, for example, refused to get off the tracks until the sale of tickets to Berlin was resumed. As of 7 August, Kruglov expected the Americans to renew the program through at least the following week.[54]

After the unrest in the GDR during summer 1953, the East German state security service was transformed into one of the most coercive and effective in the Soviet bloc. It has been suggested that without the uprisings—and without American efforts to exploit the unrest to increase pressure on the Soviet Union and its East German surrogates—this toughening of the GDR regime might not have happened. Indeed, in the view of some historians, the cause of German reunification itself was delayed by these events. Similarly, some have speculated that had Beria succeeded in inheriting Stalin's mantle, his determination to reform outmoded and inefficient domestic and foreign policies would have had a liberalizing effect on the Soviet approach to the German question.

Unfortunately, whatever Beria's position may actually have been with regard to the future of the GDR, the role of SED, and the need to reach a compromise with the West on the nature of a reunited Germany, it is our view that he went about achieving these goals in a way that virtually guaranteed failure. During the brief interregnum, Beria, in spite of his awareness of how the Soviet power game was played, behaved in a reckless, headstrong, and naive manner: reckless, because he should have known the extent to which the SED regime was disliked by East Germans and how strongly they would resist the abrupt changes of the kind attributed to him. Even if he had championed these changes merely as one more weapon in the power struggle after Stalin's death, he dreadfully underestimated the population's strength in thwarting them. The headstrong Beria ignored the obvious—that the Soviet military would vigorously resist any experimentation that could jeopardize its hold on this piece of German territory, which represented sacrifices made during and since the war. And he should have understood the extent to which the Soviet intelligence services valued their stake in Germany as a base for foreign operations. Finally, he was naive to believe that he could prevail in his attempt to succeed Stalin by achieving total control of the security forces. He should have anticipated that his opponents had been hard at work planting their cronies in the system—and, for that matter, in the armed forces. By attempting to rid MVD of his enemies and build a brand-new service, he had made it nearly impossible for MVD and its East German friends to cope with the June explosion that his political machinations had set in motion.

10

The Mysterious Case of Otto John

The story of Otto John, president of the Office for the Protection of the Constitution (Bundesamt fuer Verfassungsschutz, BFV)—the West German counterespionage agency—is a fitting sequel to the events of June 1953, but in fact it spans the entire time frame of this book. A veteran of the wartime resistance, suspected of Gestapo ties yet involved with British intelligence, John became in 1950 the first postwar West German counterintelligence chief while harboring deep misgivings about the policies of the government he served. These views and his own emotional, quixotic nature attracted KGB attention, and an attempt was made to recruit him. The recruitment did not work out as planned, but John's experience offers a fascinating example of KGB operational frustration. This is the first time material from the KGB's John file has been made public.

By July 1954 the two sides of the Cold War in Germany seemed deadlocked. The newly formed KGB and its East German counterparts continued their investigations into the causes of the 17 June 1953 uprising; the West German Bundestag had met in West Berlin on 17 June 1954 to reelect Theodor Heuss as federal president. Four days later, the disappearance in Berlin of Otto John, president of BFV, was made public. A few hours after that ADN, the East German official news agency, announced that John had requested and received political asylum. Thus exploded the most sensational bombshell of the Cold War in Germany. The scandal of the John case was heightened by the key role attributed to the flamboyant gynecologist-surgeon and jazz trumpeter Wolfgang ("Wo-Wo") Wohlgemuth, who had disappeared with John—either as guide or abductor.

Three days after his disappearance, the first of John's statements from the East, an attack on Adenauer's policies, was transmitted by East German radio. The consternation of the West was complete when, scarcely three weeks later, John appeared at a press conference in East Berlin attended by Western correspondents. In a comprehensive statement John gave as the reason for his action his impassioned desire to preserve German unity. He described Adenauer as a confirmed separatist whose government included unreconstructed Nazis in high places. For three-quarters of an hour John fielded questions from his audience. It was a masterful performance: John convinced all present— including his former chief in British intelligence, Sefton Delmer—that his defection had been voluntary and that his views were utterly sincere.

Allied intelligence and security agencies in Germany that had been in regular contact with John were shocked; they scrambled to help prepare a "damage report" about what sensitive information in his possession might have been given over to the Soviets. American services were particularly upset because John had just paid a visit to his counterparts in Washington, where he had been given the usual series of briefings and had been invited to social events normally attended by chiefs of friendly services. BFV had never been privy to BOB operations, so there was no need to take special precautions. But BOB's East German agents needed reassurance that their operations had not been compromised.[1] Media reverberations ranged from screaming headlines in the West Berlin dailies to articles in the American press that highlighted John's recent visit.[2]

Immediately after his sensational press conference, John dropped from sight. But by the end of 1954 he began touring East Germany under the auspices of the Committee for German Unity, an East German propaganda organization. In his appearances he pleaded for a neutral, united Germany friendly to the USSR. And so it went for more than a year—until 4:52 P.M. on 12 December 1955, when John suddenly reappeared in West Berlin, having been spirited away from his East German bodyguards-cum-captors by the Danish journalist Henryk Bonde-Henryksen, his friend. Within two hours, John and Bonde-

Henryksen had been flown out of the city under pseudonyms to Cologne. There, after a few hours of deferential interrogation, John was formally arrested as a traitor. He was tried, found guilty, and sentenced to four years in prison.

Since John's sentencing there has been an unremitting struggle on the part of various people—including successive presidents of the FRG and, preeminently, John himself—to clear his name through the courts. These attempts have failed; every appeal has been turned down. In 1965 John published *Twice Through the Lines*.[3] In it he insisted that he had been abducted to East Berlin under the influence of a drug administered by Wohlgemuth. He further claimed that his entire performance in East Berlin and the Soviet Union had been under duress, but that he had managed to reveal no secrets to the Soviet or East German authorities. John's version of his case was contested four years later in the book *Das Ende einer Legende* (The end of a legend) by West German journalist Hans Frederik. Frederik's book contained a lengthy interview with an official spokesman for the KGB, "Colonel Karpov." In what was an unprecedented move, Karpov volunteered KGB's version of the John case, denying that John had been abducted or placed under any form of duress during his sojourn in East Germany and the Soviet Union. The KGB—through Karpov—also denied that John had been in any need of rescuing: he and Bonde-Henryksen had crossed into West Berlin without hindrance. After the breakup of the GDR and demise of MfS, it was learned that Frederik had been an East German agent whose book on Otto John had been published under the direction of MfS.[4] Incidentally, "Colonel Karpov" was none other than Vadim Vitoldovich Kuchin, one of the best-qualified German specialists in Karlshorst. It was he, using the name Vladimir Appolonovich Karpov, who in 1969 had supposedly contacted Frederik and issued KGB's denial that John had been drugged and kidnapped.

SVR Archives Provide Another Version

These are the bare bones of the John case. It remains the longest-running mystery play of the Cold War in Germany. Upon arriving in Moscow in summer 1993 to begin work on this book, we were surprised to discover that John had been there three weeks earlier in his Odyssean quest to clear his name. Hence we received unsolicited the first of several Russian versions of the John case. The details were fresh in the memories of the retired KGB officers concerned because they had just completed videotaping a German television documentary on the issue. The title of the documentary on the eighty-seven-year-old John was "I Don't Want to Die a Traitor."[5] In addition to an edited summary of the KGB John file, which we were allowed to read,[6] we obtained the guidelines that had been prepared by the Russian Foreign Intelligence Service for those retired officers who were to appear in the documentary.[7]

The file summary was a more detailed version in intelligence service jargon of the story told by "Colonel Karpov" in 1969. From it we learned that in KGB correspondence John had been referred to by the code names Proton and Keller. The guidelines emphasized several points that the Russians hoped would have a positive effect on German public opinion. They hoped the program would stress the "positive role of the USSR concerning the unification of Germany at the beginning of the 1950s," as well as "the efforts of the Western Allies at that time not to permit the rebirth of a strong and unified Germany" and the measures then taken "by the intelligence services of the United States, Great Britain, and France to oppose the normalization of German-Russian relations." When the television program was aired, it did not follow this script. It became evident that the Karpov version was not the whole story, and that because of the tale's potential effect on relations with Germany, Russian intelligence officials wished to include their own version.

Before examining the John case more fully in an intelligence context, let us review the circumstances surrounding John's abrupt departure on the evening of 20 July 1954. The North Korean invasion of South Korea in June 1950, launched without warning, had thrown the West into panic lest the same exercise be repeated in Germany. In response the Western Allies had reinforced the North Atlantic Treaty Organization (NATO), which had been created in 1949 in the wake of the Berlin blockade. For a credible defense against a Korean-style assault, NATO needed West Germany. Thus German rearmament had become a key issue overnight.

The prospect of German rearmament under former Wehrmacht generals caused political turmoil in the West at large, and in West Germany in particular. The stoutest of democrats blanched at the prospect. For those like John, who had risked life and limb to resist the Nazis and whose brother had perished at the hands of the Nazis in the same cause, the specter of a new Nazi military machine was horrifying.

Otto John, moreover, was no ordinary antimilitarist. He not only had connections during the war to the German anti-Nazi resistance movement; he also had ties to Allied intelligence. When the 20 July 1944 plot on Hitler's life collapsed, John had fled to England with British help. For the remainder of the war he had worked for British intelligence, broadcasting in German on the radio program *Soldatensender Calais.* From 1945 through 1949 John was involved in investigating German generals as a consultant to the British War Crimes Commission, and he conducted interrogations for the British prosecution at the Nuremberg war crimes trials. He gained special notice as the chief German assistant to the British prosecutor in the trial of Field Marshal Erich von Mannstein, who was charged with seventeen counts of war crimes. John's work in the von Mannstein trial was bitterly resented in Germany—and not only by former Nazis. Over the years of discussion of the John case—in and out of parliament and the courts—the basic criterion applied to whether he and others like him were members of the resistance was whether such members were under the command or tutelage of a foreign power. Thus Otto John's British connection further prejudiced his position even before his appointment to BfV.

As the 1950s unfolded, John became obsessively fearful of a return to Nazi power in West Germany. Because he felt his warnings to the Adenauer government and the Western Allies of Nazi infiltration had been ignored, John decided to take his case to the Soviets, whom he knew to be sympathetic. Was this decision made on his own, or was he guided by forces he never fully understood?

The initial SVR answer to this question, contained in the summary of the case shown to us in September 1993, seemed contrived. Had John really gone voluntarily to East Berlin to meet with Soviet representatives? If so, what was he led to expect, and how was he persuaded not to return? When the television program appeared on the Hessischer Rundfunk in late November, our doubts multiplied. The former head of the KGB apparat in Karlshorst, Yevgeny Pitovranov, made an effort to put a good face on the story, but the program's producer, backed by testimony of other former KGB officers on the same program, contradicted the bland version of events favored by SVR. In response to our continuing doubts, SVR provided us with a written summary of the actual John dossier.[8] When we combine this with the results of our own inquiries, a fascinating case history of Cold War espionage emerges that has as its focus the role of KGB.

John as a Spy for the West

The Soviet dossier on Otto John did not begin with his appointment as BFV president in 1950. It begins in 1939, when John worked for the German Airline Lufthansa, and traces his relationship with Adm. Wilhelm Canaris, chief of German intelligence (Abwehr). Canaris saw John's frequent travels to Lisbon and Madrid as an opportunity to maintain contact with foreign supporters.[9] According to reports in the SVR dossier from the prewar NKVD residency in Berlin, by 1939 John was in contact with the American correspondent Louis Lochner. There were also reports that the German opposition with which John was associated saw Lochner as a link to Franklin D. Roosevelt.[10]

Soviet sources in British intelligence, notably Kim Philby, described John's clandestine ties to the British service and his extensive reporting on German progress on atomic weapons, submarine deployment, and on the rocket and missile testing facilities at Peenemünde. But for the Soviets, John's information on the Nazi war machine was a trifle compared with the insights his reporting gave into the activities of the non-Communist resistance to Hitler. Cited in the Soviet dossier are reports received by British intelligence on visits by John to Lisbon in December 1942 and a year later, when he described the plans and problems of the anti-Nazi resistance he claimed to represent. Probably thanks to Philby, the view was expressed in the SIS document transmitted with the reports that "there was no basis for changing the opinion that John's actions and conversations were approved by the Gestapo if not dictated by them."[11]

This information that Philby provided to NKGB from the "depths of British intelligence," fueled by SIS's apparent suspicion of John's Gestapo connections, brought him to Soviet attention and revived Soviet fears that, were German resistance to get rid of Hitler, Germany might conclude a separate peace with the Allies. Although the basis for SIS's apparent conviction that John was under Gestapo control is not evident from the KGB dossier, it certainly reflects the deep-seated suspicions of British motives—doubts that were prevalent throughout the Soviet government and that found resonance time after time as the John story unfolded.[12]

After the failure of the plot on Hitler's life, John eluded the Gestapo and escaped to Portugal. From there he was taken to England with SIS help. In spite of lingering suspicions of Gestapo links—which would have explained his ability to flee Germany—the Soviet dossier states that John was interned briefly in a comfortable apartment in the center of London and by Christmas 1944 had completed the transition from informant to collaborator with British intelligence. After preparing extensive reports on the situation in Germany and on leading German political figures, and after helping to identify key Nazis, John was placed in the psychological warfare department under Sefton Delmer, where he worked on the radio program *Soldatensender Calais.* It was here that John met Wolfgang Gans Edler Herr von und zu Putlitz, a former German diplomat with a checkered past who also worked in Delmer's unit and who later played an important role for the Soviets in the John operation.

The Soviet dossier provided little information about the circumstances of John's work in war crimes and his move to the Federal Republic. It did note his appointment as the first president of BfV—due, it was claimed, to "English influence." Soviet interest in John was rekindled in 1951, not only because of his BfV position but also because unidentified sources provided new information about his political attitudes. Peter Deriabin, who at the time was a desk officer in the Austro-German department of MGB foreign intelligence, suggests that among the sources was an agent in BfV itself.[13] The existence of a Soviet agent in BfV at this time was confirmed for Hans Frederik in his interview with the KGB's "Colonel Karpov," although it is unclear whether Frederik's MfS-driven book can be believed.[14] John was described by these sources as both an advocate of German unity who approved Soviet efforts in that direction and an outspoken critic of Adenauer's policies and of the presence of former Nazis in his government.

KGB Berlin began to increase its coverage of John, though it proceeded cautiously, suspecting that he was still a British agent. Soviet sources reported that John was spineless in his resistance to the influence of others, inconsistent in his actions, intemperate in his use of alcohol, and lacking discernment in his choice of friends. The Soviets also had another perspective on John through his collaborator at *Soldatensender Calais,* the effete aristocrat von Putlitz, who confirmed the Soviet picture of John's circumstances, background, and unhappiness with the Adenauer government. The KGB officer who directed the operation was Vadim Vitoldovich Kuchin, alias Karpov.[15]

The Soviets Try to Recruit John

According to the dossier and "Karpov's" 1969 account, the first break in the case came in late 1953, when Max Wonsig, who had been an agent of Soviet intelligence in Germany since 1946, informed his case officer that a certain playboy gynecologist in West Berlin, Wolfgang Wohlgemuth, was a close friend of Otto John's. "Wo-Wo" Wohlgemuth fancied himself a Communist—a "cocktail party partisan," in Berlin parlance—and he was bent on doing something for the Soviet cause. Wonsig's sister, who was a nurse, had worked under Wohlgemuth in a Berlin hospital and had arranged for her brother and the doctor to meet. (John had met Wohlgemuth during the war in Berlin's famous Charité hospital while his brother, a war casualty, was under Wohlgemuth's care.) Wonsig described the relationship between John and Dr. Wohlgemuth, emphasizing John's dissatisfaction with the Adenauer regime and his desire to meet with Soviet officials. Wonsig also offered to introduce Wohlgemuth to a KGB officer. This report "hit Karlshorst like a thunderstorm," offering as it did the prospect of developing a relationship with the head of West German counterintelligence at a time when KGB was still reeling from the near collapse of the East German regime during the June 1953 riots. The recruitment of West German counterintelligence chief John offered an opportunity to recoup.

According to the 1969 Kuchin (Colonel Karpov) account, Wonsig and Wohlgemuth first met at an East Berlin bar. But SVR archival material places the first meeting in a Karlshorst safe house on 21 January 1954, after which Wohlgemuth visited John in Cologne. Wohlgemuth described John as politically indifferent, disillusioned with life, and still nostalgic for his prewar existence. Asked by Kuchin whether John might be brought to the point of furnishing secret documents, Wohlgemuth said that it would take time but that it could be done. Wonsig's continuing role in the development of the operation was allegedly limited to putting the KGB in touch with Wohlgemuth; he was not trusted to do more.

KGB was now faced with devising some way of meeting directly with John. Wohlgemuth proposed the use of his apartment in West Berlin; Karlshorst turned this idea down. John himself rejected the suggestion of a clandestine tryst in Switzerland, saying that he would have no assurances that he would be dealing with serious Soviet officials. Wohlgemuth was told to tell John that he would be introduced in the Soviet sector to an "important political figure to discuss the question of progressive groups in West Germany capable of working in a united Germany." But John was constrained by the nature of his position—he could not simply go to Berlin and disappear for a few hours.

The occasion that lent itself perfectly to the purpose was the memorial ceremony in Berlin-Ploetzensee on 20 July, the anniversary of the failed plot against Hitler. John had every right to be there; indeed, his absence at such a ceremony would have prompted comment. To KGB it was the perfect moment to begin recruiting Otto John. The proposal satisfied John, and the meeting with the Soviet official was set. When General Pitovranov was informed of this, he responded with the Russian equivalent of "I'll believe it when I see it." Accordingly, on the evening of 20 July, John rode in Wohlgemuth's car to East Berlin, where he transferred to a KGB operational car and was taken by Kuchin to a safe house in Karlshorst.[16] The extract of the Soviet dossier emphasized that John's trip to the Soviet sector of Berlin was entirely voluntary and was based on his desire to meet with representatives of the USSR.[17]

The first sentence of the official report by Pitovranov—transmitted via secure telephone to KGB Chairman Ivan Aleksandrovich Serov, then in Kiev, and Aleksandr Semyonovich Paniushkin, head of the KGB's First Chief Directorate—must have made quite a splash in Moscow. It read: "On 20 July the President of the West German Office for the Protection of the Constitution (political police), Otto John, was brought to Democratic Berlin by the West Berlin doctor Wolfgang Wohlgemuth, a confidential contact of the intelligence department of the Inspectorate."[18] The report went on to describe John's motives for going to East Berlin and his desire to establish contact with the Soviets for a common struggle. Also noted was John's readiness to answer KGB questions. John supposedly "wished to maintain contact with us to discuss political problems and joint actions against the Nazis of West Germany." But Pitovranov believed John's present position was insecure; he noted that John had refused to provide information on the activities of Bonn institutions and the agent operations of his own "office," claiming that he did not have access to such material. "Therefore," Pitovranov concluded, "we considered the recruitment of John both inexpedient and unrealistic. We have taken the decision to persuade him not to return to West Germany and to make an open break with Adenauer that would be accompanied by a corresponding political declaration by him."[19]

For all its bureaucratic precision, Pitovranov's report to Serov and Paniushkin was a bit too pat. The decision not to recruit John was certainly a wise move professionally. John had refused the Soviet pitch, and the Soviets had refused his. John was ready to cooperate only to the extent of accepting any information the Soviets could give him about former Nazis in the Adenauer government. He asked for—indeed, demanded—such information. This proposition had no appeal for the Soviets, who realized that John would not know how to use such information without entrapping himself in a totally insupportable position vis-à-vis the Adenauer government. KGB also saw John as a highly emotional complex of explosive sensitivities. He lacked the equanimity that is the basic requirement of an undercover agent. The result was a stand-off.

The KGB dossier pointed to yet another aspect of the decision not to proceed with the John recruitment: KGB suspected that John was still collaborating with British intelligence. The goal of the British operation might have been to place John in a position to control, or at least influence, the many unofficial Soviet-German contacts used by KGB to further Soviet policies in Germany. KGB was not alone in suspecting John of being a British cat's-paw: the KGB dossier produced a 24 August 1954 letter sent to the US High Commissioner in Germany, James B. Conant, by FBI Director J. Edgar Hoover. The letter noted that "it appears that our allies, despite the information which they received in good time from the State Department concerning our doubts about Dr. John's sincerity, gave him their full support."[20] But this letter could not have affected the deliberations of Pitovranov and his officers during the night of 20–21 July 1954. Were there other reports, or was the FBI angle introduced as a reflection of the continuing KGB obsession with British intelligence, thus justifying their actions that night?

Was John Kidnapped?

It is quite possible that John was fully prepared to accompany Wohlgemuth to the East Berlin rendezvous. He had, after all, taken the precaution of emptying his pockets of anything that might have been considered sensitive (such as his notebook, his official identity card, and the key to his Cologne office safe).[21] Nevertheless, wasn't it in the interest of Wohlgemuth, Wonsig, and the Soviet officers concerned to get John to East Berlin by whatever means necessary without doing him permanent psychic or physical harm? Wohlgemuth was a doctor of medicine. John had arrived in his office in a state of inebriation and dejection. What could have been easier for Wohlgemuth than to administer a pill, powder, or draught—say a preanaesthetic medicine that produces a state of benumbed euphoria—to render him helpless for half an hour? That was all that was needed. For Wohlgemuth to have done less would have seemed downright foolhardy under the circumstances. Why take chances of John's changing his mind at the last minute? And what about Wonsig?

Here we have the testimony of Boris Nalivaiko, with a lifetime of experience in KGB German operations, who delivered his statement on television: "I must say, as an espionage professional, it fills me with pride to this very day that in the end it was one of the members of my group who participated in the operation that succeeded in bringing Otto John to the territory of the GDR." Nalivaiko added, before he was interrupted by his KGB chaperon, that the agent was a German who had been liberated by the Soviets from a concentration camp, and his code name was Kaefer (bug).[22] This was the clue that brought the KGB agent Max Wonsig to light. Shortly after the documentary was broadcast on 28 November 1993, a former neighbor of Wonsig's contacted the television station. Wonsig had died eleven years earlier, but the neighbor mentioned Wonsig's niece, who later confirmed and augmented the account of Wonsig's role in the abduction of Otto John. Her version is contradicted by the Russian archival material, which also attacks Wonsig's personal and operational past. According to the archives, Wonsig was dropped by KGB because of his extreme lack of principles and his cheating in financial matters. KGB contact with him was sporadic; he was at some point turned over to MfS.[23] This assessment is hard to square with the praise of Wonsig by Nalivaiko. Even Kuchin (alias Colonel Karpov), in his 1969 account to Frederik, was positive in his characterization of Wonsig's role in bringing Wohlgemuth to KGB. Finally, there is the strange testimony at the John trial concerning Wonsig's own claims to have played an important role in the case.[24] Given this conflicting record, it becomes impossible to say with certainty whether John went voluntarily to his KGB tryst or was "assisted" by Wohlgemuth and/or Wonsig.

The second part of Pitovranov's message to Serov deals with a far more important aspect of the manner in which KGB Karlshorst dealt with John as soon as it became apparent that recruitment was not a viable option. Because it would have been embarrassing to allow John simply to return to West Berlin after his sojourn in Karlshorst, it was decided to keep him in East Germany. Using John to further Soviet policies on Germany may have fit well with Soviet interests and John's mood. Recall Pitovranov's words: "We have taken the decision to persuade him [*sklonit' ego*] not to return to West Germany." But Pitovranov claimed that "the possibility of medical or other psychological pressure never arose and was never considered for a person of John's rank." Pitovranov later reiterated this claim on television: "I swear by all that is holy to me, that we do not on the whole have medication for such purposes, no preparations with which we could influence someone."[25]

This position was contradicted by another participant in the television program, KGB officer Vitaly Gennadievich Cherniavsky, who had worked directly with Kuchin on the John operation. He asserted that "John had come to us in East Berlin voluntarily to have political discussions with Soviet representatives. We wanted to recruit him, but he turned us down. Because it was necessary that John remain in East Berlin, we put a sleeping pill in his coffee. He was put out with this medication while he was already in East Berlin, and after sleeping for about thirty hours, he was worked over by specialists from the KGB with psychological pressure. He finally said that he would cooperate with us."[26] According to Cherniavsky, one of the gimmicks used to apply psychological pressure was a fake newscast by a well-known East German announcer indicating that John had already defected to the Communists in East Berlin.[27]

Like Nalivaiko, Cherniavsky was no novice in the intelligence world when he worked on the John case. When he was assigned to the KGB Berlin apparat in summer 1953 under diplomatic cover, Cherniavsky had assumed the alias Chernov. As chief of the apparat's First Department, he would have had responsibility for the West German section, which explains why he had detailed knowledge of the John case.[28] The chief of that section was Kuchin. The appearances of Pitovranov and Nalivaiko in the famous television program were arranged through Col. Igor Prelin of the Association of Foreign Intelligence Veterans, which occasionally fronts for the SVR, but Cherniavsky made contact on his own. He had financial problems and a wife who needed constant medical care, and he certainly knew a great deal about the John case.[29] Therefore, his claim that suasion was used to ensure that John remained in East Berlin and agreed to cooperate with his KGB captors is not entirely illogical. John was exhausted and had been drinking heavily; it probably would have taken very little to put him out.[30] Once the die was cast and return impossible, it is likely that John consented to play what he conceived would be an important role in the cause of German unity. His decision, however reached, was greeted with relief in KGB Berlin and Moscow.

The Soviets Are Dissatisfied

Naturally, not everyone in Karlshorst and Moscow was happy with the outcome of the operation, and many more became disenchanted as efforts were made to debrief John on Bonn political circles in general and his own service in particular. On one issue all agreed: John was convincing when he told Pitovranov that he did not know the names of individual agents. But this did not satisfy an irate Serov. He accused Pitovranov of not knowing how to conduct an interrogation and said he would send Aleksandr Mikhailovich Korotkov, recognized throughout the First Chief Directorate as the KGB's top German expert. Korotkov did come, and he spent much time both questioning John and helping to shape the propaganda campaign being planned. If we put aside the question of agents' names, was there nothing else of value John could have imparted to his KGB interlocutors? The Soviet material on this point and the statements made to the German author Frederik by Kuchin in 1969 suggest that John did reveal information of interest to the Soviets. The KGB summary notes that John apparently presented the Soviets with written reports on the structure, tasks, working methods, and personnel of BfV. Frederik's account includes a photocopy of a document that purports to be a brief typewritten report on Guenther Nollau of BfV.[31] But the Frederik book was a KGB-MfS production, and the statements attributed to John may not be wholly accurate.

The first 1993 KGB summary we were given repeats Kuchin's claim. Still, the 1994 review of the KGB file indicated that John had provided rather general and not very useful information on the work of BfV and the Western Allies' special services to forestall the reunification of Germany and to use West Germany as an advance post against the USSR. None of what he said was news to KGB. Most of it had been reported through their own sources; John's statements merely confirmed that "BfV controlled the entire political life of the Federal Republic."

Extracts or copies of the KGB interrogation reports of John were not made available to us, so it is impossible to know just what information he did provide. Although KGB continued its efforts to pry secrets from John throughout his stay in the USSR, from 25 August to 7 December 1954 John's true value to the Soviets was that he gave them a measure against which to evaluate reporting on West Germany from other KGB sources. His reliability also helped them conduct their ongoing propaganda campaign in support of the Soviet version of German reunification—a campaign in which John himself was intended to play a role.

John's "Defection" Becomes a Soviet Propaganda Tool

The propaganda campaign envisaged by Pitovranov began with the 22 July 1954 announcement by the East German news service, ADN, of John's request for political asylum in the GDR, which was accompanied by his statement attacking the Bonn regime. John later claimed that the statement was virtually dictated to him by the Soviets, whereas according to the KGB file, John initiated and carried it out on his own. Either way, this was only the opening volley in the campaign; the main battle would be the public press conference planned for early August. General Korotkov played an important role in readying John for this occasion. On 29 July, Pitovranov reported to Moscow that the John case was "widely discussed by the delegates to the SPD Congress in West Berlin, where the majority considered that John went to the GDR voluntarily. Several delegates believed that the reasons for John's move to the GDR were his opposition to Reinhard Gehlen and the possibility of John's being removed from his BfV post."[32]

The dramatic buildup of propaganda continued. KGB files reflect that on 4 August Otto Grotewohl read a letter from John to the GDR parliament (Volkskammer) in which he thanked members for granting him asylum. Grotewohl ended his address by remarking that "John came to the GDR with the recognition that it is better to defend the German people against a hostile regime and war than to be responsible for defending a regime of this sort." The press conference, held on 11 August, was indeed a "masterful performance" and was so reported to Moscow.[33] Great pains were taken to conceal KGB's hand, and only John knew that the Soviet "diplomat" prominently present and quietly observing the proceedings was none other than Cherniavsky, alias Chernov.

Following the press conference, a few contrived East German propaganda stunts were arranged, including a grotesque meeting in Dresden between John and Friedrich von Paulus, former commander of the Sixth Army at Stalingrad. John claims he was also introduced to Ernst Wollweber, the East German minister of state security, at a dinner hosted by Pitovranov, but there is no confirmation of this from KGB files. On 25 August, John was flown to the Soviet Union, accompanied by Kuchin. This was apparently a special flight, because John recounts that one of the other passengers was Pitovranov's mother, who had been staying with the general in Karlshorst. A Berlin Base source employed in the Pitovranov household confirmed that the mother had visited her son in 1954. After a brief stop in Minsk for frontier controls, the plane landed at a military airfield near Moscow.[34] Until John's departure from the Soviet Union in December, Kuchin was his principal interlocutor, assisted by "Vadim Konstantinovich," a KGB officer whom John found very sympathetic. This period gets scant treatment in the KGB file summary received in 1993 and in extracts of the file provided later. We learned only that John was held in "safe houses in Berlin and went on holiday to Moscow and Gagra."

We are left, therefore, with John's account. After Kuchin had apparently failed to obtain from John the cooperation sought by KGB, Aleksandr Mikhailovich Korotkov arrived in Gagra with his German-speaking wife, ostensibly on vacation. The sessions with Korotkov, as described by John, were long and intensive, including questions on the Rote Kapelle Soviet espionage ring and the German resistance generally, a subject with which Korotkov was very familiar. Korotkov also probed deeply into the history of John's relations with the British, demanding that John tell him "what duties you were given by the British and who your boss in London is." When nothing came of this, according to John, he was flown back to Moscow, where Cherniavsky took over. Just before his departure, John was treated to lunch with Paniushkin, who made small talk and wished him luck in his work for German reunification. Apart from John's own testimony, there is no description from KGB sources of these meetings with officers at the very highest level of KGB's foreign intelligence.[35] At that time, Korotkov was a deputy chief of the First Chief Directorate for the European area, so for him to have spent this much time on the John case is indicative of its importance in KGB eyes.

Paniushkin's parting statement to John that "reunification is a great task for you" may have been an exercise in KGB irony. In any case, it soon became apparent after John's return to East Berlin in December 1954 that the Soviets had lost interest in him. A major shift in Soviet policy toward Germany was in the offing that resulted in Moscow's recognition of Adenauer's government. Consequently, John was turned over to the East German MFS, which became responsible for his housing and safety; as the KGB file summary stated, this was done "to prevent terrorist actions against him by the Western special services," not because he was a prisoner. A sinecure was found for John in an office of the East German Unity Committee in Humboldt University, not far from the Brandenburg Gate. Here he churned out pieces on unification and addressed meetings throughout East Germany on the subject. Except for occasional, routine visits from his old friend Kuchin, John saw little of the Soviets. In the Kuchin (Karpov) account of the John affair, when plans were being made for the visit of Konrad Adenauer to Moscow in September 1955, John allegedly proposed that he also be present behind the scenes, eliciting information for KGB from the Bonn delegation. KGB rejected this offer because the Soviets did not wish to risk a flap during the visit, but Karpov indicated that John had helped provide background on individual delegates.[36] There is no information from the KGB file on this incident, nor does John mention it in *Twice Through the Lines.*

John Escapes to West Berlin

John found himself increasingly at loose ends in East Germany; the campaign for a neutral united Germany had run its course. Rather than an asset, John was gradually becoming something of an embarrassment to the Soviets and the East German authorities. He could not convincingly be kept under wraps: he had to be accorded a certain amount of freedom in meeting the press—particularly the foreign press. It was in this framework that his friendship with Bonde-Henryksen came into play. Berlin was Bonde-Henryksen's beat. He had interviewed John in spring 1955, and they had remained in intermittent contact since then. John felt that with Bonde-Henryksen's help he could slip over into West Berlin. Of course, the KGB and Kuchin accounts insist that John was free to leave whenever he wished. Be that as it may, by November, John and Bonde-Henryksen were actively considering various escape options, apparently encouraged by the moral support of Prince Louis Ferdinand of Prussia.

Bonde-Henryksen was a patriot and had been a member of the Danish underground; hence he was closely connected both to Danish intelligence and to the German resistance of which John had been a member. One of Bonde-Henryksen's oldest friends, who had advanced to the position of chief of Danish military intelligence, was Col. Hans Lunding. Immediately after the war Lunding had been an undercover liaison to the Americans and British at the headquarters of Admiral Doenitz, the last head of state of the Third Reich. Lunding was also well known to John, having met him as president of the BFV at intelligence conferences. It was Lunding who concocted the artful plan to rescue John from East Germany.[37]

In summer 1955 a World Youth Festival was to take place in Helsinki. Lunding's idea was to elicit Soviet permission for John to attend the affair in neutral Finland. John would fly from Schoenefeld Airport in East Berlin to Helsinki via Czech Airlines, with a scheduled stopover in Copenhagen. In the airport transit lounge, John was to go the washroom and enter the cubicle on the far right side. Adjacent to the toilet bowl was a secret door; on the other side of the door Danish agents would be waiting. According to Bonde-Henryksen, the Soviets decided against the expedition "at the last minute," presumably because they mistrusted the Copenhagen stopover.[38]

The alternative escape plan worked out by John and Bonde-Henryksen was conceived when John noticed that the main entrance to Humboldt University, where he had been given an office, was under major repair. John discovered that it was possible to make one's way through the scaffolding into or out of the building. The MFS guards, on the other hand, apparently assumed that it was impassable and that John could exit only through the back door. Just before leaving the university area with his guards, John claimed he had forgotten something inside the building. Leaving his briefcase with the guards, and asking them to be alert because he had left a sizable sum of money in the case, he reentered the building, left by the front door, and joined Bonde-Henryksen. The ruse worked like a charm: the trip through the Brandenburg Gate to freedom in Bonde-Henryksen's light green Ford with its Danish insignia took exactly seven minutes. The check by East German police, who were accustomed to seeing the Danish journalist come and go, was cursory during this relatively quiet period in Berlin.

According to Bonde-Henryksen, the operation was planned in close coordination with Berlin representatives of West German intelligence authorities, who in turn kept Gerhard Schroeder, the Federal interior minister, informed. The most actively involved member of the Federal government was State Secretary Franz Joseph Strauss, a schoolmate of John's wife. It was Strauss who told John, through Bonde-Henryksen, that "he should avail himself of every opportunity to escape—I can guarantee that nothing will happen to him." But this promise was not kept.[39]

Nothing has surfaced in KGB archives on this subject other than the repeated assertion that John was in fact free to leave whenever he chose. But logic suggests that with the newly appointed Ambassador to the Federal Republic about to arrive in Bonn, the Soviets were perfectly happy to let the Germans deal with this problem on their own. The fall-out of adverse publicity that John's return would create would benefit the Soviets without further undercover involvement. On the other hand, Bonn authorities were anxious to deal with the legal problems posed by the case as quickly as possible.

John's return to West Germany was bound to be a scandal for the Adenauer government because some form of prosecution was nearly inevitable. Here a relic of the Third Reich in West Germany was to play a major role. For although it was not true that the Bonn legislative and executive branches were full of Nazis, the West German judiciary certainly was. At war's end the majority of German judges and prosecutors were Nazi party members.

Not only were the dispensers of the law tainted with the recent past, in some ways the laws themselves were relics of the Third Reich. So when Otto John came home for the second time, he ran into the drawn knives of the only Nazi underground in existence—that ensconced in the West German judiciary. This fact continues to trouble Germans. In a 1993 letter to the editor of a West German newspaper, a reader wrote: "There was a trial in Karlsruhe. John was sentenced to four years' imprisonment for treason, while the prosecuting attorney had demanded only two years' imprisonment. Was the object of the exercise to show what sort of people they were, the assassins of the 20th of July? Convicts?"[40] The answer came a few days later from the last living member of the Federal court that had sentenced Otto John, Guenther Willms: "Otto John was sentenced to four years' imprisonment not for treason, because this could not be proved. The severity of the sentence arose from the judges' finding that the deed committed was judged to be 'an unprecedented breach of loyalty on the part of a high official of the Federal Republic.'"[41]

The real case against John was his public assertion that the Federal Republic of Germany was—in terms of Realpolitik—no more the sole legitimate German state than was the so-called German Democratic Republic (East Germany). In essence, John revealed that the emperor—the West German government—had no clothes. The state had to do something about John's transgression. Four years' imprisonment was perhaps the least severe sentence the Federal Republic could have then imposed to keep its very substance from unraveling. To be sure, West Germany was far stronger as an institutional civic society than East Germany. But when the great struggle ended and the Federal Republic emerged victorious as the sole German state, many believed that the government could afford to put the case of Otto John in perspective by rehabilitating the man before he died a "traitor." Instead, John's conviction was upheld in December 1995 by the highest court, which rejected his fifth appeal, citing inadequate evidence to alter the verdict.[42] The case was finally closed when John died on 26 March 1997.

PART III

BOB Tries Harder

11

The Berlin Tunnel: Fact and Fiction

N o operation in BOB's history cost as much time or money as did the effort to penetrate key Soviet and GDR communications via a tunnel deep below the Soviet sector. And since the night of its choreographed discovery in April 1956, few clandestine operations have ever received so much attention. Not all of this attention has been wholly accurate, and none of it has been complete. In volume 26 of the State Department's *Foreign Relations of the United States for 1955–57*, published in July 1992, the reader is referred to David C. Martin's *Wilderness of Mirrors* "for a detailed account of the construction of the tunnel and its uses."[1] This account was based on an unclassified, heavily sanitized version of a CIA report of the operation prepared in 1957 and released in 1977; it also drew from interviews with persons who claimed to have been involved with the tunnel operation. Under the circumstances, it is not surprising that the account contained several errors that have been repeated and distorted further in subsequent publications. Soviet versions of the operation, particularly the role of George Blake and the events surrounding the "discovery" of the tunnel in April 1956, have provided a mysterious background against which some have attempted to shape the tunnel story to their own ends.[2] Now, for the first time, the full story can be told based on archival material from both CIA and KGB files and testimony from officers from both services who were actually involved.

One of the most common and persistent misconceptions about the tunnel is that Gen. Reinhard Gehlen, founder of the postwar Federal German Intelligence Service, came up with the idea and assisted in its development. This claim was raised most recently in an article by Thomas Huntington. It was denied persuasively by William Hood, a retired CIA senior officer who was in Vienna during Operation Silver (a similar tunneling operation against Soviet communications) and who was later Chief of Operations of CIA's East European division. There is no suggestion from the available records, or from the memories of individuals who participated in the project from its earliest inception, that CIA's tunnel operation ever involved the Gehlen Organization.[3]

Another myth, appearing in Burton Hersh's *The Old Boys: The American Elite and the Origins of the CIA,* is that the project was started by the US Army's G-2 commander and then taken over by CIA. This version has Bill Harvey arriving in Berlin in 1954 to take control of a structure "originally designed as quartermaster warehouses." Actually, Harvey arrived in December 1952 as the new chief of Berlin Base with the tunnel already in mind. The West Berlin contractor who built the structure, with its deep basement and ramps for forklifts, was actually given the cover story that the deep basement was part of a new, cost-effective design for quartermaster warehouses. But the warehouse cover was part of Harvey's original concept, and the US Army fronted for CIA in making the contractual arrangements. The project was coordinated with the G-2 of the US Army, Gen. Arthur Trudeau, and top levels in Europe were briefed by Allen Dulles. Army cooperation throughout the operation was superb.[4]

Another confusing error emerged from a claim in *Wilderness of Mirrors* that CIA had made a technical "breakthrough" called the echo effect that enabled it to recover clear text from encoded teletype messages. The echo effect allegedly was used successfully in linetap operations in both Vienna and Berlin. This claim apparently arose from interviews with the late Carl Nelson of CIA's Office of Communications.[5] But there must have been some misunderstanding, because the so-called echo effect played no role in processing telegraphic circuits at Washington headquarters.[6]

Related to the echo effect mystery was the allegation that the British Secret Intelligence Service (SIS), with whom CIA collaborated on the

Berlin tunnel, was never told of the echo effect, so that SIS officer George Blake, who betrayed the tunnel project to the Soviets, had never learned of it. Our examination of minutes of SIS-CIA meetings in December 1953 provided to KGB by Blake revealed that SIS was fully aware of the problems inherent in processing telegraphic material and that these issues were to be worked out between the two services. The same minutes also specified that "encrypted material would naturally have to go to GCHQ [General Communications Headquarters] and NSA [National Security Agency]." The echo effect was never a factor.[7]

Blake began reporting to KGB before the tunnel was even completed, and many have written that Soviet awareness of the tunnel meant that the information uncovered by its use was either insignificant or false. Former CIA officer Victor Marchetti launched this attack in 1972 by claiming that the tunnel "produced literally tons of trivia."[8] Although in *Wilderness of Mirrors* Martin tiptoes around the possibility of Soviet disinformation, by 1984 Chapman Pincher was stating flatly that the tunnel "produced nothing but a mass of carefully prepared misinformation."[9]

In 1989 the three authors of another book on Cold War espionage, *Widows*, proclaimed that "the material from the famed tunnel was doctored from the beginning."[10] But KGB seemed not yet ready to boast of its purported role. George Blake's own story, for example, *No Other Choice*, which appeared in 1990 and was presumably checked by KGB, said nothing about KGB disinformation. In March 1991, Kondrashev, Blake's former case officer, wrote an article for the Border Guards' monthly journal *Pogranichnik* describing Blake and his part in the exposure of the tunnel. It contained no reference to disinformation.

But three publications in 1992 seemed to cement the idea that the Soviets had tricked the American intelligence community. In *Berlin, Then and Now*, Tony Le Tissier alleged that "the Soviets were able to set up their own special team to occupy and mislead Western intelligence resources."[11] In *Eclipse: The Last Days of the CIA*, Mark Perry stated that because the tunnel had been "betrayed to the Soviets . . . the Agency was forced to discard many of the secrets it had deciphered because they were useless."[12] And David Wise in *Molehunt* related his view that the tunnel "harvested little information of value."[13]

By 1993, however, KGB seemed prepared to jump on the disinformation bandwagon. In that year a book appeared about Lee Harvey Oswald, written by KGB counterintelligence veteran Oleg Nechiporenko, who had served in Mexico City when Oswald had visited the Soviet embassy there. Unexpectedly, in his introduction Nechiporenko described the tunnel operation and its betrayal by Blake, asserting that it was "diluted by Soviet intelligence with a healthy dose of disinformation." Because Nechiporenko never had the remotest connection with the tunnel or with KGB German operations, this bit must have been deliberately inserted by KGB.

The most unusual view of the disinformation question to emerge from accounts of the tunnel can be found in Peter Grose's *Gentleman Spy*. Incorporating nearly all of the myths about the tunnel described above, including the view that the British (and Blake) were never told about the "American code-breaking technology," Grose speculated that the product may indeed have been genuine. The Soviets could have allowed it to pass unhindered to convince the West that it harbored "no aggressive designs."

The Real Story of the Tunnel's Development

Actually, none of the Western writers on this subject were in a position to judge the issue.[14] The caricature drawn of Bill Harvey during this period fails to capture the essence of the man's performance as chief of CIA's largest and most active operational organization in Europe and, simultaneously, as the driving force behind the tunnel. The real tunnel story began in early 1951, when Frank Rowlett told Bill Harvey of his frustration over the loss to American intelligence caused by the Soviet shift from wireless transmissions to landlines, which had begun in the late 1940s.[15] But continued study revealed that the Soviets were using two types of landlines in their zones of occupation in Austria and Germany. One, which involved overhead lines strung on telephone poles, used new speech secrecy devices. These were attractive targets, but they were virtually inaccessible. Operated by MGB's Government Signals Directorate (Upravlenye pravitelstvennoi sviazi) and reserved for high-level MGB, military, and Communist Party customers, they were heavily guarded by roving patrols looking for problems or linetapping. BOB eventually tried to tap these lines, but success was limited.

Both CIA and SIS were therefore interested in the possibilities of tapping the second type of landline: buried cables. The cables followed traditional communications pathways established by the former Austrian and German imperial governments; Vienna and Berlin were their hubs. Portions of the lines were used by the Soviet occupation forces, although CIA and SIS were uncertain about the extent of this use and the intelligence potential of the messages passing through them. Based on these early studies, OSO's Staff D, which was responsible for clandestine operations against foreign communications abroad, stationed representatives in both Austria and Germany to find out more about the cable systems. In Vienna, SIS efforts were the first to succeed, and by 1952, CIA had agreed to coordinate its program with that of SIS in order to avoid overlapping efforts.

The Key Players

By this time, Harvey's tunnel had begun to take shape, conceptually at least. The Staff D man in Frankfurt, known as Fleetwood (a Harvey sobriquet), quickly discovered that his main target area would be Berlin. His partner was Walter O'Brien, a Chicago lawyer and onetime professional baseball player who had served as an infantry officer in World War II. Called Landsman by Harvey, O'Brien had arrived in OSO headquarters in Karlsruhe in September 1951 and had been kept busy by Gordon Stewart dealing with legal matters. This was not why he had signed on with CIA, and his quick temper and profane, colorful descriptions of his current activity soon drew the attention of the Staff D man. O'Brien was easily vetted for the higher clearances needed for Staff D operations. Because he spoke fluent German, he was assigned to Berlin with a cover position as chief of the counterespionage (CE) branch. His real job was to develop contacts in that element of the West Berlin post office responsible for operating long-distance telephone lines. They could help him recruit agents in East Berlin with information on Soviet use of such lines.

Aside from Gen. Lucian B. Truscott, head of the combined OSO and OPC German Mission, and Gordon Stewart, Truscott's deputy for OSO operations, as well as the Staff D representative, no one in CIA Germany was aware of the project. Neither Peter Sichel nor his successor as chief of BOB, Lester Houck, was briefed on the special responsibilities of their CE branch chief.[16] This extremely tight security continued throughout the life of the operation. For example, David Murphy was selected as Berlin deputy base chief in summer 1954, but he was not briefed by Harvey on the tunnel until after he had arrived in Berlin.

O'Brien's "cover" turned out to be a misnomer: real and important issues needed to be handled by CE branch. What had been a counterespionage backwater involved mostly in double-agent operations and support operations (like hiring messengers and handling communications to East Berlin) had turned into a cauldron of security investigations arising from MGB and MfS operations against OPC-supported groups like the Free Jurists. In addition, O'Brien became directly involved in handling the first penetration of the new East German intelligence service. Nonetheless, he made considerable progress on his Staff D tasks as he and Fleetwood solidified relationships with West Berlin contacts and began to work with East Berlin specialists in long-distance lines who had access to information on the entire East German long lines system and its interface with Soviet military communications.[17]

O'Brien was able to recruit an official in the long-distance department of a key East Berlin post office (Berlin-Lichtenburg) who began providing books specifying which subscribers utilized cables in its area. The bulky books, approximately $18 \times 10 \times 2$ inches each, were brought by the source to a point near the sector border; O'Brien would meet him, drive off to the old BOB headquarters on Foehrenweg in Dahlem, and photograph the information in the photo lab set up in the attic. This first recruitment in the East Berlin post office was followed by others; BOB was therefore able to collect more information on the cable system, learn which cables were assigned to the Soviets, and then cross-check the data to ensure accuracy. The process continued throughout 1952.[18]

Meanwhile, as summer 1952 drew to a close, Harvey prepared to move to Berlin. At about the same time, Frank Rowlett was to move to CIA, where as chief of Staff D he would direct the tunnel project from Washington headquarters.[19] The tip-off that this move to Berlin was no ordinary assignment for Harvey was his integration into the State Department's Foreign Service as special assistant to the director of the Berlin Element of the High Commission Germany. For Berlin this was a first. Until then all BOB officers, including the base chief, had been under US Army cover. Because Harvey's true role required that he travel frequently, he needed the extra security of a diplomatic cover. Even regular army travel in the air corridors was not necessarily safe in those days. With Harvey in place as chief of BOB, O'Brien now reported directly to him on his landlines project.[20]

After his arrival, Harvey increased the pressure on O'Brien's agents to come up with technical details on Soviet landlines. The size of this agent net and the kinds of access the agents could provide also expanded under Harvey. By this time, BOB had begun interviewing refugees coming through the refugee camp at Marienfelde in West Berlin. By talking to persons who had been involved in long-distance telephone operations, it was possible to find new sources who could be recruited independently from those agents who had been recruited through contacts at the West Berlin post office.[21]

Nevertheless, the original recruitments in the East Berlin post office were still vital. Among them was a woman referred to as the *Nummer Maedchen,* the numbers girl. She worked in that part of the post office where specific long-distance cables were assigned for official use and users were shifted from one cable to another. A highly classified operation, this switching office maintained cards on current Soviet or East German users of each cable, which was an essential element in deciding which cables to tap. Her material was so extensive that it seemed too good to be true, but a comparison of her information with that from other sources, and later from the tunnel itself, proved its veracity.

Among the more recently engaged sources was a lawyer in the GDR Ministry of Post and Telecommunications, the ministry responsible for the entire East German telephone net. He was an expert on the international postal service and gave BOB an overview of Soviet utilization of the East German communications systems. BOB also had sources in switching offices in district centers like Erfurt, Dresden, and Magdeburg. One of these individuals copied the cards listing current cable users and taped them to his behind. Meetings with him always began with an embarrassed "excuse me," followed by a rapid lowering of his drawers and the sound of ripping tape. Another immensely useful source was the principal Russian-language interpreter for the same GDR Ministry of Post and Telecommunications, who was involved in many of the technical dealings between the Soviets and the ministry. As BOB's planning for the tunnel advanced, it became necessary to obtain precise details on the physical location of the Soviet cable lines to be tapped. For this, another source in the ministry was able to obtain copies of the official maps showing the exact location of the cables. Without this agent network, it would have been impossible to undertake the tunnel project.[22]

By spring 1953 it was time to confirm what the voluminous reporting on Soviet utilization of East German cable lines had clearly indicated: Soviet military and civilian authorities in East Berlin were making extensive use of buried cable lines for their communications needs. Between 11:00 P.M. and 2:00 A.M. an agent in the East Berlin telephone office would switch, or "patch," the Soviet telephone traffic—whether voice or teletype—onto a cable attached to a West Berlin circuit, where the communications would be recorded for a brief period by a German-speaking CIA technician posing as an employee of the West Berlin office.[23] The information obtained by BOB was judged to have produced "unique material of high interest." Even at this stage, CIA technicians realized that demodulation equipment would have to be designed to separate the channels. The comment in *Wilderness of Mirrors* that the equipment used in this early testing process "was able to pick up the clear text of enciphered messages" is inaccurate. The statement "at this point we knew it could be done" in the 1977 declassified report referred not to the "echo effect" but rather to the discovery that the cables were worthwhile targets that could be tapped. This confusion probably derived from the author's misunderstandings of Carl Nelson's statements, some of which were obvious exaggerations. On the same page, for example, we are told that "in Berlin, Nelson found the blueprint of the city's telephone and telegraph system." If only it had been this simple.[24]

Devising the Tunnel Entrance

During spring and early summer 1953, as CIA continued to make test recordings and collect technical data from agent sources, consideration was given to where the tunnel should be located and how it could be disguised. During this period, responsibility for these aspects fell squarely on Harvey, who worked with Fleetwood in Frankfurt. For a man who had arrived in a totally new operational environment just a few months earlier without knowing German, the challenges must have been daunting. Further, although the tunnel was his main concern, Harvey and BOB were caught up in the aftermath of the 17 June uprising, which not only complicated BOB's operations but also placed a heavy load on the base for reporting on current conditions in the GDR. At the same time, O'Brien's CE branch was overwhelmed by orders to investigate how the Soviets had been able to roll up the paramilitary stay-behind organization affiliated with the Free Jurists. One of the newest members of the CE branch assigned to the task was Hugh Montgomery, who had served in X-2 of OSS in Austria and Germany at the end of the war, including a stint in Berlin. In 1952 he had joined CIA, and in summer 1953 he found himself back in a Berlin safe house, interviewing survivors of the Free Jurists' stay-behind debacle and their relatives, trying to understand who knew whom in these groups.[25]

It was not long before Harvey called Montgomery in and told him he would be working with O'Brien on a special operation involving East German telecommunications. Montgomery was then introduced to the West Berlin long-distance lines agents and took over some of the East German sources. He also worked on expanding BOB's agent coverage of the GDR cable system by debriefing refugees. Although Montgomery suspected that his activity was related to plans to tap the cable lines under active study, he was not briefed on the tunnel until fall 1953. In the months to come, Montgomery was to be a key link for Harvey between the base and activity at the tunnel site.[26] It was this team—Harvey, O'Brien, and Montgomery in Berlin and Fleetwood in Frankfurt—that did the bulk of the tunnel's development work in 1953–54. There were also frequent meetings in Frankfurt with Frank Rowlett, who arrived from Washington for on-the-spot briefings by his field team. O'Brien remembers Rowlett, an incredibly fast typist from his many years of work with cipher machines, bending over his typewriter and taking detailed notes as the team described their activities.[27]

By August 1953 detailed plans for the tunnel were in place. Rowlett visited Germany for a final review and to assist in preparing a formal proposal for DCI Allen Dulles.[28] The proposal was sent to Dulles under a cover memorandum from General Truscott. In it Truscott emphasized the need for the "highest possible degree of security" and for confining knowledge of the plan to "those individuals who can make a specific contribution to the success of this operation." The project's purpose was "to collect covertly the Soviet intelligence known to be passing over certain underground telecommunications cables that are adjacent to and accessible from the US Sector of Berlin." Details of the traffic carried on these lines were outlined, with a note that the description was based on "reliable technical information collected over a period of several years." Access to these cables would be achieved "through the construction of a subterranean passage approximately 1,800 feet in length, one-half of which will be in Soviet territory."[29]

Although perfect cover for the tunnel entrance was not possible, some premise was needed for the construction under way. Once construction was completed, it would be possible to maintain "absolute internal security within a physically enclosed area housing the operation." The plan was to build three warehouses along the sector border as part of a supposed US Army "emergency equipment dispersal system." Contractual arrangements for constructing the warehouses were to be handled by the military in Berlin as a normal Post Engineer Project. The scheme was ingenious but expensive. To cut costs, the three "warehouses" were eventually reduced to just one. The report also described how an engineering unit would occupy the completed site and start extending the passageway. The end of the report described the need for the director of CIA to obtain approval from the highest levels of the military establishment and advised that the military commanders be informed of the project on a " 'your eyes only' basis."[30]

The Soviets Learn of the Tunnel Plan

Dulles approved the project. On 22 October 1953 Harvey and Fleetwood were in London for one of many meetings with SIS concerning the tunnel. In spite of the rigorous security measures in force, KGB soon became aware of the tunnel plans through its source at SIS, George Blake.

A great deal has been written about George Blake since the 1950s, much of which goes beyond the scope of this book. We shall confine our account to statements about Blake's reporting on the tunnel and KGB's response to the information he provided. Blake first came to the attention of Soviet foreign intelligence when he was interned in North Korea after the capture of Seoul in June 1950. Vasily Alekseevich Dozhdalev, who spoke excellent English, went to Korea to meet and perform an in-depth assessment of Blake. Dozhdalev recommended follow-up, and Nikolai Borisovich Rodin, a.k.a. Korovin, was sent to secure Blake's agreement for future cooperation and to make arrangements for subsequent contact. Later Blake was referred to in KGB documents by the code name Diomid. When the British internees were released in spring 1953, Blake was among them. After his return to London, Blake spent his holidays in Holland, where he was met by Rodin. There the two planned for later meetings in the United Kingdom.[31]

Meanwhile, a decision had been made in Moscow to select a case officer to handle Blake in London. For a case of this importance it had to be someone not known to British counterintelligence. He also had to have the background to carry out whatever embassy cover duties were assigned to him. At the same time, the officer should have operational experience, particularly in surveillance and countersurveillance techniques. The job fell to Sergei Aleksandrovich Kondrashev, a coauthor of this book and at the time a young officer who had only recently been assigned to the foreign intelligence directorate.[32] To prepare himself for the London assignment, Kondrashev began reading the Diomid file, studying London city plans, and reviewing reports on British surveillance. His work against the US embassy in Moscow was helpful in this regard because he was familiar with American efforts to evade surveillance.

As a result of Rodin's meeting with Blake in the Netherlands, KGB became aware that Blake was to be assigned to the Y Section, which, in Blake's words, "was concerned with highly secret operations of a technical nature against the Russians."[33] Although "Harvey's Hole" went forward, its progress was henceforth monitored by Diomid.

In October 1953, Kondrashev arrived in London as an embassy first secretary responsible for cultural relations. His job included everything from arranging a tour of the celebrated violinist David Oistrakh to getting tickets for VIPs to attend sports events. He also served as interim KGB resident until Sergei Leonidovich Tikhvinsky arrived to replace Nikolai Borisovich Rodin. But Kondrashev's main responsibility was the Diomid operation: within the residency, he was the only one who knew the name of his source, or his position.[34]

Kondrashev's first meeting in England with Diomid came in late October. This conference was a chance for the two to get acquainted, to work out plans for further meetings, and to discuss Blake's need for a camera to photocopy the many documents passing through his hands.[35] Blake also passed Kondrashev a preliminary list of SIS telephone taps and microphone operations against Soviet installations. These included data on Operation Silver in Vienna (the SIS tunnel project there) but nothing yet on Berlin.[36]

Handling Blake in London was not easy. Moscow Center controlled every step of the operation; the residency was given absolutely no initiative and could not deviate from prescribed procedures. Once Blake failed to appear at a regularly scheduled meeting and missed the alternate meeting that had been arranged in advance. When informed of Blake's failure to make these meetings, Moscow advised waiting for the next scheduled meeting. When Blake still did not show up, Kondrashev suggested that he try to intercept Blake on his way to the office.

Moscow rejected this idea and insisted that Kondrashev wait for yet another meeting. This time Blake was at the appointed meeting place, a London cinema, and he explained his previous absences to Kondrashev. Blake had worried that the Petrovs, KGB officials who had recently defected to Australia, knew about his contact with the Soviets. He wanted to be sure that his SIS superiors were not on to him. Except for this one interruption in their schedule, Kondrashev met with Blake without incident until Blake left London in 1955.[37]

En route to meeting Blake, Kondrashev always selected a pretext for leaving the embassy that was obvious enough to foil British surveillance. For an important 18 January 1954 meeting, for example, it was the departure of a delegation of Soviet chess players. True to his cover as cultural affairs officer, he escorted the group to the airport. The remainder of the day he spent shopping and watching movies. During this time, Kondrashev was checked for surveillance twice by a residency officer at prearranged points in his itinerary. The meeting with Blake took place on the top deck of a bus. After receiving material from Blake, Kondrashev got off several stops later at a prearranged location and was picked up by a residency officer parked nearby.[38]

Blake had passed Kondrashev a carbon copy of the minutes of an CIA-SIS conference on the Berlin tunnel that had been held 15–18 December 1953 in London (see appendix 9). Blake was listed as one of the SIS participants. A coded cable reporting that the meeting had taken place was sent immediately to Moscow, but it was not until 12 February that a full report was submitted. The reports in the Blake case were prepared and written by Kondrashev himself, photographed, and then sent to Moscow in the diplomatic bag as undeveloped film. But in the case of the 18 January meeting report, and perhaps others, the carbon copies were so barely legible that Kondrashev forwarded them directly to Moscow without photocopying. The report was signed in Kondrashev's code name, Rostov. It affords us a fascinating look at KGB tradecraft.[39]

In his comments on the material, all of which apparently referred to British intercept or audio operations in various areas, Kondrashev wrote, "The information on a planned intercept operation against internal telephone lines on GDR territory to a radar station is of interest."[40] The minutes that followed listed the participants and covered, in separate attachments, tentative plans for processing the material as well as a discussion of the technical problems of placing the taps and bringing the circuits through the tunnel to the terminal area. It was proposed that the speech-processing unit be located in London, whereas the handling of telegraphic material would require further study. It was agreed that all encrypted material would go to General Communications Headquarters (GCHQ) and the National Security Agency (NSA), the cryptologic services of Britain and the United States.[41]

Although Blake's name is listed among the SIS participants in this meeting, Harvey does not appear as one of the CIA participants. This is strange, because in *No Other Choice*, in describing this important meeting, Blake makes much of the "Texan" Bill Harvey and his "Wild West approach to intelligence." We know that Kim Philby, the SIS officer uncovered as a KGB spy, blamed Harvey in large part for his downfall. One wonders if these stereotypical references to Harvey were made up and inserted under Philby's influence.[42]

Harvey did attend some meetings in London, but he missed most of them. After all, he had a large base to run, and his courtship of General Truscott's aide, C. G. Follick, occupied his free time. It was not unusual for him to wait for the summary by Rowlett, who normally headed the American delegation in London meetings. After the big December meeting Rowlett spent 19–22 December in Frankfurt getting Harvey up to speed. The same routine was normally followed, although Harvey was present at a London meeting on 4 March 1955, just before the crucial cable tapping was to begin. According to CIA officer Cleveland Cram, Harvey opened the Americans' part of this meeting by noting the need for secrecy and expressing the hope that there were no Philbys present—in a pointed allusion to Kim Philby. The Scotsman George Young, identified by Blake as SIS chief of the Y section, agreed, adding, "We don't want to be caught with our kilts up, Bill."[43]

The Soviets Protect Their Source

After officers in Moscow received Kondrashev's February 1954 reporting on the tunnel and other audio operations, KGB's top priority became protecting Blake. According to Kondrashev, only three persons in the First Chief Directorate were aware that a source existed. The head of the directorate realized that Blake's information pertained to the communications security responsibilities of KGB's Eighth Chief Directorate, so he would invite the chief of that directorate to drop by his office where he could read, but not retain, a copy of the report. He was not, of course, given the identity of the source. Within the First Chief Directorate, a directive was sent to department chiefs on 9 April 1954 from Arseny Vasilievich Tishkov, directorate deputy chief for operational-technical matters, regarding the handling of information from agent sources concerning audio operations.[44] Tishkov was considered one of the most experienced officers in the field, which is why he was chosen to supervise operations based on Blake's reporting. He had the authority to take any action necessary to protect the source. In his words: "The measures worked out for removing, neutralizing, or utilizing these audio surveillance operations for disinformation against the adversary must be based on well-thought-out cover for the sources of such information, in order not to compromise the real source, and in order to ensure that such measures are not taken at once against all operations, but gradually. . . . In working out and implementing such measures, it is necessary to observe the strictest secrecy. Proposals for dealing with this material are to be reported to me, and all measures on this question will be implemented only with my permission."[45]

This memorandum highlighted the terrible catch-22 that the Soviets were in. They knew about the tunnel, but they were unable to do anything about it immediately for fear of compromising Blake. On the basis of this Tishkov directive, area departments and residencies could not take any action against hostile audio operations without first securing Tishkov's approval. As Kondrashev knew, Tishkov would turn down any proposal that posed even a slight risk of betraying Blake. KGB was experienced in the exploitation of audio devices as channels for disinformation, but it always took care to protect sources. As for the communications lines being tapped by Operation Gold, the Berlin tunnel, Kondrashev stated unequivocally that they were not used for disinformation. To do so, he said, would have involved too many people and would have risked Blake's security.[46]

An example of the care with which KGB treated Blake can be seen in its handling of information he provided on Operation Silver, SIS's tap operation in Vienna. Although Blake reported on the existence of the operation right after he began working for the SIS technical group in September 1953, it was not until a year later, 20 September 1954, that KGB Chairman Serov sent a report to USSR Defense Minister Nikolai Aleksandrovich Bulganin on "an English intelligence document . . . obtained clandestinely (*agenturnym putem*) on the activities of the Soviet occupation troops in Austria and Hungary for the second half of November 1953." The report was prepared from "monitored telephone conversations of Soviet officers and enlisted personnel stationed in Austria and Hungary." It is significant that this ninety-page document was not passed to the Soviet military until after the Vienna operation was terminated by SIS. It was certainly not sourced to Blake.[47]

The Soviet military leaders were surprised by the quality and extent of information that the Western Allies obtained on the Soviet occupation forces in Austria and Hungary by monitoring conversations of Soviet officers and enlisted personnel. Nevertheless, they took no action against the intercept operation planned for the Berlin area lest the source be endangered. Another factor in the decision not to disclose the tunnel plans outside of a narrow circle was the fact that the intercept activity had not yet begun, and Blake could continue to keep the Soviets advised of any progress. As a result, no one in Germany was briefed, not even Yevgeny Pitovranov, head of the KGB apparat in Karlshorst, until after Blake's connection with the technical section in London had ended in spring 1955.[48]

Construction Begins

Meanwhile, unaware that their brainchild had been compromised to the Soviets, the Americans and British moved steadily to complete the Berlin tunnel. On 20 January 1954, CIA Director Dulles gave his formal approval, and on 9–10 February remaining technical agreements were reached, including one to place the telegraph processing unit in Washington. Construction of the warehouse, with its unusually deep basement and ramps to accommodate forklifts, went forward under German contractors in Berlin. Meanwhile, the US Army engineers chosen to dig the tunnel began experimenting in New Mexico with a mock-up of the project. George Blake recalled that the British also dug a test tunnel at a military compound in Surrey, where soil conditions resembled those in Berlin. He also thought that the tunnel was built by British mining engineers—whereas the "surface work, the building of a military depot over the tunnel, removing the sand and the logistics connected with it, were done by the Americans."[49] Blake's insistence on these points is odd because he should have known better—even if the minutes of the December 1953 meetings that he passed to the Soviets make no reference to how the tunnel would be constructed. In fact, the US Army engineer detachment constructed the tunnel; the British drove the vertical shaft from the end of the tunnel to the target cables, and British telecommunications experts made the actual tap. British technical expertise in this special area was paramount.

After the warehouse was built, the engineer detachment arrived on 28 August to occupy the site and wait for tunnel construction equipment to arrive. By 2 September construction of the initial vertical shaft to the tunnel level had begun. On 8 September, at eight feet beneath the basement floor, about sixteen and a half feet below ground level, water was detected, and pumping began. The discovery of water was an unwelcome surprise: the engineers had believed the water table would be thirty-two feet beneath the surface. (The oft-repeated story that the engineers had struck the drainage field of the warehouse's own septic tank is an unlikely tale made somewhat more believable by the fact that later, beyond the sector border, they dug into the cesspool of a bomb-damaged house.[50]) After a week of testing and continued pumping, the excavation could safely proceed above the water table the diggers had encountered. The engineers kept the tunnel at sixteen and a half feet, and by 17 October they had progressed beyond the concrete foundation of the warehouse wall.[51] Digging the tunnel was dirty work, and because the army detachment was supposed to be manning a classified electronics intelligence station, not grubbing about in the muck, it wouldn't help the cover if they were regularly seen in dirty fatigues. The army laundry did not provide enough secrecy, so a washer and dryer were installed on site.[52]

Meanwhile, the detachment settled down to a routine of security precautions that lasted well beyond the construction phase. A concealed and continuously manned observation post was established in the warehouse that overlooked the course of the tunnel. A log was kept of personnel and vehicular movements in the area, and it was reviewed regularly to detect pattern changes. Visits to the tunnel area by persons other than detachment members were made in closed trucks to avoid observation, and microphones were placed along the fence line of the installation to alert the detachment to intruders and to pick up any conversations by patrolling East German police. It was anticipated in October 1954 that the tunnel excavation would be completed by the end of January 1955.[53]

In November, Harvey went to Washington to report on the tunnel's progress and to seek approval for emergency measures to be taken should the operation be discovered. It was agreed that the target area

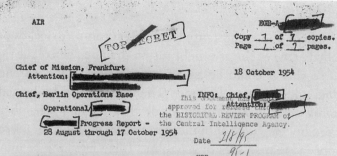

AIR

EXB-A

Copy 7 of 7 copies.
Page 1 of 7 pages.

TOP SECRET

Chief of Mission, Frankfurt
    Attention:

18 October 1954

Chief, Berlin Operations Base

    Operational/

INFO: Chief,
    Attention:

Progress Report –
28 August through 17 October 1954

Synopsis: Set out below is a progress report concerning developments in the ▮▮▮▮▮ operation from 28 August 1954 through 17 October 1954. This dispatch contains no requests for action, all action requests being handled separately as they arise. It is primarily for the purpose of documenting progress and problems to date.

1. On 28 August 1954 the ▮▮▮▮▮ detachment took over the site under the command of ▮▮▮▮▮ The basic shipment of equipment began arriving on the site on that date and was completely stowed by the end of the following day, 29 August. The period between 29 August and 2 September 1954 was consumed in shaking down in the new installation. On 2 September ▮▮▮▮▮ and his crew began actual excavation. On 7 September the last of the necessary equipment arrived on the site and was securely unloaded and stowed.

2. On 8 September at approximately 8 feet below basement floor level, i.e., approximately 16½ feet below the surface of the ground, small amounts of water were encountered. This development was completely unanticipated inasmuch as all geologic and other data previously collected reflected that the water table in this area was at approximately 32½ feet. Further investigation reflected that immediately below the water there was a layer of heavy clay almost impervious to moisture which also was completely unanticipated since the geologic data had reflected that the soil composition in the area was composed completely of sand without either clay or rock formations. Pumps were procured and immediately placed into operation, and insofar as could be determined, the water flow was approximately 400 gallons per day in a hole 12 feet in diameter.

3. It being impossible for obvious reasons to conduct test borings outside the installation along the intended route of approach to the target, efforts were made to do as much testing as possible within the necessary limitations of security to, determine the exact significance of the water. A test bore hole was sunk at the other end of the warehouse installation which revealed a similar phenomenon, i.e., the presence of water and a clay layer, except that at that location, approximately 50 yards away, water was first encountered at 16 feet instead of 16½ feet. In the

17 October 1954 This document is part of an integrated file. If separated from the file it must be subjected to individual systematic re-
hmr:mpd

TOP SECRET

CONTROL

US OFFICIALS ONLY

Distribution:
3 – COM (Copies 1, 4, 5)(w/1 attach. a/s)
3 – Chief, ▮▮▮▮▮(thru COM –
    Copies 3, 6, 7)
(Copies 1,3,4,5,6, 7 hand-carried to COM 18 October by ▮▮▮▮▮

Dispatch, 18 October 1954, from chief, Berlin Operations Base, progress report for 28 August–17 October 1954, on Berlin tunnel operation.

would be kept under constant visual observation. A steel door would be installed between the preamplification chamber, where the signal was isolated so that it could be amplified and sent to the warehouse for recording, and the tunnel proper. The door would be locked except when individuals were actually inside the "preamp" chamber, which was linked by telephone with the warehouse. As a further precaution it was proposed that an area of the tunnel forty feet long be mined with plastic explosive in a garden hose hidden behind the tunnel's liner plate. If the charge were set off, the tunnel would collapse without causing a surface explosion. Although the fuses for these explosives would be stored nearby, the mined area was engineered so that it could not be detonated accidentally. These plans were approved orally by CIA Director Dulles on 29 November 1954.[54]

The tunnel was actually completed at the end of February 1955, and the tap chamber was finished a month later.[55] The three cables were tapped separately between May and August 1955, and a recording of each was begun immediately thereafter. Arrangements were also made for a team of linguists to be on site to listen in on key circuits with the help of a BOB-built machine called the eggbeater. This on-site capability to monitor selected circuits in real time became an important factor in site security when the Army cook at the site (who did not know about the tunnel) got lost while driving from Berlin to Frankfurt am Main. (Travel by car was still permitted for nonsensitive military personnel, and to have forbidden it for the service staff at the site would have aroused suspicion.) The cook took the Autobahn east toward Frankfurt an der Oder by mistake and was quickly taken into custody by the East German border police (Grepo). When he was reported overdue at the Helmstedt checkpoint on the Autobahn through the Soviet zone, live monitoring began at the site while the US Military Police went through their drill of recovering a stray soldier. The on-site monitors were able to follow Grepo's actions in releasing the man the same day.[56]

The Berlin tunnel complex is depicted in fig. 11.1. Its endpoint, the tap chamber, was connected with the main tunnel by a vertical shaft. Next came the chamber containing the preamplification equipment. A heavy, torch-proof steel door was erected between the vertical shaft of the tap chamber and the preamp chamber. It was on this door that an official-looking inscription in German and Russian was placed warning trespassers to keep out. In addition, a sensitive microphone was

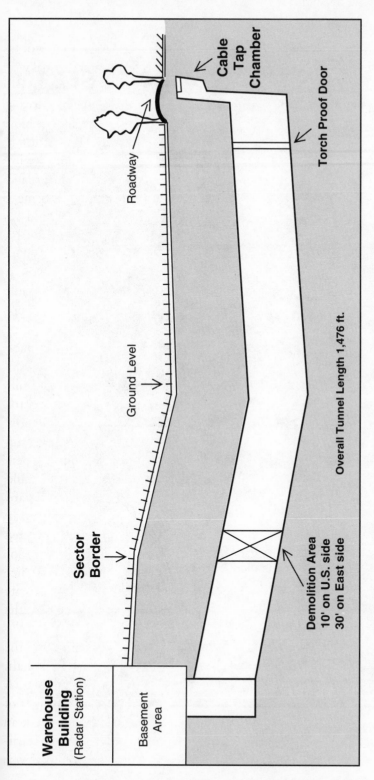

Fig. 11.1 Berlin tunnel, engineering drawing (not to scale; vertically exaggerated).
Source: appendix A, "The Berlin Tunnel Operation," Clandestine Services History (CSHP-150), CIA-HRP.

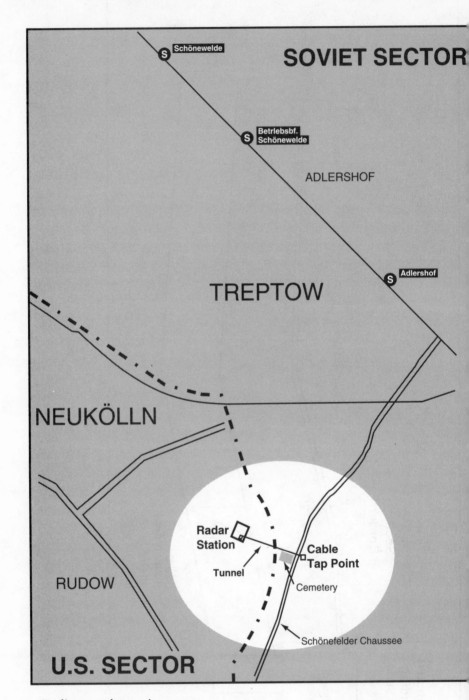

Berlin tunnel overview.

installed in the tap chamber to permit security personnel at the site to monitor any activity there. The tap and preamp chambers had been heavily insulated, but no recording or monitoring was done there. In fact, apart from periodic inspections of the equipment, every effort was made to avoid creating undue noise in this area—which was, after all, located well within the Soviet sector.[57]

As planned, the door from the preamp chamber to the tunnel proper was also made of heavy steel. Sandbags lined both sides of the tunnel itself in order to increase insulation and provide a shelf for the power and signal cables, as well as for the ducts leading from the air conditioning equipment in the warehouse. Along the floor of the tunnel was a wooden track used to wheel out carts full of dirt. The track was actually built from the packing boxes in which the steel tunnel liners had been delivered. Within the warehouse was the air conditioning and dehumidifying equipment, the eggbeater, and the recorders.[58]

What Did the Soviets Know?

In a May 1995 interview, Blake repeated his claim, made in *No Other Choice,* that he left the technical section in London in January 1955 and was later sent to the Berlin SIS station. Once there he was no longer involved in the tunnel, the activities of which were run separately from the regular station. Blake felt that by this time the operation was pretty much in the hands of CIA. As far as Blake knew, the material obtained from the tap was not processed in Berlin but rather was sent by British aircraft every other day to London. Blake assumed that if intelligence pertaining to Berlin was obtained from the tunnel, London would send it to Peter Lunn, head of the Berlin SIS station, who had been aware of the tunnel from its inception.[59] But it seems reasonable to assume that Blake could have alerted the Soviets to the fact that the tunnel had begun to produce intelligence as of May 1955. When Blake arrived in Berlin, he was first met by Nikolai Borisovich Rodin, the KGB officer who had recruited him. Rodin advised him not to reveal his knowledge of the tunnel to anyone, including KGB officers. Afterward, Vasily Alekseevich Dozhdalev took over and continued as Blake's case officer during Blake's tour in Berlin.[60]

When Pitovranov was advised of the tunnel operation, he followed standard KGB procedure for an operationally sensitive area: he placed the "radar station" under observation and initiated discreet investigations into the background of residents in the neighborhood of the reported cable tap. In late 1955, KGB Moscow sent a team of technical specialists to Karlshorst under Vadim Fyodorovich Goncharov (alias Gorelov). Goncharov was only partially informed of his mission. According to him, the team's purpose was to work with the Signals Directorate of the Group of Soviet Forces Germany (GSFG) to protect the security of GSFG communications. Goncharov described various actions by the Western special services to eavesdrop on Soviet communications, saying that these "forced us to pay attention to the necessity of carrying out defensive measures against possible leaks of information."[61] Goncharov's group was given only general information about the tunnel; they were not told the source. But an attempt by Western services to tap a Soviet cable near the border of the American sector was an obvious possibility to the team: they knew KGB was tapping an American line near Potsdam.

After Pitovranov had been alerted to the existence of the tunnel and the Goncharov team had arrived, measures were taken to make Soviet telephone conversations more secure. According to Goncharov, a check of conversations at the military communications center in Karlshorst "revealed violations of the most elementary norms of security. During conversations codes were often not used . . . which led to leaks of secret information. We then taped the conversations between GFSG headquarters and the commanders of military units." Pitovranov showed the results to the chief of GSFG, Marshal Andrei Grechko, who "initially couldn't believe that so much could be gleaned from telephone chatter. After listening to a tape sample, he was convinced and gave the appropriate instructions to his commanders on telephone security."[62]

When the KGB technical unit arrived in Karlshorst in late 1955, they did some preliminary searching for the tap in the Alt Glienicke area and elsewhere along the border using KGB equipment. Over these great distances (fifty to sixty kilometers) the apparatus found nothing wrong, but when they began to work from a local German telephone office and tried checking smaller segments, they discovered the location of the tapped cable. Recognizing that physically uncovering the tunnel would require more personnel than was available to KGB Karlshorst, and wishing to make its discovery appear to be the result of a routine Soviet Army check of its lines, Pitovranov obtained Grechko's permission to create a special military signals company. The officers and enlisted personnel were recommended by their commanders for hazardous duty and screened by KGB. The group was issued appropriate equipment and trained by Goncharov's people. A detailed plan was prepared for locating and uncovering hostile taps on Soviet landlines anywhere in the Berlin area. The timing of the operation was to be designated by Moscow.[63]

The Soviet Story of How the Tunnel Was Found

In early 1956, the tunnel was still producing valuable information. Unknown to the West, Khrushchev and Bulganin were considering how best to shut it down. Khrushchev apparently wanted the discovery of the tunnel to be made into a major propaganda event. He was dissatisfied with the international situation, feeling that neither Soviet diplomatic recognition of the Bonn government nor the withdrawal of Soviet forces from Austria following the state treaty had advanced Soviet interests as anticipated. The situation in the Middle East had become increasingly tense as Soviet and Western interests collided. But Khrushchev was planning a state visit to London in late April, and he did not wish to disrupt relations with the British. He thus ordered KGB to find a way to reveal the tunnel's existence that would not endanger their source, George Blake, yet would achieve maximum publicity—publicity that would emphasize the American role while downplaying British involvement. Consequently, KGB Karlshorst drew up a plan for the "accidental discovery" of the tunnel and a subsequent press conference. In order to ensure emphasis on the accidental nature of the discovery, drafts of messages by Grechko, Soviet Ambassador in East Berlin Georgy Pushkin, and Pitovranov were prepared in advance. On the basis of these cover messages, lower echelons would put the intended spin on the diplomatic, technical, and propaganda follow-up necessary. These officers would have no idea that the tunnel's discovery had been the work of a KGB penetration of the Anglo-American project.[64]

In an interview with a *Globus Novosti* correspondent on 21 January 1993, Pitovranov stated that the signal troops began searching with detection instruments and finally began to dig. Although in his interview Pitovranov was uncertain about the date, it was in fact the night of 21–22 April 1956. Asked how they knew where to dig, Pitovranov said that "from advance information by our friend [Blake], we determined the shortest possible route to the Schoenefeld highway from the American cover installation. And we concentrated on that point." At

2:30 A.M. Pitovranov, along with KGB officers Sergei Vasilievich Patrikeiev and Nikolai Sergeevich Miakotnykh, went to the airfield at Schoenefeld, not far from the tunnel site, to await the outcome.[65] These officers were logical choices to accompany Pitovranov on this occasion. Patrikeiev was his deputy for intelligence, and Miakotnykh was chief of the British department of the Second Chief Directorate. (He had reportedly been involved in the 1953 flight of Donald Maclean's wife to Moscow, where she joined her husband, the KGB source in the British Foreign Office.[66])

A lieutenant ran up to Pitovranov's party and said, "The colonel is asking for you." They went to the site, where the colonel reported, "We've found it!" and began to descend into the installation. Pitovranov recalls that he warned them to be careful because it might be mined, but the engineers continued into the hole and proceeded along the entire length of the tunnel. Then, in Pitovranov's words, "at about 6:00 A.M. the colonel invited us down to take a look, which we did. Everything was well equipped, as though they intended to be there for a thousand years. There were coffeemakers and everything needed to prepare food. The equipment was neatly arranged, American and partly English. The organizers of the project must have been convinced we'd never get to them here."[67]

As Goncharov tells the story, they began to dig that night. "Gradually we began to open things up. The cables were laid at a depth of 80 centimeters, and perpendicular to the building where the Americans were supposedly observing aircraft. In the place where we uncovered the cable we encountered a manhole. We opened the hatch and climbed down into the tunnel, the entrance to which was blocked by a massive iron door. On it was a sign in German and Russian. It read 'By order of the CINC GSFG [chief of GSFG] entrance to the tunnel is categorically forbidden.' This was evidently done to convince any Soviet or German communications personnel that they could go no further, that beyond were special communications lines to which access was forbidden." Naturally, the working group expected that this door would be locked from the inside, but apparently the "American specialists so little expected they would be discovered that the door had not been barred shut."[68]

After they opened this first door, Goncharov said they were astonished to see people sitting there. Why were Americans there, on GDR soil? According to Goncharov, the "Americans could have extended the tap lines to our lines of communications further into the basement of the building that they had built. But this is a distance of about 400 meters and they would have had to bring the cables that far and provide for amplification. To make their work easier, they did this closer, on our territory, and set up this large, camouflaged door, behind which was an entire control point *(kontrol'nyi punkt)*. But they never expected that this door would be discovered, so they left it open for hours."[69]

When the Soviet working party entered the control point, Goncharov insists they saw operators sitting with earphones on, tape recorders spinning away, while others were drinking coffee. Taken aback at the sight of the Soviets, the operators threw down their earphones and fled through the tunnel toward the American sector. Without thinking, Goncharov continued, the Soviet group rushed after them. They stopped when they encountered a barricade of sandbags within the American sector at the entrance to the basement of the building. On the barricade, a crudely lettered sign had been placed with the words "You are entering the American sector." Seeing this, the Soviets returned to the control point, examined the recording equipment, unplugged it, and then disconnected taps to the Soviet circuits at the distributing frame.[70]

The True Story Revealed

It is unlikely that poor memory alone could have caused Pitovranov and Goncharov to provide accounts of the tunnel's discovery so fanciful in their description of the physical installation and the timing of the events of the night 21–22 April. What really happened was that for several days prior to 21 April unusually heavy spring rains had begun shorting out the long-distance cables. This problem was reported over engineering circuits being monitored at the tunnel site, as well as by BOB's penetrations of the GDR post and telegraph system. On 19 April the tunnel tap was checked and appeared in order. Meanwhile, all during this period, and right up to the early morning of 22 April, Soviet military signals centers continued normal operations.[71]

At ten minutes before 1:00 A.M. on 22 April, American personnel at the warehouse observation post, using night vision equipment, detected forty or fifty men in the vicinity of the tap chamber digging at three- to five-foot intervals. (They were probably personnel from the special signals detachment described by Goncharov.) Bill Harvey was alerted through the BOB switchboard. By 2:00 A.M. the Soviets had discovered the top of the tap chamber, and Russian speech was heard. The Soviet officer overheard was a Captain Bartash, a GSFG signals officer who later received an award from Marshal Grechko for discovering the tunnel tap. Harvey had Hugh Montgomery come immediately to the site to assist duty linguists in monitoring the real-time conversations from engineering circuits—and more important, from the still-live microphone. As Harvey stood impatiently by, the tape was stopped at key points and the German and Russian conversation interpreted for him. The excitement level was so high that the linguists occasionally forgot to press the "stop" button: the result on the recording is a mixture of German or Russian and English.

By 2:50 A.M. the Soviet working party could see the tap cables leading down to a trap door in the floor of the tap chamber above the shaft. At 3:00 A.M., the first East German long-distance lines specialists appeared, barricades were erected to keep away the curious, and a German-speaking Russian voice announced that a decision on how to proceed would have to wait until morning. Meanwhile, the tunnel tap continued to monitor ongoing discussions between the chiefs of the GSFG signal center at Wuensdorf and the signal center in Karlshorst for any sign that they knew what was happening at the tunnel. At this point, they were busy talking about communications problems connected with the move of certain air warning facilities.

By 6:30 A.M., it had become apparent that the GSFG Signals Directorate had learned that something was amiss: its chief, Lieutenant Colonel Zolochko, had left Wuensdorf for the tunnel site. When he arrived, along with others carrying circuit diagrams and cable occupancy data, the Americans listening in heard, "The cable is tapped." Five minutes later, the Karlshorst Signal Center chief was instructed to use the overhead lines facilities of the East Berlin KGB Government Communications Directorate (UPS) regiment to bypass the tapped portion of the cable line. Although this was a perfectly logical reaction, the fact that up until then the KGB's UPS was deliberately kept out of the tunnel search operation in spite of their expertise in communications security suggests that, for source protection reasons, KGB was still eager to have the tunnel discovery appear to be a military operation in no way linked to KGB.

At the site, the working party was still in the tap chamber and had not yet descended into the shaft connecting it with the tunnel proper. The tap continued to function as before. From 8:00 to 9:00 that morning, numerous calls were recorded on the tapped lines, as Grechko's staff tried to locate Col. Ivan Kotsiuba, acting Soviet commandant of Berlin. Kotsiuba was to play a central role in initiating the prearranged diplomatic scenarios surrounding the tunnel's "discovery."

Not until 12:30 P.M. on Sunday, 22 April, did the East German technicians remove the trap door over the vertical shaft. Then, unable to open the massive steel door leading to the preamp chamber, they dug a hole through the adjacent wall from which they could view the chamber. They were bowled over by what they saw: "*Donnerwetter!* Look at that . . . it goes all the way under the highway! How did they do it? It's fantastic!" They then enlarged the opening to permit access to the chamber. At this point, or even before, Harvey instructed Montgomery to find Gen. Charles L. Dasher, the US Commandant, and ask his permission to arm—and if necessary, detonate—the explosive charges lining the tunnel. Montgomery, looking somewhat the worse for wear, finally located Dasher at a reception in the Wannsee Yacht Club being given for Gen. Maxwell Taylor, the US Army Chief of Staff, in Berlin on an official visit. After hearing Harvey's message, Dasher asked if there was a possibility that Russians might be killed or injured. When told "possibly," Dasher said that he would not approve unless Harvey could guarantee in person that no one would be hurt. Clearly, no such guarantees could be given, so this option was abandoned.

By 2:20 P.M., the opening was large enough for the Soviets to enter, unlock the door, take movie cameras in, and begin exploring. Earlier that day, when it became apparent that there would be no way to collapse the tunnel using the explosives, Harvey had ordered sandbags and barbed wire to be placed at the spot in the tunnel where the sector border crosses. As in Goncharov's version, a crude, hand-lettered sign was placed on the sandbags in German and Russian bearing the message "You are now entering the American sector." Just beyond this point the tunnel dipped slightly, blocking the line of sight from the Soviet side. Harvey had set up an unloaded .50-caliber heavy machine gun as a visual deterrent, but because of the angle it was not visible from the Soviet side. At about 3:00 P.M. footsteps were heard moving through the tunnel toward the American side. Harvey pulled back the bolt on the machine gun, making a loud and distinctive noise. He heard the footsteps stop and then hurry away. At 3:35 P.M. the tap cables were cut, and at 3:50 the microphone went dead. The tunnel had lasted eleven months and eleven days.

The Soviets Carry Out Their Publicity Campaign

As part of the Soviet "accidental discovery" scenario, diplomatic and publicity responses were ready to go as soon as the Soviets started digging. On 22 April, the day of the discovery, a message signed by Vladimir Semyonov in the Foreign Ministry was sent to Soviet Ambassador Pushkin via secure telephone. It directed the Soviet Berlin commandant to send a protest to the US commandant about the tunnel. The message added, "Additional instructions concerning journalists and others will be given tomorrow."[72] On Monday, 23 April, a joint message was sent to Moscow signed by Grechko, Pushkin, and Pitovranov, in that order, which described the tunnel, reported the reaction of the American commandant to the protest, and presented their "recommendations for your approval." These recommendations had been worked out in advance in Moscow and formed a vital part of the scenario. They were:

1. The chief of staff of Soviet forces must protest in writing to the headquarters of American forces in Europe, with this to be published in the press.
2. Invite correspondents accredited both to East and West Berlin to inspect the installation.
3. Give approval to German friends to speak out on this question, but not before publication of this in the press.
4. Send a group of our specialists to study the equipment.
5. Despite the fact that the tunnel contains English equipment, direct all accusations in the press against the Americans only.[73]

Khrushchev that day was being received by Queen Elizabeth II at Buckingham Palace, and the last paragraph of the instructions was in keeping with the thrust of the planned postdiscovery propaganda spin.

The Soviets held their press conference at the tunnel the next day, but they needn't have bothered. In the West the tunnel operation was hailed by the media as a "striking example of the Americans' capacity for daring undertakings."[74] Still, it is fascinating to observe how the Soviets' interest in making the most of the tunnel discovery led to fairly widespread confusion about the events of 22–23 April 1956. On 28 April the official East German newspaper *Neues Deutschland* used a distinctive sketch to describe the tunnel. In June 1956, KGB published an illustrated "guide" with a similar sketch (fig. 11.2). Almost twenty years later virtually the same sketch, somewhat better drawn and with explanatory text in Russian, was found in svr archives (fig. 11.3). Each of these sketches incorrectly depicts the tunnel as originating in the area of the motor pool garage or the power-generating building, not the "warehouse" or "radar station." Obviously, the Soviets' decision to blur the real source of the tunnel on the American side was based on their desire to protect Blake.

But as soon as this version circulated in the propaganda exercise it took on a life of its own.[75] An article entitled "Spies for Sale" in a 1978 London compendium on espionage presented its version of the tunnel's discovery: "But on April 22, 1956, the Russians suddenly burst in at the far end. The electric alarm system did its job. The Russians found the tunnel deserted although all the equipment was still in place. The operators *had left so quickly that the Russians found a coffee pot still bubbling in a deserted chamber* [our emphasis]." Accompanying the article was a detailed drawing purporting to show the "recording equipment" and "recreation area" adjacent to the tap chamber. In this sketch, the tunnel was depicted as originating in the barracks, even farther away from its true location in the "radar station."[76] In our view, these publications reflect the well-rehearsed KGB story of the tunnel's "discovery"—a story that portrays heroic Soviet technicians surprising the hapless Americans and forcing them to abandon their earphones and recorders to flee ignominiously down the "spy tunnel." This version was still being circulated in the Western press in 1997.[77] It is true that everyone in the West, and even senior East German telecommunications personnel, were convinced that the Soviet counteroperation had been accidental.[78] But no one who was there had any illusion that the Soviet "discovery" was glamorous. Fourteen hours of hard work, most of it performed by East German specialists, had to be done before the tap could be fully uncovered and cut off.

Was It All Deception?

Did the Berlin tunnel provide CIA and SIS with important information, or did KGB's knowledge of the project mean that only disinformation was obtained? Alternatively, did KGB's overriding desire to protect Blake as a source in SIS mean that much real information was sent through landlines tapped by the tunnel? Many top KGB officials were not even aware of the tunnel's existence until long after its presence was

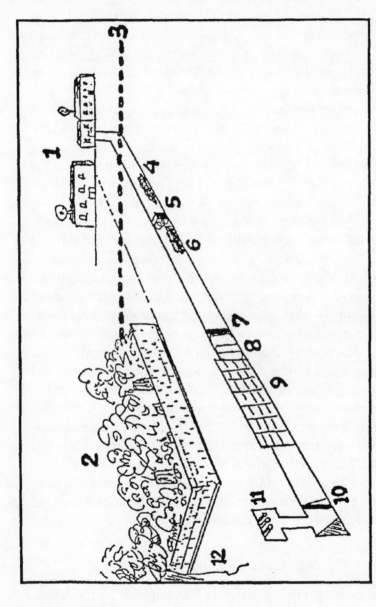

Fig. 11.2 KGB published an illustrated "guide" in June 1956 that included this sketch. (1) American radar station at Rudow. (2) Rudow Cemetery. (3) Border between West and East Berlin. (4) Sandbags. (5) Barbed-wire entanglement. (6) Sandbags. (7) First steel door. (8) Air-conditioning unit. (9) Amplifiers. (10) Second steel door. (11) Shaft to Soviet telephone lines. (12) Shönefelder Chaussee.

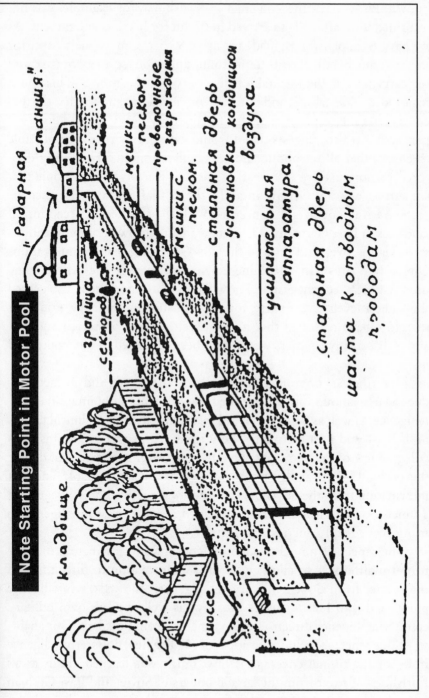

Fig. 11.3 Berlin tunnel, sketch from SVR Archives.

known. Pitovranov, the KGB chief in Karlshorst, for example, was not informed until after Blake arrived in Berlin for his new assignment. As we have seen, plans were made for using Soviet Army signals cover for investigating hostile threats to the communications security of GSFG and for carrying out the inevitable "discovery" of the tunnel. This was a major KGB undertaking, and one that convinced CIA and SIS that the discovery was the result of cable faults caused by heavy rains. This complex scenario also suggests that it would have been virtually impossible to ensure that all telephone and telegraphy circuits carried only doctored or nonsensitive information without alerting many people that something was up. Deception aside, the KGB's foreign intelligence directorate was not overly concerned with the planned interception of landlines in East Germany. They knew that their own communications went via the overhead lines of the KGB Government Communications Directorate (UPS). In telephone conversations over these lines, they used a speech secrecy system known as V Ch. This system also served the highest levels of the party, foreign ministry, and military. KGB must therefore have reasoned that its own security was protected and that any truly sensitive matters would have been restricted to UPS-controlled lines.

Nevertheless, one must conclude that the tunnel did in fact produce a large amount of badly needed and difficult to obtain military intelligence, as well as coverage of political and scientific-technical targets in the USSR and East Germany like Wismut. Appendix 5 contains a detailed review of the items obtained. It must be remembered that during this period U-2 or satellite photography was not yet available, and that information from the occasional defector was received only irregularly. Tunnel production therefore represented a bonanza of intelligence to many British and American analysts.

One aspect of tunnel production continues to fascinate: KGB's apparent indifference to allowing sensitive information to filter through the tunnel from Soviet military intelligence—the GSFG's intelligence points and GRU Headquarters Moscow, as well as KGB's own military counterintelligence directorate serving GSFG from Potsdam. Our analysis of this aspect is included in appendix 5. The final counterintelligence irony of the tunnel coverage is how much was learned about KGB's Karlshorst apparat from the large numbers of Soviet and East German officials who called officers there and forced them to reveal much detail about themselves.

Of course, there were winners and losers on both sides of this story of the tunnel, and the question of how deceptive Soviet communications were will probably never be put completely to rest. But certainly the intelligence that BOB obtained from its tunnel taps was not all a "mass of carefully prepared misinformation." Was the voluminous information on the Soviet military and on Soviet intelligence and security components "diluted with healthy doses of disinformation by the KGB," as suggested by some? Perhaps, but to date no evidence has been advanced to support this view.[79]

12

Redcap Operations

hroughout the West the 1950 North Korean invasion had created fears of similar hostile action against West Germany that
could lead to general war. Intelligence on Soviet plans and intentions was urgently needed, yet tighter Soviet security had
stemmed the flow of voluntary defections, which by 1952 had
become CIA's primary source of information about the Soviet regime.
In response, with the approval of top American officials, CIA created its
worldwide program of "defector inducement"—called Redcap after the
railroad baggage porters who eased their clients' passage.[1] First priority went to efforts to recruit Soviets as sources or, as the Redcap slogan-
eers put it, to encourage them to "defect in place." Failing that, those
who insisted on defecting outright would be brought to the West,
where their intelligence knowledge could be tapped. Many OSO professionals viewed this widely advertised program with skepticism and irritation because they had been trying all along to recruit Soviets as
sources—and in their view defection was a second-best alternative because the source's connections were lost. But Americans love nothing
better than a well-organized promotional campaign, and the professional voices were quieted in favor of the more bureaucratically correct
Redcap program.

Berlin, a Key Center of Redcap Operations

Pressures to recruit Soviets or get them to defect were greatest in Berlin because it was situated in the middle of the largest concentration of Soviet troops anywhere in the world. BOB's own Redcap branch consisted of several staff officers and some gifted contract employees—foreign-born American citizens so fluent in German and Russian that they could pose as either Germans or Russians. The officers first questioned East German refugees to find out who in East Germany might have contact with Soviets. When such information was uncovered, BOB made every effort to establish clandestine contact and persuade the person in East Berlin to visit West Berlin.

Unfortunately, using former East German residents was not a terribly productive way to get to Soviet personnel. From the moment they arrived in East Germany, Soviet workers were indoctrinated to avoid and distrust the local population, any of whom could be "imperialist agents." Furthermore, as cooperation between MfS, East German security, and Soviet military counterintelligence improved, both services were on the lookout for friendships between Soviets and the Germans with whom they worked. Even at parties arranged by the authorities, the Soviets tended to cling to each other and remain aloof from the German staff. Almost the only context for close relationships between Soviets and East Germans was the black market: some Soviets, for example, enlisted their German drivers to find special things for them on the side. But these straightforward business affairs seldom gave the Germans any real insight into the Soviets' personal lives.

Whisper Sweet Somethings to Me: East German Women in Action

At least 95 percent of the social contacts reported were between East German women and Soviet men. The majority of these women were prostitutes to whom the Soviets turned only for sex. In fact, the women were already well known to the local police, who reported to MfS and Soviet military counterintelligence any affair that appeared to be more than casual. Contacts between Soviet personnel and German women employed in Soviet installations were also restricted to cool working relationships. If an office romance bloomed and was detected by any of the many Soviet and MFS informants there, either the Soviet was sent home and the German woman fired or the affair was tolerated long enough to see whether a Western service was involved.

It didn't help BOB's recruitment efforts that East German women were ostracized by their coworkers, family, and neighbors for consorting with the enemy. Those who did so openly in the framework of official German-Soviet friendship meetings were usually diehard Communists, and even they were under constant Soviet surveillance to ensure that they did not exploit their Soviet contacts.

BOB, then, had to struggle to find women who could overcome these obstacles. But the effort to find female agents who could work effectively in this difficult environment could also have a comic side. One Redcap case officer spotted a young professional woman who he thought might be perfect, but for some reason he changed his mind. The spurned candidate, however, refused to accept her fate. To prove how capable she was, she followed her case officer, copied down his license plate numbers, located his home and office, and through him was able to identify many BOB officers by their true names. When she proudly presented her huge file of information to BOB, the case officer and his supervisors were shocked. When they finally determined that hers was not the work of an opposition service, the woman was helped to quietly resettle in West Germany.

Even if women were found and trained for the job, there was no guarantee that the Soviet target would visit West Berlin: in fact, as soon as this was suggested, most Soviets left their East German "girlfriends." Their fear of the West, and of crossing the sector border, was so deeply ingrained that they found the idea impossible to consider. To help assuage this fear, BOB enlisted the help of the National Labor Union (NTS), an émigré organization that distributed leaflets in both German and Russian explaining how easy it was to cross from East Berlin into the Western sectors. BOB also attempted to create a similar capability in another émigré group, Union of the Struggle for the Liberation of the Peoples of Russia, or SBONR.[2]

The Real Story of "Sasha" Orlov

Although collaboration with SBONR failed, BOB turned to Igor Orlov, an independent agent and ex-SBONR member, for help. Orlov's specialty was recruiting and running German women in defection inducement operations. Pressures on BOB to produce were intensifying, and it was felt that Orlov could make a difference. Over time, this decision would affect the lives of several BOB officers in ways that no one could have foreseen.

So that he could reside in West Berlin, Orlov was given a new name and persona: Franz Koischwitz. But his case officers still called him Sasha, his name since Vlassov Army days. Although many versions of the Sasha story have been told, this account is buttressed for the first time by documentary evidence.

Just before Orlov's independent operations in Berlin got under way, a sinister incident occurred that, in the words of his first case officer, "put a considerable crimp in the relationship." Vladimir Kivi, another ex-SBONR member who was to work with Orlov as an independent Redcap operator, vanished without a trace two or three months after his arrival from Munich. Kivi, a tall, blond, blue-eyed Estonian, was quiet, even-tempered, and very efficient. Like Orlov, he had worked with the Germans during the war and then with the Gehlen Organization.[3] There was no sign of a struggle in his apartment; his clothes and effects were still there. The Berlin police were notified, but their investigations produced nothing. Given the frequency of Soviet-inspired kidnappings in postwar Berlin, it was assumed that Kivi had been abducted. Although the incident evoked concern in BOB that another operation might be involved, there seemed to be no reason to pin the blame on Orlov.[4]

By spring 1952 an operation involving one of Orlov's East German agents began to show promise. The woman's romantic relationship with a Soviet officer, which had been interrupted during the officer's winter leave in the USSR, was reestablished when she received word from him of his return to Karlshorst. Although professing both love for the woman and anti-Communist sentiments, he remained reluctant to visit West Berlin. To persuade him, Orlov, armed with a photograph and a letter from the woman introducing him as her cousin, went himself to the officer's apartment in the Karlshorst compound and announced that she was pregnant. The only way to keep her from complaining to the Soviet Kommandatura, Orlov explained, was to meet with her wealthy West Berlin aunt, whose counsel the girl had always followed.[5]

Orlov's visit to the Karlshorst apartment of a Soviet officer was considered a dangerous "breach of procedure" by his BOB case officer, who cautioned Orlov against trying it again. The Soviet officer still refused a West Berlin meeting, but he maintained contact. After several failed attempts to persuade him to cross the sector border, on 12 August the officer declared he would do so only if the "cousin"—Orlov—would escort him. Accordingly, a rendezvous was set for 18 August 1952 near a subway station in East Berlin, just inside the sector border. Shortly after they were seen entering the subway together, they appeared at a BOB safe house, where the officer introduced himself as Lt. Col. Nikolai Stepanovich Svetlov, a group chief within the information department of the Soviet Control Commission in Karlshorst. The department dealt with the overt Western press and had no intelligence connections.[6] The BOB case officer probed for names of personnel and for more detail on Svetlov's duties, but it was obvious that he had little of interest to offer.[7]

After stating that he would be on leave in the USSR until October 1952 and emphasizing that he had no intention of defecting, Svetlov asked what he should do to appease his pregnant girlfriend and her irate aunt. He was told that they could probably be silenced if he agreed to turn over his leave papers for BOB's inspection before departing; they would be returned to him within an hour or so.[8] This request came from CIA's Munich operations base, and Orlov's BOB case officers knew why they had asked: by counterfeiting the difficult-to-find leave papers of a Soviet officer, including the leave ticket *(otpusknoy bilet)*, the one-time pass for crossing the Soviet frontier *(razovyi propusk)*, and the authorized requisition *(trebovanie)* for train travel, CIA would acquire another cover for infiltrating its agents into the USSR. BOB excitedly cabled mission headquarters in Frankfurt on 19 August asking that technical experts be available between 21–24 August "with all equipment necessary for photographing, comparing paper samples, etc."[9] But on 22 August Svetlov announced that he could hand over only his leave ticket. He claimed that because he was traveling in a group, the senior officer in the group had kept the other passes. Still, the leave ticket was photographed and Svetlov's office telephone number noted.[10]

Svetlov never appeared again, and he was never reached at his Karlshorst office number.[11] In spite of BOB's high hopes, the case fizzled. In retrospect, incidents like Orlov's bizarre visit to Karlshorst (which would be risky under any circumstances, but especially so for a former Soviet intelligence officer, ex-Gehlen collaborator, and now CIA agent) should have sounded warnings. Instead, the case helped secure Orlov's position within BOB, even though during the following year none of his cases panned out. But at CIA headquarters and at the German Mission, continuing, routine checks into his past revealed possible security breaches. Some accused Orlov of making up reports while he was associated with the Gehlen Organization, for example, and others charged him with doctoring documents during his SBONR period.

Compounding these past problems were new accusations directed at Orlov since his arrival in Berlin: he was described as a skirt-chasing heavy drinker who tended to talk too much when intoxicated. Some of these charges were proved false, and many were disputed by case officers who had worked with him. Nonetheless, by 20 April 1954, BOB had been ordered by the German Mission to drop Orlov. BOB demurred, and on 21 July CIA's Eastern European division reviewed the controversy in a long dispatch. Although it dismissed many of the accusations against Orlov and advanced other reasons for his poor performance, it also recommended that Orlov and his wife be fired. Shortly after BOB received this dispatch, Orlov was involved in a car accident and charged with drunken driving.[12] But BOB, ignoring these warning signals, recommended that Orlov stay on until some of his ongoing Soviet defection operations were completed. These cases, the first such in more than a year, looked promising: somehow Orlov's cases seemed to progress to full-blown defection operations more rapidly than most.

The first case involved a twenty-one-year-old West Berlin woman whom Orlov had met in a West Berlin bar on April Fool's Day 1954. By mid-May she had been recruited and had begun to cruise the dance cafes near Karlshorst for likely defectors. She met a promising young Soviet, Anatoly, and made a date for 2 June. Anatoly failed to show, but another man, Aleksandr—a money order clerk in the Karlshorst military post office—appeared in his place. The romance blossomed during June, and by 12 July Aleksandr had made his first visit to West Berlin. The speed of these developments raised eyebrows in BOB. The case officer, in his first dispatch describing the events, suggested it might be a KGB provocation.[13]

At BOB's instructions, the woman began giving Russian émigré newspapers to Aleksandr. She claimed she had found an émigré organization, TSOPE (Tsentral'noe ob"edinenie poslevoennykh emigrantov) that would help him should he decide to stay in the West, and on 2 August she gave him a letter in Russian from the TSOPE office.[14] On 23 August, Aleksandr came to West Berlin and met for four hours with a Russian-speaking member of the Redcap branch who was posing as the TSOPE representative. The representative was allowed to inspect Aleksandr's identity documents, which had been issued only four months earlier. Their date of issuance actually coincided with his transfer from his tank unit to the postal unit in Karlshorst. He was, the documents proclaimed, Sgt. Aleksandr Mikhailovich Smirnov. Smirnov declined to remain in place in his unit as a Western source, saying he wanted more than anything to move to the West so he could marry his German sweetheart.[15] But he did agree to turn over lists of field post numbers, copies of regulations on military censorship, postal forms, stamp pad inks, passes, permits, and so forth—all of which were needed by CIA to help their agents get into the USSR.[16]

On 4 September the girlfriend announced that the sergeant would make his break the next night.[17] He did so on 6 September, bringing with him only two unclassified, outdated Soviet Army service manuals, four postal money order forms, and an illegible handwritten list of persons who had recently sent money home. He was interviewed by the "TSOPE representative," who opined that the sergeant was a genuine defector and not a KGB plant.[18] On 7 September he was flown with his girlfriend to the Defector Reception Center (DRC) near Frankfurt.[19] Here the woman ended the romantic charade, declaring that she never wanted to see the sergeant again. Smirnov was immediately subjected to a series of interviews and polygraph tests whose results were complicated by his claim that he was heartbroken. By November, little progress had been made in resolving doubts about Aleksandr's story— particularly his shaky account of having been transferred in April 1954 from a tank unit to the Karlshorst post office.

Aleksandr had little useful information, but he could do simple radio repairs and he played a great game of chess. CIA decided not to involve him in a complicated counterintelligence interrogation and simply resettled him in West Germany. He worked for the NTS radio station until May 1958 and then took a private-sector job. On 8 November 1958, he was visited by a Russian-speaking woman. Their conversation must have unnerved him, because he drew his pay, bought a heavy overcoat, and on 15 November disappeared. CIA assumed that he had redefected.[20]

Orlov's other case was also initiated by one of his young women, who met a charming young Soviet soldier in an East Berlin dance hall in December 1953. This relationship lasted until April 1954, when a second Soviet moved in and the first chap disappeared. The "bait and switch" in this case, although played out over a longer period, paralleled that in the Sergeant Smirnov case. As further lure, the Orlov agent described a fictional wealthy grandmother in West Berlin who had recently died, making her an heiress. To give the story more credibility, the woman gave the Soviet officer money to repair a friend's car, which he had crashed. The Soviet soldier apparently decided to move with the woman to West Berlin and help her claim her fortune. In June 1954 the Soviet was enticed into a BOB safe house in West Berlin, where he was introduced to the woman's "uncle," a Russian-speaking Berlin officer ostensibly representing TSOPE. Meetings between the officer and the "uncle" continued off and on until October, when the officer agreed to remain in place until 1 January 1955. But on 22 December the Soviet suddenly announced to his West Berlin contacts that he would not defect because he realized that the girl would never marry him. At a follow-up meeting on 29 December, the Soviet agreed to remain in contact with the BOB officer during his upcoming transfer to the USSR and accepted secret addresses to which he should write. Communications were to reach him via his mother in letters mailed to her from inside the Soviet Union.[21]

On the surface at least, it appeared as though BOB and Orlov had achieved another success: the transformation of a defection inducement operation into the recruitment of a source willing to report to CIA from inside the USSR. But in 1959, an analysis by CIA Headquarters of the case from its inception through four years of correspondence with the agent in the USSR questioned its value and raised the possibility that the agent had been under Soviet control from the beginning.[22]

After the Svetlov case in 1952, these two 1954 operations were the only ones in which Orlov participated that produced results. With both of them finished by the end of 1954, attention turned again to Orlov's future.[23] By this time, his affiliation with BOB was no secret to the Berlin police and others. Further, BOB had come to realize that because of tighter East German security, his boy-meets-girl operations against the Soviet military were no longer feasible. Even BOB finally admitted that Orlov would have to go, perhaps to the United States.

The decision made, CIA Washington headquarters wrestled for more than a year with the problems of arranging his entry into the United States. In a 9 October 1956 message to CIA Washington, annoyed BOB leaders emphasized that after Orlov's apartment lease expired, he could not stay in Berlin: he would have to wait in West Germany for passage to the United States.[24] BOB had washed its hands of Orlov.

In hindsight, Orlov's true loyalties and the nature of the cases he produced seemed suspect even before he left Berlin. There had been other signs that something was amiss. In 1953 he had been introduced to an East German who had seemed an ideal candidate for supporting Redcap operations in East Germany. A former employee of a police motor vehicle office and later a taxi driver, this man could provide blank East German drivers' licenses and car registration forms. He was paid for these documents and signed receipts for the funds and for the tiny, easily concealed camera that BOB issued to him. In April 1953 the Soviets caught him and he was sentenced to prison.[25] After his release three years later, he came to West Germany and in June 1956 described to CIA interviewers the circumstances of his arrest. During his interrogation by Soviet officials, they had shown him the originals of receipts that he had signed while working for Orlov—documents that only he, Orlov, and BOB had handled. Rather than refer the case to BOB for its reaction, CIA gave the ex-agent a polygraph test and concluded that he was lying. There is no record that the results of the interview were ever passed along to BOB, despite the fundamental questions it raised about Orlov's credibility.[26]

Even more damning for Orlov was the case of a CIA double agent from the émigré department of the Karlshorst KGB apparat. In late 1956 he reported hearing startling news from his KGB case officers concerning Vladimir Kivi, the ex-SBONR member who had disappeared shortly after coming to Berlin with Orlov in October 1951. The KGB officers told the double agent that Kivi had been "apprehended by the Soviets in Berlin; he was still alive, but in the Gulag."[27] Considering how difficult it would have been for Orlov to be a double agent with an honest partner, these revelations should have alarmed BOB.

In spring 1957, Orlov and his family were finally admitted to the United States. In the absence of any firm evidence that he was anything but the victim of bad luck with his cases and a changing operational environment in Berlin, he was given additional assessment and training in Washington. After his stint in the United States, he returned to Europe to help with various operations in Germany and Austria. He was returned to the United States at the end of 1960, and his association with CIA was finally terminated without prejudice.

Less than a year later, the defection of KGB officer Anatoly Mikhailovich Golitsyn in Helsinki returned Orlov to the spotlight. Golitsyn has been the subject of scores of books and articles since his defection.

He had been in the foreign intelligence directorate since 1945. From 1951 to 1953 he served in the American section of MGB's counterintelligence department in Moscow, after which he received an assignment in Vienna working on émigré cases. In spring 1962, during his first debriefings after defecting, he described an agent who he thought was code-named Sasha, who had been recruited by the MGB émigré department in 1950 or earlier but in 1953 had been transferred to the American section—Golitsyn's section—of the counterintelligence department. His name began with K and ended in "sky."[28] At that time, according to Golitsyn, Sasha worked for an American intelligence unit in West Berlin and passed information on his unit and associates to the KGB. Once he had even informed KGB that the Americans were planning to send an agent into the USSR documented as a Soviet soldier.

Golitsyn embellished his story in later years, and it is now difficult to separate what he learned in his MGB service in 1953 from what CIA debriefers showed him in the 1960s to jog his memory. Nevertheless, it was a remarkably long time before anyone made the connection between Golitsyn's description and Orlov. About eighteen months after his defection, Golitsyn was shown a list of names and identified Victor Zharov as the agent who had been sent into the Soviet Union "documented as a Soviet soldier." This was not accurate. Zharov had been in Berlin working as a refugee debriefer for the BOB Redcap branch. But he had associated with both Orlov and his wife, and a subsequent file check revealed that involvement and cast suspicion on Orlov.[29]

How did Orlov elude CIA investigators for so long? The name Orlov had used since Vlassov Army days was Aleksandr Kopatsky (in German transliteration, Kopazky), and he was known to friends and his CIA case officers as Sasha, the diminutive for Aleksandr. After serving in the Vlassov Army he had joined SBONR, which meant that KGB's émigré department was most likely first responsible for his case. His case would naturally have been transferred to the KGB counterintelligence department's American section after BOB had placed him in Redcap operations. The Svetlov case, which Orlov kept alive by making a personal visit to Karlshorst, did involve CIA interest in obtaining Soviet military documents for CIA agents entering the USSR documented as Soviet soldiers. Orlov was fully informed of BOB's desire to obtain Svetlov's leave documents. Because he was aware of the USSR operations program in the Munich area from his earlier SBONR connections, he also knew that they might be used to document other American agents. Taken together, these factors should have made it immediately clear that Orlov was the man described by Golitsyn.[30] Instead, the hunt for "Sasha" lasted several years, casting suspicion on many innocent CIA officers in the process.

When we asked for information on Orlov from the SVR archives, officials told us: "There is no information on the collaboration of Igor Orlov, Aleksandr Kopatsky, or Franz Koischwitz with Soviet intelligence." They went on to state that a person "presenting documents identifying him as Igor Orlov, a citizen of the United States, had visited the Soviet embassy [in Washington] on 10 May 1965."[31] This person had said that he had been born in Moscow and that "at the close of the war he had found himself in Germany in the American zone, working as a civilian employee at an American Army installation. He married a German citizen. In 1961 he left for the United States with his family, and in 1962 he became an American citizen." According to the report, this visitor had claimed that the FBI was interrogating him and his wife, "attempting to obtain an admission that he collaborated with Soviet intelligence while he was in Germany during the 1940s and 1950s."[32]

The visitor reportedly inquired into the possibility of being "granted asylum in the USSR or being reunited with his family." According to the report, in view of the confused answers the visitor gave to questions concerning his time in Germany and his departure for the United States in 1961, and because "he received his American citizenship much too quickly" (within one year), the Soviet officials only gave him information for how he could apply for asylum or search for relatives; no one offered to help him wade through the bureaucracy and make it happen. He was told to prepare the necessary documents and send them by mail or deliver them in person. "The visitor did not appear at the embassy again, and the documents never arrived." The report concluded with the statement that "a file check of the name I. Orlov, including one for Germany, showed no material on him."[33]

Reportedly, Orlov did visit the Soviet embassy in Washington in spring 1965. Two separate KGB sources later identified him as a KGB agent. In light of what we now know about Orlov, the SVR response to our inquiry was obviously disingenuous.

BOB's Deputy Chief Has a Close Call: Redcap Vienna

An interesting and important Redcap operation took place in Vienna in early 1955 while negotiations over the Austrian State Treaty were still stymied by Soviet insistence that action on the treaty be linked to progress on a German peace treaty. David Murphy was just settling into his new post as deputy chief of BOB when he received orders from CIA Washington to proceed to Vienna to participate in an operation targeting Boris Nalivaiko, who in 1947–48 had been deputy chief of the Committee of Information (KI) residency in Berlin.

As the "Soviet consul from Berlin," Nalivaiko had been present at a December 1951 US-Soviet meeting in Bremerhaven, in connection with the return to the United States of Lend-Lease icebreakers. His interest in making foreign securities investments at the time suggested that he might be vulnerable to blandishments from the capitalist West. Nalivaiko claimed that he had accumulated nearly 80,000 West Marks and was seeking a secure and profitable haven for his funds. He also seemed unusually familiar with various consumer goods and their costs. At the same time, he expressed the conviction that the USSR would one day improve, but if the country "ever collapsed, he would collapse with it."[34] He seemed a good candidate for defection. Posing as Col. Francis Manning, a Washington official "in a position to discuss Nalivaiko's future," Murphy was to be introduced to Nalivaiko by Robert Gray, whom Nalivaiko had known in connection with the Malinin case as an American journalist in Berlin.

Gray and Nalivaiko met at the Vienna municipal park, where Nalivaiko agreed to be introduced to Manning at the Gartenbau Cafe, a site chosen by the Soviets. A junior Vienna mission officer spotted a known KGB officer watching the exchange at the park and expressed doubts about going ahead with the Gartenbau meeting, but CIA's Vienna Mission decided to proceed.[35]

Until this time we have had only the CIA record of the operation, embellished by numerous unofficial accounts and commentary.[36] Now we have Nalivaiko's story of the Gartenbau incident in both an unclassified Russian periodical and in his classified memoirs. Both confirm many details of this story, but the classified version describes the KGB side of the affair.[37] Nalivaiko noted that one of his missions in Vienna was to investigate the disappearance of Pyotr Deriabin, a member of the KGB residency. The residency claimed that it was not seriously concerned about the defection because Deriabin's knowledge was limited to his own section, which dealt with the security of official Soviets in Vienna.[38] Nonetheless, Nalivaiko made the rounds of Allied consular officials in search of information about Deriabin. At this point, Gray called Nalivaiko and insisted on seeing him. After receiving approval from the KGB resident, Nalivaiko, wearing a concealed tape recorder, dined with Gray in the company of both men's wives. Gray warned Nalivaiko that he was in trouble with Moscow and faced recall. Nalivaiko was not convinced. He in turn asked Gray about Deriabin but received no response.[39]

Each step in the operation was cleared with Moscow by the Vienna KGB resident.[40] Moscow was in favor of playing along with the CIA attempt to recruit Nalivaiko so that it could strike a decisive blow against the Americans. The Soviets also hoped for a propaganda advantage that could be used in negotiations under way for a peace treaty with Austria. The only sticking point was that KGB wanted to delay final action until February, when the Soviets would take their turn as the chief authority in the international sector.

After meeting with Gray at the Viennese park, Nalivaiko insisted—in step with the KGB plan—that Manning would need to show proof that he was empowered to act. Security would be assured at the cafe meeting by having two officers from the KGB residency pose as customers. A third officer, charged with protecting Nalivaiko from harm, was sent specially from Moscow for the event so that he would not be known to the Americans. On Friday, 4 February, Moscow gave its final approval. Nalivaiko called Gray, agreed to a meeting with Manning, and named the site. The trap was ready.[41]

Although completely unaware of KGB plans, as a precaution selected CIA officers entered the cafe before the meeting to observe the proceedings. Gray and "Manning" arrived next. According to Nalivaiko's account, he entered the cafe at 6:00 P.M. Gray, who was seated to the right of his companion Manning, saw Nalivaiko and waved. Their table, in Nalivaiko's words "chosen professionally," was against the back wall next to a potted palm, the entry to the cloakroom and kitchen, and the exit to the street.

When Nalivaiko joined them, the group ordered beer. After a few moments of nervous small talk, Nalivaiko asked Manning to show him proof of his authority. Manning flashed a letter made up for the occasion. Nalivaiko seized the document in his right hand and with his left threw his beer at Gray. Nalivaiko then attempted to thrust the document into his pocket while he and Manning tussled over it. Suddenly Manning was struck by Nalivaiko's bodyguard and surrounded by the other Soviets in the cafe. Meanwhile, Nalivaiko, turning to the cafe's many startled Austrian patrons, shouted that the Americans had taken "provocative actions . . . against a Soviet consul."[42]

While Nalivaiko protested, the KGB agents demanded that Manning come with them. Tempers flared as Manning (Murphy) pretended not to understand Russian, a denial that one KGB officer kept insisting was false. This nasty standoff was finally defused by one of the CIA Vienna mission officers assigned to the stakeout. This officer, a native of the city, telephoned the police station next door, complaining that "honest citizens could not enjoy their coffee without the Americans and Russians raising a ruckus."

Moments later, in Nalivaiko's words, "surprisingly, the door opened wide and into the cafe burst fifteen men, as tall as grenadiers, in black overcoats and helmets, with two enormous dogs on leashes. It was the Austrian police." They were followed by the international military police, "four in a jeep," who checked the documents of their respective conationals and, after admonishing both parties, released everyone. The Americans had been tricked, but KGB, for all its meticulous planning in the selection of the Gartenbau Cafe, had overlooked the location of the Viennese police station—the one factor that foiled the Soviets' attempt to seize Murphy and Gray.

Because of Viennese publicity Murphy was spirited out of Vienna and returned to Berlin. It is difficult to assess the propaganda advantages the Soviets may have gained, if any, from the Gartenbau episode. In any event, it was driven from the front pages by news from Moscow on 8 February that Georgy Malenkov had been replaced as chairman of the USSR Council of Ministers by Marshal Bulganin.[43] War hero Georgy Zhukov was named minister of defense. As for influencing the Austrian treaty, in early March the Soviets backed down on their insistence that action in Austria be linked to progress on a German peace treaty. This change in Soviet policy toward Germany came as a surprise to many Soviet leaders, who thought of neutrality for Austria as a trump card in the game started by Khrushchev.[44]

A Defection in Pakistan: Smirnov's Predictions

In spring 1955, A. A. Smirnov, a thirty-three-year-old third secretary of the Soviet embassy in Karachi, Pakistan, defected to American authorities and was flown to the United States, but he then changed his mind.[45] It was decided to return him to Soviet control via Berlin. But before Smirnov was returned to the Soviets he was interviewed by Murphy and voiced some perceptive, even prophetic, views on Berlin and the German question:

> I believe that many great and important decisions will be made this year [1955] in regard to Germany. No thinking man in Soviet circles believes that the twelve or so planned German divisions present any threat to the safety of the Soviet Union. As soon as West Germany is armed, however, there could be a change in attitude toward the occupying powers. Under these conditions, the Soviet Union might agree to free elections throughout Germany provided that there were a complete withdrawal of both Allied and Soviet forces from all of Germany. The hardcore Communists in East Germany, being well organized and financed, could be counted on to send a considerable number of Communists into the new government. . . . Actually, the form of government is immaterial as long as the Soviet Union could separate the newly united Germany from NATO. One means of attempting this separation would be for the Soviets to return the expropriated German territories now in possession of the Soviet Union and Poland.[46]

Although Smirnov was repeatedly asked to remain in the West, he remained adamant about leaving. He was returned to Soviet control on 17 May 1955. But his comments were made just as BOB was hearing fascinating rumblings from sources in East Berlin of possible policy changes.

Growing Discord Between the USSR and East Germany

Smirnov's comments on Soviet intentions toward Germany seemed to reflect Moscow's hopes rather than realistic expectations. But his ideas were of special interest to BOB because they reflected themes that were emerging from other intelligence reports during summer 1955. Although CIA had dismissed the possibility that the Soviets would withdraw their troops in exchange for guarantees of a reunited but neutral Germany on Soviet terms—a plan that seemed to pose greater disadvantages to the Soviets than advantages[47]—Smirnov was certainly right that 1955 was a critical year for Cold War Germany. By 5 May, the Western Allies had recognized the sovereignty of the Federal Republic of Germany, and on 9 May the FRG was accepted as a member of NATO.

At the same time, the West invited the USSR to a four-power summit conference in Geneva that summer. This invitation may have inspired the Soviet government to ask Konrad Adenauer, chancellor of the FRG, to come to Moscow to discuss diplomatic, trade, and cultural relations between the two countries.

This apparent Soviet about-face toward the Adenauer government was seen by many in the West as a blow to the prestige of the East German leadership. At about this time BOB began receiving reports from sources on the staff of the SED Politburo that indicated growing problems in USSR–East German relations. During a May 1955 conference of Warsaw Pact nations, for example, Walter Ulbricht was said to have submitted proposals for sealing the borders between the GDR and West Berlin, but these were flatly rejected by the Soviets. Instead, the Soviets previewed their intended proposal to Chancellor Adenauer that "a reunited Germany be given certain economic concessions in territories east of the Oder-Neisse, without any changes in territorial sovereignty." The East Germans were also told that "the GDR would not be represented in Moscow by a special delegation during the Adenauer visit."[48]

At a 6 July meeting of the SED Politburo, Georgy Pushkin, Soviet ambassador to the GDR, in reply to a question on the future of the GDR government, reportedly called the issue "an internal German matter" and said, "The GDR government has been of little use in solving problems related to the German question. The SED Politburo should get rid of the idea that the USSR considers the GDR as important strategically and politically as the SED seems to think it is. The population and raw material resources of the GDR are of no consequence to the USSR in the overall international picture." Believing that he had sufficiently shocked the SED Politburo with these comments, Pushkin concluded his remarks with the standard line that the "Soviets would agree to reunification based on free elections only if such a Germany were to have a 'social democratic government.'"[49] At a meeting on 16 July, Khrushchev accused SED of having "failed to comprehend the change which Soviet policies had undergone" and of having undertaken "actions that hindered East-West détente."[50]

Washington was preparing for the Geneva summit when these reports were received, and the State Department and White House were fascinated, if somewhat baffled by them. Such tension between the Soviets and their East German friends was difficult to believe, as was the

likelihood that the Soviets would approve extensive economic concessions for a reunited Germany from former German territories now controlled by Poland. Some at CIA labeled the declarations deliberate lies.
In any case, none of these dramatic Soviet offers were in fact made during the Geneva conference or the Adenauer meetings in Moscow. Perhaps the only hopeful note for the West during the meetings was that
the Soviet delegation endorsed the notion that German reunification
should be undertaken by the Germans themselves.

13

BOB Concentrates on Karlshorst

BOB's Redcap program had always tried to extend its operations into major Soviet garrison areas throughout East Germany in spite of tighter Soviet and East German security measures. But BOB's effort was poorly organized; each branch tried independently to develop operations against those Soviet components that interested it most. The result thus depended not on the experience of branch personnel but on the nature of their operations. Those in the atomic energy group, for example, were seasoned operators working against a specific target. But the separate counterintelligence branch (CE), successor to X-2, was still occupied with unproductive Soviet double agents and overwhelmed by its mandate to investigate security flaps in the covert action programs.

From their operations, individual branches produced bits and pieces of information on those Soviets in East Germany of special concern to them. Each branch used its own organizational scheme to arrange the material it acquired on Soviet individuals and installations. The scientific and technical branch had the best scheme, but it received considerable help from its Washington desk in developing and organizing material. There was general agreement that BOB desperately needed a system that could incorporate these data into a centralized repository accessible to all officers working on Soviet operations. CIA documents and eyewitness testimony show how this was done and the way in which it affected these operations.

The Target Room

A number of related developments finally led to the consolidation of BOB's Soviet information. Most important, it became accepted that it was useless for BOB even to try to recruit and maintain East German agents in or near Soviet installations in East Germany; Soviet security was too tight. Besides, by 1953–54 the interesting Soviet targets were being moved into the Soviet compound in Karlshorst.[1] This compound, an important post since the war, had become the Soviet center of Germany: MGB and KGB foreign intelligence, Soviet military intelligence (GRU), and key targets of BOB's atomic energy effort had all been moved there. An area of about one square mile contained the offices, service facilities, and residences of the most important Soviets in Germany.

Finally, the move from the old BOB offices in Foehrenweg to a much larger building in the US compound on Clayallee gave BOB staff the incentive and the space needed to place all Soviet operations in a single branch. The "target room" created there held an amazing array of information about the Karlshorst compound, including listings of Soviet personnel, their telephone numbers at work and at home, their addresses and places of work, and the license plate numbers on their cars. Along with the descriptions of offices and residences, notebooks with floor plans were maintained on apartments used by KGB as safe houses for training "illegals"—Soviet spies who were documented as foreign citizens and sent abroad—and for meeting with agents from West Berlin and elsewhere. To update the 1943 Berlin city map then in use, BOB coaxed the US Air Force into providing aerial photographs of Karlshorst. These more accurate layouts were used when debriefing refugees and other sources about the compound.

By spring 1955, the target room had become the focal point of an expanded operation to develop East German sources with access to the compound. Although the Soviet compound had long since been cleared of all German residents except for a highly select contingent of GDR officials, the Soviets still had to rely on German employees to maintain this town within a town. BOB started looking for German employees with compound passes who either worked there or visited regularly.

There were a great many people in this category: repairmen from public utilities, couriers, trash removers, and so forth. These individuals could provide detailed and often documentary information on the Soviets with whom they worked. Even the cleaning women at the hotel where Soviet officials stayed were able to provide registration slips that the visitors had filled out using their real names. BOB used information like this to test the veracity of a confessed Soviet spy: one wrong answer to a question like "Was Ivan Ivanovich in Karlshorst on 12 May?" could break the cover story of even the most seasoned operative. One East German agent for BOB worked in a military administrative office that handled housing and maintenance for GRU workers in the compound. There was a potbellied stove in the office in which the Soviets were supposed to burn documents. But they were careless, and the agent was able to retrieve partially burned documents and deliver them to his BOB case officer.[2] And then there was the source in the Karlshorst branch of the GDR postal system who was responsible for receiving and forwarding undeveloped personal film from Soviet officers for processing. He provided not only identifications and descriptions but also the occasional snapshot to be filed in BOB's "mug books."

BOB also used information collected in the target room to find out which German Karlshorst compound employees were KGB or Mfs informers. Twenty-five percent of these employees were thought to report directly to KGB or Mfs, and KGB was certainly capable of manipulating them to oppose BOB's operations. Because of the extensive target room database, BOB could also test the reliability of its own newly recruited agents.

BOB's Creative Countermeasures

BOB acquired a respectable surveillance capability of the compound even though the restricted area was always under guard. As photo surveillance capabilities improved, pictures of Soviets residing in Karlshorst were added to the mug books. In one case, BOB concealed a camera in the lunch box of a German worker who parked his truck opposite the entrance to KGB headquarters, placed the lunch box on the ledge behind the driver's seat, and took photos of KGB officers streaming in and out during their lunch break while he munched his sandwich.

Agents who had access to Soviet offices or residences were also used by BOB to wire the compound for sound. The veteran KGB counterintelligence officer Valentin Vladimirovich Zvezdenkov, who served in Karlshorst in the 1950s, described how KGB technicians discovered a transmitter in a chandelier in the office of KGB apparat chief Aleksandr Korotkov. The impulsive Korotkov wanted to leave it there so he could say a few choice words to the Americans, but he was talked out of the idea. Later KGB learned from the boastful electrical supply firm manager that voices picked up by the Americans' transmitter could be received three kilometers away. This incident so unnerved KGB security that it was retold in somewhat altered form in security lectures to other Soviet units in Karlshorst, including GRU.[3]

The chandelier setup was a favorite BOB operation. On another occasion, one of BOB's agents, an electrician, overheard that his firm was to acquire new fixtures for remodeled offices in KGB headquarters. One fixture was a large wooden chandelier. The agent did not know for which room it was slated, but it seemed appropriate for a very large office or conference room. He brought the disassembled chandelier to West Berlin, where a cavity was hollowed out in one arm and a listening device and transmitter were installed. The device was returned to the KGB storage area to await installation by the firm. Weeks went by and nothing happened. The agent later reported that the chandelier had been returned to the firm without the transmitter. The BOB officer in charge of the case sensed danger and urged the agent to defect, but the agent refused, claiming that because so many others had access to the storeroom, suspicion would not fall on him. Still concerned, the case officer put the agent on ice: they held only short, infrequent meetings during which every effort was made to detect hostile surveillance. For six months nothing happened, and then the agent stopped showing up at meetings in West Berlin. BOB later learned that after the discovery of the transmitter each of the workers with access to the storeroom had been placed under continuous MfS surveillance. The agent was observed meeting his BOB case officer on 8 August 1957 and arrested a week later. Sentenced to prison for espionage, the agent served nine years. He was finally released in 1966 under the "prisoners for ransom" program and allowed to resettle in West Berlin, where he told BOB his story.[4]

Soviet security programs continually frustrated BOB's efforts. Even as BOB was getting its target room in order and trying to expand its agent network in Karlshorst during 1954, a large-scale Soviet effort was under way to dismiss "redundant" members of the German staff. These German personnel were replaced either by Soviets or by Germans who had been vetted by MFS. As German employees were fired, they were given stern warnings by Soviet security personnel not to divulge information on the compound to anyone and to report any attempts to lure them to West Berlin. Sometimes even these warnings were inadequate. In one case, a very knowledgeable ex-employee fled to West Berlin and was later targeted for kidnapping by KGB. But one of the employee's former colleagues, who had been forced to participate in the kidnapping plan, shortcircuited it by defecting to BOB first.[5]

On 16 September 1957, BOB's GRU source, Pyotr Popov, reported that some areas of Karlshorst were to be returned to German control. In addition, all Germans living in the compound were to be evacuated, the size of the compound was to be reduced, stronger fences were to be built, and a regiment of KGB troops were to be brought in as security guards.[6] But the East Germans resisted the order because it would have meant that a number of politically important GDR officials would be moved. In addition, a double wire fence was deemed too expensive, so the Soviets compromised on a three-meter-high wooden fence.[7] As of February 1958, BOB estimated that there were about four hundred German nationals who still had regular access to the compound.[8]

As KGB tightened its security in the Karlshorst compound it relied more than ever on MFS, the East German security service, to pressure the remaining Germans employed there to serve as informants. Their main job was to report any suspicions that fellow employees had been recruited by a Western service. This greatly complicated BOB's task of infiltrating Karlshorst, and its response was to try to persuade US intelligence and counterintelligence services in Berlin to avoid uncoordinated operations into the Soviet compound. But similar attempts to persuade the West Berlin Intelligence Service (Bundesnachrichtendienst, BND) to desist from operations that could threaten BOB's sources eventually aroused the interest of Heinz Felfe, an active KGB agent who led BND's Soviet counterespionage branch. (For details about Felfe's activities see appendix 6.)

Updating Target Room Information

The information produced by the Berlin tunnel was an unanticipated counterintelligence bonanza, and it greatly enhanced BOB's ability to respond to requests for information on Soviet intelligence activities.[9] Although during the tunnel's operation its information was kept separate from target room holdings to ensure secrecy, after it was discovered all of its findings were integrated with target room files.

The tunnel material underscored the need for this sort of depth and accuracy in the Karlshorst database. After the tunnel was closed in April 1956, new sources were sought who could update the database. One such source began in spring 1955 and lasted until fall 1960. The agent was a gregarious and astute East Berliner who worked in the Soviet office that handled unaccompanied Soviet freight shipments from Berlin to Moscow. In the normal course of his duties he obtained the name of the Soviet shipper and the addressee in Moscow. Because each Soviet unit in Berlin-Karlshorst handled the paperwork for these shipments in its own way and used its own vehicles to bring shippers to the freight office, it was possible to identify the Soviet office to which the shipper was assigned, whether KGB, GRU, Soviet embassy, Soviet trade delegation, or Soviet Army advisers to the East German National People's Army.[10]

Further, these were not ordinary shipments. It was always easy for BOB's man to know when a shipper was returning permanently to Moscow, because the boxes often included such items as furniture, musical instruments (even grand pianos), and household appliances, which almost always required special packaging. By developing a reputation as a friendly, helpful fellow, the agent got to know the Soviet drivers and even some of the shippers themselves, and while chatting with them acquired information on their past postings and new assignments.[11]

During this operation, the agent identified a great many officers and other personnel by their real names: 1,331 from KGB, 156 from GRU, 431 from the Soviet embassy in East Berlin, 199 from the trade delegation, and 170 Soviet military advisers. The high number of KGB personnel makes sense because the KGB vastly outnumbered other personnel working or residing in Karlshorst. As the agent's early reports (in 1955–56) were checked against target-room holdings, it became clear that he was reporting accurately. He cemented his reliability by being able to pick out photos of known KGB or GRU officers from among several pictures spread before him.[12]

But by summer 1960, the agent and his wife were getting jumpy. Although the case had been run with great care and without involving other base agents, the case officer, who had served in Germany since war's end, sensed that the time had come to withdraw the couple. When BOB proposed to the two that they be resettled in West Germany, their relief was palpable. In September 1960, out they came. A happy ending to an operation of this kind was rare.[13]

The tunnel operation had also revealed the first significant information about a new part of a Soviet directorate: the Special Department (Osoby otdel—OO) of the Directorate of Counterintelligence (UKR). Commanded by Col. Leonty Vasilievich Shatalov, OO was responsible for the security of all Soviet Army personnel and installations in the Karlshorst area. Some of the tunnel information, like the addresses of the OO's various elements and residences of its personnel, could be checked against existing target room holdings.[14] But it took the arrival of the "banana queen" and her extensive debriefing by BOB to flesh out the true significance of this unit.

The Banana Queen

During summer 1956, BOB learned of the defection of a young woman describing herself as "a KGB officer from Karlshorst" who had been involved in an operation against a US military intelligence unit in West Berlin. After a preliminary interview at the debriefing center in West Germany, BOB brought the woman to Berlin for further questioning. Learning about what she knew turned out to be a long and difficult process. She was full of fascinating anecdotes of her work for Soviet counterintelligence in Karlshorst and elsewhere in East Germany, most of which could be checked against tunnel material. But when inconsistencies emerged and she was questioned further, she would lean toward a bowl of fruit on the table, take a banana, and carefully and deliberately peel it. Such was her concentration that she appeared to be oblivious to her surroundings. For this performance, which left her male interlocuters spellbound, she was dubbed the banana queen. But this coquettish maneuver failed to influence her principal interrogator, an experienced Russian-speaking woman who specialized in the Soviet intelligence services.[15]

To make sense of the banana queen's information on Karlshorst, BOB interviewers tried to find out how she had obtained it. Their questions toward this end revealed a kaleidoscopic account of the effects of war and the Soviet occupation on a very young, shrewd, and vain woman whose principal talent was persuading men to accept without question whatever role she happened to be playing at the time. Born in the Soviet Union, she became involved with Soviet military counterintelligence at war's end, serving as an interpreter and assuming a variety of identities as part of ongoing investigations of Soviet Army personnel suspected of illegal activities. Although she would often act the part of a KGB officer, she was always an agent, never a full-fledged member of state security. During the mid-1950s she was assigned to the Potsdam counterintelligence directorate of the Group of Soviet Forces, Germany (GSFG). In general, she worked in support of Col. Leonty Shatalov's Special Department in Karlshorst. One of the counterintelligence operations in which she participated involved contact with an employee of a US military organization in West Berlin whom Shatalov wished to recruit, and it was this case that prompted her defection.[16]

Target room files confirmed most of the information the banana queen provided during her BOB interviews. Occasional inaccuracies could invariably be traced to her status as an agent: the Soviets never gave her the details she would have had as a KGB staff officer. Nevertheless, her portrait of the interaction between the Potsdam headquarters of the GSFG's counterintelligence directorate, the directorate's Special Department in Karlshorst, and the KGB's Karlshorst apparat under Pitovranov added depth and detail to the tunnel reporting.[17]

Life in military counterintelligence in Karlshorst in 1955–56, as portrayed in her stories, was never dull. Any incident that raised suspicions, no matter how far-fetched, had to be investigated, and the banana queen was involved in many of these operations. One senior lieutenant on his way home on leave, for example, was carrying forty gold watches, according to the train conductor. The military counterintelligence officers in charge immediately suspected espionage, which drew the attention of the counterintelligence directorate in Potsdam. The lieutenant was taken off the train and interrogated, but he managed to convince everyone that he had saved enough to buy the watches (which were not actually gold) for resale at home in the USSR. Another case concerned the suspected poisoning of Soviet troops by subversive agents or via balloons sent by the Americans. But further investigation showed that the soldiers had contracted rabies after killing and eating a rabid fox.[18]

While discussing the Special Department in Karlshorst, the banana queen spoke at length on what she called the agent section. Her description confirmed other reports that UKR GSFG was running active counteroperations against the Western Allies' operations to lure Soviet Army personnel. Although at times the Soviets prohibited their mili-

**house Building
adar Station)** **Motor Pool** **Barracks
Mess Hall**

Photo from SVRA Tunnel "Album" (captions by D. Murphy)

Berlin tunnel, surface installations.

CIA director Allen Dulles, right, presents to William Harvey the Distinguished Intelligence Medal for the Berlin tunnel operation. At left is Gordon Stewart.

George Blake, in white, addresses young KGB officers at the Dzerzhinsky Club in Moscow, 1990. At left is Kondrashev.

From left, Norman Borodin, Ivan Agayants, Sergei Kondrashev, and Iskhak Akhmerov, 1968.

Frank Wisner, London, 1960.

Sergei Kondrashev stands directly behind Nikita Khrushchev during the June 1961 Vienna summit meeting with John F. Kennedy. Sitting between the Soviet and US leaders is Austrian president Adolf Schaerf.

Gen. Albert Watson II, saluting, is driven through Checkpoint Charlie into
Berlin, 25 October 1961, after filing a protest over East German border restric-
(UPI/Corbis-Bettmann)

East German soldiers stand guard at the Friedrichstrasse border crossing, 4 December 1961, while workers build tank traps and reinforced wall. (UPI/Corbis-Bettmann)

tary counterintelligence from conducting agent operations in West Berlin and West Germany, such operations were common during the 1950s and 1960s.[19]

The banana queen's most extensive and interesting assignment for Shatalov's Special Department (OO) was her participation in the security investigation of Capt. Yevgeny Netsvetailo, a case officer in a Karlshorst intelligence unit. Her testimony provided BOB with a textbook example of how KGB military counterintelligence ran a case against an officer in military intelligence. This officer was suspected of being a double agent because he was too successful. His operations all worked flawlessly, yet his extramarital affairs often embarrassed his chiefs. In conducting the operation, OO used several informants who worked with Netsvetailo. Also needed, however, was an agent who could develop closer relations with the man. The banana queen was a natural choice.

Her cover was that she was an interpreter for the Soviet advisers to the GDR National People's Army. She was introduced to Netsvetailo as someone who spoke German and could pose as his wife either in agent meetings in East Berlin safe houses or during trips to West Germany. During one such trip, Netsvetailo contacted an intelligence directorate radio operator who was to be withdrawn for some reason. She was told to destroy her radio, and Netsvetailo and the banana queen took her back to Karlshorst. The banana queen was expected to report to OO on Netsvetailo's actions on all these occasions. But by April 1956, OO had decided to end the banana queen's involvement in the Netsvetailo case because her operation with the employee of the US military intelligence unit had higher priority. To end the relationship within the framework of the cover OO had devised, it was arranged to have an OO informant see the couple dancing at an East Berlin restaurant and report it.[20] Netsvetailo, who had no idea the queen was an OO plant, was properly chastened for his improper behavior in public, and the affair ended with the appropriate notation in the OO case file.

Not all the work of KGB military counterintelligence was as frothy as depicted by the queen. Kondrashev recalls a case in which the directorate in Potsdam and the apparat in Karlshorst cooperated in an operation to lure a Western intelligence service into trying to contact a Soviet military code clerk. In this operation, Kondrashev, who claims credit for the idea, worked directly with the deputy chief of the directorate, which had operational control of the case. A trustworthy officer was chosen and trained as a code clerk. He was set up in a military unit as cover with a code room that had special cipher machines. The ultimate purpose of the operation was to pass military disinformation, and it had the approval of Soviet Army Chief of Staff M. V. Zakharov. Kondrashev recalls that UKR succeeded in having the officer recruited by either the Americans or the British, but he claims that in the long run the Soviet military was unable or unwilling to provide accurate military information as cover for the release of selected disinformation.[21]

Everyone Is After the Emigrés

Another KGB activity that involved BOB during the mid-1950s was the work of the émigré department of the Karlshorst apparat. This department, one of the largest in the apparat, was responsible for infiltrating the many émigré organizations that had located in West Germany and elsewhere in Western Europe after the war. Since the Russian Revolution and the exodus of thousands of émigrés, all of whom were thought to be enemies of the new Soviet state, state security had been obsessed by the threat posed by their anti-Soviet actions. When a massive new wave of émigrés was thrown up in the wake of the German defeat, this fear reappeared, stronger than ever, particularly because KGB was well aware of CIA support for many émigré organizations. As a result, recruiting informants in these groups became a high priority for KGB Karlshorst.

Frequently the émigrés whom KGB had recruited turned themselves over to Western authorities. Other agents were discovered through Western counterintelligence coverage of the same émigré groups. By "doubling" these agents—getting them to work against their KGB controllers—BOB could identify department chiefs, individual case officers, and operational support facilities and could determine KGB goals for specific groups or individuals.[22] The double agents also revealed how worried KGB was about CIA's political and propaganda activities among Soviet émigrés. In countering these activities, KGB concentrated on contacting high-level personnel within organizations and institutions supported by CIA. What surprised BOB was how ready KGB Karlshorst was to take risks to meet and recruit such individuals in West Berlin.

A favorite operational site was the Soviet war memorial in the Tiergarten. Although it was in the British sector, the memorial was guarded by Soviets and was therefore a safe spot for making initial contacts with potential émigré agents. After the ice was broken and KGB was confident that a solid recruitment was in the offing, the case officer and potential agent would venture out into unprotected areas of West Berlin like the botanical gardens or various cafes and restaurants. A favorite meeting place was the restaurant Haus Wien, located in a brightly lit section of the fashionable Kurfuerstendamm. On several occasions CIA asked BOB to monitor the West Berlin meetings, both to identify the Soviet case officers involved and to learn details that could be later asked of the double agent to check his or her veracity and loyalty. In some cases BOB was asked to consider arresting one or more of the KGB officers so that they could be held for questioning as a prelude to a defection pitch. But no such arrest was ever made. This would have been impractical, for the officers carried Soviet official identification and always came to West Berlin in groups of two or three. More to the point, such an arrest would have doomed the double-agent operation and caused a monumental political flap.[23]

In the post-Stalin period, KGB tried to attract new émigré agents with the promise that past evils in the Soviet system had vanished. This approach had even greater resonance after Khrushchev's "secret speech" of February 1956 denouncing Stalin.

As soon as the émigré was securely indoctrinated, meetings shifted to safe houses in Karlshorst. In addition to debriefings by the agent's KGB handler, sessions were arranged with specialists who taught ciphers and one-way voice link communications. In one case, a radio training officer assigned agents to get details on the transmitting power of Radio Liberty to Soviet forces in East Germany.

As the KGB contact with émigré agents matured, they arranged meetings with them in West Germany and Switzerland. The émigré department took advantage of the summit and foreign ministers conferences in Geneva during summer and fall 1959 for agent meetings. It was also fairly standard practice for émigré agents to be introduced to the chief of the department. Pitovranov's successor, Aleksandr Mikhailovich Korotkov, seemed particularly fond of these encounters and listened with interest to descriptions by his countrymen of political life in the Federal Republic.

Because these émigrés were normally astute observers not only of their own milieu but also of the West German scene, they passed along useful information on Soviet attitudes toward current issues. Some of these viewpoints were almost certainly fed to them by their KGB case officers. On the other hand, in certain circumstances, like when the agents were treated to special trips to Moscow, some useful intelligence was obtained on Soviet internal problems and politics.[24]

The Karlshorst émigré department was a large, busy unit, but it was neither the largest nor the most vital in KGB. Honors for this role went to the illegals department of the Karlshorst apparat, whose activities in East Germany supported Soviet illegals operations throughout the world.

14

The Illegals Game: KGB vs. GRU

F rom the outset, both Soviet military intelligence and state security's foreign intelligence relied heavily on "illegals"—intelligence officers documented as foreign citizens and sent abroad—
to conduct their foreign operations. Indeed, illegals figured in
many of the most important successes of Soviet intelligence
during World War II and the Cold War. Before the Allied victory over
Germany, Soviet illegals operations had depended on agent networks in
Austria and Germany to supply the documentation needed to transform Soviet officers into foreign citizens.[1] But from 1945 on, East Germany became the most important center for KGB illegals support. In
appendix 7 we describe how the Third, or illegals, Department of the
KGB apparat grew into the largest of KGB Karlshorst; we explain its
work; and we examine BOB efforts to follow its activities.

For the KGB illegals directorate the most important event of 1957
was the loss of "Colonel Abel," one of their most senior and accomplished illegal operators.[2] But for Berlin Base it was the year when Lt.
Col. Pyotr Semyonovich Popov—BOB's source in Soviet military intelligence in East Germany—was transferred from the GSFG intelligence
directorate unit at Schwerin to the illegals section of GRU Operational
Group (Opergruppa) in Karlshorst. The account of the confrontation
between KGB and CIA that Popov ignited reveals much about how tense

the situation in Berlin had become—and how essential BOB and KGB were to their own sides in the Cold War.

Although extensive material has been published in the West on the Popov case, this is the first time documents from CIA files have been made available to support the recollections of officers who participated directly.[3] Although no SVR archival material has been released, Maj. Gen. Valentin Vladimirovich Zvezdenkov, the KGB officer primarily responsible for the KGB aspects of the case both in Karlshorst and Moscow, has spoken extensively with us.[4] The contrasts between the KGB perspective and the CIA account are startling and result in great measure from Popov's strategy while under interrogation to deceive KGB about the full extent of his relationship with CIA.

The case began on New Year's Day 1953 in Vienna, when Popov dropped a secret letter into the car of a US foreign service officer. The note offered to trade information for money, which he needed to pay for an abortion for his mistress. The letter was passed to CIA Vienna, which quickly arranged a meeting with Popov that confirmed his identity and great potential value as a source in Soviet military intelligence. CIA case officer George Kisevalter then took over and continued to handle the operation for the six and a half years before Popov's arrest by KGB.

According to the KGB version of the story—as told later by Popov in an effort to exonerate himself—during a February 1953 meeting between Popov and "Bash" (one of the GRU's Austrian agents), Popov was "detained by two persons posing as Austrian policemen. He was taken to the American military police barracks," where he was interrogated and then recruited by threats of a blackmail exposé of his Soviet intelligence status. KGB also suspected that Popov's love life might have made him vulnerable for recruitment. Although later KGB Vienna's counterintelligence people heard from a source in the Austrian police that there was a "traitor in the Soviet Group of Forces in Austria with the rank of lieutenant colonel," the hint could not be confirmed.[5]

After the withdrawal of the Soviet occupation forces from Austria, many GRU officers, including Popov, returned to Moscow for leave and reassignment. He had been briefed by CIA on signal sites and other communications arrangements needed to reestablish contact in Moscow, but a mix-up occurred: CIA did not know that Popov was to be assigned to the GDR. He arrived there at the end of September 1955 and was sent to Schwerin, the location of an intelligence point of the intelligence directorate (RU) of GSFG. On 10 January 1956, Popov made contact with a member of the British Military Mission visiting the nearby port of Stralsund. He passed him a letter with a notebook containing intelligence information addressed to the CIA case officer who had handled him in Vienna. The liaison officer's description of Popov and the contents of the letter and notebook left no doubt that Popov had arrived and was again seeking contact. The letter was passed to SIS Berlin, which turned it over to BOB Chief Bill Harvey and his deputy, coauthor David Murphy, who by this time was in charge of BOB's Soviet operations. They immediately alerted CIA headquarters, which gave BOB background on the case and got Kisevalter ready for a new posting to Berlin.[6]

In this way, SIS was alerted to the existence of a sensitive, productive CIA source in Soviet military intelligence in East Germany. Some have speculated that George Blake, KGB's source in SIS who was by now on duty at SIS Berlin, became aware of the case, if not the precise identity of the source. But Blake denies having learned about Popov's meeting with the British Mission.[7] Indeed, Kondrashev has insisted that Blake never mentioned Popov.[8]

In any case, right after receiving the Popov message from SIS Berlin, Harvey and Murphy began planning regular communications with Popov.[9] The British Mission officer, with "remarkable presence of mind," had arranged for Popov to be met in Stralsund on 24 January. With only ten days left to make the meeting and establish the basis for future contacts with Popov in East Germany, Harvey and Murphy asked Col. "Al" Bellonby, chief of the US Military Liaison Mission, to include Stralsund in a tour by a team of his officers on that date. Relations between CIA and the military had not improved much since the early postwar days, but Bellonby had the highest respect for Bill Harvey. The proposition received high-level clearance, the meeting was held, and the East German phase of the Popov operation went forward.[10]

Popov's version of events under KGB interrogation was that CIA sought him out in his new location and forced him to renew his relationship with the agency. According to KGB, a "young woman . . . placed a letter from Grossman [Kisevalter's alias] in Popov's mailbox after Popov refused to accept the letter from her on the street." To reinforce KGB's impression of him as a lady's man, Popov also claimed to have seduced this female courier.[11] But in fact, BOB entrusted subsequent meetings with Popov in the Schwerin area to an elderly male BOB support agent whose reliability had been tested and whose demeanor would not arouse any sort of excitement—or suspicion. He made courier runs about once a month until December 1956. During this part of the operation Popov passed along the first solid evidence of the contents of Khrushchev's secret speech, as well as extensive information on the agent nets run by the RU GSFG.[12]

But the meetings with BOB's elderly courier and the secret messages from Popov sometimes relayed through other channels were as frustrating as they were valuable. Kisevalter had arrived from Washington by this time and was tucked away in a small office at BOB, supposedly reviewing Berlin tunnel material for leads. Both he and Popov were eager for personal meetings to resolve the normal misunderstandings that crop up in guarded, indirect communications. Besides, the warm personal relationship that had blossomed between Kisevalter and Popov in Vienna had helped the source stay on course. Kisevalter had become Popov's friend, father figure, confidante, and adviser—no one else could have managed the case as well.[13]

Arranging for trips to East Berlin or RU GSFG Headquarters in Wuensdorf as cover for crossing into West Berlin was never simple, but Popov managed to make three visits while still in Schwerin. Some of them were hair-raisers for the BOB case officers. When Popov arrived in West Berlin for one meeting, for example, he had forgotten the location of the safe house. He had left the notebook with his emergency telephone numbers in Schwerin, so he returned to Karlshorst, where he called his wife in Schwerin to get the numbers. He then crossed over to West Berlin, called the BOB switchboard, spoke to his case officer, and finally reached the meeting place. Even after his transfer to East Berlin, he had problems with the Berlin transit system. Once he went to an East Berlin station and boarded an express elevated train that passed through West Berlin to Potsdam. When Popov got off he was accosted by a Soviet military policeman who then called his sergeant. Although the sergeant allowed Popov to board a train back through West Berlin, he also reported the incident, and Popov was reprimanded for having gone to West Berlin without permission. On another occasion Popov arrived early for a meeting, so he casually went around the corner to a bar for a couple of beers.[14]

In a meeting in West Berlin at the end of March 1957, Popov produced an intelligence bombshell that was to have serious repercussions

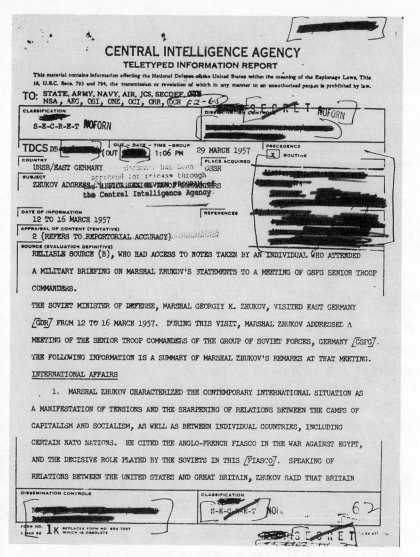

CIA teletyped information report, 29 March 1957, regarding Zhukov address to GSFG troop commanders. KGB deduced that the source of the report was Popov, who was later executed as a spy.

for his security. Marshal Georgy Zhukov had just completed a visit to GSFG, during which he had addressed senior troop commanders. His speech touched on several sensitive areas, like the need for caution in revealing Soviet military secrets to the East German People's Army, details on the Soviet military intervention in Hungary, and specifics on Soviet military contingency strategies (a plan to reach the English Channel on the second day of war, for example). Zhukov covered GSFG combat readiness and discipline as well as new Soviet weapons developments, and he attempted to play down the atomic capabilities of the US Army. The text of this speech was given to CIA by Popov and distributed by CIA on 29 March 1957 under tight controls and very limited distribution.[15]

The report was sent to London under equally tight controls. Because the content dealt with the Soviet Army in Germany, the report made its way to the SIS station in Berlin. Naturally the source of the report was disguised. But the Popov case was of course known to SIS, and SIS and CIA had continued to communicate about various aspects of the case.[16] Thus, when the report finally reached SIS Berlin, it was probably seen by George Blake, who was responsible for Soviet operations. Blake made clear in his autobiography that he gave everything of interest that crossed his desk to KGB. Presumably he passed along the Zhukov report.[17]

KGB's account of how it became aware of the Zhukov report is sharply different: a "friendly service" provided a copy of a report of the Zhukov speech that the Americans had received from one of their agents. KGB counterintelligence investigators assumed that the source had been at the meeting at which Zhukov spoke, and Popov's name was on a list of attendees. This finding was matched with the earlier KGB Vienna report that had been shelved awaiting further evidence. It was then decided to have Zvezdenkov, an experienced counterintelligence operative, start an investigation in Karlshorst without identifying Popov as the suspect. Zvezdenkov was to be supported by the KGB apparat, but his reports on the investigation would go directly to the top of KGB.

The report on Zhukov's speech had an explosive effect at KGB headquarters, and not only because it revealed a high-level American penetration somewhere in GSFG. For Georgy Zhukov, the greatest Russian war hero, had himself become a highly controversial figure. He had returned from "exile" after Stalin's death and had been named first deputy minister of defense. Upon replacing Bulganin as defense minister in

February 1955, Zhukov had moved to reduce the size and influence of political organs in the Soviet military. This effort alienated members of the sacrosanct Chief Political Directorate and also many in the Central Committee. In May 1956 he had prepared a devastating attack on Stalin's wartime leadership for a CPSU plenum that was never held, an action that further alienated powerful hardliners like Molotov in the Presidium. Further, even though Zhukov supported Khrushchev in his June 1957 showdown with the Molotov-Malenkov group, relations between the two were never congenial: Khrushchev fired Zhukov in October 1957. The revelation that Zhukov's secret speech was known to the West came at a time when the Presidium was racked by internal conflict. The pressures on KGB to investigate the leak must have been enormous.[18]

Meanwhile, Popov had been pulling strings with a friend in GRU personnel to arrange a transfer to the GRU Strategic Intelligence Operational Group in Karlshorst. By April the new assignment was approved. Murphy, who had been monitoring meetings with Popov, was introduced to him in anticipation of his move. But Kisevalter remained in charge; it would have been impossible for any newcomer to achieve the level of trust and confidence that Kisevalter had with Popov.

At the end of June, Popov arrived in Karlshorst, was placed in the illegals section of the Opergruppa, and went to work almost immediately. The nature of his activities confirmed that the GRU Opergruppa took Berlin's role in illegals support just as seriously as did KGB. During this summer Popov dispatched two illegals, received two returning to Moscow via Berlin, and handled one who was undergoing training for ultimate assignment in a German-speaking area. In addition to the information he provided on the illegals he handled, Popov gave BOB a complete description of the GRU Opergruppa's organizational structure, as well as its personnel and offices in Karlshorst.

In a bizarre twist to this story, an Asian journalist showed his BOB contact a detailed report on Zhukov's GDR trip, which he claimed had been given to him by Yevgeny Pitovranov, chief of the KGB Karlshorst apparat.[19] This report contained many of the same items in the Popov report. But the journalist's BOB case officer was unaware of the Popov case and attached no special significance to the Zhukov piece. For some time the journalist had been receiving briefings in the Soviet embassy from an East Berlin official (identified by him as Pitovranov) for the purpose of promulgating the Soviet position in Western and Third

World media. Was the Zhukov report a routine handout, or was Pitovranov trying to provoke a reaction through the journalist, whom he continued to use as a regular press outlet?[20]

Had Zvezdenkov done a review of security cases in Berlin over the year 1956–57, he would have known that Western services were zeroing in on Karlshorst. BOB had targeted an RU GSFG unit there, using leads furnished by a defected KGB OO Karlshorst agent who herself was involved in investigating that unit. BOB had also attempted to persuade the chief of the East German military intelligence service to defect; this service was under the tutelage of Popov's GRU Opergruppa. In September 1957 Popov reported on Soviet plans to step up the continuing reduction of numbers of Germans in the Karlshorst compound. He also reported that KGB sweep teams were routinely searching for transmitters in GRU offices, probably as a result of KGB discovery of the BOB chandelier bug in Karlshorst. According to Zvezdenkov, a special surveillance team was sent from Moscow to begin spot surveillance of Popov. Organized from Second Chief Directorate officers who had served in Karlshorst, the team concentrated on covering Popov in East Berlin. Surveillance by this team in West Berlin was considered too risky.[21]

In October, Popov was responsible for dispatching a female illegal, Margarita Tairova, via Paris to New York, where she was to meet her husband, another GRU illegal. CIA had informed FBI of her arrival, and she came under surveillance by FBI, which spotted her meeting with her husband. The couple later reported to GRU that they had felt watched but had eluded their surveillants and had used their emergency escape plan. Soon after this incident, Popov went on home leave to the USSR, returning in January 1958. He had detected no threats to his own situation, though he noted that in the wake of Zhukov's removal the atmosphere at GRU Headquarters was gloomy. But according to Zvezdenkov, KGB was very concerned about the number of GRU illegals, including the Tairovas, whom Popov might have compromised and was fearful that Popov had reported extensively on GRU personnel stationed abroad.[22]

After Popov's return from leave his BOB operation continued, seemingly undisturbed. In March, Popov reported on the presence in Karlshorst of GRU Gen. P. P. Melkishev, who was there to meet his ace Swedish spy, Stig Wennerstroem.[23] Melkishev's presence at the Opergruppa in connection with a case so sensitive might suggest that GRU had no suspicion that it faced security problems, but signs were appearing of a developing KGB investigation. At about the same time, for example, Popov told his BOB case officers that Capt. Yevgeny Netsvetailo had been transferred to the Opergruppa from an RU GSFG intelligence point in Karlshorst. Netsvetailo was the same officer who had been investigated in spring 1956 by Colonel Shatalov's KGB Military Counterintelligence unit in Karlshorst—an investigation in which the banana queen played a key part. It would have been standard procedure for Shatalov's people to use Netsvetailo as an informer within the GRU Opergruppa afterward.[24]

During May and June 1958, Popov went on home leave. In July an old friend of his, Ivan Markovich Stakh, appeared at his birthday party. Popov and Stakh, a KGB First Chief Directorate officer, had met as classmates at a refresher course of the Military-Diplomatic Academy in Moscow. The wives of both men were from Kalinin, northeast of Moscow, and both men stayed there while taking the course. They became friends during the long commuter train rides between the two cities. Stakh turned up in East Berlin in 1958 for an operational meeting, reported into the Karlshorst apparat, and then looked up his good friend Popov. Was this meeting coincidence, or had it been planned by KGB?[25]

More sinister was the sudden interest taken in Popov by Lt. Col. Dmitry Fyodorovich Sknarin, who was responsible for counterintelligence coverage of the Opergruppa. Normally, Sknarin contented himself with socializing with the Opergruppa senior staff, but in mid-July he suddenly began participating in the volleyball games played by GRU officers. This behavior was so obviously uncharacteristic that one GRU officer remarked, "It isn't enough that they have informers among us, he [Sknarin] even comes to observe us himself!" Once, after Sknarin had missed a few games, he was kidded by some GRU officers who wanted to know why he failed to appear for physical training.

As these signs of KGB interest in the GRU Opergruppa multiplied, they were all dutifully reported by Popov. He was not indifferent to them, nor was he unaware of the role of Shatalov, Sknarin, and other military counterintelligence personnel in Karlshorst. He knew that they were subordinate to the GSFG counterintelligence directorate in Potsdam and that they were responsible for the security of all military units, including GRU, in the Berlin garrison. He was also aware of the distinction between the KGB military counterintelligence unit and the KGB apparat under Pitovranov and later Korotkov. He was even able to describe the role of the apparat in performing file checks on GRU agent candidates. Popov was not an innocent in regard to the attentions being paid to the Opergruppa, but as so often happens in the world of counterintelligence, he harbored an unrealistic hope that they would never reach him.

As the weeks passed, Popov's life seemed on track, although he continued to worry about his lack of operational accomplishments. To assist him, BOB had one of its American student agents pretend to respond to Popov's pitch to become a GRU agent. Although it might have seemed a good idea at the time, it may have backfired. Later another GRU officer was assigned to work on the case with Popov. Because Popov spoke no English, it seemed a logical move by GRU. But BOB should have seen the signal of GRU's doubts about the legitimacy of the American student's recruitment.[26]

KGB's concern over the Tairovas' being followed in New York had not resurfaced since Popov had originally been questioned about it. Then, on 8 November, Popov called BOB for an emergency meeting. Agitated, he said that a message had arrived from Moscow posing questions about his Yugoslav girlfriend, with whom he had continued to correspond while in East Germany. Unbeknownst to Popov, the woman had turned against Communism as a result of the Soviet suppression of the Hungarian "freedom fighters," testified against the Austrian Communist Party's role in election frauds, and by August 1958 had informed the Viennese police of her earlier relationship with Popov.

The problem escalated in October, when the police were called to prevent an intoxicated GRU officer from entering the woman's apartment in Vienna. The ensuing flap and a GRU file check on the woman again brought her relationship with Popov to official attention. In his response to Moscow, Popov was required to write a letter of self-criticism. In it he minimized the number of letters he had written and claimed operational justification. Popov and the members of the BOB "Popov team" hoped that would be the end of it.[27]

Popov's involvement in the work of the Opergruppa seemed perfectly normal during the following days. He was even made duty officer for the night of 15–16 November, a job that gave him access to all of the unit's files. (This may have been a trap.) The next morning a cable arrived from GRU Headquarters directing Popov, as the principal case officer, to hand-deliver to Moscow the file on the American student.

According to Zvezdenkov, by this time the GRU had been advised by the KGB of the necessity of removing Popov from Berlin.

Still, neither Popov nor his BOB case officers thought it particularly odd that Popov had been called to Moscow to discuss an ongoing case. There was certainly no talk of Popov's defecting. Popov would undoubtedly have resisted, but had BOB known that he was in imminent danger, it would have urged him to defect. Actually, the main topic Popov wanted to discuss with BOB was Khrushchev's 10 November statement abrogating the provisions of the Potsdam Declaration concerning Germany and four-power control of Berlin. As the BOB officers began putting on their coats at the end of the meeting, Popov was still trying to decide what presents to take to his friends in Moscow.[28]

Nothing more was heard from Popov in Berlin. On 8 December, KGB Chairman Ivan Serov was transferred to head GRU. We know that Khrushchev had been seeking to replace Serov in KGB, but the timing seemed to relate to the Popov case. On the same day, a reliable BOB source reported that Valentin Zvezdenkov, the veteran KGB counterintelligence officer who we now know was controlling the Popov investigation, left permanently for Moscow. The same source told BOB that on 17 December Popov's wife processed baggage for return to the USSR.

On Christmas Day 1958, Popov signaled for a meeting in Moscow. The site chosen indicated that it would a quick "brush" meeting, one at which he would simply pass a message. He failed to appear, but the meeting took place on the alternate date, 4 January. At this meeting the message passed stated that he had been dismissed from GRU, placed in the reserves, and sent home to Kalinin to await a new assignment. Zvezdenkov explained that this action was taken by GRU at KGB insistence to keep Popov away from classified GRU information while giving KGB time to determine how the Americans would handle the case in Moscow and whether Popov had accomplices. KGB surveillance continued, but Popov was not aware that he was being followed.

Popov signaled for a second meeting on 21 January; he passed no message but was given one from CIA. This meeting was observed by KGB agents, and afterward he was watched around the clock. KGB agents reported that as of 3 January 1959, the "American radio-intelligence center in Frankfurt am Main" began to broadcast coded messages to an agent in the USSR.[29]

Then KGB got a break. To ensure that Popov would have the new communications instructions before leaving Moscow, a coded message had been prepared by CIA to be mailed to his home in Kalinin in the event that he did not request a second January brush contact. Through a mix-up, the back-up letter was mailed even though Popov had in fact asked for the meeting.[30] The letter was intercepted, photographed, reinserted in the envelope, and put back in the mail. The code was then deciphered by KGB technicians. The text, dealing with matters like radio broadcasts, new addresses abroad to which he could write, and requirements following up Popov's reporting on nuclear submarines, made clear his intelligence involvement on behalf of CIA. His ability to elicit information on Soviet nuclear submarine production from unsuspecting naval officers confirmed that he remained a serious security threat. KGB and GRU leaders decided to arrest him during his next visit to Moscow.[31]

During the evening of 18 February, Zvezdenkov was at the KGB club when a breathless officer interrupted him with the news that the chief of the surveillance department needed to speak with him right away. It seems that Popov had met a lover near Serebrianny Bor, a wooded area northwest of Moscow. Surprised by her irate husband, he had departed the premises at high speed—leaving his surveillance behind. Agents eventually caught up with him, but the incident convinced KGB that it could not risk Popov's escaping to the West. He was taken into custody that night, and his Kalinin house was searched. There KGB found his communications gear and the text of a letter he had prepared to pass at the next Moscow meeting. He was taken to Lefortovo prison and the interrogations began.[32]

Popov appeared for a third brush contact on 18 March, looking fit and dressed as a full colonel in the transportation corps. He passed a message written in the usual pocket-sized notebook. The message said he been assigned to a transportation unit in the Sverdlovsk region and then explained that he would not use the Berlin letter drop that had been proposed to him at the previous contact. It also asked for a Moscow address and included a few bits of military information far below his usual standard. Apart from the mediocre quality of the military data it contained, danger signals in this message and in one received from Sverdlovsk at the Berlin drop raised suspicions that Popov was under Soviet control. The message in the notebook was written conventionally, front to back, whereas previously Popov had deliberately written from back to front. Moreover, this message, unlike his others, was not numbered.[33]

These suspicions were well founded. During his interrogation Popov had quickly confessed but had insisted that he had acted under duress and had little involvement with the Americans. KGB, meanwhile, was faced with the necessity of recovering those GRU illegals still located abroad under various false identities. Because Popov seemed genuinely contrite, they decided to run him as a double agent during the several months needed to organize the safe return of the GRU illegals to the USSR. Popov apparently believed that his cooperation would lessen the severity of his punishment, so Zvezdenkov felt he would not signal CIA that he was under KGB control. The proposal was approved, even though it would mean allowing Popov to meet his CIA contact in Moscow. To minimize the number of these contacts, Popov was to be notionally assigned to Alapaevsk in Sverdlovsk oblast. His conditions of confinement were relaxed to avoid giving him the appearance of a prisoner. Although Popov was to be kept under close but covert guard during the first contact with CIA on 18 March, it was risky. To Zvezdenkov's relief, all went well.

A second meeting with his CIA contact took place in Moscow on 23 July: Popov was given detailed CIA requirements on Soviet missile launch sites. (Apparently the KGB officers who selected this area in the Urals for Popov's notional assignment were unaware of the missile site construction under way there. CIA analysts jumped on this opportunity and came up with very specific questions.)[34] On 18 September, Popov received new instructions from CIA for future contacts in Moscow on bus 107. By this time however, KGB had assured the security of the GRU illegals, so a decision was made to end Popov's charade at the next meeting, in October.[35]

For CIA, meanwhile, the further exchanges with Popov during the summer heightened suspicions concerning his status. Then, at the 18 September meeting in a restaurant men's room, Popov succeeded in passing a real message that he had prepared without KGB's knowledge. The message was printed in pencil in Popov's handwriting on eight small pieces of paper, tightly rolled into a cylinder the size of a cigarette. It was wrapped in cloth and suspended inside Popov's trousers by a string. From the contents of the message, which in style was completely consistent with the Popov his case officer had known over many years, it seemed probable that it had been prepared over a period of several days. In this message Popov explained that he had been arrested in February and that he had attempted to minimize the extent of his CIA work, picturing himself a "victim of your [CIA's] aggression."[36] Popov also confirmed CIA's suspicions that the meetings held with him since February had been under KGB control. He was promised that if he cooperated they would run him as a double agent in Berlin. Although Popov said his treatment had improved after the July meeting, KGB Colonel Zvezdenkov, whom Popov named as the officer heading the investigation, had told Popov it was too early to talk about sending him to Berlin to continue to play this double-agent operation there.[37]

In his secret message, Popov theorized that KGB was preparing for a propaganda coup regarding his case, to be announced during upcoming talks between Khrushchev and President Eisenhower. He pleaded with CIA to intervene on his behalf and emphasized the need to conceal the existence of this secret message from KGB, which seemed well informed on the US embassy. Popov knew that KGB still mistrusted him. In a section of his secret message devoted to Marshal Zhukov, Popov reported that immediately after his arrest he had been grilled intensively by two general officers about Zhukov's speech to Group of Soviet Forces, Germany, officers in March 1957. One of the examining officers was Maj. Gen. Oleg Mikhailovich Gribanov, chief of KGB's Second (counterintelligence) Directorate.

Why was the letter so important when CIA already suspected that Popov was under Soviet control? Above all, it was an extraordinary act of courage and exemplary tradecraft on Popov's part. The letter not only confirmed American suspicions about Popov but specified what KGB knew and didn't know about the details of his collaboration with CIA. Equally important, it revealed KGB plans for a well-timed propaganda exploitation of the case. The single most significant detail in the letter, though, was that the interrogators had focused on Zhukov. The West's acquisition of the Zhukov speech had of course sparked KGB suspicion of Popov. But Zhukov's star was falling, and the familiar intertwining of Kremlin politics and counterintelligence issues may also have driven the interrogation. What better way to denigrate a general whose popularity galled Khrushchev than to pressure Popov into revealing some link between Zhukov and the American spy?[38]

The American student recruited by Popov with BOB's help met with his GRU handler on 14 October 1959. It was a sensitive meeting: CIA already knew that Popov had been compromised but wanted to preserve the student in his double-agent role for as long as possible. The BOB case officer explained the situation and left it to the student to decide whether he would make the meeting. He did, and it went off without incident. Then, at a brush meeting on bus 107 in Moscow on 16 October, KGB brought the game to an end in a blaze of publicity by arresting Popov and detaining the CIA officer found with him on the bus. Popov's forebodings had been correct. The arrest of BOB support assets who had been involved in the Popov case had already begun. Thus ended the illegals game for BOB.

Popov's case went to a closed trial before the Military Collegium of the Soviet Supreme Court on 6–7 January 1960. According to the KGB account, "Considering Popov's sincere confession . . . [and] his desire to cooperate fully to reduce the damage caused by his treason and to save people devoted to him, KGB requested that the collegium not give the death penalty to Popov." Nonetheless, Popov was found guilty and sentenced to death. He was executed by firing squad in June 1960. With the Americans and the Soviets in the middle of a Berlin crisis in 1960, there was little room in Moscow for clemency. The final decision was probably made by Khrushchev himself.[39]

The United States owed Popov a great deal. For several years he was the nation's best guarantee of "early warning," and he produced the most valuable intelligence on the Soviet military of any source in that period. Because of him Soviet military intelligence became an open book. He identified more than 650 GRU officers and provided hundreds of leads to GRU agents. The KGB account pays tribute to his accomplishments by quoting the conclusions of CIA analysts that "the reporting of one man had direct and significant influence on the military organization of the United States—its doctrine and tactics—and permitted the Pentagon to save at least 500 million dollars in its scientific research program."[40] Finally, Popov showed immense courage in preparing and passing to CIA the secret warning that he was under KGB control. The origins of that courage and his motivation to sound the alarm can perhaps be found in a comment Popov made to George Kisevalter just before leaving Vienna in 1955: "This is what I like about your organization: you find time to drink and relax, and you have respect for the individual. With us, of course, the individual is nothing, and the government is everything."[41]

PART IV

Tests of Strength

15

KGB and MfS: Partners or Competitors?

Since the Berlin Wall has come down, the opening of East German Ministry of State Security files has produced an avalanche of publications on MfS organization and operations. But the Soviet side of the Stasi story has not yet been revealed. It is told here for the first time, based on KGB documents and accounts by KGB officers who worked directly with MfS.

During its nascent years, the East German security service and its Soviet tutors were thwarted by the twin shocks of Beria's attempts to "reform" Soviet state security and of the 17 June uprising. While BOB was doggedly digging the tunnel, enjoying its unprecedented product and using it to support a variety of operations against the Soviets in Karlshorst, state security veteran Yevgeny Petrovich Pitovranov was trying to rebuild Stasi and integrate it into the Warsaw Pact security system. To achieve these goals, Pitovranov had to contend with criticism from the new KGB chairman, Ivan Serov, in Moscow and with Walter Ulbricht's attempts to use Stasi to quash his own political opponents.

After Beria's downfall, Pitovranov was called in by Nikolai Shatalin, then a deputy minister of internal affairs, and told he was being sent to Berlin to take over: "Following the putsch, things need fixing," Shatalin said.[1] Pitovranov, well suited for this position because of his extensive experience in Soviet domestic security and counterintelligence, was

285

extremely critical of the German service and its performance during the riots. In a 7 August 1953 letter to USSR Internal Affairs Minister Sergei Kruglov, he commented that "the events of 17 June and their consequences demonstrated the scope of hostile work against the GDR but were a complete surprise to our security forces and those of the GDR." Furthermore, the GDR state security departments "were in no condition to cope with hostile underground forces." Pitovranov noted, for example, that "the GDR security forces had only four informants in the 8,000 strong SPD organization in East Berlin and possessed no agents in the trade unions and none in churches." He claimed that "in consideration of the weakness of the German security system and the stirring up of hostile elements in Germany," his Karlshorst apparat must itself work against those forces "organizing hostile subversion in the GDR."[2]

Pitovranov then explained to Moscow that the Karlshorst apparat would have to undertake certain tasks "on a temporary basis until normal conditions in the GDR are restored." He proposed using the apparat's existing Fifth Department, already responsible for working against hostile elements penetrating the GDR state apparatus, to create "a secret-political department composed of three sectors" to cover "leading organs of the bourgeois political parties" in the GDR as well as "West German and West Berlin subversive centers and their underground organizations on GDR territory."[3] Pitovranov also intended to assign additional personnel to the senior district advisers elsewhere in the GDR "to combat the underground, depending on the conditions in each district."[4] He suggested adding a group of inspectors to "provide critical assistance and timely control over the work of the district offices." In conclusion, Pitovranov noted that both High Commissioner Semyonov and First Deputy Yudin had approved his proposal, and he requested a decision from the minister.[5]

In sum, Pitovranov's reaction to the situation he faced in summer 1953 was, first, to declare the East German security services incapable of dealing with the problem, and second, to increase the strength of his own apparat to cope. This position ran counter to efforts undertaken before 17 June to build up MfS as a formally independent entity, one ready to take over responsibility for state security in East Germany. Although there can be no doubt that the June events shook the Soviets badly, this do-it-ourselves approach also reflected the split within KGB over the future of East German state security. Would MfS become a truly independent partner, or remain a KGB auxiliary?

Although Pitovranov took immediate steps to improve the Karlshorst apparat's ability to deal with the situation after 17 June, he realized that something still had to be done to improve relations with the East German service. Much of the difficulty stemmed from the way the Karlshorst apparat was organized. Each of its departments was responsible to a comparable department in the Moscow headquarters of the foreign intelligence directorate—political intelligence, counterintelligence, scientific and technical intelligence, communications intelligence, émigré affairs, and illegals operations. In Karlshorst these departments not only ran their own operations (about which the East Germans were unaware) but also acted in an advisory capacity to an analogous element of MfS. In both conducting unilateral operations and advising their MfS opposite numbers, the Karlshorst departments followed directives from their respective Moscow controllers.

But compartmentation between these departments was very strict, both in Moscow and Karlshorst. Whereas in Moscow routine responsibility for administration of the apparat, as well as direction of its political intelligence operations against German targets, came under the German department of the First Chief Directorate, this department was not privy to the activities of the others. Orders would go to Karlshorst from the counterintelligence department, for example, without the German department being informed.

In Karlshorst, Pitovranov, as the senior officer, was theoretically responsible for all KGB activities in his area and could change or even countermand these directives. But doing so would have been difficult—the chief's office in Karlshorst was not an operational staff but was primarily responsible for administration and conducting logistical support, maintaining files, and doing name checks for each element. The situation became even more complex if an operational directive from Moscow to one of the Karlshorst department heads was signed by the chairman or a deputy chairman of KGB. In this case, the chief of the apparat would inform the KGB chairman of any possible negative consequences to the directive and place the whole responsibility for the operation on Moscow. It was a situation not unfamiliar to the chief of any large CIA station.

This chaotic state of affairs seriously hindered work with the East Germans. When Pitovranov arrived, each of the departments in Karlshorst was responsible for training that element of MfS which corresponded to its specialty. The results were uneven and undermined the overall training and readiness of MFS. Arguments often arose between officers responsible for advisory work and those handling cases solely under MGB control. Those who wanted to take over an MFS operation against an American agent network in East Germany often accused advisers "of working for Gehlen and not MGB."[6] Given these circumstances, Pitovranov decided to create a separate advisory group. To head his new department, he chose Vasily Ilich Bulda, a tall, tough Ukrainian who had been desk officer for the Karlshorst apparat in Moscow and earlier an officer in its counterintelligence department.[7] Pitovranov also brought in other veterans such as Khachik Gevorkovich Oganesian and Vasily Fedorovich Samoilenko to strengthen the apparat team responsible for rebuilding the East German service.[8]

To deal with the criticism leveled at the Karlshorst organization in a way that would not offend Moscow bureaucrats, Pitovranov asked each of the foreign intelligence directorate's components—such as counterintelligence, for example—to send a representative to the new advisory department.[9] Thus the advisory department would comprise representatives from each speciality. The advisers had offices in MFS headquarters and were paid by MFS. The advisers still considered themselves responsible to their respective apparat departments, but the new arrangement made it easier to integrate the apparat's overall approach to MFS. Nevertheless, the apparat continued to run unilateral operations.[10]

Pitovranov, while introducing Bulda to Walter Ulbricht, promised that KGB would no longer recruit sources within MFS, a practice about which the SED chief had complained.[11] Pitovranov also expressed hope that as the East Germans acquired more skill and competence MFS could be freed from tight KGB controls, allowing a reduction in KGB advisory personnel in both East Berlin and the districts. KGB advisers, for example, typically reviewed applications for MFS staff employment and investigated candidates' backgrounds.[12]

At the same time, Pitovranov cautioned Ulbricht that as the KGB presence diminished, the SED Politburo and Central Committee would have to assume much more responsibility for directing and controlling the East German services. A key issue was the need for East Germans to recruit more agents in the West. In cases where MFS officers lacked experience, Soviet advisers were to take over MFS leads on Westerners of interest to KGB. This marked the beginning of a new drive for intelligence on the West, an effort that had suffered since the KI residencies had been dissolved in 1951–52 and incorporated into the Karlshorst apparat.[13]

Serov Defends the Germans

The new approach irked someone in Moscow: on 5 April 1954, Ivan Aleksandrovich Serov, now chairman of the newly created Committee of State Security (KGB), sent Pitovranov a cautionary letter stating that "the condition of German operational work depends first of all on the level of leadership they receive from the advisory department, which, as you know, is functioning unsatisfactorily and is not providing adequate assistance to the German MVD organs." Serov added, "We cannot agree . . . with your statement that 'the overwhelming majority of the officials of the GDR MfS are so far unable to work independently.' If this mood were to spread among the Soviet advisers and the leadership of the East German state security, it would affect their work."[14]

To support his claim that the GDR state security services already had enough experienced personnel, Serov highlighted measures undertaken by German state security in "eliminating antidemocratic formations and nests of spies within the territory of the GDR, as well as the penetration of West Berlin spy centers by several agents."[15] But other KGB counterintelligence officers disapproved of the mass roundups of Western agents, many of whom were simply backup sources for the West in case the borders were closed. The arrests were made to generate publicity, and although they may have boosted SED's morale, they did not represent good counterintelligence policy. One officer stated that he knew of 130 agents of the Gehlen Organization in the GDR who came on the air with their radios only once every two or three months to indicate that they were still there. He urged that these agents not be arrested because new, unidentified agents would simply be sent to replace them. He argued, "Why not leave them in place . . . [given that] we knew who and where they were?"[16]

Serov also criticized Soviet advisers for not knowing about valuable agents run by the Germans, for not giving their German operations officers concrete guidance on cases, and for not being familiar with the status of work in these German units. In Serov's view, Karlshorst officers seldom visited advisers in outlying areas to provide them with practical assistance in dealing with their GDR colleagues. The Serov letter then came down hard with his main concern: weakness in the work of the GDR state security organs against hostile intelligence centers in West Berlin. He insisted that "almost nothing had been done to recruit individuals working directly for the intelligence services of the enemy, nor have they recruited any agents from among the officials of these services."[17]

To combat this problem, Serov suggested that Soviet case officers recruit agents within the Western services whose information was not only valuable for KGB but also could be used to check the accuracy of discoveries by the GDR's state security organs. KGB's top leadership was trying in this case to straddle a contradiction typical in relations between KGB and the East European services still under its control. Moscow wanted its officers to be able to take over the best East German leads while it encouraged MfS to expand its own coverage.[18]

Pitovranov, with Serov's guidance, ordered the creation of "active, offensive operations against hostile intelligence and other subversive organs and services in West Berlin." KGB wanted to give this responsibility to the "Special Department for West Berlin, created at KGB recommendation in the Berlin District Directorate of GDR State Security." It would recruit "broad agent networks capable of systematically informing [KGB] of the situation in West Berlin, reporting in timely fashion of hostile actions being prepared against [it], and ensuring that measures are carried out to disorganize the actions of subversive centers and organizations of the adversary in West Berlin." This special department was also to create "agent nets from among the residents of West Berlin working in the GDR and from GDR residents working in West Berlin."[19]

After designating which East German service departments were to be involved in the program, the KGB plan listed those hostile intelligence services of primary interest. Seven American installations were named, including the radio station RIAS.[20] The American listing had many errors, and although there were several entries for the French, the British were not even mentioned. This was a curious omission, perhaps indicating a concern for George Blake's security. The coverage of installations allegedly affiliated with the Gehlen Organization appeared extensive, even though KGB was also running sensitive penetrations of that group (as the case of Heinz Felfe confirms).[21]

In time, the GDR security and intelligence services grew in size and effectiveness. As this happened, the name of the KGB apparat in Karlshorst underwent several changes during the 1950s to keep pace with the developing relationships between KGB and the GDR services. On 10 May 1954, KGB Berlin was called the Inspectorate for Security Questions under the High Commissioner (Inspektsiia po voprosam bezopasnosti), and corresponding inspectorates were created in each of the Bezirk (district) centers. In 1955 the unit was renamed Apparatus of the KGB Senior Adviser attached to the GDR Ministry of State Security (Apparat starshego sovetnika KGB SSSR pri MGB GDR). A short time later it reverted to the designation Apparatus of the KGB Representative in Germany, which it bore until 1992. The advisory department under which KGB had controlled and directed MfS operations gave way to a coordination and liaison function known as "K i S," from the Russian Koordinatsiia i sviaz' (coordination and liaison). Variations of these name changes also occurred in KGB district offices.[22]

The district offices, found in each Bezirk center, were a vital part of KGB's presence in the GDR. Usually located in buildings controlled by the Soviet military komendatura, their strength depended on the size and importance of the district but seldom exceeded twenty officers. Their mission was threefold: to serve as liaison between KGB and the district MfS directorate, to develop and run operations against KGB targets independently of MfS, and to provide support to the unilateral operations of the Karlshorst apparat. In addition, the districts were required to submit regular status reports on the political situation in their areas. The reports tended to be uniformly upbeat and uncritical; to report critical comments would have invited follow-up and investigation. In order to accomplish these tasks, the KGB district offices maintained a network of support agents and contacts at local GDR government offices, police departments, commercial firms, and educational institutions. Visits between Karlshorst and district KGB officers were frequent, control by the apparat was tight, and district chiefs attended weekly staff meetings in Karlshorst.[23] But the transition from the role of adviser to that of liaison was not always easy. Although KGB tried to assign and retain district officers who got along well with their German counterparts, friction often developed. KGB officers were often impatient with the growing reluctance of German officials, particularly those in MfS, to follow orders "without question." This shift in attitudes was apparent at all levels of Soviet-German interaction.[24]

The Ulbricht Factor

In all Communist countries during these years, control of the security and intelligence services rested with the party leadership. Khrushchev had firm control over KGB, for example, and Ulbricht maintained power over MfS. This political dynamic dominated KGB Karlshorst's relations with MfS. The difficulties of negotiating with SED, aggravated by dissension within KGB itself, became acute in the period leading up to the raising of the Wall in 1961 and affected Karlshorst's performance at this critical time.

Ulbricht was obsessed with defeating his opposition within the ruling SED, even though these elements had never posed a serious challenge to his leadership. In fact, Ulbricht had eliminated a strong rival, State Security Minister Wilhelm Zaisser, following the 17 June uprising and Beria's arrest. But he was unnerved that he had been unable to put his own man, Erich Mielke, in Zaisser's place: instead, he had to be content with the appointment of Ernst Wollweber. Although Mielke, as MfS counterintelligence chief, must have borne some responsibility for the June events, this had not been the chief obstacle to his appointment: his contentious relationship with some Soviet leaders was probably the main reason he had failed to get the job. By late 1954, Ulbricht had begun his crusade to oust Wollweber. He was determined to change his minister of state security and to solidify his personal authority over this vital component of state power. To accomplish these goals he needed KGB help, and he lost no time trying to secure it.

Karlshorst KGB Chief Pitovranov recalls being invited to dinner at the Soviet embassy in East Berlin by Ambassador Georgy Pushkin. Ulbricht, their guest, expressed his view that Wollweber was a weak security minister. "We must consider how to strengthen this important sector," Ulbricht said. Pitovranov agreed that Wollweber was "simply not up to the job" but insisted that "the Soviet side had not been involved in selecting [him]."[25]

Pitovranov's protests that the Soviets had had nothing to do with Wollweber's 1953 appointment did not convince Ulbricht, possibly because he knew of Wollweber's close ties to the Soviets over the years. Ulbricht persisted, asking Pitovranov what kind of intelligence and counterintelligence service the Soviets had created if it could not be kept informed of the activities of the SED "opposition." Ulbricht cited a meeting at the Restaurant Volga in East Berlin a few days before that had been attended by such party rivals as Wollweber, Otto Grotewohl, and Karl Schirdewan but about which he had not been informed. Ulbricht also decried his failure to hear of slurs made against him by Schirdewan during a flight from Peking with Soviet Politburo ideologue Mikhail Suslov.

Pitovranov first told Ulbricht that Soviet Chekists were forbidden to investigate the leadership of the Communist Party and government in the USSR and that MfS officers probably were bound by a similar rule. He then made light of these attacks on Ulbricht: "Look here, Schirdewan is a child. He just needs a smart slap on the rear."[26]

Not mollified, Ulbricht asked Pitovranov what he would think of Erich Mielke as a successor to Wollweber. Pitovranov remarked that Ulbricht had asked this question before and had been told that it was up to the SED Central Committee. Ulbricht persisted until Pitovranov gave his views. Pitovranov said, "Mielke is a hard and energetic worker who has performed good service in the past. But there are some aspects of his more distant past that are hard to understand. His brother died in West Berlin, but Mielke never reported this to the SED Central Committee. We do not know the reasons for his silence." Sensing that Ulbricht felt he had to have the approval of KGB to appoint Mielke to this job, Pitovranov went on to say that he did not trust Mielke: "He is crafty and insincere to everyone, including the Soviets, even though he plays the role of a good friend. It would be best if you chose one of your best district first secretaries to be minister and then made a professional like Mielke or Markus Wolf his deputy." It was evident that Pitovranov was fond of Wolf; he called him a decent, completely disciplined person with a good head on his shoulders. But it was well known that there was no love lost between Mielke and Wolf, so Pitovranov's suggestion was never seriously considered.[27]

The matter of Mielke's appointment did not end with the embassy dinner. Before Pitovranov left Karlshorst for a new Moscow assignment, KGB Chairman Serov called him to say that he and KGB veteran Aleksandr Korotkov, a longtime Soviet friend of Ulbricht's, were arriving on other business and would see Pitovranov off. Shortly thereafter, Pitovranov learned what the "other business" was about: the two had met with Ulbricht and had agreed that Mielke would be made GDR minister of state security. According to Pitovranov, Serov and Korotkov returned to Moscow shortly thereafter, loaded down with gifts from a grateful Mielke.[28]

Meanwhile, Ulbricht had been causing problems for the Soviets on other fronts. On 7 February 1955 Serov advised the Central Committee about problems with Ulbricht that had been reported by KGB Karlshorst. Evidently Ulbricht had directed GDR state security organs to increase repressive measures taken against "persons suspected of wrecking and sabotage." In the case of the Ministry of Agriculture, Ulbricht had insisted that "at least 10–12 percent of those working there were enemies" and had "ordered suspects in the ministry to be searched and arrested even if there was no proof of their criminal activity." Ulbricht wanted similar action taken against other ministries, particularly the Ministry of the Construction Industry and the State Secretariat for Coal. When State Secretary Wollweber emphasized the necessity of observing the law, Ulbricht countered, "It would be expedient to instruct the prosecutors, as a temporary measure, to sanction arrest and detention, not for twenty-four hours as the law provided but for two weeks." Serov made clear that "our German friends have been warned by the inspectorate that in dealing with such questions as searches and arrests or a two-week detention of suspects, as demanded by Comrade Ulbricht, it is necessary to use discretion lest innocent people be implicated and an atmosphere of uncertainty be created for leaders in ministries, thus creating a pretext for flight to the West."[29] Serov's letter to the Central Committee may have been in part an effort to demonstrate his support of "socialist legality" and the reforms of the Stalinist-style security organs that had been under way since Beria's ouster. It probably also had its origins in the generally negative view of Ulbricht held by some in Moscow.[30]

In spite of Ulbricht's preference for Mielke, Wollweber hung on, and in November 1955 the State Security Secretariat was once more made an independent ministry with Wollweber as minister. During Wollweber's tenure, the East German service (with Soviet help) had some noteworthy counterintelligence successes. In addition to the operations referred to by Serov in his 5 April 1954 letter, KGB archives reveal that in July–August 1954, Operation Strela (Arrow) resulted in the arrest of 359 persons, among whom were 203 members of the Gehlen Organization and other West German intelligence services. Seven agent radio sets were also captured. Then, in April 1955, a massive operation called Vesna (Spring) was carried out against American, British, and West German intelligence organs, as well as other subversive organizations. As a result, 640 agents were arrested, and four American, five British, and three West German agent nets were liquidated. Thirteen portable agent radio sets, secret writing materials, arms, and other equipment were confiscated.[31] In addition to these counterintelligence successes, Markus Wolf's intelligence group was making its mark. It was to become Hauptverwaltung-Aufklaerung (HVA). It looked as though Stasi, along with other parts of the GDR's national security establishment, was coming of age.

MfS Joins the Warsaw Pact

On 18 January 1956, the GDR announced the creation of a Ministry of National Defense, and the formations of the Barracked People's Police (Kasernierte Volkspolizei) became the National People's Army (National Volksarmee, or NVA). In January, NVA was formally placed under the command of the Warsaw Pact forces led by Soviet Marshal Konev. The East German security and intelligence service, MfS, was in turn brought into a more formal relationship with the other Soviet bloc security services, and thereby invited to a conference of these state security services in Moscow presided over by Serov on 7–11 March 1956. MfS would now be given a say in how the East European services were to operate within the GDR. Serov also had another reason for participating in the conference: he was growing increasingly concerned over evidence that nationalistic sentiments were gaining strength in Hungary and Poland.[32]

The conference agenda covered these points:

1. The necessity of uniting the strength of the intelligence services of the countries participating in this conference against the "principal aggressor governments of the United States and England."
2. Determination of the main direction of intelligence work for each country participating in the conference.
3. The conduct of joint measures against the principal "aggressor states."
4. Exchange of information and reports on the hostile activities of the intelligence services of the adversary against countries in the "democratic camp"[that is, the USSR and its allies].
5. Coordination and mutual assistance in the areas of signal intelligence and operational-technical services.[33]

All the agenda items except the second were discussed in the plenary sessions. The main direction of intelligence work in each country was considered in bilateral meetings between representatives of KGB and the relevant service. The first item was handled by Chairman Serov, who reviewed the international situation for the conferees and emphasized the large sums being spent by the American and British intelligence services for "total espionage." Serov identified "intelligence collection on atomic technology, the aviation industry, the navy, docks, sea lanes, the oil industry, and various military units, as the main areas of concentration of services working against the Soviet Union." In this connection, Serov emphasized the "necessity of struggling against the careless handling of secret documents and the need to improve counterintelligence work in the armed forces." He underscored the "significance of counterintelligence work in the paramilitary police, which in his opinion were in a sorry state a year ago."[34]

Serov also "warned of the enemy's use of nationalist groups to split the politico-moral unity of the people's democracies." He said that "the main base for recruitment of hostile agents was reactionary émigré organizations. By leaning on these organizations, provocations and antidemocratic actions are carried out against the countries of the democratic camp. For this reason it is essential to exchange experiences and coordinate actions."

To disrupt American and British intelligence, the Soviet delegation urged "the acquisition of sources in the leading circles and political parties of capitalist countries who could obtain documentary information on a wide range of basic intelligence questions. . . . It was of special importance to determine the condition of mobilization plans, because in the current situation, when wars are no longer declared, every hour has decisive significance." Also important, according to the Soviet delegation, was "exposing and exploiting the contradictions between imperialist states in the political, economic, and military areas." The Soviets also expressed interest in such areas as active measures, counterintelligence, scientific-technical collection, and the creation of illegal residencies.[35]

The leader of one delegation complained that the absence of direct communications with the GDR MfS had slowed work against hostile centers in West Germany and West Berlin. The GDR delegation explained the special problems of West Berlin and the FRG and made several proposals to improve coordination, including "the exchange of political and operational material (of a general nature), the application of concentrated blows against the hostile centers in West Germany, and the coordination of activity on the GDR's borders with Poland and Czechoslovakia." In his concluding remarks, Serov agreed that the state security services of the people's democracies must maintain contact with the GDR MfS, and that a special group should be established in Berlin to ensure such contact.[36]

The bilateral talks between KGB and the GDR delegation were conducted by Maj. Gen. Aleksandr Semyonovich Paniushkin, the head of foreign intelligence, now KGB's First Chief Directorate. In the Soviet delegation's view, MfS needed to direct its main effort against West Germany and West Berlin, but so must the USSR, Poland, Czechoslovakia, and Hungary. The level of work and the targets to be covered, in their view, should be determined separately for each state. The GDR should create illegal residencies in the most vulnerable targets, and the counterintelligence organs of the people's democracies should concentrate on interfering with émigré organizations in West Germany.[37]

During this discussion, the GDR delegation stated that it needed to conduct operations in France in order to cover the Saarland adequately. This point was of particular interest to BOB, which had been able for several years to observe MfS HVA's efforts in the Saar through reporting from an illegal resident whom it had doubled at the outset of the operation.[38] The bilateral talks ended with a request from the GDR side to define more precisely how cooperation with the state security organs of the people's democracies would be achieved. It was then agreed that operational groups from the people's democracies could not function within the territory of the GDR unless they had the approval of the GDR MfS.[39] This demonstration of bloc solidarity was more apparent than real. Although no hint of dissension is found in KGB accounts of the conference, events were unfolding that were to severely test this solidarity and the loyalty of some East European parties to the Soviet Union.

Khrushchev's "Secret Speech" Sparks Controversy

The trouble began during the Twentieth Party Congress in February 1956. In a twenty-thousand-word speech, Khrushchev denounced Stalin and his reign in terms that his listeners never could have imagined. The speech had repercussions throughout the Communist world. After it, the KGB party organization received a letter from the Central

Committee describing the speech and presenting reactions to it in various countries. KGB officers generally refrained from expressing their opinions on sensitive internal political questions in front of fellow officers lest they be reported, but after the "secret speech" nearly everyone openly wondered what was happening to the country. At the same time, "the chiefs of the East German state security organs seemed even more perplexed than the Soviet officers." Furthermore, as the Karlshorst apparat received negative assessments from East German leaders of the new anti-Stalinist line in the speech, particularly those critical of the failure of Khrushchev to have warned them in advance of this abrupt shift, the decision was made by Pitovranov not to forward the reports to Moscow.[40]

In Berlin, Lt. Col. Pyotr Popov, BOB's source in the intelligence directorate of GSFG, reported on the official briefings and muted personal reactions of fellow officers. The Berlin tunnel, which was in full operation in March 1956, also provided insights. General Grechko had attended the Congress, and he spoke of it to family members on lines that were tapped by BOB.

During the months immediately following the secret speech, Khrushchev abandoned plans to apply military pressure on Poland and accepted new leadership there. But Hungary was another matter. As of 1 November, Imre Nagy, who had become chairman of the Hungarian Council of Ministers following the open revolt that had begun in Budapest in October, was still negotiating through Yuri Andropov, Soviet Ambassador to Hungary, for the full withdrawal of all Soviet troops. When these assurances were not forthcoming, Nagy repudiated the Warsaw Pact and announced Hungary's neutrality. On Sunday morning, 4 November, massive numbers of Soviet forces entered Hungary and crushed hopes for independence.

Perhaps the most violent European reaction to repression of the Hungarian uprising occurred on 5 November in West Berlin. West Berliners, always nervous about Soviet actions and what they meant for their own freedom, were shocked that the Soviets had agreed to withdraw from Hungary and then reintroduced their forces. One hundred thousand angry West Berliners marched in protest along the Avenue of the 17th of June (the former Charlottenburger Chaussee), and for a short while it looked as though they would continue right though the Brandenburg Gate and into East Berlin. At this crucial moment the newly elected mayor of West Berlin, Willy Brandt, dissuaded the crowds from this course. His leadership on the occasion catapulted him into international prominence.

This outburst by the politically sensitive West Berliners was not mirrored by marches in the East. Residents of East Berlin and the rest of the GDR had learned their lesson from the 1953 uprising and remained calm. Indeed, KGB Karlshorst had every reason to be satisfied with the performance of its protégé, MfS, during this period. But the two security forces continued to test the boundaries of their relationship throughout the Cold War.

Korotkov Replaces Pitovranov in Karlshorst

It was not surprising that Aleksandr Korotkov replaced Pitovranov in the Karlshorst post. The two men were cut from different cloth. Pitovranov had served primarily in counterintelligence within the USSR, whereas Korotkov had been in Germany before the war and immediately thereafter. As the first postwar foreign intelligence resident in Berlin, Korotkov had worked closely with Walter Ulbricht. The temperaments of Pitovranov and Korotkov were as different as were their service backgrounds. Pitovranov was a careful, precise, reserved individual who weighed his words carefully before speaking. Korotkov, on the other hand, was a shouter: he was quick to lose his temper and vent his feelings on whoever happened to be nearby. His quick temper never prevented him from objectively assessing other officers and gaining their trust, but it did not endear him to the higher echelons of KGB and the Communist Party of the Soviet Union (CPSU).[41]

The conflicting positions of Pitovranov and Korotkov on the Mielke candidacy highlight differences among the views of KGB officers about the future of KGB's relationship with MfS. Would KGB continue to exploit the East German service, or would MfS keep striving for independence? Indeed, how serious was the conflict between KGB and MfS? Most of the leading officers of KGB's Berlin apparat knew that it would be very difficult for the Soviets to acquire reliable sources in West Germany comparable to those of MfS. So KGB encouraged the development of MfS's foreign intelligence service, or HVA, as long as KGB could profit from its successes.[42] By using the refugee channels to place East Germans in West Germany, HVA had developed extensive penetrations of the Bonn government. HVA agents, many of whom produced huge numbers of classified documents, were in the FRG's most sensitive agencies, like the counterintelligence service (BFV), the Foreign Office, and the Defense Ministry, as well as in the Christian Democratic Union (CDU) and Social Democratic Party (SPD), the major political parties. Although many KGB officials in Karlshorst and Moscow attributed this success to the HVA chief, Markus Wolf, other MFS officers, such as Wolf's deputy, Horst Jaenicke, also deserved credit.[43]

The KGB apparat always appreciated valuable information from new HVA sources, even though normally KGB did not know their identities. On the other hand, in cases where the reporting was considered vital, it was often possible for KGB to ensure that it was receiving the source's full reporting by referring the matter to one of their trusted contacts within MFS.[44] The case of Willy Brandt's assistant, Guenther Guillaume, is a good example. Guillaume was an MFS/HVA agent whose reporting was of such extraordinary importance that KGB used its own sources in HVA to verify the authenticity and completeness of the information. When received, these reports were sent by an officer-messenger from Andropov personally to Gromyko because they often contained details of interest to him. It was, after all, information of the best quality on the situation in Germany and on discussions with the Western powers. After Gromyko read them, they were sent back to KGB via the courier. When publicity over Guillaume's arrest forced Brandt's resignation, Brandt was assured by Brezhnev in a personal letter that the "Soviet side had no knowledge of . . . this time bomb." At the time, many wondered whether KGB criticized HVA for this flap, given its negative effect on Soviet–West German relations. In fact, the professional KGB reaction was limited to unhappiness over the loss of a source of this quality.[45]

After his arrival in Karlshorst in fall 1957, Korotkov witnessed Ulbricht's elimination of his SED opposition and saw further evidence of growing GDR assertiveness. At the Thirty-Fifth Plenum of the SED Central Committee in February 1958, oppositionists Karl Schirdewan and Ernst Wollweber were relieved of their party and government positions.[46] Wollweber had evidently incurred Ulbricht's special dislike; BOB reported that later in 1958 Ulbricht began to threaten court action against him, tried to have him thrown out of his home in the Karlshorst compound, and had his outpatient privileges canceled at the Soviet hospital there.[47]

Also during the Thirty-Fifth Plenum, "KGB advisers' interference in GDR internal affairs in flagrant violation of GDR sovereignty" was discussed. Soviet Ambassador Pushkin was accused of having permitted this interference to occur. That something of this sort could be discussed at an SED Central Committee indicates SED's growing independence from the USSR on internal security matters. Popov noted that, following this plenum, his group was told that SED had forbidden GDR intelligence and counterintelligence from exploiting East German sports organizations for operational purposes. The same cautions, also based on developments at the Thirty-Fifth Plenum, were expressed concerning the Leipzig Fair.[48]

Strained KGB-MfS Relations Provoke a Bureaucratic Tug of War

Although Ulbricht had eliminated his opponents in the party, his friend Korotkov would soon face a challenge to his position in Karlshorst. The pretext for this challenge was a familiar question: To what extent should KGB rely on the East German services? This issue became paramount in the struggle that erupted between Korotkov and Aleksandr Nikolaevich Shelepin, head of the Komsomol (Communist Youth League), whom Khrushchev had appointed to replace Serov as KGB Chairman in December 1958.[49] The story of Korotkov's death and of the acrimonious struggle between his Karlshorst apparat and Shelepin, ostensibly over relations with the MfS, has never been told. It covers the period 1959–61, during which the Berlin situation reached crisis proportions, culminating in the erection of the Wall. As in 1953 during the Beria interregnum, leadership squabbles weakened KGB Karlshorst at a critical moment.

In late 1958, KGB Chairman Serov was transferred to head GRU, military intelligence, a step down. The reason for his transfer given later by KGB higher-ups was that GRU needed to be strengthened after Popov, a CIA agent, was discovered in GRU's Strategic Operational Group in Karlshorst. But this was not the real reason. Neither was Shelepin's KGB assignment engineered by the Politburo solely to erase the Stalinist image clinging to Serov or to engage KGB more directly in "the strategic, political economic and ideological struggle with the capitalist powers," although certainly these were factors. In the eyes of many, the chief reason underlying Serov's dismissal was Khrushchev's realization that Serov knew too many secrets.

Many KGB officers resented Shelepin's efforts to rid KGB of anyone suspected of having ties to Serov, and they disapproved of his intentions to use the service as a springboard for his own ambition. They also feared that his plans to involve KGB directly in the "political struggle" would mean a return to the Stalinist past, when the service was dragged into the leadership's internal power maneuvers. Shelepin was also disliked because he cut back the number of rest homes and sanitoriums available to the service and reduced KGB pay and benefits. Although many acknowledged that Shelepin had improved KGB's internal counterintelligence organization and procedures, nearly everyone complained that service interests had been subordinated to those of the party leadership when it was discovered that many key KGB posts were going to party and Komsomol officials handpicked by Shelepin.[50]

Shelepin had a tremendous capacity for intrigue. One of his first actions in office was to look for ways to eliminate Korotkov's influence. Korotkov had been around too long and was too outspoken for Shelepin's taste, yet as chief in Karlshorst he occupied a key KGB post. Shelepin's plot was helped along by Aleksandr Mikhailovich Sakharovsky, deputy KGB chairman and head of the First Chief Directorate, who had little love for Korotkov—the two always managed to mind their manners in public but in fact were very antagonistic. When Shelepin took over, stories began to circulate of the privileges Korotkov had enjoyed in Karlshorst as a result of his relationship with Serov.

Shelepin began by asking for a written status report from Korotkov on the Karlshorst apparat. The bureaucratic tug of war that ensued over Sakharovsky's efforts to obtain this famous report revealed much not only about Korotkov, but also about how the Karlshorst group interacted with the East German MfS.[51]

In addition to pressing Korotkov for a status report, KGB's counterintelligence resources were employed to monitor the activities of the German department in Moscow, the Karlshorst apparat, and Korotkov, including all contacts between Korotkov and his friends and colleagues.[52] But none of these actions produced the report Shelepin had requested. As the deadline drew near, Sakharovsky called in Leonid Yemelianovich Siomonchuk, chief of the German department, and ordered him to write the report. The latter objected, reminding Sakharovsky that the Karlshorst apparat was composed of separate departments, each of which responded to different command elements in Moscow.

Siomonchuk's response provides additional insight into the bureaucratic realities of the relationships between Karlshorst and KGB

Moscow: "How can I write a report about the activities of the entire apparat, which is responsible personally to the chairman, when I am aware only of what goes on in the German field? I don't know anything about operations against the main adversary, the United States, in counterintelligence, on the Soviet colony, illegals, and so forth. Why not have your deputy call in all of the department and directorate chiefs and tell them what to write?" This was done, but they, too, protested that they could not write such a report in Moscow. Only Korotkov would know the details of operations in his area. Aleksei Alekseevich Krokhin, who headed the illegals directorate, argued that Korotkov was doing what he had been directed to do in the illegals line, "but why should he have to explain to us?"[53] This was not an unreasonable reaction given Korotkov's long experience in illegals operations. Ivan Anisimovich Fadeikin, an old German hand with past service in Karlshorst who headed the Thirteenth Department, suggested that they call Korotkov on the secure telephone and explain what was needed.[54] Siomonchuk put in the call, described the situation, and was told by Korotkov that he would send in the report on Monday.[55]

On Monday there was no report, but Korotkov announced he would return to Moscow to make his report in person. To ensure a report that would be acceptable to Shelepin, one was drafted by Siomonchuk and appropriately amended by Sakharovsky. In essence, their report blandly asserted that work with the German "friends" had improved over the past year and that the level of information received was better. This draft was presented to Shelepin by Korotkov at a meeting attended by the senior officers of the First Chief Directorate. Shelepin sharply criticized Korotkov for it, commenting that he should not just work with the Germans but also attend to the affairs of his own apparat. To this Korotkov replied, "In that case, I'll pack my suitcase and leave." Shelepin responded by ordering a new investigating commission to examine the situation in Karlshorst.[56]

When the commission's report was finally completed, Shelepin discussed the results with Korotkov. Shelepin repeated the same admonition that had led to the commission's creation: "Pay more attention to supervising the apparat, working with your own people, and coordinating this work with military counterintelligence. After all, we have an army there and are concerned for its security. You must use your territory for our own intelligence work and not rely on the German 'friends.' We must have our own assets."[57]

Realizing that this idea had come from Sakharovsky, Korotkov replied that to do this he would have to have a suitable deputy. He asked that Siomonchuk, the German department chief, be assigned to Karlshorst. But Siomonchuk protested the Karlshorst assignment, saying he had had enough of overseas posting. He also noted that the position taken in the commission's report was wrong because in reality everything had to be done through the Germans. He said that KGB no longer had enough personnel who knew German and the area well enough to carry out these operational tasks unilaterally: "It is stupid to assume that one can recruit the citizens of a friendly, allied country without the permission of the host service." If KGB were to try it, Siomonchuk predicted, conflicts would arise within parties and governments. Ignoring Siomonchuk's protests, Shelepin simply said, "Tell Korotkov that you will be working with the Germans. He has nothing to do with it."[58]

Korotkov returned to Berlin but was recalled to Moscow yet again by Shelepin for consultations in the Central Committee on 27 June 1961. After the discussions, Korotkov went to the offices of the German department of the KGB First Chief Directorate, described his visit to the Central Committee, and telephoned Serov. Later that day the two old friends went to the KGB sports complex at the small Dinamo Stadium in Petrovka, where they played tennis. There Korotkov suffered a heart attack and died. Korotkov's running battles with KGB Chairman Shelepin, which had crippled KGB Karlshorst at the onset of the Berlin crisis, had taken its toll. Mielke came to the funeral in Moscow with several of his deputies, including Bruno Beater and Markus Wolf. Wolf, who was fluent in Russian, delivered a eulogy on behalf of MfS.[59]

16

Khrushchev's Ultimatum

Well, are you ready to leave Berlin?" GRU Lt. Col. Pyotr Popov intended this as a joke, but neither George Kisevalter nor David Murphy was in the mood for levity. It was 17 November 1958. Popov had called an emergency meeting to announce his imminent departure for Moscow on what everyone hoped would be a brief visit—but all realized that it could be the end of the operation. There were other worries as well. One week before, Nikita Khrushchev had announced that because of violations of the Potsdam Agreement, the Western Allies had forfeited their right to remain in Berlin. The USSR would turn over those functions it still exercised in Berlin to the GDR, Khrushchev explained; the Western Allies would have to make their own arrangements with the East Germans.

After his little joke, Popov explained that he considered the threat to abrogate the Potsdam Agreements genuine because the decision to do so had been under consideration for some time. But Moscow, though ready to carry through on its threat, was anxiously awaiting American reactions to Khrushchev's speech. Even Popov's GRU unit had received firm instructions to submit "daily reports concerning the reactions of people in the occupation forces and the West Berlin population."[1]

Kisevalter was eager to use the limited time available in the 17 November meeting to review emergency communications plans with Popov, but Popov insisted on describing the changed atmosphere at the Soviet colony in Karlshorst following Khrushchev's speech. Everyone there seemed convinced that a major turning point in relations with the West over Germany had arrived. Popov summarized the situation this way: "The essentials of this matter are clear. We are going to turn over the sovereignty of East Berlin to the East Germans, and this will be a political move to force the Western powers to negotiate with the East Germans. Secondly, the GDR will try to reduce . . . your influence in West Berlin." He added that the East Germans would know exactly how many troops the West maintained in Berlin and would give permission only for a certain number to cross their territory. Popov also thought it possible that all Soviet troops would be withdrawn from East Berlin, thus presenting the West with a situation where "we have withdrawn our troops from Berlin and you have not."[2]

Popov's prediction was not far off the mark. Khrushchev's speech was followed by the Soviet note of 27 November 1958, which proposed that West Berlin become a demilitarized, free city—but if this were not done within six months, the Soviets would transfer their Berlin responsibilities to the GDR. The United States immediately responded to the Khrushchev ultimatum, making clear that it would not "acquiesce in a unilateral repudiation of its rights and obligations in Berlin by the Soviet Union."[3] This ultimatum, and its implied threat to Allied rights in West Berlin, created a crisis that dominated the lives of West Berliners and Allied forces in the area for months to come. But the situation should not have surprised the West. For some time the Soviets had been looking for a way to give the GDR responsibility for dealing with the Western Allies on Berlin and to disavow any responsibility for actions taken to force the allies from their territory.

Beginning in late 1957 and continuing through 1958, East German authorities had begun preparing for the time they would assume responsibility for dealing with West Berlin and the Allied presence there. In October 1957 the GDR brought in new East German currency to replace the old. In the process, the borders between East and West Berlin were virtually sealed off to prevent speculators from shuttling between East and West Berlin, making profits on currency fluctuations. This again demonstrated that, with a sufficient commitment of manpower, movement across the sector borders could be stopped. Reports were also received that passenger traffic from Potsdam to East Berlin via the elevated rail lines (S-Bahn) that crossed West Berlin would be routed over the Berlin Outer Ring. That meant that GDR citizens living in the Potsdam area and forbidden from entering West Berlin (including government officials and party members) would have to commute to their East Berlin jobs via slow steam-driven trains on the outer ring around Berlin. In addition, East German controls already in effect over non-Allied train and truck movements between Berlin and West Germany were intensified: mail cars were removed from trains for inspection, freight shipments were confiscated, and individual passengers were searched.[4]

At every opportunity, the Soviets and GDR authorities tried to force the United States to deal with the GDR on issues that had been the province of the Soviet military. When a US Army helicopter landed by mistake in East Germany on 7 June, for example, the Soviets turned over the passengers and crew to GDR officials. This meant that the US Military Mission had to deal with GDR authorities to secure the release of those on board. Diplomatic efforts to persuade the Soviets to intervene failed: the release of the personnel and helicopter was finally obtained through negotiations between the American Red Cross and the East German Red Cross. The quick action by the Soviets and East Germans in transforming a chance incident into a highly publicized test of wills showed how serious the Soviets and the East Germans were about transferring control of East Berlin to the GDR.[5]

To prepare for this transfer of power, Walter Ulbricht also took steps to crack down on the opposition to his leadership within SED—opposition that had been simmering since the 17 June 1953 revolt. Many dissidents hoped that the arrival in February 1958 of the new Soviet ambassador, Mikhail Georgievich Pervukhin, who had a reputation as an economic specialist, might make Ulbricht behave more pragmatically. Such delusions were soon dashed. Given the GDR's forward position vis-à-vis West Germany—a member of NATO—the Soviets needed stability in East Germany above all, and if Ulbricht could provide it, they would stick with him no matter how outrageous his policies. In commenting on BOB intelligence reports about the disappointment of many "middle- and lower-level party functionaries" over the downfall of opposition leaders, the State Department's Berlin Mission doubted that "these unsettling effects will be of great moment in the near future" and expected "party discipline to be maintained." The Fifth SED

Congress, in July 1959, confirmed this evaluation. BOB's perennially optimistic sources in the group around Schirdewan still hoped for change, but everyone accepted that the opposition to Ulbricht was going nowhere. The Soviets and East Germans were free to pursue their goals for West Berlin.[6]

Soviet Scare Tactics

In January 1958 the Soviets initiated a series of actions that affected the movement of Allied military trains and military truck convoys between West Berlin and West Germany. By insisting on the right to inspect military vehicles and to stamp the travel orders of passengers on military trains, the Soviets appeared to claim the right to determine who could travel and what could be shipped.[7] BOB personnel were prohibited by CIA from using the Autobahn, so they had their cars driven to Helmstedt by military drivers and then took the train. This vacation travel was essential in relieving tension. Such travel harassment by the Soviets just before Khrushchev's 10 November speech managed to create a climate of worry and isolation that greatly increased the shock of the ultimatum for BOB.

As harassment intensified, train travel became an unnerving experience. The military train from Berlin always arrived at the Soviet border checkpoint at Marienborn, just east of Helmstedt, at about midnight. The train commander would give the Soviets the passengers' documents to check. Each identity document number had to conform to the travel order; any mistakes could result in delays of the train. More than once, a Nazi swastika drawn in the dust of the side of a passenger car furnished an excuse for a delay. Because American passengers could not leave their cars during the trip—by Soviet order, even the window shades of each compartment had to be lowered—it was a mystery who had drawn the forbidden emblems. A passenger who raised the shade while stopped at the Marienborn checkpoint risked staring down the barrel of a Soviet submachine gun. US authorities did steadfastly resist Soviet demands to board the trains, enter compartments, and check individual passengers against their documents. Still, fear that the Soviets might force the issue increased the BOB chief's anxiety each time a group of his officers left by train for the West.

Although most people tried to appear calm, the atmosphere among the American military and intelligence communities was becoming very tense. All sorts of rumors spread from household to household. One particularly vicious story was that if the Allies tried to evacuate their dependents, West Berliners, enraged at being abandoned, would stone these women and children to death at the train station. No one really believed that this bizarre scenario could happen, but it did add to the unspoken fears of young American families in Berlin.

As the crisis continued through 1959, consideration was given to providing BOB personnel with authentic military cover. After all, BOB had been pretending to be a military department. It might become necessary for BOB personnel to wear field uniforms and weapons, use military equipment, or even participate in defensive operations organized by the US military. The days when Bill Harvey insisted that all new arrivals draw a weapon were long past. When an administrator at the base warned that many base officers had no idea how to fire a machine gun, he was told by his military counterpart, with utter seriousness, "Don't worry, there'll be a sergeant there to show them."

Inside BOB, the most difficult problem was how to make sure that all classified files would be destroyed if the base were evacuated. Paper had been accumulating since the base was activated in 1945. Harvey kept thermite grenades on top of his office safes, and elaborate incendiary devices were set up on the roof of BOB's office building in the US compound, all intended for rapid file destruction. CIA's Technical Services Division gave BOB demonstrations of the rooftop devices, but they were never put to the test.[8] Even so, these emergency preparations, which were intensified as the deadline for the ultimatum approached, alarmed everyone within the BOB family. All knew that there was little chance of concealing their CIA affiliation if the worst happened.

The Soviet proposal to give GDR officials the responsibility for staffing rail and highway control points had been anticipated by the Western Allies. By the beginning of 1958 they had decided to accept East German personnel at checkpoints, but they would consider the East Germans as agents of the Soviets, who would bear the ultimate responsibility for ensuring the unrestricted movement of personnel to and from Berlin. But would the Western Allies use limited military force to maintain unrestricted access to Berlin? As of 3 September 1958 the British and French governments still refused to discuss this issue. It is unclear how much the Soviet decisions announced in November were influenced by the Western Allies' decision to accept East Germans at checkpoints and their waffling over contingency planning. Although foreign reactions to the ultimatum must certainly have been a major intelligence target, no SVR archival material could be found.[9]

During 1958, KGB continued to stress its concern about West German rearmament, but the problem of West Berlin was uppermost in both Soviet and East German thinking. The new GDR passport law of 11 December 1957, by introducing drastic penalties for "flight from the republic" *(Republikflucht)*, reduced the overall number of refugees from East Germany but sharply increased the proportion leaving through West Berlin. In spite of continuing efforts by GDR authorities, the Western sectors remained the principal escape hatch. Both Soviet and East German officials were frustrated by the increases in the refugee flow, particularly among the intelligentsia. Each side blamed the other, yet the Soviets were still unwilling to allow the GDR to take any actions to halt the flow that might spark a confrontation with the West.[10] Out of this frustration came the Soviet characterization of West Berlin as a "center of hostile activity against the GDR and other socialist countries," which found its echo in the 27 November ultimatum.[11] This, the Soviets contended, was the real threat to GDR stability. By stressing this theme in their propaganda, the Soviets evidently hoped to convince the populations of the NATO states that defense of their rights in West Berlin was not worth risking war.

This propaganda ploy was not new. In 1953 the "subversive centers" in West Berlin had been blamed for the anti-SED strikes and riots of 17 June. In 1954 Pitovranov, newly appointed KGB chief in Karlshorst, used the same arguments when urging the East Germans to expand and improve their agent operations against these same "centers." In 1956 the Western and GDR press was filled with stories of the "defection" of a US military intelligence principal agent, who reportedly brought along a field safe filled with documents. *Neues Deutschland* ran a series on the phony case, replete with names of alleged agents, as part of a campaign directed at US intelligence in West Berlin (leaflets were distributed in West Berlin at the same time, warning Germans not to visit American intelligence installations).[12] On 27 January 1958, the KGB proudly reported to Yuri Andropov, then in the Central Committee, that the West Berlin senate was investigating the Fighting Group Against Inhumanity, a subversive organization working for the West that by then was nearly on its last legs. By summer 1958, the leaders of both the Fighting Group and the Free Jurists had been forced to resign.[13]

KGB Active Measures Dubs West Berlin an Espionage Swamp

Top priority in the massive diplomatic and media campaign supporting the Khrushchev ultimatum was to present West Berlin as an "espionage swamp." Responsibility for this task went to KGB and its Karlshorst apparat. KGB counterintelligence officer and West German specialist Yuri Yakovlevich Litovkin was assigned to the Karlshorst apparat to run this program (BOB confirmed his presence in Karlshorst in May 1959). It got under way in early 1958 when KGB sought the support of the East European intelligence services. According to Michal Goleniewski, CIA's source in Polish intelligence, the other agencies refused to participate because their sources in the Western services would be exposed.[14] Nevertheless, the campaign went forward, well in advance of the November ultimatum, and reached its climax in spring and summer 1959.

Another indication of these preparations was a 21 June 1958 KGB memorandum concerning Bill Harvey, prepared in Moscow for a "comrade" whose name was not given. The memorandum covered the period 1957–58 and reported the existence in West Berlin of "a unit of the CIA of the USA, actively working against us. This unit [is] headed by the American Bill Harvey, known by the nickname 'Big Bill.' . . . One of his assistants is Dave Murphy." The memo also contains a clue that it may have been used in the "espionage swamp" campaign: "The available material provides a basis for assuming that 'Big Bill' and his coworkers carry out active intelligence work against the countries of the Socialist camp, for which they have a large agent network."[15]

It might seem unbelievable to readers of intelligence literature produced in the West that a propaganda campaign of this magnitude, coordinated with a major initiative of Soviet foreign policy, could have been in preparation months before the appointment of Aleksandr Shelepin as chairman of KGB in December 1958. Shelepin has been widely acclaimed as the initiator and creator of KGB "active measures," or "disinformation."[16] This stress on Shelepin's role has been most vividly portrayed in Anatoly Golitsyn's *New Lies for Old.* There Golitsyn describes a massive, long-term Soviet deception program and claims that the Sino-Soviet split, the breakaway of Romania's Nicolae Ceaușescu, the Prague Spring, and the actions of Soviet dissidents were all carefully planned active measures designed to confuse and weaken the West. Some still share these views and consider everything that has occurred in the former Soviet Union and in Eastern Europe since 1989 to be part of the same master plan, or, as Golitsyn called it, the New Methodology. But most scholars and intelligence specialists, after rejecting the concept of a spurious Sino-Soviet split, have altogether dismissed the idea that the disintegration of the Soviet empire was an event orchestrated by KGB.[17] On the other hand, many former KGB officers are convinced that the Soviet Union's collapse was actually orchestrated by the West.[18] (For additional background on active measures, see appendix 8.)

There seem to be two opposing views of the circumstances whereby Department D, the first widely known disinformation component of KGB, was created in 1959. One, represented by Golitsyn, ascribes the change solely to Aleksandr Shelepin, who he claims sought to enlist KGB actively "in the strategic, political, economic and ideological struggle with the capitalist powers." In another view, the formation of Department D probably owed more to bureaucratic and operational necessity than to the New Methodology. In fact the reason for creating a separate department for disinformation within the First Chief Directorate was to improve the efficiency of active measures. According to the directorate's chief, Aleksandr Sakharovsky, active measures proposals, some of them harebrained, came in from various residencies and were reviewed by the individual geographic departments for approval or rejection. There was no overall plan, no central coordinating point. This was to be the role of Department D, which would not normally run its own operations but instead coordinate agents from the individual departments and their residencies. The assistance, expertise, and in some cases approval of other ministries and the military was needed to conduct such active measures operations as deception, disinformation, compromise, or exposure.

In fact, one of the principal reasons for creating Department D was to help the Soviets carry out their growing number of active measures operations against West Germany and to support Soviet policy on East Germany and East Berlin. Indeed, there was so much pressure to keep up with the demand that German specialist Sergei Kondrashev was assigned to Department D as deputy chief.[19]

Serious Accusations

During the 1960s, active measures against West Germany expanded. Captured German documents from World War II were used to try to link

West German officials with the worst aspects of the Nazi regime. State Secretary Hans Globke; the inspector general of the Bundeswehr, Gen. Adolf Heusinger; and Refugee Minister Theodor Oberlaender—all were implicated. Again using Gestapo records, Department D launched rumors accusing Chancellor Adenauer of earlier ties to French intelligence. At the same time, as a backdrop to these operations, waves of individual actions intended to discredit West Germany were undertaken. Many incidents of anti-Semitic violence and vandalism, for example, were blamed on West German neo-Nazis, reported in detail in the Soviet and East European press, and passed to the Western media by KGB agents.[20]

One of the best examples we have of KGB active measures operations affecting West Germany is a campaign involving Defense Minister Franz Joseph Strauss that peaked during 1962 and led to Strauss's resignation in October of that year. One element of the campaign was a report on the situation in West Germany during 1961 prepared in February 1962 by a "government organ" of one of the NATO countries and received by KGB from a friendly East European intelligence service. On 20 September 1962, KGB Chairman Semichastny sent a summary of the report to Deputy Minister of Foreign Affairs V. V. Kuznetsov and to Defense Minister R. Ya. Malinovsky, with copies to the governments of the GDR and the Czechoslovak Socialist Republic through KGB liaison.[21]

The report described the effects of the Berlin crisis on West German foreign and defense policies during 1961. Emphasizing that the FRG was to remain in NATO, it noted that the Berlin events had made the West Germans more assertive: "the era of complete submission to Allied commands . . . is over." This shift, according to the report, could be seen in Adenauer's recent visits to Washington and in the increasingly "independent actions" by Defense Minister Franz Joseph Strauss in both Europe and America.[22]

Key elements of "West German defense doctrine" cited in the KGB summary are "the creation of deterrent forces *[sil ustrasheniia],*" maximum forward positioning of forces as "basic defensive dogma," complete and lasting integration of the NATO forces with the goal of putting these concepts into practice, and finally, the "inadmissibility of discrimination toward the Bundeswehr [West German Army] by other allied forces concerning organization, equipment, and determination of operational missions."[23] The negative implications of these Strauss policies for various plans to reduce tensions in Europe were pointed out,

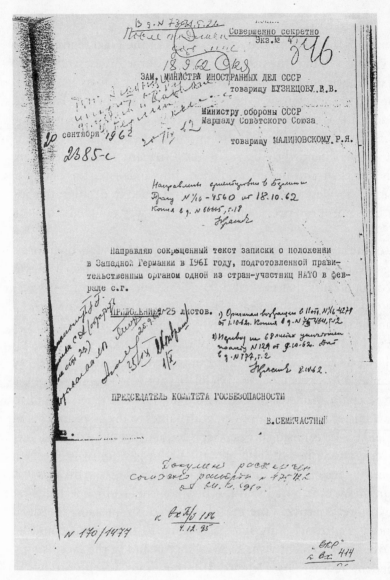

Report, 20 September 1962, from KGB chairman Vladimir Semichastny to Deputy Foreign Minister Vasily Kuznetsov and Minister of Defense Rodion Malinovsky, describing the impact of the Berlin crisis on West German foreign and defense policies. The report probably originated with an East European service and was sent to KGB Moscow, where it was translated and disseminated. From notations on the report it appears to have been used in the KGB active measures campaign against West German Defense Minister Franz Joseph Strauss.

followed by the comment that although reciprocal controls for warning of attack were not excluded, the FRG Defense Ministry had insisted categorically that such "controls extend over the territory stretching from the Atlantic Ocean to the Urals."[24]

There are frequent references in the report to Defense Minister Strauss and his attempts to acquire nuclear weapons for the FRG and to cast doubt on the American atomic monopoly: "Like General de Gaulle, Strauss is no longer satisfied with verbal assurances," but because "he does not wish to enter into conflict with an ally as necessary as the United States, he cannot take the path being followed by France." But Strauss let it be understood among his followers that failure to achieve agreement on atomic weapons "will inevitably push the FRG into the embrace of France."

It must have been evident that the report, even though several months old, could be of great assistance in the anti-Strauss campaign. Coauthor Kondrashev, then first deputy chief of Department D, noted that he personally selected this analysis for dissemination.[25] The fact that it was sent to both the East Germans and the Czechs also supports this thesis because the services of both countries cooperated extensively with KGB in anti-German disinformation operations.[26]

Evidence of the report's role in the ongoing campaign can be seen in the marginal notation from Aleksandr Sakharovsky, chief of foreign intelligence, to Ivan Agayants, chief of Department D, instructing him to "prepare a proposal and send it to Berlin." Agayants relayed the order to deputy Kondrashev, who signed it. This campaign to denigrate Strauss was a classic example of that element of active measures designed to "compromise anti-Soviet officials of foreign governments," in vogue since the Committee of Information and before.

But for BOB it was the mounting crescendo of attacks from the East on "subversive activities" in West Berlin that hit hardest. Under that broad rubric, the KGB-directed active measures campaign listed such things as RIAS, the popular American radio station in the American sector. Inevitably, there were discussions among the Allies about "concessions" that might be made to the Soviets to quiet these accusations. In December 1958, for example, Ambassador Llewellyn Thompson cabled suggestions from Moscow that included "termination of overt Western activities in Berlin such as operation of the radio station." In February 1959, British Undersecretary of State Hoyer Millar commented to US Secretary of State John Foster Dulles that "one concession the West might make would be to cut down propaganda and related activities in West Berlin."[27]

In the immediate wake of Khrushchev's November ultimatum, Western governments seemed unaware both of the Soviet bloc's enormous propaganda and intelligence presence in East Berlin and of the need to counter the Soviet characterization of West Berlin as an espionage swamp. But even by the end of 1958 BOB was earnestly preparing for a counterattack on both the diplomatic and propaganda fronts. Further, on 31 December 1958 the Allies formally rejected the Soviet position on Berlin. Their position was underlined by the 92 percent participation in the Berlin city elections that month: SED received only 1.9 percent of the vote and earned no seats in the Berlin Senate. The stage seemed set for a major confrontation between East and West.

17

BOB Counters the Soviet Propaganda Campaign

A
S BOB's target-room analysts were assembling material for a counterattack on the Soviet and East German "espionage swamp" campaign, another part of Khrushchev's offensive required immediate BOB attention: his promised withdrawal of Soviet forces from East Berlin. In a pamphlet circulated in West Berlin, the Soviets threatened that the "Soviet Komendatura would be closed down and guard troops withdrawn from East Berlin as part of the handover of its functions to the East Germans."[1] The NATO allies, of course, were expected to follow suit and withdraw forces from their sectors of West Berlin. But for the Allies to have followed the Soviet example would have meant leaving West Berlin's people defenseless against the GDR security services. Allied unanimity was being severely tested. And the question of whether the Soviets really intended to withdraw quickly became a test of BOB's coverage of the Soviet East Berlin headquarters in Karlshorst.

An 11 February 1959 situation report by BOB suggested that the Soviets were preparing to remove the last vestiges of their military forces from East Berlin. KGB and military intelligence personnel were rapidly shifting to nonmilitary cover, a pattern initially reported by Popov. New facilities for the Soviets, including dependent housing and barracks, were being constructed outside Berlin. Military communications facilities were to be removed from Karlshorst. Also, Soviet air force instructors were training GDR personnel to control traffic in the air corridors over Berlin. Since 1945 the Berlin Air Safety Center, headquarters for this effort, had been staffed jointly by Soviet and Allied personnel, without any East German presence.[2]

Some of this information probably was deliberately planted by the Soviets to impress the West. A Soviet official told a BOB source in SED that "the Karlshorst Compound is in the process of almost complete turnover to the East Germans."[3] But BOB's Karlshorst sources could not confirm this sea change, even though their reporting during April and May showed that the Soviets were continuing to cut back in East Berlin. It was true that the last KGB German employees were replaced by Soviet citizens, the KGB motor pool was placed under Soviet embassy auspices, and the KGB apparat's administrative officer directed all suppliers and contractors to forward their invoices to the Soviet embassy instead of KGB.[4] The Soviet long-distance telephone and telegraph exchange in Karlshorst was to be dismantled, but the exchange in the Soviet embassy in central Berlin (unused since its installation in 1954) would stay.[5]

Still, there was no firm indication that these cutbacks reflected a final Soviet decision to withdraw. In fact, a 20 April report suggested the opposite. Although the Soviet military units in East Berlin had not yet been allocated funds for 1959, no unit commander or administrative officer had received orders to leave.[6] Also, although a KGB communications intelligence unit was moved from Karlshorst compound to Potsdam, it now appeared that the KGB's Eleventh Signals Regiment (responsible for all high-security Soviet communications in Berlin) would remain in the Weissensee area of the city.[7]

By the end of June, it became clear that the Soviets had no immediate intention of withdrawing their military from East Berlin and abandoning Karlshorst. All Soviet Army maintenance and construction funds for Berlin (frozen since January 1959) were released to individual units, and arrivals and departures of Soviet personnel stabilized. By the end of August there had been no significant change in the strength of the Soviet colony in Karlshorst. On 1 September the school for Soviet children reopened. Except for the drastic reductions in local employees and the more central role of GDR MfS in controlling compound security, the situation in Karlshorst had returned to normal.[8] Had the declaration that the USSR would withdraw from East Berlin been serious? Given the on-again, off-again nature of Khrushchev's negotiations on Berlin during 1959–60, we will probably never know.

Even while trying to establish the truth about this more pressing matter, BOB was not allowed to lose sight of its efforts to counter Soviet complaints about espionage in West Berlin. It was true, as reported by KGB in January 1958, that the West Berlin senate was investigating the Fighting Group Against Inhumanity, one of the "subversive" organizations at the top of the KGB list. According to a CIA report, although the senate's investigation would indeed respond to public criticism of West Berlin's nongovernmental resistance groups, the main objective in their investigation was to offset Soviet charges of Western intelligence activity by exposing simultaneously "illegal Communist [Soviet and GDR] activities in West Berlin, including . . . the East Berlin offices responsible for their direction."[9] Indeed, as part of this exposé it was reported that the senate planned an exhibit of materials from East Berlin intelligence services, including East German military intelligence.

The Karl Linke Case

Sure enough, on 22 January 1959, the opening salvo in the spy wars counterattack was fired. The West Berlin tabloid *Berliner Zeitung* carried the headline: "Espionage Chief of the Zonal Army Defects to West Berlin!" Next day, the front page carried a full-length photograph of Maj. Gen. Karl Linke, head of the GDR's military intelligence. Opposite ran the headline: "East Berlin—Europe's Biggest Espionage Center" and in smaller type, "His Deputy's Defection Cost Him His Career." The same issue carried details of a press conference in West Berlin at which Linke's deputy, Lt. Col. Siegfried Dombrowski, discussed East Berlin espionage. *BZ* reported that Dombrowski brought with him Linke's diary, which detailed a visit to Soviet military intelligence headquarters in Moscow. The story was picked up by the press throughout Western Europe and North America. It provided impressive detail on the East German military intelligence service and the Soviet advisers in GRU who initiated and directed its operations, as well as commentary on both Soviet KGB and GDR Mfs activities centered in East Berlin.[10]

How was BOB, working in concert with West German officials, able to respond so rapidly to the need to counter Soviet attacks on West Berlin espionage activity? The explanation begins more than two years earlier. In September 1956, one of BOB's best Karlshorst sources, whom we shall call Frau K., reported that she had been offered a position as housekeeper for Gen. Karl Linke of the East German National People's Army. She had worked earlier for KGB Gen. Yevgeny Pitovranov. His recommendation smoothed her way into the new job, which she began in December 1956. Linke was chief of East German military intelligence. A prewar member of the German Communist Party, Linke had left for the USSR and acquired Soviet citizenship when Hitler came to power. Returning to Germany at war's end, he was eventually assigned to the paramilitary Barracked People's Police, forerunner of the National People's Army. He became chief of the political directorate of the GDR Ministry of the Interior before being assigned to the army intelligence position.[11]

Both Linke and his wife were fervent Communists and deeply suspicious. Mrs. Linke also suffered from a painful illness that made her extremely irritable. The couple, concerned that Frau K. might turn out to be a Western agent, set traps for her when she started working for them. They would, for example, arrange papers on the general's desk in a pattern so they could tell if Frau K. had moved them. On one occasion the wife even forced Frau K. to strip and submit to a search. By April 1957 these indignities and continual quarrels with Mrs. Linke brought Frau K. to the point of leaving her job and seeking refuge in West Berlin. But as Frau K.'s distaste for her employers grew, the Linkes became more pleased with her work and even apologized for their suspicious treatment of her.[12] Still, the wife's general disposition improved little; working for her often made Frau K.'s life miserable.

Meanwhile, Frau K. was learning that General Linke, though he had made a fetish of security, was anything but secure in his daily habits. He left lists of telephone numbers and other service papers on his desk, and more important documents were locked in a desk drawer for which a key could easily be duplicated. Recognizing that Frau K.'s position gave her access to potentially useful information, the case officer persuaded her to remain in the job for at least six more months; in return, BOB would help her resettle in the West. The operation developed an odd pattern: at every meeting, Frau K. would complain vigorously of her treatment at the hands of the general's wife, after which the case officer would calm her down while simultaneously reviewing the material she had brought him from Linke's desk.[13]

The intelligence from the case was extraordinary, and its value was enhanced when much of the best information on the relationships between Linke, his organization, and the Soviet GRU advisers was confirmed by Berlin tunnel reporting and later by Popov. But the most revealing evidence of the nature of Linke's relationship with GRU came in his report for the East German Defense Ministry on the March 1957 conference at GRU Headquarters in Moscow, during which such matters as strategic intelligence, clandestine communications, and reports evaluation were discussed. He named the GRU officers who gave the presentations and listed which of the "principal missions" of the East German service were of special interest to the Soviets. In addition, Linke was told by a GRU officer that often "it is a good idea to recruit Germans under the guise of the British or French intelligence services." He was also advised that "sources who are not completely clean should not be dropped, just be handled specially"—that is, doubled.[14]

All in all, Linke's report provided a fascinating picture of the relationship between the East Germans and their Soviet "friends" in military intelligence. To have acquired it from the head of the service himself, fresh from a Moscow conference, was rare indeed. Perhaps the most important part of the report for BOB was the insight it gave the Americans into GRU attitudes toward KGB. In discussing the relationship between MFS and Linke's service, one GRU officer advised Linke that whereas "a good relationship is necessary, so is full independence! Under no circumstances do we permit our state security service [KGB] to gain insight into our [GRU] intelligence work." When one considers how KGB handled the investigation of Pyotr Popov, BOB's source in GRU Karlshorst, the advice given Linke by GRU Moscow appears to have been wishful thinking.

In fact, Popov confirmed much of the information contained in the Linke conference report and provided a more realistic version of the relation between GRU and the East German service. Clearly, problems had developed that were not unlike some of the difficulties KGB faced with the East German MFS. For example, GRU advisers had been obtaining from the Linke group "spotting reports" on Germans in whom GRU was interested as agent candidates. These had been detailed reports, not merely names and addresses. But by January–February 1958, the reports had become more difficult for GRU to obtain. Linke's people wanted to recruit these candidates themselves and so were cutting back on the number of reports passed to GRU.[15]

By June 1957, a crisis had developed in Linke's case. Frau K. had called an emergency meeting because while making copies of a new telephone directory of Linke's organization she had made a small ink mark on the original, which she had had to return to the desk drawer. This incident, which intensified her fears of being discovered, came on top of the news that during most of the summer Frau K. would have no access to classified documents. Linke, who would be away on leave in the USSR, leaving his house to his children and grandchildren, had insisted that Frau K. take an unpaid leave while he and his wife were away. She could return in September 1957, but that was when BOB had promised her she could leave the job and come West. Everyone at BOB agreed that there was no way Frau K. could be persuaded to remain in place any longer.[16]

When BOB reviewed the information that Frau K. had obtained about Linke personally, his service, its personnel, and its relations with GRU, it was obvious that he would never be able to explain to his superiors a security compromise of this magnitude. It was decided, therefore, to take advantage of the time that Frau K. had left, during which the demon wife would be conveniently absent visiting her daughter, to try to recruit Linke or bring about his defection. Furthermore, using Frau K. to deliver the proposal meant the operation could be conducted in complete security, an important factor in persuading Linke to cooperate. The recruitment letter was to stress the chance of a fresh start, a new identity, Western medical treatment for his chronically ill wife, and a guaranteed income. Of course, if recruitment or defection failed, BOB knew that its possession of the sensitive information it had obtained from Linke could be used at some point in the future to discredit and disrupt the East German military intelligence service and its relations with its Soviet patrons in GRU. But as of summer 1957, no one at BOB had any inkling of the "ultimatum" to come or the Soviet propaganda campaign that followed.[17]

The recruitment operation began with Frau K. asking to begin her summer vacation on 30 June, after Linke's wife would have left but before Linke departed to join her. Because Linke had no intention of paying Frau K. during his absence, he could not very well object. The simplest plan would have been for Frau K. to leave the letter where Linke could not miss it and then depart for West Berlin. But doing so would have left BOB uncertain of Linke's reaction and made it difficult to respond securely to any requests from him for future contact. So BOB pushed its operational and technical capabilities to the limit by preparing transmitters for Frau K. to install in Linke's home. A team of support agents was to pass the transmitters to Frau K. Another support team would simultaneously establish a monitoring point close enough to the Karlshorst compound to pick up the transmitters' signal.

On Thursday evening, 27 June, Frau K. was given the transmitters by a support agent, and she took them to her apartment. The next evening she met her case officer in West Berlin, where she was given the recruitment letter and final instructions for how to place the transmitters. The following morning, a Saturday, Frau K. reported for work as usual. After Linke left for his office, she installed the transmitters in the study and removed from the desk a classified telephone directory, the original of Linke's report on his Moscow trip, and a bundle of letters written in Russian and German. Frau K. hid them in her dress and, after activating the transmitters and placing the letter right in the middle of Linke's desk, prepared to leave. Suddenly the telephone rang. It was Linke calling to say that he had forgotten to give Frau K. the extra key so that she could reenter the house after she had completed her morning shopping. (Frau K., of course, had no intention of doing the shopping that morning.) Linke promised to send his driver immediately with the key. Fearing that Linke himself might return and discover that something was up, Frau K. returned the documents to the desk and hid the letter in the kitchen. To her relief, the chauffeur arrived alone and simply handed over the key.[18]

Alone again, Frau K. once more took the documents from the desk, secreted them in her clothing, and went out, leaving the key on the table and closing the front door behind her. The letter! In her fright she had forgotten to retrieve it from the kitchen and replace it on the desk. At this point, Frau K. could have been forgiven if she had abandoned the mission and left the scene. Instead, dedicated to finishing the job, she stopped a passing janitor from the Housing Administration who knew her. She told him that she had come out to do her shopping but had forgotten her key, and this Good Samaritan lent her a ladder. Frau K. climbed over the fence and through the living room window, replaced the letter on the general's desk, left by the front door with as much dignity as she could muster, and returned the ladder to the janitor. She arrived in West Berlin at 11:30 A.M., disheveled but triumphant. She never returned to East Berlin; BOB assisted her in resettlement.

Later that day, the support agent handling the reception equipment at the clandestine monitoring point near Karlshorst reported that he was receiving the carrier wave but heard no transmission. Several tapes were checked through 30 June, but nothing was heard. Although BOB sources reported that General Linke had left his VIP Karlshorst villa, evidently in disgrace, nothing definitive was heard until more than a year later. On the evening of 5 August 1958, Linke's deputy Dombrowski defected to BOB with his wife and sons. In addition to extensive knowledge of East German military intelligence and related matters, Dombrowski provided the first concrete information on the aftermath of the Frau K. operation.[19] Dombrowski's statements and his potential value as a source were confirmed when a few weeks later Popov reported that a "Lt. Col. Dombrowski had gone over to the West." When Kisevalter commented that Dombrowski was only the deputy for administration, Popov responded, "This man may not have engaged in operations, but he had attended conferences and, of course, knows all about the personnel in [East] German intelligence."

According to Dombrowski, he and Linke had been in the office on that fateful 29 June 1957 afternoon until 1:30 P.M., after which Dombrowski went on leave. Linke's last official day in the office was less than a month later, 22 July 1957, when he issued an order transferring authority to his deputy. On 25 July an order was published from GDR Defense Minister Willi Stoph stating that Linke had been placed on indefinite leave due to failing health. Only the acting chief, the secretary who had typed an extra copy of the classified telephone list on Linke's orders, and three Soviet advisers were aware of the real reasons for Linke's departure.[20] But by the end of September, the entire service knew the true story and had expressed indignation among themselves that a cover-up had been organized for Linke: anyone else would have been expelled from SED and given ten years in prison.

Although housing assignments were unchanged because of the housing shortage and red tape, there was a wholesale change of intelligence service telephone numbers in mid-July, and families with domestic servants were told to fire them. To guard against further attempts by American intelligence to contact senior East German officers, surveillance of their residences was begun. The wholesale personnel review occasioned by the Linke flap resulted in the dismissal "without prejudice" of only eight low-level employees for various petty reasons. Nothing apparently happened to the Soviet advisers, who continued in their duties.[21]

It was CIA Headquarters' awareness of the Linke case and the Dombrowski defection that prompted its 20 November 1958 cable to BOB urging that these operations be included in preparations for a "spy center" counterattack in coordination with West Berlin authorities. The result was a press conference on 22 January, augmented by press handouts that combined the material from the Linke case with Dombrowski's own knowledge. Both measures added sensational proof to Western charges that East Berlin was a hotbed of Soviet and East German espionage.[22]

BOB's Counterattack Irks Gromyko

> Gromyko, who sat stony-faced through the recital, seemed ... to be at a loss as to how best to reply.
> —*Foreign Relations of the United States, 1958–60*

While the first phase of BOB's riposte to Soviet and East German attacks on West Berlin as an espionage center rippled through the Western press, a somewhat less flamboyant but equally important effort was under way by BOB's Soviet and East German counterintelligence analysts.[23] As preparations began for the Foreign Ministers' Conference on Berlin scheduled for Geneva in May 1959, State Department officials expressed concern that the issue of "subversive activities" in West Berlin might be formally raised by the Soviets during the deliberations. To deal with this, BOB began to assemble the best counterintelligence information available on the true extent of espionage and covert action based in East Berlin and conducted by the Soviets, East Germans, and representatives of the East European services. Documents covering this issue were prepared at BOB, made available directly to the Berlin Mission, and sent to CIA Headquarters for use by the State Department. Before the Geneva conference began, William Bundy, who led the CIA intelligence support team to the American delegation, visited Berlin to familiarize himself with local conditions and BOB's material.[24]

On 1 June the Allied foreign ministers gathered at Soviet Foreign Minister Andrei Gromyko's residence for an informal meeting. US Secretary of State Christian Herter, who had recently replaced John Foster Dulles, opened the discussion by reading from BOB papers on "subversive activities and inflammatory propaganda originating in East Berlin and directed against West Berlin and the Federal Republic." What followed was a detailed description of the Soviet, East German, and East European intelligence services located in East Berlin. Herter interrupted his reading twice: once to quote from East German radio broadcasts that attacked him personally, and the second time to quote from personal attacks in the official East German press on the West German Foreign

Minister Heinrich von Brentano. According to the record of the meeting, "Gromyko, who sat stony-faced through the recital, seemed . . . at a loss as to how best to reply. He opened by saying that our people who had worked on these papers had obviously done much work." Further, he backpedaled by saying that "questions of propaganda and subversion were not one of the principal questions to be considered. This problem ranked fourth or fifth or even sixth."[25] In a letter to President Eisenhower describing the meeting, Herter said that he thought some of the passages "shook Gromyko up a bit" and predicted that in future sessions of the conference, "we may hear very little more about it."[26]

The exchange between Herter and Gromyko produced a resounding response in the Western press. In addition to the priceless quote "Gromyko . . . sat stony-faced," the press carried a number of specific items from the BOB material, including a description of the KGB's massive headquarters in the St. Antonius Hospital in Karlshorst. The *New York Herald Tribune* headline of 7 June told the story: "BOTH SIDES PLAY THE SPY GAME—Reds Better Financed and More Active; Danger Seen if West 'Tones Down' Work."[27] This barrage of articles and attention ended, for the time being, Soviet efforts to introduce into serious diplomatic negotiations the issue of intelligence gathering in Berlin. The spy issue was resurrected as the Berlin crisis sharpened and as new KGB active measures were launched, but it never again had the same influence on world opinion. Unfortunately, we do not know just how Gromyko conveyed his displeasure to Shelepin over the way the KGB "spy center" campaign backfired on him personally.

In a curious way, the Soviet and East German assault on the intelligence agencies in West Berlin had favorable but unforeseen consequences. The failure of American intelligence and counterintelligence agencies to coordinate their refugee screening and operations not only had worked to the advantage of Eastern counterintelligence but also had complicated relations between the American intelligence community and the West Berlin government. After the stories about East Berlin espionage were released, US agencies realized the urgency of the problem and were willing to coordinate their efforts. But as this new era of cooperation dawned, many in BOB wondered whether it was not already too late to counterbalance the increasing effectiveness of MfS's internal security and counterintelligence elements. New BOB operations were becoming much harder to develop, and existing cases were sustained only with great difficulty.

18

Bluffs, Threats, and Counterpressures

For BOB, 1959 had been a good year. Its Karlshorst sources had provided the information that the Western Allies needed to call Khrushchev's bluff on his threatened military withdrawal from East Berlin. Using its files and recent operational accounts, BOB had been able to provide detailed intelligence on the real extent of Soviet East German intelligence and subversive operations based in East Berlin. This information, used in publicity campaigns and by the US Secretary of State at meetings with Soviet Foreign Minister Gromyko, blunted Soviet attacks against West Berlin as an espionage swamp and removed the issue from the diplomatic agenda. BOB Chief David Murphy, feeling satisfied about BOB's successes, was looking forward to leaving Berlin in summer 1960. His successor, William Hood, was already in place, serving as deputy chief.

BOB Prepares for the Paris Summit

The decision by the Four Powers to hold summit talks on Berlin in May 1960 meant that BOB had to begin in January to put together briefs for the US delegation on intelligence-related issues. One such brief was an intelligence report dated 5 May confirming that Soviet forces still showed no signs of leaving East Berlin.[1] Because no one was sure to what extent the espionage swamp issue might again play a role, an update was also needed on the shape of the US intelligence community in West Berlin. New agreements among the American services meant that they were coordinating clandestine operations with BOB and had eliminated redundant operations. For the first time since the end of the war, BOB could provide policymakers with precise information about all US intelligence activities in Berlin.

The issue of refugee screening and debriefing was still controversial in 1960. US intelligence agencies relied heavily on refugees to provide not only information relating to Allied security but also fresh intelligence on the GDR and leads to potential agent candidates. But American interactions with refugees were often perceived by West Berlin and FRG authorities as interference in refugee screening and resettlement. Streamlining the debriefings helped assuage this criticism. By April, a month before the summit was to begin, the percentage of refugees selected for screening had fallen dramatically. Further, the new debriefing system devised by BOB gave the intelligence services a much more efficient pattern of security screening.[2]

The presummit reports also focused on the relation between intelligence activity and any new summit agreements regarding the stationing of Allied forces that might dilute Allied responsibility for the security of West Berlin. Were this to happen, the legal basis for security screening of refugees—indeed the very conduct of intelligence and counterintelligence operations—might be jeopardized. BOB also warned that any agreement to reduce the size of the US garrison in West Berlin would cause sharp cuts in the size of US intelligence agencies there because they relied completely on the US military presence for cover and logistical support.[3]

In addition, BOB emphasized the negative effects of a separate Soviet peace treaty with East Germany. Allied leaders, of course, were primarily concerned that such a treaty would allow the Soviets to use their East German colleagues to interfere with access to West Berlin. In BOB's view, other aspects of the treaty could also affect the Allied position in West Berlin.

In a 2 May 1960 dispatch to CIA Headquarters written just before he left to join the US summit delegation in Paris, Murphy argued that "a more likely result [of a peace treaty] will be the creation of an 'international frontier' between East and West Berlin. This will provide the SED regime for the first time with a 'legal' basis for eliminating the present uncontrolled movement across the sector borders. In doing so they would not only reduce the refugee flow to insignificant proportions but also prevent the exposure of thousands of East Berliners to the 'demoralizing ' influences of West Berlin." In addition to stabilizing Ulbricht's Germany, Murphy cautioned, "we can be sure that the level of intelligence activity will drop sharply. Refugee screening will cease almost entirely and it will become more and more difficult to maintain contact with those assets we now have." Prescient words.[4]

KGB Presummit Reporting

Murphy's pessimism stemmed from an appreciation—buttressed by BOB's reporting—of the nearly desperate situation of the Ulbricht regime. CIA analysts did not always agree. For example, a 3 May 1960 National Intelligence Estimate presented a more optimistic picture of the situation in East Germany than that contained not only in contemporary intelligence reporting but also in documents recently uncovered in East German and Soviet archives. NIE makes the incredible statement that "the current outflow of refugees probably only has a minor effect on [East German] economic growth although it does from time to time accentuate shortages of specific skills."[5]

Compare this assessment with comments in August 1958 to the CPSU Central Committee from Yuri Andropov, a future KGB chairman. He noted that the percentage of intelligentsia among refugees had increased by 50 percent since 1957. Andropov repeated his warnings in November 1959. A month later, Soviet Ambassador Mikhail Pervukhin neatly paraphrased Murphy's comments on West Berlin's role as a showcase for Western democracy by noting that the "uncontrolled border . . . prompts the population to make a comparison between both parts of the city, which unfortunately, does not always turn out in favor of Democratic [East] Berlin."[6]

Soviet officials seemed concerned, but we have no comparable reporting of information that the KGB Karlshorst apparat may have obtained on the deplorable political and economic situation in East Germany. Given the high level of interest in East Germany displayed by Soviet embassy reporters and by Andropov in the Central Committee, it seems reasonable to assume that KGB chairman Shelepin would have pushed apparat chief Aleksandr Korotkov to provide such reporting. We cannot account for the absence of this kind of material. Perhaps the lapse was the result of Moscow Center's dispute with Korotkov over how to deal with MFS.[7]

Apparently other KGB residencies did not provide much better information. The only KGB report we obtained from SVR archives reflecting presummit preparations was a copy of a survey done by West German military intelligence in April 1960 that contained West German views on "the international political situation and the activities of the Eastern Bloc on the eve of the Summit." But the survey was not disseminated in Moscow until 16 November 1960.[8] In any case, when CIA's U-2 was shot down over Sverdlovsk, Khrushchev canceled the May summit.[9] Perhaps he had been warned that Eisenhower would have nothing new to say on Germany. There was a suggestion of this sentiment in Shelepin's 1960 annual report, but the original KGB report could not be located in SVR archives.[10]

KGB did provide an excellent report of the summit breakup that was taken from an August 1960 memorandum by a "West European diplomat stationed in West Berlin," but it, too, was not disseminated until 18 November. The report emphasized the East German leaders' frustration over the GDR's poor economic performance. The report's author scathingly compared East Berlin's problems with successes in West Berlin and concluded by predicting in elegant terms that the Soviets would soon resolve the stalemate.[11]

Other KGB reports convey little of the magnitude of the summit failure and its effect on the countries concerned. One, for example, covered the political difficulties faced in West Germany by FRG Minister for All-German Questions Ernst Lemmer, particularly with respect to his relations with various refugee groups and with Adenauer personally. On Berlin, Lemmer was quoted as expressing the view that the USSR would take no aggressive action but would move "gradually," which according to him could be more dangerous, because West Berlin "could not withstand difficult situations, particularly a new blockade."[12]

The next two reports from the same file were provided to KGB by their "Hungarian friends" and testify to the Hungarian service's good contacts in the Vatican and the Italian government. Both were disseminated by Moscow Center on 9 September 1960. The first described talks on disarmament held by FRG Bundeswehr Gen. Adolf Heusinger with the Italian government.[13] The other concerned a statement made by Chancellor Adenauer to the apostolic nuncio in Bonn that "the US had completed preparations for transfer of 'Polaris' missiles to the armed forces of the FRG. However, the transfer could not be accomplished until the decision of the Western European Union (WEU) forbidding the FRG to possess offensive weapons could be annulled." Adenauer asked the Vatican to assist him in persuading WEU member states to rescind the decision. On 8 July, the request was reviewed and approved by the Commission of Cardinals on Foreign Affairs, and Papal Legate Testa was authorized to discuss it with Adenauer during a forthcoming visit to the FRG.[14]

When the summit collapsed in May, some feared that the Soviet "spy center" campaign would be rekindled. The strategy was revived to some extent, but this time its focus was narrowed to CIA. The effort seemed to lack its previous punch, perhaps because the Soviets feared the campaign might backfire: on 28 September, Shelepin distributed to Moscow a copy of a periodic report by West German counterintelligence describing the arrests of more than five hundred persons accused of spying in the FRG for Soviet and satellite services with bases in West Berlin.[15]

Another KGB reaction to the U-2 flight was the preparation of an active measures campaign aimed at discrediting CIA Director Allen W. Dulles, whom Khrushchev rightly saw as the man behind the spy plane affair. The KGB proposal was sent to the Secretariat, CPSU Central Committee, by KGB Chairman Shelepin.[16] This document must have been prepared in Department D of the First Chief Directorate because it used a number of the intelligence and counterintelligence assets of the directorate.[17]

One aspect of Shelepin's proposal that related directly to BOB operations concerned the American practice of "covering officers of West German intelligence services with documents of American citizens." This excerpt shows how important the active measures campaign was to the Soviets. To enhance it, KGB was willing to risk revealing information about ongoing, sensitive cases—in this case the involvement of Heinz Felfe, KGB's penetration of the West German intelligence service—by placing a West German officer in the US Headquarters Compound in Berlin to handle liaison with BOB on the Karlshorst operation.[18]

SED Threatens a Coup d'Etat in West Berlin

In July 1960, BOB reported on SED plans to provoke incidents and foment unrest in West Berlin as a way of supporting Khrushchev's claim that the Berlin situation "could give rise to dangerous accidents." On paper, at least, the Ulbricht regime could easily undertake such actions. There were six thousand SED members in West Berlin itself, and large numbers of East Berlin's workers' militia *(Kampfgruppen)* could be sent quickly into West Berlin via the elevated railroad system, which was controlled by the GDR.[19]

BOB had become concerned nearly a year earlier, in 1959, when the GDR attempted on 7 October (the GDR national holiday) to fly the new GDR flag on railroad property throughout West Berlin. Five thousand Kampfgruppen, posing as railroad employees, were sent in to accomplish this feat.[20] The display of GDR flags was seen at the time by the ever-sensitive West Berlin population as a challenge to the authority of city leaders and to the Western Allies. The West Berlin police were directed to remove the flags, and in some areas major clashes occurred.

Afterward, the US commandant urged that the Allies use troops to assist the police if such a situation came up again. To implement this approach, a plan was needed to coordinate the actions of the West Berlin police and Allied forces.[21]

To assist the planning effort, BOB prepared a report for the US commandant on the capabilities of the East Germans for large-scale subversive actions in West Berlin. It soon became evident that the US Army's contingency planning had been predicated on a possible attack by regular Warsaw Pact forces. In this scenario, US troops were to take up defensive positions around the US community to safeguard American lives and property. Few provisions had been made for supporting the West Berlin police in their defense of such civilian establishments as city hall, police headquarters, and radio stations. Hostile elements could easily enter from East Berlin and simply ignore Allied installations while they concentrated on seizing civil centers of control. This could result, under certain circumstances, in the East Germans' taking control of the city. Although such a frightening outcome seemed unlikely, the events of October 1959 demonstrated that it was not impossible.[22]

Significantly, BOB reports from SED sources on this possibility, the first of which was disseminated on 9 July 1960, did not predict Soviet "military" action against West Berlin but rather the creation of conditions whereby the East Germans could seize control of vital civilian installations. Distribution of the reports accelerated joint planning between the US commandant and the police, but it also alarmed Washington. Perhaps because the scenario represented a new factor in the

Berlin equation, some at CIA Headquarters suggested that BOB's source was parroting Soviet disinformation as part of a KGB scheme to raise the level of concern over the Berlin crisis. But no evidence has been found to support these suspicions.

The question then asked by Washington was whether the Soviets would ever approve of such actions by East Germans. BOB first made clear that no US intelligence unit in West Berlin had sources that could reliably answer that question. Still, because one had to "assume that such plans existed," might not Ulbricht press Khrushchev to allow him to proceed with this strategy if the situation seemed ripe? Ulbricht was growing increasingly desperate because thousands of GDR citizens continued to pour into West Berlin seeking refuge. It could be "difficult for the Soviets to resist allowing Ulbricht to pluck what appears to be a ripe plum if it is done in the right way." It should be made absolutely clear to the Soviets, BOB urged, that Allied troops in West Berlin would reinforce the police in any situation that threatened public security.[23]

Khrushchev Threatens Action if Bundestag Meets in West Berlin

On 8 July 1960, Khrushchev suddenly threatened to sign a separate peace treaty with East Germany if the West German parliament, the Bundestag, were permitted to hold a session in West Berlin as it previously had done.[24] Events since the onset of the Berlin crisis in November 1958 made the Allies wonder whether it was worth pursuing a new session in the face of Khrushchev's threat. Both the French and the British sought ways of canceling or delaying the Bundestag meeting without giving offense to either the FRG or West Berlin.

KGB reported a communication about this issue sent by the British ambassador in Moscow, Sir Patrick Reilly, to the Foreign Office in mid-July 1960. Noting that Khrushchev had not made his statement in a "categorical form," Reilly went on to "emphasize that the Western powers should not underestimate the 'threat' contained in it." It is possible, Reilly wrote, that "the intention of the FRG to hold a Bundestag session in West Berlin may have been taken by Khrushchev as a challenge which could not remain without an answer." Reilly also noted that FRG's Moscow Ambassador Hans Kroll had himself recommended that the Bundestag not meet in West Berlin. In conclusion, Reilly warned that doing so "could lead to very serious consequences." This report, though excellent, was not disseminated by KGB Chairman Shelepin to V. V. Kuznetsov at the Foreign Ministry until 3 October, by which time it had been rendered moot by other events affecting West Berlin.[25]

GDR's September 1960 Travel Controls: Portent of the Wall?

Concern over Khrushchev's threat prevailed, and the Bundestag meeting did not take place. But the East Germans seemed determined to carry out some harassment of the West German government. They chose two long-scheduled meetings in Berlin—of West German organizations representing former prisoners of war and persons expelled from former German territories in the East—as a pretext for instituting new travel controls on the West. Claiming that the meetings represented a "provocative misuse of West Berlin by the FRG, condoned and supported by the Western Allies," the GDR announced on 30 August that as of "midnight that same day controls to travel to East Berlin would be imposed on West German residents and continue through midnight 4 September." The action came without prior warning and took the Western Allies, West Germans, and West Berlin authorities "completely by surprise."[26]

Given the circumstances, BOB strongly believed that these controls were aimed at creating a de facto international frontier between East and West Berlin. In an analysis cabled to CIA Headquarters on 13 September 1960, never before published, BOB described the results of this action: more than one thousand West Germans were denied permission to travel to East Germany on grounds imposed unilaterally by the GDR. Others were refused entry to East Berlin from West Berlin. Most important, the increased controls immediately and dramatically reduced the numbers of refugees arriving in the West: only 3,041 refugees made it to West Berlin during the week of 31 August–6 September, compared with 4,544 the week before.[27]

In effect, BOB reported, the East Germans had succeeded in "establishing effective control of movement between East and West Berlin via vehicular and pedestrian crossing points." GDR control of West German travel to Berlin had been facilitated by the introduction of a new questionnaire about one's possible Nazi background and wartime activities that travelers had to complete at the border. At the same time, the GDR instituted a "widespread . . . campaign in East Germany and East Berlin to condition residents of these areas to accept increased travel controls as necessary for . . . protection against West German revanchists."[28]

In addressing the long-term implications of this short-term action, BOB repeated its view that the present situation, "wherein thousands of East Germans flee to West Berlin each week and other thousands visit the Western sectors, was intolerable to the East German regime."[29]

BOB expected the GDR to use its repressive actions to demonstrate that it could institute measures against West Berlin on a step-by-step basis and in the process weaken ties between Berlin and the FRG and sow discord among the Allies. More important, BOB feared, they might "create doubts in the minds of West Berliners that the Allies are willing or capable of withstanding East German pressure on Berlin."[30]

BOB then highlighted the Achilles heel of both Soviet and Allied positions on Berlin: the idea of four-power control of Berlin. The Soviets had contended that East Berlin was the capital of the GDR, a position in violation of the four-power status of the city. The Western Allies, meanwhile, had "been walking a tightrope strung between their legal position that Berlin enjoys four-power status and the reality that West Berlin has become for all purposes a Land of the Federal Republic." According to BOB, this awkward situation provided the Soviets and East Germans with opportunities for "manipulation and exploitation." But resolving the dilemma by giving the FRG greater responsibility and an even more visible role in West Berlin while still requiring France, Britain, and the United States to defend the Federal Republic's presence in West Berlin would not be popular with the public in Britain and France.[31]

BOB's alternative would involve a "new, sustained and vigorous emphasis of Berlin's four-power status and the concept that Greater Berlin (including East Berlin) represents an area held in trust by the four powers as the future capital of a reunified Germany." The BOB analysis described the sensitivity of both the Soviets and East Germans on this score. At one point the SED leadership had even considered moving the capital of East Germany to Leipzig. But after SED had committed itself to maintaining its center in East Berlin, it risked an embarrassing loss of prestige and administrative chaos if it moved its capital. Hence SED's anxiety over the 1959 speculation concerning free elections in Berlin and United Nations status for it. By adopting BOB's suggestion, which would have the support of the West Berlin population, the Allies could throw the Soviets and SED off balance at a time of great vulnerability.[32]

When Murphy discussed this analysis in Washington at CIA Headquarters and the State Department, he found general agreement with BOB's pessimistic assessment of the implications of the GDR's travel controls but little enthusiasm for BOB's policy suggestion. The 1948 division of Berlin had been accepted de facto by successive US administrations. There was little understanding of Soviet and East German vulnerability on the issue. Consequently, no one believed that resurrection of the issue of four-power status could derail the Soviets and East Germans, who were trying to resolve the problem of GDR stability by altering the status quo in West Berlin.

But Murphy did hear firm support for the continued presence of Allied troops "to prevent the taking of West Berlin by force." Washington's main concern was to ensure that the Soviets, in their search for stability and an end to West Berlin's role as an escape hatch and "showcase of democracy," not be allowed to permit their East German friends to take actions that could humiliate the West, and particularly the United States, which was then preoccupied by a presidential election campaign. Even within CIA's Eastern Europe division, it was acknowledged that there was little one could do about East Berlin or Berlin as a whole. These discussions foreshadowed similar dialogues less than a year later about the Western response to the Wall.

KGB Reporting on the September 1960 Controls

On 3 November 1960, KGB distributed a report based again on a memorandum prepared by the representative of a West European government in West Berlin. After commenting on the GDR's September controls, the official described the action by the East Germans on 10 October—residents of West Germany were required to obtain "special permission" to visit East Berlin—as well as the retaliatory Allied action that denied interzonal documentation to East Germans wishing to travel in countries that did not recognize the GDR. The report suggested that Ulbricht obtained Soviet approval for these actions either at the "Bucharest meetings" or while he was in the Soviet Union in August. Of special interest in light of the controversy over the four-power status of Berlin, the report described the protest made to the Soviet commandant, Gen. Nikolai Zakharov, over imposition of the September controls. Zakharov dismissed the protest, claiming that the GDR enjoyed "full sovereignty in its territory." He also complained that the

"Western Allies were making available to these revanchist groups land and air communications that were intended solely for the occupation troops."[33]

Even more interesting was the description of a meeting in West Berlin between Mayor Willy Brandt and representatives of foreign governments (except those of the Soviet bloc and the occupying powers). Brandt reportedly said that they should expect a "whole series of measures by the East German authorities to separate the two sections of Berlin and destroy the connections between the FRG and West Berlin." In Brandt's opinion, each measure individually would appear so insignificant that the occupation powers would not be able to respond. Noting that the Western commandants had refrained from interfering when the city administration was split in 1948 and during the 1953 uprising in East Berlin, Brandt felt that the East Germans could be counting on the Western Allies' continued passivity. The East Germans, he explained, could feel that they enjoy "a certain freedom of action" because their actions were "directed solely against the FRG and West Berlin" and did "not affect the occupying powers and their communications." As a further example of West Berlin's concern, the report cited the senate's recommendation that the number of occupation troops be increased as an "impressive demonstration" to the Soviet Union of the Western powers' determination to defend West Berlin. "In the given situation," concluded the West European official, "an incorrect assessment of this determination could lead to fatal consequences."[34] If KGB received other reporting along this line, it could only reinforce its view that to achieve its goals in Berlin the best course was to move one step at a time, carefully assessing the consequences of each action and doing their best to ensure that Walter Ulbricht stayed in line.

Another view of the Berlin situation disseminated to Gromyko by Shelepin on 10 December 1960 originated in an 11 October report from the ambassador of a West European country in Moscow to his government. Here again, the lengthy delay suggests that the reporting was obtained by a KGB source in the ambassador's capital and forwarded through KGB channels to Moscow Center, where it was translated and disseminated by the Information Service. Noting that the Berlin question continued to occupy a central position in Soviet policy, the ambassador commented that Bonn's decision to break off trade with the GDR had aroused deep misgivings in Moscow, perhaps because of a fear that the FRG would take "analogous measures against the USSR." The

West German cancellation of the Interzonal Trade Agreement (IZT) with the GDR on 30 September 1960 appears to have surprised Khrushchev. He realized that the Soviet Union could not easily make up for the economic losses the GDR would suffer should trade with West Germany end. Despite the vital importance to both Khrushchev and Ulbricht of information on the issue, KGB was evidently unable to give Moscow advance warning of West German intentions in this regard. In fact, the report, not disseminated by Shelepin until December 1960, contains the only reference to the cancellation of the IZT agreement in any of the KGB reporting made available to us. The immediate crisis ended by mid-December, just as the 10 December report was being read by its recipients, when the FRG finalized a new IZT agreement with the GDR as well as new trade agreements with the USSR.[35]

The West European diplomat concluded his report by asserting that the publicized exchange of notes between the USSR and the United States on German rearmament, as well as Khrushchev's statements at the session of the United Nations General Assembly in New York, were all intended "to concentrate attention on the Berlin question." He insisted that "no other question is of more concern to the interests of the Soviet Union and the European satellite countries as they watch with alarm the rapid rebirth of the economic and military might of the FRG. For Khrushchev, resolution of this problem is linked to his personal prestige. He deludes himself with the hope he will succeed where his predecessors failed—that is, force the Western powers to give up on Berlin, and with this to move the frontier of the Soviet bloc to the Elbe." The scarcity of reports from KGB sources during this critical period, reports that might have informed the Soviet leadership that the West was unlikely to give up on Berlin, reflects KGB Moscow's continued resistance to disseminating unwelcome reports to Soviet leaders.[36]

In a December 1960 briefing of president-elect Kennedy by President Eisenhower and his cabinet, Secretary of State Christian Herter commented about Berlin: "This [situation] is acute and dangerous, and Mr. Khrushchev has heavy pressure to get the Berlin question settled and stop the movement of refugees to the West from behind the Iron Curtain." To a pragmatic politician like John Kennedy, this formulation must have sounded like the preamble to a proposal to help Khrushchev find a way out of his dilemma. Still, the year ended quietly in Berlin, and discussions elsewhere on the Berlin issue were amicable and relaxed, whether between US Ambassador Walter Dowling and Soviet

Ambassador Pervukhin in East Berlin or between participants at the last, very subdued NATO ministerial meeting of 1960.

Within BOB itself, the hectic pace of the growing Berlin crisis had caused Allen Dulles to cancel Murphy's plans to return to Washington for a tour at headquarters in 1960. William Hood left Berlin for another assignment, and John Dimmer was named deputy in his place. Although Dulles never went to West Berlin after becoming director of Central Intelligence, Murphy met him when he traveled to Western Europe and briefed him on the current state of Berlin play.

These briefings were impromptu affairs. One began on Dulles's aircraft on a flight from Frankfurt to the Hague and continued at the ambassador's residence. The Dulles party arrived in the middle of a reception being given for Chief of Naval Operations Adm. Arleigh Burke. When the guests caught sight of Dulles, they abandoned the receiving line and crowded around him, probably hoping to hear secret pearls of wisdom on the continuing Berlin crisis. Dulles, always jovial, managed to extricate himself from his admirers and retire to his quarters to ready himself for the rest of his Berlin briefing later in the evening. In this session, Dulles was told that case officers were increasingly occupied with preparing their people for the inevitable moment when ever more stringent East German security and ever tighter controls on movement across sector borders would severely restrain if not eliminate the opportunities for intelligence gathering that the United States had enjoyed in Berlin since 1945. Ultimately, this preparation for the inevitable was BOB's real job.

PART V

Concrete Diplomacy:
The Berlin Wall

19

Facing the Inevitable

Regardless of the complexity of the policy issues affecting West Berlin's future, it was evident to BOB that it would have to move faster to prepare its agents in the East for the inevitable closure of the sector borders. Nevertheless, for BOB, 1961 still began on a high note. David Murphy and his BOB crew were waiting for the appearance of the mysterious Heckenschuetze, "Sniper," whose identity had been a matter of intense speculation in CIA ever since his first letter had been received in the West in March. Later communications had contained references, albeit often obscure ones, to possible penetrations of Western intelligence services by KGB and Polish intelligence. Sniper reported on two of the most important Soviet spies to affect BOB's operations: George Blake, KGB's spy at SIS who compromised the Berlin tunnel, and Heinz Felfe, KGB's man in the West German Intelligence Service (BND), which was responsible for Karlshorst operations. Although investigation of Sniper's reporting had already begun, no decisive action could be taken on his leads until CIA knew who he was. But now it seemed likely that the enigma would finally be resolved. The excitement at BOB was palpable.

An emergency telephone number at the BOB switchboard had been established for Sniper, and the operators had been warned that if they missed his call they would be on the next boat home. The call came, placed by a person who claimed to be acting on behalf of a Herr Kowalski. Arrangements were made to set up a dead drop—a hiding place where materials could be left by an agent for later retrieval—for Sniper in Warsaw. A drop was made and the contents successfully recovered. Now the final act was about to begin. Because no one had ever seen Sniper, BOB decided that a clandestine street-corner meeting was out. Instructions to Sniper had to be simple, and the BOB reception team had to establish its credentials immediately. The American Consulate was finally chosen as the site for this crucial meeting. The consulate was open to civilians but was adjacent to the military section of the American compound on Clayallee, which was guarded by military police. A suitably impressive office was found and microphones were installed.

At 5:30 P.M. on 4 January, a call came from the go-between announcing that Kowalski would arrive in a half hour. Departing from his usual conspiratorial manner, the caller commented that Kowalski, on whose behalf he was ostensibly acting, had asked that Mrs. Kowalski be treated with special care. The switchboard operator relayed the message to the Sniper team, and the BOB reception plan went into high gear. The chief of BOB's Eastern European branch, who would first receive Sniper, moved to the consulate's entrance. "Bob," the officer who had just flown in from West Germany to act as the Washington "special representative," went to the consular office. The switchboard was kept on alert, in the event that Sniper changed plans. The safe house to which the Sniper party would be taken after initial contact in the consulate was readied, and the BOB operational car that would take them there was parked near the main entrance of the consulate. A Polish-speaking officer was to drive the car in order to pick up any bits of what BOB anticipated would be Polish conversation between Sniper and his wife. When everything was set, David Murphy, head of BOB, and John Dimmer, his new deputy, left the BOB office and walked over to the listening post. They were filled with anticipation, heightened with the tension always felt in high-profile cases.[1]

At 6:06 P.M. a West Berlin taxi pulled up to the consulate and discharged a man and a woman, each carrying a small bag. They looked up apprehensively at the consulate entrance and moved tentatively toward the steps. The couple was immediately greeted by the BOB branch chief and ushered into the consulate, then introduced to the Washington "special representative" and taken down the corridor to the consular office. Here they were informed that they would be granted

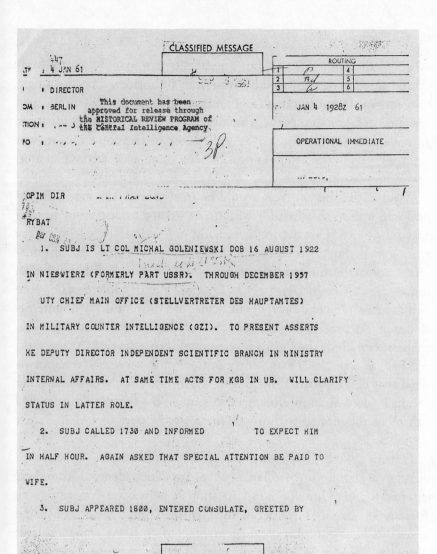

CLASSIFIED MESSAGE

447
4 JAN 61

DIRECTOR

OM BERLIN

TION

TO

JAN 4 1928Z 61

OPERATIONAL IMMEDIATE

OP IM DIR

RYBAT

1. SUBJ IS LT COL MICHAL GOLENIEWSKI DOB 16 AUGUST 1922

IN NIESWIERZ (FORMERLY PART USSR). THROUGH DECEMBER 1957

UTY CHIEF MAIN OFFICE (STELLVERTRETER DES HAUPTAMTES)

IN MILITARY COUNTER INTELLIGENCE (GZI). TO PRESENT ASSERTS

HE DEPUTY DIRECTOR INDEPENDENT SCIENTIFIC BRANCH IN MINISTRY

INTERNAL AFFAIRS. AT SAME TIME ACTS FOR KGB IN UB. WILL CLARIFY

STATUS IN LATTER ROLE.

2. SUBJ CALLED 1730 AND INFORMED   TO EXPECT HIM

IN HALF HOUR. AGAIN ASKED THAT SPECIAL ATTENTION BE PAID TO

WIFE.

3. SUBJ APPEARED 1800, ENTERED CONSULATE, GREETED BY

Berlin cable (operational immediate), 4 January 1961, reporting the safe arrival of Lt. Col. Michal Goleniewski, Polish intelligence official previously known to CIA only as Sniper.

asylum in the United States, but only if the man would identify himself and agree to be debriefed by American authorities. This seemingly innocent request produced an embarrassing pause, after which the man explained in German that the woman was not his wife but his mistress. He requested asylum for her as well. Most of the conversation was barely audible in the listening post, where agents were becoming anxious. Who was this guy?[2]

Assured that his mistress would be treated well, the man asked if she could wait in the corridor because he wished to discuss matters of great sensitivity. This accomplished, the tempo and precision of the meeting picked up. The man explained to the CIA officers that his mistress, an East Berlin resident, knew him only as a Polish journalist, Roman Kowalski. In fact, he was Lt. Col. Michal Goleniewski, who until January 1958 had been deputy chief of Polish military counterintelligence. At present he was director of the independent scientific-technical branch of the Polish foreign intelligence service. At the same time he was acting as a KGB source in the Polish service. He acknowledged that he had written the Sniper letters and that he was the caller who had posed as an intermediary. Agents in the listening post sighed with relief and smiled with joy as these words were recorded. Sniper was for real.[3]

Goleniewski, his mistress, and their escort officer (the "special representative") left Berlin on 5 January 1961 for Wiesbaden and from there departed for the United States.[4] As soon as he was on American soil, Goleniewski's debriefings began. He identified hundreds of Polish and Soviet intelligence officers and agents, including Blake and Felfe. But before the briefings could be completed, Goleniewski grew increasingly difficult to manage, and ultimately he refused to cooperate. A mental illness, characterized by his conviction that he was heir to the Imperial Russian throne, clouded his many contributions to Western counterintelligence during the Cold War.[5]

Sniper's Revelations Inspire BOB to Clean House

The jubilation felt in BOB at the successful exfiltration of Goleniewski could not erase the unhappiness and anxiety caused by his revelations about Blake and Felfe, both of whom were arrested by the end of 1961. This concern was compounded by growing awareness of widespread security problems within the BOB support agent structure. Support agents mail letters, establish or service dead drops, do background checks, and conduct surveillance, among other duties. All intelligence services need such agents, but in a divided city like Berlin, with its distinctly accented German, they had to be natives. For this reason their assignments had to be carefully chosen, by weighing risks against the danger of compromise, and they had to be "clean"—that is, free from any suspicion of hostile control. Further, their tasks had to be accomplished in East Berlin, an area dominated by MFS, an internal security service that by the early 1960s was all too good at intercepting Western agents and doubling them back. BOB could little afford internal spies at a time when East Berlin was rapidly being shut off from Western access.

To appreciate BOB's dependence upon these agents, it is essential to understand how they were recruited and supported. Over time, BOB had developed a centralized "operations support" branch that controlled the recruitment, training, and handling of support agents. It was not a glamorous placement—no counterintelligence breakthroughs or exciting reports were produced that could earn case officers praise and promotions. As a result, these jobs often went to junior officers on their first overseas assignments. Because their German language proficiency, however competent, was not up to developing and recruiting the kinds of street-smart Berliners who were ready to risk prison for mailing a letter in East Berlin, some support agent networks relied as well on local intermediaries, or "principal agents." Principal agents, most of them native Berliners, used their circle of friends and relatives to find agents who could do the job. In many cases, they provided continuity and exercised significant independence because any of their BOB case officers with talent were quickly snapped up by other branches.

Given the frenetic pace of agent operations in Berlin, the demand for information always exceeded the supply of agents. But when the need arose in the Popov case for a "clean" courier, one was available: an elderly East Berlin pensioner—code named the Old Man—with a niece in West Berlin. Through a friend he had been introduced to a BOB principal agent, a gregarious Berlin native known to a succession of BOB case officers as Fatso, who had been in contact with BOB since the early 1950s. Fatso had been set up in a small service business in West Berlin, but his primary job was recruiting likely support agents. Some, like the Old Man, were East Berlin residents; others had lived in the Soviet sector but later moved to West Berlin. Which ones were chosen for what support task depended on the nature and duration of the job. In the case of the courier runs to Popov in Schwerin, the agent had to have legitimate GDR documentation and be free to travel—hence the selection of a pensioner. The Old Man was a natural, and he performed admirably.

After KGB's dramatic 16 October 1959 arrest of Popov on bus 107, BOB needed to warn the Old Man that "something had happened to the person whom he had met during 1956–57." "Hans," the officer chosen to convey this message, was newly assigned to the support branch but already spoke German with native fluency and was an adept student of Berlin life and customs.

But CIA had by this time begun to mistrust Fatso. Prodded by Washington headquarters, BOB had begun to review the operational history of the agents in the Fatso entourage after one of them was arrested in December 1958. The agent had been told to recover a briefcase containing a camera from the baggage room at the Ostbahnhof (Eastern Railroad Station) in East Berlin. It had been deposited there by another agent, a photographer who used it for a Karlshorst photo-surveillance mission. BOB's review included an examination of all operational actions in which the arrested agent had participated.[6] Although no evidence was obtained indicating that Fatso had been recruited by MfS, the review demonstrated that it would be hazardous to continue to use him as a recruiter of support agents; many of his people knew one another, which made effective operational compartmentation difficult, if not impossible. As a result, Fatso was dropped by BOB in August 1959; he had been a fixture on the BOB operational scene for too many years. Some of BOB's old-timers felt a twinge of regret mixed with nostalgia, but to most it seemed a correction long overdue. They were optimistic that the worst was over. They were wrong.

Fatso's Mistakes Further Shake Up BOB

When Hans advised the Old Man that although the person he had met in 1956–57 (Popov) did not know his true name or his place of residence, he also explained that there could be no guarantees that he, the Old Man, would not fall under suspicion. Hans assured the Old Man that if he wished, he would be given financial assistance to resettle in West Berlin and find an apartment. The Old Man sighed and thanked Hans for his offer, but said that at his advanced age he did not want to move from his lifelong home in East Berlin. Hans had no choice but to accept this decision, and he made arrangements for future contact. But before ending the meeting, he made clear to the Old Man that further contact with Fatso was out, as was any further operational activity. Fatso, Hans explained, was known to MfS, and any involvement with him would be dangerous.[7]

After that meeting, BOB lost track of the Old Man. It was later learned that he had been arrested in November 1959, tried for contact with "American spies," and sentenced to prison. He was released in May 1962 and continued to live quietly in East Berlin, but he took advantage of one of the few Wall-era holiday visiting periods to see his niece. While in the West, he contacted BOB and told of his arrest.

By the end of 1960, just as BOB desperately needed support agents to help prepare its Eastern spies for tightened border controls, MfS pulled a caper that, although unsuccessful, shed considerable light on the parlous state of BOB's operational support structure. On 24 November, Fatso received a letter from one of his former agents who had been dropped earlier by BOB on suspicion of contact with MfS. Attached to it was a second letter from an MfS officer containing an artfully phrased recruitment pitch, "thanking" Fatso for his "cooperation," and inviting him to a "face to face" meeting.[8]

No longer employed by BOB, Fatso had been given a low-security telephone number and told to call if anything untoward occurred that could affect his or BOB's security. When he received the letters, Fatso immediately contacted BOB and turned them over. In the second letter, Stasi thanked Fatso profusely for his "good services." He had, according to the letter, "warned our people ... about the completion of an assignment at the Eastern Railroad Station," making it possible for them to catch "agent S ... in the act." The result of this was the "detention of the agent R." What did this MfS pitch imply, and what did BOB learn from it?[9]

Agent S was the BOB support agent who had picked up the camera in the East Berlin railroad station and had been arrested in December 1958. When the East Germans said that Fatso had "warned our people," they were referring to "Guenther," another longtime BOB support agent who had actually been under Stasi control for many years, though neither Fatso nor BOB knew this. MfS was in a quandary. Guenther had been selected initially by BOB to recover the camera, but if he did, MfS would miss the chance to nab a clean BOB support agent and expand its knowledge of BOB's support operations. But in fact the "Karlshorst photographer" was also under MfS control, and at MfS's instructions he delayed bringing the baggage claim check to West Berlin until it was too late for BOB to contact Guenther, who had deliberately made himself unavailable. A substitute had to be found quickly by BOB, and "S," a West Berlin resident, turned out to be the sacrificial lamb.[10]

The reference to the role of "S" in detecting "R" was obviously intended to add a twist that would put more pressure on Fatso to cooperate. "R" was the Old Man who had been arrested in 1959, after the windup of the Popov case. From their interrogation of "S," the East German investigators probably learned that he had been a longtime friend of the Old Man's niece and her husband, both West Berlin residents. The MFS must have hoped that by introducing this link to the Popov case they would make it harder for Fatso to disclose the recruitment pitch to BOB. But who was Guenther, in whom the MFS reposed such confidence in planning the operation underlying this pitch?

Guenther, a West Berlin resident and acquaintance of Fatso, was recruited by Fatso in 1954 as a support agent.[11] Arrested in June 1956 during a letter-mailing mission in East Berlin while carrying a false East German identity document supplied by BOB, he was forced to sign an agreement to work for MFS and given a cover name. He was then released and told to tell his American "boss" that he had delivered the letter, then to return to East Berlin for regular meetings with MFS. Of course, he told Fatso and the BOB case officer, he had no intention of reporting back.[12] An attempt to polygraph Guenther failed, apparently because of his health problems. He was therefore put on ice and given no further operational assignments in East Berlin, but he remained in contact with Fatso. In spring 1959, however, Guenther was reactivated. He was fitted for a disguise and wig because of BOB's desperate need for people still willing to perform operational tasks in East Berlin. His health had improved, but apparently he still could not be subjected to a polygraph to resolve the question of his possible MFS ties, so he was not actually given any assignments.[13] Finally, on 30 September 1959, as a result of the overall security review of operations support branch cases, Guenther was dropped "without prejudice" by BOB for security reasons related to the June 1956 incident.[14]

But that was not all. Stasi also included in its letter to Fatso warm thanks for having alerted them to caches of two agent radio sets in November and December 1959. This was during the time following the Khrushchev ultimatum, when BOB's Soviet branch was trying to provide alternate communications for its agents. Even though Guenther had been formally dropped from BOB's agent rolls, he was called upon to dig the holes in which the radio equipment would be hidden. Obviously Guenther should never have been used, regardless of the pressure on the case officer to get the radios to his agents. Stasi learned from Guenther what nights the radios were buried and compared the dates with license plate records for vehicle crossings at the sector border. Eliminating those with valid reasons for visiting West Berlin, Stasi soon arrested the independent BOB agent who had furnished the car to transport the bulky radio equipment.[15]

The MfS letter to Fatso demonstrated that action had to be taken immediately to prevent local agents, who may have been doubled, from knowing enough to jeopardize the safety of other BOB agents in East Germany. The need to provide alternate communications had never been greater, yet to continue using the same coordinated approach among the branches would only give MfS a road map to remaining good agents. As a defensive measure, BOB abolished its central support branch. Henceforth, each case officer in the area branches had to find his own operational support agents and make sure these agents were not being used in other cases. This was a tough dictum because it meant that at a time when the pressures to prepare for the inevitable were greatest, the tempo of BOB operations had to slow down.

Planning for an Uncertain Future

While BOB was doing everything possible to ensure that it could communicate with its Eastern agents if tightened sector border controls made meetings in West Berlin impossible, it also had to reckon with the fact that finding and recruiting new sources was becoming extremely difficult. The military services, whose clandestine operations were now being coordinated by BOB, were the first to feel the pinch, but the situation affected the entire intelligence community. As the problems in operational support activities suggest, the principal reason for concern was the increasing effectiveness of the East German secret police. MfS outshone not only KGB but the Gestapo of Nazi days as well. Stasi's army of internal informants, highly effective record system, and good counterintelligence coverage of targets in West Berlin all contributed to its ability to smother new cases before they had a chance to develop. Refugees who had held positions of importance, the usual source for new BOB leads, came under MfS suspicion as soon as unusual absences from office or organization were noticed. An immediate MFS investigation followed, including a check on family members, neighbors, coworkers, and anyone else who might receive an invitation to West Berlin.

In addition, earlier KGB publicity describing the "espionage swamp" in West Berlin had dampened prospective agent recruiting. East Germans, even those whose records showed them to be staunchly anti-Communist, were reluctant to become involved with intelligence activities. To do so meant risking an unauthorized visit to West Berlin at a time of heightened security both at sector borders and on elevated and underground railroads.

BOB planned to provide sources with emergency impersonal communications in the event that meetings with agents in West Berlin were no longer possible, but case officers knew just how tough this would be. Smuggling two-way radio sets into East Berlin was enormously risky and complicated. And training agents to operate these radios was difficult—most of them were simply unable to master it. Case officers were also aware of the dangers associated with two-way radio communications. If possession of such equipment came to the attention of the agent's family members or circle of friends, odds were excellent that the word would get out to an MFS informer. And if an agent did go on the air, MFS was growing ever more adept at intercepting and locating the sources of such broadcasts.

Because of these doubts and difficulties, BOB focused on trying to train agents to write coded messages to their BOB case officers. A major campaign was instituted in West Berlin, West Germany, and throughout Western Europe to find people who would agree to receive letters from East Germany and pass them along to BOB. Coincidentally, KGB was involved in a parallel effort. During the Berlin crisis, fearing it would have difficulties maintaining contact with its agents in West Berlin and West Germany, KGB created its own network of letter drops in Western Europe for emergency use.[16]

Messages to a BOB agent from a case officer were sent in code via one-way voice broadcasts. The agent needed only a standard shortwave civilian radio, not a two-way radio set. Although this meant that the opposition could easily intercept and record such transmissions, it would still have no clue of the recipient's whereabouts. Or so the theory went. BOB discovered to its chagrin that the East German postal authorities regularly checked to determine which citizens were illegally listening to radio receivers on which they had not paid their radio tax.

Naturally, BOB agents paid their taxes. But it turned out that while making their checks on these Schwarzehoerer, illegal listeners, the radio authorities' technical vans could also determine the frequency to which the listener was tuned. BOB finally determined that a Grundig model, available in East Germany, was sufficiently shielded to prevent emissions from giving away the frequencies in use; but finding such solutions was possible only through trial and error.

Instructing agents in these one-way voice link (OWVL) techniques was much easier than training them to use a radio set. For one thing, the material needed to handle secret writing and the decoding of broadcasts was much easier to conceal than a radio set. Moreover, OWVL, by its very nature, seemed to reassure the agents that this was indeed only an emergency precaution, designed to add flexibility to their communications without eliminating meetings in West Berlin. The agents had been showered with East German press articles and films showing captured radio operators, and the very idea of radio communications frightened them.

During 1960 and 1961, BOB case officers literally worked night and day to learn how to manage these impersonal communications and then convince agents in the field that the system would work. Even though they were assisted by communications technicians, the case officers had to learn the drill because, in the final analysis, it was they who would have to persuade the agent of the need for emergency communications. It was tedious and often exasperating work, made more difficult by the fact that the agents themselves, who had already risked prison to cross the sector border to bring their case officer intelligence information, resisted being pressured to learn codes.

The East German branch, whose agents were still providing good intelligence on internal GDR affairs, did particularly well during this demanding period before the Wall was erected. The branch was headed by a tough, uncompromising chief, "Fritz," who had little patience for fools and laggards. Even before the central operations support branch was abolished, the East German group had begun to get organized so that it could arrange its own network of agents. Some of these agents, mostly "little old lady pensioners," offered their apartments as safe houses for a modest fee. These new agents were completely independent and had no ties with the earlier support structure. Their use during the months before the Wall went up helped throw MfS counterintelligence off the trail at a critical period for BOB.

Always searching for new angles to improve agent communications, Fritz saw an advertisement in a US electronics catalogue for a still somewhat primitive infrared apparatus that was more like a toy than a serious communications device. Because the East German branch had agents who lived within sight of buildings on the west side of the sector border, he wanted to order it and try it out. An infrared device, even with limited range, would have been perfect. He was told that because it was made in the United States, CIA Office of Communications policy would permit its purchase for use in operations only after it was tested and approved. Nothing ever happened. Had BOB been able to find this equipment locally, it would have tested it on its own. Perhaps this reluctance to test new technologies was why Bill Harvey delighted in referring to communications research and development officers as "wafflebottoms."

Other Intelligence Priorities

In spite of its intense preoccupation with improving the emergency communications of its agents in the East, BOB, especially the East German branch, continued to inform the American government about changes within the upper echelons of SED and the GDR government. The decline of GDR prime minister Otto Grotewohl is a good example. In June 1959, BOB described the relationship between Ulbricht and Grotewohl as cool. According to BOB sources, Grotewohl had actually participated in the anti-Ulbricht activities of Karl Schirdewan and his friends in 1957–58. Ulbricht was aware of Grotewohl's involvement but reportedly did not act because he feared that the Soviets would stand by Grotewohl as they had in previous disputes. He was, after all, their "showpiece Socialist," whose defection from the German Social Democratic Party right after the war had made possible the creation of SED. The two men had been at odds since Ulbricht's insistence in the late 1940s that Grotewohl, in the name of "socialist morality," end his affair with his secretary. In the violent argument that ensued, Grotewohl had a nervous breakdown and was treated in the Soviet hospital in Karlshorst. The Soviets then took Grotewohl's side. The Soviet ambassador to East Germany instructed Ulbricht to let Grotewohl divorce his wife and marry the secretary.[17]

In September 1960, Ulbricht created the GDR State Council as a device to streamline control and put decision making in his own hands.

BOB reported that Grotewohl, who had suffered an apparent stroke earlier in September, was nevertheless required to attend the ceremonies in honor of the council's creation, after which he entered a sanitorium near Moscow. In December 1960 members of Grotewohl's staff expressed doubt that he would ever resume his official duties.[18]

In early January 1961, Grotewohl was scheduled to return to the GDR, but his Soviet doctors ordered him to remain in the Moscow-area sanitorium. Meanwhile, East German media still issued statements in Grotewohl's name, giving the impression that he was still functioning as prime minister.[19] According to BOB sources, Grotewohl actually returned to the GDR in early March 1961 but did not resume his official duties. Even though the East German media continued to publish his "appointments" in order to convey an impression of "business as usual," Grotewohl actually remained in seclusion at his villa in the new GDR government leaders' enclave in Wandlitz. Although he retained his position until his death in 1964, his influence was nil. He was replaced as prime minister by Willi Stoph.[20]

What About Insurrection in East Germany?

In March 1961, David Murphy visited CIA headquarters in Washington. The new administration was in place, the abortive Bay of Pigs landing was still a month away, and Berlin seemed likely to be the next crisis spot. The refugee flow continued unabated. More than five thousand people had fled East Berlin during the long Easter weekend. The Cuban adventure had not yet given covert action a bad name, and Henry Kissinger, who had come to Washington from Harvard to advise the administration on the Berlin issue, had requested a "survey of clandestine activities which might possibly be undertaken in support of the US position on Berlin." A reply was prepared in CIA's Eastern European division, to which a note had been added: the review was "informal and does not represent a recommendation by the Agency that these actions be undertaken."[21]

The survey was predicated on the assumption that the "Soviet Union intends to . . . complete the integration of East Berlin into East Germany and to make the Western position in West Berlin so tenuous that the West will eventually see no alternative but to withdraw from Berlin and recognize . . . East Germany as a sovereign state." The suggestions included actions designed to increase economic pressures in

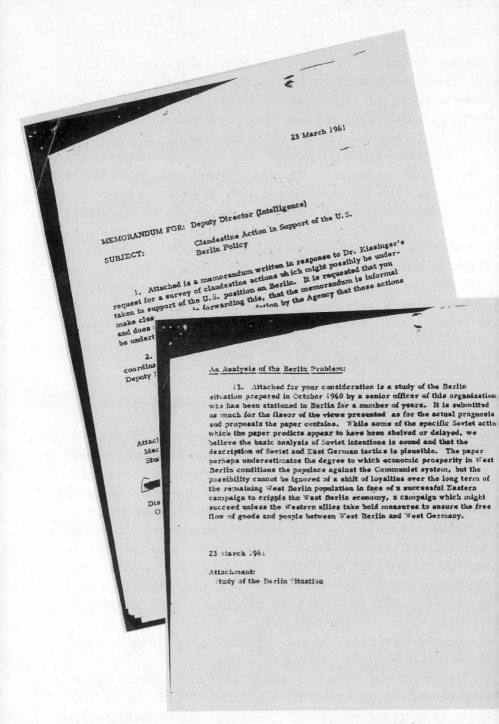

23 March 1961

MEMORANDUM FOR: Deputy Director (Intelligence)

SUBJECT: Clandestine Action in Support of the U.S.
Berlin Policy

1. Attached is a memorandum written in response to Dr. Kissinger's request for a survey of clandestine actions which might possibly be undertaken in support of the U.S. position on Berlin. It is requested that you make clea̲ ... ... in forwarding this, that the memorandum is informal and does ... ...tion by the Agency that these actions be undert...

2.
coordina...
Deputy D...

Attach...
Mem...
Stud...

Dis...
O...

An Analysis of the Berlin Problem:

13. Attached for your consideration is a study of the Berlin situation prepared in October 1960 by a senior officer of this organization who has been stationed in Berlin for a number of years. It is submitted as much for the flavor of the views presented as for the actual prognosis and proposals the paper contains. While some of the specific Soviet actio̲ which the paper predicts appear to have been shelved or delayed, we believe the basic analysis of Soviet intentions is sound and that the description of Soviet and East German tactics is plausible. The paper perhaps underestimates the degree to which economic prosperity in West Berlin conditions the populace against the Communist system, but the possibility cannot be ignored of a shift of loyalties over the long term of the remaining West Berlin population in face of a successful Eastern campaign to cripple the West Berlin economy, a campaign which might succeed unless the Western allies take bold measures to ensure the free flow of goods and people between West Berlin and West Germany.

23 March 1961

Attachment:
Study of the Berlin Situation

Memorandum, 23 March 1961, from Gordon M. Stewart, chief, Eastern European Division, to deputy director, intelligence, regarding clandestine action in support of US Berlin policy. CIA responds to Henry Kissinger's questions on insurrection in East Germany.

East Germany. A final category was included under the heading "What about insurrection?" These proposals, aimed at increasing "East German instability," would have to be "gauged accurately" because the intent was not "to incite the populace to insurrection" but to "stimulate ... concessions to the populace." Given the efficiency of the East German police state and the dearth of agents available to implement such actions (organizations like the Free Jurists and the Fighting Group Against Inhumanity had virtually ceased to exist), the ideas were extremely unrealistic. Other elements in this category included "encouraging an increase in the flow of refugees with critical skills" and "encouraging selected West German political leaders to develop contacts with East German politicians ... for the transmittal of ideas and plans." As for the refugee flow, East German propaganda was already blaming the West. Consequently, securing West German approval and assistance for actions as politically sensitive as those recommended seemed doubtful at best.[22]

The other actions suggested were for the most part similar to those contained in the "Long Range Plan for Berlin" (drawn up by CIA's Eastern European division on the basis of BOB recommendations made after the GDR had tightened border controls in September 1960). They involved increasing the Western presence in West Berlin, culturally as well as militarily; encouraging worldwide interest in maintaining West Berlin's freedom; and countering Communist propaganda about the city. All these were feasible. The suggestions were prefaced by the caveat that they would require cooperation of the West German government. Clandestine actions—like encouraging boycotts of East German firms or harassing East German trade representatives abroad—were considered "to place the Communists under economic pressure," but the memorandum recognized that without a consensus by NATO countries on this issue, covert operations "would almost certainly be ineffective."[23]

As for possible insurrection, the reaction was firm and to the point. Having raised the issue as a question, the Eastern European division drafters stated flatly that "insurrection is not a feasible clandestine action operation except in a situation in which open military action between the Soviet Union and the West is actually imminent."[24] If the first category of suggestions in this memorandum urging actions to "increase East German instability" echoed earlier covert action concepts, the unequivocal rejection of "insurrection" as an option was a signal

CENTRAL INTELLIGENCE AGENCY

This material contains information affecting the National Defense of the United States within the meaning of the Espionage Laws, Title 18, U.S.C. Sec. 793 and 794, the transmission or revelation of which in any manner to an unauthorized person is prohibited by law.

CLASSIFICATION — DISSEMINATION CONTROLS

SECRET — CIA INTERNAL USE ONLY

COUNTRY	GERMANY	REPORT NO.
SUBJECT	IMPLICATIONS OF NEW EAST GERMAN MEASURES AGAINST WEST BERLIN— SITUATION REPORT AS OF 7 SEPTEMBER 1960	DATE DISTR. 13 SEPTEMBER 1960
		PRECEDENCE
		REFERENCES
DATE OF INFO.		
PLACE & DATE ACQ.	GERMANY, BERLIN	
APPRAISAL	COMMENTARY	FIELD REPORT NO.

This document has been approved for release through the HISTORICAL REVIEW PROGRAM of the Central Intelligence Agency

Date 3/8/94

94-1

HRP

THIS IS UNEVALUATED INFORMATION. SOURCE GRADINGS ARE DEFINITIVE. APPRAISAL OF CONTENT IS TENTATIVE.

SOURCE

STAFF OFFICERS OF THIS ORGANIZATION STATIONED IN BERLIN SINCE 1952-54.

PREPARED FOR INTERNAL USE OF THIS ORGANIZATION AS BACKGROUND INFORMATION ON THE CONTROL MEASURES TAKEN BY THE EAST GERMAN REGIME DURING 31 AUGUST - 4 SEPTEMBER 1960. THOUGH BASED ON ALL AVAILABLE DATA, THE VIEWS EXPRESSED ARE THOSE OF BASE OFFICERS. THIS REPORT WAS PREPARED BEFORE THE NEW EAST GERMAN MEASURES WHICH TOOK EFFECT ON 9 SEPTEMBER 1960.

1. UNDER THE PRETEXT THAT TWO LONG SCHEDULED MEETINGS IN WEST BERLIN MANIFESTED FEDREP REVANCHIST PLANS AGAINST ITS EASTERN NEIGHBORS AND THEREBY REPRESENTED FURTHER PROVOCATIVE FEDREP MISUSE OF WEST BERLIN CONDONED AND SUPPORTED BY THE WESTERN ALLIES, THE SED REGIME ON 30 AUGUST ANNOUNCED THAT CONTROLS ON TRAVEL TO EAST BERLIN OF WEST GERMAN RESIDENTS WOULD BE IMPOSED AS OF MIDNIGHT AND CONTINUE THROUGH MIDNIGHT 4 SEPTEMBER. THIS ACTION CAME WITHOUT PRIOR WARNING

CLASSIFICATION — DISSEMINATION CONTROLS

SECRET — CIA INTERNAL USE ONLY

		OCI	ONE	OCR		DD

CIA information report, 13 September 1960, BOB staff analysis regarding implications of new East German measures against West Berlin.

that in Central Europe, at least, CIA had no illusions about overthrowing a Soviet-supported Communist regime through externally mounted clandestine operations. But this hope that somehow local revolts by East German citizens could be instigated by CIA "on demand" lingered on in the minds of some policymakers and was raised again later in the summer.

Will America Give Nuclear Weapons to NATO?

KGB reporting for this period emphasized relations with the new Kennedy administration in Washington. But delays in getting this information to Khrushchev must surely have lessened its value to the Soviet leader. On 24 April 1961, for example, KGB prepared an analytical memorandum on Kennedy's foreign policy. It described FRG leaders' concern that the Kennedy administration was interested in relaxing tensions in US-Soviet relations. Adenauer feared that any relaxation in US-USSR tensions might produce decisions on Germany and Berlin detrimental to FRG interests. To exert pressure on Kennedy not to pursue such a course, the FRG hinted that it would also like to improve relations with the USSR: the FRG would not play the "heavy" for Western European policies.

Another FRG concern was the Kennedy administration's "new military policy," in which the United States announced that it would abandon plans to "transform NATO into a 'fourth atomic power.'" According to this new policy, no atomic weapons would be transferred to the FRG. A KGB memorandum quoted the FRG defense minister as saying, "The new American policy raises questions about the very creation of the Bundeswehr [FRG Army] and delivers an irreversible blow to troop morale." The memorandum concluded that the FRG will "continue to press for atomic weapons for the Bundeswehr."[25]

Other interesting KGB reports found in the SVR archives underline Soviet interests at this important juncture. At the end of March, the Italian ambassador in Moscow reported to Rome that the Soviets were doubling their efforts to reach an agreement with Bonn because of concern that signing a peace treaty with the GDR alone would only lead "to an increase in dissatisfaction among Germans." The ambassador also noted that "the Soviet threat to cut off communications between West Berlin and West Germany could turn against the USSR, but despite this, the Soviet government persists because its allies, and above all the GDR government, are pushing it." The report concluded by noting Soviet concern over "the rearming of Western Germany and the support being given to the FRG by its allies."[26]

Reinforcing earlier reports of FRG concern that the Americans and Soviets might resolve their differences at West Germany's expense, KGB reported a conversation held in late April between the FRG ambassador in Paris, Herbert Blankenhorn, and an unidentified source. The report claimed that if NATO possessed atomic weapons, then "the threat of atomic war breaking out would force the Russians to refrain from unilateral actions concerning West Berlin." "Unfortunately," Blankenhorn reportedly said, "we have information which leads us to believe Kennedy adheres to a different point of view on this question." In Kennedy's entourage it was felt that the "Berlin conflict" must not be allowed to transform itself into a world war. NATO must not be given atomic weapons, and the Berlin conflict should remain "local in character." In spite of these differences, Blankenhorn asserted that "the FRG would approve US foreign policy actions and expects complete and unconditional support from the United States in the Berlin question." This report was passed along to the Soviet Foreign Ministry on 3 May 1961.[27]

The emphasis in KGB reporting on access by the Bundeswehr to atomic weapons continued during spring 1961. On 6 May, KGB reported in detail on Adenauer's discussions with members of the NATO investigative group led by Dean Acheson. Adenauer was reportedly concerned that the Kennedy administration, which was concentrating on Latin America in the grim aftermath of the Bay of Pigs disaster in April, considered Europe of secondary importance. He worried that in a European conflict with the USSR, unless NATO had its own weapons the Allies would intervene too late and the Soviets could conquer all of Europe. Adenauer stated, "If this problem is not resolved, NATO will face the danger of collapsing, and several European countries will be forced to resort to the creation of their own deterrent forces."[28]

According to the KGB report, Acheson assured Adenauer that "in the event of a conflict with the Soviet Union, the United States will intervene immediately." But atomic weapons, he said, would be used only as a last resort. As a result of his conversation with Adenauer, Acheson reportedly gained the impression that West Germany would continue "its intrigues among NATO member countries on the question of . . . atomic weapons." When the KGB report is compared with Acheson's own report of the five hours he spent alone with Adenauer and his interpreter on 9 April 1961, KGB emphasis on Adenauer's concerns about NATO's nuclear capabilities seems overdone.[29]

Overall, KGB reporting obtained for this period deals less with the Berlin crisis and the difficult problems of USSR relations with its GDR partner than with the question of West German access, via NATO, to atomic weapons. Our search of the SVR archives unearthed no reports formally disseminated by KGB for the critical period of January–June 1961 on the Berlin crisis or plans under way in Moscow and East Berlin to resolve it. Why? The reason appears to be the very personal, secretive manner in which Khrushchev conducted Berlin policy. KGB officials at all levels were extremely reluctant to pass along any reporting from residencies abroad that might contradict Khrushchev's views or appear to criticize the way he was handling the Berlin situation.[30]

Even though Berlin was of major concern to Khrushchev and Ulbricht, they were determined to keep their real plans secret. Although many observers have believed that the 28–29 March 1961 meeting of the Warsaw Pact Political Consultative Committee in Moscow was crucial in Soviet planning for the Wall, Berlin was not even listed on the official agenda. According to newly released documents, the agenda, approved at the 15 March 1961 meeting of the Presidium of the CC CPSU and circulated to Warsaw Pact member states in preparation for the session, dealt only with Warsaw Pact military matters.[31] Ulbricht chaired the meeting, and after work on the agenda was completed he and other delegates spoke to the Berlin problem in familiar terms, expounding on the dangers of subversives' uncontrolled movement from West to East Berlin.[32] The massive flight of the GDR population was portrayed as a result of Western provocations, and there was unanimity on the need for strengthening controls along the border. In his speech, Ulbricht specifically linked the massive flight of the GDR population through West Berlin to FRG rearmament, claiming that this loss of East German manpower was of benefit to the West German effort. Significantly, Ulbricht also insisted on the need to "guarantee the invulnerability" of the GDR economy in the event that West Germany should respond to East German measures to correct the Berlin situation by violating the interzonal trade agreements.

These discussions were fully reflected in the protocol of the 28–29 March meeting, but there was no mention of specific measures to close the sector borders or build a wall. Such preparations were being undertaken in complete secrecy and would never be disclosed at such a session.[33] Also, Khrushchev, knowing that the border closing would provoke hostile reactions in both East Germany and the West, was anxious to avoid premature disclosure of Soviet involvement. Most important, before committing himself irrevocably to such action, Khrushchev clearly wished to test the position of the new Kennedy administration on Berlin, although no time had yet been set for a meeting between the two men.

On 19 May 1961 the Soviet ambassador in East Berlin, Mikhail Pervukhin, sent a letter to Foreign Minister Gromyko to update him on the Berlin problem before the Vienna summit. At one point in his letter, Pervukhin emphasized that the "friends would now like to establish enough control over the sector border between Democratic and West Berlin so that they could, as they say, 'close the door to the West,' reduce the flow of the population from the Republic, and weaken the actions of economic diversion against the GDR, which have been carried out directly from West Berlin." This forceful statement suggests that the East Germans were in fact making preparations to "close the door."[34]

The Vienna summit soon launched the next and most virulent phase of the Berlin crisis. The implications of the meeting were still reverberating throughout capitals in both East and West on 27 June, when "Sasha" Korotkov, called back from Berlin to Moscow to explain the performance of his Karlshorst apparat, died. The apparat would now be without its veteran leader in the critical days ahead.

20

Countdown to the Wall

The Vienna summit in early June 1961 was a pivotal event in the Berlin crisis, which had festered since November 1958, when Khrushchev issued his first ultimatum to the Allies: either settle the Berlin problem on his terms within six months or he would sign a peace treaty with the GDR ending Allied rights in Berlin. In Vienna, Khrushchev made the same threat again. Kennedy, still smarting from the Bay of Pigs debacle, emerged from the meetings determined to take whatever measures were needed to defend the Allied position there. Planning these actions, including proposals for covert paramilitary operations by CIA in the GDR, dominated administration activity on Berlin for the next several years. In spite of warnings that East Germany would be forced to act to cut off the flight of refugees to the West, this aspect of the Berlin problem was ignored. The countdown to the Wall continued.

During David Murphy's visit to Washington in March 1961, it had been decided that William Graver would replace him as base chief when he left BOB in early summer. An old Berlin hand, Bill Graver had been at BOB from 1954 until 1958, heading operations against East German targets. After his return to Washington, he became chief of the branch at CIA headquarters responsible for supporting BOB activities. Graver, who literally towered over his colleagues, was known in BOB as "der

Lange," the Tall One.[1] Until Graver took charge at BOB, John Dimmer, who had been deputy and chief of operations at BOB for nearly a year, was to sit in. With the Vienna summit about to begin, BOB case officers were still concentrating on the difficult but essential task of providing their agents with emergency means of communication for use if the sector borders were closed.

Sergei Kondrashev was still deputy resident in Vienna. Known to the American diplomatic community as Laughing Boy because of his unusually jovial manner, Kondrashev was a practiced linguist who was extremely popular on the diplomatic circuit—as was his wife, Rosa, who many thought was the daughter of a high-ranking GRU general. (Her father was actually a senior KGB official.) Kondrashev wore well-tailored clothes—a legacy of his London tour, where he had handled George Blake—and was unique among Soviet diplomats then posted in Vienna for his ability to discuss political subjects in fluent English, German, or French without having to fall back on Soviet ideological cant. The summit was the high point of his Vienna tour. Everyone marveled at the manner in which he would break into conversations during social events that were being translated by the official Soviet interpreters, sometimes correcting a word or phrase. He especially enjoyed interrupting conversations with the beautiful Jacqueline Kennedy. The regularly assigned interpreters were clearly annoyed, but KGB deputy resident Kondrashev enjoyed special privileges.

The first summit session was held at the American ambassador's home on 3 June. It became a sparring match in which Kennedy and Khrushchev tested one another's limits. The next meeting took place at the Soviet embassy. The atmosphere cooled when talk turned to Berlin. Khrushchev revealed plans to sign a peace treaty with the GDR, unilaterally if necessary, after which "all rights of access to Berlin will expire because the state of war will cease to exist." When Kennedy asked "whether such a peace treaty would block access to Berlin," Khrushchev said that it would, for "the USSR considered all of Berlin to be GDR territory." Reverting once more to a six-month ultimatum, Khrushchev declared that when an interim arrangement expired in December, access to West Berlin would end and Western troops would have to be withdrawn. (Khrushchev's bluff this time was based on his view that the Allied garrisons, unwilling to come to an agreement with the GDR about their presence, would have to be withdrawn.) He added that "to save prestige" token contingents of these troops might remain, joined by Soviet troops—all of whom would be subject to GDR control. Khrushchev again made clear that his decision to sign a peace treaty "was firm and irrevocable"; he would do so in December if the United States "refused an interim arrangement." Kennedy ended the summit with the famous observation that "It [would] be a cold winter."[2]

Ever since this encounter, there has been much speculation about what Khrushchev thought of Kennedy. According to Kondrashev, who was present, Khrushchev spoke on this point to the senior officers of the Soviet embassy immediately after the meeting. Contrary to widespread reports that he felt scornful of Kennedy, Khrushchev told his entourage: "We have here a president who has a profound understanding of the world situation. He knows what he wants and vigorously defends his position."[3] This accolade notwithstanding, the countdown to the Berlin Wall had begun. Immediately after the Vienna sessions, Kennedy stopped off in London for a meeting with Prime Minister Harold Macmillan to discuss the Soviet challenge. The two leaders agreed that the West must stay in Berlin regardless of any Soviet-GDR treaty, and they considered the wording of a formal reply to Khrushchev. Foreign Secretary Lord Frederick Home said after the meeting that Kennedy "feared that Mr. Khrushchev was being forced into some action over Berlin by his difficulties with the GDR. . . . Refugees were still coming to West Germany at the rate of about a million per year." The prime minister added: "It was a very poor advertisement for the Soviet system that so many people should seek to leave the communist paradise."[4]

Certainly Walter Ulbricht felt pressed to solve the refugee problem. He addressed a press conference in East Berlin on 15 July to praise the Soviet position. During the question-and-answer period that followed, he made a curious remark that hinted at things to come. Asked by a West German correspondent whether a Berlin Free City meant that "a state boundary will be erected at the Brandenburg Gate," Ulbricht replied, "Nobody has the intention of building a wall." Ulbricht's comment later became much analyzed, but at the time it was barely noticed by US officials. They were completely wrapped up in the problem of how to cope with the potential threat to their position in West Berlin.[5]

The Unsettling Question of Refugees

For the remainder of June 1961, the Kennedy administration concentrated on establishing the policy and administrative framework needed to prepare for the expected crisis over access to Berlin. Former Secretary of State Dean Acheson became a major player, and in his first Berlin report to the president on 28 June he counseled toughness: it was imperative to let Khrushchev know in no uncertain terms that he could not succeed in pushing the Allies out of West Berlin. He emphasized that the American military should be ready to use force if access to West Berlin were challenged.[6] Two days later, National Security Adviser McGeorge Bundy issued National Security Action Memorandum No. 58, paragraph 7 of which asked the secretary of state and the director of central intelligence for advice on "preparations to be taken to create a capability for inciting progressively increasing instability in East Germany and Eastern Europe, at such time after 15 October as it may be ordered." Bundy also asked for suggestions about "bringing this capability to the attention of the Soviets before they make their critical decisions about Berlin." It seems that some policymakers still had an exaggerated view of CIA capabilities in the GDR.[7]

CIA's Eastern Europe division had no such misconceptions. In a meeting at CIA headquarters on 22 June 1961, former BOB chief Bill Harvey expressed it this way: "It is unrealistic to believe that we could infiltrate into the East Zone a sleeper net of sufficient size, reliability, and skill to . . . play a part in organizing resistance groups [as well as] remain in a state of readiness until called up in connection with military operations. Our abilities are not equal to this task when balanced against the defensive capability of the [East German] Ministry of State Security."[8]

There was complete agreement with Harvey's statement within the Eastern Europe division; most of those present still recalled vividly the collapse of the paramilitary program in East Germany that had been linked to the Free Jurists. The suggestion that steps be taken to "increase the refugee flow" were rejected unanimously. If the military contingency actions envisaged under the Acheson plan were implemented, they alone would increase the flow. If other acts were undertaken in this regard, the group's sense was that "we might very well precipitate a Berlin crisis by forcing the East to blockade the city."[9]

As part of its preparations for the planned 13 July National Security Council meeting, CIA reported, "The Soviets probably believe that the West has at present only a limited capability to stir up dissidence in East Germany." The report went on to state that if "private western warnings and clandestine activities convinced Moscow that a Berlin crisis could provoke a covertly supported wave of disorders in the Satellites, then the Soviets might be inclined to proceed more cautiously in their moves against Berlin." This naive faith in "sending the Soviets a signal" was misplaced in the Berlin situation.[10] It is difficult to imagine what more the Americans could have done to confirm the Soviets' contention that all unrest in East Germany, including the refugee flow itself, was the result of conscious action by Western governments.[11]

As if to demonstrate the point, KGB chairman Aleksandr Shelepin sent a detailed forty-nine-page report on the subject to Foreign Minister Andrei Gromyko.[12] Dated 13 July 1961, the report covered the activities of "revanchist and militarist organizations in West Germany and West Berlin" directed against the GDR. The report reflected KGB's view that such groups were increasingly active and emphasized that "the activities of these organizations are supported by the Bonn government." According to the report, Adenauer had told a July 1960 audience, "If the German people stand loyally on the side of the West, the day will come when 'East Prussia' will be liberated."[13]

At the time it was often difficult to separate objectivity from "ideological correctness" in KGB reporting, but as we have seen, particularly during the active measures campaign against "espionage swamp West Berlin," the Soviets were well informed about the Allied intelligence presence. A KGB report on CIA's Berlin Base for 1960–61 notes that "the largest field organ of the Central Intelligence Agency in Europe operates in West Berlin." Under military cover, "it is known to the American intelligence community as the 'Berlin Operations Branch of the Army Detachment.'" Further, "the CIA branch in West Berlin functions as an independent organ, subordinate directly to Washington." Its chief was listed as "Dave Murphy."[14]

Although the Americans continued to concentrate on the access crisis that they anticipated would occur in fall 1961 after the signing of a peace treaty, the Soviet embassy in East Berlin saw the problem of the refugee flow in much sharper focus and recognized the dilemma of pursing a peace treaty while that flow intensified. On 7 July Ambassador Mikhail Pervukhin sent a letter to Foreign Minister Gromyko in which he emphasized that the peace treaty and control of communications between the FRG and West Berlin would not only underline the GDR's sovereignty but also "create conditions for solving the GDR's much more acute problem, the exodus of the population to West Germany."[15]

Displaying a firm grasp of the realities of the Berlin situation, Pervukhin commented candidly on the difficulties the GDR might face in assuming responsibility for control of the air corridors, but he urged the Soviet military and the GDR to work out joint procedures for "detecting and intercepting aircraft in violation." As for military road traffic, he urged the Soviet military to start checking the documents of all individuals and examining all cargo before the GDR peace treaty took effect. (The Soviets had tried to introduce such changes at the onset of the crisis in 1958, but Allied resistance had made them back off.) Pervukhin also suggested that the GDR begin charging the Allied military higher rail transit fees than those paid in the FRG.[16] He recommended separating the East and West parts of the city rail system, too, but warned that this would be difficult and expensive to accomplish.

During all this time, the US government still focused on maintaining access to West Berlin and responding to a potential military attack. Nevertheless, a 12 July telegram from US Ambassador Walter Dowling in Bonn that reported "growing uneasiness among the Soviet zone population" hit home. The message predicted that the "refugee flow may increase to an actual flood unless additional, harsher restrictive measures are taken against travel from the zone into East Berlin and thence across the sector border." The telegram ended by questioning whether the United States could remain on the sidelines if this happened, as it had on 17 June 1953. Such inaction would, in Dowling's view, "mean the end of our prestige and influence in Germany."[17] The response, dated 22 July, points out that "if the GDR tightens controls between the Soviet Zone and East Berlin, there is not much the United States could do." The Kennedy administration seemed in no mood to challenge the right of the Soviets or the GDR to close sector borders.[18]

Information Is Slow to Reach Khrushchev

On 20 July 1961, KGB Chairman Shelepin sent a personal message to Khrushchev that largely reflected KGB reporting on the May NATO Council meeting in Oslo, during which the foreign ministers of the United States, Britain, France, and the FRG had also met separately to discuss Berlin.

The report represented an enormous effort by many highly placed KGB agents who were, in Shelepin's words, "employed in the foreign ministries, general staffs, and other government agencies of the Western powers as well as the NATO structure." It gave Khrushchev important insights into Western Allies' military plans to be activated if access to West Berlin were challenged. Touched upon were plans for an airlift and the integration into NATO war plans of Live Oak, the code name for an American, British, and French military effort created to deal with the Berlin crisis. The Shelepin report also reflects discussions among the Allies about when or under what conditions to use nuclear weapons. According to KGB sources, the Western powers had still not given final approval to specific actions to be taken against the USSR, GDR, or other signatories to a peace treaty. NATO members were concerned that they had only two choices if the Soviets interfered with Allied rights to be in West Berlin: giving in or "unleashing war." The report concluded that the foreign ministers of the four powers—United States, Britain, France, and the FRG—would therefore work out positions to be taken in the event of negotiations with the USSR. These powers would hope to use the negotiations to "delay the conclusion of a peace treaty with the GDR."[19] But as thorough as the report was, it is difficult to understand what Shelepin hoped to gain by sending it to Khrushchev so long after Khrushchev's summit with Kennedy. Although individual items in the report could have been received from residencies by telegram and thus have reached Khrushchev earlier, it may be that Shelepin simply wanted to impress Khrushchev.[20] Whatever the reason, it seemed that KGB's problems of getting information where it was needed—and fast—had not changed much since the days when "Iron Pants" Molotov created KI.

KGB also obtained an excellent report reflecting deliberations on the Berlin crisis within the West German Socialist Party (SPD) during June and July. In addressing the SPD leadership in June, Deputy Chairman Herbert Wehner noted that Western leaders, while proclaiming their "firm intention to remain in Berlin," were saying nothing about achieving the "unification of Germany." In the view of neutral countries, especially India, and some circles in the West, Wehner said, this Western position was "not quite sound." Wehner declared that "one must not rely only on the Western powers," and he recommended "a worldwide propaganda campaign calling for the 'self-determination' of Germany and the maintenance of the 'freedom' of Berlin." But again, it would have been helpful if Gromyko had been given this detailed report in early August, when decisions about closing the border were being made. In fact, Shelepin sent it to him on 31 August.[21]

Further indications that the Western powers were willing to sacrifice freedom of movement in all of Berlin came in discussions with President Kennedy during a meeting of the Interdepartmental Coordinating Group on Berlin on 26 July, the day after his speech to the nation on Berlin. Acheson expressed the view that the Western negotiating position might include at some stage "a discouragement of movements of population as distinct from acts of genuine political refuge." This was an extraordinary proposal, considering the thousands of East Germans pouring daily into the Marienfelde refugee center in West Berlin.[22] Acheson later modified his position by proposing "a general undertaking to discourage excessive movements of population, so long as reasonable freedom of movement is permitted within the city, including freedom to live in one part and work in another without economic or other penalty."[23] But the Soviets and East Germans could never have accepted this plan.

In any event, President Kennedy's 25 July 1961 speech dealt only with US vital interests in West Berlin and covered the various military and other measures the United States would take to meet any Soviet challenge to those rights. There was no mention of freedom of movement in Berlin as a whole, another "signal" to the East that efforts to control their borders in Berlin would not be resisted. With regard to the Kennedy Berlin speech, we have another example of Shelepin's tardiness in delivering information to Soviet leaders. He waited until 26 August to advise the Central Committee that KGB had intercepted a number of letters from West Germany containing Russian translations of Kennedy's speech on Berlin. He was proud to announce that the letters, which he characterized as misleading, were being withdrawn by KGB and destroyed. But in fact, these translations were accurate. Did Shelepin suppress details of these letters because he was aware that they had been prepared and mailed by an anti-Soviet émigré organization in West Germany, presumably an important KGB Karlshorst target? We may never know.[24]

The Soviets Anticipate a Peace Treaty with the GDR

By now the West was preparing for the ministerial consultations on Berlin that would begin in Paris on 5 August. An American delegation charged with holding some early meetings with the Allies left Washington on 27 July. KGB Moscow also expected a drawn-out crisis. In a

29 July memo to Khrushchev, Shelepin proposed that the Soviets create "a situation in various areas of the world that would favor dispersion of attention and forces by the United States and their satellites, and would tie them down during settlement of the question of what a German peace treaty would mean for West Berlin." The program would be undertaken to "show to the ruling circles of the Western powers that unleashing a military conflict over West Berlin can lead to the loss of their position not only in Europe but also in . . . Latin America, Asia, and Africa."[25]

The proposal was apparently approved by Khrushchev. From Shelepin's shopping list of active measures, Defense Minister Rodion Malinovsky and Deputy KGB Chairman Pyotr Ivanovich Ivashutin chose a few designed to convince the West that the Soviets were "prepared to launch an attack in retaliation for Western armed provocations over West Berlin." The two thought it was especially important to deceive the West about Soviet military capabilities: perhaps the West could even be persuaded that the USSR had flight-tested an aircraft with a nuclear engine.[26]

A parallel program initiated as a result of Shelepin's list was in fact an extension of a campaign that had been under way for some time: discrediting the West German military leadership by tainting it with a Nazi past. This campaign had only a marginal effect—although the Soviets were pleased with the result. In March 1962, KGB learned that NATO Secretary Dirk Stikker had expressed to the council his concern about Soviet attacks on Gen. Adolf Heusinger and declared that NATO should publicly defend Heusinger. After some debate, the council finally agreed to issue such a statement in the name of the secretary-general.[27]

KGB reports from this time reflect the Soviets' continued optimism that an independent peace treaty could be reached with the GDR. The closing of Berlin sector borders is never mentioned. Although KGB expressed some concern over possible "countermeasures concerning visits to West Berlin by citizens of the USSR and other socialist countries," a KGB memorandum of 3 August repeats the formula that "*upon conclusion of the peace treaty,* the borders between East and West Berlin will become a state frontier" (our emphasis). Because the "majority of refugees leave the GDR for the West through West Berlin," KGB recommended measures like halting movement between East and West Berlin by rail and subway, strengthening the military presence at the border, reducing the number of crossing points, and paring down the number of East Berliners working in West Berlin. Unlike Pervukhin, whose 7 July letter to Gromyko recommended that movement between East and West Berlin not be further restricted because of the difficulties inherent in making a change, KGB, with minor reservations, had by this time come down on the side of tightening sector border controls. But some of KGB's ideas—like reaching a profitable arrangement with the West Berlin Senate to allow some East Berliners to continue working in West Berlin—were unrealistic. Such proposals demonstrate how little practical input Moscow Center was getting on the crisis from Karlshorst since Korotkov had died.[28]

KGB did follow Pervukhin's lead in warning of the economic consequences of the planned actions, but it pointed out that the GDR could respond by shutting down the FRG's communications with West Berlin and by preventing deliveries of raw materials, food supplies, and manufactured products. KGB also warned that the peace treaty might incite certain East Germans—those "under the influence of Western propaganda"—to protest. The report particularly notes how a worsening of the food supply or the general economic situation would exacerbate this problem. Observing that "the period of preparation for signing the peace treaty will be accompanied by an increase in the flight of GDR residents to the West," KGB suggested that the Soviets sign the peace treaty "in the shortest possible time." If it is assumed that the term "peace treaty" had by this time become a code phrase for actions to strengthen controls on the sector border, then it would appear that at Moscow Center at least, there was some recognition of the need for more immediate action than the leisurely approach suggested in Shelepin's 29 July active measures proposal.[29]

The possible effects of West Germany's canceling of interzonal trade, as noted in KGB's 3 August memorandum, had been a consistent preoccupation of the Soviets and East Germans ever since the FRG had taken this action to protest the September 1960 restrictions on the travel of West German citizens to East Berlin. The theme was sounded again by Ulbricht in his speech to the meeting of the Warsaw Pact Political Consultative Committee (PCC) in March 1961. At the Thirteenth Plenum of SED's Central Committee, held 3–4 July 1961, Ulbricht stalwart Erich Honecker also called for emergency economic measures to be taken if the trade agreement with the FRG were disrupted because of a peace treaty.[30] Indeed, we now know that as early as 1 June the USSR Council of Ministers had adopted a decree calling for "immediate assistance to the GDR in the event of a rupture of trade relations" with the FRG. This concern was heightened with a 29 July 1961 letter sent to the Central Committee by Mikoyan and Gromyko regarding the possibility of a cutoff of interzonal trade and recommending countermeasures. After pointing out that retaliatory threats by the USSR or GDR to halt trade with the FRG would be ineffective, this letter, like the KGB memorandum, urged suspension of civilian transport between West Berlin and the FRG.[31]

Another action by Soviet leaders was clearly linked to the impending closure of the sector borders. The Presidium directed the Foreign Ministry, Defense Ministry, and KGB to prepare as quickly as possible a large-scale propaganda campaign that would reveal alleged preparations by Central Treaty Organization countries along the USSR's southern rim (Iran and Turkey, for example) to attack the USSR with nuclear weapons. Soviet measures to close the borders in Berlin could thus be portrayed as a defensive response to "aggressive" Western plans.[32]

On 5 August, at Ulbricht's request, the first secretaries of the Communist and workers' parties of the Warsaw Pact countries met in Moscow to discuss the Berlin question.[33] They did not discuss specific measures to close the borders, although all the delegates, including the East European leaders present, supported the need for action. Poland's Wladyslaw Gomulka condemned the "open border between our Berlin and West Berlin." If discussions took place between Khrushchev and Ulbricht concerning the details and timing of border closure, they were held in private with only their closest advisers in attendance. Khrushchev undoubtedly approved of Ulbricht's plans, but he still wished to keep secret the extent of Soviet involvement.[34]

While the Warsaw Pact conference was under way, other players in governments East and West continued to act as though the longer-range crisis of a treaty and its aftermath were still the major concern. On 8 August the KGB's First Chief Directorate sent to GRU Chief Gen. Ivan Serov a report from French sources detailing plans by US Air Forces Europe for carrying out an "air bridge" (*vozdushnyi most*) if land access were blocked by the USSR or GDR. The report also covered plans for air support of an expected attempt by a small Allied force to reopen land access to West Berlin along the Helmstedt-Berlin Autobahn. This was the so-called "ground probe" called for in Live Oak plans.[35]

In Paris, the consultations on Berlin held 4–9 August with the foreign ministers of the United States, United Kingdom, France, and West

Germany ended with agreement that negotiations with the USSR on Berlin could take place in October or November, but no decision was reached on when a public announcement would be made of Western readiness. The West seemed oblivious to the fact that events in Moscow and East Berlin were rapidly overtaking their planning. The only time a Western foreign minister seemed on target during these important months was when when FRG Foreign Minister Heinrich von Brentano conveyed the concern of Willy Brandt, mayor of West Berlin, over the effect that GDR harassment was having on the East Germans. Their situation could worsen "if the Berlin door were to close." Von Brentano's remarks caused Secretary of State Dean Rusk to remark that "an attempt to seal off the refugees . . . might lead to an explosion and precipitate the problems under consideration sooner than expected." How right he was.[36] A full three weeks after the ministerial consultations in Paris ended, KGB chief Shelepin duly sent Khrushchev a detailed and accurate report on these meetings. But by then the events of 13 August had made its contents obsolete.[37]

The Berlin Wall Surprise

According to former ambassador to the GDR Pyotr Abrasimov, who replaced Pervukhin, the formal decision to construct a concrete wall was made on 6 August 1961 by the Presidium of the CPSU Central Committee and the Politburo of the Central Committee of SED. Abrasimov commented that "the GDR by itself would never even have thought of doing this—it never would have been permitted such independence."[38] Abrasimov's account is a bit exaggerated. In fact, there was no need for a special session of the Presidium on 6 August; in approving the protocol of the meeting on 5 August of Warsaw Pact party secretaries, the Soviet leadership knew that it had sanctioned the border closure. On 7 August, the SED Politburo met in extraordinary session in East Berlin, where Ulbricht informed his colleagues of Khrushchev's "decision to close the border on the night of 12–13 August." Moreover, the Volkskammer (East German parliament) was to meet on 11 August "to ratify the decision to move promptly toward a peace treaty." According to MfS archives, Erich Mielke, minister for state security, met with his subordinates later on 11 August to advise them of the Volkskammer decision and of an operation—code-named Rose—that would be undertaken in the next few days for which "all preparatory work is to be carried out under the conditions of strictest secrecy."[39]

Secrecy also prevailed in Moscow. Despite the abiding concern felt by both Soviet and East German leaders that the West might retaliate by halting FRG-GDR trade, it was not until 12 August, as action got under way in East Berlin to carry out the border closing, that the Presidium of the CC CPSU, chaired by Khrushchev, met in special session to deal with this pressing issue. Final approval was given to decrees that would provide "immediate assistance to the GDR in the event of a rupture in trade relations with the Federal Republic of Germany." This was a serious measure involving the State Planning Commission (Gosplan), the Ministry of Foreign Trade, and other ministries in the creation of a "special material reserve" necessary for the "normal functioning of GDR industry."[40] The Presidium obviously anticipated that the imminent border closing, which was never mentioned in the protocol of the meeting, might move the West to invoke trade sanctions. But because implementing such a sweeping decree would greatly broaden the circle of those in the know, it evidently seemed necessary to wait until virtually the last minute to take this final action. As we have seen, this same precaution was taken regarding the CENTO propaganda campaign.

The border closing operation, run from a small staff under SED Politburo member Erich Honecker, began late Saturday, 12 August.[41] Sometime after midnight, public transportation between sectors was halted. The East Germans erected barbed wire fences along the entire sector boundary. Berlin had been physically divided.

The events of that August 1961 weekend have been described in countless publications. But questions persist. First, was the 13 August action part of the original USSR-GDR plan for a peace treaty in 1961, as presented to Kennedy in June, or was it primarily a GDR initiative, eventually agreed to by Khrushchev, the timing and scope of which was dictated by the immediate need to halt the flow of refugees? Both views are partly correct. Khrushchev would have preferred his own approach—a peace treaty with the GDR—because, had his threats succeeded, it might actually have altered the status of West Berlin, a goal he continued to pursue even after the Wall was raised. Ulbricht, while agreeing that this outcome would have been desirable, hedged his bets by preparing to seal off of East Berlin and halt the refugee flow.

Although he at times discussed his thinking with key Soviets, he probably never revealed the full extent of his secret plans. We do not believe that during this time the proposed peace treaty was simply a code word for the Wall. When it became evident to Khrushchev that the West was not going to agree to his proposals for changes in West Berlin, and the refugee problem reached proportions that threatened to destroy the GDR regime, he gave Ulbricht's plan his full support.

Next, could the East Germans possibly have made these preparations without involving the KGB apparat in Karlshorst and Moscow Center? Evidence from SVR archives suggests that the East Germans did act autonomously. KGB active measures plans, as well as their reporting focus, suggest that until very late in the game KGB still believed that the peace treaty was in the offing. Ulbricht even kept the GDR bureaucracy out of the loop until the last minute by placing the responsibility for planning and executing the 13 August action with Erich Honecker, an SED stalwart.

Would not Erich Mielke, the minister for state security, have known of the plan by Ulbricht and have informed his KGB friends? It is important to remember that Mielke's fundamental loyalty was to Ulbricht, not to the Soviets. It is certainly likely that Mielke was one of the few East German officials who knew of the plans for 13 August, but there is no reason that he would have informed the Karlshorst KGB. Mielke was aware of KGB's tangled relationship with his service—a relationship that had resulted in the removal (and perhaps contributed to the death) of Aleksandr Korotkov, whom Mielke had trusted more than he trusted most KGB officials.

Finally, were US officials in West Berlin and Washington surprised when the sector borders were closed because their intelligence services had failed to tell them what was happening? It must be remembered that the Americans were themselves trying to figure out how to stem the tide of refugees that summer. Further, the United States had made clear on many occasions, through official and unofficial channels (like Senator William Fulbright's famous statements on American television on 30 July to the effect that the Russians had the power to close the border in any case without violating any treaty), that freedom of movement in all Berlin was not a vital American interest.[42]

Peter Wyden, in his book *Wall*, pinpoints why no intelligence agency operating in a denied area could ever be expected to learn in advance of a secret undertaking like the 13 August border closure: "No wonder

Western intelligence could learn nothing about the DDR's [GDR's] preparations for erecting the Wall. All advance moves were kept just about invisible. . . . Only some twenty trusted leaders knew what was about to happen." The barbed wire and posts that were first erected to test Western reactions were issued to troops "as part of their equipment for 'exercises.'"[43] The construction of the actual Berlin Wall did not begin until after it was clear that no Western reaction was forthcoming.

Did any of the US intelligence agencies have credible advance information of the forthcoming closure? If the circle of persons who knew what was to come was not widened until Friday, 11 August, and if the action did not get rolling until Saturday afternoon, our answer must be no. BOB's strength in its coverage of the Soviet compound in Karlshorst proved to be its weakness here: only an agent close to Ulbricht could have picked up indications in the week before the closure that the Wall was about to go up. In 1961 former KGB officer Oleg Gordievsky just happened to have been assigned to East Berlin as a Foreign Ministry trainee, which was standard procedure for graduates of the Institute of International Relations regardless of their future career assignments. He arrived on 11 August, and the only untoward event in his apartment in Karlshorst was an attack of bedbugs. It was not until the afternoon of Saturday, 12 August, that he and his colleagues were advised to remain in their quarters that night. When they awakened the next morning they discovered that the sector border had been closed.[44]

What would have been the NATO allies' reaction if a tested, reliable source had reported in advance that the closure would take place on 13 August? The case of GRU Col. Oleg Penkovsky is often cited in this regard. Penkovsky had earlier relayed exceptionally comprehensive information on the plans of the Soviets to deal with any Allied efforts to open access to West Berlin by force following the signing of a separate peace treaty. Penkovsky also learned, CIA later found out, "the details of the plan to build the Wall four days before it was executed" but "had no way of conveying the information to his Western contacts."[45] This meant that Penkovsky had acquired such information on 8 or 9 August, well after the decision had been taken in Moscow and Berlin to proceed. Anyone who believes that this message could have been received, processed, and (for source protection) given very limited distribution in time to achieve the consensus needed for real action within the Kennedy administration, not to mention among the NATO allies, has a lively imagination.

21

The Berlin Wall:
Winners and Losers

The first order of business for CIA following the border closure was to convince President Kennedy that West Berliners' fury at Allied passivity during this crisis could, unless appeased, seriously interfere with his plans for addressing the peace treaty threat. BOB, meanwhile, was busy dealing with the effects of the Wall on its operations: it rapidly activated emergency links with its sources, shifted its operational priorities, and reduced its staff, all while providing intelligence support to Gen. Lucius Clay, back in Berlin as Kennedy's personal representative. As 1961 ended, BOB strained to maintain contact with agents in the East and tried to sway East German border guard troops with targeted propaganda.

David Murphy had arrived in San Francisco on home leave on Saturday, 12 August 1961. The next day he received a frantic telephone call from CIA headquarters in Washington: "They've closed the sector border. Get here as soon as possible!" As soon as he arrived, Murphy reported to the offices of the Eastern European Division. There he heard for the first time news of the serious "intelligence failure" connected with the East German action on 13 August. Apparently no one in the White House had been prepared for the outburst of anger and frustration that had sent hundreds of thousands of West Berliners into the streets to protest both the barbed wire along the sector border and the lack of a Western response. For residents of West Berlin, Western inaction constituted betrayal. How could the Kennedy administration have failed to anticipate their reaction? Since the Berlin crisis had begun in 1958, there had been a steady drumbeat of warnings from the State Department's Berlin Mission and from BOB that the Western position in West Berlin depended almost entirely on the support and trust of the city's population.

As news bulletins reporting the mass demonstration at the Berlin city hall poured in, the president received an urgent appeal from Willy Brandt, who needed help to avoid a crisis of confidence in the Western powers resulting from "doubts as to determination of the three powers and their ability to react."[1] Messages from US officials in Berlin emphasized that West Berliners had interpreted the lack of Western response to the border closing to mean that the West was an unreliable ally in resisting future Soviet and East German pressures against the city. As he read the incoming cables, Murphy received instructions from Richard Helms, then chief of operations, deputy director of plans, to report to the director's office. There Allen Dulles told Murphy that they would both be attending a meeting at the White House to consider the American response to the problem of West Berlin morale.

When the two arrived, the meeting had already begun. The president was there, as were all the other members of the Berlin Steering Group. It was a full house, and one could sense the group's frustration tinged with irritation over the events unfolding in West Berlin.[2] Dulles introduced Murphy as the former Berlin Base chief who had just returned from Berlin. The president, evidently aware that Brandt had emphasized in his appeal the four-power status of Berlin, and determined to make his own position clear, made sure Dulles and Murphy realized that "our writ does not run in East Berlin." It was evident that Kennedy did not wish to hear Murphy argue that the border closure was unacceptable. But he did welcome insight into the problem of West Berlin morale. Dulles and Murphy told the president how Berliners, East and West, had always thought of their city as a single entity in spite of the changes that had occurred since the war. Families stayed in touch, birthdays and anniversaries were celebrated together, and visits from sector to sector continued. Consequently, the ban on all movement came as a shock to West Berliners. They now needed reassurance that they would not be abandoned by the United States and its allies. This explanation apparently made sense to the president. He responded by ordering Defense Secretary Robert McNamara to augment US forces in Berlin (one of the few specific requests in Brandt's letter) and by sending Vice President Lyndon Johnson and General Clay to Berlin.[3]

These measures did reassure West Berliners somewhat. Afterward, the West Berlin authorities seemed to be more interested in designing popular retaliatory gestures against the Soviets and their East European allies than in complaining about inertia in the West. On 17 August, for example, Mayor Brandt forbade employees of the West Berlin senate to meet representatives of the USSR or other socialist countries who resided or worked in East Berlin. As for personnel of the Czechoslovak, Polish, or Yugoslav military missions in West Berlin, meetings by West Berlin officials with them "must remain within a businesslike and official framework." Brandt also urged representatives of foreign consulates and other offices in West Berlin to avoid inviting representatives of the USSR and other socialist countries to official receptions.[4]

But in spite of these efforts to stabilize the situation, the events that followed made clear that a "peace treaty" and some resolution of the West Berlin situation in the Soviets' favor remained a Moscow priority. Indeed, the GDR decree announcing the closing of the sector border, and subsequent decrees concerning border control regulations, all stated that they would "remain in effect 'until the conclusion of a peace treaty.'" The number of crossing points originally established on 13 August was reduced from thirteen to seven. Foreigners—including members of the West Berlin occupation forces—were limited to one point, West Germans to two.[5]

There was no doubt that the Western powers' position in West Berlin was still threatened. On 23 August and 2 September, the Soviets sent messages to the Western Allies declaring that there was no "legal basis for the operation of commercial aircraft" in the air corridors, and on 4–5 September the Soviets threatened to walk out of the Berlin Air Safety Center. The GDR paralleled these actions by accusing the United States of misusing both the air corridors and ground access and by protesting the "reinforcement of the US Berlin garrison on 20 August." The GDR insisted that it would "eventually demand control over all traffic to Berlin." Soviet actions against the air corridors seemed imminent, but these threats were not carried out for several months.[6]

Increased harassment of American personnel visiting East Berlin reinforced the view that the Soviets were still determined to sign a separate peace treaty with the GDR and to drive the Western Allies from West Berlin. Although the Kennedy administration was equally determined to maintain its position in the city, and was particularly worried about any challenge to the air corridors, the president and his advisers were also sensitive to Western European concerns that in concentrating on military preparations for a "peace treaty" crisis the United States had ignored an opportunity to negotiate with the Soviets. As a result, the administration began to search for ways to approach the Soviets; at one point, the United Nations was considered as a possible go-between for resolving the Berlin problem.[7]

Meanwhile, the United States continued to prepare for war. On 8 September, President Kennedy signed a National Security Action Memorandum that increased the numbers and readiness of conventional forces in Europe.[8] A new report dated 16 September from Colonel Penkovsky contained alarming information that added urgency to these military preparations. According to Penkovsky, "Soviet and satellite forces will be brought to a high state of combat readiness in exercises of 'unprecedented scope' during early October and lasting for one month." Immediately after the October CPSU Party Congress, a "separate treaty will be signed." The report then implied that a challenge to Allied access would follow immediately after the treaty was signed. The Soviets reasoned that the West "will swallow the second pill"—the first having been the border closure in Berlin.[9]

The Soviet View of the Berlin Wall Crisis

The Soviets were convinced that the West had no interest in negotiating over Berlin. On 4 September, KGB chief Aleksandr Sakharovsky sent information on the Western position concerning negotiations on Berlin to Vladimir Semyonov in the Foreign Ministry. Reportedly, "in working out their positions relative to the intention of the USSR to conclude a peace treaty with the GDR, the United States, Britain, and France devote[d] their primary attention to the problem of West Berlin and entirely neglect[ed] the question of a peace treaty." Although they were determined to convince "public opinion of the West's intention to exhaust all diplomatic possibilities in defending their 'vital interests,' ...

the refusal of the Western powers to enter into negotiations can be traced to the fact that their allies and neutral countries would not support the actions they plan." Western plans, according to this report, were to engage the Soviets militarily if their movement to West Berlin was contested, although the Western Allies would likely react initially with an airlift so that the USSR or GDR could be more easily blamed for having started the military action. This KGB report is a reasonably accurate representation of the Western position at this time.[10]

There was additional KGB reporting on the question of possible negotiations under way between Secretary of State Rusk and Foreign Minister Gromyko during the session of the United Nations General Assembly in New York. KGB kept the Foreign Ministry advised of reactions to these events; one example is a report obtained from their East German "friends" and sent to Semyonov by Gen. Mikhail Kotov, deputy chief of the First Chief Directorate. This information, obtained by Markus Wolf's MFS / HVA from sources in the West Berlin senate, described the firm conviction of West Berlin leaders that "whether or not a peace treaty is signed with the GDR, the United States, England, and France will not leave West Berlin." They also believed, according to the report, that the air corridors linking West Berlin with the FRG are "inviolate because the Western powers have given the Soviet Union to understand that 'encroachment' (*posiagatelstvo*) on the air corridors would lead to a new world war." On the other hand, the report stated that the Allies had informed the senate that "concessions would have to be made concerning the legal and fiscal links between West Berlin and the FRG."[11]

But muddying the Soviet intelligence waters was a 30 September KGB report on an Adenauer cabinet meeting held on 30 August. Although the source's reliability was "being checked," and the information was already a month old, KGB Chairman Shelepin sent it to Vasily V. Kuznetsov at the Foreign Ministry. In it Adenauer was quoted as expressing satisfaction that "at the foreign ministers conference in Paris, they had basically been successful in defending the FRG position with decisive support from France." He reportedly declared that "Kennedy, along with Macmillan and de Gaulle, does not want Berlin to lead to an armed conflict. The Americans and English still hope that future negotiations will lead to acceptable results. France is constrained by Algiers and by the reorganization of its armed forces." Adenauer concluded that "all the Western powers agreed that in the event of such a conflict it would be impossible to hold West Berlin, and no one could foresee the outcome of the initial, limited, local actions."[12]

This report contains errors and omissions suggesting a lack of attention in KGB's Information Service. The only "foreign ministers conference in Paris" about which Adenauer could have been speaking on 30 August were the ministerial consultations held in Paris on 4–9 August, just before the closing of the Berlin sector borders. It is unbelievable that Adenauer would not have mentioned this momentous event. Further, between 30 August and the report's KGB distribution on 30 September, another foreign ministers' conference had been held in Washington and the Rusk-Gromyko talks at the United Nations General Assembly had begun, all of which dealt with the possibilities for negotiations. One would have expected a comment to this effect from the KGB officer preparing the report.[13]

For Khrushchev, the closing of the sector borders had been a triumph. It had prevented the possible collapse of the GDR, thereby appeasing Ulbricht, and at the same time it had avoided provoking Western countermeasures. An attachment to a Central Committee decision called the 13 August action a "great success." Because of it, "the channels from West Berlin for the conduct of subversive and diversionary activity against socialist countries were closed." During negotiations, "the Western powers never raise the question of controls at the West Berlin border. Moreover, US representatives have admitted . . . that the measures of 13 August met the vital interests of the GDR and other socialist countries."[14]

The KGB apparat in Karlshorst might not have sounded the same exultant note of success. As of mid-September it was still trying to determine the effects of the action on its partners in MfS, on the general population, and on its own operations. With that in mind, a KGB apparat officer met on 23 September with a trusted contact within MfS who had attended a conference of senior MfS officials to review the results of the border closing operation. After opening with a statement that everything was normal, the MfS source went on to say that during "the first days after the closing, the MfS organs and the People's Police were heavily involved in apprehending persons who . . . expressed themselves negatively about the border closing. . . . More than seven thousand people were detained, most of whom were soon released, because there was no basis for their arrest. About one thousand persons were arrested. The results of the investigations in these cases are not yet known."[15]

The mfs agent also reported that "some department chiefs expressed dissatisfaction over the fact they were not brought into the preparations for closing the border. As a result, several operational matters (communications with agents in West Berlin and so forth) were not taken into consideration, and now it is difficult to correct the situation."[16] This complaint resonated in kGB Karlshorst. kGB was concerned that its operations would be impaired if Western countermeasures inhibited visits to West Berlin by Soviet citizens. But kGB and mfs soon realized that they were better off with the Wall. The sector borders had quickly become an international frontier. Movement in either direction was controlled by East German border guards in a manner that had become familiar along the entire Iron Curtain. In fact, these new controls gave both kGB and mfs the opportunity and the time to screen West Germans and foreigners more thoroughly for operational use in the West. At the same time, East Germany's secret police faced far fewer internal security problems: the Wall sharply reduced the refugee flow and over time virtually eliminated the uncontrolled movement of persons between East and West Berlin.

BOB Takes Stock

The mfs assessment that the situation in the East had "stabilized" since the Wall had gone up was not entirely accurate. According to BOB, the GDR was far from sanguine about its ability to keep the population in line now that the West Berlin "safety valve" had been closed, and it had undertaken a variety of measures to deal with potential unrest. Thirty thousand or more East Berliners who held jobs in West Berlin until 13 August, for example, were "ordered to take on menial jobs" elsewhere in East Germany. Permitting these very unhappy people to remain in Berlin would have constituted a security threat and morale problem.[17]

The GDR also began to force youths ages 18–23 to join the National People's Army and the security forces. Young men had never been drafted before because they were the least politically reliable of anyone in the GDR population: they made up nearly half of the refugee flow. The GDR introduced conscription less to increase military manpower than to improve internal security by imposing military discipline on the young men and moving them away from their families and neighborhoods. The draft, which was enacted despite severe labor shortages throughout the GDR economy, contributed to the depressed mood of the population, who had been suffering food shortages and a rise in the prices of consumer goods following local "elections" in mid-September. But BOB concluded that "no evidence existed of an 'organized resistance' or likelihood of 'spontaneous uprisings on a wide scale.'"[18]

For CIA's Berlin Base, the operational world had been turned upside down by the new sector border controls, which effectively ended the possibility of GDR citizens visiting West Berlin without interference. Berlin's status as a unique operational asset in the Cold War had ended. Even so, in a 14 September letter to Washington headquarters, the new BOB chief, Bill Graver, sounded a hopeful note. "Traffic is still crossing the border in both directions," he wrote, but he cautioned that it was still too early to predict the extent to which loopholes could be found in the controls. Surprisingly, there were still thirty to forty refugees crossing from East to West Berlin each day (as contrasted with Bavaria, for example, where because of the much tougher zonal border controls, in the period 13–31 August only one hundred refugees had registered). Some of the escapes were dramatic and widely publicized. Others ended tragically.[19] But by early November, the number of escape attempts had dwindled as the East Germans solidified the Wall and extended their controls to the area adjacent to it. This meant that only "legal travelers," persons with valid reasons for visiting East Berlin, could be used operationally. The physical barriers and constant foot and vehicular patrols along the border had made "black," or illegal, border crossings impossible.[20]

Given the new situation, BOB began reordering its priorities. Most important was the need to initiate and sustain two-way communications with those agents who had been so trained before the border closed. By early November, BOB was in touch with more than twenty-five agents who had received alternate communications before the border closing. Next came the reactivation of agents who for whatever reason could not be given a two-way radio or letter-drop location before 13 August. New secure methods had to be devised for contacting them, giving them the necessary communications materials, and training them in their use. Planning for this would require courier missions even more carefully planned and executed than those initiated after earlier crackdowns. The tough new operating conditions meant that security slips could simply not be tolerated.[21]

BOB also examined possibilities for recruiting new sources to report on the GDR from among "legal travelers"—East-West traders, for example, or others who were still able to move easily through the checkpoints. These sources gave BOB the "quick response" capability it needed to cover East Berlin during periods of heightened tension—coverage that guided the US Command in West Berlin as it tried to judge Soviet or East German reactions in such circumstances. The officer on whom Graver relied most to inform him was "Fritz," the same tough-minded East German branch chief who had pressed for alternate communications with BOB agents as soon as the implications of Khrushchev's 1958–59 "ultimatum" had become clear. He was now deputy chief of base for operations, responsible for all intelligence operations.[22]

Graver's efforts paid off. In the year after the Wall was erected, BOB was able to establish two-way contact with more than thirty sources in the East. To sustain these agents, BOB mounted over fifty support missions with no losses. In this same period, BOB published 262 field reports based on reporting from these sources. One example was a 3 August 1962 report on the growing food shortage in East Germany. But BOB was under no illusions; it recognized that over time these sources would succumb to feelings of isolation and fear and break contact. Others would eventually be tracked down by MfS. Nevertheless, at a time of crisis, BOB had an intelligence capability in the GDR that no other Western service could match.

On the covert action side, Graver insisted that there could be no return to the anti-Communist group operations of the 1950s. But he liked the idea of using noninvasive "actions which could be undertaken to harass the East German regime, dramatize the Berlin issue worldwide, and bolster West Berlin morale." These strategies were in line with those suggested earlier in the "long range plan" for Berlin by CIA's Eastern European division and BOB in 1960–61, but they were adapted to the new circumstances imposed by the Wall. Graver's proposals were also a response to the special interest of Robert Kennedy, the attorney general, in stimulating "worldwide protest over the East German action."[23]

The East German border guards along the Wall became a principal target for actions designed to irritate the GDR and frustrate its control of the Wall. BOB encouraged border guard defections and ensured that they received plenty of media coverage—coverage that made heroes of the defectors and told those remaining at their posts, in Willy Brandt's famous phrase: "Don't allow yourself to be degraded" (*Lass dich nicht zum Lumpen machen*). A BOB officer who arrived for his first tour just after the Wall had gone up remembers the border guard operation well. Natively fluent in German, he was put to work immediately debriefing border guard defectors and writing their stories in German in an appealing human-interest style that was snapped up by the local press and replayed elsewhere. The US military was understandably eager to interrogate each defector at length, but BOB could not wait until these interrogations were complete or the story would die. By placing a BOB officer on the debriefing team, BOB was able to get the material to the press while it was still newsworthy. To get similar features on divided Berlin to worldwide audiences, BOB created and supported an extensive network of agents in the international media.[24]

It required no special insight to realize that BOB had become overstaffed. No matter how hard it worked at maintaining contact with its sources in the East, at trying to develop new assets, or at mounting an expanded covert action effort geared to the new circumstances, far fewer officers were needed than before the Wall had gone up. Reduction in BOB staffing also involved consolidating the several operations branches into two branches and creating a separate covert action branch that was staffed by transferred officers. Although it was tough to let these individuals go, personnel reductions and transfers began almost immediately and continued into 1962.

Some of the transferred officers were reassigned to a task force in West Germany to tackle the problem of how to support resistance in East Germany in the event of a military confrontation over access to West Berlin. This program arose from the realization that CIA did not have, nor could it create, clandestine assets in the GDR with two-way communications solely to foment resistance "on demand." The task force was poised to select and train volunteers from among the most recent East German refugees. If circumstances warranted, they would be infiltrated into the GDR to collect intelligence on Warsaw Pact troop movements and provide direction to local resistance. Murphy, now deputy chief of CIA's Eastern European division, briefed Henry Kissinger on CIA's limitations in supporting East German resistance. Nevertheless, because the Kennedy administration's main concern was still the possibility of armed conflict arising from a bilateral peace treaty between the USSR and the GDR, the president's closest advisers persisted in believing against all evidence and expert advice that resistance in the GDR could be counted on as a formal part of Allied contingency planning.[25]

Even as late as 9 August 1962, in a briefing of Kennedy, "covert action" was presented as a viable aspect of an overall four-phase program. In phase 1, covert action would be in "preparation," whereas in phase 2 it would be limited to fostering "passive resistance." In phases 3 and 4, during which military operations would begin, the United States "would propose to encourage isolated acts of active resistance" but "avoid encouraging an uprising, unless general war seemed imminent."[26] These projections were highly unrealistic. This was the GDR of 1962, not the Europe of 1942, where growing resistance to the Nazi occupier was beginning to play an important role in support of Allied plans and operations.

The Wall changed everything, and Graver had to cope with a whole new set of circumstances. None was more challenging than the relationship he would have to establish with Gen. Lucius Clay, the newly appointed presidential representative "with rank of Ambassador on Temporary Assignment to Berlin." Clay's 1961 Berlin appointment grew out of his brief visit there in August with Vice President Johnson in the immediate aftermath of the border closing. His assignment was seen by many, particularly in the military and civilian command structure, as more symbolic than substantive.[27] Clay, however, believed that he had a vital role to play in restoring West Berlin morale. He remained an imposing figure. Allen Dulles and his immediate successors in Berlin had taken nearly three years to win Clay's trust a quarter-century earlier—finally succeeding during BOB's reporting during the blockade of 1948–49—but Graver was so adept at making his information indispensable to Clay that the two soon had a solid working relationship.

To illustrate how well the two got on, Graver often told the story of Attorney General Robert Kennedy's visit to West Berlin in early 1962.[28] For BOB staffers, Kennedy's visit offered an opportunity to demonstrate how they had responded to his urgings to boost the morale of West Berlin and tell the Berlin story throughout the world. John McCone, director of CIA, had advised BOB of the visit and insisted to Graver that BOB be given time to brief Kennedy on the West Berlin covert action program in which the attorney general had expressed great interest. Although an extremely tight schedule had been planned for Kennedy, Clay's intervention secured the BOB briefing.

Graver reciprocated on behalf of BOB by helping to arrange Robert Kennedy's successful meeting with two articulate East German students. They had been studying in West Berlin but were on summer vacation in the GDR when they were trapped by the Wall, and their fellow West Berlin students rescued them. Graver and the students met with Kennedy early in the morning—perhaps too early—at the West Berlin residence reserved for the American ambassador in Bonn and visiting dignitaries. When they were ushered in to Kennedy's sitting room, they heard the shower running in the adjacent bathroom. Minutes later, RFK emerged in his underwear, pulling on his shirt as the conversation began. The students were overwhelmed, and later told Graver, "A German minister would never have been able to do that!"[29]

The Political Situation in Germany, East and West

Just before Clay arrived in Berlin on 19 September, elections were held in West Germany. Adenauer was reelected chancellor but with a smaller majority than he had enjoyed sixteen years earlier. The German Socialist Party (SPD) made impressive gains, and KGB became interested in the party's plans. On 28 September, KGB Deputy Chairman Pyotr Ivanovich Ivashutin sent a report to the Central Committee of CPSU describing a meeting in Bonn of the SPD Central Leadership, the SPD parliamentary faction, and the SPD Party Council on 19–20 September. The purpose of the meetings was to discuss the results of the election, the gains made by the Social Democrats at the expense of Adenauer's Christian Democrats, and SPD's chances of forming a new government. SPD Chairman Erich Ollenhauer spoke out for a coalition of the three major parties.[30]

Brandt reportedly supported him, commenting that in the "near future the foreign policy situation of the FRG will become even more complicated," requiring a new government "formed on the broadest possible basis." In KGB's report, Brandt added that according to his information the Allies were ready to make a compromise with the USSR on the Berlin and German questions "at the expense of the FRG." In return the Allies would achieve an advantageous settlement on West Berlin. According to the KGB source, Brandt also noted that in the "atmosphere of uncertainty" prevalent in West Berlin, it might be acceptable to "transform the city into the seat of the United Nations." In conclusion, the meetings resolved to accord candidate Brandt the authority to act in any manner the complex situation demanded.[31]

Another KGB report, this time from a "proven source," described the nearly parallel views of senior officials in the Adenauer government on Allied plans for negotiations with the Soviet Union. In early October, Foreign Minister Heinrich von Brentano and Defense Minister Franz Strauss reportedly advised Adenauer of concessions the West was prepared to make. They included de facto recognition of the GDR and the Oder-Neisse frontier and refusal to provide the Bundeswehr with atomic weapons. In return, the GDR would grant Allied forces access to West Berlin. In view of this, von Brentano and Strauss recommended that the FRG "tacitly agree to the de facto recognition of the GDR inasmuch as it would be impossible to avoid in the future" and agree to discussions with the GDR on civilian access to West Berlin, but drag out discussions on the eastern frontier. As for a disengagement zone between NATO and Warsaw Pact forces, or forbidding the arming of the Bundeswehr with atomic weapons, the ministers warned Adenauer to "decline this on the grounds it would weaken NATO."[32]

This stress on atomic weapons for the Bundeswehr is a recurrent theme in KGB reporting, yet KGB seems never to have distributed—or perhaps even received—US statements on the subject. President Kennedy's letter to Chancellor Adenauer dated 13 October 1961, for example, stated: "As far as the nuclear weapons component of European security is concerned, . . . it has been the long-established policy of the US Government not to relinquish control of nuclear warheads to any nation not owning them and not to transmit to any such nation information or material necessary for their manufacture."[33] The Soviets were certainly sensitive to any suggestion that the West Germans might acquire nuclear weapons, but reports from KGB sources often confused possession of nuclear delivery systems—artillery, aircraft, and surface-to-surface missiles—with possession of nuclear shells, bombs, or warheads, which in fact could not be released to West German forces except under NATO authority.[34] Perhaps this confusion was intentional; because the Soviets professed to believe that NATO would eventually give the FRG nuclear capability, they were actively pursuing their antinuclear campaign. They must have been pleased with a report of a meeting in October of SPD chairman Ollenhauer with the chairman of the "Committee for the Struggle Against Atomic Death" and trade union representatives. Ollenhauer commented that in the absence of a popular movement against nuclear armaments, it appeared inexpedient to create one artificially, but the trade unionists favored expanding the Committee's activities. This was agreed to during a subsequent meeting of the SPD Presidium.[35]

Tests of Nerves

Meanwhile, General Clay had just barely settled into his new quarters at the Wannsee guest house when he became embroiled in a controversy with the US military commands in Heidelberg and Paris over the isolated Steinstuecken enclave adjacent to the US sector.[36] To show the flag, Clay flew in by helicopter, spent some time chatting with the residents, and returned with a refugee who had been hiding there. West Berliners were ecstatic about this sign of American support. In his account of his actions to Secretary of State Dean Rusk, Clay observed: "I am sure that there is determination in Washington and we must make it clear to the people of West Berlin and to the East German and Soviet forces that it exists here too."[37]

The next major crisis, the tank confrontation at Checkpoint Charlie, the Friedrichstrasse control point, was sparked by General Clay's recommendation on 29 September that if the East Germans closed the crossing point to Allied traffic the barrier should be destroyed by tank or heavy equipment. Discussions of this theoretical situation and various alternatives continued among officials in Washington, Berlin, and all points between (like Bonn, Heidelberg, and Paris) until 23 October, when Allan Lightner, Jr., the senior State Department official in Berlin, was held up at the Friedrichstrasse crossing point by East German police who demanded to see his identification. He refused and sat there for a full hour before being told by the American MPs that he was to return to the American sector. When the matter was raised with Gromyko in Moscow by Ambassador Llewellyn Thompson, the Soviet foreign minister asserted that the GDR was within its rights.[38]

After this incident, Soviet tanks were brought into the Friedrichstrasse area to bivouac a few blocks from Checkpoint Charlie. In response, American tanks were deployed along the same street on their side of the boundary, although they returned to Tempelhof each evening at 5:00. On 26 October the Soviet tanks entered Friedrichstrasse and moved up to the border adjacent to the checkpoint. The American tanks were quickly brought back from Tempelhof. The faceoff that followed was one of the most dramatic moments of the Cold War in Berlin.

BOB quickly determined the tanks' nationality by having a BOB officer under diplomatic cover stroll along Friedrichstrasse on the East Berlin side of the border, listening to the Russian conversation of the tank crews. When Clay was absolutely sure that these tanks were indeed Soviet—operated by Soviet crews and not East Germans—he announced at a press conference that their presence demonstrated Soviet responsibility for the actions of the East German police.[39] At 5:55 P.M. Berlin time, Clay called President Kennedy with a status report and to advise him that no further attempts to help civilians cross into East Berlin would be undertaken until Monday, 30 October.[40] Meanwhile, the number of Soviet tanks in the vicinity of the crossing point kept increasing. What followed thereafter is unclear. Several sources, including General Clay himself, have stated that at about 11:00 P.M. Berlin time Clay received a call on an open telephone line. Bill Graver was in the Emergency Operations Center when the call came through. Clay's military aide picked up the telephone, heard a very familiar New England voice, turned beet red, and held out the instrument to the general. It was President Kennedy. According to Graver, Clay first said that the situation was calm. He then added that he had just been handed a report of tanks on the move, but that they didn't appear to be near Friedrichstrasse. "I'll call if movement occurs," Clay concluded.[41]

According to the State Department, "no other record of this conversation has been found."[42] But KGB seemed to confirm both calls. A combined KGB report was sent to the Central Committee by Shelepin on 31 October. The first part of the report describes how Clay first gave Kennedy a situation report, then promised to undertake no further probes until Monday. Kennedy asked what the British and French do at the checkpoints. Clay replied, wryly: "The French . . . send their people through the checkpoint with a military escort. As for the English, they have been presenting their identity documents for fifteen years." In what appears to have been the 11:00 P.M. call, Kennedy recommended that "it would be best to send over only people in uniform until we hear from Thompson." Clay agreed, and remarked that "seven more Soviet tanks have arrived at the control point. I think, Mr. President, that this is a test of nerves." Kennedy expressed confidence that Clay had strong enough nerves.[43]

By midnight on 27 October there were as many as thirty Soviet tanks present, but the next morning they began to withdraw. There is no single documented account of the circumstances that finally resolved the crisis. The popular American version is that Clay and the United States "scored an impressive victory."[44] But the US victory was perhaps more apparent than real. On 23 December, East German border guards demanded that US civilian officials accompanying the US commandant in Berlin, Maj. Gen. Albert Watson II (en route to a Karlshorst meeting with the Soviets) identify themselves. Watson refused to allow this and was denied access to East Berlin. He countered by barring Col. Andrei Solovyov, the Soviet commandant, from West Berlin. On 30 December, Solovyov responded that he regretted the American confrontation, but he argued that the East Germans were following orders.[45]

Watson's decision to bar the Soviet commandant from West Berlin caused a diplomatic furor that lasted into 1962. On 13 March, KGB's Karlshorst apparat reported to Soviet officials in Berlin, alleging that French Commandant Jean Lacomme was replaced by Edouard K. Toulouse because of Lacomme's pliant attitude toward his American counterpart. French authorities had been "dissatisfied with the actions of the Americans, who violated the principle of 'joint responsibility' and attempted to command their English and French allies." Indeed, the KGB report continued, when the Americans asked General Toulouse to bar the Soviet commandant from the French sector, he declined, saying he would have to "forward the proposal to the French embassy in Bonn."[46]

The commandant issue turned moot during summer 1962 when the Soviets abolished the position of Soviet commandant. A 7 September KGB situation report, based on information from sources of the "friends" (MfS) and the Karlshorst apparat, stated that the "abolition of the Soviet kommandatura was received with a certain anxiety by ruling circles in West Berlin."[47] Meanwhile, American civilian officials continued to visit East Berlin but identified themselves with their diplomatic passports.

The US administration was also ambivalent about continuing to exercise its rights to move troops along the Autobahn. In late November news stories attributed to Soviet sources appeared in the Western press labeling American troop movements along the Autobahn "provocative." In the Americans' view, these movements were "routine and the normal exercise of long established rights." KGB, always alert to squabble between the Western Allies, reported to Gromyko and the Central Committee that Clay had asked British and French commanders in Berlin to follow the American example "in organizing demonstrative transfers of their troops along the . . . Autobahn." According to KGB, the request was refused by both the British and French. This report was accurate. President Kennedy initially wanted "to avoid giving the Soviets any opportunity to divide the Allies by a plausible claim that trouble originated in a US provocation." But on 9 December, the president decided to continue US troop movements, lest this "give the Communists the impression they [had] succeeded in intimidating us."[48]

Meetings of the ministers of the United States, Britain, France, and the FRG in Paris on 10–12 December were the last major diplomatic events of 1961. There they discussed negotiations with the USSR on the Berlin question. But the outcome was not heartening for the NATO allies. France was reluctant to negotiate with the USSR, and no one could ignore the fact that the Soviet position had not changed since 1958.[49] The only KGB report on these meetings described a speech by FRG Foreign Minister Gerhard Schroeder before the December 1961 NATO Council in Paris. The speech reportedly followed the standard FRG view on negotiations with the Soviet Union on Berlin and Germany.[50]

This report was not actually disseminated until 28 April 1962. By itself, therefore, it could not have influenced the Soviets' analysis of the disarray among the Western powers evident during these important December meetings. Nor could this reporting on the NATO Council meeting have been factored into the Soviet decision to begin serious interference with Western flights in the air corridors in early February. The stalemate would continue.

By December 1961 what had begun as a tangle of barbed wire strung on concrete posts had become a series of formidable and exceedingly ugly barriers along the sector borders, as well as along the boundary separating West Berlin from the East German countryside. West Berliners and members of the Allied forces who had come to know Berlin well since the war were angered and sickened not just by the hideous patchwork of brick, concrete, and wire: even more disturbing was the deathly quiet along once busy streets—a silence broken by day by the incessant noise of new wall segments being built, and at night by the occasional burst of automatic fire from a nervous border guard who thought he saw movement just beyond the Wall. Worst of all was the complete absence of life in the part of East Berlin adjacent to the Wall. Even those East Berliners who could be seen in the distance scurried along, not daring to look toward the West lest a furtive glance be interpreted as treason.[51]

In their determination to eliminate the possibility of East Germans' crashing cars or trucks through checkpoints, by year's end the East

Germans had reinforced all vehicular crossing points with concrete structures that channeled traffic and slowed it to a crawl. The Brandenburg Gate was also closed off with an unusually thick lower wall that was apparently built to thwart the passage of tanks. (According to the Soviets the lower wall and landscaping served to "beautify" the area and provide an appealing background to the East Germans' view of the Brandenburg Gate.) The weather that year was especially cold. At any temperature, Christmas was hardly a festive occasion for Berliners on either side of the Wall: the holiday was a painful reminder that they were cut off from friends and relatives. Nevertheless, as a gesture of solidarity with the people of East Berlin, West Berliners celebrated the holiday by erecting Christmas trees along the Western side of the Wall. Looking back on the events of August 1961, it seemed clear who had won this round.

Epilogue

The Berlin Wall represented an important tactical victory for KGB because it kept BOB at a distance in East Germany, but the struggle for Berlin continued for many years. Within the decade, Willy Brandt's Eastern policy (Ostpolitik) had resulted in full recognition of the GDR by the West, the virtual abandonment of reunification plans, and the signing of the Four-Power Treaty, which preserved West Berlin as a separate entity. It was the ultimate irony for the Soviets that these changes were the work of a Social Democratic chancellor. From Lenin through Khrushchev, Soviet leaders had rejected Social Democrats as legitimate advocates of social and economic change. The Andropov-sponsored mission to meet Brandt aide Egon Bahr—which had become the basis for Ostpolitik and had created a channel between Brandt and Brezhnev—had been a last, desperate attempt to bridge the chasm separating Soviet orthodoxy from Social Democracy. That Brandt was forced from office by the arrest of Guenther Guillaume, a spy in his administration sent by the very East German service that KGB had created, seemed a shabby sequel to these diplomatic breakthroughs.

In spite of the GDR's new diplomatic status, East Germans were disappointed after Ostpolitik was initiated. The East German economy had constant problems, even though it enjoyed both a special trading relationship with West Germany and inclusion in the Common Market. The country was forced to exchange West German prisoners, many of whom had been victims of the intelligence wars, for billions in hard currency. Further, as the last decade of Soviet power began, the Communist system in East Germany began to disintegrate. Some believe that, had he lived, Yuri Andropov, who had served as KGB chief longer than any of his predecessors (or successors), might have kept the Communist system afloat longer with his tough, perceptive leadership. But the glasnost and perestroika introduced by his successor, Mikhail Gorbachev, accelerated the dismantling. By summer 1989, the Polish Communists had joined a noncommunist government and the Hungarians had opened their borders to the West, allowing thousands of East German "tourists" to pour through. Once again, East Germans were voting with their feet to leave the Soviet bloc.

During this summer, Kondrashev, special consultant to KGB chairman Vladimir A. Kriuchkov, was vacationing in the GDR as the guest of Minister of State Security Erich Mielke, as he had done for many years. But this time, on the day before Kondrashev was to return to Moscow, Mielke surprised him with an urgent question. "Sergei," asked Mielke, "what does Gorbachev think he is doing? Does he realize that if your policy with regard to Poland and Hungary continues that the GDR will not be able to contain the social forces it releases? Gorbachev and your leaders should understand that the German Democratic Republic will be crushed!" Mielke asked Kondrashev to give this message verbatim to Kriuchkov for immediate relay to Gorbachev. When Kondrashev was assured that Mielke's message had been given personally to Gorbachev, he asked whether there had been a reaction. Kriuchkov replied, "There was none."

During his October visit to East Berlin, Gorbachev made it clear that Soviet troops would not help the GDR suppress its growing internal opposition. On 18 October 1989, Ulbricht's successor, East German party chief Erich Honecker, was removed, and by year's end the Brandenburg Gate was opened. By 3 October 1990 Germany was once more a single country. The former occupying powers set September 1994 as the date for withdrawing Western troops from West Berlin and for removing Soviet forces from East Berlin and East Germany. The KGB apparat in Karlshorst, headed by Maj. Gen. Anatoly Novikov, closed down in 1992, well before the deadline. When the US Army celebrated its last Fourth of July in Berlin in 1994, BOB was deactivated at a ceremony attended by CIA Director R. James Woolsey, David Murphy, and other former base chiefs.

How could the GDR, the keystone of the Soviet position in Eastern Europe, have collapsed? Perhaps no government in contemporary history had intelligence on its adversaries that was as accurate as that provided to Moscow. Its often documentary information was obtained from sources with access to decisionmakers at the highest levels. The Western powers, by contrast, received little comparable information on Soviet plans, capabilities, or intentions. Our analysis of the newly released KGB archival material reveals that the Soviet treasure trove of intelligence never shaped Soviet policy as it could have. Nowhere was this disparity between information and influence more evident than in East Germany. Forced to accept without question the dictates of their leaders, agents wrote and rewrote their reports to conform to the prevailing Soviet ideology. Further, Soviet leaders were unable (or unwilling) to exploit their intelligence advantage to urge GDR administrators to change their policies. When Gorbachev finally did this, the end came swiftly for East Germany and the Wall, and it was followed by the collapse of the Soviet Union itself.

APPENDIXES

More Detail from CIA and KGB Archives

Appendix 1. The Merger of KPD and SPD: Origins of SED

Central to Soviet plans for Germany was the work of a cadre of German Communists who had entered the country with the Red Army in April 1945. A year later they had succeeded in forcing the German Communist Party (KPD) and the German Social Democratic Party (SPD) to merge in the Soviet zone into a single party, the Socialist Unity Party (SED). Although the merger was an apparent success, the Soviets were dissatisfied with political conditions in East Germany.[1] When the first free postwar elections were held throughout Berlin in October 1946, "an unprecedented 92.3 percent of the eligible voters had gone to the polls," but SED received just 19.8 percent of the popular vote and won only 26 out of 160 seats in the city council. This was a last time a free election was held in East Berlin until March 1990, after the Wall came down.[2]

None of the political actions carried out by the Soviets and their Communist allies created more resentment and eventual resistance than did the forced merger of SPD with KPD. The deep-seated animosity between German Communists and socialists had its roots in the very origins of the Soviet and German Communist parties; both began as splinters from their respective social democratic parties. In the new Soviet Union, the social democrats were eliminated. In Germany, KPD and SPD, which became the strongest of the working-class parties, survived until Hitler's rise to power. Had the parties joined in opposition to the Nazis, they might have slowed Hitler somewhat but instead the German Communists, at Stalin's insistence, had branded SPD members "social fascists" and had cooperated with the Nazis to overthrow Weimar. Most SPD members in Berlin and the Soviet zone remembered this betrayal vividly and rejected any suggestion of a reconciliation with KPD.[3] Efforts by the Soviet occupation authorities to crush the remnants of SPD opposition and attempts by the West German SPD to prop up its East German counterpart involved both KGB and CIA in a recurring subplot of the Cold War.

In summer 1945, the merger had stalled. Otto Grotewohl, the SPD leader who later led the fight in the Soviet zone for the merger, vacillated. KPD, its leaders possibly recognizing that it represented only a minority of the population, was likewise unenthusiastic about joining forces with SPD. But the final reasons for the delay in accomplishing the merger in the Soviet zone probably had less to do with the Soviets' concern for SPD than with their desire to wait until it became clear that a merger involving SPD in all four occupation zones was not going to be easy. By November it was apparent that most SPD members, in both West and East Germany, were against the merger. SPD split, and Grotewohl became chairman of the SPD Central Committee for Berlin and the Soviet zone. But the Soviets, now committed to the merger, strongarmed all parties to bring it about. By pressuring SPD leaders and promising them important posts in a future united German government with immediate material benefits, like better housing and improved rations, the Soviets persuaded Grotewohl and others to campaign for the merger. A former officer in the SMA secretariat recalls that Marshal Georgy Zhukov himself played an active role in persuading Grotewohl to cooperate. Grotewohl was rousted from bed, feverish from a recurrence of malaria, and taken to Zhukov who, in the words of this SMA officer, "made a Christian of him."[4] This officer's testimony confirms an April 1946 BOB intelligence report describing a series of late-night sessions at Karlshorst, during which Grotewohl was pressured to agree to the merger.[5]

In March 1946, General Clay stated that the merger would not be recognized in West Berlin unless a majority of SPD members voted for it. A plebiscite was arranged, but the Soviets, after some hesitation, banned it in their sector just one day before the scheduled vote. Some SPD organizations in East Berlin districts tried to hold the plebiscite despite the ban, but their polling places were shut down by Soviet troops. The final result of the voting was 29,610 against, 2,937 for the merger, which was nonetheless consummated on 21 April 1946.[6] Still, this action did not immediately result in an effective workers' party along Soviet lines: SPD influence remained strong, and SED members still spoke not of the "dictatorship of the proletariat" but of "democracy." Undaunted, the Soviets moved forcefully, almost instinctively, to fashion this party in their own image.[7]

After the merger, membership in SPD once more became illegal in the Soviet zone and the Soviet sector of Berlin. There was no formal decree outlawing the party, as in Hitler's time, but SPD was effectively banned. In May 1946, SPD organizations from the three Western occupation zones met in Hanover, where they elected Kurt Schumacher, an old German Social Democrat and survivor of Hitler's prisons, as chairman of the West German SPD. The sole link between SPD members in the Soviet zone and the main party was the SPD Eastern Bureau (Ostburo), whose offices in West Berlin and West Germany struggled to maintain this contact and to support Soviet zone members in their resistance to SED and its policies.

On 23 December 1946, SED leaders met with Marshal Vasily Sokolovsky and Political Adviser Vladimir Semyonovich Semyonov to complain about their problems. Col. Sergei Ivanovich Tiulpanov, chief of SMA's Propaganda (later Information) Directorate, was apparently not present. The SED group consisted of Wilhelm Pieck, Walter Ulbricht, Otto Grotewohl, and Max Fechner. The official memorandum of these conversations was found in SVR archives. A unique document, it encapsulates in unedited form the extent to which each of the Soviet actions during the crackdown caused intense dissatisfaction in the Soviet zone and thereby complicated SED's execution of the very policies the Soviets wished to pursue. SED leaders presented a lengthy list of grievances—continued dismantling of factories, extraction of reparations from current production, and rapes and robberies carried out by soldiers and officers of the Soviet Army.[8] All of these abuses were being exploited politically by the Social Democrats, whose mouthpiece, *Der Telegraf,* had published lurid news accounts.

In defending Soviet actions at the meeting, Sokolovsky speculated on one source of doubt in the new SED: "When the party was unified, people entered it who were not pleased by the democratization [sovietization] of Germany." In response, Grotewohl complained that SED was considered a party of the occupation forces. Fechner added that "the results of the elections in Berlin were bad. It was a big mistake to allow the Social Democrats to function in Berlin." Sokolovsky replied that it was hard to say who had won and who had lost on this issue. "If we had not agreed to allow SPD to function in Berlin, then SED would have been prohibited in Berlin. As far as the zone is concerned, we do not intend at present to permit SPD in the Soviet zone. Everything depends on how well SED is strengthened in the zone."[9]

The Soviets, by insisting on the SED merger and alienating SPD members in their zone who resisted, not only added to the atmosphere of tension in East Germany but also mobilized scores of opponents whose attitudes and actions posed serious problems for occupation authorities and SED itself. But the anti-SPD campaign was only one of several parallel political actions undertaken by the Soviets in 1945–46 that resulted in further turmoil and increased resistance to the occupation. Marshal Zhukov's order of 10 June 1945 authorizing "democratic and anti-Fascist parties" not only gave a head start to the German

Communist Party but opened the way as well for the founding of so-called bourgeois parties: the Christian Democratic Union (CDU) and the Liberal Democratic Party (LDP). These parties, along with SED, constituted the Anti-Fascist Front (later to be called the National Front), which was launched four days after Zhukov's order.[10] As in other Soviet-occupied countries in Eastern Europe that were being transformed into "people's democracies," these parties were intended not to challenge the existing political structure but only to lend an aura of respectability to the civilian governments being imposed by the Soviets at local and provincial levels, and later in the German Democratic Republic. The newly constituted parties were vaguely modeled on the German Democratic (liberal) Party and the Center (Catholic) Party, which had existed in the Weimar period.[11] That association helped undermine Soviet plans for these new parties: many of the people who joined them had in fact either participated in or had memories of their Weimar counterparts and although a few accepted their scripted roles, many adopted a militant anti-Soviet stance. These anti-Soviet rumblings in turn attracted to these "bourgeois" parties individuals who resented the occupation government. Thus, to the Soviets' surprise, these parties became centers of opposition to the Soviet occupation.

The Soviets Get Even with Germany for Wartime Wrongs

During the December 1946 meeting between Sokolovsky and SED, party leaders criticized the seemingly contradictory Soviet policies on industrial dismantling and reparations. The Soviets continued to dismantle machinery despite repeated promises to stop. SED leaders complained that coal mining machinery was being dismantled in Saxony even as the people there faced severe fuel shortages. Furthermore, they pointed out, the disorganized way the Soviets carried out the dismantling aroused even more resentment than the dismantling itself. These actions were turning the most qualified workers against the Soviets and SED and were giving the Western press ammunition for attacks against the party.

At this point, Marshal Sokolovsky interjected: "We'd like to spit upon the mercenary Western press!"[12] This emotional rejoinder reflected the confusion of most Soviets on this subject. After viewing the destruction of the USSR by German invaders during the war, the Soviets felt they had a right to take everything they needed from Germany to rebuild their own country. Few gave much thought to a future in which the Soviets would be asked to limit their demands on the German economy in order to support SED. Linked to the problem of dismantling was the question of reparations for war damages inflicted by Germany. It was difficult to understand, SED leaders said, why a plant should be taken apart when it could make products for civilian use, a portion of which could be allocated to reparations.

One example of a poor dismantling strategy involved the Zeiss factory in Jena. There a confrontation occurred between the dismantlers and the SMA Industrial Directorate that greatly upset the workers. On Marshal Sokolovsky's orders, officers were told to appease the workers but to continue some dismantling.[13] "Why," Ulbricht asked Sokolovsky, "could [the workers] not have been told right away [that dismantling was to continue], to avoid the unhappiness and dissension?" Sokolovsky dodged this question, replying only that "we were restoring production at Jena for peaceful needs."[14]

The Soviets failed to develop a comprehensive, consistent, and fair dismantling system in large part because of Soviet leaders' divergent views on how best to exploit the German economy. Some supported existing dismantling procedures; others wanted the Soviet Ministry of Foreign Trade to play the principal role; and still others, such as Beria, insisted on controlling those elements of the East German economy that could contribute to the Soviet atomic program. Contributing to this dissent was the primitive Soviet view of how a modern industrial society functioned. Having participated in Stalin's forced industrialization of the 1930s, Soviet officials were slow to understand that an electronics plant in Jena could not produce finished goods without receiving parts from an intricate web of suppliers throughout Germany. This obtuseness, as well as the chaos brought about by Soviet bureaucratic disagreement, infuriated even the most apolitical East German plant directors and added to discontent in the Soviet zone.

Still another irritant for SED was the question of the eastern borders of Germany. At the Potsdam Conference, the former German territories of Silesia, Pomerania, and the southwestern portion of East Prussia had been placed under Polish administration. Although technically the future of these areas was supposed to be decided by a peace treaty, it had become evident by 1946 that they had become a de facto part of Poland. As a result, thousands of Germans had been expelled from these heavily industrialized regions and were living in the Soviet zone, where they constituted a highly vocal and bitterly anti-Soviet minority. SED tried desperately to distance itself from the Soviets on the frontier question. As with the problem of reparations, SED wanted to emulate the local focus of the French Communist Party, addressing the frontier question from a "German viewpoint." Their inability to do so fueled the dissension of thousands of unhappy Silesians throughout East Germany.[15]

In spite of the intense emotions aroused by Soviet actions, thousands of people in the Soviet zone probably would have remained passive during the difficult postwar occupation had it not been for the continuing incidents of rape and pillage by Soviet Army personnel. Since the end of the war, stories of such atrocities had been told and retold in virtually every East German household until they had achieved the status of folk legend. But many of the stories were true, and these degrading acts were still happening in late 1946, infuriating the citizenry. Each of the SED leaders at the December meeting with Sokolovsky expressed concern over this emotionally charged issue. They realized that an army that had only a year and a half earlier finished a long war was not, as Grotewohl delicately put it, a "ladies' seminary." Even the venerable German Communist Pieck protested that the incidents were complicating these leaders' political work. Sokolovsky replied: "We are withdrawing half of our army and as a result disorders will occur. We are returning repatriates, former prisoners of war, others who were treated badly by the Germans, and that must be understood psychologically. People are returning home, and they will not find their places because they were destroyed by the Germans. Of course, they are venting their anger on people. It's an inevitable evil. We, of course, do not encourage this, we fight it, but we cannot assign 100,000 people to watch over another 100,000." Ulbricht was not convinced. He complained that German police were often incapable of restoring order because they did not have the right to fire upon Red Army soldiers. "Can't something be done?" he asked Sokolovsky.[16] The grim emphasis that the SED leadership placed on the issue of rape and robbery in talks with the head of SMA demonstrates that it must have been a very serious problem, one that was rapidly eroding SED support even among long-time Communists.

SED leaders raised only some of their many grievances at the December 1946 meeting with Sokolovsky. But the problems they addressed represented issues of grave concern to people in every walk of life in the Soviet zone—abuses that were evoking antipathy among the population toward the Soviet occupiers and their German partners. The Soviets, through inconsistent, arbitrary, and harsh policies, had undercut their postwar plan. Ex-Nazis and other opponents were now joined in hatred of the regime by large segments of the population and by the handcrafted SED that was supposed to represent Soviet interests. Efforts by KGB to counter this opposition and operations by CIA Berlin to reveal its underlying causes sparked the first intelligence confrontations of what was rapidly becoming a very Cold War.

In the October 1946 parliamentary elections in the East German provinces, the combined votes for LDP and CDU had exceeded those for SED. The implications of this vote must have shocked Moscow. In his 23 December 1946 meeting with the SED leaders, Marshal Sokolovsky insisted that "we will ensure, and let there be no doubt about this, the creation of a government that will see Germany develop on a democratic course." Invoking the names of past and present West German politicians who were particularly disliked by the Soviets, Sokolovsky continued: "We will not allow reactionaries in a future German government. . . . The participation of [Karl] Schumacher, [Heinrich] Bruening, and others like them in a German government is excluded. We have never counted on [Jakob] Kaiser, and never will."[17] The incongruity of the Soviets' total rejection of the "bourgeois" parties in West Germany and their insistence on retaining caricatures of similar parties in their own zone was a serious error and caused continuing security problems. Many leaders of the outlawed German parties successfully fled to the West, but hundreds of other supporters throughout the Soviet zone were harassed, persecuted, and imprisoned for believing in a future for Germany that clashed with Marshal Sokolovsky's views.

BOB's Coverage of the Merger

BOB's early start in covering the Christian Democratic Union (CDU) enabled the base to continue to follow that party as it resisted Soviet and SED efforts to make it a proper "anti-Fascist" coalition partner. In spite of Soviet opposition, CDU fostered expansion of church-related youth activities throughout the zone. At the same time, CDU urged young people to resist the recruitment efforts of Erich Honecker,[18] leader of the SED-sponsored Free German Youth (Freie Deutsche Jugend). CDU also actively opposed SED antireligious campaigns. Local CDU organizations in the Soviet zone protested SED school reforms and the exclusion of religious studies. BOB covered Soviet reactions as well as these CDU activities, taking note, for example, when the CDU lord mayor of Martin Luther's city of Wittenberg was removed as "politically unreliable." The Soviets' view was that no member of CDU should be permitted to occupy a position of leadership unless he adopted the SED line. BOB's contacts in CDU continued to report on Soviet harassment of CDU members and attempts to curtail CDU activities.[19]

As the 23 December 1946 meeting between Sokolovsky and the SED leaders illustrated, the biggest problem for both SED and the Soviets was how to deal with members of the German Social Democratic Party (SPD) in the Soviet zone who remained opposed to the merger with KPD. Their concern was aggravated by the fact that SPD members in the Western occupation zones and in West Berlin continued to support and assist these recalcitrants. BOB reports described SPD complaints about Soviet manipulation of trade union elections, accounts of Soviet troops occupying East Berlin polling places to prevent the March 1946 referendum on the merger from taking place there, and details on the harassment of individual SPD members in the Soviet zone by SED activists, Soviet MGB units, and Communist-controlled trade union activists, in order to force them to support the merger. Even after the SPD-KPD merger was rammed through in the Soviet zone, BOB observed that SED was harassing members of independent SPD organizations still functioning in East Berlin.[20]

BOB soon recognized that the success or failure of the forced merger between German socialists and Communists was an important factor in the equation of Soviet power in their own zone. If the merger didn't work, then Soviet plans for the "consolidation of its position in eastern Germany" would suffer a serious setback. They had staked everything on being able to create from this merger a single party on the model of the Soviet Communist Party. To obtain access to information on the merger, it would be necessary to establish contact with SPD's Eastern bureau (Ostburo). This organization acquired information while it helped resettle SPD members who had left the Soviet zone and while it lent support to those who opted to stay and resist. The work of the Ostburo was controlled by SPD headquarters in Hanover, in the British zone. It naturally attracted the attention of BOB and other Western intelligence agencies. The Ostburo was willing to provide information to these services because it hoped to influence Allied governments' policies on Germany.

BOB's sole interest at this time was expanding its intelligence coverage of the Soviet zone. Consequently, when US officials were asked by the Ostburo for a contact with American intelligence, BOB was interested.[21] BOB did not direct Ostburo activities, nor could it have. Neither did it use SPD as a source of leads to possible agent recruits in the Soviet zone. Instead, BOB concentrated on obtaining useful information on the status of Soviet and SED efforts to expand SED and contain the opposition to the merger.

But the Ostburo provided the same material to other Western intelligence contacts, whose efforts inevitably overlapped with BOB's. Both BOB and the Berlin region of the US Army's Counterintelligence Corps (CIC), for example, were receiving the same reports. In addition, BOB discovered that some of the Ostburo reporting seemed "padded," even fabricated. This should not have been surprising, given the Ostburo's desire to maintain the impression that a vigorous SPD resistance still existed in the Soviet zone. Knowing that tough Soviet countermeasures against all forms of political opposition were working, BOB might have tried to persuade the SPD Ostburo operation to adopt more professional techniques. But this idea was never seriously considered because SPD, protective of its independence, would not and most probably could not make meaningful improvements in its security.[22]

The Soviets, meanwhile, knew about the relationship between SPD's Ostburo and Western intelligence services and considered it a threat to Soviet security. In MGB's view, based on documents of the period, when Kurt Schumacher was elected the leader of SPD, it stopped being a political party and became an espionage and subversive organization working for the British and American intelligence services. In February 1946, Schumacher was said to have ordered SPD in Berlin and the Soviet zone to work actively against the merger of SPD and the Communist Party: as a result, SPD members in Berlin voted against the proposal. In April 1946, after SPD and KPD were united in the SED, Schumacher organized the Ostburo, which according to MGB, "created illegal organizations of SPD in the Soviet zone through which subversive work was carried out against SED and the Soviet occupation authorities."[23]

The MGB report that described SPD's role placed elements of SPD underground organizations in each of the major cities of the Soviet zone. Here they were believed to be engaged in "penetrating SED [so as to] occupy leading posts in the party in order to break it up from within, and to gain positions in local German government agencies." The report also accused SPD of colluding with CDU to oppose SED candidates in the 1946 elections. SPD and CDU members in the Soviet zone were said to have attacked SED for "not being a German political party but a creature of the Soviet Military Administration."[24]

As the Soviets gradually eliminated members of CDU and the Liberal Democratic Party (LDP) who resisted the subordinate role written for them by SED, the influence of these parties waned—and so did their value as sources of accurate inside information on Soviet intentions. In addition, much of the information on these fringe parties was duplicated in the press. As long as the fate of these parties was a concern of much larger and increasingly active political groups with the same or similar names in West Germany, such press coverage continued and affected Western public opinion. But it could not help predict Soviet actions.

Appendix 2. Double Agents, Double Trouble

In 1946, BOB's double-agent cases that had begun in late 1945 continued under the guidance of Henry Hecksher. They were time-consuming operations, but Hecksher was new to SSU and eager to demonstrate his prowess. One of the double agents, code-named Zigzag, was Karl Krull, a former Berlin attorney and member of Abwehr who had volunteered his services to OSS in summer 1945. Zigzag led Berlin Base X-2 officers to his former Abwehr colleagues, some of whom had already been approached by the Soviets. A few of these, faced with arrest or cooperation, were persuaded by Berlin Base to become American agents. With the help of Zigzag, for example, Berlin Base agents approached former Abwehr officer and Berlin attorney Hans Kemritz, who was offered the choice of either cooperating or being arrested. He chose to cooperate but noted that he had already been recruited by the Soviets.[1] After arresting him in May 1945, the Soviets had subjected him to long interrogations concerning his Abwehr connections and had released him on the condition that he work for them.

Given the cryptonym Savoy by BOB, Kemritz was doubled against his Soviet case officer. This led to a fascinating but risky operation that gave BOB advance information on Soviet plans against individuals of counterintelligence interest. Through Savoy, CIA also attempted to nab the Soviet agents who were recruiting former Abwehr officers. Using his attorney's offices in East Berlin, and acting under his Soviet handler's instructions, Savoy invited former Abwehr colleagues for "business meetings." When they left Savoy's office, they were picked up by the Soviet recruiter and offered the same option: cooperation or arrest.[2] Over the lifetime of the Savoy case, several unsuccessful attempts were made to lure the Soviet case officer, known as Captain Skurin, to the Western sectors.

Security was a constant problem. Complaints were becoming more frequent from persons in the West who suspected Savoy's complicity in several kidnappings by the Soviets.[3] As one case officer observed, "Quite aside from the strain this places upon our relations with US law enforcement agencies, the resultant increase in the number of persons becoming aware of Savoy's status ... carries in itself the germ of serious repercussions."[4] By August 1946, Savoy's BOB case officer commented in a review that "Savoy is about the most notorious agent of the MVD in Berlin ... and at the moment, [he] is unable to contribute any startling new intelligence." His recommendation that the case be dropped was ignored.[5]

Soviet captain Skurin told Savoy on 3 September 1946 that "he was no longer allowed to lure [ex-Abwehr] officers released by the Americans and the British into the Russian Sector for arrest," but concern for Savoy's security continued.[6] At a 16 October meeting, Skurin grilled Savoy on the number of persons in West Berlin who knew of his Soviet intelligence relationship, and then learned that Savoy had been making carbon copies of his Soviet reports. Skurin demanded and received the file of carbons that Savoy had kept in his East Berlin office. Only later did Savoy remember that the same file contained copies of some reports intended only for BOB, including a psychological assessment of Zigzag.[7] Because of this bungle, Savoy was resettled in the US zone. He lived quietly there until he was arrested on 4 November 1950 by West German authorities responding to complaints from survivors of persons fingered by Savoy and later incarcerated by the Soviets. The Berlin court subsequently advised that the "American Commissioner of Land Hesse has taken over the prosecution of Dr. Kemritz and has turned him over to the qualified American district court."[8] This situation led to the so-called Kemritz law, which held that one could not be prosecuted for having obeyed the instructions of an occupying power.[9]

Savoy was out of play, but the operation to get at Skurin continued. A replacement for Savoy was found in a former agent of Skurin's, "Ford," who had engaged in tasks similar to those given Savoy. Ford was approached and successfully doubled, and he sustained the flow of reports on Skurin.[10] In a new attempt to entice Captain Skurin into West Berlin, BOB found an attractive woman, code-named Gambit, who had an appropriately interesting German intelligence background—in the Reichsicherheithauptamt, a security office created under Reinhard Heydrich during the Nazi regime.[11] Employment with the US military was obtained for her under an assumed name. As BOB had planned, Skurin located her despite the alias. He gave Ford the job of persuading her to visit him in East Berlin.

BOB preferred to lure Skurin to the West.[12] A 17 March 1947 progress report was decidedly upbeat in its summary of the operation: "Skurin is the MVD captain in Berlin, two of whose agents, Savoy and Ford, have been working for OSO as double agents for quite some time. He is now extremely interested in getting in touch with another OSO agent, Gambit. Since, through these agents, OSO has been well informed concerning Skurin's operations during the past year, Berlin Station is now working on a plan to have Skurin defect to OSO or to remain in place to report on Soviet intelligence activities. The present plan is that if Skurin does not defect willingly, OSO will threaten to inform his superiors concerning the excellent penetration job which has been accomplished in his office."[13] Accordingly, Gambit agreed to meet Skurin in the French sector, which had become neutral ground. Skurin never bought the scam, probably because he was aware of or suspected Gambit's double role for BOB.

Another aspect of the Skurin operation included efforts to encourage the defection of a young Ukrainian woman who had been Captain Skurin's German interpreter. Doocia, as the counterintelligence branch referred to her (in an American variant of the Russian diminutive Dusia), had been brought to Germany during the war and had become Skurin's interpreter when hostilities had ended. BOB interest in Doocia began in February, when she told double-agent Savoy that nearly half the female secretaries employed by NKVD since the May 1945 surrender had been returned to the USSR because "they knew too much." In April Doocia told Savoy that she had seen her name on a list of Ukrainian interpreters scheduled for early return to the Soviet Union. Savoy believed she was reluctant to return. This news triggered a series of moves orchestrated by Hecksher through Savoy to entice her into West Berlin for recruitment or defection.[14]

At the same time, Hecksher was advised by German mission headquarters that in order to carry out a successful secret defection, they needed to solve the problem of "disposal of the body"—a reference to the fact that because of the Clay-Sokolovsky agreement, Doocia would have to be resettled outside of Germany.[15] Although the idea of luring Doocia to West Berlin remained active during the summer, nothing seemed to work. In retrospect, it seems that Savoy may have drawn a fanciful picture of this young woman and of the likelihood of her defection. BOB never knew whether Savoy's portrait was accurate or whether it was devised to please his BOB case officer and enhance his own status.

Appendix 3. The Mysterious Case of
Leonid Malinin, a.k.a. Georgiev

Perhaps the strangest, most fascinating BOB counterintelligence case had to do with Maj. Gen. of State Security Leonid Alekseevich Malinin. While researching this book, we found this intriguing reference to a KGB Major General Malinin in *Secret Servant,* the 1987 memoirs of former KGB officer Ilya Dzhirkvelov: "Some thirty generals were reduced in rank, including KGB Major General Malinin. I took part in a court martial at which he was charged with having committed an abuse of his official position when on duty in Germany after the war."[1] Robert Conquest's *Inside Stalin's Secret Police* relates that on 11 July 1945 an L. A. Malinin was accorded the military rank of major general along with other NKVD and NKGB officials.[2] When we interviewed Tom Polgar in October 1993, he volunteered that Henry Hecksher had been in contact with a "Lieutenant General Malinin, whom he met at dinners at the home of James Riddleberger, deputy political adviser." According to Polgar, during the course of several dinners, Malinin spoke frankly about conditions in Russia. When asked how it was that he was able to speak so freely about presumably secret matters, Malinin replied, "Just because you don't know about it doesn't make it secret."[3] In a subsequent interview, Peter Sichel said he recalled such a contact, but that it was kept secret by base chief Dana Durand.[4]

When asked about this case, Kondrashev provided SVR archival material on Malinin that greatly surprised his coauthors. Malinin was in fact the KI resident in East Berlin and had indeed had contacts with Americans, for which he was eventually punished.

Although BOB did make contact with Malinin and code-name him Desoto, it had no idea that he was the KI resident. George Belic initiated the relationship on 9 December 1947 at a dinner given by "a member of the OMGUS Press Section." Malinin seemed prepared to discuss a wide range of political topics, so Belic arranged for him to be invited to a dinner party given by Ambassador Robert Murphy on 16 January 1948. Durand and other officials attended, with Belic serving as interpreter.[5] Subsequent meetings with Malinin occurred at dinner parties hosted by James Riddleberger and attended by Hecksher, among others.

While Malinin was in contact with American officials in West Berlin, he apparently was also active under the name Georgiev, or Georgiev-Malinin, in contacts with various East German politicians. He was reported in Western press articles to still be active under these names as late as spring 1949, although as of June 1948 his presence in Berlin could no longer be confirmed.[6] There is a hint of this aspect of the case in Durand's statement that this operation, "if it can be continued, has carried us into the highest echelon where intelligence, deception and policy converge in a single (or perhaps dual) personality." In a note written for the file while at Washington headquarters, Hecksher commented that Malinin's case "strikes me as particularly significant inasmuch as he engaged in what we would call political action on a very high level. The conspiratorial aspects of his work were underscored by the fact that he, vainly, tried to operate under an alias."[7]

The Soviet version of General Malinin's contacts with the Americans and his eventual trial and dismissal can be reconstructed based on archival reports including Malinin's personnel file, a classified monograph held in a special collection of the Andropov Institute, and interviews with retired KGB officers who knew Malinin. We were surprised to learn, first, that Malinin was not simply a Soviet deputy political adviser but also the foreign intelligence resident, having replaced Aleksandr Korotkov in 1946. It was his first assignment abroad, but Malinin had been in state security since the late 1920s.[8]

According to a report in Soviet archives, during the second half of 1947 an unidentified Soviet official met Robert Gray, a member of the "American Information Bureau," and his wife, Galina, a Russian who had left the USSR in the 1930s. The Grays said they had met General Malinin and had expressed a desire to invite him to a "Russian" dinner. As a result of their discussion, Gray sent Malinin a written invitation, which Malinin accepted. At the dinner "Malinin was introduced to an American, 'George Bell,' with whom he held an extensive conversation apart from the guests. The dinner lasted until long after midnight." According to the Soviet official, who was present at the dinner and who accompanied Malinin on their return to East Berlin, Bell had tried to establish that generals Malinin and Georgiev were the same person. Malinin denied this, claiming that "General Georgiev" really existed but visited Berlin from Moscow only occasionally. The Soviet official suspected that Bell was an American intelligence officer and that Gray was subordinate to him.[9]

In January 1948, General Malinin advised the Soviet official that he had received a call from Bell, who had said that Ambassador Murphy would like to meet him. Malinin said that "he would try in every way to avoid this meeting, since it was likely that Bell would invite persons who knew him as Georgiev, thus causing a breach of his security." Two weeks later, Malinin told the Soviet official that if Gray asked about Malinin, he was to be told that the general "was in Potsdam and almost never visited Berlin." On 17 March 1948 the Soviet official reported that "he had been invited to the Grays', and, as he expected, George Bell was also there, trying hard to determine the whereabouts of General Malinin." The file indicates that after this event, the residency was directed to break off all contact with Gray and Bell.[10]

The deputy resident, Boris Yakovlevich Nalivaiko, continues the story in his memoirs, which were published in a classified edition by the Andropov Institute. It turned out that he had in fact been developing Gray as an operational prospect but that nothing had come of it because he did not speak English and Gray had a limited command of Russian. When Nalivaiko told Malinin of his intention to break off contact, Malinin suggested that someone else meet Gray for a second assessment. So when Gray suggested that Nalivaiko invite someone from his side, Malinin suddenly proposed that he come along. It was at this event that Gray introduced "Bell" to Malinin. Nalivaiko thought Malinin was going so that he could sound out the West's position on German questions. Unfortunately for Malinin, the next day an article appeared in "American newspapers" in which a highly placed Soviet representative was quoted as not excluding the possibility of a meeting between Stalin and Truman. Because Malinin's account of the meeting (sent to Moscow in his capacity as resident) reached Moscow the same night, it was not hard to figure out the source. Other officers have said that Malinin was thought to have talked of Stalin's plans to adopt a harder line on Germany. In any case, Malinin was recalled and replaced as resident.[11]

But replacement was not enough for Stalin, who had heard of the case. Stalin ordered Molotov, head of the Committee of Information (KI), which had taken over Soviet foreign intelligence, to punish Malinin. As a result, he was tried by an officers' court for the crime of

> entering into personal contact with the well-known American intelligence officer [Robert] Murphy, without the permission of the Center, and carrying out political discussions that gave a false impression of Soviet foreign policy, specifically of the possibility of the Soviet Union's signing a separate peace with Germany. He also gave the Americans grounds for circulating false information in the foreign press concerning secret meetings of USSR representatives in the United States and Berlin and of preparations for meetings of the heads of state of these countries.
>
> Malinin was also accused of failing to organize the work of the residency of the Committee of Information in Germany in a correct manner, did not acquire valuable agents capable of clarifying Anglo-American policy in Germany, and at the same time took no actions to rid agent networks of spies and provocateurs infiltrated by foreign intelligence. He permitted the crudest violations of operational security in agent work, and compromised himself and a number of operational workers in the residency. The entire period of his leadership was in fact a total loss to the intelligence activities of the Committee of Information in Germany.[12]

Because the accusation was based on newspaper stories, not on convincing testimony, the organizers of the court had decided to try Malinin for abuse of his official position. Nalivaiko claimed that in his testimony he "attributed everything to the inexperience of the resident [Malinin] in making such meetings despite efforts by the court to indict him for political shortsightedness, bordering on criminal action." Nevertheless, in the report of the trial, the conclusion read: "There is no basis for a review of the sentence in the case of Comrade Malinin." He was reduced in rank from general to colonel.[13]

In reviewing the Soviets' story of the first meeting, whereby Bell meets Malinin through the good offices of Robert Gray and his wife, we see that it conforms to the BOB account. But clearly the Soviets were either ignorant of Malinin's subsequent meetings with ambassadors Murphy and Riddleberger and other BOB officers or chose to suppress this knowledge. In the account of the trial, however, Malinin's contact with Murphy was a major issue.[14] The "unidentified observer" in the archival account—the Soviet official who had accompanied Malinin to the first Gray dinner party and had returned with him to East Berlin—was obviously Nalivaiko. The Malinin affair was not Nalivaiko's last encounter with CIA. Several years later, his relationship with Gray climaxed in the notorious Gartenbau Cafe incident in Vienna.

Appendix 4. MGB at Work in East Germany

In a report submitted to MGB Minister Viktor Abakumov, MGB chief in Germany Nikolai Kovalchuk stated that 549 people had been arrested for espionage in Germany during the first half of 1948. Of that number, 391 agents were American, 121 were British, 31 were French, and 6 were from "other services." During the first quarter of the year 211 had been arrested, 338 in the second quarter.[1]

The preponderance of "American" agents in this report may be misleading. In one case, code-named Nit, the MGB operational sector in Thuringia reported the arrest of 88 spies on 20 July 1948. The "underground organization" that the Soviets had discovered had been created by a German staff at the request of American intelligence. It was known as Immer Bereit Sein (Always Ready), and it collected military intelligence throughout the Soviet zone. Its headquarters was in Frankfurt am Main, and it was staffed by former German officers. According to SVR archives, the leader of the organization in East Germany was Walter Kammer, a former Wehrmacht officer known to his subordinates as Number 94.[2]

This story was confirmed to American intelligence when an interpreter from the Soviet operational sector in Thuringia defected soon after the event. He was a displaced person who had been brought to Germany from the Soviet Union during the war. Like many others, he had been forced to work for MGB as an interpreter but had been scheduled for return home, where he expected prison or exile. According to his testimony, two members of Immer Bereit Sein had tried to recruit someone in Eisenach for their network but the person had reported the approach to the MGB operational sector there, which arrested the would-be recruiters. Lengthy interrogations resulted in a list of twenty-five members of the Immer Bereit Sein in Thuringia. At 3:00 A.M. on 23 June 1948, MGB fanned out to arrest them all. Everyone arrested admitted his guilt, and some identified ex-German army captain Walter Kammer as the leader and another former officer as his deputy. When the arrest teams arrived, Kammer was not at home. His assistant was not so fortunate. In his home they found a suitcase belonging to Kammer that contained the names and addresses of agents throughout the Soviet zone. Based on this discovery, and on the initial interrogations, 123 persons were arrested. An additional forty arrests were planned for 18 and 19 July. According to the confessions of those arrested, including Kammer's deputy, Immer Bereit Sein was organized, financed, and answerable to the American intelligence community in Frankfurt am Main. As far as they knew, the German head of the group was former field marshal Heinz Guderian.[3]

The case had reached such huge proportions that a personal representative of Kovalchuk, chief of MGB Germany, and three representatives from MGB

Moscow were assigned to the MGB operational sector in Thuringia to assist and advise. On 18 July 1948 the wife of one of the arrestees came to the American sector of Berlin with the story. Her information, along with the rest of the case, was sent immediately by Berlin S-2 to the deputy director of intelligence for the European Command, with a note that Berlin S-2 could not provide the backup these operations apparently required.[4] The director in turn passed the case to the appropriate department of the US Army in Germany.[5] This operation was actually an activity sponsored by the Gehlen Organization, then funded by the United States Army. The Gehlen Organization was later taken over by CIA.[6]

Western military intelligence operations such as Immer Bereit Sein were not sophisticated or high-level. They were undertaken to compensate for the American and British intelligences' nearly total lack of knowledge about the Soviet forces. The Soviet counterintelligence response was guided by specific directives from Moscow. The Soviets dealt with "imperialist intelligence services" by engaging in various "operational games" with double agents that permitted state security agents to penetrate American and British intelligence services.[7] But in BOB's experience with its order-of-battle agents, the Soviets wasted little time playing complex double-agent games with individuals identified as American agents. Contact with the American or German handlers was sustained only long enough to ensure a complete roll-up of the net.

It should be pointed out that MGB counterintelligence often labeled all activities hostile to Soviet and SED authority as "Western intelligence." Further, individuals or groups actively opposed to the regime were considered "terrorists." According to MGB, after the defeat of the underground Nazi organization Werwolf and the arrest of many of its members, Nazi elements began creating new illegal diversionist-terrorist organizations. For the most part, the leaders were former members of the Nazi youth organization, Hitler Jugend. The organizers of the groups recruited followers by spreading rumors of war between the Soviet Union and the "Anglo-American bloc." One such group, referred to in MGB documents as Edelweis Piraten (the Edelweiss Pirates), reportedly had these tasks:

Organizing terrorist acts against the Soviet army, Soviet personnel, and activists for SED and other "democratic organizations."

Carrying out diversionary actions against industrial targets, particularly those whose products were paying off war reparations.

Upsetting the work of SMA by stirring up anti-Soviet feelings in the German population.

Spreading profascist propaganda against SED policies.

Training armed groups to fight the Soviet army in the event of a war between the Soviet Union and the Anglo-American bloc.[8]

We found no record of American intelligence operations involving the Edelweiss Pirates. Actually they were originally anti-Nazi young gangs that had risen up in opposition to the Hitler Youth and its efforts to impose ideological uniformity among German teenagers. But MGB's investigation of the Edelweiss Pirates reportedly established that some of these groups had been organized by Anglo-American intelligence services and dispatched to the Soviet zone. Between 1 October 1946 and 15 February 1947, MGB agents liquidated fourteen such groups and arrested sixty of their members.[9]

The pursuit of the Edelweiss Pirates is just one example of MGB leaders' vigilance against opposition to Soviet policies in East Germany. Because no one in MGB Germany could challenge these policies, any resistance to them by the German population was accepted as evidence of sabotage instigated by the West. For example, Kovalchuk advised Minister Abakumov on 28 January 1947 that according to an agent of the operational sector in Brandenburg, a "Union of Baltic Germans" had been created in the British zone with the sanction of the British occupation authorities. The union maintained a file on all Germans who fled the Baltic and tried to assist them in emigration. The MGB report noted that an "illegal committee" of this group existed in the Soviet zone.[10]

The Soviets were even more sensitive to pressures from Silesian refugees to redraw Germany's eastern border. On 21 December 1946, Kovalchuk reported that this agitation had increased after Secretary of State James Byrnes, in a speech at Stuttgart, emphasized that the eastern territories of Germany then occupied by the USSR and Poland could not be considered permanent short of a peace treaty. According to a report from an agent in the MGB Berlin operations sector, a group soliciting signatures from Silesian refugees for petitions to abrogate this aspect of the Potsdam agreements was headed by Rudolph Nadolny, a former German ambassador to the Soviet Union.[11] On 31 March 1947, Kovalchuk reported an increase in propaganda calling upon Silesian refugees to unite and to petition the Allied Control Commission to reconstitute Germany within its 1937 borders. Kovalchuk claimed that the involvement of the Christian Democratic Party in these actions was directed and subsidized by the Anglo-American powers.[12]

The Rudolph Nadolny Case: A Cold War Classic

According to SVR archival material released for the first time, Nadolny's story demonstrates how complicated it was for MGB intelligence and counterintelligence agencies to pursue common goals within the complex politics of the immediate postwar period. Russian historian A. M. Filitov, in his 1993 book on Germany, writes of Nadolny as one who stood for "the traditions of Rapallo,"[13] whereas many Western observers felt that Nadolny was an "agent of influence"—the Soviet intelligence term for an individual who is used to influence public or official opinion. Writing about Nadolny's actions in April 1949, General Clay said, "Whether or not Nadolny, who lived in East Germany, was an agent of the Soviet Military Administration as some believed, the views he presented would have been an aid and comfort to the Communist program had they received any real reception in western Germany."[14] Had Nadolny in fact been a Soviet agent of influence, he would probably have been handled by the MGB Foreign Intelligence residency in Berlin under Korotkov or his successor, Maj. Gen. Leonid Alekseevich Malinin.

Nadolny's case shows that not all Soviet actions in this period were completely coordinated. The political action operations of the foreign intelligence residency were often at odds with SMA's Information Directorate, and both were the objects of investigation by MGB's counterintelligence sectors in East Germany. Nadolny offered his services to the Soviet Ministry of Foreign Affairs soon after the end of hostilities in 1945. On 29 August 1945, this ministry sought an update from the Ministry of State Security on Nadolny's activities since 1933 and whether it would be wise to use him in a political role in the Soviet zone.[15]

On 3 October 1945, MGB responded with a report on Nadolny signed by the head of the foreign intelligence directorate. The report covered Nadolny's career through 1937, including his tour as German ambassador in Moscow from 1933 to 1934. Although he had been a firm opponent of the Soviet political and economic system and one of the first diplomats to join the Nazi Party, Nadolny had opposed Hitler's policy of hostility toward the USSR. From the file it was also apparent that Nadolny had met with Malinin, the MGB foreign intelligence resident in Karlshorst.[16]

In a 6 December 1946 report from Deputy MGB Minister Pyotr Fedotov, then chief of foreign intelligence, a source reported on Nadolny's desire to speak with General "Georgiev" (the alias that we know the Berlin resident, General Malinin, often used when dealing with German political figures) and Ambassador Semyonov. The proposed topic was a plan by the United States, Britain, and France to sign a peace accord with the individual provinces in their zones rather than with a central German government. Nadolny also noted that the Western powers intended to embarrass the provincial governments in the Soviet zone if they recognized the new German-Polish border. When the report was released, it confirmed that Nadolny had been in contact with the foreign intelligence residency and that both Moscow and the residency were aware of his political orientation and possible usefulness in the field.[17]

But to MGB representatives in Germany, Nadolny seemed a loose cannon. An MGB report to Minister Abakumov dated 23 November 1946 (about a year after the exchange between the Foreign Ministry and the MGB's foreign intelligence directorate), provided much more detail on Nadolny and indicated that Kovalchuk's people had been following him. The report covered Nadolny's postretirement activities in Iran on behalf of Hitler's Foreign Minister Joachim von Ribbentrop, where he had cultivated right-wing circles as a way of strengthening German influence in that country. Kovalchuk also described letters sent to the Soviet High Command immediately after the capitulation in which Nadolny and others had opposed the decisions of the Potsdam Conference. For example, in July 1945, Nadolny had joined with Andreas Hermes of the Christian Democratic Union and others in giving a virtual ultimatum to SMA. In it they had called upon the Soviet Union to, among other things, return livestock, free all arrested persons, restore access to bank accounts, satisfy the fuel requirements of the German population and German industry, and stop evicting Sudeten Germans from Czechoslovakia. Nadolny had also urged the Soviets to again allow the German Red Cross to assist the German people.[18]

The Kovalchuk report reveals extensive counterintelligence coverage of Nadolny by MGB agents in Berlin during 1945 and 1946, the very years that Nadolny was apparently in contact with the Karlshorst residency under Korotkov and later, Malinin. One of the agents had even known Nadolny from their work together in Iran before the war. This coverage, including trips by agents from the Soviet sector of Berlin into the American zone, revealed Nadolny's contacts with Anglo-American authorities, pro-Western German diplomats, and anti-Soviet political parties (such as CDU and SPD) in both East and West Germany. One source quoted Nadolny as saying he opposed the political program of the newly created SED and would "never support the party." As late as 7 November 1947, just two weeks before Kovalchuk submitted his report to Abakumov, an agent reported that Nadolny remained strongly opposed to the Potsdam decision on Germany's eastern frontiers. Kovalchuk's report is a fascinating account of the differences between the foreign intelligence directorate and the counterintelligence elements that predominated in the Soviet zone in 1945–46. These differences continued to affect Soviet political goals in Germany into the KI period.[19]

MGB Political Operations

Surveillance of organizations seeking to revise the Potsdam agreements on the future eastern border of Germany represented only one part of MGB's political operations. The operational sectors were also deeply involved in penetrating and thwarting the policies of any and all groups that opposed SED. In November 1946, Kovalchuk forwarded a report from the operational sector in Thuringia concerning the arrest of the provincial secretary of the Christian

Democratic Union. This individual had campaigned actively for CDU in the fall 1946 elections and, in the words of the report, had worked actively against SED "under the cover of CDU." He was charged with "anti-Soviet agitation—the collection and publication of slanderous fabrications directed at the Soviet occupation authorities."[20] But the Soviets continued to have problems with the Thuringian CDU. In December 1947 a KI report from agent sources to MGB Minister Abakumov stated that "the Americans had organized the defection of Doctor Rudolf Paul, former minister-president of Thuringia, and his immediate associates (the majority of whom were members of resistance groups in Weimar), along with valuable documents."[21]

Although SVR archives have provided numerous examples of various MGB political or countersubversive operations, little has been made available reflecting the collection and dissemination of political intelligence reports during the period 1945 to late summer 1947. One item, a January 1947 report from Kovalchuk to Abakumov, does show that MGB was collecting a kind of political intelligence that later became a staple of KI reporting on the German problem: information that responded to specific requests from Moscow and told Stalin exactly what he wanted to hear. The report was a reaction, at Moscow's request, to an SED proposal for a German peace treaty. The SED proposal was essentially a propaganda effort made to minimize the effect of that party's very poor showing in the fall 1946 provincial elections. The ploy was to make diplomatic overtures to the West in order to divert attention from difficulties within East Germany—particularly problems with the German reunification offensive.

Following each request, the intelligence service would report on reactions within the Soviet zone and also by the West German population and the Western powers. The reports, like this January 1947 example, followed predictable patterns. First came the good news: "The progressive elements of the population responded positively to the proposed constitution, seeing in it a reflection of a future, truly democratic people's democracy in Germany." But there was always bad news as well. This report went on to state: "Together with these positive reactions, there was also sharp criticism of the proposal, primarily from the bourgeois parties and reactionary elements of the population." Agent reports that supported this claim followed, from quarters such as the Liberal Democratic Party, CDU, and the offices and residences of American Military Government officials. All of these Western views were presented as sharply critical of the constitutional project, of the procedures for its implementation, and of SED's motives in making it. A typical report ended by stating that these negative responses, at least in East Germany, were the fault not of the Soviets, but of SED for having failed properly to indoctrinate the population "in the substance and significance of the constitution for a German Republic."[22]

Upon receiving this report, Abakumov directed that it be sent to Molotov. Whatever Molotov's response, it probably mattered little because by this time

Molotov was already preparing for a new initiative in Soviet intelligence, KI. Little did he know that the problem of coordinating Soviet intelligence collection activities was not so easily solved.

Security Problems Among Soviet Personnel in Germany

Neither counterintelligence operations against Western services nor the suppression of political dissent in East Germany were as important to MGB Berlin as was the protection of those Soviet citizens who lived or worked away from military installations. The counterintelligence directorate of GSOFG at Potsdam continued to be responsible for the security of all personnel, military and civilian, assigned to units of the Soviet occupation forces. But there were thousands working at various levels of SMA and for other special organizations in the Soviet zone. This group, known in MGB parlance as the Soviet Colony or SK (Sovetskaia koloniia), was particularly vulnerable to the many new influences for which neither the Soviet government nor their previous experience in the Soviet Union could have prepared them. This vulnerability was described in poignant terms by Yuri Modin when he and his family arrived in London for their first assignment abroad in June 1947: "The difference in standard of living between ourselves and the West was such that we had the impression of having arrived on a different planet."[23] This from a member of the elite foreign intelligence directorate in Moscow and at a time when bomb-damaged London was still on rationing. No wonder the average Soviet citizens found it difficult to adjust to postwar Germany, which for all its misery and destruction seemed ahead of their country in many ways. It was the job of the MGB operational sectors and groups to recruit informants among these people, monitor their activities, and intervene if any of them appeared ready to break ranks with the system.

On 27 July 1948, more than three years after the end of hostilities in Germany, Kovalchuk sent a report on the "Results of Agent-Operational Work in the Soviet Colony of Germany for the first six months of 1948." More than two hundred Soviet citizens had been arrested, among them workers in SMA, representatives from individual Moscow ministries and Soviet joint stock companies, and former military personnel from GSFOG units remaining in Germany after demobilization. In addition, more than one hundred displaced persons had been arrested for refusing to return to the USSR. Few of these individuals were actually agents of Western services. The largest group arrested, more than 150, comprised citizens who had defected, or were apprehended while attempting to defect, to the West.[24]

When one considers that this report was filed in summer 1948, it is apparent that the Soviets were tremendously concerned about the loyalty of their citizens in Germany during these immediate postwar years. In a 3 February

1948 memorandum to CIA's assistant director for special operations, the chief of Foreign Branch M, Richard Helms, attempted to estimate the number of Soviet deserters in Germany and Austria. Recognizing that because the US policy of returning defectors meant that accurate lists were not kept, Helms in his rough estimate put the figures at 450–500 in the American zones of Austria (where defectors were never turned back) and another three hundred in Germany. He added that American military authorities estimated that 60,000 Russians had deserted to Europe and other countries outside the Soviet Union between the end of World War II and October 1947.[25] It is not unlikely that MGB General Kovalchuk may have been been downplaying the extent of his problem.

Appendix 5. Was It Worth It?
What the Berlin Tunnel Produced

The volume and content of the information CIA found supports the claim that KGB allowed valuable information to pass through cable lines tapped by the Berlin tunnel. The project tapped three cables containing "273 metallic pairs capable of transmitting a total of 1,200 communications channels," of which about 500 were active at any given time. "On average, 28 telegraphic circuits and 121 voice circuits were recorded continuously" on hundreds of Ampex tape recorders installed in the "warehouse," which during the life of the tunnel used "50,000 reels of magnetic tape."[1]

In fact, the reels were so numerous that the BOB registry chief, responsible for shipping some of them to Washington, complained about their weight. Because many insiders knew that BOB had been running operations into the Wismut uranium ore mining and processing facilities, the registry chief was informed "for his information only" that the packages contained processed uranium ore that would enable specialists to estimate the size of the Soviet atomic arsenal. Satisfied that he now knew the secret, he stopped griping.

A total of 443,000 conversations were fully transcribed from voice reels. Of these, 368,000 were Soviet and 75,000 were East German. The daily output of the telegraphic processing center was approximately 4,000 feet of teletype messages. Processing of the tunnel take continued after the tunnel's "discovery" in April 1956. Ninety thousand translated messages or telephone conversations had been disseminated as of 30 September 1958, resulting in 1,750 intelligence reports.[2] The coverage afforded by the tapped cables or the volume of production alone cannot convey the magnitude or the value of the information provided. Nor can it impart the significance of the KGB decision in 1955 to let the project continue unhindered. If, in fact, everything had been "doctored from the beginning," then KGB's play would have been perfect: it would have been able to protect its source's security and at the same time avoid the leakage of state secrets.[3]

On the other hand, the Soviets' obsession for preserving "state secrets," which led them to suspect even the innocent of violating security regulations, was equaled by Western ignorance of conditions in the USSR and its occupied areas. Western intelligence services could not keep up with the demand for information about these areas. Loss of access to Soviet wireless communications had caused Bill Harvey and Frank Rowlett to consider intercepting landlines in the first place. Moreover, it was getting ever more difficult to communicate with agents in the USSR and East Germany. By 1954–55, KGB and the East German MFS were continuing to roll up Allied and West German agent networks. Further, these agents' access to Soviet military installations was extremely limited. Soviet Army defectors were prized but were increasingly rare as Soviet military counterintelligence worked with MfS to strengthen controls over troop units. It is hard to imagine in this era of U-2 and satellite photography, but Western intelligence analysts at the time simply did not have the information needed to estimate the strength of the Soviet threat. Consequently, the US Army G-2 at the time, Gen. Arthur Trudeau, knowing what a wealth of intelligence tapping the landlines had produced on Soviet forces in Austria and Hungary, enthusiastically supported the tunnel project.

The situation was particularly critical in Germany. First, the Allied position in Berlin had been subjected to continual harassment since the Berlin blockade of 1948–49, yet Allied policy insisted on the right of the Allies to remain in their sectors of the city. Any attempt to force them to leave could have resulted in war. Second, GSFG, commanded by Khrushchev supporter Marshal Andrei Grechko, was the largest Soviet force outside the USSR. Information on its activities, equipment, and personnel, as well as those of the neighboring northern group of Soviet forces in Poland, was of vital importance in estimating Soviet capabilities for offensive action, not only against Berlin and Germany but also against Western Europe. Third, since 1946, East Germany had been a major contributor of raw materials and manufactured specialties to the Soviet nuclear energy program. Finally, Soviet efforts to stabilize the East German political situation, still restive two years after the June 1953 riots, were vital to long-range Soviet plans in Europe.

In this context, the tunnel was seen as a unique, timely, and reliable source of intelligence information on the USSR, East Germany, and Poland. The tunnel's taps offered hard data on Soviet political actions and intentions in Berlin and on its relations with the Western occupying powers, as well as indications of differences of opinion between the Soviets and East Germans on the problem of West Berlin's status. As the GDR tested the limits of its sovereignty, the tunnel provided detailed information on the nature and limitations of Soviet military and economic control over East Germany and other Soviet-occupied territories. Each incident in Berlin involving citizens of the Western powers reported by the tunnel reflected the "unpreparedness, confusion, and indecision among Soviet and East German officials" over how authority should be delegated. The tunnel warned the West that the Soviets were creating an East German National People's Army based on the existing paramilitary alert police. It also provided insights into how the Soviets implemented the decisions of the Twentieth Party Congress (during which Stalin's memory was denigrated) among the Soviet military and the scientific and technical intelligentsia stationed in East Germany. In addition, conversations overheard in the tunnel revealed much about the progress of Marshal Zhukov's efforts to diminish the influence of political officers in the Soviet armed forces.[4]

Some writers have claimed that much of the tunnel take was simply gossip. But this so-called gossip was important, too: it was by and about senior players in the Soviet hierarchy at a time when the West was coming to grips with a new set of top Soviet leaders. Although Stalin was long dead, the struggle for ultimate succession in Moscow continued, and hints regarding who was close to whom were important. Conversations of this type also furnished vital clues about political attitudes, morale, and behaviors within the upper echelons of the Soviet military and civilian hierarchy. Corruption, influence peddling, and nepotism were evident at all levels.[5]

Military-related information from the tunnel was highly prized and included reports on the reorganization of the Soviet Defense Ministry, on increased Soviet–East European military cooperation under the Warsaw Pact, and on a reduction in the strength of the Soviet armed forces. The tunnel data also identified several thousand Soviet officers. These identifications confirmed wartime holdings and formed the basis for establishing new biographic records on many officers who had entered the armed forces after the war. Parallel to this, the tunnel provided details on Soviet ground force units in the USSR not previously identified or not located by other sources since wartime, as well as on several thousand field post numbers used by the Soviets to conceal the real designations of military units, a gold mine for order-of-battle analysts. Analysts also received detailed training and readiness plans for Soviet units stationed in East Germany and Poland.[6]

Reports made from the tunnel taps revealed "the development of an improved nuclear capability in the Soviet Air Army in East Germany and the re-equipping of this army with new bombers and twin-jet interceptors with airborne radar." They also described, for example, "the doubling of Soviet bomber strength in Poland and the creation of a new fighter division there. Over one hundred new Soviet Air Force installations were identified and located in the USSR, East Germany, and Poland, including a number of key aircraft factories." As for the Soviet Navy, the tunnel reported new information on the organization of the Soviet Baltic Fleet, its bases, and its personnel.[7]

The tunnel's main contribution to scientific-technical information was the identification of personalities associated with the Soviet atomic energy program, which was then under the USSR Ministry of Medium Machine Building. Several hundred personnel, as well as the location of the ministry's installations in the USSR, were fingered. This information could not have come at a better time. Hundreds of German scientists who had participated in the Soviet atomic program and related weapons development were being released, and the tunnel information provided a way to crosscheck their statements during debriefing. Of special interest to BOB, as well as to the intelligence community, was new information obtained through tunnel taps on the organization and activities of the Wismut uranium mining operation, information that included links to KGB components responsible for security there.[8]

One might have expected KGB to have been indifferent to political, military, and scientific security leaks that might have resulted from their decision to let the tunnel project proceed rather than endanger their source, George Blake. More fascinating were the secrets revealed about Soviet military intelligence and counterintelligence units (especially the latter, because it was an arm of KGB) or about numerous East German security components with whom the KGB apparat had contact as advisers. Because these services, taken as a whole, represented the single largest counterintelligence problem faced by NATO, the detailed information the tunnel provided on them was of special significance.

Hardest hit were the Soviet military intelligence units in East Germany. Of the telephone lines tapped, twenty-five carried conversations of the Soviet general staff's Chief Intelligence Directorate (GRU) and the intelligence points or units subordinate to the intelligence directorate (RU) of the Group of Soviet Forces Germany (GSFG). More than 350 GRU and RU officers were identified in East Germany, along with details on the organization, agent operations, and activities of the individual units involved. This information was invaluable for analyzing reporting from double agents being run against RU intelligence points in East Germany by CIA and friendly Western services. When in 1955–56 CIA source GRU Lt. Col. Pyotr Popov was assigned to the Schwerin point of RU GSFG, tunnel information was of vital assistance in guiding this operation's case officer because it provided invaluable details about the personnel and activities of the various intelligence points of the GSFG's RU. As GRU inspection commissions arrived in East Germany from Moscow, the resultant increase in unguarded telephone conversations provided additional insights into RU activities.[9]

Additionally, the tunnel produced a wealth of detail on the "special designation" (*osobogo naznacheniia*—OSNAZ) communications components subordinate to the RU GSFG Directorate. These units were responsible for intercepting the radio transmissions of Western military forces in West Berlin and West Germany. They also provided radio communications support for agents reporting to the directorate's various intelligence points. Tunnel information covered the whole range of clandestine radio operations from agent training techniques and facilities, to agents' radio sets (models, specifications, problems encountered in their use, and so forth), to details on the operation of the directorate's main radio station, which was used to maintain contact with agent networks. Included in this reporting were the names of officers assigned to these units, the cover names of many of the agents involved, and information on KGB cooperation with this aspect of military intelligence operations. Details on the procedures and problems of agent radio communications by Soviet military intelligence in East Germany—whose sources operated not only in West

Germany but also throughout the NATO countries of Western Europe, were a bonanza to Western counterintelligence specialists at the time.[10]

In all the tunnel coverage of the GSFG intelligence directorate, there were many taped phone conversations between that directorate and the Chief Intelligence Directorate (GRU) of the General Staff of the Ministry of Defense in Moscow, which resulted in extensive reporting on GRU itself. In addition, intercepted conversations between Soviet military intelligence personnel often provided surprising information on GRU units far removed from East Germany—for example, the intelligence directorate of the Transcaucasian Military District, whose headquarters were at Tbilisi and whose sixteen intelligence points covered the borders with Iran and Turkey.[11]

The counterintelligence directorate of the GSFG, which had its headquarters in Potsdam and was then commanded by Maj. Gen. Georgy Tsinev, was also the focus of extensive reports.[12] The directorate controlled special departments throughout the GSFG responsible for the security of military personnel and installations. The tunnel also reported on the directorate's Third or Operations Department, which ran agents against Western intelligence units in West Berlin and West Germany. The conduct of agent operations against Western targets had earlier been a bone of contention between state security's foreign intelligence directorate elements in Karlshorst and those of the counterintelligence directorate in Potsdam. Tunnel taps revealed Third Department operations to be a large, scattergun effort in which many low-level agents concentrated on exposing Western agents. This activity involved frequent communication with the KGB apparat under Pitovranov in Karlshorst as well as with KGB advisers to MfS, much of which was recorded in the tunnel.[13]

Periodic inspections of counterintelligence operations by Moscow chiefs also got the Soviets talking by phone. In March 1956, for example, the deputy chairman of the KGB and chief of the KGB's Third Military Counterintelligence Directorate, Lt. Gen. Pyotr Ivanovich Ivashutin, participated personally in the work of the commission and was particularly interested in the Third Department's operations. This bit of information, discussed via landlines and picked up by tunnel recorders, was used by BOB to check the knowledge of a defector from the Potsdam directorate in 1956. Looking back on these conversations, it seems unlikely that either Ivashutin or Tsinev was ever aware of the tunnel's existence.[14]

The one Soviet intelligence unit that probably felt it had the least to fear from the tunnel taps was the Karlshorst apparat of KGB's First Chief Directorate. At least this must have been the judgment in Moscow when it was decided to allow the tunnel operation to proceed. Overlooked in this calculation was the fact that Pitovranov's unit was still compelled to communicate with countless other Soviet and East German units by landlines covered by the tunnel. Although Pitovranov's men practiced good telephone security, they could not control the practices of the others. This was true, for example, of the KGB officers at Wismut. Some of these officers were responsible for controlling courier operations, whereas others were to provide security for the scientific and technical personnel at the project. The Wismut unit reported directly to Pitovranov or his deputy.[15] Another group that contributed to the tunnel's knowledge of Pitovranov and his apparat was the department that controlled advisers to MfS. Even Pitovranov's penchant for hunting wild boar at night with infrared telescopic sights was discovered through tapped landline conversations: Maj. Gen. Pavel Dibrova, Soviet Berlin commandant (the one who missed the tunnel's "discovery"), complained over the phone that Pitovranov might accidentally kill some of the local population.[16]

This description of the tunnel's contribution to Western awareness of Soviet intelligence and security in East Berlin and East Germany would be incomplete without some reference to a KGB intercept operation being run against the Americans. Col. Vadim Goncharov (alias Gorelov), the KGB Second Special Department officer who had been sent to arrange military cover for the "discovery" of the tunnel, told us the story of how KGB tapped an American cable near Potsdam. At some point, the Americans stopped using the cable, and KGB was not sure why. The reason was simple: the intercept operation was directed, supported, and staffed by a KGB intercept unit in Karlshorst whose conversations were being intercepted by the tunnel. Although the unit's phone security was very tight, the conversations, coupled with other BOB intelligence on Karlshorst, made it possible to identify the group, its physical location, and the vehicles it used in its operations.[17]

Appendix 6. BOB's Attempts to Protect
Karlshorst Sources Backfire

On 5 May 1958 Bill Harvey hosted Maj. Gen. Ralph Osborne, the us Army's military intelligence chief in Europe responsible for all us Army intelligence and counterintelligence activities in West Berlin.[1] Normally, when Harvey entertained high-level visitors, he took them into his BOB office, sat them in chairs in front of his desk, and gave them a rousing version of his signature speech, "We're here to protect the United States against its enemies." That done, the group would proceed in convoy to Bill's house for lunch, where the martinis were dry and plentiful. By the end of lunch the visitors were usually convinced that "these CIA guys weren't so bad after all." The scenery changed when Bill moved from his fortresslike white stucco villa on Lepsius Strasse to a larger, more dignified mansion on Milinowski Strasse, but the program seldom varied.[2]

Osborne's visit was different: his session with Harvey was a serious affair. It began in the BOB offices at 9:00 A.M. sharp on 5 May 1968 and lasted until well after noon. The topic of the meeting was the Soviet compound in Karlshorst and the need to resolve conflicts of interest between BOB and army counterintelligence over operations in that area. By spring 1958, tighter security measures in the Karlshorst compound, spearheaded by MfS, had made operations there much more difficult, but reporting from Karlshorst sources was still essential for keeping BOB case officers informed about conditions there. As the number of German employees who worked in the compound or otherwise had regular access to it had diminished, it had become harder to recruit new agent candidates to replace those who had been lost. They either were fired, fled to West Berlin in panic (one step ahead of Stasi), or became fed up with conditions in East Berlin and left as refugees. If coverage of the Soviet compound was to continue, BOB had to gain the cooperation of the army's Counterintelligence Corps (CIC) and its Berlin military intelligence component. To accomplish this, BOB had to get these military agencies up to speed about the importance of Karlshorst. This was the reason for the meeting at BOB.[3]

Harvey chaired the meeting, and David Murphy gave the Karlshorst briefing. Because the briefing was in BOB's offices, it was possible to show General Osborne examples of the card files, dossiers, and charts of the Soviet intelligence elements in Karlshorst and to review many operational cases from which both CIA and the military would have profited had there been effective coordination. Harvey urged that BOB be given primary responsibility for covering Karlshorst. According to this plan, all refugees who had information on this target would be automatically sent to BOB, and all CIC or military intelligence operations in the area would be coordinated in Berlin with BOB. In return, BOB would respond to requests from the army for information on Karlshorst and the Soviet units located there.[4]

BOB officers who attended the 5 May session guessed that although BOB's proposal may have made sense to Osborne, he was unlikely to accept it given his subordinates' likely opposition.[5] These forebodings proved true: the BOB proposals were rejected. Only after six months had passed and the Soviet and East German media had begun to characterize West Berlin as an "intelligence swamp" did all American intelligence units review their activities and eventually submit to CIA coordination and oversight.[6]

As part of its efforts to establish primacy among agencies conducting operations in Karlshorst, BOB also sought cooperation on this score from the Gehlen Organization. This organization was named after former Wehrmacht general Reinhard Gehlen. Gehlen had headed German military intelligence on the Russian front during World War II, and afterward had offered his archives and experience to US army intelligence. His organization was later taken over by CIA, which supported it until it became the Federal Intelligence Service (BND). The Gehlen Organization had long conducted operations in East Germany and had been a major KGB counterespionage target, so BOB was aware of the security risks it faced in trying to work with BND on Karlshorst. But BOB officers never realized that because of one man, Heinz Felfe, KGB would share many of the secrets of this fateful partnership. Felfe, one of KGB's most productive agents in BND, was certainly well placed. A Dresden native and ex-member of the Nazi Security Service (SD), Felfe had been held by the British after the war and had worked briefly as a British spy. In 1951 he was introduced to KGB by fellow-Dresdener and former SD officer Hans Clemens, who was also a member of the Gehlen Organization. Soon thereafter Felfe joined Gehlen's group and began his career as a KGB agent in the future West German intelligence service.

From 1951 to 1961 Felfe rose to a position in BND headquarters in which he virtually dominated BND's Soviet counterintelligence operations. He also became aware of intelligence activities by many of BND's liaison partners, including BOB. Felfe caused considerable damage to BND and to West German and Allied security until his arrest in November 1961. But how BND coped with this problem and the broader implications of Felfe's betrayal is not within our scope.[7] Our concern is Felfe's effect on BOB's Karlshorst program.

The Double Life of Vladimir Shchukin, KGB Case Officer

In June 1956, BOB Deputy Chief Murphy visited Gehlen's headquarters in Pullach, near Munich, and briefed Felfe and other BND officials on the Karlshorst target. At that time, BND had an agent in East Berlin, code-named Lena, who was a member of the German National Democratic Party and a director of the party's publishing house, Verlag der Nationen.[8] Lena's political intelligence was of great interest to Gehlen. During the operation, Lena reported to BND that KGB had recruited him as a source of political information on West Germany. Rather than drop the case, BND continued to run Lena as a double agent. Lena began to provide BND with voluminous material on KGB Karlshorst, including telephone numbers, car license plates, descriptions of safe houses, and KGB personnel. During the June briefing, Felfe asked Murphy to have this information checked in BOB files. Murphy agreed, and an avalanche of requests for file checks followed. Replies derived from sensitive cases or tunnel material were carefully eliminated as a matter of routine, but not because BOB then entertained any suspicion of Felfe.

At the time, the most perplexing aspect of the Lena case was that Lena's KGB case officer had apparently given Lena his full name, Vladimir Konstantinovich Shchukin. This was extremely unusual. Case officers from KGB apparat in Karlshorst, regardless of their rank or specialty, normally used aliases (as did Felfe's KGB case officers). In October 1956, while investigating at BND's request the license number of the car Shchukin used to meet with Lena, BOB found that this car had been parked in front of the home of KGB German expert Vadim Vitoldovich Kuchin, who had figured prominently in the Otto John case. BOB also noted that Shchukin and Kuchin had visited an industrial fair in West Germany together in May 1955, using their diplomatic passports.[9] While researching the John case, we noted that Kuchin's assistant in Moscow during John's stay there had been Vadim Konstantinovich Umnov, known as Vadim the Younger. John had returned from Moscow to East Berlin in December 1954, and Shchukin had arrived in Karlshorst in February 1955. Were Umnov and Shchukin one and the same person?

Umnov had been scheduled for a Karlshorst assignment in fall 1953, but his appointment was canceled when traces of tuberculosis were discovered in his lungs. It makes sense, then, that Umnov was assigned as Kuchin's Moscow assistant in the John case; he was otherwise on medical hold. When the time came for KGB to assign a case officer to Lena, they evidently decided to create the Shchukin identity for Umnov, who used it for the duration of the Lena case. Indeed, Umnov and Shchukin were the same person. This became apparent when Shchukin was assigned in the late 1960s to the Soviet embassy in Vienna, where he was chief of Line N, which handled illegals support. (After leaving Karlshorst in 1960, Umnov served in Directorate S, the KGB illegals component.) Umnov's KGB colleagues wrongly assumed that the alias was necessary because he had been compromised in his true name in an earlier foreign assignment. In reality, the Shchukin identity was necessary for the Vienna assignment because Umnov had used it not only in meetings with Lena but also for trips from East Berlin to other European countries.[10]

Coordination Eludes BND and BOB: Felfe's Role

Meanwhile, Felfe pressed his BND colleagues to complete their study on Karlshorst and to persuade BND field units to recruit "low-level observation sources [street cleaners, for example] with access to the compound." While discussing these topics in late December 1956, a BND officer concerned with Karlshorst was advised by a CIA liaison officer to proceed slowly with source recruitment so as not to interfere with BOB's extensive coverage. The officer replied that he would coordinate any such directives to BND field units with CIA before sending them to the field. But a month later the same officer was still gung-ho on recruiting new agents in the compound: he repeated his intention to advise BND field operations units of the need for sources on Karlshorst. The CIA liaison officer reiterated his earlier concerns, but in reporting these events in a letter to BOB commented that it was probably BOB's briefing of BND officials on Karlshorst the previous summer that had caused BND to get the "operational bug" on this target.[11] This reaction, as we saw from our briefings of the American military on Karlshorst, was not unexpected. Although BOB knew that Felfe had become the driving force behind the BND drive to recruit sources in Karlshorst, no sinister motives were perceived.

During this same conversation, the CIA liaison officer broached the topic of the BND "Karlshorst Study," which had been in preparation for some time. The study was to contain a list of all information available to BND on telephone numbers, license plates, safe houses, and Soviet agents. The liaison officer suggested that it be checked by BOB before being officially published. There was no immediate response, but eventually BOB did get the study. A massive effort, the document actually revealed the limited nature of operationally valid information available to BND. Written in a ponderous, almost stiflingly "correct" style, it was found, among other things, to include all of the phone numbers in the Karlshorst district (not just those within the Soviet compound), most of which were easily found in the East Berlin telephone directory.[12]

In September 1957, BOB observed that BND field units were still pursuing leads from refugees to potential Karlshorst sources without coordinating such actions with BOB. Continued pressure by BOB finally made senior BND officials agree to approach General Gehlen about giving BOB primacy in Karlshorst operations, although the officials doubted that Gehlen would agree. The cable traffic about this issue became antagonistic. One BND officer asked whether other Allied intelligence and counterintelligence services had "agreed to stay out." And Murphy remembers suggesting that if Gehlen did not agree, BOB would no longer respond to BND requests for traces regarding Karlshorst.[13]

On 10 October BOB was told that Gehlen did not agree to its proposals but had promised that no operations would be undertaken without prior coordination with CIA. Gehlen added that if BOB seemed to have better access to an agent candidate spotted by BND, BND would turn over the lead to BOB—if BOB promised to share any information the source provided. As expected, CIA's Eastern Europe division at headquarters rejected BOB's rash idea to retaliate by not providing traces, pointing out that, in view of Gehlen's responsibilities to the Federal German Government, he had made as many concessions to the BOB position as he could.[14] BOB acquiesced, recognizing that BND, as the intelligence service of a sovereign government and ally of the United States, would never officially relinquish to a foreign service its right to conduct operations in Germany affecting the security of the Federal Republic. Furthermore, as BND well knew, BOB had not persuaded its American military counterparts to agree to similar proposals.

Felfe began to push to expand BND operations into Karlshorst as a way of developing closer relations with BOB. Murphy made several visits to Pullach over the next few years, and Felfe frequently visited Berlin. This increased level of activity provided Felfe with additional justification for his Berlin visits. Meetings with Felfe were even held in BOB safe houses. To the young Karlshorst analyst picked to give him sanitized briefings, Felfe was a pompous yet surprisingly colorless man despite his correct suit and meticulous haircut. She found his attitude condescending, almost dismissive. On such trips, Felfe was normally accompanied by a CIA liaison officer. But because liaison officers are not full-time baby-sitters, he also managed to find time to visit Karlshorst for meetings with his KGB case officer. By 1959, BND's interest and operational involvement in the Karlshorst compound was so great that it had assigned an officer in West Berlin to work exclusively on Karlshorst matters. A young, energetic chap with a surprisingly relaxed manner, he was given an office within the US Headquarters Compound on Clayallee, appropriate documentation, and assistance in communicating with BND headquarters. BOB even made available to him "quick change" devices for license plates. This arrangement lasted until just after the sector borders were closed in August 1961.[15]

Felfe's career as a KGB agent ended a few months later. The information leading to his downfall came from Michal Goleniewski, a lieutenant colonel of Polish State Security who began to write secret messages to CIA in 1958 and finally defected to BOB on 4 January 1961. Goleniewski had reported that two of six BND officials who had made an official visit to Washington in 1956 were Soviet agents. As soon as Goleniewski was safely in the West and had confirmed his report, an intensive investigation of Felfe was undertaken that eventually led to his arrest, trial, and incarceration. Sentenced to fourteen years in prison, he served only six. Felfe communicated with KGB from his prison cell through secret letters to his "mother" in East Germany. On 14 February 1969 he was exchanged for twenty-one German citizens. Three of them were West Germans who had been held in the USSR; the remainder were East Germans serving time in East German prisons for being Western spies.[16]

Felfe's Memoirs

Seventeen years later, Felfe's memoirs were published as *Im Dienst des Gegners: 10 Jahre Moskaus Mann im BND* (In the opponent's service: Ten years as Moscow's man in BND). The work represents a carefully prepared series of "revelations" woven around Felfe's career in BND. The author portrays himself as a dedicated Marxist-Leninist, and to prove it he scatters throughout the book such words and phrases as "the secret war against socialism," "imperialist," and "neocolonialism." In fact, the manuscript was a joint KGB-Mfs venture. KGB put Felfe in touch with Mfs, which assigned Herbert Brehmer to run the project. Brehmer and Felfe spent several months in Moscow in a KGB apartment where they were provided sanitized KGB file material to include in the manuscript. When the draft was finished, it was turned over to KGB for their review. According to Felfe, KGB insisted on the party jargon.[17]

In the chapter "My Operations," Felfe discusses his role in fostering closer relations with BOB on Karlshorst operations. Making clear that BND had learned nothing important about the Karlshorst compound until he had assumed control of the program, code-named Diagramm, Felfe describes the "extensive" results of Diagramm and how they were published in a five-volume handbook with Soviet telephone numbers, house plans, street maps, and personality information. Felfe claimed that this handbook contained everything BND and CIA knew about Karlshorst and had been distributed throughout BND and to other West German agencies such as BfV and the Federal Prosecutor's Office. This was the same document that BOB analysts had found to be ponderous and filled with extraneous nonsense.

Still, Felfe was extraordinarily proud of his masterpiece; his description of it in *Im Dienst des Gegners* has been embellished and repeated in several publications since. One of the reviewers' favorite "revelations" was Felfe's claim that he had possessed a large, multicolored plan of the KGB headquarters in Karlshorst showing "which lavatory was used by which senior officer." At one time BOB did furnish Felfe with a black and white street plan of Karlshorst annotated with the most important sites. But it was not in color, and lavatories were not its first priority.[18]

Felfe's published description of his Karlshorst operations project Diagramm is filled with exaggerations. He claims that it "forced CIA to check with BND in Pullach for data desired on KGB in Central Europe." This was not normal practice, nor did BOB release information to the Diagramm group that had been obtained from sensitive sources. But BOB's experience in working with Felfe on Karlshorst does demonstrate how dangerous it was to share operations and operational products with liaison services. Such cooperation was essential in many situations, yet each partner added potential security risks. Felfe was correct when he claimed that his role in Diagramm suited him perfectly: he more than satisfied his BND superiors without having to take serious risks.[19]

Strangely missing from Felfe's 1986 account of his manipulative handling of the Karlshorst relationship with BOB is any mention of the part played by BND double-agent Lena. Had it not been for the Lena case and the interest it sparked in BOB's Karlshorst analysts, such intensive BOB-BND cooperation might never have been undertaken.

We had hoped to obtain an assessment of Felfe from his longtime case officer, Vitaly V. Korotkov, known to Felfe as Alfred II.[20] Another source reported that this Korotkov, no relation to Aleksandr Mikhailovich Korotkov, had been stationed in Vienna with the MGB foreign intelligence residency from 1952 until his transfer to Karlshorst in 1955. After his tour there, he served at Moscow Center in the section of the counterintelligence directorate concerned with operations against West German intelligence and security services.[21] This would have been a normal assignment for Korotkov following Felfe's arrest, and he would have been the officer to handle the secret correspondence with Felfe during his imprisonment. Interest in Korotkov's views was heightened by an interview he gave to the Moscow correspondent of a Berlin newspaper in which he briefly described his relationship with Felfe.[22]

According to Korotkov, Felfe's greatest overall value was his ability to advise KGB in advance of actions planned against it by BND, BfV, or the Americans. He also provided valuable intelligence on issues like the armament of the West German Bundeswehr. This information was so important to the Politburo that it overruled a KGB decision to put the operation on ice in 1961, when it was feared that Anatoly Golitsyn's defection might have endangered Felfe's security. Korotkov referred to 1961 as "Top spy Felfe's fateful year . . . when the noose around his neck was getting tighter" and commented that the Politburo's decision to keep him in place meant "politics won and Felfe was sacrificed."[23]

Our Interview with Felfe

When we interviewed Felfe for this book, he seemed flattered by the attention. He commented that although in the past he had made frequent trips to the Soviet Union as an "honored guest," his "Russian friends had all disappeared from Karlshorst within two years after reunification even though they were given four years to wrap up their affairs." Apparently, tight surveillance drove them away in 1992. Felfe's feelings toward KGB and the Soviet Union have changed since his book was released. As Korotkov said in a *Berliner Zeitung* article, one never doubted the authenticity of Felfe's information because he had "decided to work with Soviet intelligence out of deep conviction." When the whole system came crashing down, Felfe's view of the world had to change.[24] He now takes a very sober view of his erstwhile comrades. Despite the appearance given in his book of a rabid "anti-imperialist" and true Communist, Felfe is a profoundly bourgeois character, tradition-bound and conservative. He had convinced himself that by serving the Soviet Union he was advancing the cause of Marxist-Leninist doctrine, but he has come to realize that he had incorrectly estimated the country he served. This impression of Felfe's attitude is consistent with the view of those who knew him during the 1950s. He was then essentially a self-centered person, one who liked to live well and who thoroughly enjoyed being the center of attention. During his association with the Soviets for nearly forty years, he lived within the framework of their ideology.

During our interviews, Felfe spoke freely about his past double life. He said he had never been warned by his case officers that revelations by KGB defectors may have threatened his security—in particular the statements from Peter Deriabin, an earlier defector, that "there were two Soviet agents in the Gehlen Organization code named Peter and Paul."[25] Felfe's case officer, Korotkov, never mentioned Goleniewski, although Felfe said that he had since learned that Korotkov knew that a compromise was possible as a result of this case. But Felfe believed that Korotkov was ordered by his superiors to say nothing about it because they wanted to continue to exploit Felfe. Asked about the thesis advanced by others that KGB had deliberately sacrificed him to cause problems for BND, Felfe's response was explosive: "Quatsch!" (rubbish).[26]

Felfe had no idea why Korotkov in his *Berliner Zeitung* article had implied that Golitsyn had compromised him. But Felfe did volunteer this curious statement about the Golitsyn defection: "Golitsyn provided information before he came over. Only after this information was confirmed was he accepted. Thus, the Americans learned what he had to say before he actually defected. It was an exchange deal." Insofar as one can judge, this statement must have originated in comments by Felfe's case officers after his release from prison to account for his compromise. Only by claiming that Golitsyn passed information to the Americans before his defection in December 1961 would KGB have been able to blame Golitsyn for Felfe's arrest in November.[27]

In other defection or espionage cases that Felfe brought to KGB's attention, including those involving the East German security and intelligence services, KGB officers routinely reassured him: "No one can know about you. Don't be worried." Felfe gave as an example KGB's reaction to a public speech by Erich Mielke attacking West German espionage in the GDR. In the speech Mielke allegedly cited Felfe among others. Gen. Aleksandr Mikhailovich Korotkov immediately went to Mielke and said "Hands off! This is our man." Mielke reportedly replied, "*In Ordnung!* No one [in MFS] but me knows about him and no one will ever know!"[28]

According to Felfe, the true name of Alfred I, the KGB case officer who handled him until Alfred II (Vitaly Korotkov) took charge, was Ivan Ivanovich Sumin. Until he assumed control of the case, Alfred II attended the Felfe meetings with Alfred I. Thereafter, Alfred II was alone with Felfe, except when he brought Gen. A. M. Korotkov. In discussions with General Korotkov, Felfe said, "The main theme was always politics, only politics. He was only interested in the German Federal Republic, its direction and intentions. He made no mention of CIA."[29]

Felfe insisted that when Alfred II asked him, "How can we support you so that you can look good in your job?" he refused the offer. He was determined to keep the relationship with the Soviets as simple as possible, and he was concerned lest KGB assistance complicate matters. In essence, Alfred II acceded to Felfe's wishes. Furthermore, Felfe never held discussions with Alfred II concerning CIA operations or personnel. For example, Alfred II was not informed in advance of Felfe's trip to Washington in 1956, but Felfe did send him a postcard through an accommodation address while he was there. Felfe's report on his trip was received without commentary by Alfred II. He asked no follow-up questions but was peeved that it had been the Americans, not the Soviets, who had been the first to invite Felfe to their capital.[30]

When Felfe described to Alfred II the addresses, telephone numbers, license plate numbers, and other details on Karlshorst that CIA had given to him, Alfred II interrupted him: "We are interested if someone has access to our safes. Other things are of no interest; we know what we have in Karlshorst and how it works, and we know it better than the Americans." On another occasion, Alfred II reminded him that low-level Karlshorst operations, whether run by CIA or BND, were of no interest to him. "That's your business," he added. Felfe never understood Alfred II's lack of interest in information pertaining to Karlshorst. Once, for example, Felfe told him he could pass him five thick notebooks with BND material on Karlshorst (obviously the BND Diagramm report). Alfred II's only reply was "Do whatever you want with it." On the other hand, Alfred II made sure that no action was taken by MfS against CIA or BND agents involved in Karlshorst operations if such action could endanger Felfe. Finally, Felfe claimed KGB never expressed specific interest in CIA officers, whether encountered in Berlin or at the CIA liaison office. When a name arose, Felfe was asked for standard personality data and indications of possible vulnerability—nothing more. Although Alfred II appeared disinterested, Felfe continued to report faithfully on all of his activities involving CIA and Karlshorst.[31]

To illustrate the KGB modus operandi in dealing with him on Berlin cases, Felfe cited the Lena operation. When it was reported to BND that Lena had been recruited by KGB, the case was automatically assigned to Felfe because within BND it was treated as a Soviet double-agent case. Felfe insists he never met Lena and that the KGB case officer never spoke to him about the case in advance. When he reported it, his case officer told him to "play it as he wished, it doesn't concern us." Lena was allowed to report whatever he could about Karlshorst. There was never any coordination concerning the case. Nor were there any follow-up questions by Felfe's case officer concerning BOB file checks on information reported by Lena. When asked, Felfe professed to have no idea why the KGB case officer in the Lena case used his "true name." He never met Shchukin because KGB would not have permitted it. It would have involved crossing lines of one operation with another.[32]

For most of the period during which Felfe worked with KGB, neither he nor they seemed concerned about his security. The safe house in Karlshorst where he met Alfred II was changed only once, and KGB left it to Felfe himself to determine when he could travel safely to West or East Berlin. Felfe preferred it this way. He recalls, for example, a time when he arrived in Berlin for a meeting but his case officer, who was either ill or on leave, failed to appear. This did not bother Felfe, who returned to Pullach and patiently awaited the next meeting.[33]

Our account of the Felfe case will certainly disappoint those who have believed that CIA, and specifically BOB's Karlshorst operations, were Felfe's principal target. It has often been assumed that KGB played a major role in those Karlshorst-related activities that helped advance Felfe's career. It was further believed that these actions were the result of close collaboration between KGB and Felfe and were orchestrated in advance. In addition, it was understood that because KGB had placed great value on information on CIA personnel, operations, and installations, KGB had reacted to his reporting with specific requirements.

But it is Felfe's position that although KGB claimed it was ready to help him improve his position in BND, they never advanced specific ideas. Moreover, Felfe insists that he rejected the general idea when it was offered because he feared complications that he could not control. According to Felfe, KGB never discussed BND cases like Lena that had been doubled by KGB and were his responsibility. Finally, Felfe insisted that his KGB handler never responded to his reporting on BOB Karlshorst activities, personnel, or installations with specific questions or requirements. Can Felfe be believed? Not necessarily. A closer look at his account of his relationship with KGB, based on what we have learned about the workings of KGB in East Berlin, is definitely in order.

An Interpretation of Felfe's Account

Clearly, the Felfe case was run from its inception by the German department of the counterintelligence directorate of KGB foreign intelligence through the counterintelligence component of the Karlshorst apparat. This component's main tasks were to penetrate the West German intelligence and security services and to protect Soviet interests against these services' operations. They saw in Felfe a source who was ideally situated to serve their interests and considered Felfe's exploitation of the Karlshorst scene through his Diagramm project primarily as a means of improving his stature within BND. Felfe's reporting on his BOB relationships and on Karlshorst operations probably made up only a fraction of his coverage of BND and other West German services and his political and military coverage on the West German government. Although KGB had other penetrations of BND, Felfe was considered a unique and valuable source. In cases of this kind, knowledge of the case and above all the source's identity would have been carefully protected by the responsible department. If Felfe had reported items on CIA of compelling interest to the American department of the counterintelligence directorate, there would have been no automatic disseminations of the Felfe report to that department. Instead, the chief of the directorate would pass on the information, taking care to disguise the source.[34]

One can easily understand, therefore, the KGB leadership's reluctance to see Felfe's Diagramm transformed from an engine powering his ascent to senior responsibility in BND to a device calling for his active involvement in covering BOB and its Karlshorst program. As soon as KGB began feeding specific requirements to Felfe, a highly perceptive and ambitious person, it faced the risk of alerting Felfe to its real Karlshorst and BOB interests, and any slip might have sounded an alarm within BOB.

We shall never know the whole story until SVR officials are prepared to reveal it. But it would be misguided to ignore the damage that must have been done by Felfe to BOB's Karlshorst program. Granted, KGB's chief priority in his case was undoubtedly to obtain information on BND. We can be sure, however, that the steady stream of data on BOB personnel and Karlshorst operations that Felfe passed to KGB, no matter how well sanitized, went to the American section of the Karlshorst apparat's counterintelligence department. They must have found it a very useful adjunct to their other operations directed at American intelligence units in West Berlin.

Appendix 7. KGB Illegals in Karlshorst: The Third Department

Illegals—Soviets documented as foreign nationals and sent abroad—were always an important component of Soviet foreign intelligence, and after 1945 East Germany was the most important center for KGB illegals support. The career of Aleksandr Mikhailovich Korotkov, chief of the Karlshorst apparat until his death in 1961, illustrates how important illegals work was to KGB. His experience as an illegal during the 1930s left him well poised to become the first postwar resident of NKGB's foreign intelligence directorate in Berlin in 1945, where support for illegals operations was a major concern. Even though NKGB had official access to records offices and to police files throughout the country, it still recruited its own sources for illegals support. When Korotkov left Berlin in 1947 he returned to Moscow and headed the illegals directorate of the Committee of Information (KI). Later chiefs of the Karlshorst apparat also often highlighted their work in illegals operations in their résumés. Aleksei Alekseevich Krokhin and Anatoly Ivanovich Lazarev were both former chiefs of the KGB's illegals directorate, or Directorate S. Another chief of Directorate S, Yuri Ivanovich Drozdov, got his start in Karlshorst under Korotkov.[1]

After KI was dissolved and its illegals activity had been returned to MGB, Korotkov continued in illegals work. Some of the illegals specialists had been assigned by that time to area departments, but they continued to handle illegals.[2] This shift had occurred as part of the continuing debate in MGB over whether the illegals directorate should be the only foreign intelligence component to recruit, train, document, dispatch, and control illegals. Some illegals operations were actually shifted to area departments in the early 1950s. For example, the Austro-German department, anticipating a time when travel between East and West Germany would become more difficult, began to create illegal residencies in West Germany.

In August 1953, a meeting was called by the new chief of foreign intelligence, Aleksandr Semyonovich Paniushkin, to consider proposals concerning the future of illegals operations. Among these plans was the idea of creating a separate illegals directorate within the First Chief Directorate.[3] These proposals were acted upon and the new directorate, sometimes called the "special directorate" or Directorate S, was born. Over the years it remained an important and highly sensitive element of KGB operations. Its activities in East Germany, controlled from Karlshorst, continued to play a vital role in the training and documentation of KGB illegals.

The Runge Case

The KGB illegal Yevgeny Yevgenievich Runge, code-named Max, defected to CIA's Berlin Base in October 1967 in a highly publicized case—defections were rare after the Wall was erected. Runge named a number of West German citizens as KGB agents. But missing from the public record was the extent to which he was able to describe the workings of the Third Department in Karlshorst, as well as the interrelationship between the illegals directorate and other components of KGB in Moscow and Karlshorst.[4] A close examination of Runge's career also reveals a fascinating cross-section of the work and personalities of KGB's German illegals activities and the extent of BOB's knowledge of those Karlshorst illegals officers with whom Runge had worked in the 1950s and 1960s. Also, for the first time we have Kondrashev's description of the Runge case as he saw it from his position as chief of the German Department in KGB Moscow.

Runge, an ethnic German, was born in 1928 in the eastern Ukraine. He escaped forced evacuation to Central Asia when World War II began, acquired German citizenship during the German occupation, and was brought to German-controlled areas by retreating German forces.[5] After various adventures, including a brief stay in an American prisoner-of-war camp, he found himself in the Soviet zone at war's end and began attending school in East Berlin. There Runge was encouraged by officers in the Soviet Repatriation Office to continue his education in the new GDR. He did not realize it then, but the officers were seeking candidates for illegals work, and Runge seemed a natural. He was informally approached by Terenty Fyodorovich Novak, a highly decorated state security officer who had served with Soviet partisans operating behind German lines during the war. Novak was under cover in the Soviet consulate at the time. In his biography, Runge described his first visit to the Karlshorst compound in 1953, where he was introduced to the illegals directorate chief, Korotkov, and to Boris Yakovlevich Baryshnikov, head of the illegals department in Karlshorst.[6] Runge was told that his qualifications were needed in the illegals program, where he could become a "real" intelligence officer.[7] Runge was then formally recruited and met his first illegals case officer, Nikolai Nikolaevich Balashov, who supervised his training in illegals tradecraft and communications. While in training, he continued his college education and in 1954 graduated from the Political Economy Institute of Humboldt University in East Berlin. In 1955 Runge was sworn into KGB as a junior lieutenant.[8]

Balashov's supervisor in the illegals department in Karlshorst was Yevgeny Fyodorovich Mikhailov, an illegals officer specializing in German operations who later became the Moscow Center officer responsible for Runge's activities in West Germany. Fluent in German, Mikhailov toured German prisoner-of-war camps in April–June 1953 to interview candidates for agent work in West Germany. Mikhailov was reportedly close to illegals chief Korotkov, who was responsible for sending him to Karlshorst in September 1953.[9]

Documentary support for Runge's transformation into a West German citizen was obtained by Karlshorst from the Polish service and from an illegals department agent in the West Berlin police force. In 1956, at KGB's direction, Runge married Valentina Rusch, a Soviet agent operating in West Germany. Her case officer was Yevgeny Ivanovich Mosvenin, a senior illegals support officer. Rusch recalls that the wedding took place the day before her birthday. A small reception was attended by her new husband, her case officer, Runge's case officer, and their boss, Yevgeny Fyodorovich Mikhailov.[10]

The couple settled in Cologne and opened a small business as cover. Here Runge handled two agents. One, a waiter at diplomatic receptions, occasionally installed listening devices in rooms used by high officials. Runge was taken to meet this source when the source came to visit relatives living in the GDR. The Karlshorst illegals support officer who introduced them was Dmitry Ivanovich Svetlakov, then serving under cover of the second secretary of the Soviet embassy in East Berlin.[11] The second agent, whom KGB code-named Arnold, was a steward at the French Military Liaison Mission in Bad Godesberg who provided sensitive documentary materials pertaining to NATO and Franco-German military cooperation.

In 1956, while Runge was handling these sources, the Hungarian revolt occurred, and the Soviets prepared for possible Western military intervention. Because Arnold might be able to obtain insights into options being considered by NATO, Runge was asked to report immediately any information of this kind. He and his wife were also instructed to report on any American troop movements along the Bavarian-Czech borders. KGB could reach Runge in an emergency via one-way radio link, but his only communications to KGB consisted of messages by mail that he sent to addresses in East Berlin and Vienna.[12] These messages took from two to three days to be received, so he was also given a telephone number in Vienna by his Moscow case officer, Yevgeny Mikhailov, to be used only in the event of a military crisis—instructions repeated during the Cuban missile crisis of 1962.[13]

With the exception of this "war emergency" phone number, Runge's communications system remained the same during his entire tenure in West Germany. KGB broadcast to him weekly via shortwave radio signals disguised as amateur radio transmissions. The times and frequencies were entered in a signal plan, and the text of the broadcasts was enciphered in Morse code numerals that Runge deciphered with a miniature pad that he used only once. He then used a simple conversion alphabet to convert the numerical text into Russian. Replies to KGB, which were letters sent to his accommodation addresses, contained secret messages. The writing was straightforward except for descriptions of such sensitive matters as names, addresses, meeting places, and times, which were enciphered by another one-time pad. Interestingly, Runge was never given any concealment devices in which to hide his signal plans, one-time pads, or secret writing carbons; he had to devise his own.[14]

In January 1960 Runge was recalled to Karlshorst for security reasons: the West Berlin policeman who had helped register Runge's West German documents with the West Berlin police had been arrested. After closing down their modest business in Cologne, his wife followed Runge to Moscow. In fall 1960, after KGB had concluded that his cover had apparently not been compromised, Runge was directed to move from Cologne to Frankfurt am Main. By spring 1961, he was ordered to break off contact with agent Arnold.[15]

Before returning to West Germany and establishing himself in the Frankfurt area, Runge was given a new assignment: handling Heinz Suetterlin. Code-named Walter by KGB, Suetterlin had been recruited by MfS but turned over to KGB, a transfer of which he been unaware until he was introduced to his KGB case officer, Leonid Prokhorov, who was using the cover of a third secretary with the Soviet embassy in East Berlin.[16] Prokhorov gave Walter the names of several prospective candidates, and Walter zeroed in on Leonore Heinz, code-named Lola by KGB, a Foreign Office secretary. He managed to meet, court, and then marry her, after which he persuaded her to deliver documents to him. According to Runge, this assignment made sense because Walter held a "strange fascination for women."[17]

Lola's operation had produced correspondence from West German missions abroad, primarily in developing countries; instructions from the FRG Foreign Office; and BND's monthly intelligence summaries. But despite the large volume of reports that she provided, and the genuineness of the documents themselves, the material contained little on the FRG's relations with its major allies in NATO or with socialist countries, or on FRG plans for actions against the USSR. According to Runge, KGB was unwilling to believe she could remove this much material and suspected deception.[18] In any event, she clearly needed guidance on what to collect. Walter had been unable to provide such guidance, so Moscow was eager to bring Runge into direct contact with Lola. But the cover Walter had used to justify his need for these documents was a rather vague world peace movement. How would Lola react to meeting KGB officer Runge, even if he spoke perfect German? Finally, an introductory meeting was set for 12 December 1966. Runge thought Lola was receptive, but in his report to Moscow sent via a Vienna letter drop, Runge said he thought he detected hostile surveillance of Walter. As a precaution, Runge did not appear for a planned 23 December meeting with him.[19]

Runge's message caused KGB to thoroughly review his activities and the Lola case. Runge was ordered to Budapest, where his longtime handler Yevgeny Mikhailov had been assigned. Runge refused because a bona fide West

German citizen might have a long wait for a Hungarian visa in 1967; for an illegal, a sudden visit to Budapest might arouse unwelcome suspicion. Moscow then ordered him to return to Moscow via Karlshorst. His wife, Valentina, also returned immediately after receiving a telegram from East Berlin announcing that her husband was ill. Valentina flew to West Berlin and was met by KGB case officer Balashov, who escorted her to Moscow.

On 3 February, Runge and Valentina met in Moscow with a person who introduced himself as Sergei Aleksandrovich Kondrashev, who Runge thought was chief of the Austro-German department. Kondrashev was accompanied by the illegals directorate officer responsible for the Runge operation. When Kondrashev told Runge that KGB suspected Walter was a double agent for West German counterintelligence, Runge protested that he considered the case still clean and salvageable. To support his claim, he pointed out that nothing had happened to Walter since the 12 December meeting. The more Runge protested, the more KGB suspected his loyalty. In any case, Runge and Valentina's West German operation was finished.[20]

Because Runge was thought to have been compromised by his association with Walter and could not return immediately to West Germany, Valentina was entrusted with the job of dismantling their cover business there. Runge handled the administrative aspects of the liquidation from Karlshorst and while there assisted the Third (illegals) Department of the apparat, which at that time was headed by Boris Yakovlevich Nalivaiko.[21] On 15 May 1967, at the suggestion of First Chief Directorate Chief Sakharovsky, Kondrashev met Runge in East Berlin to discuss a possible future assignment (earlier security concerns having ostensibly been resolved). A major issue was Runge's refusal to leave his son in a boarding school in the USSR; he wished instead to take him on assignment in West Germany. His insistence aroused suspicion, but some KGB officers nevertheless thought his request should be granted.[22]

Runge, Valentina, and their son defected in October 1967. According to the KGB file, a reliable source reported that "Runge's reasons for defection were KGB's decision to cut him out of the 'W' case without telling him, his unwillingness to leave on a new foreign assignment without his son, and his disillusionment with Communism." KGB considered Runge "lacking in discipline and guilty of violation of security rules; he also made exorbitant financial demands."[23]

Meanwhile, unbeknownst to Runge, the Walter-Lola operation had indeed continued. Walter's former case officer Leonid Prokhorov had met him in Vienna in August 1967. But Walter and Lola were jailed in West Germany when the Soviet operation was discovered. Released in 1972, Walter made his way via Yugoslavia to Dresden in East Germany. His hopes for quiet retirement in the GDR ended with reunification. He still received his pension nevertheless, this time from his old adversaries in Bonn.[24] Lola, the source in the Foreign

Office, committed suicide in her cell on 15 October 1967.[25] At KGB Center, letters of reprimand were placed in the personnel files of those KGB officers responsible for supervising the Runge case.

Although Runge was an illegal (which meant that officially he was never to be briefed on matters outside his own operations), by 1967 he had become a trusted officer with impressive successes to his credit. He also had become familiar with the illegals component at Karlshorst where his illegals career had begun. While in Karlshorst in 1967 he learned that Berlin had remained one of the major centers abroad for supporting KGB illegals activities despite tightened controls following the erection of the Wall in 1961. According to General Lazarev, the Directorate S chief who met with Runge during summer 1967, the GDR remained the only country in the Socialist bloc where the names of living persons were still used by illegals operating abroad. The persons whose names were used in this way were kept under observation to ensure the security of the illegal using their background, even though in most cases they had no idea their documentation was being exploited by KGB.[26]

KGB's Third Department

The Third Department also had its representatives, or Line N officers, in each KGB district group throughout the GDR.[27] These officers searched for persons whose background might be used to support illegals' legends. Checks were made through KGB agents in GDR repatriation offices and camps to acquire the names of persons entering the GDR from West Germany or foreign countries, or even better, of someone applying for permission to move to the GDR. After vetting the person and determining that he seriously intended to move to the East, the candidate was recruited under various pretexts and sworn to secrecy but never told that his name and background would be adopted by a KGB illegal living somewhere abroad. The work was extremely time consuming and labor intensive, which explains why the Third Department in Karlshorst was always the largest component in the KGB apparat.[28]

Another part of the Third Department's work involved document preparation and forgery; a staff of document specialists was maintained in Karlshorst for this purpose. The department also handled support agents in the GDR—Runge called them *praktikanty,* or probationers—who helped provide illegals' cover stories or documentation and who trained candidates for illegals work. The GDR was extremely valuable to Directorate S as a secure place where illegals could live under East German cover and familiarize themselves with conditions outside the USSR.

The testing and training of illegals candidates in the GDR, in which Runge participated, was taken very seriously, and recruits were thoroughly tested before they left on assignment. In one training scenario, Runge was given the cover of an anti-Soviet, pro-capitalist West German businessman who was visiting East Germany and was given the names of alleged contacts of potential interest to KGB in both West Germany and the United States. Illegals trainees were furnished a tip about the presence of a "West German" in the GDR, and it was up to them to make contact and develop the operation. The whole procedure was made as realistic as possible: in his role as the West German, Runge challenged the trainee's views on current events, tempted him with women and/or alcohol, and made it difficult for him to obtain information on his intelligence potential. In this way, Runge tested the trainee's political reliability, his moral character, and his operational competence and ingenuity. When the exercise was over, Runge would grade the candidate. These evaluations were discussed with the head of the illegals department, Nalivaiko, and with representatives of other Karlshorst departments. According to Runge, of the thirty to forty trainees with whom he worked, some were German agents who had been selected for illegal assignments, whereas others were Soviet illegals who had completed their training in Moscow and were undergoing on-the-job training in the GDR. It was sometimes difficult to distinguish between the two groups because the Soviets' "knowledge of the German language was excellent."[29]

While Runge was in Karlshorst in spring and summer 1967, Boris Nalivaiko, the chief of the apparat's Third Department, was preparing to return to Moscow for an assignment in Moscow Center. His place was taken by his deputy, Marius Aramovich Yuzbashian, who remained until 1970, when Nalivaiko returned to Karlshorst for his last foreign assignment. Nalivaiko wrote in his memoirs that when he went back "the agent-operational climate had not undergone any basic changes." When he left Karlshorst for the last time in 1974, Nalivaiko reaffirmed the importance of East Germany to KGB illegals operations, noting that as of that year Moscow had pronounced the Third Department's work "most satisfactory."[30]

Appendix 8. Soviet Active Measures: A Brief Overview

Anatoly Mikhailovich Golitsyn's position that Soviet active measures really began with Aleksandr Nikolaevich Shelepin and Department D in 1959 is not surprising. Golitsyn's initial debriefing on the subject in 1962 was considered "the only reasonably complete discussion of the subject [*dezinformatsiia*] ever received from a Soviet source."[1] Western counterintelligence specialists were of course aware of Soviet use of deception and disinformation from the early years of the Soviet state, but they did not have a coherent organizational history of the program. According to SVR archives, a "special bureau for disinformation" was created in the state political directorate (Gosudarstvennoe politicheskoe upravlenie—GPU) on 11 January 1923. It was directed by the Central Committee of the Russian Communist Party "to break up the counterrevolutionary plans and schemes of the enemy." The tasks of this group resembled those given future disinformation units but at this time were largely directed at internal as well as foreign opponents of the new regime.[2]

For that time it was not an unsophisticated approach to active measures. The new disinformation unit was first ordered to establish records of reports received by GPU, the intelligence directorate of the Red Army, and other offices concerning information available to foreign intelligence services on Russia, as well as records of the kinds of information sought by the enemy. Analysis of these factors would then permit the creation of disinformation to be passed to the enemy, giving an inaccurate picture of the internal situation in Russia, in its armed forces, and so on. Actually, KI, from its inception in 1947, had been deeply involved in active measures operations that continued the Chekist tradition of exploiting intelligence to further Soviet aims. In his September 1947 note to Stalin on KI, Molotov includes in the primary tasks of the new organization measures to "unmask the anti-Soviet activity of foreign circles, influence the public opinion of other countries, and compromise anti-Soviet officials and public figures of foreign governments." These tasks remained in force when KI was transferred to the Ministry of Foreign Affairs and KI residencies were enjoined to "create agent networks in influential press and propaganda organs."[3] It was the KI disinformation component, therefore, that was responsible for carrying out active measures between 1947 and 1951, the early years of the struggle between East and West over the future of Germany. Nevertheless, when the foreign intelligence element of state security returned to MGB from KI, the disinformation unit did not return with it.[4]

When this shift occurred, the remnants of KI, now called Small KI (*malyi komitet*) were retained under the Ministry of Foreign Affairs. But attached to Small KI was a disinformation component, known as Service 2 or Service D, housed within Small KI's offices on Moscow's Gogolevsky Boulevard. It operated as an extension of the First Chief Directorate of the KGB for active measures operations, but its activities were concealed from most of Small KI's staff.[5] An important task of the service was to use foreign intelligence reports as a basis for disinformation that would then be passed to the foreign press through trusted channels as a way of "exposing and compromising" policies hostile to the USSR.[6] At the same time, Service D also participated in elaborate clandestine propaganda operations launched by KGB's First Chief Directorate. An example was the scheme to exploit the hoped-for defection of West German intelligence officer Friedrich Heinz. This operation was masterminded by Yevgeny Pitovranov, KGB chief in Karlshorst, to counter Western efforts to create a European Defense Community. Later, this disinformation unit was subordinated to a more formal, yet still secret, Foreign Ministry department that coordinated foreign policy objectives with active measures operations. Carrying out active measures from this semiofficial unit must have been complicated by the need to coordinate its activities with intelligence received from such First Chief Directorate components as the geographic departments, the information department, and counterintelligence.

Nevertheless, it was this cumbersome bureaucracy, working closely with the German department, that prepared and launched the effective attacks on West Berlin as an "espionage swamp." The campaign was timed to reach a climax just prior to the four-power meetings on Berlin—which Khrushchev confidently expected would take place before the expiration of his November 1958 ultimatum. These attacks were the first phase of a much broader active measures program in support of Soviet goals on Berlin. The latter phases were undertaken by Department D after its creation by Shelepin in January 1959. Headed by longtime European specialist Ivan Ivanovich Agayants, the new department brought together officers from various parts of the First Chief Directorate to create and coordinate disinformation programs. The West Berlin espionage swamp campaign constituted a major activity. But it is not identified in Golitsyn's *New Lies for Old* as one of the disinformation operations of the New Methodology—or master plan for disinformation about future events in the Communist world. Instead, during the period of the Berlin crisis, 1958–60, Khrushchev, the Central Committee, the Soviet government, and KGB's Department D are pictured by Golitsyn as having devoted their energies primarily to Soviet-Yugoslav relations.[7]

Appendix 9. Operation Gold

Note: The original January–February 1954 document, received by Kondrashev from George Blake, was yellow-green carbon and could not be removed from the file. The following is based on a transcription by Kondrashev.

Operation "Gold"

SIS/CIA MEETINGS ON STOPWATCH/GOLD HELD IN LONDON ON 15TH, 16TH, 17TH & 18TH DEC. 1953.

1. Meetings were held in London on 15th, 16th, 17th and 18th December 1953 to discuss processing and technical requirements for the STOPWATCH/GOLD operation. The following were present:

Mr. McKenzie	
Mr. Young	
Mr. Milne	
Col. Gimson	SIS
Mr. Blake	
Capt. Montagnon	
Col. Balmain	
Mr. Taylor	
Mr. Urwick	

Mr. Rowlett	
Mr. Wheeler	
Mr. Nelson	CIA
Mr. Cook	
Mr. Leichliter	

2. The discussions were carried out in two main groups, one dealing with processing and the other with technical matters. Attached at Tab "A" are the agreed minutes covering the processing talks and at Tab "B" are the agreed minutes covering the technical discussions.

3. The discussions were of an exploratory nature. It was agreed that a further meeting should be held after each side has had a chance to examine the results of these discussions. It is believed that such a meeting could be held on or about 1st February 1954 at which it will be necessary to come to firm conclusions on the future conduct of the operation.

TAB "A"

PROCESSING TALKS

TARGET INTELLIGENCE

1. The last available information on the target was taken as a basis for discussion. This information, which is dated up to July 1952, shows that there were three cables, Nos. 150, 151, and 152. It is known that cable 150 was earmarked by the Russians as a reserve cable. It is not certain, therefore, whether any pairs in this cable are in use.

CIA reported that there are indications that cable 150 may be in use on the target sector. The question of the tap chamber being constructed in such a way as to enable cable to be tapped also will be actively taken up. Cables 151 and 152 are believed to contain 81 Russian speech circuits, of which 19 are voice frequency telegraph circuits. It was pointed out that this information is far from recent and that changes are likely to have taken place, but that as these are the only figures available, they would have to serve as a basis for further discussion. It was agreed that both sides would keep the target intelligence under close review to establish any changes which have taken place, or may take place in the future, particularly with regard to cable 150.

PRELIMINARY ESTIMATE FOR PERSONNEL

2. Using present British experience as a basis it was estimated that 81 speech circuits would produce 162 reels per day, each lasting 2.5 hours. The processing of these reels would require 81 transcribers, 30 collators, 27 cardists, 10 people in the Signals Section, and 10 Russian typists, making a total of 158. These figures would have to be increased if the processing party were not integrated.

FORWARD SIGNALS TEAM

3. It was agreed that the first priority was to provide a Signals team for the field consisting of approximately 2 Signals Officers, 6 transcribers, 1 Russian typist, and 1 secretary. This team will be regarded as an advance party of the base Signals Section or Sections. Based on the information available at the meeting, this should ideally be a joint Anglo-American team, which will require fitting cover. The key personnel should be trained and available in Berlin by mid-August. Therefore recruiting should start in January and training in May 1954. It was pointed out that the principal qualifications for the two Signals Officers are a knowledge of telecommunications and Russian. SIS is prepared to provide half this team. Further examination by CIA of this question is necessary.

LOCATION AND FORM OF PROCESSING ARRANGEMENTS

4. In discussing the location and the form which the processing unit or units might take, it was agreed that the important factors to bear in mind are:
(i) The disruptive effect of any move of experienced British personnel to any location outside London.
(ii) The additional cost, delay and security risk which would be involved in the transit of tapes were the unit located in Washington.
The experienced British personnel now in London are largely non-mobile, but if it were decided to move such of them as were willing. . . . . [one line in the document was cut off]
5. In addition to these two main considerations the pros and cons of various courses of action were debated and listed, the lists being attached to these minutes to cover:
Appendix 1. Four possible sites for the processing staff.
Appendix 2. Three possible forms for the processing arrangements.
In listing these pros and cons, it was noted that they expressed the views only of London and Washington headquarters' officers, and that the CIA and SIS representatives in Germany may well have other and stronger arguments for locating the processing in Germany. Their views should therefore be given consideration before the final decision is reached.

REQUIREMENTS OF AN INTEGRATED PROCESSING PARTY

First phase

6. With reference to an integrated processing party it was agreed that such a party should initially consist of approximately 5 people in the Base Signals Section, 25 transcribers, 6 collators, 4 cardists, and 5 Russian typists. Recruiting of the transcribers should be completed by the 1st July 1954, when they should start their training. In view of the possibility of the operation not being successful, which should be known by the 15th September 1954, the preliminary training of transcribers should be confined to material of the lowest practicable sensitivity.

Second Phase

7. This party of approximately 45 would have to be increased gradually to meet the volume of work but this would only be done when the quality and quantity of the intelligence in the cables is known. It is proposed that this party might have one head and would need two administrative officers, one for the American staff and one for the British, and two staff officers on the Intelli-

gence side to look after the respective customers' interests. All the other members of the party could be mixed according to availability. If such an integrated party were agreed upon, its organisation would require further working out.

NON-INTEGRATIVE PROCESSING PARTIES

8. Paragraphs 6 and 7 consider the personnel which would be needed in a single integrated processing party, i.e., Course 3 in Appendix 2. Non-integrated parties—in whatever form—would require an upward revision of the estimates given above.

BRITISH EXPERIENCE IN SELECTING THE PERSONNEL

9. When considering the type of candidates for the transcribing team, it was pointed out that selection need not be restricted to persons with a Russian or Slav background. British personnel who had acquired a knowledge of Russian in universities, had proved, in practice, to be equally good at transcribing as native Russians. This would enlarge the recruiting field and diminish security risks. It was also thought possible to get Service Officers seconded to the unit. The question of the secondment of enlisted personnel had so far not been investigated, but it was thought possible that a small number of national servicemen, employed on monitoring duties, might become available. Apart from the usual Police and MI5 vetting, SIS had in the past not considered the fact of having relatives behind the Iron Curtain, in itself, as a security objection but rather whether the candidate had recently been in contact with them and each case had been considered on its own merits. There had been no psychologist tests or examinations, other than the . . . . . . [one line of the text is missing].

TELEGRAPH MATERIAL

10. It was agreed that the problem of how to handle telegraph material required further study. The encrypted material would naturally have to go to GCHQ and NSA, but unencrypted material need not necessarily be dealt with in that way. Other alternatives should be investigated, such as:

a) to have it done by the speech traffic processing party itself

b) to set up a separate party

c) to have a GCHQ and/or NSA party attached to the processing party for this work.

SIS and CIA will keep this problem under review for consideration at the next meeting.

TAB "B"

1. We are all agreed that we should plan to attack all circuits which are likely to appear off the three cables. This applies to both physical, derived and carrier facilities.

GENERAL

2. Careful review by the respective technical staffs associated with this project has disclosed that there is essentially complete agreement on the technical problem involved and on its solution.

3. As regards the terms and definitions, it would be convenient to use those contained in the "Combined Glossary of Communication Terms—APC 167."

4. It was the consensus that previous arrangements and agreements providing for exchanges of technical data and general information have been found advantageous and should be continued in the same manner in connection with this project.

APPROACH AREA

5. An endeavour will be made to make available the side circuits, phantom circuits and carrier pairs at the unit which will couple to the target cables. Following the coupling unit there will be a first distribution frame, this being used to effect coupling with the preamplifiers which may or may not be sufficient to cater for all of the circuits in the cables. Clearly apparatus and power facilities will be required for complete coverage, but only a detailed survey of the cable traffic will permit determination of the precise number and type of preamplifier equipment which is necessary.

6. Following the preamplifiers there will be a second distribution frame (which may in fact be integral with the first) to provide for interconnection between the preamplifiers and the cables to the terminal area. It is clearly desirable that the cables through the main length of the tunnel shall be large enough to accommodate all of the physical and derived circuits and should include screened pairs to cater for possible carrier systems which may be working on unloaded pairs in the target cables.

[Four more pages of technical description are not copied].

Notes

The following acronyms and terms are found frequently in the endnotes:

AVPRF   Arkhivy vneshnei politiki rossiiskoi federatsii (Foreign Policy Archives of the Russian Federation), which contain material from the Soviet Ministry of Foreign Affairs.

CIA-HRP   Central Intelligence Agency Historical Review Program. Established by the Historical Review Group of CIA's Center for the Study of Intelligence (CSI). All CIA documents cited or reproduced were released by CIA/CSI/HRG.

             All cables and dispatches specified as originating from Berlin were from Berlin Operations Base (BOB). Where the information has been declassified for release, the recipient of cables, except where noted, was "Director" (CIA Headquarters), and the recipient of dispatches was "Chief, EE" (East European Division). CIA information reports originated in CIA Headquarters and were disseminated there. Berlin information reports, whether by cable or dispatch, were disseminated locally and sent to CIA Headquarters for dissemination there as CIA information reports.

CWIHP   Cold War International History Project, Woodrow Wilson International Center for Scholars, Washington, D.C.

FRUS   Foreign Relations of the United States is prepared by the Historian of the Department of State and published by the US Government Printing Office.

KBS   *Veterany vneshnei razvedki Rossii* (Kratkii biograficheskii spravochnik) [Veterans of foreign intelligence of Russia (short biographic handbook), ed. T. V. Samolis (Moscow: SVR Press, 1995)].

NARA   National Administration of Records and Archives. Records Group (RG) 226 contains the OSS records that were transferred to NARA by CIA.

SVRA   Archives of Sluzhba vneshnei razvedki (the Foreign Intelligence Service of the Russian Federation).

TsKhSD   Tsentr khraneniia sovremennoi dokumentatsii (Center for the Preservation of Contemporary Documentation).

Interviews, except where otherwise specified, were conducted by David E. Murphy.

455

Chapter 1. CIA's Berlin Base

1. USSR Foreign Policy Archive, AVPR SSR, Fond Sekretariata Molotova, opis 5, por. 332, papka 29. This document was obtained by Kondrashev.

2. Kondrashev. When People's Commissar for State Security Vsevelod Merkulov reported to Stalin, Molotov, and Beria on the 27 Dec. 1943 Fitin-Donovan meeting, he noted that Fitin was accompanied by his deputy, Gaik Ovakimian.

3. See, most recently, Christopher Andrew and Oleg Gordievsky, *KGB: The Inside Story* (New York: HarperCollins, 1990), 323–325; and Anthony Cave Brown, *Wild Bill Donovan: The Last Hero* (New York: Times Books, 1982), 422–423.

4. Their activities on behalf of NKVD/NKGB have since been confirmed by Venona, one of several code names for an Army Signal Intelligence Service cryptographic activity that succeeded in breaking NKVD/NKGB messages. The contents of these messages were released publicly by the National Security Agency during 1995 and 1996. See Venona Historical Monograph 2, "The 1942–43 New York–Moscow KGB Messages," and Venona Historical Monograph 3, "The 1944–45 New York and Washington–Moscow KGB Messages."

5. For example, in drafting one such dissemination, NKGB used two OSS reports. See SVRA file 36514, vol. 1, pp. 279–83. The first, dated 6 Dec. 1944 from Allen Dulles in Bern, concerned Hitler's health and plotting against him by his lieutenants Himmler, Goebbels, and Bormann. The second, also from Dulles, on 22 Dec. 1944, reported on Himmler's frantic efforts to seek contact with the Western Allies. The draft set forth first the information from OSS, then NKGB's evaluation. Regarding the report on Hitler's health, NKGB added an encoded letter to London from the British ambassador in Stockholm appearing to confirm the OSS report. It was obtained in London from NKGB agent sources. On the basis of reporting from its sources in the Swedish Ministry of Social Security, NKGB concluded that Hitler had recently resumed command of the German Army and had rejected suggestions for peace proposals. In addition, NKGB sent to Stalin a copy of OSS Daily Political Summary no. 40 of 16 Feb. 1945, noting specifically that it was "received in Washington from agent sources." See SVRA file 36514, vol. 2, pp. 89–90, doc. 13/5.

6. SS Sturmbahnfuehrer Wilhelm Hoettl, chief of SS foreign intelligence operations in southeastern Europe, volunteered his services to OSS, described the remnants of his networks, and led OSS to his radio communications center in western Austria. Col. Andrew H. Berding, chief of X-2, OSS German Mission, reported the affair to William Donovan on 8 June 1945 through Allen Dulles, then chief of the newly formed OSS Mission in Germany. Berding recommended that the information obtained from Hoettl be passed to the Soviets and that the Soviets be invited to participate in joint exploitation of the network. Separately, Berding urged that conditions be imposed on the offer to NKGB, such as a prohibition on Soviet interrogation of Hoettl or his people and joint operation of the communications center. Berding to Donovan, 8 June 1945, "Hoettl Case," and 8 June 1945, "Hoettl Case: Additional Observations," NARA RG 226, entry 108. See also Berding to Donovan, 27 June 1945, "Documents Pertaining to Hoettl Case," NARA RG 226, entry 108.

7. Lt. Gen. P. M. Fitin to Maj. Gen. John Deane, 1 Aug. 1945, NARA RG 226, entry 108. See also Brown, *Wild Bill Donovan,* 753–54.

8. Ambassador Hugh Montgomery, interview, McLean, Va., 9 Nov. 1993. Montgomery was a member of the OSS detachment charged with destroying the communications center.

9. Not content to wait, Frank Wisner, head of the secret intelligence branch and future CIA deputy director of plans, sent three OSS officers through Soviet lines to Berlin to seek potential agent recruits from officials of a firm owned by one of the officers before the war. This mission was the first OSS report on life in Soviet-occupied Berlin. See Wisner to Shepardson and Penrose, 17 May 1945, NARA RG 226, box 20, entry 108B.

10. Omar Bradley, *A Soldier's Story* (New York: Holt, 1951), 551. Because of this dearth of information on the Soviet occupation forces, the US military insisted that BOB engage in a protracted effort to collect such data.

11. The building was designed by Hitler's architect, Albert Speer, with air raid protection in mind: it blended in with the larger of the surrounding villas and had three stories below ground.

Construction began in 1936, and in 1940 Field Marshal Keitel and his staff in the High Command moved in. Keitel lived across the street in a villa owned by Max Schmeling, the German boxer.

12. In addition to his oral briefing, Dulles gave Clay a lengthy memorandum that not only described the problems faced by the SSU German Mission but also contained his thoughts on the future place of a new Germany in Europe. NARA RG 226, folder 847, microfiche 1642, roll 74.

13. Jean Edward Smith, *Lucius D. Clay: An American Life* (New York: Holt, 1990), 261–62.

14. Robert Murphy, *Diplomat Among Warriors* (New York: Pyramid, 1964), 290. A. N. Buchin with N. N. Yakovlev, *170,000 Kilometrov s G. K. Zhukovym* (Moscow: Molodaia Gvardiia, 1994), 135. In his book *Clay*, Smith strongly defends Clay's view in 1945–46 that it was possible to cooperate with the Russians, and he points to broad US support for Clay's opinion (pp. 287–95). In our view, given the realities of Soviet politics at the time, Clay's position was extremely naive.

15. Weekly Letter, Berlin Operations Base, 17 Nov. 1947, CIA-HRP.

16. Durand, a balding former professor in his middle forties with a dashing black moustache, flashing dark eyes, and a quizzical, often sardonic expression, was a charter member of the X-2 branch of OSS and one of the original group to learn Ultra from the British in 1943. See Robin Winks, *Cloak and Gown: Scholars in the Secret War, 1939–1961*, 2d ed. (New Haven: Yale University Press, 1996), 262–263. Durand had long been on the list of officers scheduled for a Berlin assignment. His selection as chief of the most operationally active yet politically sensitive post within SSU Mission Germany may have appeared a natural consequence of the appointment of the German Mission's X-2 branch chief, Crosby Lewis, as chief of mission—a signal, perhaps, that the dominance in the mission of such SI officers as Wisner and Helms was over.

17. Dispatch to Foreign Branch M from Chief of Base Berlin via Chief of Station, Karlsruhe. Dana Durand "Report on Berlin Operations Base," 8 April 1948 (Clandestine Services History Program—CSHP 24), CIA-HRP.

18. Memorandum, Bastedo to Dulles, 25 Dec. 1944, "Status of Planning for the German Unit." NARA RE 226, box 207, folder 2915, entry 146. See also Wisner to Shepardson and Penrose, 17 May 1945.

19. For its headquarters, SMA selected the former German Army Combat Engineer School (Pionierschule) in the Karlshorst area of Lichtenberg district. It also became home to Soviet intelligence in East Berlin. A pleasant neighborhood of modest homes and apartment houses that was once famous for its race track, the area suffered relatively little bomb damage. The entire area around SMA headquarters was taken over and fenced off into a Soviet-controlled compound.

20. NARA RG 226, box 169, entry 108.

21. The Soviets allowed CDU, a postwar party with its roots in the Center Party of pre-Hitler Germany, to organize in East Germany because they anticipated that it would become a pliant member of the newly created Anti-Fascist Front (later, National Front).

22. NARA RG 226, box 152, entry 88; NARA RG 226, box 169, entry 108.

23. That this reporting was hitting home was confirmed by a statement in a monthly progress report for SI Production Division, SSU Washington, which stated: "In December 1945, Berlin had clearly become the best intelligence producer on Soviet political activities affecting the CDU in the Soviet Zone." NARA RG 226, box 202, folder 2820, entry 146. (Tom Polgar, interview, 19 Oct. 1993, and Peter Sichel, interview, 14 Dec. 1993.)

24. The report was cited in a 29 Dec. 1945 message from Murphy to the State Department describing the CDU situation. FRUS 1945, vol. 3, pp. 1079–91.

25. BOB sources reported on a special conference in Mar. 1946 of Marshal Zhukov, SMA specialists, a Moscow ministerial delegation, and representatives from East Germany industry to examine "difficulties in the industrial reparations program" and to accelerate production of industrial cranes badly needed for reconstruction of Soviet cities. But plant managers could not be sure of retaining the necessary machinery because often new dismantling orders came after production had begun. In one case, a factory scheduled to produce for reparations to the USSR had carefully salvaged machinery left over from its first dismantling experience only to have the renovated equipment removed as well. SSU Intelligence Dissemination No. A-67697, 20 Mar. 1946,

"Russian-German Conference Regarding Reparations Programs," NARA, RG 226, microfiche 1656, roll 2.

26. Lucius D. Clay, *Decision in Germany* (New York: Doubleday, 1950), 158.

27. Henry S. Lowenhaupt, "On the Soviet Nuclear Scent," *Studies in Intelligence* [CIA in-house journal] 2 (fall 1967), CIA-HRP.

28. Memorandum, 31 Aug. 1951, "Survey of the Office of Special Operations, Section on Germany," para. 4, CIA-HRP. See also Memorandum to DDCI from the Acting Assistant Director for Special Operations, 6 Oct. 1951, "OSO Relations with CIC," CIA-HRP. The withdrawal of production personnel from Tewa was successful because of cooperation by the US Army's CIC in Germany. Although this action had a negative affect on Tewa production, the Soviets had probably acquired their own manufacturing capability by this time.

29. Memorandum, 13 Jan. 1953, to Chief, Foreign Intelligence Staff, EE Division, on the effort of the Berlin Operations Base to "penetrate the Soviet Atomic Energy Program via their procurement programs in East Germany." CIA-HRP.

30. Operational Dispatches, BOB to Headquarters, 5 May 1953, 5 June 1953, and 7 Oct. 1953, CIA-HRP.

31. Henry S. Lowenhaupt, "Chasing Bitterfeld Calcium 1946–1950," *Studies in Intelligence* 17 (spring 1973), CIA-HRP.

32. Pitovranov, interview with Kondrashev, 1 Nov. 1994.

33. Lowenhaupt, "On the Soviet Nuclear Scent."

34. Durand, "Report."

35. Bradley, *Soldier's Story*, 464.

36. Durand, "Report."

37. These descriptions of operations undertaken as part of the order-of-battle collection program are taken from interviews with officers who served in Berlin and at German Mission Headquarters at Heidelberg during the period, as well as from Durand, "Report."

38. Richard Cutler, unpublished manuscript "OSS Recollections." See also Polgar interview.

39. Durand, "Report."

40. Dispatch to Chief, EE Division, 26 May 1956, CIA-HRP.

41. Ibid.

42. Ibid.

43. Ibid.

44. Polgar interview.

45. Frank Wisner anticipated the problem of X-2's role in the OSS German Mission: "Another matter which causes me much concern is the apparent unwillingness of the X-2 Branch to get on the team. It is my conviction that the nature of SI and X-2 work within the American area of occupation will have so many points in common that it would be a ridiculous mistake for the two branches to continue to operate separately as in the past." See Wisner to Shepardson and Penrose, 17 May 1945.

46. Polgar interview; Whitney Tucker, interview, 20 June 1996.

47. Durand, "Report."

48. Ibid.

49. Belic was the son of a colonel in the White Russian Army who was killed while fighting in southern Russia with General Deniken's forces. George and his mother made their way to the United States, where he graduated from the Georgetown School of Foreign Service. He served as an intelligence specialist in the US Navy during the war, including a posting to Soviet-occupied Bucharest in 1945. See Tom Bower, *The Red Web: MI6 and the KGB Mastercoup* (London: Atrium, 1989), pp. 92–93, for this background on George Belic.

50. In December 1946, the German Mission helped transfer Granovsky from Sweden to Germany. Granovsky's description of NKGB operations in the Ukraine, in the newly acquired territory of Ruthenia ceded to the USSR by Czechoslovakia, and in the Soviet zone at war's end provided BOB with its first solid information on the organization, personnel, and methodology of NKGB. Memorandum, Chief Foreign Branch M, 11 Mar. 1949, CIA-HRP. See also Anatoli Granovsky, *I Was an NKVD Agent* (New York: Devin Adair, 1962).

51. According to Durand, "Report," one who did was Capt. Alexander Sogolow, a member of the Berlin Command intelligence office. A huge man with an engaging smile and a twinkle in his eye, Sogolow had left Russia with his family in the early 1920s via Berlin and spoke native Russian and excellent German. In *Molehunt* (New York: Random House, 1992), David Wise discusses Sogolow's career in connection with past CIA security investigations (see pp. 172–74). More sympathetic and evocative of the real "Sasha" Sogolow is David Chachavadze's treatment in his *Crowns and Trenchcoats* (New York: Atlantic International, 1990), which includes a description of Sasha's funeral at Arlington National Cemetery.

Sogolow was of great help to BOB in Soviet defection operations and was responsible for giving BOB one of the best cases in the Soviet field it ever had—one that later provided vital information during the blockade. But Sogolow's reputation for encouraging defectors was not lost on the Soviets. In January 1948, the Soviets lodged a formal complaint to the American commandant regarding his activities, and he was ordered back to the States—pronto. After Sogolow returned to the United States, he joined CIA and was sent to Germany, where he was stationed in the Munich area rather than Berlin.

52. Don Huefner, interview, 19 Aug. 1993. See also Bower, *Red Web*, 93.

Chapter 2. KGB Karlshorst

1. Kondrashev, who was assigned to the Pavlovsky operation not long after joining the MGB's Second (internal counterintelligence) Directorate.

2. Ibid.

3. According to Kondrashev, Pavlovsky, who was half Jewish and lived in constant fear that he would somehow become a victim of Stalin's anti-Semitic purges, remained in the service for a time but later died in a psychiatric hospital. In later years, coauthor Kondrashev visited East Germany, accompanied by his daughter. Wanting to provide something special for her visit, GDR Minister of State Security Erich Mielke said he would arrange for them to stay at an MfS guest facility near Berlin. It was, said Mielke with a knowing smile, a place that the "Soviet friends" had used right after the war. When Kondrashev arrived at the guest house, it was the same "Dammsmuehle" castle.

4. Kondrashev. For example, Nikita Khrushchev appointed Aleksandr Shelepin chairman of KGB to reduce or eliminate the influence of people like Ivan Serov. Later, Leonid Brezhnev used cronies Semyon Tsvigun and Georgy Tsinev to keep an eye on new KGB chairman Yuri Andropov.

5. This date was for years celebrated by KGB officers at home and abroad as the birthday of KGB's foreign intelligence service. It is still so celebrated by the new Russian Foreign Intelligence Service (SVR).

6. Following his dismissal, Yezhov was initially transferred to the People's Commissariat for Water Transport. He was attacked publicly by Stalin at the Eighteenth Party Congress in March 1939 and arrested on 10 Apr. In the style of Soviet purge practices, the official record of his investigation accused him of being an agent of Polish and German intelligence and of having contact with circles in Poland, Germany, England, and Japan that were hostile to the USSR. The investigation of Yezhov was completed 1 Feb. 1940. On 3 Feb. his case was heard by the Military Collegium of the Supreme Soviet. During his trial, Yezhov denied the charges and claimed force had been used against him. He was shot on 4 Feb. See Robert Conquest, *Inside Stalin's Secret Police* (London: Macmillan, 1985), 76–85. For additional background on Yezhov's career, see Grigorii Tsitriniak, "Rasstrel'noe Delo Yezhova: Shtrikhi k portretu palacha," *Literaturnaia Gazeta* (Moscow), 12 Feb. 1992.

7. SVRA. Memoirs of P. M. Fitin, chief of foreign intelligence 1939–46. It was written for a classified collection dedicated to the sixtieth anniversary of Soviet foreign intelligence and intended at the time for restricted circulation. For Fitin's background, see KBS, which indicates that Fitin was one of more than two hundred young Communists with higher education assigned by the Central Committee to perform intelligence jobs in 1938 to overcome the damage caused to foreign intelligence by the purges. Fitin rose rapidly within a year to become, at age thirty-one, the chief of foreign intelligence, a department that he guided throughout the hectic years of the war.

For his time, he came as close to being an intelligence professional as could have existed under Stalin. As a result he was frequently at odds with his own chief, People's Commissar for State Security V. N. Merkulov.

8. Ibid. In Sudoplatov's 1994 book *Special Tasks* (Boston: Little, Brown, 1994), he confirms that he had been Fitin's deputy. Of Fitin, Sudoplatov recalls only having had him sign requests for release from prison or the camps of various ex-NKVD officials who were needed in the Fourth Directorate during the war. He makes no further mention of Fitin until they were gathered together at "table number nine" in May 1945 during the grand victory celebration in St. George's Hall in the Kremlin. This is strange, considering the close, intensive interaction between the two during the war.

9. For example, Yakov Tishchenko, a fluent German-speaker who was in charge of the Belorussian section of the Fourth Directorate, recalls being sent to besieged Leningrad for two months on a special operation and then, after the surrender of the Sixth German Army at Stalingrad, interrogating senior German officers. Afterward, he was detached from the Fourth Directorate and sent to Scandinavia under diplomatic cover. Using the alias Razin, Tishchenko later played a role in the development of Soviet intelligence in Germany. See *Memoirs of Yakov Fyodorovich Tishchenko alias Roshchin alias Razin,* unpub. manuscript, Moscow, 1992, provided by Kondrashev.

10. Amy Knight, *Beria: Stalin's Lieutenant* (Princeton, N.J.: Princeton University Press, 1993). Some of these groups, such as the Volga Germans, were considered security risks and were moved soon after the outbreak of the war. Others, including the Chechens and Crimeans, had been under German occupation and were deported after the territories had been retaken by the Red Army. All of these deportations were carried out under deplorable conditions.

11. Kondrashev. Also, during a discussion with the authors on 6 July 1994, Gen. Anatoly Oleinikov, Russian counterintelligence service representative in Berlin and an officer with extensive military counterintelligence experience, confirmed that the changes were indeed related solely to the issue of power and that the special departments continued to function in the same manner as they had before they became Smersh.

12. If there is any question about how Stalin felt about the loyalty of Soviet POWs who had seen the West firsthand, note his order of 11 May 1945 to the commanders of the first and second Belorussian fronts, the first, second, third, and fourth Ukrainian fronts, and to comrades Beria, Merkulov, Abakumov, etc., concerning the establishment of holding camps. These camps would be created within each front for Smersh to detain and investigate former POWs and displaced civilians. D. Volkogonov, *Triumf i Tragediia,* bk. 2, pt. 1 (Moscow: Novosti, 1989), 394.

13. Robert Stephan, "Smersh: Soviet Military Counterintelligence During the Second World War," *Journal of Contemporary History* 22 (1987): 585–613. Whatever Stalin's intent, according to army Gen. Pyotr Ivashutin, who was chief of counterintelligence of the third Ukrainian front during the war years, military counterintelligence "was transformed from a purely counterintelligence organ into a powerful intelligence and counterintelligence service, occupied not only with the search for enemy agent nets but also conducting operations in the rear of the enemy." Ivashutin believes that the practical results of Smersh activity were greater than those obtained by NKGB and that this accounted for Abakumov's advancement. See K. A. Stolyarov, *Golgofa: Dokumental'naia Povest'* (Moscow: Fizkul'tura i sport, 1991).

14. Kondrashev. See also CIA-HRP Dispatch, OSO Chief of Station, Karlsruhe, to Chief FBM, 26 July 1949, Appendix F, "Structure and Personnel of the CI Directorate of the Group of Soviet Occupation Forces in Germany."

15. Christopher Andrew and Oleg Gordievsky, *KGB: The Inside Story* (New York: Harper-Collins, 1990), 346–52. A KGB official history is given by Gordievsky as the source for his information on NKGB/NKVD operations in Poland. See also "Activities of General Ivan Serov in Poland," Intelligence Report, 8 Nov. 1958, CIA-HRP.

16. By the end of 1945 there were ten such camps receiving prisoners from Smersh units and later the new NKGB operational sectors. See Achim Killian, *Einweisen zur voelligen Isolierung: NKWD-Speziallager Muehlberg/Elbe, 1945–48* (Leipzig: Forum Verlag, 1993). One Soviet source states that during 1945 more then ten thousand "Nazi criminals" were arrested and sentenced in

the Soviet zone of Germany. Kondrashev's notes from drafts of a new history of Soviet foreign intelligence under preparation in SVR in 1994 support this claim.

17. SVRA file 36514, vol. 2, doc. 14/15, Report for the State Defense Committee, "Illegal Nazi Organization," p. 295.

18. A military engineer before the war, Sidnev was transferred on party orders to state security, where he served in a special department of the Leningrad military district and then became chief of the special department of the Karelian front. In 1944 Sidnev was deputy chief of Smersh of the First Belorussian Front, and in April 1945 he was transferred to the Berlin position at Serov's request. According to his official personnel file, Sidnev was simultaneously deputy chief of the Smersh directorate of the Group of Soviet Occupation Forces and chief of the Berlin operational sector. The information on Sidnev's career and assignments up to 1947 is taken from his personnel file and was obtained by Kondrashev from state security archives in Omsk.

19. Ibid. See also A. N. Buchin with N. N. Iakovlev, *170,000 Kilometrov s G. K. Zhukovym* (Moscow: Molodaia Gvardiia, 1994), 144–46.

20. In February 1945 Vadis sent back to Moscow a captured German document describing the Warsaw uprising of July 1944. The German report blamed the British for the uprising and noted that the Poles were disillusioned by the failure of the Allies to come to their aid. Vadis obviously knew that this was what Moscow wanted to hear. See SVRA, Report, Lt. Gen. A. Vadis, Chief of the Directorate of Counterintelligence Smersh, First Belorussian Front, Feb. 1945.

21. CIA-HRP Dispatch, OSO Chief of Station, Karlsruhe, to Chief FBM, 26 July 1949.

22. *Sovetskaia voennaia entsiklopediia,* vol. 6 (Moscow: Voenizdat, 1978), 142–43.

23. Georgy Aleksandrovich Korotia, who in 1945 was the chief of a department in the Berlin *opersektor,* interview with Kondrashev, 17 Dec. 1994. Indeed, as can be seen in Norman M. Naimark's *The Russians in Germany: A History of the Soviet Zones of Occupation, 1945–1949* (Cambridge: Belknap Press of Harvard University Press, 1995), 378–97, based on research in the archives of the Soviet Military Administration, the dividing line between the personnel and activities of Soviet internal affairs and state security in Germany was difficult to determine, even in official correspondence. For example, on p. 393, when Naimark cites complaints in 1947 by Maj. Gen. I. S. Kolesnichenko, chief of Soviet Military Administration in *Land* Thueringen, of "NKVD" (still so-called by Kolesnichenko, even though by then it had become the MVD), the operations in question were in fact being conducted by the MGB Operational Sector for *Land* Thueringen.

24. AVP USSR. Fond Sekretariata V. M. Molotova, opis 7, por. 416, papka 30. These advisory posts were much sought after, and there was stiff competition for them between the Foreign Affairs Commissariat *(Narkomindel)* and NKGB/NKVD. For example, the political adviser attached to Marshal Rokossovsky's second Belorussian front was Amaiak Zakharovich Kobulov, the younger brother of Bogdan and a member of Beria's inner circle who had served as NKVD resident in Berlin before the war. Costello and Tsarev in *Deadly Illusions* (New York: Crown, 1993) note that Amaiak obtained his Berlin posting because of his ties to NKVD leaders, not because of his operational competence. On p. 441 the authors quote from Amaiak Kobulov's official file 15852, vol. 1, made available from SVR archives.

25. Kondrashev. From the history of the work of foreign intelligence against the German target now being compiled in SVR.

26. Ibid.

27. *Dva generala.* Classified publication on the careers of Ivan Ivanovich Agayants and Aleksandr Mikhailovich Korotkov (Moscow: SVR Press, 1992), 60 copies.

28. Sobolev was the first political adviser appointed in early summer 1945. He was replaced by Semyonov in 1946. See Robert Murphy, *Diplomat Among Warriors* (New York: Pyramid, 1964).

29. CIA-HRP Dispatch, OSO Chief of Station, Karlsruhe, to Chief FBM, 26 July 1949. Also Kondrashev.

30. V. M. Chebrikov et al., *Istoriia sovetskikh organov gosudarstvennoi bezopastnosti* (History of the Soviet organs of state security), 1980, SVRA.

31. Sudoplatov et al., *Special Tasks,* 238. John J. Dziak, *Chekisty* (Lexington, Mass.: N.p., 1988). Among state security personnel, the departure of Merkulov, Bogdan Kobulov, and others from MGB

was universally looked upon as a demotion, and Abakumov was generally perceived as having won a struggle with Beria.

32. David Holloway, *Stalin and the Bomb: The Soviet Union and Atomic Energy, 1939–1956* (New Haven: Yale University Press, 1994), 134, 148.

33. CIA Information Report, 2 Dec. 1953, "Notes on the Administration for Soviet Property in Germany," CIA-HRP.

34. SVRA file 60345, vol. 3, doc. s/6147, pp. 186–88. This 7 June 1947 report from Kovalchuk to Minister Abakumov is an example of positive intelligence collection. It forwards a mix of reporting from various sources in the Berlin operational sector predicting the outbreak of war before the end of 1947. Kondrashev reports that an American officer is quoted as saying, "We do not wish to see the spread of Bolshevism in Europe and the whole world. Only America can put a stop to it."

35. Information Report, OSO Information Control, "Re-Organization of the Russian Intelligence Services in Germany," 11 Sept. 1947. CIA-HRP.

36. SVRA file 60345, vol. 2, Report by "VCh" (speech secrecy system) from Kovalchuk to Abakumov, 19 Dec. 1946, no. 0167.

37. Kondrashev.

38. Yuri Modin's descriptions of his work in supporting and handling the reports dissemination of the "Cambridge" cases during the war and immediate postwar period indicates that he was terribly overloaded: delays in dissemination must have been inevitable. During the Paris talks on the Marshall Plan in June 1947, for example, Modin describes Molotov's rage at not having been sufficiently well informed in advance by MGB intelligence sources. See Yuri Modin, *Mes camarades de Cambridge* (Paris: Robert Laffont, 1994), 129–30, 150. See also Scott D. Parish and Mikhail M. Narinsky, *New Evidence on the Soviet Rejection of the Marshall Plan, 1947,* Mar. 1994, Cold War International History Project, working paper 9, p. 45, which describes the importance of Cambridge Group sources to Molotov during this vital conference.

39. SVRA, extracts from the "History of Foreign Intelligence of the Organs of State Security of the Soviet Union," 1982, p. 269. Completed under the chairmanship of then KGB Chairman Kriuchkov, the work is classified Top Secret, and all copies are numbered. The text of the 1947 Molotov-Stalin memorandum and a statement of KI tasks taken from the decree could not be located in SVR archives. They were obtained by Kondrashev from notes retained by a KI veteran. See also extracts from the 30 Sept. 1947 decree establishing KI, and the 1949 decree transferring KI to the Ministry of Foreign Affairs. This decree states: "The Committee of Information does not become a part of the Ministry of Foreign Affairs (MID) in an administrative, financial or organizational sense, but remains an independent organization. The Committee of Information is a secret organization and is financed from special funds of the Council of Ministers of the USSR."

40. Before KI, for example, when Yuri Modin was preparing for his assignment to Great Britain, where he was to handle sources like Guy Burgess and John Cairncross, he was told that he would not be given a diplomatic position because the Ministry of Foreign Affairs had not approved. Apparently, relations between the intelligence directorate and the ministry were not good. Instead, he was assigned as a code clerk, a terrible cover position for meeting and handling these important British sources. Normally, code clerks would not have had any knowledge of a foreign language, nor were they permitted any contact with foreigners. A Soviet code clerk who broke this mold would have immediately attracted the attention of the British security service. If this was the best MGB could do in arranging cover for the handler of its best sources, one can see why some were relieved to participate in the KI experiment.

41. Australian Archives, Australian Capital Territory, Commonwealth Research Services, A6283 XR1, item 7, p. 2. Some parts of MGB's foreign intelligence directorate had already moved into this compound.

42. SVRA, "History of Foreign Intelligence."

43. Kondrashev.

44. Ibid.

45. Sudoplatov et al., *Special Tasks,* 237. Competent or not, it must have been hard for Vyshinsky to avoid some responsibility. The 1949 decree specifically states that "in an opera-

tional-political sense, the Committee of Information is subordinate personally to the foreign minister."

46. SVRA, "History of Foreign Intelligence." Unfortunately, it was not possible to obtain the texts of these decrees dealing with operative matters from SVR archives even though they were referred to in official histories.

47. SVRA, "History of Foreign Intelligence." See also Australian Archives, Australian Capital Territory, Commonwealth Research Services, A6283 XR1, item 7, p. 14, paras. 85–86.

48. Kondrashev.

49. Abakumov was replaced temporarily by Sergei Ogoltsov, and then by Ignatiev, a Central Committee functionary whom Stalin could control. Although Abakumov was removed from office on 4 July 1951, he was not arrested until 12 July. Instead a commission was formed to inquire into his case. After his arrest, Abakumov was accused of having suppressed crucial testimony in the "doctors' case," an alleged anti-Soviet plot by several Kremlin doctors, many of whom were Jewish. Another product of Stalin's paranoia, these doctors' arrests in January 1953 were to have served as justification for new purges. Abakumov was also accused of corruption. A large quantity of valuables, including hundreds of meters of dress fabric, silver plate, a hundred pairs of shoes, and even secret documents, were allegedly found in his home at 11 Kolpachny Pereulok in Central Moscow (until recently the home of SVR's public affairs bureau). In spite of this evidence, Abakumov's case was not decided until 1954.

50. Pitovranov, interview with Kondrashev, 21 June 1994. See also Stolyarov, *Golgofa*. This publication contains a section entitled "General-Polkovnik Abakumov: Fakty i kommentarii," which is referred to by the publisher as "the first truthful representation of the circumstances and reasons for the death of a great Soviet counterintelligence officer." Pitovranov was selected for state security in December 1938 as a result of the Nov. 1938 decision of the Central Committee to bring new blood into those departments badly hit by the Yezhov purges. At the time of his selection, Pitovranov was a student and leader of the party organization in the Moscow Electromechanical. This ceremonial farewell was vintage Stalin, who used such occasions not only to indicate his approval of the one he honored but also to send a message to others.

51. Ibid.

52. Ibid.

53. Pitovranov interview.

54. Ibid. Although Pitovranov did take charge of foreign intelligence, he held the post only for a few months before Stalin's death in Mar. 1953—at which time he was reduced to deputy chief of counterintelligence in the state security component of Beria's new Ministry of Internal Affairs (MVD). But Pitovranov later served in senior KGB positions in Germany and elsewhere.

55. Ibid.

56. Boris Nalivaiko, *Memoirs*. These memoirs are held in the SVR Special Collection.

57. Of Cossack origin, Tishchenko was born in the Far East and served there in the Civil War. An early member of the Foreign Department of OGPU, Tishchenko was stationed in Harbin, Manchuria, until 1930, when he was assigned to Berlin. In 1935 he was transferred to Vienna as resident. In 1938 he was recalled to Moscow in connection with the ongoing purges of senior foreign intelligence personnel. He somehow escaped prison and execution, but he was dismissed from the service. During World War II, Tishchenko was recalled to active duty. He initially served in the Fourth (partisan) Directorate, was then designated resident in Stockholm, and in 1945 was assigned to Helsinki as resident where his cover was deputy chief of the Allied Control Commission. See *Memoirs of Yakov Fyodorovich Tishchenko*. Biographic details from these memoirs were supplemented by Kondrashev (Tishchenko was his father-in-law).

58. SVRA. Extracts from *Memoirs of Vasilii Petrovich Tishchenko*.

59. Ibid.

60. Ibid. These official diaries should not be confused with Halder's personal unofficial diaries, which were written in shorthand and hidden with a neighbor in Aschau, West Germany. The personal diaries were seized by US forces and later published by Hans-Adolph Jacobsen in three volumes in German, and in one volume in English. For the English version see *The Halder War Diary, 1939–1942* (Novato, Calif.: Presidio, 1988).

61. *Razvedchik,* no. 3 (1989). This internal publication of KGB is now published by SVR.

62. When KI was dissolved, Ilichev was assigned to the Third European Department of the USSR Ministry of Foreign Affairs, responsible for Germany and Austria. See SVRA, "Decision on the Creation of Three KI Residencies in Berlin," from "History of Foreign Intelligence."

63. Ibid.

64. Australian Archives, Australian Capital Territory, Commonwealth Research Services, A6283 XR1, item 7, p. 12.

65. SVRA, "Decision."

66. A principal target in the USIG group was Yevgeny Ilich Levin, who remained a prominent figure in KGB scientific and technical operations for many years. After USIG was abolished, Levin's cover was reportedly shifted to deputy chief, scientific-technical section of the Soviet trade delegation in East Berlin. Levin later became better known as the senior KGB official attached to the State Committee for the Coordination of Scientific Research Work and as Oleg Penkovsky's boss. See CIA-HRP, Dispatch, To Chief EE from BOB, 8 Aug. 1955, "Status of Effort to Locate Soviet Atomic Energy Representatives in the DDR." See also Jerrold L. Schecter and Peter S. Deriabin, *The Spy Who Saved the World* (New York: Scribners, 1992).

67. SVRA, "Decision."

Chapter 3. The Berlin Blockade Challenges Western Ingenuity and Perseverance

Source of epigraph: Peter Sichel, interview, 14 Dec. 1993.

1. FRUS, 1947, vol. 2, p. 908.

2. Memorandum, DCI to the president, 16 Mar. 1948, Harry S. Truman Library, Papers of Harry S. Truman, President's Secretary's Files. The memorandum refers to a 22 Dec. 1947 CIA report on the possibility of Soviet steps to force the Western powers from Berlin.

3. Enciphered telegram from Berlin, no. 20430, 9 Jan. 1948, SVRA file 38179, vol. 4, pp. 268–72.

4. Enciphered telegram, no. 06/20233, 6 Jan. 1948, SVRA file 38179, vol. 4, pp. 266–67. General Clay, *Decision in Germany* (New York: Doubleday, 1950), 208, notes that the Soviets demanded a separate set of plates to permit the new currency to be printed in Leipzig in their zone. The United States rejected this; Clay cited as the reason the earlier experience in providing plates to the Soviets for printing Allied military marks.

5. SVRA file 38179, vol. 4-a, pp. 136–37.

6. William R. Harris, "March Crisis, Act I," *Studies in Intelligence* [CIA in-house journal] 10 (fall 1966): 8, 15, CIA-HRP. Harris devotes much of his article to examining how this 5 Mar. message was handled procedurally within the intelligence community and the precedents that were established as a result.

7. Soviet demands for removing the cable maintenance teams were not intended solely as pre-blockade harassment: the Soviets were responding to a real threat. The presence of these Western teams attracted not only disgruntled East Germans in their vicinity but disaffected Soviet military personnel as well. For example, a member of a signal team in the Weimar area—who was badly injured when his vehicle was deliberately rammed by unidentified Soviets—later helped BOB establish contact with Soviets he had known in the area. Sichel interview.

8. William R. Harris, "March Crisis 1948, Act II," *Studies in Intelligence* 11 (spring 1967), 9–10, CIA-HRP. Harris based his speculation that the positions and movements of certain Soviet officers during the period were intended to deceive the West on data that are now known to be invalid. For example, he places Zhukov in Berlin from January through March 1948. Actually, Zhukov spent January in the hospital because of a heart attack and in February left Moscow for his new assignment commanding the Urals Military District. Harris also fingered Lt. Gen. L. A. Malinin as head of MVD security forces in Germany and Maj. Gen. P. M. Malkov as deputy to Marshal Sokolovsky. But Malinin was KI resident and had already been recalled because of his unauthorized contacts with US officials (he was tried and sentenced in June 1948); Malkov served as head of the SMA Directorate of Internal Affairs. Harris also claimed that "the Soviets had centralized their intelligence organizations in Germany under . . . Col. Gen. B. Z. Kobulov." In fact,

Kobulov was the representative of the USSR minister of internal affairs in Germany, which was responsible primarily for exploiting Wismut and other industries for the Soviet atomic bomb program.

9. Report, 13 May 1948, based on enciphered telegrams from the Berlin KI residency, SVRA file 38179, vol. 5-a, pp. 213–15.

10. Askold Vsevolodovich Lebedev, interview with Kondrashev, 23 Aug. 1994.

11. ORE 41–48, 14 June 1948, CIA-HRP.

12. Progress Report, Chief of Operations to Assistant Director for Special Operations, 30 June 1948, CIA-HRP.

13. Memorandum, R. H. Hillenkoetter to the secretary of defense, 30 June 1948, "Current Situation in Berlin," CIA-HRP.

14. Memorandum, R. H. Hillenkoetter to the secretary of defense, 28 June 1948, "Situation in Berlin," CIA-HRP.

15. Ibid.

16. CIA Information Report, 15 July 1948, "Russian Unilateral Dismissal of Berlin Police Officials," CIA-HRP.

17. CIA Information Report, 21 Feb. 1949, "Possible Removal of Police President Paul Markgraf," CIA-HRP.

18. Memorandum, R. H. Hillenkoetter to the president, 10 Dec. 1948, CIA-HRP.

19. CIA Information Report, 30 Dec. 1948, "Soviet Measures to Further Tighten the Sector Blockade in Berlin," CIA-HRP.

20. CIA Information Report, 7 Feb. 1949, "Indoctrination of Police in the Soviet Sector of Berlin," CIA-HRP.

21. CIA Information Report, 7 Feb. 1949, CIA-HRP.

22. CIA Information Report, 7 Mar. 1949, "SED Preparations for Illegal Work in Western Berlin," CIA-HRP.

23. CIA Information Report, 7 Mar. 1949. "Progress of the SED Membership Purge," CIA-HRP.

24. Confidential interview, 3 Nov. 1993. Tom Polgar, interview, 19 Oct. 1993; Sichel interview. CSHP 098, July 1971, "Illegal Border Crossing Program," pp. 16–18, CIA-HRP.

25. This was one Korean model that the Soviets followed in Germany. In 1946–47 in North Korea, the Soviet Army created "police officer training schools" that served as cover for paramilitary units. In early 1948 the units were formally designated the North Korean People's Army.

26. The 5 December 1948 elections were held despite the blockade and SED's campaign against participation. More than 86 percent of eligible voters in West Berlin participated, and SED was soundly defeated.

27. CIA Information Report, 23 Mar. 1949, "Berlin East Sector Police Presidium—Paramilitary Police," CIA-HRP.

28. Gordon Stewart, interview, 6 Nov. 1993.

29. Sources of epigraphs, respectively: FRUS, 1948, vol. 2, p. 931; Report from Berlin, 3 June 1948, SVRA.

30. This report from the MGB Berlin Operational Sector, which Lt. Gen. Kovalchuk would most certainly have forwarded to MGB Moscow, is an example of continued MGB Germany political reporting in competition with the KI residency. SVRA file 60345, vol. 23, pp. 46–55.

31. The Soviets offered food and heating fuel at sharply reduced prices but in return asked that recipients pledge not to accept food from the Allied airlift. Only about 1 percent of West Berliners accepted the offer. See Robert P. Grathwol and Donita M. Moorhus, *American Forces in Berlin, 1945–1994: Cold War Outpost*, Department of Defense, Legacy Resource Management Program, Cold War Project (Washington, D.C., 1994), 48.

32. SVRA file 60345, vol. 23, pp. 46–55.

33. Grathwol and Moorhus, *American Forces in Berlin*, 42, 52.

34. SVRA file 38179, vol. 4, pp. 325–27. Bauer, a prewar member of the German Communist Party who went into exile in France, fought in the Spanish Civil War and was interned in Switzerland during World War II. After the Nazi collapse he returned to Germany and initially headed

the KPD faction in the Hessian parliament. He moved to East Germany in 1947 and later became chief editor of the Soviet-controlled radio *Deutschlandsender*. See *Der Spiegel* 38 (13 Sept. 1971).

35. SVRA file 38179, vol. 4, pp. 325–27.

36. *New York Times,* 19 Sept. 1972. Bauer himself did not long remain a source for the Berlin KI residency. In August 1950 he was arrested and charged with having cooperated with Noel Field, who had been tried by a Budapest court as an American agent. Bauer was condemned to death by a Soviet court, but the sentence was changed to twenty-five years' imprisonment. He was released from the Gulag in 1955 and returned to West Germany, where he became an adviser to Willy Brandt. He died in September 1972.

37. Report from KI resident, Berlin, to Moscow, 3 July 1948, SVRA file 35887, vol. 2, pp. 15–16.

38. SVRA file 44331, vol. 1, pp. 63–66. Kondrashev notes the desire of the German participants in the meeting to use interzonal trade as a weapon against the West German Communist Party (KPD), evidence of their refusal to accept the growth in the USSR's influence following the 1945 victory and of their desire to isolate West Germany from East Germany.

39. The "Kremlin meetings" refer to discussions on the Berlin question held in Moscow between Molotov and the ambassadors of the three occupying powers. On 3 August the three ambassadors then met with Molotov and Stalin.

40. SVRA file 35887, vol. 2, pp. 43–45.

41. FRUS, 1948, vol. 2, pp. 999–1006.

42. SVRA file 40712, vol. 2, pp. 46–49. Given the rapidity with which this document was delivered to Moscow and disseminated to Stalin, it is likely that the source was Guy Burgess, aide to Hector McNeil, undersecretary for foreign affairs.

43. SVRA file 40712, vol. 1, pp. 346–51.

44. FRUS, 1948, vol. 2, p. 925.

45. SVRA file 40712, vol. 2, pp. 77–80. The discussions and actions taken by the Western foreign ministers in their Paris meeting are described in FRUS, 1948, vol. 2, pp. 1173–79. A Russian translation of the Bevin notes bears the notation that on 2 October 1948 they were used in a briefing of Molotov and Zorin.

46. SVRA file 40712, vol. 2, pp. 160–63.

47. Ibid.

48. Ibid. FRUS, 1948, vol. 2, p. 1179, notes that "Mr. Marshall, with Gen. Clay's assistance, gives his colleagues detailed information on the operation of the airlift." In *Decision in Germany,* Clay describes Foreign Minister Bevin's concern at "the slow build-up of the airlift" and his response that the daily tonnage would soon be doubled (p. 376).

49. Ibid.

50. Lebedev interview.

51. Georgy Alekseevich Korotia, interview with Kondrashev, Moscow.

52. SVRA file 40712, vol. 1, pp. 7–11.

53. The Western Union (later the Western European Union) comprised France, Great Britain, Belgium, Luxembourg, and the Netherlands. Created in March 1948 following the Prague Coup, it was a first step toward a common European defense.

54. FRUS, 1948, vol. 3, pp. 276, 290–91.

55. SVRA file 43274, vol. 1, pp. 151–56.

56. Ibid., pp. 160–62. Kondrashev believes that this report provides evidence of the reluctance of the German people and German politicians of the period to participate in any degree of remilitarization, including the creation of the so-called labor units.

57. Ibid., pp. 182–183. Kondrashev believes that this report and others like it confirmed to Soviet intelligence and the Soviet leadership the American desire to rearm Germany against the wishes of its people and of other countries. In his logic, European countries were under the influence of the Soviet Union at the time because of the Soviets' role in the victory over Germany and because of their common prewar mission against Nazism.

58. SVRA file 43274, vol. 1, pp. 122–23.

59. Ibid., pp. 223–25.

60. SVRA file 40712, vol. 2, pp. 329–31.

61. Ibid., pp. 507–9.

62. In a 2 February 1949 press conference, Dean Acheson intimated that concerning the other three questions (on whether the USSR would join the United States in declaring that neither had any intention of going to war, on gradual disarmament, and on a possible Truman-Stalin meeting) Stalin's responses were trivial—that they were intended to frame the Berlin question and make clear that it was the principal concern. See Dean Acheson, *Present at the Creation: My Years in the State Department* (New York: Norton, 1969), 267–68.

63. SVRA file 40712, vol. 3, pp. 268–69.

64. FRUS, 1949, vol. 3, p. 751.

65. SVRA file 43297, vol. 4, pp. 30–31, no. 1791, 9 June 1949.

66. Report 18972/i/1091, 9 June 1949, SVRA file 35837, vol. 2, pp. 164–66.

67. SVRA file 43297, vol. 4, p. 123, 17 Oct. 1949. This report was translated from the German. In view of the reference to the "ambitious Reuter," it may have a source in the office of West Berlin mayor Ernst Reuter.

68. SVRA file 43207, vol. 4, p. 134. A notation on the report indicates that it was used in a summary on Berlin and disseminated to "seven addressees."

69. FRUS, 1949, vol. 3, pp. 422–25.

70. Report 1773, SVRA file 43274, vol. 1, pp. 308–12.

71. SVRA file 40712, vol. 1, pp. 325–26.

Chapter 4. The Korean War

1. See "The Cold War in Asia," CWIHP *Bulletin* 6–7 (winter 1995–96).

2. Vladimir O. Pechatnov, *The Big Three After World War II: New Documents on Soviet Thinking About Post War Relations with the United States and Great Britain*, Working Paper 13, CWIHP (July 1995), 19.

3. Report, Resident Valerian (code name for KI resident Razin), 22 Oct. 1949, SVRA file 44330, vol. 1, pp. 226–27.

4. Dispatch, Resident Valerian, Berlin KI Residency, no. 1201, 29 Aug. 1949, SVRA file 44330, vol. 1, pp. 139–42.

5. Enciphered telegram, from Berlin, no. 601/22233, 20 Oct. 1949, SVRA file 43297, vol. 4, pp. 114–15.

6. KI Report, no. 3719/s, 23 Oct. 1949, SVRA file 44333, vol. 1, pp. 214–16.

7. KI Report, no. 4280/z, 12 Dec. 1949, SVRA file 44353, vol. 1, pp. 419–22.

8. Report, Zorin to Stalin, no. 40–11—eh, 9 Nov. 1949, SVRA file 44333, vol. 1, pp. 370–72.

9. SVRA file 43297, vol. 4, p. 134. Cable from Paris residency, no. 22647, 24 Nov. 1949. European residencies during the KI period were discouraged from using telegrams to forward information reports unless the message was extremely important and time sensitive.

10. KI Report, no. 4278/z, 12 Dec. 1949, SVRA.

11. Dispatch from Berlin, no. 1207, SVRA file 43274, vol. 1, pp. 285–88.

12. KI Report, no. 1407/3, 29 Apr. 1950, SVRA. Within the Committee of Information this report went to Graur of KI Disinformation and also to Ivan Ivanovich Agayants, resident in France until 1949 and then chief of the Second (European) Directorate of the Committee of Information. Nine years later, this same Ivan Agayants would become the first chief of KGB's disinformation department. There was no distribution to Stalin or the Politburo; it went only to Vyshinsky and Gromyko.

13. Dean Acheson, *Present at the Creation: My Years in the State Department* (New York: Norton, 1969), 308.

14. Frank A. Ninkovich, *Germany and the United States: The Transformation of the German Question Since 1945* (Boston: Twayne, 1988), 84.

15. Kathryn Weathersby, "New Russian Documents on the Korean War," CWIHP *Bulletin* 6–7 (winter 1995–96). Weathersby describes and discusses many of the documents declassified by the presidential archive in Moscow on the "decision-making behind the outbreak . . . of war in

Korea." The same issues of the *Bulletin* also contain translations from the Russian presidential archives of meetings between Stalin and Mao Tse-tung during December 1949–January 1950, along with several commentaries on the transcripts by scholars in the field.

16. Kathryn Weathersby, *Soviet Aims in Korea and the Origins of the Korean War: New Evidence from Russian Archives,* Working Paper 8, CWIHP (Nov. 1993), 22–24. In her excellent study, Weathersby, quoting from the testimony of retired North Korean People's Army Lt. Gen. Yu Song-chol, notes that in addition to the deliveries of arms and ammunition for the attack, the Soviets replaced the existing team of advisers with Soviet Army officers "with extensive combat experience" and prepared an operational plan for the invasion.

17. Acheson, *Present at the Creation,* 405.

18. The following quotation by Louis J. Halle in *The Cold War as History* (New York: HarperPerennial, 1991), first published in 1967, vividly conveys the shock felt in Europe at the news of the North Korean invasion: "Communist forces had attacked across the line that separated the two sides in the Cold War. . . . The satellite Army of the Communist half of Korea, in a stroke that achieved complete surprise, invaded the non-Communist half. Immediately it became plausible that the same thing might happen at any moment along the line that divided the two Germanies" (p. 189).

19. Ninkovich, *Germany and the United States,* 85. The situation was not comparable in Korea, where by late 1947 the Soviets had reduced their forces to two divisions and by 1948 had withdrawn them completely. See the study *North Korea Today,* prepared by Assistant Chiefs of Staff, G-2, US Army Forces in Korea (Nov. 1947). The authors were David E. Murphy and William J. Spahr.

20. *North Korea Today.*

21. Murphy happened to be in Pyongyang on a visit to the US liaison team with Soviet Headquarters, North Korea, when the People's Army was unveiled.

22. Matthew B. Ridgway, *The Korean War* (New York: Doubleday, 1967), 8. See also Weathersby, "New Russian Documents." In message no. 2, p. 36, Kim Il Sung asked for arms for three divisions in addition to the existing seven. Stalin approved.

23. FRUS, 1950, vol. 4, p. 697.

24. Norman M. Naimark, *"To Know Everything and to Report Everything": Building the East German Police State, 1945–49,* Working Paper 10, CWIHP (Aug. 1994), 22–24.

25. Report, no. 4749-i, 24 June 1952, SVRA file 70465, vol. 1, pp. 124–30.

26. Intelligence Memorandum, CIA to President Truman, 21 Aug. 1950, "Increased Capabilities of Paramilitary Forces in Soviet Zone Germany," Harry S. Truman Library, Records of the National Security Council. See also CIA/ORE Report, 9 Sept. 1950, "Probable Developments in Eastern Germany by the End of 1951," CIA-HRP.

27. *Die Welt,* 26 June 1950.

28. Acheson, *Present at the Creation,* 436–37.

29. William G. Hyland, *The Cold War* (New York: Times Books, 1991), 55.

30. KI Report, no. 3128/s, 31 Aug. 1950, SVRA file number n.a., pp. 272–73.

31. FRUS, 1950, vol. 4, pp. 706–9.

32. Yuri Modin, *Mes camarades de Cambridge* (Paris: Robert Laffont, 1994), 207.

33. Kondrashev.

34. KI Report, no. 27/z, 4/5 Jan. 1951, SVRA.

35. FRUS, 1950, vol. 4, pp. 730–33.

36. Modin, *Mes camarades de Cambridge,* 210.

37. National Intelligence Estimate NIE-17, 27 Dec. 1950, "Probable Soviet Reactions to a Remilitarization of Western Germany," CIA-HRP.

38. FRUS, 1950, vol. 4, pp. 698–99.

39. FRUS, 1951, vol. 3, p. 1331.

40. National Intelligence Estimate NIE-4, 1 Feb. 1951, "Soviet Courses of Action with Respect to Germany," CIA-HRP.

41. Ibid.

42. "Evaluation of the Information Work of the Berlin Residency, 1 Apr. to 30 June 1951," SVRA file 58286, vol. 1, pp. 14–31. The Russian term *dezinformator* does not necessarily imply the source was passing disinformation, merely that his information was not accurate.

43. NATO appointed General of the Army Dwight David Eisenhower Supreme Allied Commander, Europe, on 19 Dec. 1950.

44. FRUS, 1951, vol. 3, pp. 445–46.

45. KI Report, no. 733/z, 7/8 Feb. 1951, SVRA, file number n.a., pp. 70–73.

46. KI Report, no. 141/z, 9 Jan. 1951, SVRA, file number n.a., pp. 18–19. According to FRUS, 1950, vol. 4, McCloy was summoned by Adenauer on 16 Dec. 1951 to discuss Brussels. He heard Adenauer's familiar views on West German foreign policy and apparently did brief him on "positions which the US should take at Brussels regarding further steps as to Germany."

47. KI Report, no. 5508/z, 26 Sept. 1951, SVRA file 45513, vol. 4, pp. 117–22.

48. KI Report, no. 4064/z, 28 July 1951, SVRA, sent to Stalin and Politburo addressees.

49. KI Report, no. 4388, 11–12 Aug. 1951, SVRA file 45513, vol. 1, pp. 242–44.

50. KI Report, no. 3634/z, 13 July 1951, SVRA file 45513, vol. 3, pp. 199–204.

51. KI Report, no. 2208/s, 5 May 1951, SVRA file 45513, vol. 3, pp. 1–4.

52. FRUS, 1951, vol. 3, pp. 1079–81.

53. SVRA file 45513, p. 224, 24 July 1951.

54. Memorandum, General Truscott to DCI, 6 July 1951, CIA-HRP.

55. MGB Information Report, no. 7619/s, 28 Dec. 1951, SVRA file number n.a., pp. 423–25.

56. KI Report, 13 Nov. 1951, SVRA file 45513, vol. 4, pp. 286–90.

57. "Evaluation of the Information Work of the Berlin Residency, 1 Apr. to 30 June 1951," SVRA file 58286, vol. 1, pp. 14–31.

58. KI Report, no. 5/2/2716, 26 July 1951, SVRA file number n.a., pp. 225–26.

59. Report, no. 5680/s, 2 Oct. 1951, SVRA file 45513, vol. 4, pp. 139–42.

60. Report, no. 950/i, 9 Nov. 1951, SVRA file 45513, vol. 4, pp. 223–27. By this date, MGB had absorbed the foreign intelligence component of the Committee of Information. The report was signed by the new minister of state security, Semyon Denisovich Ignatiev. The distribution of this report within the foreign intelligence component still reflected the previous KI organizational structure.

61. Ibid.

62. Ibid.

63. Report no. 6212, based on a dispatch from the MGB Paris residency, SVRA file 43297, vol. 5, pp. 223–25. This unique document, a draft of the final report, translated from the French, bears the notation at the bottom of the first page "With all the usual reservations concerning the genuineness of the signatures and the sincerity of the signatories."

64. Ibid.

65. Ibid.

Chapter 5. Cold Warriors in Berlin

1. Michael Warner, ed., *Under Harry Truman* (Washington, D.C.: CIA, 1994), doc. 38. See also Arthur B. Darling, *The Central Intelligence Agency: An Instrument of Government to 1950* (University Park, Penn.: Pennsylvania State University Press, 1990), 261.

2. SVRA file 38179, vol. 5-a, pp. 213–15, 12 May 1948.

3. NARA NND 740/32 SANACC (State–Army–Navy–Air Force Coordinating Committee) 395, "Utilization of Refugees from the Soviet Union in U.S. National Interest," 17 Mar. 1948.

4. DCI Hillenkoetter, Memorandum for Executive Secretary, National Security Council, "Utilization of the Mass of Soviet Refugees," 19 Apr, 1948, CIA-HRP. This hardheaded view of émigré groups almost certainly reflected the view of many in OSO as of 1948.

5. Warner, *Under Harry Truman*, doc. 43.

6. Darling, *Central Intelligence Agency*, 280.

7. Warner, *Under Harry Truman*, doc. 47.

8. Don Huefner, interview, 17 Feb. 1995. David Murphy, who had worked in Soviet operations with OSO beginning in February 1947, was dropped into this boiling pot in fall 1950, when he was chosen to head a combined OSO-OPC Soviet operations base in Munich. It was a rare instance of OPC's agreeing that independent agent operations into the USSR made little sense given the limited pool of agent candidates and the effectiveness of Soviet counterintelligence. See also Warner, *Under Harry Truman*, xxi.

9. The energetic Henry Sutton later became identified with the notorious Bund Deutsche Jugend (BDJ), an OPC project conceived of as both a West German antidote to the GDR's Free German Youth organization and a stay-behind organization in the event West Germany was invaded from the East. See Burton Hersh, *The Old Boys* (New York: Scribners, 1992), 360–61.

10. Peter Coleman, *The Liberal Conspiracy: The Congress for Cultural Freedom and the Struggle for the Mind of Postwar Europe* (New York: Free Press, 1989), 16. See also Michael Warner, "Origins of the Congress for Cultural Freedom, 1949–50," *Studies in Intelligence* [CIA in-house journal] 38 (summer 1994): 29–38.

11. C. G. Harvey, interview, 15–16 Nov. 1993, Indianapolis. WAC Col. C. G. Follick, also on de Neufville's staff, later became an aide to General Truscott and in February 1954 married Bill Harvey, who at that time was Berlin Base chief. C.G. had entered Central Intelligence Group as a personnel officer and then served in the headquarters of OSO's Latin American division. Her insistence on an overseas posting led to her assignment with OPC Germany.

12. Richard Helms, "Richard Helms Remembers the Early Days of the CIA," *Central Intelligence Retirees Association (CIRA) Newsletter* 19, no. 3 (fall 1994): 4.

13. Gordon Stewart, interview, 6 Nov. 1993; Peter Sichel, interview, 14 Dec. 1993; Tom Polgar, interview, 19 Oct. 1993. Stewart was OSO chief of Station Germany; Peter Sichel was chief of OSO Base, Berlin; and Tom Polgar was the OSO aide to Gen. Lucian B. Truscott, first CIA senior representative, Germany.

14. Paul Haefner, interview, 22 Apr. 1994, McLean, Va.

15. KI Report, no. 1245/z, 19 Apr. 1950, signed by Zorin, SVRA file 45513, vol. 1, p. 172.

16. FRUS, 1950, vol. 4, pp. 824–25, 829–30, 844–47, 849, and 861–62.

17. KI Report no. 3509/z, 7 July 1951, signed by Zorin, file n.a. See also FRUS, 1951, vol. 3, pp. 2008–11. On 15 August, in an apparent effort to discourage visits to West Berlin by festival participants (about 500,000 had taken advantage of the hospitality centers since the festival had opened on 5 Aug.), eleven thousand FDJ members invaded the French and US sectors of Berlin. They attempted to demonstrate but were dispersed by West Berlin police. One hundred fifteen were arrested. Interrogation revealed a plan for invading West Berlin under the pretext of "accepting Mayor Reuter's invitation to visit West Berlin." See FRUS, 1951, vol. 3, pp. 2012–14.

18. Letter to DCI, 10 Feb. 1959, "Letter to DCI from Rainer Hildebrandt," CIA-HRP.

19. Report 237, 18 Dec. 1952, SVRA file 68881, vol. 2, pp. 89–117.

20. Dispatch, COB Berlin to C/EE, 6 Apr. 1959, "Press Reaction to the Dissolution of the *Kampfgruppe gegen Unmenschlichkeit*," CIA-HRP. Hildebrandt may have had the last word. In Stephan Kinzer, "Germany Warms Up to 'a Fossil of the Cold War,'" *New York Times*, 24 Aug. 1993, which describes Hildebrandt's attempts to preserve his Museum at Checkpoint Charlie, he is portrayed as a vigorous, albeit aging, human rights activist.

21. Haefner interview, 22 Apr. 1994.

22. After Trushnovich disappeared, the East German news announced that he had "fled voluntarily" after "breaking with the American secret service and the NTS." In 1992, the Russian Foreign Intelligence Service (SVR) provided the victim's son, Yaroslav A. Trushnovich, with personal effects found on the body and the results of an autopsy performed by Soviet Army doctors. The 5 Oct. 1992 SVR letter of transmittal confirmed that the kidnapping was carried out "by members of the Soviet special services which brought about his death."

23. The 9th Department, of which Khokhlov was a member, was the organizational successor to Special Bureau Number One, created by Pavel Sudoplatov. It later was designated the 13th Department and then Department V. The department was abolished after the defection of Oleg Adolfovich Lyalin in England in 1971, and its functions were absorbed in Directorate S (illegals) of KGB's First Chief Directorate.

24. George Blake was born in Rotterdam, became a member of the Dutch underground during the war, and later joined SIS. Sent to Seoul, Korea, as SIS chief of station, he was captured when the war began. He spent three years in captivity in North Korea, where he was recruited by Soviet intelligence. Blake provided the KGB with the information that compromised the Berlin Tunnel, a story told in chapter 11. See also David Chavchavadze, interview, Dec. 1993, Washington, D.C. George Blake discusses NTS in *No Other Choice* (London: Jonathan Cape, 1990), 23. Blake, interview with Kondrashev, 7 Apr. 1995, Moscow.

25. Kondrashev.

26. Dispatch, C/EE to COM Frankfurt and COB Berlin, 21 July 1954, CIA-HRP. Subsequent record checks indicated that Kopazky was dropped because he "fabricated reports." In the intelligence jungle of 1946–51 in the Munich area, padding reports to improve one's payments of cigarettes, coffee, and such was virtually standard procedure for émigré practitioners of the intelligence game.

27. William Sloane Coffin, Jr., *Once to Every Man: A Memoir* (New York: Atheneum, 1977), 86. See also Memorandum to Operational Clearance Officer from Chief, Foreign Division S, 29 May 1951, CIA-HRP.

28. Later, the SBONR rejectees attempted unsuccessfully to reactivate the project. These efforts resulted in a flurry of accusations and counteraccusations involving Orlov.

29. Cable, Berlin to Headquarters, 4 Sept. 1951, CIA-HRP. See also C/EE Dispatch to COM Frankfurt and COB Berlin, 21 July 1954, CIA-HRP.

30. SVRA, MGB Report no. 6498/i, 2 Oct. 1952.

31. Kaverznev report I/2375, 18 Dec. 1952 to S. I. Ogoltsov, SVRA file 68881, vol. 2, pp. 89–117. At the time, Ogoltsov had been appointed chief of the combined Chief Intelligence Directorate of MGB, under which came the First (foreign intelligence) Directorate and the Second (counterintelligence) Directorate. He lasted in this position only until Stalin's death the following March.

32. SVRA file 85793, vol. 19, pp. 5–71. Material taken from a section of a KGB report on West Berlin dealing with "subversive organizations."

33. Ibid.

34. Cable, Berlin to Director, 9 Feb 1954, CIA-HRP. C. D. Jackson, a former president of the National Council for Free Europe, was an enthusiastic leaflet ballooner, having participated in the first launching of RFE balloons toward Czechoslovakia in August 1951. See Sig Mickelson, *America's Other Voice: The Story of Radio Free Europe and Radio Liberty* (New York: Praeger, 1983).

35. Source of epigraph: SVRA file 85793, vol. 19.

36. Dispatch, COB Berlin via COS Karlsruhe to Chief, Foreign Division M, 16 Aug. 1950; dispatch, Chief, BOB, to Chief of Station, Karlsruhe, 9 Apr. 1951, CIA-HRP. Polgar interview.

37. Ibid.

38. The plan was drawn up by Yevgeny Ignatievich Kravtsov, head of the Austro-German department, approved by Lt. Gen. Pyotr Vasilievich Fedotov, deputy chief of the foreign intelligence directorate, and countersigned by the directorate chief, Sergei Romanovich Savchenko. Creation of the kidnapping team and local planning was left to the head of the MGB apparat in Karlshorst, Lt. Gen. Mikhail Kirilovich Kaverznev. See Peter Deriabin, *The Secret World* (New York: Doubleday, 1959), 188–93. The working conditions at Wismut and their political effects on the SED regime are described in detail in Norman M. Naimark, *The Russians in Germany: A History of the Soviet Zone of Occupation, 1945–1949* (Cambridge: Belknap Press of Harvard University Press, 1995), 238–50.

39. SVRA file 70465, vol. 1, pp. 138–39.

40. Ibid.

41. There are several reasons for suspecting that this secretary had already become an agent of the MGB. The post-Linse kidnapping investigation revealed that the circumstances of her earlier arrival in West Berlin as a refugee and of her employment with the Free Jurists were suspicious. In addition, the MGB report to Molotov et al. on the Linse case and the campaign against the Congress of International Jurists has a portion excised immediately following the name of the secretary. Furthermore, the twenty-four hours that elapsed between her "defection" and the

publication of her accusatory letter would not have been adequate to debrief her and then prepare the letter. Also, defections from West to East in the Berlin of the early 1950s were rare.

42. Berlin OPC dispatch, 8 Aug. 1952, "International Congress of Jurists and Soviet Zone Show Trials," CIA-HRP.

43. SVRA file 70465, vol. 1, pp. 176–79, MGB Report no. 5577/i, 11 Aug. 1952. In describing the abduction of Dr. Linse, Soviet documents normally used either *vyvod* (removal) or *izyatie* (withdrawal). It is surprising that the word *pokhishchenie* (kidnapping, or abduction), which implies a criminal and not a political act, was inserted in the MGB report.

44. Ibid. Incidentally, according to Report, Chief, EE Division, to the DDP, 5 Aug. 1952, CIA-HRP, a resolution by the Netherlands delegate to the Congress was adopted condemning the kidnapping of Dr. Linse.

45. See 11 Aug. 1952 MGB report on Linse. See also Walter Sullivan, "U.S. Again Protests Berlin Kidnapping," *New York Times,* 7 Aug. 1952.

46. "Soviet Returns Food U.S. Sent to Dr. Linse," *New York Times,* Berlin ed., 11 Dec.1952.

47. West Berlin Police Report, Berlin, 13 Nov. 1952, "Background Material on the Kidnapping of Dr. Linse." This report was made available to the press by Dr. Johannes Stumm, president of the West Berlin Police. See "Kidnapped German in Jail in East as Soviet Chief Feigned Ignorance," *New York Times,* 14 Nov. 1952.

48. Dispatch, to COB Berlin, 24 Feb. 1956, "Walter Linse"; Dispatch to EE Division, 6 June 1956, CIA-HRP.

49. Report, Kaverznev to Ignatiev, 3 Mar. 1953, SVRA.

50. "Soviet Says Kidnapped German Died in a Russian Prison in 1953," *New York Times,* Berlin ed., 8 June 1960. In its article on the German Red Cross story, the *New York Herald Tribune* recalled that the Linse kidnapping was "as brutally efficient as it was brazen" ("Kidnapped Linse Died in Red Jail," 9 June 1960).

51. Confidential interview, 1 Mar. 1995, and Walter O'Brien, interviews, 15 Aug. 1994, 23 Mar. 1995, former BOB CE branch chief.

52. Warner, *Under Harry Truman,* doc. 73.

53. Ibid., docs. 78 and 79.

54. Memorandum for Chief, EE, from Henry Hecksher, "Amendment No. 3 to Project," 12 May 1952, CIA-HRP.

55. Report, Kaverznev to Ignatiev, 3 Mar. 1953, SVRA. Referred to by Kaverznev as Department D, the new unit was to create agent nets in East Germany to support military operations "planned by the Americans."

56. Memorandum, C/EE to DDP, 12 Oct. 1953, "German Mission Investigation of the Arrest of Soviet Zone Members of the CIA-Sponsored Stay-Behind Resistance Network," CIA-HRP.

57. Memorandum, Thomas Polgar (then in EE Division at CIA Headquarters) to C/EE Division, 15 Aug. 1957, CIA-HRP.

58. Berlin ADN (East German News Service) to East Germany, 25 June 1958.

59. *Der Spiegel,* 16 July 1958, pp. 35–36.

60. Harro Lippe-Gaus, "Theo Friedenau and His Investigating Committee," *Frankfurter Allgemeine Zeitung,* 19 July 1958.

Chapter 6. East German State Security and Intelligence Services Are Born

1. Comparisons are inexact, but it is generally accepted that the East German Ministry of State Security was far larger than the Nazi Gestapo. For example, the Gestapo employed one official for every 10,000 citizens, whereas by the time of the regime's collapse, MfS had one officer for every 200 East Germans.

2. Kondrashev, memorandum, 28 Mar. 1994, drawn from KGB German department historical material.

3. Ibid.

4. For a detailed description of the development of East German police and security services from 1945 to 1949 see Norman M. Naimark, *The Russians in Germany: A History of the Soviet*

Zone of Occupation, 1945–1949 (Cambridge: Belknap Press of Harvard University Press, 1995), 353–97. Be aware that many of the activities attributed therein to "NKVD/MVD" were in fact the work of the operational sectors and groups of the USSR Ministry of State Security (MGB), under the direction of the minister's representative in Germany, Lt. Gen. Nikolai Ivanovich Kovalchuk, who also held the rank of deputy MGB minister because of the importance of the position.

5. Maj. Gen. Melnikov to Abakumov, no. MK/23959, 10 Oct. 1949, SVRA file 68881, pp. 37–41.

6. Letter no. 12, 7 Jan. 1950, SVRA file 68881, pp. 153–55. The content of the Chuikov-Semyonov letter was repeated to the chief of the MGB Second (counterintelligence) Chief Directorate, E. P. Pitovranov, by MGB Apparat Berlin. The distribution of this communication to Stalin suggests that it had considerable importance. In addition to Stalin, it went to Molotov, Beria, Mikoyan, Kaganovich, Bulganin, Vyshinsky, Vasilevsky, Abakumov, Sokolovsky, Shtemenko, Gromyko, and Zorin.

7. Melnikov to Abakumov, no. MK/23959, SVRA file 68881, pp. 37–41.

8. Transcription, "V Ch" from MGB representative in Berlin, Maj. Gen. Melnikov, to Chief, MGB USSR Second Chief Directorate, E. P. Pitovranov, 5 Feb. 1950, SVRA file 68881, p. 171. V Ch was a telephone speech secrecy system in use in the USSR and Soviet occupied areas. This message, like some others, was prepared in advance and transcribed by a stenographer at the receiving end. More often, V Ch was used for urgent business and either no record was kept or brief notes were taken that were often later destroyed.

9. This is Kondrashev's view. He worked with Mielke until the collapse of the GDR regime.

10. Kondrashev.

11. SVRA file 68881, vol. 1, pp. 184–87.

12. Kondrashev. For background on dismissals of Austrian CP agents see CIA Information Report, 22 Mar. 1954, CIA-HRP.

13. SVRA file 68881, vol. 1, pp. 214–21.

14. Ibid.

15. Ibid.

16. Ibid.

17. For example, Herbert Wehner, then a member of the German Communist diaspora in Moscow, reported on his German comrades to the Comintern official, Georgi Dimitrov, who would in turn hand them over to the NKVD. Kondrashev.

18. Kondrashev.

19. SVRA file 68881, vol. 2, pp. 89–117.

20. Ibid.

21. Ibid. Ogoltsov had been named acting minister after Abakumov's arrest in 1951 but then was replaced by Semyon Denisovich Ignatiev. From December 1952, as deputy minister, he was responsible for the Chief Directorate of MGB, which in accordance with Stalin's decision of Nov. 1951 combined the foreign intelligence and counterintelligence directorates.

22. SVRA file 68881, vol. 2, pp. 89–117.

23. SVRA file 68881, vol. 3, pp. 1–4.

24. Ibid.

25. SVRA file 68881, vol. 3, pp. 21–28, sec. 9.

26. Decision of the KI Collegium, "O Sozdanii Predstavitelstva Kollegii Pri Vneshnepolitich-skoi Razvedke GDR," 19 July 1951, SVRA.

27. Kondrashev.

28. Peter Siebenmorgen, *"Staatssicherheit" der DDR* (Bonn: Bouvier Verlag, 1993), 111–12.

29. Markus Wolf, Chronology, 11 Oct. 1973, CIA-HRP.

30. For background on this case see Comment by EE Division Desk Officer, 14 Mar. 1952, CIA-HRP.

31. Dispatch, EE Division to BOB, 17 Sept. 1952, CIA-HRP.

32. Ibid. Also Walter O'Brien, interviews, 15 Aug. 1994, 2 Mar. 1995. O'Brien was chief of BOB's counterespionage branch and principal handler of this source.

33. Richard Meier, *Geheimdienst Ohne Maske* (Bergische Gladback, FRG: Gustav Luebbe Verlag, 1992), 157–59.

34. Dispatch, EE Division to BOB, 9 Apr. 1957, CIA-HRP.

35. Extract from report of IWF Staff Meeting, 2 Feb. 1953 (first meeting chaired by Markus Wolf following his appointment as chief), CIA-HRP.

36. Extract from report, "Special Staff Meeting, IWF, 7 Mar. 1953," CIA-HRP.

37. Memorandum, Acting DDP, Richard Helms, to DCI, 10 Apr. 1953, CIA-HRP. In the interval before the arrests were to take place, BOB attempted, vainly, to secure by telephone the defection of two of the Soviet advisers.

38. David J. Dallin, *Soviet Espionage* (New Haven: Yale University Press, 1955), 334–43, plus numerous articles from the period in the Ullstein Archive, such as the article in the 22 Apr. 1953 issue of *Der Spiegel*, which named Wolf.

39. Berlin Dispatch to EE Division, 16 Jan. 1953, CIA-HRP. This dispatch, which described the contents of six rolls of film passed to BOB by the source on 5 January 1953, included the details of information obtained by IWF on various aspects of interzonal trade—for example, reported discussions between the East German Deutsche Notenbank and the Bank of England. The latter was allegedly interested in direct contact with GDR trading circles but wished to "keep these discussions secret."

40. Kondrashev.

41. Wollweber, a sailor who took part in the 1917 Kiel mutiny of the Imperial German Navy, became a member of the German Communist Party and a member of the party faction in the Reichstag. He gained fame after Hitler seized power by organizing maritime sabotage operations. Arrested by the Swedes in 1940, he was released as a result of Soviet intervention and spent the remaining war years in the Soviet Union. See Dallin, *Soviet Espionage,* 372. See also Pavel Sudoplatov et al., *Special Tasks* (Boston: Little, Brown, 1994), 25.

Chapter 7. Stalin Offers Peace, but the Cold War Continues

1. Gerhard Wettig, "Stalin and German Reunification: Archival Evidence on Soviet Foreign Policy in Spring 1952," *The Historical Journal* 37, no. 2 (1994): 411–19. This article relies heavily on documents found in AVPRF. According to the 10 Mar. 1952 note, "the conclusion of a German peace treaty will establish stable conditions of peace for the German people, will be conducive to the development of Germany as a united, independent, democratic and peace-loving state in accordance with the Potsdam decisions."

2. CIA National Intelligence Estimate, NIE-53-1, published 1 May 1952, CIA-HRP.

3. Wettig, "Stalin and German Reunification."

4. SVRA file 45513, vol. 5, pp. 93–98.

5. Ibid., pp. 103–5. This report on the 18 Dec. 1951 cabinet meeting may have been taken from a 23 Dec. 1951 note from Transport Minister Seebohm to FDP Land chairmen in which he adds the thought that "Adenauer will find himself in a horrible dead end since the German people will be content if remilitarization never takes place."

6. SVRA file 53272, vol. 1, pp. 162–98. Zorin's comments suggest that one of the purposes of the 10 Mar. 1952 "peace treaty" proposal was to delay or block action on West German participation in European defense.

7. SVRA file 45513, vol. 5, pp. 285–88.

8. Report no. 4285/1, 11 May 1952, SVRA file n.a., pp. 324–40.

9. At the Nineteenth Party Congress, which opened on 5 Oct. 1952, the Politburo was abolished and an enlarged Presidium was created. See also SVRA file 45531, vol. 6, pp. 192–93. The report was signed by USSR Minister of State Security Ignatiev. The source was not given.

10. SVRA file 45513, vol. 6, pp. 133–45.

11. *New York Times,* 15 July 1952.

12. The minutes of this meeting were taken from the Archive of the President of the Russian Federation (APRF). Both the minutes of the 7 April 1952 meeting sourced to APRF, fond 45, opis

1, delo 303, list 179, and the notes taken by Wilhelm Pieck at this meeting are cited in the CWIHP *Bulletin* 4 (fall 1994), 34, 35, 48.

13. CIA Information Reports on East Germany from 3, 5, and 10 Dec. 1952; 26 Jan. 1953; and 4, 6 Mar. 1953, CIA-HRP.

14. Report no. 1586/i, 13 Mar. 1953, from E. P. Pitovranov to G. M. Pushkin, with copies to Siomonchuk and the Fifteenth (information) Department of the Intelligence Directorate (RU) of the Chief Intelligence Directorate (GRU), SVRA.

15. Georgy Alekseevich Korotia, interview with Kondrashev, 17 Dec. 1994, Moscow. Korotia served in Germany in various capacities in the field of counterintelligence.

16. SVRA file 45513, vol. 6, pp. 133–45.

17. These exclaves (enclaves, according to the GDR) were parcels of territory that had legally belonged to Berlin even though they were outside the city's boundaries. Perhaps most famous of these was the village of Steinstuecken near the American sector border. Access was maintained to this exclave even after the creation of the Wall in 1961, first by helicopter and later by a narrow road, surrounded on both sides by barriers.

18. Ibid.

19. Memorandum, to DDP, 9 July 1952, "Evacuation of Berlin," CIA-HRP.

20. Memorandum, Lyman B. Kirkpatrick, Assistant Director, Special Operations (ADSO), via Deputy Director (Plans), to DCI, 23 June 1952, "Berlin Coordination," CIA-HRP.

Chapter 8. Soviet Intelligence Falters After Stalin's Death

1. In William J. Tomson's words, "Unauthorized pursuit of a *rapprochement* with Tito had been one of the charges against Beria in 1953. By 1955, however, Khrushchev decided he must come to terms with Tito." See Tomson, *Khrushchev: A Political Life* (New York: St. Martin's, 1995), 155.

2. Beria's reputation as a secret police chief is so firmly embedded in the history of the Soviet era that it is difficult to remember that from 1946 until Stalin's death he was absorbed with developing first the atomic and then the hydrogen bomb. He was, of course, aware of Stalin's manipulation of the services and their leaders (Abakumov's case was an example), and he undoubtedly recognized that his turn might come. Still, he was not sufficiently familiar with service personnel and problems to have embarked on the crash program undertaken in Mar.–June 1953 to reshape and dominate the state security apparatus.

3. The "Boy Diplomat" was Richard Helms, then chief of operations, DDP; "The Black Prince" was James Angleton, chief of the CI Staff; and the "Bishop" was Gordon Stewart, then deputy chief of the German mission. This and other background on Harvey comes from his wife, C.G., and CIA retirees who served with him in Berlin.

4. Report no. 768/i, 23 Feb. 1953, SVRA file 45513, vol. 7, pp. 105–6. Volkogonov notes that Stalin had not felt well during the last week of February 1953, and in fact had not been himself since his return from Sochi a month or so earlier. Stalin's infirmity may explain why Ignatiev omitted him from the list of recipients. Dmitrii Volkogonov, *Triumf i tragediia: Politicheskii portret I. V. Stalina* (Moscow: Novosti, 1989), bk. 2, pt. 2, p. 191.

5. Report no. 1572/p, 13 Mar. 1953, SVRA file 45513, vol. 7, pp. 120–21. See also Pavel Sudoplatov et al., *Special Tasks* (Boston: Little, Brown, 1994), 341. Directorate designations can cause confusion here. In December 1952, after the abolition of the Committee of Information, Stalin created within MGB a Chief Directorate of Intelligence (GRU) of which the First Directorate was foreign intelligence and the Second Directorate was internal counterintelligence. When Beria amalgamated MGB and MVD into MVD, the foreign intelligence directorate was designated the "Second Chief Directorate" of the new MVD, and counterintelligence became the "First Chief Directorate," thus marking a break with NKGB-MGB tradition in which foreign intelligence had always been the "first" directorate.

6. Report no. 1684/r, 19 Mar. 1953, signed by Ryasnoi, SVRA file 45513, vol. 7, pp. 130–32. See also Peter Deriabin, *The Secret World* (New York: Doubleday, 1959), 216–17, and Sudoplatov et al., *Special Tasks*, 359.

7. Amy Knight, "Beria the Reformer," *New York Times,* 3 Nov. 1993. See also James Richter, *Reexamining Soviet Policy Towards Germany During the Beria Interregnum,* Working Paper 3, CWIHP, June 1992, p. 13. In his study of this period, Richter drew on "Delo Beria" (Stenographic report of the July 1953 Plenum), *Izvestiia TsK KPSS 1–2,* Moscow (Jan.–Feb. 1991): 140–214, esp. 147–208, which reflects the events leading up to Beria's arrest from the point of view of the new, collective leadership.

8. Kondrashev, bill of indictment *(obvinitel'noe zakliuchenie)* on case no. 0029-53. According to Kondrashev, the transfer of the investigative files relating to the indictment was made because of numerous requests received by the prosecutor for information on their cases by those individuals or their relatives who were somehow involved.

9. Ibid., vol. 8, p. 29; vol. 3, pp. 140–41.

10. Report no. 708/i, signed by MGB Minister Ignatiev, 19 Feb. 1953, SVRA file 45513, vol. 7, pp. 97–99. This same source advised that leading SED officials like Rudolf Herrnstadt and Gerhard Eisler were already under surveillance and that purges were planned against others in the GDR intelligentsia. Here again, the report was distributed to Beria, Malenkov, Bulganin, and Khrushchev but *not* to Stalin.

11. Report, no. 44/B, to the Presidium of the CC CPSU, signed by L. Beria, 6 May 1953, SVRA file 3581, vol. 7.

12. Ibid.

13. Ibid. The sentence noting that the CC SED "falsely" assumes "that as long as free circulation exists between West Berlin and the GDR, such flights are inevitable" strongly suggests that even then the SED leadership was attempting to influence the Soviets to close the border, an action that would not be taken until August 1961.

14. Ibid.

15. Evidence for the proposals made by Beria suggesting the abandonment of "socialism" in the GDR comes from Molotov as cited by James Richter, *Reexamining Soviet Policy Towards Germany.* The Molotov quotations are taken from Feliks Chuev, *Sto Sorok Besed s Molotvym* (One hundred forty conversations with Molotov) (Moscow: Terra, 1991). No documentary record of what actually occurred at this meeting has been located that would clarify Beria's position and that of others on the German question.

16. "Ein Dokument von grosser historischer Bedeutung vom Mai 1953," *Beiträge zur Geschichte der Arbeiterbewegung* 32, no. 5 (1990): 648–54. As cited by James Richter, *Reexamining Soviet Policy Towards Germany,* 9.

17. Kondrashev, who added, "If it could be shown that such reports had actually reached certain leaders, who then did nothing, the very existence of such reports would have constituted an accusation. At this point, it is difficult to imagine who could have wanted such reports destroyed other than the victor in this duel to the death, Nikita Sergeevich Khrushchev."

18. Bill of indictment, p. 118, vol. 7, pp. 65, 74, 64.

19. Ibid.

20. Ibid.

21. Dispatch, SR Division to German Station, 9 Sept. 1953, CIA-HRP.

22. Bill of indictment.

23. Ibid.

24. Deriabin, *Secret World,* 169–70. Deriabin, who was in the German department of the foreign intelligence directorate at this time, recalls hearing that Beria intended later to rebuild the MVD apparat in the GDR to a new strength of 3,600.

25. Vasily Ilich Bulda, interview with Kondrashev, 5 Jan. 1995, Moscow.

26. Biographic Summary, undated, "Medvedev, Pavel Nikolaevich (Col)," CIA-HRP.

27. Bulda interview, 5 Jan. 1995.

28. Yevgeny Viktorovich Berezin, interview with Kondrashev, 4 May 1995, Moscow.

29. Leonid Yemelianovich Siomonchuk, interview with Kondrashev, 24 Oct. 1994, Moscow.

30. *Sovetskaia voennaia entsiklopediia,* vol. 3 (Moscow: Voenizdat, 1976), pp. 48–49, and vol. 8 (Moscow: Voenizdat, 1980), pp. 486–87.

31. Nadja Stulz-Herrnstadt, ed., *Rudolf Herrnstadt—Das Herrnstadt-Dokument: Das Polit-buro der SED und die Geschichte des 17. Juni 1953* (Hamburg: Rowohlt, 1990), 74. Herrnstadt was an important witness to the events of 17 June and their relation to the Beria case, not only because of his position within the SED Politburo but also because of his ties with the Soviets arising from his wartime work with Soviet intelligence. He was married to a Russian and spoke Russian fluently.

32. The events, actions, and editorials described in this paragraph are taken from James Richter, *Reexamining Soviet Policy Towards Germany*, and Christian F. Ostermann, *The United States, the East German Uprising of 1953, and the Limits of Rollback*, Working Paper 11, CWIHP, Dec. 1994.

Chapter 9. The Events of June 1953

1. Yevgeny Pitovranov, interview with Igor Vladimirov, of RIA "Novosti" and published in *Globus*, 17 Jan. 1993.

2. "The uprising of the construction workers in Berlin was almost completely unexpected. Unexpected because at that time neither the state security organs of the GDR nor our Berlin *apparat* had received any signals from sources concerning the preparation of these events." From an unpublished manuscript prepared by Kondrashev in connection with the fortieth anniversary of the 17 June 1953 events.

3. A description of these events from the Soviet viewpoint is contained in "The Report to the Soviet Leadership (To Comrade V. M. Molotov, N. A. Bulganin): On the events of 17–19 June 1953 in Berlin and GDR and certain conclusions from these events." Dated 24 June, it was signed by V. Sokolovsky, V. Semyonov, and P. Yudin. The document is quoted in "New Documents on the East German Uprising of 1953," in the Cold War International History Project *Bulletin* no. 5 (spring 1995), with an introduction and commentary by Christian Ostermann.

4. SVRA. This report was selected by Kondrashev from a file to which he obtained access in December 1996. The file came from a former KGB archival repository in the Urals area. Beginning in March 1953, the file no longer contained documents for the period mid-March to mid-June 1953, roughly from Stalin's death until the 16–17 June events in East Berlin. Kondrashev believes they were destroyed.

5. See Ostermann, "New Documents on the East German Uprising of 1953," for a recent treatment of these events. Two important documents cited in this article are the 24 June 1953 report to Molotov and Bulganin by Marshal V. Sokolovsky, High Commissioner V. Semyonov, and Deputy High Commissioner P. Yudin, and the 20 July 1953 report to the SED Central Committee on the events.

6. According to Ostermann in his "New Documents on the East German Uprising," the report of this cruise came from the East German Ministry of State Security, which must have been Kuchin's source.

7. Ibid. The official 24 June 1953 Soviet "after action" report claims that East German state security had information as of 14 June that strikes were planned but did not pass this on to the Soviet Control Commission. Kuchin's report contradicts this.

8. Ibid. In their letter, the workers claimed that "the increases in work norms had become necessary because the GDR government had decided to return property to the capitalists and kulaks but had insufficient funds to cover this [action]."

9. Ibid.

10. Ibid.

11. Ibid.

12. Ibid.

13. Col. I. A. Fadeikin, by V Ch to MVD Moscow, 12:25 P.M., 17 June 1953, SVRA.

14. Christopher Andrew and Oleg Gordievsky, *KGB: The Inside Story* (New York: Harper-Collins, 1990), 423.

15. Fadeikin to MVD Moscow, 17 June 1953.

16. Ibid.
17. Ibid.
18. Ibid.
19. Ibid.
20. See Ostermann, "New Documents on the East German Uprising."
21. This "telephonogram" sent by the speech secrecy system V Ch was the first of several that would be sent by Semyonov, or by Semyonov together with Marshal Sokolovsky or General Grechko, during the 17 June events and their immediate aftermath. They are taken from AVP SSSR, fond Secretariat Molotov, opis 12a, por. 200, papka 51, MID SSSR, Secretariat of the Minister V. M. Molotov, 1953, Secret, 17.6.53–20.6.53 and were cited in Hope Harrison, "The Bargaining Power of Weaker Allies in Bipolarity and Crisis: Soviet-East German Relations, 1953–1961," Ph.D. diss., Columbia University, 1993. We are grateful to Ms. Harrison for providing the Russian texts of these messages.
22. Particulars with regard to Marshals Sokolovsky and Govorov are taken from the Voennyi entsiklopedicheskii slovar' (Moscow 1983).
23. Harrison, "Bargaining Power."
24. CIA Information Report, "Closing of the Berlin Borders," 18 June 1953. CIA-HRP.
25. Tom Polgar, interview, 13 Oct. 1993, and interviews with other former BOB officers who served in Berlin at the time.
26. Christian F. Ostermann, The United States, the East German Uprising of 1953, and the Limits of Rollback, Working Paper 11, CWIHP, Dec. 1994, pp. 18–19. Apparently, this story first appeared in Thomas Powers, The Man Who Kept the Secrets (New York: Knopf, 1979), and has been repeated in numerous books, Ph.D. dissertations, and articles since. A more recent article on this subject by Christian Ostermann repeats the same charge but in an end note refers to a 17 Mar. 1995 letter to the author from Tom Polgar, who "claims that 'no cable seeking permission to provide the rioters with arms was ever sent.' Hecksher 'would never have sent such a foolish cable. Had he done so, the then Chief of Station . . . would have relieved Hecksher and sent him home.'" See Ostermann, "Keeping the Pot Simmering: The United States and the East German Uprising of 1953" German Studies Review 19, no. 1 (Feb. 1996): 61–89.
27. Polgar interview; Peter Sichel, interview, 14 Dec. 1993; and Gordon Stewart, interview, 6 Nov. 1993. In addition, Murphy interviewed, either personally or by telephone, and corresponded with eighteen former base officers who served in Berlin at the time.
28. Memorandum, 18 June 1953, from Frank G. Wisner, Deputy Director for Plans, to John Bross, "Developments in East Germany: Overt and Covert Propaganda," CIA-HRP. The "high-level consideration" referred to by Wisner which took place earlier on the 18 June was the meeting of the National Security Council. At this meeting, Allen Dulles stated that "the United States had nothing whatsoever to do with inciting these riots and that our reaction so far had been to confine ourselves . . . to expressions of sympathy and admiration" (FRUS, 1952–54, vol. 7, p. 1587).
29. Nadja Stulz-Herrnstadt, ed., Rudolf Herrnstadt—Das Herrnstadt-Dokument: Das Politburo der SED und die Geschichte des 17 Juni 1953 (Hamburg: Rowohlt, 1990), 87–88. But in their 24 June report to Molotov and Bulganin, Semyonov and Sokolovsky downplayed this aspect and placed the blame more specifically on Ulbricht.
30. SVRA file 68881, vol. 2, pp. 328–29.
31. Ibid.
32. Ibid.
33. Ibid. When the Goglidze group was sent to Karlshorst, many of the senior apparat personnel returned as well. As we can see in the cases of Vasily Morgachev, formerly an adviser to the IWF (later Markus Wolf's HVA) and Col. Yevgeny Kravtsov, then chief of the German department, these special units compromised some of the MVD's most experienced officers in German affairs.
34. Ibid.
35. Ibid.
36. Ibid.

37. Ibid. The exact status of Amaiak Kobulov at this juncture is not clear, but from the wording of the document it seems that he had not yet been formally named chief of the apparat. Because this position carried with it the rank of deputy MVD minister and would have required Presidium approval, he may not yet have made it, and with Beria's demise, never would.

38. Ibid.

39. Enciphered telegrams sh/t No 17794/1384 of 28 June 1953 from Paris, SVRA file 6881, pp. 204–6.

40. Ibid. The source of this report was a French journalist who happened to be in Berlin on 17 June and allegedly visited the Soviet sector with a colleague, Arno Scholtz, editor of the SPD newspaper *Der Telegraf.*

41. Archives of the General Department, Secretariat CC CPSU.

42. 24 June report to Molotov and Bulganin. One of these recommendations, the liquidation of the GDR ministry of state security and its transfer to the ministry of internal affairs, did survive Beria's departure.

43. Amy Knight, *Beria: Stalin's First Lieutenant* (Princeton, N.J.: Princeton University Press, 1993), 194–99.

44. Memorandum No 965/t, 29 June 1953. SVRA file 55331, vol. 1, pp. 269–87.

45. Pavel Sudoplatov et al., *Secret Tasks* (Boston: Little, Brown, 1994), 370. See also CIA Information Report, 30 July 1956, "Arrest of S. A. Goglidze and Amayak Kobulov in Berlin," CIA-HRP.

46. 30 June 1953 telephonogram to MVD Moscow from Fedotov and Fadeikin in East Berlin. SVRA.

47. An excellent description of the key elements of this plenum can be found in Knight, *Beria: Stalin's First Lieutenant,* 203–10, which was taken from issues 1 and 2 (1991) of *Izvestiia TsK KPSS.*

48. *Pravda,* 10 July 1953.

49. Stulz-Herrnstadt, *Rudolf Herrnstadt.*

50. CIA Information Report, 24 Feb. 1955, "Organization of the Soviet Intelligence Organs," pp. 7, 8, CIA-HRP.

51. Ostermann, *The United States,* pp. 25–33.

52. SVRA file 70485, vol. 2, Kruglov to Molotov, Report 411/k, 7 Aug. 1953.

53. Memorandum from John A. Bross, Chief, EE Division, for the DCI, 11 Aug. 1953, "Proposal for Establishing Food Depots along Zonal Boundaries," CIA-HRP.

54. Kruglov to Molotov, Report no. 411/k, 7 Aug. 1953, SVRA file 70435, vol. 2.

Chapter 10. The Mysterious Case of Otto John

1. Berlin Operations Base's own report on the John case was summarized in an undated memorandum for the CIA Headquarters Foreign Intelligence Staff, CIA-HRP.

2. Robert S. Allen, "CIA Faces Are Red Over Dr. John," *New York Post,* 11 Aug. 1954.

3. Otto John, *Twice Through the Lines* (New York: Harper and Row, 1972). A preface to the original German version, *Zweimal kam ich heim,* published in 1965, was written by Bonde-Henryksen.

4. Hans Frederik, *Das Ende einer Legende* (Munich: Selbstverlag, 1971). See also Guenter Bohnsack and Herbert Brehmer, *Auftrag: Irreführung: Wie die Stasi Politik im Westen Machte* (Hamburg: Carlsen, 1992). "Fredy," as a West German publisher, was given manuscripts to publish under various pseudonyms by Department X, the active measures element of HVA/MfS. He also appeared as the author of some items, including the John book.

5. Christoph Maria Froehder, *Ich will nicht als Verräter sterben: Der Fall Otto John,* transcript of Hessischer Rundfunk TV broadcast, 28 Nov. 1993.

6. Summary of Material Concerning Otto John *(Spravka po materialam v otnoshenii IONA Otto),* prepared by SVR in summer 1993 from the John file in SVRA. Provided by Kondrashev.

7. Undated (probably early Aug. 1993) SVR memorandum containing guidelines for retired KGB officers being interviewed by German TV on Otto John case. Provided by Kondrashev.

8. File Summary, S. A. Kondrashev, 24 Apr. 1994, based on a review of the John file, SVRA file 76863. The summary contains numerous extracts from documents in the file.

9. Canaris opposed Hitler and allowed Abwehr to be used to support resistance to the Nazi regime. He was removed from his post in February 1944 and executed by the SS in early April 1945.

10. Lochner did know Otto John well. When he left Germany in 1942, Lochner went to Spain, but his German wife remained in Berlin. John, who made frequent trips to Madrid for Lufthansa, helped Lochner and his wife maintain contact. Robert Lochner, interview with Bailey, Mar. 1995, Berlin.

11. SVRA file 36514, vol. 1, pp. 187–91. See Phillip Knightley, *The Master Spy* (New York: Knopf, 1989), 108–9, for comments on Philby's views of the German wartime resistance and John in particular. Through its penetrations of OSS, NKGB may also have learned of OSS's interest in John as a representative of German resistance. See Juergen Heideking and Christof Mauch, *American Intelligence and German Resistance* (Boulder, Colo.: Westview, 1996), doc. 34, 27 Jan. 1944, pp. 191–92, in which Allen Dulles notes that "for a number of reasons" he has not discussed these resistance matters with British intelligence, and doc. 44, 1 June 1944, pp. 222–23, in which John provides an OSS representative in Madrid with a letter for former Chancellor Heinrich Bruening from a resistance group composed of remnants of the German Socialist and Catholic Center parties.

12. The extent of this Soviet paranoia concerning SIS is best illustrated in Genrikh Borovik, *The Philby Files* (London: Little, Brown, 1994). He described how NKGB foreign intelligence directorate officials handling Kim Philby were afraid to tell Stalin that there were no active SIS agent networks in the USSR—given that for years Stalin had accused scores of officials of collaboration with "English intelligence."

13. Peter Deriabin, *The Secret World* (New York: Doubleday, 1959), 196–97. According to Deriabin, "In 1952 a Soviet agent who had been planted inside the Office for the Defense of the Constitution came up with further tantalizing information. He suggested that John, the well-known resistance fighter, had actually had some dealings with the Nazis."

14. Karpov, on page 543 of Frederik's account of their interview, described a Soviet source in BfV as John's secretary, Vera Schwarte. Before working for John, Schwarte had worked in Abwehr for Canaris. She had begun to work for the Soviets after the war and had been sent to the West under refugee cover to seek a job with John. See also Dispatch to Acting Chief Station, Karlshorst, 28 Mar. 1951, "Wera Schwarte," CIA-HRP, detailing her Canaris connections, arrest and imprisonment by the Gestapo, and subsequent detention by the "Russians" in December 1945. This information was given to Peter Sichel by source "Gertie" on 18 Jan. 1946. In his *Twice Through the Lines,* John himself noted that Kuchin was able to show him copies of BfV reports "not yet three weeks old," which he believed indicated a Soviet penetration of BfV. But John did not suggest who he thought the source might be.

15. Kondrashev recalls that Kuchin's German was so fluent that once, when he took over an agent from another KGB officer, the agent complained about being turned over to a German. Because of suspicion and resentment voiced by many senior KGB officials over Kuchin's expertise in things German, he never rose above the rank of colonel.

16. In the account given to Hans Frederik by Kuchin/Karpov, it was said that John was taken to "a villa in Weissensee." But because KGB had moved from Weissensee to Karlshorst a few years earlier, the version in the dossier extracted by Kondrashev is probably correct.

17. SVRA file 76863, vol. 1, p. 5. Per Kondrashev, the statements concerning the circumstances of John's trip to East Berlin were taken from Kuchin's V Ch (secure telephone) conversations.

18. Inspectorate *(Inspektsiia)* was one of the several cover terms used to designate the KGB apparat in Berlin-Karlshorst.

19. SVRA file 76863, vol. 1, p. 68.

20. Report, transmitted by enciphered telegram, 10 Sept. 1954, no. 2/1277, SVRA file 76863, vol. 1, p. 109.

21. Willi Frischauer, *The Man Who Came Back: The Story of Otto John* (London: Frederick Mullet, 1958), 171.

22. Froehder, *Ich will nicht als Verräter sterben.*

23. SVR Memorandum on Max Wonsig provided by Kondrashev.

24. Frischauer, *Man Who Came Back,* 254. Testifying was Alexander von Hase, whose father had been commandant of the Berlin Garrison in 1944 and had been executed as a member of the 20 July plot.

25. The claim concerning the absence of medical or psychological pressure was made by Kondrashev in amplification of statements contained in the John dossier summary. For Pitovranov's statement, see Froehder, *Ich will nicht als Verräter sterben.*

26. Froehder, *Ich will nicht als Verräter sterben.* According to Kondrashev, only Kuchin and Cherniavsky were involved—no "psychological experts."

27. Christoph Froehder, interview with Bailey, 3 June 1994, Frankfurt am Main. Kondrashev later spoke with Cherniavsky, who said he was misunderstood. According to George Bailey, however, Cherniavsky stood by his position that John went voluntarily to Karlshorst but did not so remain. Cherniavsky repeated that position to German journalists Ernst Leiser in 1995 and Wolf Gephardt of *Focus* magazine in 1996 and in a letter written to John in February 1995.

28. *Novoe Vremia* 42 (1992).

29. Froehder interview, 3 June 1994. An interesting sidelight on doing business in the Moscow of 1993 was Colonel Prelin's offer to sell the KGB John file for DM 30,000. Froehder turned it down.

30. In his 1969 account, given to Hans Frederik to counter John's version of events, Kuchin/Karpov stated that John was completely drunk, vomiting so badly that a doctor was called to administer medication to sober him up. Thus, one man's "hangover cure" is another man's "sedation."

31. Frederik, *Das Ende einer Legende.*

32. SVRA file 76863, vol. 1, p. 21.

33. SVRA file 77403, vol. 1, p. 272. The results of the press conference appeared in SVRA file 76863, vol. 1, p. 47.

34. John, *Twice Through the Lines.* The information on Pitovranov's mother was taken from BOB Debriefing Report, 22 Sept. 1955, CIA-HRP.

35. Ibid. Aleksandr Semyonovich Paniushkin was chief of KGB's First Chief Directorate at the time.

36. Frederik, *Das Ende einer Legende,* 549–50.

37. Henryk Bonde-Henryksen, interview with Bailey, 13 Feb. 1994, Bonn.

38. Ibid. There is no information from the SVR archives to indicate that KGB ever became aware of the Helsinki caper.

39. Ibid.

40. Hans Scherer, "Letter to the Editor," *Frankfurter Allgemeine Zeitung,* 24 Sept. 1993, p. 13.

41. *Frankfurter Allgemeine Zeitung,* 4 Oct. 1994.

42. Berlin (Deutsche Press Agentur), 13 Jan. 1996.

Chapter 11. The Berlin Tunnel

1. David Martin, *Wilderness of Mirrors,* 1st ed. (New York: Ballantine, 1981), 76.

2. When this book went to press, references to the tunnel were found in at least eighteen works of nonfiction and one novel by Ian McEwan, *The Innocent* (New York: Doubleday, 1990), which was made into a film by the same title in 1993. Heinz Höhne and Hermann Zolling, in *The General Was a Spy* (New York: Coward, McCann, and Geoghegan, 1974), were first with the Gehlen story (see their appendix B). See also the article "Spies for Sale: Post-War Germany" in Tim Healey, *Spies,* Timespan Series (London: Macdonald Educational, 1978). The Gehlen theme was repeated in Rhodri Jeffreys-Jones, *CIA and American Democracy* (New Haven: Yale University Press, 1989), and again in Peter Grose, *Gentleman Spy: The Life of Allen Dulles* (Boston: Houghton Mifflin, 1994).

3. Thomas Huntington, "The Berlin Spy Tunnel Affair," *American Heritage of Invention and Technology* 10, no. 4 (spring 1995): 44–52. William Hood, telephone interview, 28 Apr. 1997. See also Frank Rowlett, interview, 21 Oct. 1993; Walter O'Brien, interviews, 15 Aug. 1994, 29 Mar. 1995.

4. Burton Hersh, *The Old Boys: The American Elite and the Origins of the CIA* (New York: Scribners, 1992), 378. See also Dispatch, Chief of Mission, Frankfurt, to DCI, 17 Sept. 1953, "Special Intelligence," CIA-HRP. The warehouse cover is described in the field project outline contained in the attachment to this dispatch.

5. Martin, *Wilderness of Mirrors*, 76.

6. Rowlett interview.

7. Ibid. See also George Blake, *No Other Choice: An Autobiography* (London: Jonathan Cape, 1990).

8. Victor Marchetti and John D. Marks, *CIA and the Cult of Intelligence* (New York: Dell, 1975), 34.

9. Chapman Pincher, *Too Secret Too Long* (New York: St. Martin's, 1984), 252.

10. William R. Corson, Susan B. Trento, and Joseph Trento, *Widows* (New York: Crown, 1980), 29.

11. Tony Le Tissier, *Berlin: Then and Now* (London: International Battle of Britain Prints, 1994), 372–73.

12. Mark Perry, *Eclipse: The Last Days of the CIA* (New York: William Morrow, 1992), 28–29.

13. David Wise, *Molehunt* (New York: Random House, 1992), 25.

14. Oleg M. Nechiporenko, *Passport to Assassination: The Never-Before Told Story of Lee Harvey Oswald by the KGB Colonel Who Knew Him* (New York: Birch Lane, 1993). See also Grose, *Gentleman Spy*.

15. Rowlett interview.

16. O'Brien interviews.

17. Ibid.

18. Ibid.

19. Bill Harvey always referred to Rowlett as the "Mountain Boy," another Harvey nickname to which Soviet intercept operators must have grown accustomed during the years of the tunnel operation.

20. Ibid.

21. Ambassador Hugh Montgomery, interview, 9 Nov. 1993, McLean, Va.; and O'Brien interviews.

22. Ibid.

23. Ibid.

24. Ibid. See also Martin, *Wilderness of Mirrors*, 77.

25. Ibid. See chapter 5 for background on the covert paramilitary project involving the Free Jurists.

26. Ibid.

27. O'Brien interviews.

28. Dulles's interest in the tunnel can be seen in a 16 Sept. 1953 note from Richard Helms, Chief of Operations, DD/P, CIA-HRP, advising Rowlett to see the DCI as soon as he returned from his German trip. In the margin Rowlett has written, "Have done."

29. Dispatch, "Special Intelligence."

30. Ibid.

31. Kondrashev.

32. Ibid.

33. Blake, *No Other Choice,* 6.

34. Kondrashev monograph on the tunnel operation based on his review of SVR archival material, 25 Feb. 1995, p. 2.

35. Kondrashev. Although KGB laboratories would one day produce very sophisticated cameras, they were behind the West at the time. If any of the models it used were found in an agent's possession, it would immediately arouse suspicion. Consequently, Moscow decided a Minox would be preferable, and one was subsequently given to Blake.

36. Blake, *No Other Choice,* 16–18. Yuri Ivanovich Modin was identified as the KGB officer who made the first meeting with Blake in order to conceal Kondrashev's part in the case. The rea-

son for not naming Kondrashev publicly in *No Other Choice* was that he was participating at that time in the conferences on human rights under "Basket Three" of the Helsinki Accords then under way in Madrid: KGB did not want to embarrass the Soviet side in these sensitive discussions. Certainly, KGB was aware that the British knew of Kondrashev's role in the Blake case. See also the Russian edition of Blake's autobiography, Dzhorzh Bleik, *Inogo vybora net* (Moscow: Mezhdunarodnye otnosheniia, 1991), 16.

37. Kondrashev tunnel monograph. Concerning the Petrov case, Kondrashev was able to obtain a copy of the Royal Commission Report on Espionage through what he termed "a friendly contact among QC's who had sympathy with our cause." Another complication may have arisen from a trip made by Kondrashev to Holland in this same time frame in connection with his cover job as head of the cultural section of the embassy. The visit concerned performances of the Beriozka folk dance ensemble in Great Britain and Holland, although Kondrashev profited from the trip by casing possible meeting sites with Blake.

38. SVRA, Diomid file, 12 Feb. 1954. In *No Other Choice*, Blake noted that meetings always took place not far from underground (subway) stations.

39. SVRA, Diomid file. An article appearing in the London *Sunday Telegraph* early in 1997 displayed a copy of a rough sketch of the tunnel area that it attributed to George Blake, claiming that he had passed it to KGB. See Jacqui Thornton and Ian Thomas, "Revealed: The Map of Blake's Betrayal," *Sunday Telegraph* (London), 23 Feb. 1997. In an interview with Kondrashev in Moscow on 11 Mar. 1997, Blake denied ever having done a sketch for KGB of the kind portrayed in the article. According to Kondrashev, Blake did use his Minox camera to photocopy an SIS schematic drawing of the tunnel plans, but no trace of this photo could be found in SVR archives.

40. The Russian term *podslushivanie* as used in this report can be interpreted as clandestine audio operations involving either the interception of existing communications channels or the use of technical devices like microphones to eavesdrop on conversations.

41. Attachment to Kondrashev's 12 Feb. 1954 report of 18 Jan. 1954 meeting with Diomid, SVRA, Diomid file.

42. George Blake, interview with Kondrashev, 7 Apr. 1995, Moscow. That Philby was "engaged in a vendetta against the West," particularly against those he considered responsible for his exposure, is evident in analyses of his memoirs. See, for example, E. D. R. Harrison, "More Thoughts on Kim Philby's *My Silent War*," *Intelligence and National Security* 10, no. 3 (July 1995): 514–25.

43. Cleveland Cram, interview, 28 Feb. 1995, Washington, D.C.

44. According to the SVR *Biographic Handbook* (1995), Tishkov was appointed deputy of KGB School 101 and in 1960, its chief. There is no mention of his role as deputy for technical matters to the chief of the First Chief Directorate, a position that has been confirmed by CIA sources (Biographic Summary, 6 June 1972, CIA-HRP).

45. SVRA, Diomid file, p. 293.

46. Kondrashev.

47. SVRA, Diomid file, p. 317; Memorandum, KGB Chairman Serov to Defense Minister Bulganin, 20 Sept. 1954.

48. Kondrashev, tunnel monograph.

49. Blake interview.

50. Martin, *Wilderness of Mirrors*, 82–83.

51. Dispatch, Chief, Berlin Operations Base, to Chief of Mission, Frankfurt, 18 Oct. 1954, CIA-HRP.

52. C. G. Harvey, interview, 15–16 Nov. 1993. The officer, known to Harvey as the "Great Stone Face" because of his taciturn manner and laconic speech, had previously been involved in the Vienna landlines operation.

53. Dispatch, Chief, Berlin Operations Base, to Chief of Mission, Frankfurt, 18 Oct. 1954, CIA-HRP.

54. Memorandum for the Record, 29 Nov. 1954, CIA-HRP.

484 ▪ *Notes to pages 222–37*

55. The technical details of construction and the tap procedure have been described in exhaustive detail elsewhere. See Huntington, "The Berlin Spy Tunnel Affair." On page 50, Huntington pays tribute to David Martin's "superb account of the operation contained in his 1980 book *Wilderness of Mirrors.*" Huntington's description of the construction process was indeed well done, but he repeated some of Martin's misunderstandings, notably regarding the "echo effect."

56. F. E. Kindell, telephone interview, 21 Mar. 1995, and F. E. Kindell, letter, 26 May 1995.

57. These descriptions of the various components of the tunnel operation and their functions are taken from official histories that were cross-checked with F. E. Kindell, chief communications engineer at the Alt Glienicke site, and Ambassador Hugh Montgomery, who served as a principal assistant to Harvey during the entire life of the tunnel.

58. Ibid.

59. George Blake, interview with Kondrashev, 24 May 1994.

60. Kondrashev.

61. Vadim Fyodorovich Goncharov, interview with Kondrashev, 21 Nov. 1994, Moscow.

62. Ibid.

63. Ibid.

64. Kondrashev.

65. See Igor Vladimirov, "Ulbrikht prosil menia nazyvat' ego prosto Val'terom" (Ulbricht asked me to simply call him Walter), *Globus,* 21 Jan. 1993.

66. Memorandum from CIA Staff through Chief, CI Staff, to Chief, SR/CI, 26 Nov. 1962, CIA-HRP.

67. Pitovranov, interview with Kondrashev, 1. Nov. 1994.

68. Goncharov interview.

69. Ibid.

70. Ibid.

71. This account is taken from voice and telephone circuits recorded up to the moment the tap cables were cut at 3:35 P.M. on the afternoon of 22 April; from the transcripts of the conversations of Russians and East Germans picked up by the microphone in the tap chamber, which was not disconnected until 3:50 P.M.; and from interviews with Montgomery, who was at the site at the time. The data from the voice and telegraph circuits were taken from appendix A, "The Berlin Tunnel Operation," Clandestine Services History (CSHP-150), CIA-HRP. The transcripts were also released in full by CIA-HRP.

72. Telephonogram by V Ch, Semenov to Pushkin. SVRA.

73. Telephonogram by V Ch, Top Secret (declassified), no. 1365, no. 3990-M, 23 Apr. 1956. SVRA.

74. *New York Herald Tribune,* 27 May 1956.

75. Le Tissier, *Berlin: Then and Now,* 373. See also *Neues Deutschland,* 28 Apr. 1956.

76. Healey, *Spies.* Credit for the sketch is given to Popperfoto. The error in all of these sketches in not locating the origin of the tunnel in the warehouse could relate to KGB concern for source protection, because presumably only someone with inside knowledge would have known where the tunnel began on the American side. But the "bubbling" coffee pot relates so closely to the Goncharov-Pitovranov claims that it suggests the whole story was fabricated.

77. Thornton and Thomas, "Revealed."

78. Berlin Cable to CIA Washington, 10 May 1956, CIA-HRP. BOB sources reported that the head of the Main Administration for Long Distance Telephone Lines in the East German Ministry of Post and Telecommunications believed that the "Soviets had stumbled upon the tap chamber accidentally while seeking out faults in their circuits."

79. Joseph C. Evans, a retired CIA officer who was "involved in the [tunnel] operation from conception to conclusion" and who went on to become a CIA counterintelligence specialist and known writer on counterintelligence, reaches the same conclusion. In "Berlin Tunnel Intelligence: A Bumbling KGB," *International Journal of Intelligence and Counterintelligence* 9, no. 1 (spring 1996), Evans refutes various claims that tunnel intelligence was disinformation and emphasizes the value of the intelligence product.

Chapter 12. Redcap Operations

1. The abortive CIA effort to induce B. Y. Nalivaiko to defect was part of this program.

2. The comments on the origins of the defector recruitment program derive from numerous sources, but for the specifics on East Germany in the early 1950s we are indebted to a former member of the BOB Redcap branch and his monograph on the subject. See Memorandum for the File Forwarded to CIA Washington by BOB Dispatch, 11 Dec. 1953, "Relation Between Soviets and the German Population and Their Bearing on REDCAP Operations," CIA-HRP.

3. Memorandum, Deputy Chief, Foreign Division S, to Staff C, 8 Aug. 1951, "Request for Operational Clearance," CIA-HRP, signed by Dana Durand, who by this time was deputy chief of the Soviet Russia Division and would replace Harry Rositzke when the latter departed for Munich in 1952. See also confidential interview, 18 Apr. 1994, and undated handwritten personal history statement by Vladimir Kivi. CIA-HRP.

4. Ibid.

5. Dispatches, BOB, 2 Apr. and 5 May 1952, CIA-HRP. Orlov's case officer termed Orlov's actions in visiting Karlshorst a "breach of procedure," which it certainly was considering that Orlov was a former Soviet intelligence officer who had collaborated with the Germans in wartime, then with Gehlen, and was now an agent of the CIA.

6. Cable, Berlin to Director, 27 Aug. 1952, CIA-HRP.

7. Dispatch, BOB to Chief, EE, 5 Sept. 1952, CIA-HRP.

8. Ibid.

9. Cable, BOB to Mission Headquarters, Frankfurt, 19 Aug. 1952, CIA-HRP.

10. Cable, Berlin, 24 Aug. 1995, CIA-HRP. Using active-duty military documentation for agents to be parachuted into the USSR was never a serious option. Posing as an officer or NCO on leave was fraught with administrative complications and required that the agents have an up-to-date military background, which few candidates had.

11. Dispatch, BOB to Chief, EE, 13 Apr. 1953, CIA-HRP.

12. Dispatch, Chief, EE Division, to Chief of Mission, Frankfurt, 21 July 1954, CIA-HRP. This three-cornered battle over Orlov may have had more to do with the personalities of the senior officials involved than with the specifics of the case. The German Mission case was being vigorously pressed by Lester Houck, a former BOB chief who had become a senior staff officer at mission headquarters. He had been replaced by Bill Harvey after serving only briefly in Berlin. Harvey, of course, was totally immersed in his tunnel project yet was determined to defend his troops in any conflict with higher headquarters. The author of the EE Division dispatch, Peter Sichel, EE chief of operations, had been the Berlin chief for many years and probably enjoyed telling both Harvey and Houck that they were wrong on this case.

13. Dispatch, BOB to Chief, EE, 10 Aug. 1954, CIA-HRP.

14. TsOPE was the émigré "roof organization" created by OPC in Germany.

15. Cable, Berlin to Director, 21 Aug. 1954; Cable, Berlin to Director, 25 Aug. 1954; and Cable, Berlin to Director, 26 Aug. 1954, CIA-HRP.

16. Memorandum, 27 Aug. 1954, CIA-HRP.

17. Cable, Berlin to Frankfurt and Director (CIA-HRP), 4 Sept. 1954, CIA-HRP.

18. Cable, Berlin to Director, 8 Sept. 1954, CIA-HRP.

19. Cable, Frankfurt to Director, 8 Sept. 1954, CIA-HRP.

20. Cable, Frankfurt to Director, 27 Nov. 1958, CIA-HRP.

21. Memorandum, for the Chief, Soviet Russia Division, 24 Dec. 1959, CIA-HRP. This memorandum was a recapitulation of the entire operation from its inception.

22. Ibid.

23. Dispatch, BOB to Chief, EE, 4 Mar. 1955, CIA-HRP.

24. Cable, BOB to CIA Headquarters, Washington, 9 Oct. 1956, CIA-HRP.

25. Dispatch, BOB to Frankfurt, 4 May 1953, CIA-HRP.

26. Dispatch, BOB to Chief, EE, 8 Apr. 1953; Memorandum, EE Division to Staff C, 15 June 1953, CIA-HRP.

27. Dispatch to Chief, EE, 2 Jan. 1957, CIA-HRP. The Emigré Department wanted this source to report to them on the activities of SBONR, of which he remained a member. CIA no longer

used the organization for intelligence operations, but it did maintain an interest in SBONR's anti-Soviet propaganda capabilities. KGB, of course, with its paranoid preoccupation with emigration, saw SBONR as an active target.

28. The German transliteration of Kopatsky is Kopazky, which is how "Sasha's" name was spelled in all German records.

29. A graduate of an early OPC paramilitary program that was later abandoned, Zharov was first considered by Combined Soviet Operations Base in Munich for an air drop operation into the USSR. Instead, a decision was made by the German mission in October 1952 that he be sent to Berlin for training as a Redcap refugee debriefer (Cable, Frankfurt to Berlin and CSOB Munich, 28 Oct. 1952, CIA-HRP). His case officers realized that he had no aptitude for nor interest in such work (he had also been given a poor evaluation by Orlov, which greatly distressed him). By mutual consent he left Berlin and later emigrated to the United States. See Dispatch, Berlin to Chief, EE, 1 Aug. 1955, CIA-HRP, which confirmed his work at BOB. There were other factors suggesting that Zharov may not have been a KGB agent. In the early 1970s a copy of the 1969 KGB "wanted list" was brought to the West by a KGB defector. The list contained an entry for Viktor Yefimovich Turko or Turkov, also known as Zharov, stating that "from September 1951 he underwent training in an American intelligence school near Munich for dispatch into the USSR, in 1952 he continued training for eight months in the USA, after which he returned to West Germany. He first lived in a safe house in West Berlin, then in a private apartment under the name Heinrich *Mueller*. Later, as Walter *Berger*, he worked as an official member of 'CIC' in the department of political diversion."

30. A major element contributing to the confusion over "Sasha" was Golitsyn's assumption that the Sasha whose file he had read in 1953 was also the KGB's source (code-named Sasha), recruited in 1959, who was serving in an American intelligence unit in Berlin and of whom he had become aware in 1960 while assigned to the treaty organizations branch of KGB's Information Service. This could not have been Orlov because he had left Berlin in 1956. See David Murphy, "Sasha Who?" *Intelligence and National Security* 8, no. 1 (Jan. 1993): 102–7.

31. Whether by error or design, the SVR report omitted the location of the "Soviet Embassy."

32. During the first meetings with Kondrashev on this book in 1993, Murphy and Bailey discussed the extensive Western literature on CIA and KGB operations and cited the case of Igor Orlov as one directly related to CIA's base in Berlin. It was hoped that by obtaining material from SVR archives, we could correct the inaccuracies, distortions, and erroneous conclusions surrounding this case that have appeared in unclassified publications. The question was raised again in Moscow meetings in February 1994 and again on 5 July 1994 in a Berlin session. On 18 February 1995 Kondrashev provided this report from the SVR counterintelligence directorate.

33. SVR counterintelligence directorate report on Orlov provided by Kondrashev.

34. Dispatch, Berlin to Chief, EE, 30 Oct. 1952, CIA-HRP.

35. Tennent H. Bagley, "Bane of Counterintelligence: Our Penchant for Self-Deception," *International Journal of Intelligence and Counterintelligence* 6, no. 1 (1993): 14–16. The officer in question was Yuri Litovkin, who was later stationed in Karlshorst as part of one of the few "active measures" units stationed abroad.

36. Memorandum for DDP from Chief EE, 7 Feb. 1955, "Defection Attempt in Vienna on 5 February 1955, Boris Yakovlevich Nalivaiko," CIA-HRP.

37. See Boris Ia. Nalivaiko, *Tri desiatiletiia na perednem krae* (Three decades in the forward area), SVR Red Banner Andropov Institute, 1993, p. 44 (thirty copies, classified memoirs retained in the SVR special collection *[spetsfond]*, SVRA). An unclassified version, which omits many KGB aspects, is B. Nalivaiko "Konsul Bezhat' Otkasalsya," *Novoye Vremya* 37 (1993): 50–53.

38. At the time of his defection, Deriabin was one of the most knowledgeable KGB officers to defect to CIA. He provided the basis for CIA's early knowledge of the German-Austrian Department in Moscow and the KGB residencies in Vienna and East Berlin.

39. Peter Deriabin, *The Secret World* (New York: Doubleday, 1959), 263–64.

40. Fyodor Grigorievich Shubnyakov was still resident when Kondrashev arrived in Vienna in early 1957. He was a veteran of internal counterintelligence who was given the Vienna assignment as a preretirement posting.

41. Nalivaiko, *Tri desiatiletiia na perednem krae.*
42. Ibid.
43. Ibid.
44. In response to a question about the absence of KGB reporting on this and other 1955 events, it was noted that "the files in SVR archives for the year 1955 are very thin, and documents on the most interesting points are scarce." Kondrashev.
45. *New York Times,* 5 June 1955. Memorandum, for Chief, SR Division, 19 Apr. 1955, CIA-HRP. The author of this memorandum, and Smirnov's escort officer, was Alexander Sogolow, legendary friend of would-be Soviet defectors. Murphy first met Sogolow in 1949.
46. Interview transcript, 6 Apr. 1955, CIA-HRP.
47. National Intelligence Estimate NIE 11-3-55, 17 May 1955, p. 45, CIA-HRP.
48. Draft of a proposed memorandum on BOB reporting to be forwarded by the State Department to Ambassador Bohlen in Moscow, 19 Aug. 1955, CIA-HRP.
49. Ibid. Kondrashev doubts that Pushkin ever made such statements.
50. Ibid. In a May meeting with French premier Guy Mollet, Khrushchev was reported to have insisted that if Germany were to be reunited, "we also require that the social and economic achievements of East Germany shall be retained" (*Manchester Guardian,* 12 June 1956).

Chapter 13. BOB Concentrates on Karlshorst

1. See chapter 2 for background on the Karlshorst district and the establishment of the principal Soviet occupation headquarters there after war's end.
2. Dispatch, Berlin to Chief, EE, 9 Aug. 1954, CIA-HRP.
3. Ibid. Also V. V. Zvezdenkov, interview with Kondrashev, 17 Nov. 1995. Zvezdenkov died on 11 Oct. 1996 in Moscow. In September 1957, Popov reported a similar story heard during a security briefing. In this case the American agent-electrician had been given access to a chandelier to be hung in an Opergruppa safe house but was foiled by Soviet counterintelligence. See Dispatch, Berlin, 1 Oct. 1957, Extract from Popov meeting transcript, pp. 15–16, para. 60, CIA-HRP.
4. Dispatch, Berlin to Chief, Soviet Bloc Division, 25 Jan. 1967, CIA-HRP.
5. Dispatch, Berlin to Chief, EE, 9 Aug. 1954.
6. Dispatch, Berlin to Chief, SR Division, 1 Oct. 1957, CIA-HRP. Extract from Popov meeting transcript, p. 2.
7. Berlin Cable Intelligence Report, 25 Oct. 1957, CIA-HRP.
8. Dispatch, Berlin to Chief, EE (Attn.: Chief, SR), 4 Feb. 1958, CIA-HRP.
9. In February 1956, when the tunnel, Popov case, and other Karlshorst operations were demonstrating that Soviet intelligence in East Germany was active against targets in Western Europe, Bill Harvey drafted a special "Eyes Only" cable to Dick Helms and Jim Angleton. The cable proposed that because of the unique circumstances in Berlin, BOB become coresponsible with Washington for handling Soviet counterintelligence affecting the European area. One can imagine the reaction; Harvey never received a reply.
10. Dispatch, Berlin, 2 Dec. 1960, CIA-HRP.
11. Ibid.
12. Ibid.
13. Ibid. The value of true name identifications grew in the 1950s as increasing numbers of Karlshorst-based KGB officers began traveling to West Germany and elsewhere in Europe with diplomatic passports to make agent meetings. The passports were normally issued in true name, and in some cases it was only an earlier identification from the CIA "baggage forwarder" that confirmed the KGB affiliation of these travelers.
14. See appendix 5 for a description of the tunnel material on the KGB military counterintelligence components in Potsdam, Karlshorst, and elsewhere in East Germany.
15. Dispatch, Berlin, 22 Mar. 1957, Attachment A, "Positive Information on Soviet Intelligence Services in Germany," CIA-HRP.
16. Ibid.
17. Ibid.

18. Ibid.

19. Ibid.

20. Ibid.

21. Kondrashev. When asked for more information, Kondrashev stated that he was unable to obtain additional details or archival material on this case.

22. One of the most active KGB Karlshorst officers in the émigré field during the 1950s was Arkady Andreevich Fabrichnikov. Using the alias Arkady Andreevich Avramenko, among others, he was identified by a combination of double-agent reports, tunnel information, and reporting by BOB Karlshorst sources. See Dispatch, to Berlin Base, 30 Sept. 1957, CIA-HRP. After his service in Karlshorst he returned to Moscow, where he served in émigré operations at the First Chief Directorate's counterintelligence directorate. He later became a senior officer in the KGB's Second (internal counterintelligence) Directorate. Biographic Information Report, 2 Aug. 1974, CIA-HRP.

23. Cable, Berlin to Director, 7 Nov. 1955, CIA-HRP.

24. CIA Information Report, 27 Mar. 1959, CIA-HRP.

Chapter 14. The Illegals Game

1. Kondrashev emphasized that Germany and Austria were important sources of documentation and support for Soviet illegals long before World War II. He recalls hearing his father-in-law, Yakov Fyodorovich Tishchenko, a.k.a. Razin and Roshchin, speak of handling sources in the police and in printing plants in both Berlin and Vienna before the war.

2. The German "connection" also figured in the case of "Colonel Abel." This was the alias given to his FBI arresting officers in 1957 by the KGB illegal Vilyam Genrikhovich Fisher. A Soviet illegal during the prewar period, after the war Fisher was given a new identity and in 1948 entered the United States via a displaced persons camp in Germany and Canada. Fisher/Abel, KGB code name Mark, was the first illegal to be arrested in the United States after the war. He was not, as some have speculated, merely a "sleeper agent" but had served as controller of Helena and Morris Cohen, illegal agents who had handled valuable sources in the US atomic weapons program. Fisher/Abel's downfall was his assistant, KGB illegal Reino Hayhanen, who was recalled by Moscow for drinking problems. Hayhanen defected in Paris in May 1957 after receiving instructions from a KGB officer in the residency to proceed to Moscow by train via West Berlin and Karlshorst.

3. Aspects of the Popov case have been covered extensively in the book *Mole* (New York, Norton, 1982), whose author, William Hood, was chief of operations in the CIA Vienna mission until the Austrian State Treaty was signed.

4. Valentin Vladimirovich Zvezdenkov, interviews with Kondrashev, Nov. 1995, Moscow.

5. Ibid.

6. "Popov: The Conformist Who Failed," undated monograph, p. 27, CIA-HRP.

7. This charge was made by H. Montgomery Hyde in *George Blake: Superspy* (London: Constable, 1987) but rejected by Blake in *No Other Choice* (London: Jonathan Cape, 1990), his memoir published in 1990. Blake repeated this denial to Kondrashev during their 1995 interviews.

8. According to Kondrashev, the working file *(rabochee delo)* on the Blake case was preserved by special decision because of its importance. The file contains a listing of persons *(spisok prokhodiashchikh lits)* on whom an agent had reported in the course of the operation. Kondrashev insists that Popov's name was not included. Throughout the discussions of the Popov case, Kondrashev emphasized that in KGB's view, George Blake was in no way linked to or responsible for the compromise of Popov.

9. "Popov: The Conformist Who Failed," p. 28. Although word of the Popov assignment did appear in tunnel traffic, it was processed and disseminated as a routine report because, for obvious reasons, no steps had been taken to flag Popov's name to transcribers.

10. Ibid., p. 29.

11. Zvezdenkov interviews.

12. "Popov: The Conformist Who Failed," p. 31.

13. Jerrold L. Schecter and Peter S. Deriabin, *The Spy Who Saved the World* (New York: Scribners, 1992), 43, contains a background sketch of George Kisevalter and comments on his work with Popov. One sentence reads: "He liked to drink, and his drinking bouts with Popov after operational sessions were well known in the Clandestine Service." That Kisevalter liked to drink cannot be disputed. But he engaged in no "drinking bouts with Popov" during or after operational meetings in Berlin. Murphy either monitored or was present at all but a few of these meetings. He also checked the tapes of the meetings he missed.

14. "Popov: The Conformist Who Failed," pp. 37–38. According to Zvezdenkov, had KGB military counterintelligence followed up on this report of Popov's unauthorized transit of West Berlin, the case could have been resolved much sooner.

15. CIA Information Report, 29 Mar. 1957, "Zhukov Address," CIA-HRP.

16. Murphy recalls a visit to London in mid-March 1957 to discuss disposition of the leads from Popov to RU agents in the British Zone.

17. See Blake, *No Other Choice,* 203, in which Blake tells his defense lawyer that he "had photographed almost daily every important and interesting document which had passed through his hands."

18. The discussion of Zhukov's reign as defense minister is taken from William J. Spahr, *Zhukov: The Rise and Fall of a Great Captain* (Novato, Calif.: Presidio, 1993). See also "Chego stoiat polkovodicheskie kachestva Stalina?" (What is the worth of Stalin's qualities as a military leader?), *Vestnik Arkhiva Prezidenta Rossiiskoi Federatsii* 2 (1995): 143–59.

19. CIA Information Report, Subject: Zhukov Comments on Soviet Military Capabilities, 30 Apr. 1957, CIA-HRP.

20. Kondrashev acknowledges the practice of briefing media contacts but doubts that a KGB official of Pitovranov's stature would have been used in this connection.

21. Zvezdenkov interviews. Evidently as part of the "macho" image Popov was intent on creating for his interrogators, he claimed that at one time he and his CIA case officer, "Grossman," visited a West Berlin bordello.

22. Ibid.

23. Thomas Whiteside, *An Agent in Place* (New York: Viking, 1966), 72–73.

24. For background on the "banana queen" and her role in the Netsvetailo investigation, see chapter 13.

25. Extract from Popov meeting transcript, p. 4, Berlin Dispatch, 8 Aug. 1958, CIA-HRP.

26. "Popov: The Conformist Who Failed," pp. 40–42.

27. Ibid., pp. 45–46.

28. Berlin Dispatch, 24 Nov. 1958, p. 8, CIA-HRP.

29. Zvezdenkov interviews.

30. "The Popov Case," 22 Sept. 1980, pp. 8–9, CIA-HRP. The story of the mistakenly mailed letter and its interception by KGB has been told and retold in numerous publications, such as Tom Mangold's *Cold Warrior* (New York: Simon and Schuster, 1991), 251–52, and David Wise's *Molehunt* (New York: Random House, 1992), 169. It served as a linchpin for the theory that the account of the interception that was passed on by such KGB sources as Aleksandr Cherepanov and Yuri Nosenko was concocted by the KGB. According to this theory, KGB used the intercepted letter as the reason for Popov's downfall so as to protect the existence of a mole within CIA.

31. Zvezdenkov interviews.

32. Ibid.

33. "The Popov Case," pp. 12–13.

34. *Raketnye voiska strategicheskogo naznacheniia: Voyenno-istoricheskii trud* (Moscow: RVSN, 1992), 57. Construction activity linked to missile launching and support facilities began in the Sverdlovsk area as early as 1957 and was still in progress in 1959.

35. Zvezdenkov interviews.

36. "The Popov Case," pp. 12–13. Other publications have referred to this message as having been part of a bandage. The origins of this story are unknown.

37. Berlin Dispatch, 18 Sept. 1959, Attachment K, Russian text, "cylindrical letter," CIA-HRP.

38. Indeed, the second general who interviewed Popov may well have been Filip Ivanovich Golikov, whom Khrushchev had recently appointed as head of the Soviet Army's Main Political Administration, an institution that Zhukov had consistently opposed. Spahr, *Zhukov,* 256–58.

39. Berlin Dispatch, 18 Sept. 1959, Russian text, "cylindrical letter," CIA-HRP.

40. Ibid. Other Western sources have quoted the figure "half a billion." See Hood, *Mole,* 13, later cited by John Ranelagh in *The Agency* (New York: Simon and Schuster, 1987).

41. "Popov: The Conformist Who Failed," p. 21.

Chapter 15. KGB and MfS

1. Shatalin was the CPSU Central Committee functionary chosen to attack Beria's moral character at the July 1953 plenum. See *Izvestiia TsK KPSS* 2 (1991): 158.

2. SVRA file 45783, vol. 3, pp. 151–54.

3. Ibid.

4. When the traditional provinces (Laender) were abolished, the MfS structure at the Land level was also abolished and district directorates of MfS were created. On the Soviet side, the operational groups in the provinces were dissolved and advisory groups, consisting of a chief adviser and his assistants, were created in each district.

5. SVRA file 45783, vol. 3, pp. 151–54.

6. Georgy Alekseevich Korotia, interview with Kondrashev, 17 Dec. 1994. The officer in question was head of the counterintelligence department of the apparat.

7. Vasily Ilich Bulda, interview with Kondrashev, 5 Jan. 1995. When introduced to Minister Ignatiev by Pitovranov as head of the advisory department, Bulda recalls Ignatiev quoting Stalin: "No matter what happens, we must hold on to the GDR." See also Memorandum, undated, "Bulda, Vasily Ilich," CIA-HRP.

8. For details about Oganesian, see Biographic Outline, undated, CIA-HRP. Oganesian, of Armenian origin, served in Austria until 1953 and then until 1959 as a senior adviser with an office in Mielke's MfS headquarters on Normannenstrasse in East Berlin. From Feb. through Aug. 1960 he was on temporary duty in Teheran, and from 1960 to 1963 he was deputy chief of the Thirteenth Department. This brings Oganesian into the same orbit of the Thirteenth Department and Teheran as Ivan Anisimovich Fadeikin, another KGB senior officer with a Karlshorst background. For background on Samoilenko, see Biographic Memorandum, 29 Nov. 1956, CIA-HRP. Samoilenko was assigned as senior adviser in Karl-Marx Stadt (Chemnitz) from 1953 to 1955, then was transferred to a senior advisory position in Karlshorst. He left the GDR in 1957.

9. The chief of this department was normally designated by the German department, but if the chief of the apparat picked him, as when Pitovranov selected Bulda, then the choice had to be approved by the department.

10. Bulda interview. For example, Vadim Vitoldovich Kuchin, one of KGB's leading German specialists, who for many years was chief of the advisory department, was deeply involved in the Otto John operation.

11. Ibid. How much this assurance was worth is hard to say. We know that MGB had sources in the newly created East German MfS and that for years thereafter KGB relied on "trusted contacts" within MfS to obtain information that they could not be sure of receiving via regular liaison channels.

12. Ibid.

13. Ibid. According to Bulda, who had arrived in Karlshorst before the June 1953 riots, the diminution of effectiveness of intelligence collection was not surprising. The MGB apparat continued to function pretty much as it had since the war's end, when its targets were Nazi diehards and opponents of SMA and the new SED regime.

14. Serov to Pitovranov, 5 Apr. 1954, SVRA file 504456, vol. 1, pp. 2–6.

15. Ibid.

16. Korotia interview. Although this was solid counterintelligence theory, Korotia accepted the Soviet view that these agents had been put in place as part of the preparation for the events of June 1953.

17. Serov to Pitovranov, 5 Apr. 1954.

18. Ibid.

19. SVRA file 504456, vol. 1, pp. 1–9.

20. RIAS (Radio in the American Sector) was begun by the American Military Government. It broadcast in German to a large East German audience. It was not an intelligence agency, but its broadcasts of information on East Germany greatly irritated the Soviets, who demanded several times that it be shut down.

21. SVRA file 504456, vol. 1, pp. 1–9.

22. These descriptions of name changes are taken from unpublished extracts by Kondrashev from classified SVR material entitled "Rabota razvedki po nemetskoi linii" (The work of intelligence against German targets).

23. Debriefing reports, 8 Oct. 1967, 15 Feb. 1968, CIA-HRP.

24. Ibid. For example, Nikolai Semyonovich Govorukhin, formerly a member of the Third (illegals) Department of the Karlshorst apparat, had a difficult time with his MfS contacts when he was made chief of the KGB district office in Schwerin.

25. Yevgeny Petrovich Pitovranov, interview with Kondrashev, 19 Aug. 1994, and personal reminiscences. Pavel Sudoplatov et al., *Special Tasks* (Boston: Little, Brown, 1994), 25, attribute Ulbricht's decision to comments made to him by Khrushchev after Serov allegedly advised Khrushchev of Wollweber's reporting on "ideological divergences" within SED.

26. Pitovranov interview.

27. Igor Vladimirov, "Ulbrikht prosil menia nazyvat' ego prosto Val'terom" (Ulbricht asked me to simply call him Walter), *Globus,* 21 Jan. 1993. In this article, Pitovranov added that he realized later that Andropov did not agree with his views on Mielke. Nor does Kondrashev.

28. Pitovranov interview. Kondrashev cautions that no "special significance" should be attached to such gifts, which he says were limited in nature.

29. SVRA file 84834, vol. 4, pp. 81–82. Serov knew whereof he spoke. A file in the SVR archives contains an extract from a speech by Ulbricht at a closed session of the GDR Volkskammer on 12 Oct. 1954. After praising state security for its successes against the Gehlen Organization, Ulbricht urged the party to take a leading role in its work. Insisting that these "enemy organizations must be destroyed," he concluded with the order that "party secretaries everywhere must become involved with these questions and work closely with the comrades of state security." See SVRA file 504456, vol. 1, part 3, pp. 42–43.

30. SVRA file 84834, vol. 4, pp. 81–82. See also Filipp Denisovich Bobkov, *KGB i vlast'* (Moscow: Veteran MP, 1995), 134–35, for a description of Khrushchev's speech to the KGB leadership in summer 1954 in which he emphasized "socialist legality."

31. Kondrashev extracts.

32. Kondrashev, who later became a member of the KGB task force sent to Hungary to deal with the revolt of October–November 1956.

33. Report of Warsaw Pact Intelligence service conference, SVRA file 504456, vol. 1, pp. 70–78.

34. Ibid.

35. Ibid.

36. Ibid.

37. Ibid.

38. Ambassador Hugh Montgomery, interview, 24 Mar. 1995.

39. Report of Warsaw Pact Intelligence service conference, pp. 70–78.

40. Kondrashev.

41. Kondrashev.

42. The GDR foreign intelligence service, first created in 1951, was by now MfS's Main Administration A (Hauptverwaltung A), or HVA, by which acronym its exploits became famous until the collapse of the GDR.

43. Kondrashev knew Horst Jaenicke well and had the highest possible opinion of his work, professional standing, and personal character. Kondrashev believes that Jaenicke was torn between loyalty to the service and his awareness of GDR leaders' inability to resolve the future of the divided country.

44. Kondrashev.

45. Kondrashev. See also Valentin Falin, *Politische Erinnerungen* (Munich: Droemer-Knaur, 1993), 265–66.

46. Berlin Cabled Information Report, 17 June 1959, CIA-HRP.

47. Cable, Berlin, 23 June 1958, CIA-HRP.

48. Dispatch, Berlin, 7 Mar. 1958, CIA-HRP.

49. An important witness to these events is Leonid Yemelianovich Siomonchuk, then chief of the KGB's German department. He was interviewed by Kondrashev in Moscow on 12 Sept. 1994.

50. Kondrashev. See, for example, Bobkov, *KGB i vlast'*, 173–84. Bobkov criticized Shelepin for replacing veterans with young, inexperienced party careerists and for having undertaken numerous poorly conceived organizational changes. But his primary objection to Shelepin was his readiness to use the service to advance his own career. For another view, see CIA Information Report, 26 Mar. 1971, "Close Associates of Shelepin and Semichastny During Their Tenure as Chief of the KGB; Impact of Shelepin on the KGB," CIA-HRP. Anatoly Golitsyn's position is contained in his *New Lies for Old* (New York: Dodd, Mead, 1984).

51. Siomonchuk interview.

52. Ibid.

53. A. A. Krokhin served as resident in Paris from 1950 to 1954 before he became chief of the illegals directorate. He returned to Paris as resident from 1966 to 1971. See KBS, 74–75.

54. The Thirteenth Department was the latest designation of the Ninth Department, which in turn was the successor to the First Special Bureau. The First Special Bureau was created in 1946 as a sabotage and special tasks agency based on the wartime Fourth Directorate. This department always controlled a group within the Karlshorst apparat. According to M. S. Dokuchayev, former head of foreign counterintelligence and deputy chief of the Ninth (Guards) Directorate, Fadeikin was his chief when he was assigned to the Thirteenth Department. See *Moskva. Kreml'. Okhrana* (Moscow: Bizness-Press, 1995), 23. The official SVR biographic sketch on Fadeikin omits this period in Fadeikin's career—see KBS, 143–44.

55. Siomonchuk interview.

56. Ibid.

57. Siomonchuk interview. On its face this was a strange remark to a man whose apparat had been handling some of the KGB's best penetrations of Western intelligence services and other targets in the West.

58. Ibid.

59. Kondrashev.

Chapter 16. Khrushchev's Ultimatum

1. Dispatch, Berlin to Chief, SR, 24 Nov. 1958, from Popov meeting transcript, pp. 8–12, CIA-HRP. According to Popov, KGB sought to place additional apparat personnel under cover of such Soviet elements as the embassy and trade delegation that would remain in Berlin even after military control had been transferred to the East Germans. BOB had earlier become aware of KGB's increasing use of nonmilitary cover, but it had interpreted this change as stemming from KGB's desire to enable its officers in Karlshorst to travel to West Germany and elsewhere in Europe—not as a shift away from the use of military cover. Popov also complained that GRU, which relied totally on military cover, had not prepared for these changes.

2. Ibid., p. 10, CIA-HRP.

3. FRUS, 1958–60, vol. 8, p. 133.

4. Office of Current Intelligence memorandum, 1 Nov. 1957, "The Berlin Situation," CIA-HRP.

5. FRUS, 1958–60, vol. 9, pp. 713–30.

6. FRUS, 1958–60, vol. 9, pp. 711–13.

7. Current Intelligence Weekly, 5 Feb. 1959, pt. 3, "Communist Tactic Against West Berlin," CIA-HRP.

8. David Martin, *Wilderness of Mirrors* (New York: Ballantine, 1990), 68. Fear of a "Russian invasion" was very real to those who were in Berlin following the ultimatum. The reminiscences in these paragraphs are those of David Murphy.

9. FRUS, 1958–60, vol. 8, pp. 36–38.

10. Hope M. Harrison, *Ulbricht and the Concrete "Rose": New Archival Evidence on the Dynamics of Soviet–East German Relations and the Berlin Crisis, 1958–1961,* Working Paper 5, CWIHP, May 1993. It was ironic that whereas most refugees left for economic reasons, many, including members of the intelligentsia, left because the decisions of the Fifth SED Congress had demonstrated Ulbricht's determination to achieve socialism on the Soviet model. Because the Soviets could not openly criticize these decisions, their response, as in a 28 Aug. 1958 letter to the CPSU by Yuri Andropov, was to claim that SED officials "did not know how to relate to the intelligentsia and needed help" (p. 17).

11. FRUS, 1958–60, vol. 9, pp. 711–13.

12. Kondrashev. Actually the "defector" was a KGB agent who enabled KGB operatives to remove the strong box and bring it back to Karlshorst by truck through the American zone.

13. Report no. 1/16–291, 27 Jan. 1958, signed by F. Mortin, SVRA file 79541, vol. 10, pp. 125–27.

14. Part 6, "Production," undated memorandum, Goleniewski case, Paragraph D.3, p. 42. CIA-HRP.

15. SVRA file 505891, pp. 65–78, Memorandum no. 23/1/1537, 21 June 1958. According to Kondrashev, the existence of the tunnel was such a closely guarded secret that "officers working in the counterintelligence (KI) line of the Berlin apparat had no access whatsoever to information on it."

16. In "The Organizational and Operational Tradition," the first segment of *Soviet Strategic Deception,* ed. Brian D. Dailey and Patrick J. Parker (Lexington, Mass.: D. C. Heath, 1987), John J. Dziak emphasizes Shelepin's role in laying the groundwork for and creating the new disinformation department. Richards J. Heuer, Jr., in his "Soviet Organization and Doctrine for Strategic Deception," pp. 21–54 of the same volume, states that " 'Service A' is the current designation for the component that began in 1959 as Department D."

17. Anatoly Golitsyn, *New Lies for Old: The Communist Strategy of Deception and Disinformation* (New York: Dodd, Mead, 1984). Kondrashev completely rejects the thesis that the Sino-Soviet split was faked. He notes that a principal reason for his temporary transfer to the KGB Border Guards as chief of their intelligence directorate was the tense situation that developed after the bloody clashes on Damanski island in 1969. It was his inspection of the entire frontier that convinced the Soviet leadership that the Chinese forces were preparing for conflict. In fact, as early as 1963, KGB chairman Semichastni had advised the Central Committee of Beijing's "gradual takeover of Soviet islands" on the Amur and Ussuri rivers. See Mikhail Prozumenshchikov, "Postepennoe osvoenie sovetskikh ostrovov," *Istochnik* 6 (1995). This view of the Sino-Soviet split is reflected in other source reports, one of which noted that as the split worsened, a secret Chinese section was created in Service A in the late 1960s to conduct active measures against Beijing. The section included almost half of the entire strength of the service, which at that time was at least one hundred (Memorandum, undated, "Department 'A' [Disinformation]," CIA-HRP).

18. Kondrashev.

19. Kondrashev. Kondrashev was appointed deputy chief of the Department in 1962 and became chief in early 1968.

20. Kondrashev.

21. SVRA file 87597, vol. 26, pp. 346–71. The handwritten notations on the report offer further clues about its origins and the procedural reasons why its distribution was delayed. The document, some sixty-eight pages in length, originated with an East European service, which in turn must have obtained it from a source in a West European government. This route can be determined from the notation made when the original of the report was returned from the translation section to the First Chief Directorate's Eleventh Department, which was responsible for liaison with friendly services (the translation section also certified that it had destroyed the draft translation). The notation that the report was sent "for orientation" to Berlin and Prague indicates that the originating service was probably Hungarian or Polish. Thus, the chain of reports

dissemination led from the "friendly" service to the Eleventh Department, from which it was sent to translation (a long process), and then to the Information Service for dissemination.

22. Ibid.

23. There is no exact Russian equivalent for "deterrence." As David Holloway points out in *The Soviet Union and the Arms Race* (New Haven: Yale University Press, 1983), the Soviets used *ustrashenie,* intimidation, when referring to Western policy, and *zderzhivanie,* restraining or holding back, when describing Soviet policy.

24. SVRA file 87597, vol. 26, pp. 346–71.

25. Kondrashev. There is further evidence of the report's connection with ongoing active measures program. It bears a notation from Sakharovsky, then chief of the First Chief Directorate to Agayants, chief of Department D: "Prepare a proposal and send it to Berlin." Below that on the report is a note from Agayants to a specific page of the report. Kondrashev's signature indicates that he received Agayants's order.

26. The anti-Strauss effort measures by Department D had apparently begun in May 1961 and ended successfully when he left the cabinet as a result of the campaign against him run by *Der Spiegel,* which utilized KGB-supplied material. See Ilya Dzhirkvelov, *Secret Servant* (London: Collins, 1987), 298–301.

27. FRUS, 1958–60, vol. 8, pp. 163, 320.

Chapter 17. BOB Counters the Soviet Propaganda Campaign

1. Current Intelligence Weekly, 15 Jan. 1959, CIA-HRP.

2. BOB, Karlshorst Compound Situation Reports, 16 Jan., 21 Jan., and 11 Feb. 1959, CIA-HRP.

3. Intelligence Report, 6 Apr. 1959, "Soviet Official's Comments on the Berlin Situation," CIA-HRP.

4. Karlshorst Situation Reports, 7 and 13 Apr. 1959, CIA-HRP.

5. Intelligence Report, 9 Apr. 1959, "Dissolution of Soviet Long Distance Exchange Facilities in Karlshorst," CIA-HRP.

6. Karlshorst Situation Report, 20 Apr. 1959, CIA-HRP.

7. Intelligence Report, 16 Apr. 1959, "Description of the Soviet Compound at Karlshorst, East Berlin"; Current Intelligence Weekly, 7 May 1959, pt. 3, pp. 1–16, CIA-HRP.

8. BOB, Karlshorst Compound Situation Reports, 1 July 1959, 15 Sept. 1959, CIA-HRP.

9. Current Intelligence Weekly, 29 Jan. 1959, "Investigation of Intelligence Operations in West Berlin," pp. 2–3, CIA-HRP.

10. Coverage of the Dombrowski press conference was complete in West Germany but was also picked up on 22 and 23 Jan. 1959 by such newspapers as the *Chicago Tribune, New York Herald Tribune, New York Times, New York Mirror,* and *Baltimore Sun.*

11. Document Transfer and Cross Reference Memorandum, 10 Aug. 1956, CIA-HRP.

12. Dispatch, Berlin, 1 May 1957, CIA-HRP.

13. Ibid.

14. English translation of Linke notes on the Mar. 1957 Moscow Conference, CIA-HRP.

15. GRU Karlshorst was reluctant to complain about this increase in independent operational activity by the East Germans lest the East Germans insist on conducting liaison directly with GRU Moscow rather than through East Berlin. If this were to happen, GRU Karlshorst would no longer receive credit at GRU headquarters for reports supplied by Linke. Berlin Dispatch, 7 Mar. 1958, CIA-HRP.

16. Cable, BOB, 22 June 1957, CIA-HRP.

17. Ibid.

18. Dispatch, Berlin, 12 Sept. 1957, CIA-HRP.

19. Cable, BOB, 6 Aug. 1958, CIA-HRP.

20. Memorandum, undated, "Effect of a CE/PP Operation on the East German Military Intelligence Chief and his Organization," CIA-HRP.

21. Ibid.

22. There is a fascinating sequel to the Dombrowski case demonstrating how difficult it is to separate fact from fiction in intelligence literature: in 1972 Heinz Hoehne and Hermann Zolling, authors of *The General Was a Spy,* claimed that Dombrowski had been recruited by the West German Intelligence Service (BND) in 1956 and had accompanied General Linke to Moscow in 1957, where he provided BND with Linke's report of the conference. Although Dombrowski had fallen under KGB suspicion, BND, according to this tale, had managed to trick KGB by having Dombrowski pass to KGB reports it had prepared in the handwriting of one of the Soviet advisers. A clever trick, but not enough, according to this account, to save Dombrowski, who was told by BND in Aug. 1958 to be ready to leave when ordered. He came to the West in Dec. 1958, and in Feb. 1959 Linke and many others were demoted or dismissed. We do not know precisely how the authors of this dramatic episode put this tale together, but certainly parts of it were taken from BOB's Jan. 1959 counterattack material, supplemented by large doses of literary license. See Hoehne and Zolling, *The General Was a Spy* (New York: Coward, McCann, and Geoghegan, 1957), 211–12.

23. Source of epigraph: FRUS, 1958–60, vol. 8, p. 804.

24. William Bundy, telephone conversation, 1 Feb. 1996.

25. FRUS, 1958–60, vol. 8, pp. 803–4. At the morning meeting of the US delegation preceding the afternoon meeting of the foreign ministers, Defense Secretary McElroy "thought we should still evaluate the importance of our activities in Berlin which are offensive to the Soviets." Herter indicated that he intended to discuss the subject with the Soviets at the afternoon meeting and was again assured by William Bundy, the CIA representative, that "our data on Communist activities could be used without compromising sources." See FRUS, 1958–60, vol. 8, pp. 798–99.

26. FRUS, 1958–60, vol. 8, p. 812.

27. *New York Herald Tribune,* 7 June 1959.

Chapter 18. Bluffs, Threats, and Counterpressures

1. BOB, Karlshorst Situation Report, 5 May 1960, CIA-HRP.

2. Dispatch, Berlin, 2 May 1960, CIA-HRP.

3. Ibid.

4. Ibid.

5. CIA Special NIE, 3 May 1960, "The Situation and Prospects in East Germany," CIA-HRP.

6. Hope Harrison, *Ulbricht and the Concrete "Rose": New Archival Evidence on the Dynamics of Soviet–East German Relations and the Berlin Crisis, 1958–1961,* Working Paper 5, CWIHP, May 1993.

7. A disagreement of the magnitude described in chapter 15 might have inhibited the free flow of information from MfS to the KGB Karlshorst apparat.

8. Report no. 1/16-5827, 16 Nov. 1960, SVRA file 83531, vol. 22, pp. 436–40.

9. Soviet radar tracked the U-2 flights over the USSR from the very beginning (4 July 1956), tried unsuccessfully to reach them with MIGs, and complained regularly about them through diplomatic channels. Popov had overheard gossip about the protests, and in reporting on this to Kisevalter and Murphy, he jokingly compared them to the repeated "serious warnings" from Mao Tse-tung to the Americans during the Taiwan crisis.

10. Vladislav M. Zubok, CWIHP, Working Paper no. 5, pp. 12–13. Raymond L. Garthoff, "The KGB Reports to Gorbachev," *Intelligence and National Security* 11, no. 2 (Apr. 1996): 224–44, discusses KGB annual reports for the years 1967, 1985, 1986, 1988, and 1989. He states that Zubok read and made notes of the 1960 report. For the most complete account of the U-2 incident and its Paris Summit repercussions, see Michael R. Beschloss, *May Day: The U-2 Affair* (New York: Harper and Row, 1986).

11. Report no. 3023-Sh, 18 Nov. 1960, SVRA file 83531, vol. 22, pp. 442–46.

12. Report no. 1/16-4875, 3 Sept. 1960, SVRA file 83531, vol. 22, pp. 75–76. In Kondrashev's comments on this report, he notes that the document was linked to the failure of the Paris summit. This claim is not illogical given the last paragraph relating to Berlin, although the report contains no direct reference to the summit's failure. It was at about this time that Lemmer became FRG minister for post and telecommunications.

13. Report no. 1/16-4968, 9 Sept. 1960, SVRA file 83531, vol. 22, pp. 60–61.

14. Ibid., p. 62.

15. Report no. 2554-Sh, 28 Sept. 1960, SVRA file 83531, vol. 22, pp. 116–45.

16. Vladislav M. Zubok, "Spy vs. Spy: The KGB vs. the CIA, 1960–62," CWIHP *Bulletin* 4 (fall 1994): 22–33. Even though the memorandum containing the KGB proposals originated with KGB chairman Shelepin, as soon as it arrived in the secretariat it became the property of the Central Committee, which retained it in their archives.

17. Ibid. For example, para. 1e of Shelepin's same 7 June proposal to Khrushchev suggests that the KGB "prepare, publish and disseminate abroad a satirical pamphlet on A. Dulles." This was actually done under the direction of Vasily Romanovich Sitnikov, who at that time was a deputy to Agayants in Department D. The publication, *A Study of a Master Spy,* was printed in London in 1961 and reportedly was written by a Labour Member of Parliament; see Paul W. Blackstock, *Agents of Deceit* (Chicago: Quadrangle, 1966), 280. Sitnikov served extensively in Germany and Austria. His assignment to Department D followed his abrupt return from Bonn, where he had spent January to July 1959. He later became an adviser to KGB chairman Andropov.

18. The proposal called for articles on these activities to be prepared for publication "in the bourgeois press, through available means"—that is, KGB agents. For example, a BND officer working on Karlshorst operations had been given an office in the US compound and "appropriate documentation" by BOB. This action was taken at Heinz Felfe's suggestion, and he would have reported this to KGB. See Zubok, "Spy vs. Spy," 27.

19. Current Intelligence Weekly, 18 Aug. 1960, CIA-HRP.

20. Ibid. The East German railroad system (Reichsbahn) in West Berlin, including the elevated express train system (S-Bahn), contained over one hundred individual installations, ranging from freight and passenger stations to repair shops, employing thousands of workers. The Soviet occupation authorities, and later the East Germans, considered it essential to retain control over these properties after the 1948 split in Berlin city administrations. The rail lines themselves offered opportunities for infiltrating large numbers of personnel into West Berlin from East Berlin and the GDR. The various railroad installations provided assembly points and operational bases throughout the city for subversive actions.

21. FRUS, 1958–60, vol. 9, pp. 94–95, 101–2.

22. Dispatch, Berlin, 1 Aug. 1960, CIA-HRP.

23. Ibid.

24. Meetings of the Bundestag had been held in West Berlin since 1954.

25. SVRA file 85531, vol. 22, pp. 167, 168.

26. CIA Information Report Telegram (disseminated electronically), 13 Sept. 1960, "Implications of New East German Measures Against Berlin: Situation Report as of 7 September 1960," which also described East German plans to force East Berliners with essential skills to quit their jobs in West Berlin. CIA-HRP. This CIA Information Report was based on a cabled commentary on the situation prepared by BOB "officers stationed in Berlin since 1952–54." Soviet documents from the period suggest that not only the West but also the Soviets were surprised by this East German action. See Harrison, *Ulbricht and the Concrete "Rose,"* 27.

27. In a telegram from Ambassador Dowling in Bonn, these control measures were regarded as significant in that the East Germans "are acting as if a separate treaty were already in effect and Soviets had in fact turned over access controls to them." See FRUS, 1958–60, vol. 9, p. 563.

28. The campaign against East Berliners working in West Berlin had actually begun before the 30 Aug. measures were invoked. See CIA Information Report Telegram, 13 Sept. 1960.

29. Ibid. Although plans for this week of special controls had reportedly already been in the works in East Berlin, BOB believed the decision to move this rapidly derived from the sharp increase in the "quantity and quality of refugees fleeing East Germany during the month of August." For example, in Aug. 1953, right after the 17 June uprising, 10,857 refugees came into West Berlin. During August 1960, 18,409 of a total 21,000 refugees came through West Berlin.

30. Ibid.

31. Ibid.

32. Ibid. This alternative would seek agreement on limiting further expansion of the FRG political presence in West Berlin, although economic and cultural ties between West Berlin and West Germany "would be increased and intensified."

33. SVRA file 83531, vol. 22, p. 295. The Bucharest meeting noted in the report was probably the conference of leaders of Communist and Workers parties, which was held after the Congress of the Romanian Party.

34. Ibid. Of interest is the absence of any KGB reporting on Willy Brandt's visit to Vienna in October 1960 during "Berlin Week," when he vigorously defended West Berlin. Kondrashev was deputy KGB resident in Vienna at the time.

35. Report no. 3227, 10 Dec. 1960, SVRA file 83531, vol. 22, pp. not cited. For background on the new IZT, see FRUS, 1961–1963, vol. 14, pp. 1–3.

36. Ibid.

Chapter 19. Facing the Inevitable

1. Cable, Berlin, 4 Jan. 1961; Dispatch, Berlin, 15 Feb. 1961, CIA-HRP. Murphy recollections.

2. Dispatch, Berlin, 15 Feb. 1961, CIA-HRP.

3. Ibid.

4. Ibid. Mary Ellen Reese, *General Reinhard Gehlen: The CIA Connection* (Fairfax, Va.: George Mason University Press, 1990), 155, states that "Howard Roman flew from Washington to West Berlin where Sniper was to make the crossing." Actually, Roman, who had been the Washington desk officer handling the case, did not meet Sniper until he and his mistress arrived at the US Air Force base in Wiesbaden, West Germany, whence they left for the United States.

5. Part 6, "Production," from an operational account of the Goleniewski case, describing counterintelligence and intelligence information he provided (in addition to the identifications of Blake and Felfe) before his illness intervened (CIA-HRP). For background on Goleniewski's Soviet relationships, see also Memorandum, 4 Jan. 1964, "Goleniewski's Work with the Soviets," CIA-HRP.

6. Dispatch, BOB, 15 May 1959, CIA-HRP.

7. Contact Report, 27 Oct. 1959, CIA-HRP.

8. Document Transfer and Cross Reference, memorandum, 29 Nov. 1960, CIA-HRP.

9. Ibid.

10. Dispatch, Berlin, 24 July 1961, CIA-HRP.

11. Cable, Berlin, 2 July 1954, CIA-HRP.

12. Contact Report, 17 July 1956, CIA-HRP.

13. Dispatch, Berlin, 2 June 1959, CIA-HRP.

14. Report of Agent Dismissal, 9 Oct. 1959, CIA-HRP.

15. Dispatch, Berlin, 19 July 1961, CIA-HRP.

16. Memorandum, 18 May 1962, CIA-HRP.

17. CIA Information Report, 17 June 1959, CIA-HRP.

18. CIA Information Report, 15 Dec. 1960; CIA Information Report, 16 Dec. 1960, CIA-HRP.

19. CIA Information Report, 6 Feb. 1961, CIA-HRP.

20. CIA Information Report, 13 Apr. 1961, CIA-HRP. See also John C. Torpey, *Intellectuals, Socialism, and Dissent: The East German Opposition and Its Legacy* (Minneapolis: University of Minnesota Press, 1995), 106–7.

21. Memorandum for DDP, from Chief, EE Division, Subj.: Clandestine Action in Support of the US Berlin Policy, 23 Mar. 1961, CIA-HRP.

22. Ibid.

23. Ibid.

24. Ibid.

25. SVRA file 84909, vol. 24, pp. 116–17.

26. Report of the First Chief Directorate, signed by Deputy Chief Mortin, no. 1/16–1888, 3 May 1961, SVRA file 84909, vol. 24, p. 83.

27. PGU Report no. 1/16–1889, 3 May 1961, signed by Mortin, sent to Foreign Ministry, attention G. M. Pushkin, SVRA file 84909, vol. 24, pp. 84, 85 (extract).

28. Report PGU KGB no. 1/16–2333, 6 May 1961, signed by A. A. Krokhin, sent to the Soviet Foreign Ministry, attention V. S. Semenov, SVRA file 84909, vol. 24, pp. 162, 163 (extract).

29. Ibid. See also FRUS, 1961–63, vol. 13, pp. 269–72.

30. Kondrashev.

31. The agenda was covered in the 15 Mar. 1961 meeting of the Presidium of the CC CPSU (Protocol no. 319) at which the Presidium approved the formal invitation to Warsaw Pact member states and to observers (China, North Korea, Mongolia, and North Vietnam) to attend the Political Consultative Committee session in Moscow on 28–29 Mar. 1961. The invitational letter set the time of the meeting, the agenda, and order of business and named the Soviet delegation (Khrushchev, Gromyko, and Defense Minister R. Ia. Malinovsky). The formal agenda consisted of a report by Marshal Grechko, commander-in-chief of Warsaw Pact military forces on readiness and equipment, and a report by USSR State Planning Commission Deputy Chairman M. V. Khrunichev on specialization of military production within the Warsaw Pact and mutual deliveries of military equipment. These reports were delivered at the morning session on 28 Mar. at which no transcript was made. See TsKhSD f. 10, op. 3, d. 5. These documents relevant to the 28–29 Mar. 1961 Warsaw Pact Political Consultative Committee meeting were declassified in late October 1996 and made available to Kondrashev.

32. Chairmen of the Warsaw Pact Political Consultative Committee meetings were named in alphabetical order, according to the Cyrillic alphabet. The chairman of the February 1960 meeting was the head of the Hungarian delegation, and Ulbricht, as head of the GDR delegation, was given this position in March 1961.

33. TsKhSD f. 10, op. 3, d. 5.

34. Kondrashev provided a copy of the Pervukhin letter from Russian Foreign Ministry archives (AVP). On this copy of the letter is a notation indicating the letter was sent to V. S. Semyonov and I. I. Ilichev. An English translation of the letter is contained in appendix D of Hope Harrison's *Ulbricht and the Concrete "Rose": New Archival Evidence on the Dynamics of Soviet–East German Relations and the Berlin Crisis, 1958–1961,* Working Paper 5, CWIHP, May 1993.

Chapter 20. Countdown to the Wall

1. Peter Wyden, *Wall: The Inside Story of Divided Berlin* (New York: Simon and Schuster, 1989), 93. In Wyden's description of Graver, it is said that he was known by the sobriquet "El Supremo." This might have been true elsewhere, but not at BOB. Everyone there, including Bill Harvey, knew Graver as "der Lange."

2. FRUS, 1961–63, vol. 14, pp. 87–98.

3. Kondrashev.

4. FRUS, 1961–63, vol. 14, pp. 98–102.

5. See Honore M. Catudal, *Kennedy and the Berlin Wall Crisis: A Case Study in U.S. Decision Making* (Berlin: Berlin Verlag, 1980), 125. Hope Harrison, in *Ulbricht and the Concrete "Rose": New Evidence on the Dynamics of Soviet–East German Relations and the Berlin Crisis,* Working Paper 5, CWIHP, May 1993, quotes Soviet diplomat Yuli Kvitsinsky as believing that Ulbricht was merely relaying an earlier comment to him by Khrushchev: "We [the Soviets] don't conceive in our dreams of erecting a wall through Berlin."

6. FRUS, 1961–63, vol. 14, pp. 138–59.

7. FRUS, 1961–63, vol. 14, pp. 162–65.

8. Memorandum for the Record by Chief, EE Division, 22 June 1961, CIA-HRP.

9. Ibid.

10. Special National Intelligence Estimate SNIE 2-2-61, 11 July 1961, CIA-HRP.

11. Ibid. For example, in his speech to the 3–5 Aug. 1961 Moscow conference of the First Secretaries of the Central Committees of Communist and Workers Parties of Member States of the

Warsaw Pact on questions related to the preparation of a German Peace Treaty, Ulbricht claimed that "both Adenauer and Brandt, in their conversations with leading US politicians, said that it was necessary and possible to find a means of organizing an uprising in the GDR with the goal of overthrowing the workers' and peasants' regime." TsKhSD, f. 10, op. 3, d.7.

12. SVRA file 84909, vol. 24, pp. 241–90.

13. Ibid.

14. SVRA file 92560, vol. 9, pp. 127–34. In a separate KGB report (SVRA file 93272, vol. 1, p. 43) Murphy is reported to have worked in West Berlin from 1955 to 1961—as deputy chief from 1955 to 1959, and as chief from 1959 to 1961.

15. A copy of the Pervukhin letter was provided from AVPRF by Kondrashev. An English translation of the same letter was included as appendix F of Harrison's *Ulbricht and the Concrete "Rose."*

16. Ibid.

17. FRUS, 1961–63, vol. 14, pp. 191–92.

18. Catudal, *Kennedy and the Berlin Wall Crisis,* 187–88.

19. Report no. 1795-sh, 20 July 1961, SVRA file 84909, vol. 24, pp. 225–33.

20. Kondrashev.

21. Report no. 2152-sh, 31 Aug. 1961, SVRA file 86304, vol. 25, pp. 13–16.

22. FRUS, 1961–63, vol. 14, p. 228.

23. Ibid., p. 252.

24. *Istochnik: Dokumenty russkoi istorii* 1, no. 14 (1995): 52–59. The archival source for the document was given as TsKhSD, f. 5, op. 30, d. 351, ll. 26–31 (27–30 s ob).

25. Vladislav M. Zubok, "Spy vs. Spy: The KGB vs. the CIA, 1960–62," CWIHP *Bulletin* 4 (fall 1994): 22–33.

26. Ibid.

27. SVRA file 87579, vol. 26, pp. 77–78. The report, no. 1/16-1874 of 3 Mar. 1962, was prepared as an Information Report *(zapiska)* by the First Chief Directorate for V. V. Kuznetsov, with a copy to I. I. Agayants, then chief of Department D.

28. SVRA file 87668, vol. 9, pp. 61–67. West Berlin greatly irritated GDR authorities, but the issue of closing off access to it was a sensitive one for KGB, which benefited from cross-border traffic. Responding to Ulbricht's desire to take "appropriate measures" regarding border crossers, on 20 July the Presidium of the Central Committee CPSU approved a proposal by Presidium members Gromyko, Mikoyan, and Kozlov directing Ambassador Pervukhin to advise Ulbricht that it "would be expedient to proceed gradually without at first applying harsh measures of administrative pressure, in order not to cause a worsening of the situation or retaliatory measures by the Western powers." TsKhSD, f. 3, op. 14, d. 491, l. 21. Obtained by Kondrashev.

29. Ibid.

30. See chapter 19 for Ulbricht's comments at the 28–29 Mar. 1961 Warsaw Pact PCC meeting in Moscow. See also *Neues Deutschland,* 9 July 1961, quoting Eric Honecker at the 13th Plenum of the CC SED.

31. TsKhSD, f. 3, op. 14, d. 947, ll. 26–42. Obtained by Kondrashev. In a clever twist, Mikoyan and Gromyko urged that only traffic from West Berlin to the FRG be suspended because that would be "a blow to West German firms that obtain manufactured products from West Berlin but would not . . . interfere with the operation of West Berlin industry or the supply of food to the population."

32. Kondrashev. To preserve security, directives to TASS, Foreign Ministry, and KGB were not issued until after this action was given formal approval at the 12 Aug. meeting of the Presidium.

33. The timing for the 3–5 Aug. meeting was conveyed to Ulbricht by Ambassador Pervukhin based on instructions from Gromyko and Andropov dated 30 June 1961. TsKhSD, f. 3, op. 12, ll. 61–64. Obtained by Kondrashev.

34. TsKhSD, f. 10, op. 3, d. 7. Obtained by Kondrashev.

35. Report, First Chief Directorate, no. 1/16-3338, 8 Aug. 1961, SVRA file 84909, vol. 24, p. 335. One source of this information was a 13 Apr. 1961 letter from the chief of the liaison

mission of the Commander in Chief of French Forces in Germany to the French Embassy in Bonn. The letter may have been obtained by the KGB agent in the French military mission code named Arnold, run for a time by the KGB illegal Lt. Col. Yevgeny Runge.

36. FRUS, 1961–63, vol. 14, pp. 281–91. During this same session, von Brentano commented that if Allied access were to be blocked, "he could not imagine continuation of interzonal trade."

37. Zubok, "Spy vs. Spy," 28. Awareness of this KGB report on the Paris conference was found in a letter from GRU Deputy Chief A. Rogov to Defense Minister Malinovsky dated 24 Aug. 1961, which explains why KGB got the jump on GRU. The GRU letter was found in TsKhSD archives. Kondrashev declared that he was unable to find the original KGB report.

38. Kondrashev, based on research in TsKhSD CPSU Central Committee files undertaken to prove or disprove the Abrasimov statement.

39. Harrison, *Ulbricht and the Concrete "Rose."*

40. TsKhSD, f. 3, op. 14, d. 494, ll. 1–2. Obtained by Kondrashev. Matériel for the "special reserve" for GDR industry was to be taken from Soviet production and where necessary from purchases abroad (the State Bank was to be allocated fifty-three tons of gold for sale abroad to pay for the special reserve purchases). Accompanying the decree was a note dated 11 Aug. from the State Planning Commission providing details on the raw materials and manufactured goods involved. Underlining the urgency of this situation was exceptional authorization from the Presidium to the Commission on Exit Visas (Komissiia po vyezdam zagranitsu) to issue exit visas for travel to the GDR within five days for specialists designated by the State Planning Commission to work with East German industry.

41. Wyden, *Wall,* 134.

42. Ibid., pp. 81–82.

43. Ibid., pp. 134–36.

44. Oleg Gordievsky, *Next Stop Execution* (London: Macmillan, 1995), 93–96.

45. Jerrold L. Schecter and Peter S. Deriabin, *The Spy Who Saved the World* (New York: Scribners, 1992), 181–226.

Chapter 21. The Berlin Wall: Winners and Losers

1. FRUS, 1961–63, vol. 14, pp. 345–46.

2. Ibid., pp. 347–49. Included in FRUS coverage of the meeting on 17 Aug. was an excerpt from an article by Murphy in *Studies in Intelligence* [CIA in-house journal] 33 (winter 1989): 79–80, in which he described the meeting. This article was reprinted in the *Newsletter of the Central Intelligence Retirees Association* 15, no. 2 (summer 1990).

3. Ibid.

4. SVRA file 86304, vol. 25, p. 5.

5. Current Intelligence Weekly, 24 Aug. 1961, CIA-HRP.

6. Ibid. See also FRUS, 1961–63, vol. 14, pp. 372, 384–85, 410.

7. FRUS, 1961–63, vol. 14, p. 393.

8. Ibid., pp. 338–39, 393, 398–99.

9. Jerrold L. Schecter and Peter Deriabin, *The Spy Who Saved the World* (New York: Scribners, 1992), 228–29. Penkovsky got this information at a birthday party for Marshal Varentsov, Chief of Soviet Rocket Forces, which was attended by Defense Minister Malinovsky and other high-ranking officials—see Special National Intelligence Estimate SNIE 11-10/1-61, 5 Oct. 1961, CIA-HRP. In the limited distribution issue of this SNIE referring to this Penkovsky report, a footnote appeared: "We have examined closely the possibility that the source could be, wittingly or unwittingly, a channel for deception material. Our present judgment, based mainly on the sensitivity and volume of the material he is providing, is that this is unlikely." Actually, massive maneuvers were never used in Germany as a cover for surprise military action, but this strategy was practiced successfully by the Soviets in the invasion of Czechoslovakia.

10. SVRA file 86304, vol. 25, pp. 33–45.

11. SVRA file 86304, vol. 25, p. 57.

12. SVRA file 86304, vol. 25, pp. 52–56.

13. Ibid.

14. Kondrashev.

15. SVRA file 87688, vol. 9, pp. 82–84. Report of a conversation with a (KGB) source *(spravka o besede s istochnikom)*.

16. Ibid.

17. Berlin Dispatch, 6 Nov. 1961, CIA-HRP.

18. Ibid.

19. Chief BOB to CIA Headquarters, 14 Sept. 1961, CIA-HRP.

20. Dispatch, Berlin, 6 Nov. 1961, CIA-HRP.

21. Ibid.

22. Ibid.

23. FRUS, 1961–63, vol. 14, p. 348. The attorney general remained concerned about the need to "stimulate worldwide protest" on matters relating to the Berlin crisis. When the Soviets resumed atmospheric testing in early September 1961, it was seen as a crude attempt at intimidation connected to the crisis. Murphy, then CIA representative on the Berlin Task Force, recalls a meeting in Gen. Maxwell Taylor's office attended by Robert Kennedy shortly after the tests began. Kennedy was furious at CIA's inability to match the capability of the worldwide Communist movement to bring thousands into the street to protest this Soviet action.

24. Heinz Lychenheim, interview, 22 Feb. 1996.

25. Ibid. Peter Ringland, interview, 7 Apr. 1995; William J. Graver, interview, 22 Apr. 1996.

26. John C. Ausland, *Kennedy, Khrushchev, and the Berlin-Cuba Crisis, 1961–64* (Oslo: Scandinavian University Press, 1996), 156–69.

27. FRUS, 1961–63, vol. 14, p. 382.

28. Most historians have focused on the extensive correspondence between Kennedy and Khrushchev during the Cuban missile crisis and its aftermath, but this special channel began almost immediately after Kennedy took office in Jan. 1961. For example, on 18 Jan. 1962, Khrushchev gave Robert Kennedy a message to which President Kennedy responded on 15 Feb., expressing among other things, "grave concern" over the air corridor harassment. The president also mentioned "the possibility of agreements on other issues, including those mentioned in your communications through my brother." That air corridor harassment was temporarily halted during Robert Kennedy's visit to West Berlin a week later is not surprising. FRUS, 1961–63, vol. 14, pp. 819–22.

29. Graver interview.

30. Report no. 2344-i, 28 Sept. 1961, SVRA file 86304, vol. 25, pp. 63, 64.

31. Ibid.

32. Report no. 1/16–4621, SVRA file 86304, vol. 25, pp. 101–2.

33. FRUS, 1961–63, vol. 14, p. 496.

34. Catherine McArdle Kelleher, "NATO Nuclear Operations," in *Managing Nuclear Operations,* ed. Ashton B. Carter, John D. Steinbrunner, and Charles A. Zraket (Washington, D.C.: Brookings Institution, 1987), 445.

35. SVRA file 86304, vol. 25, pp. 127–28.

36. Steinstuecken was one of twelve small areas that were part of West Berlin yet separated from it by intervening East German territory.

37. See FRUS, 1961–63, vol. 14, pp. 441–43; Jean Edward Smith, *Lucius D. Clay: An American Life* (New York: Holt, 1990), 658–59; and Ausland, *Kennedy, Khrushchev, and the Berlin-Cuba Crisis,* 37. These accounts of the Steinstuecken incident differ in details. Bill Graver remembers that Clay wanted to enter the enclave by car, taking the East German guards by surprise, because he was confident they would not refuse him entry to a part of the US sector. This plan leaked: he was greeted by the mayor of the Zehlendorf District with flowers, but the guards barred his way. It was then that he went in by helicopter.

38. This account of the incident involving Lightner and the prelude to the tank confrontation was taken from FRUS, 1961–63, vol. 14, pp. 532–43. See also Ausland, *Kennedy, Khrushchev and the Berlin Crisis,* 38–39, and Graver interview.

39. Graver interview.

40. The key points in this call, made at 5:55 P.M. Berlin time on 27 Oct., were repeated in a cable by US Commandant Gen. Albert Watson II to Gen. Lauris Norstad at about 7:00 P.M. Berlin time and in a Clay cable to Rusk sent at 8:00 P.M. Berlin time. FRUS, 1961–63, vol. 14, p. 543.

41. Peter Wyden, *Wall: The Inside Story of Divided Berlin* (New York: Simon and Schuster, 1989), 263–64; Smith, *Lucius D. Clay,* 661; and Graver interview.

42. FRUS, 1961–63, vol. 14, p. 544.

43. Report no. 2613-sh, 31 Oct. 1961, SVRA file 86304, vol. 25, pp. 109–10. This call must have been made in the clear on circuits routinely monitored by the Soviets. Had it been made on a secure telephone that the KGB had been able to decipher, it probably would not have been released.

44. Ibid. Also Graver interview. Khrushchev claims it was his initiative (*Khrushchev Remembers* [Boston: Little, Brown, 1970], 460), whereas Wyden, *Wall,* 266n, quotes Robert Kennedy as telling John Bartlow Martin that it was President Kennedy's "special channel" message to the Soviet leader that did the trick.

45. FRUS, 1961–63, vol. 14, pp. 619, 704.

46. SVRA file 509492, vol. 1, pp. 33, 34.

47. SVRA file 509492, vol. 1, pp. 235–239.

48. FRUS, 1961–63, vol. 14, p. 640; and SVRA file 86304, vol. 25, p. 245. See also FRUS, 1961–63, vol. 14, p. 648.

49. SVRA file 87597, vol. 26, pp. 69–70. See also FRUS, 1961–63, vol. 14, pp. 650–81.

50. Kondrashev. See also FRUS, 1961–63, vol. 14, p. 683. While the Allies were endeavoring to coordinate their military responses to possible interference with land access to Berlin, KGB had an agent, Sgt. Robert Lee Johnson, supplying them with top secret and code-word documents from the vault of the Armed Forces Courier Center at Orly Field in Paris. See John Barron, *KGB: The Secret Work of Soviet Agents* (New York: Reader's Digest Press, 1974), 214–24.

51. When Murphy visited Berlin in fall 1961, Bill Graver took him on a tour of the Wall. By then, *die Mauer,* the Wall, dominated Berlin life in many ways. Murphy visited West Berlin again in 1967; the Wall looked much the same. It would be several years before the East Germans would rebuild their "Wall of Peace" *(Friedensmauer),* using prefabricated slabs topped by a concrete cylinder.

Appendix 1. The Merger of KPD and SPD

1. In a September 1946 report by Tiulpanov to the Central Committee in Moscow, the SMA propaganda chief was very critical of the newly formed SED and its leadership. As for the bourgeois parties created as part of a "national front," Tiulpanov noted that both the Christian Democratic Union (CDU) and Liberal Democratic Party (LDP) had actually served to attract "reactionaries and anti-Soviet elements who were looking for outlets to express their discontent." See Norman M. Naimark, "The Soviet Occupation: Moscow's Man in (East) Berlin," CWIHP *Bulletin* 4 (fall 1994): 35–48.

2. Walter Henry Nelson, *The Berliners: Portrait of a People and a City* (London: Longmans, 1969), 148.

3. Karl Dietrich Bracher, *The German Dictatorship: Origins, Structure, and Effects of National Socialism* (New York: Praeger, 1970), 198.

4. Askold Vsevolodovich Lebedev, interview with Kondrashev, 23 Aug. 1994. Lebedev served with distinction in combat units until June 1945, when he was assigned to the Secretariat of the Soviet Military Administration in Germany (SVAG) under Zhukov, Sokolovsky, and later—when SVAG was reshaped into the Soviet Control Commission (SKK)—Chuikov. Lebedev later joined the foreign intelligence directorate and served in Austria, where his marriage to an Austrian interpreter brought about his dismissal in 1957. He later was employed by the special section in the Novosti Press Agency operated by Norman Mikhailovich Borodin on behalf of the KGB's active measures component.

5. BOB Intelligence Report L-1495, "Russian Methods of Influencing Top-Level Functionaries, 26 Apr. 1946," CIA-HRP. See Norman M. Naimark's *The Russians in Germany: A History of the Soviet Zones of Occupation, 1945–1949* (Cambridge: Belknap Press of Harvard University Press, 1995), 275–90, for additional details on the manner in which SMA brought about the SPD/KPD merger.

6. George Clare, *Before the Wall: Berlin Days, 1946–48* (New York: Dutton, 1989), 120. See also Jean Edward Smith, *Germany Beyond the Wall: People, Politics, . . . Prosperity* (Boston: Little, Brown, 1969), 188. Smith describes the moment on 21 Apr. 1946 when "a thousand delegates from both parties filed into the Admiralspalast in the Soviet sector of Berlin. The scene was festive. . . . Wilhelm Pieck entered the platform from the left; at the same time Otto Grotewohl of the SPD came on stage from the right. They met in the center and clasped hands."

7. In Naimark's words, "Despite protests to the contrary, Soviet sponsorship of the SED meant that the German party would have a distinctively Russian tint. Fresh from victory in war . . . Soviet communists were supremely confident . . . about the way they did things at home" (*Russians in Germany*, 284).

8. SVRA file 60345, vol. 1, p. 147. This meeting report was prepared for the Soviet leadership. Molotov normally sent a copy to the foreign intelligence chief, who retained it in SVR archives. Kondrashev speculates that the document was sent by MGB Berlin to Moscow and then retained in archives because of ongoing MGB investigations. For example, MGB believed that Max Fechner was a British agent. Their suspicions first arose because Fechner was asked several times to move from the British sector, where he had a comfortable apartment, to East Berlin. Even though he finally did move, his refusal to go gave rise to reports that he had been in contact with British intelligence. MGB later received reports that the British were aware of discussions at SED Politburo meetings, and it was suspected that Fechner was the leak.

9. SVRA file 60345, vol. 1, pp. 147–59.

10. Alexander Werth, *Russia at War, 1941–1945* (London: Barrie and Rockliff, 1964), 988.

11. Bracher, *The German Dictatorship*, 72.

12. SVRA file 60345, vol. 1. Sokolovsky's outburst was not unlike the Soviet population's reaction to the question of dismantling and reparations. When considering the scope of the destruction inflicted by the Germans on the Soviet Union, the Soviets at first felt entitled to take anything from the Germans that might contribute to Soviet reconstruction. Little thought was given to the possibility that one day German sensibilities would have to be accommodated in order to gain Germans' support of SED.

13. Gregory Klimov, *The Terror Machine: The Inside Story of the Soviet Administration in Germany* (London: Faber and Faber, 1953). Originally published in Russian as *Berlinskii Kreml'* (The Berlin Kremlin) (Frankfurt am Main: Possev, 1953), this is a very good account of the operation of the economic element of SMA in Germany by a Soviet engineer who participated in these activities and later defected to West Germany.

14. SVRA file 60345, vol. 1.

15. Ibid.

16. Ibid.

17. Karl Schumacher was chairman of the Social Democratic Party (SPD) in the Western zones of occupation; Heinrich Bruening was a Catholic Center Party politician and chancellor during the Weimar period; and Jacob Kaiser was a Christian Democratic Union (CDU) politician in postwar West Germany.

18. Erich Honecker at the time was general secretary of the East German Communist youth organization Free German Youth (FDJ). He replaced Ulbricht as first secretary of SED in 1971 and as minister president of the GDR in 1976. He was dismissed in 1989, and died in exile in Chile in 1994.

19. NARA, RG 226, microfilm 1656, roll 2, contains a representative sampling of 1946 BOB reporting on CDU. See reports A-01386, "CDU Activities in Universities in the Russian Zone"; A-69715, "CDU Reaction to School Reform" (fights exclusion of religion); A-69719, "FDJ and CDU Youth Organizations" (CDU youth told not to join FDJ); A-68575, "Russian Policy

Toward CDU Officials" (no member of the CDU should occupy a leading position); A-68704, "Russian Influence on CDU" (details Russian efforts to hobble CDU organizational efforts in their zone).

20. NARA, RG 226, microfilm 1656, roll 2. Reports on the SPD included A-67509, "Elections in the Trade Unions" (SPD attacks KPD manipulation of elections in trade unions); A-67527, "SPD Efforts to Counter Merger" (failing that to create an independent SPD); A-67797, "KPD-SPD Merger in the Russian Zone of Berlin" (SPD referendum not permitted, troops occupied polling places); A-69359, "Political Propaganda and Pressures by the KPD, FDGB and NKVD" (attacks on the SPD); and A-69723, "Party Activities in Berlin" (Russian harassment of independent SPD in Berlin area).

21. For example, when the Ostburo asked Ambassador Robert Murphy for a contact with American intelligence, the request was turned over to BOB chief Dana Durand, who gave the task of establishing this contact to Henry Hecksher and Tom Polgar. They in turn visited Kurt Schumacher in Hanover; he gave his blessing to the arrangement. Tom Polgar, interview, 19 Oct. 1993. In February 1948, Peter Sichel followed up with an interview in Berlin with SPD Ostburo official Sigmund Neumann from Hanover, to whom he was introduced by Brewster Morris of the OMGUS Office of Political Affairs. Dispatch, 12 Feb. 1948, "Meeting with Sigmund Neumann of the SPD Ostburo," CIA-HRP.

22. Polgar interview. See also Naimark, *Russians in Germany,* which provides extensive detail on Soviet and East German persecution of SPD members in the Soviet zone.

23. SVRA file 60345, vol. 3, pp. 46–82.

24. Ibid.

Appendix 2. Double Agents, Double Trouble

1. Tom Polgar, interview, 19 Oct. 1993; Whitney Tucker, interview, 20 June 1996.

2. *New York Times,* 21 June 1951. When Kemritz was charged by the West German courts several years later for having entrapped Germans wanted by the Soviets, the Allied High Commission claimed that his actions "had been at the behest of an Allied occupation authority, and therefore he could never be brought into German court on these charges."

3. Berlin Special Counterintelligence (SC) Report, 11 Mar. 1946, "Review of Agent Security," CIA-HRP.

4. Berlin SC Report, 14 May 1946, CIA-HRP.

5. Berlin SC Report, 3 Aug. 1946, CIA-HRP.

6. Berlin SC Report, 5 Sept. 1946, "Change in MVD Policy," CIA-HRP.

7. Berlin SC Report, 25 Oct. 1946, "Review of Agent Security," CIA-HRP.

8. "Security of the West," *Der Spiegel,* 20 June 1951, pp. 10–12.

9. Polgar interview. The West German press gave extensive coverage of this case, as did the *New York Herald Tribune.* In a final editorial on 25 June 1951, the newspaper reluctantly supported the decision to transfer the case to US jurisdiction on the basis that "secret agents . . . do expect protection."

10. Berlin SC Report, 8 Nov. 1946, "Personality of Ford—An Evaluation," CIA-HRP.

11. Formed in 1939 under Reinhard Heydrich, RSHA *(Reichsicherheithauptamt)* combined the functions of the Security Police (Gestapo and Kripo) and the Security Service (SD). Its deputy, Gen. Walter Schellenberg, was responsible for RSHA intelligence work abroad.

12. Polgar interview.

13. Memorandum, Special Counterintelligence Operations (SCO) to Deputy Chief of Operations, OSO, 17 Mar. 1947, "CE Operational Progress Report No. 6," CIA-HRP.

14. Berlin SC Report, 12 Apr. 1946, "Doocia—NKVD Interpreter and Secretary," CIA-HRP.

15. NARA, RG 226, entry 108. The reference to "disposal"—or resettlement—was raised because at that time if BOB had induced Doocia's defection in defiance of the Clay-Sokolovsky agreement, the German Mission would have had to relocate her outside of Germany, an expensive and time-consuming effort.

Appendix 3. The Mysterious Case of Leonid Malinin, a.k.a. Georgiev

1. Ilya Dzhirkvelov, *Secret Servant* (London: Collins, 1987), 30. Dzhirkvelov once served in that element of the Disinformation Department of the KGB First Chief Directorate under Novosti Press Agency cover that was used to place items of disinformation.

2. Robert Conquest, *Inside Stalin's Secret Police: NKVD Politics, 1936–1939* (London: Macmillan, 1985), 150.

3. Thomas Polgar, interview, 19 Oct. 1993.

4. Peter Sichel, interview, 14 Dec. 1993.

5. Memorandum, for the Director, Central Intelligence, undated, "Major General Leonid A. Malinin," CIA-HRP.

6. *New York Times,* 20 Apr. 1949; *Washington Post,* 18 Apr. 1949; *New York Herald Tribune,* Paris ed., 20 Apr. 1949.

7. Dispatch, Durand, 8 Apr. 1948, "Report on Berlin Operations Base." Routing and Record Sheet, Henry Hecksher to SR/CE, 30 June 1955, CIA-HRP.

8. Born in the Siberian city of Novosibirsk in 1907, Malinin first served in state security in the transport system. In 1935 he attended the NKVD Central School in Moscow, after which he occupied a series of senior positions in transport until 1941. During the war he served as chief of the NKVD directorate of Odessa Oblast, where he organized the evacuation of the city. From 1943 until 1944 he was chief of the NKGB directorate of Novosibirskaia Oblast. From 1944 to 1945 he occupied the same post in the Ternopolskaia Oblast in the Western Ukraine, which was a hotbed of Ukrainian nationalism. It may have been his service there that led to his appointment as resident in Berlin. Extracts from the personnel file of Malinin, Kondrashev.

9. SVRA file 38179, vol. 5a, pp. 308–13.

10. Ibid.

11. Boris Ia. Nalivaiko, *Tri desiatiletiia na perednem krae* (Three decades in the forward area), SVR Red Banner Andropov Institute, 1993 (thirty copies, classified memoirs retained in the SVR special collection *[spetsfond],* SVRA).

12. Report 160/2487, 14 Nov. 1967, SVRA.

13. Ibid.

14. William R. Harris, "March Crisis, 1948, Act I," *Studies in Intelligence* [CIA in-house journal] 10 (fall 1966): 4, CIA-HRP. Harris states that Clay "interpreted the contacting of his political adviser, Robert Murphy, by a General 'Georgiev' (who was really Lt. Gen. L. A. Malinin of the MVD) as an additional Soviet effort to gauge American plans for Germany." Although it is possible that Robert Murphy mentioned to Clay his encounters with Malinin, he never advised Dana Durand of this, which is strange considering that the contact was the result of a BOB operation.

Appendix 4. MGB at Work in East Germany

1. SVRA file 60345, vol. 23. The reports were entitled "An Account and Observations on the Work of the MGB Opersectors in Germany," and they covered the periods 1 Jan.–1 July and 1 July–31 Dec. 1948. These operations collected information on Soviet military installations via agents who would visit the target sites and physically observe, as well as sometimes sketch or photograph, the installation. Winter weather made such operations difficult, hence the number of such agents dispatched in the spring—and sometimes captured—rose sharply.

2. SVRA file 60345, "Report on operations case 'Nit.'"

3. Memorandum for the S-2, from Headquarters, Berlin Military Post, APO 742, 19 July 1948, "Military Intelligence" (regraded unclassified 11 Aug. 1994 by CRD USAINSCOM FOI/PG).

4. Memorandum, S-2 Berlin Command to Deputy Director of Intelligence, European Command, Heidelberg, 27 June 1948, "Affiliated Operations" (regraded unclassified 11 Aug. 1994 by CRD USAINSCOMNFO/1PO).

5. Letter, Headquarters European Command, 29 June 1948, "Affiliated Operations" (EUCOM declassified, 94-00016).

6. In an address reprinted in the *CIRA Newsletter* 19, no. 3 (fall 1994), the former CIA director Richard Helms commented: "During the early period we had to take over the entire intelligence apparatus of the German Wehrmacht, which had been working on the Soviet Union. It was called 'Fremde Heere Ost.' The army took this over after VE Day, ran it for a time, but it was recognized in the Pentagon that this was probably not the greatest idea for the US Army to have on its T/O [table of organization]. After much negotiation, . . . the whole affair was transferred to the Agency."

7. SVRA, *Istoriia sovetskikh organov gosudarstvennoi bezopastnosti* (History of the Soviet organs of state security), 1980, prepared by an authors' collective under the direction of V. M. Chebrikov. The Moscow guidance in the 1947–52 period was based on counterintelligence directives described in this document. Among the methods for dealing with "imperialist intelligence services" was the "dangling" *(podstavka)* of tested Soviet state security agents who would pose as willing candidates for recruitment. Also encouraged was doubling seized American and English agents and running them for the benefit of state security. During this period it was said that Chekists successfully carried out a series of operational deception gambits with the American and English intelligence services that permitted state security agents to penetrate hostile services.

8. SVRA file 60345, vol. 2, pp. 41–50.

9. See Anton Gill, *An Honorable Defeat: A History of German Resistance to Hitler, 1933–1945* (New York: Holt, 1994).

10. Report no. 3/767, Kovalchuk to Abakumov, 28 Nov. 1946, SVRA file 60345, vol. 2, pp. 248–53.

11. Report no. 3/1214, 21 Dec. 1946, SVRA file 60345, vol. 2, pp. 65–76.

12. Report no. 3/3394, 31 Mar. 1947, SVRA file 60345, vol. 2, pp. 99–106.

13. "Rapallo" refers to the 1922 Treaty of Rapallo between the Weimar Republic and the Soviet Union, the two states that had suffered defeat and political isolation following World War I.

14. Lucius D. Clay, *Decision in Germany* (New York: Doubleday, 1950), 389–90.

15. Memorandum, 29 Aug. 1946, Deputy Foreign Minister V. Dekanozov to Minister of State Security V. S. Abakumov, SVRA file 34061 (on Nadolny).

16. Report no. 1/4–24808, 3 Oct. 1946, from Deputy Minister of State Security P. V. Fedotov, SVRA file 34061.

17. Ibid.

18. Memorandum no. 00283, 23 Nov. 1946, from N. Kovalchuk to USSR Minister of State Security Abakumov, SVRA file 36401, vol. 1, pp. 29–37.

19. Ibid.

20. Memorandum no. 00206, 22 Nov. 1946, Kovalchuk to Abakumov, SVRA file 60345, vol. 1, pp. 1–4. CDU had been a bête noire for the Soviets since its creation in 1945. In his Sept. 1946 report to the Commission of the Central Committee examining the work of the Information Directorate of SMA in Germany, chief Sergei Tiulpanov admitted that "when this party [CDU] turned out to be an obvious threat and synonymous with everything reactionary, we undertook to replace [Andreas] Hermes with [Jakob] Kaiser in December 1945." See Norman M. Naimark, "The Soviet Occupation: Moscow's Man in (East) Berlin," CWIHP *Bulletin* 4 (fall 1994). When this action was reported by BOB in Dec. 1945, it was greeted as "anti-Soviet."

21. Committee of Information Report 1/5/34831, Dec. 1947, SVRA. Paul's defection was in fact arranged by CIC. Paul gave as one of his reasons for defecting a reported threat by a high Soviet official in Thuringia "that Paul and his kind would be gotten rid of following the London CFM [Council of Foreign Ministers] meeting, when 'remaining bourgeois elements will be liquidated from leading positions in the Soviet Zone.'" Ironically, by the end of 1947, pressures were mounting from the Information Directorate to remove as head of the Soviet zone CDU Jakob Kaiser, the very man whom Tiulpanov had selected to replace Andreas Hermes in Dec. 1945. See FRUS 1947, vol. 2, pp. 887, 903.

22. Memorandum no. 3/222, Kovalchuk to Abakumov, 3 Jan. 1947, SVRA file 60345, vol. 1, pp. 163–74.

23. Yuri Modin, *Mes camarades de Cambridge* (Paris: Robert Laffont, 1994), 149.

24. Report no. 5/12541, Kovalchuk to Abakumov, 27 July 1948, SVRA.

25. Memorandum, Chief of Foreign Branch M to Assistant Director for Special Operations, 3 Feb. 1948, CIA-HRP.

Appendix 5. What the Berlin Tunnel Produced

1. "The Berlin Tunnel Operation," CSHP-150, sec. 5: Production, 24 June 1968, CIA-HRP. It would have been physically impossible to accommodate the recorders in the preamp chamber as suggested by the testimony of Pitovranov and Goncharov and pictured in subsequent sketches, which were evidently supplied by KGB.

2. Ibid.

3. William R. Corson, Susan B. Trento, and Joseph Trento, *Widows* (New York: Crown, 1980).

4. "The Berlin Tunnel Operation," appendix B: Recapitulation of the Intelligence Derived, CIA-HRP.

5. Ibid. See also Information Report, 17 Apr. 1959, "The Grechko Family and Their Friends," CIA-HRP.

6. Field post numbers provided G-2 order-of-battle analysts with clues to the designation and locations of Soviet Army units.

7. "The Berlin Tunnel Operation," appendix B.

8. Ibid. For background on the Soviet uranium mining project, see chapter 1.

9. See "Soviet Russia Division Counterintelligence 1946–56," CSHP-334, pp. 207–9, which pertains to Berlin tunnel material released under CIA-HRP. See also Information Report, 22 Aug. 1956, "RU Detachments in Berlin," CIA-HRP, and Information Report, 17 Dec. 1956, "Soviet Military Intelligence GSFG: Inspecting Commissions from Moscow, (28 Mar.–21 Apr. 1956)," CIA-HRP.

10. Information Report, 9 July 1957, CIA-HRP.

11. Information Report, 13 Dec. 1957, CIA-HRP.

12. This is the same Tsinev who later became chief of KGB's Third Military Counterintelligence Chief Directorate and deputy chairman of KGB.

13. Information Report, 30 Sept. 1958, CIA-HRP.

14. Information Report, 15 Sept. 1958, "Visits of KGB Inspection Commission to GSFG: 1955–56," CIA-HRP.

15. Information Report, 7 Aug. 1958, "Relationship of the KGB to Wismut SDAG," CIA-HRP.

16. Information Report, 23 July 1958, "Lt. Gen. E. P. Pitovranov," CIA-HRP.

17. Memorandum, C/SR Division, 26 May 1958, CIA-HRP, reflecting Berlin Base correlation of the tunnel material on the Karlshorst-Treuenbrietzen-Potsdam operation with its collateral.

Appendix 6. BOB's Attempts to Protect Karlshorst Sources Backfire

1. Berlin Dispatch, 7 May 1958, CIA-HRP.

2. This description of Harvey's first home in Berlin, on Lepsius Strasse, is found in Evan Thomas, *The Very Best Men* (New York: Simon and Schuster, 1995), 131. It is somewhat exaggerated for those who actually served in Berlin, as is the comment that lunch "was served at 4 P.M." It probably depended on the guests. As for Milinowski Strasse, its red brick sedateness was enlivened by the vegetable garden and the wandering chickens, whose eggs C. G. Harvey doled out to BOB wives.

3. The problem of uncoordinated US intelligence operations in Berlin first arose in the immediate postwar period. The effort to create a single, coordinated US effort against Karlshorst was the latest episode in this long history. Interagency rivalry in Washington and West Germany did not permit genuine cooperation between CIA Berlin and its US competitors.

4. Berlin Dispatch, 7 May 1958, CIA-HRP.

5. Ibid.

6. Berlin Dispatch, 19 May 1958, CIA-HRP. That the information obtained over the years by the US Army's CIC on Soviet intelligence activities in Karlshorst was not being properly recorded or utilized was borne out in December 1958, when BOB was given a copy of CIC's Karlshorst Compound Workbook. For example, the workbook reported only six safe houses in Karlshorst during 1951–58—an incredible number considering that almost every important KGB and GRU case during that period used Karlshorst facilities (the GRU Opergruppa alone had several

safe houses that were regularly exchanged for new ones). The CIC analysts noted that such data from current CIC cases were either not recorded or never received. See Berlin Dispatch, 7 May 1959, CIA-HRP.

7. Mary Ellen Reese, *General Reinhard Gehlen: The CIA Connection* (Fairfax, Va.: George Mason University Press, 1990).

8. The German National Democratic Party was the component of the East German "Fatherland Front" that was intended to attract and serve as a political vehicle for ex-Nazis and military figures in the GDR.

9. Berlin Dispatch, 24 Oct. 1956, CIA-HRP.

10. CIA Information Report, 3 Aug. 1992, CIA-HRP. According to Kondrashev, Umnov also taught at the foreign intelligence service unit.

11. Dispatch to Berlin, 8 Feb. 1957, CIA-HRP.

12. Ibid. A few years later, BOB received a second version of the BND Karlshorst study. Neither it nor the first one supported the glowing accounts of how Felfe impressed General Gehlen and others with his Karlshorst files, maps, and charts. See Reese, *General Reinhard Gehlen*, 147.

13. Cable, Berlin, 11 Sept. 1957; Cable to Berlin, 27 Sept. 1957, CIA-HRP.

14. Cable to Berlin, 10 Oct. 1957, CIA-HRP.

15. Murphy. The "quick change" devices enabled BOB case officers to leave the US Compound office with US Occupation plates on their cars, stop in a deserted area, and change to West Berlin license plates.

16. Reese, *General Reinhard Gehlen*, 165.

17. Heinz Felfe, *Im Dienst des Gegners: 10 Jahre Moskaus Mann im BND* (Hamburg: Rasch und Roehring Verlag, 1986). According to Guenther Bohnsack and Herbert Brehmer in *Auftrag Irreführung: Wie die Stasi Politik im Westen Machte* (Mission to mislead: How the Stasi made politics in the West) (Hamburg: Carlsen, 1992), 82, the Felfe memoirs were a joint KGB-MfS active measures operation intended to discredit BND. For example, the East German service allegedly introduced an agent into the Gehlen family circle through daughter Katharina. The agent reported details from dinner table conversations that were later given to Felfe for use in his book. See also Felfe, interview with Bailey, 22 May 1996, Berlin.

18. Ibid. See also Reese, *General Reinhard Gehlen*, 147, and Christopher Andrew and Oleg G. Gordievsky, *KGB: The Inside Story* (New York: HarperCollins, 1990), 448; and Donald Hueffner, interview, 19 Aug. 1993.

19. Felfe, *Im Dienst des Gegners*.

20. Kondrashev. As for the hope that Korotkov would have additional background on the Felfe case, on 25 Feb. 1995 SVR provided a "Note by V. V. Korotkov on the Case of H. Felfe." It was worthless, representing the briefest possible summary of Felfe's own book and omitting any reference to Felfe's Diagramm operations against Karlshorst. From the contents of the note it also seemed that SVR had no interest in a new version of a book on the Felfe operation.

21. Headquarters Dispatch, June 1962, CIA-HRP.

22. Manfred Quiring, "The Man in Pullach Made His Deliveries to 'Alfred 2' as Regularly as Clockwork," *Berliner Zeitung*, 3 Nov. 1993. In his interview, Korotkov said he arrived in Karlshorst in February 1955. When Felfe's previous case officer, Alfred I, returned to Moscow, Korotkov took over and remained until about 1961, when he returned to Moscow to process Felfe's information there. Korotkov remembered Felfe as a model agent, a workaholic who "regularly delivered on the average of 12 rolls of Minox film per month." For this he received a monthly payment of DM 1,500. In 1956, Korotkov recalls, this was raised to DM 2,000 to help Felfe build a house near Munich.

23. Ibid.

24. Ibid. Because Golitsyn defected in December 1961 and Felfe had actually been arrested in November 1961, this comment in the *Berliner Zeitung* article made no sense. When Kondrashev raised this point with Vitaly Korotkov in Moscow, Korotkov said he was misunderstood.

25. Heinz Felfe, interview with Bailey, 30 Mar. 1995.

26. Ibid. See also Reese, *General Reinhard Gehlen*, 146, 156; and David C. Martin, *Wilderness of Mirrors* (New York: Ballantine, 1980), 105, 107. The thesis that KGB deliberately compromised

Felfe through Goleniewski was based on the fact that Goleniewski obtained the information in a "conversation he had with General Gribanov, the chief of KGB counterintelligence. Gribanov . . . had bragged to him that of the six Gehlen Organization officers who had gone to the United States on one of CIA's orientation tours in 1956, two were Soviet agents." See Reese, *General Reinhard Gehlen*, 155. The reference to Gribanov, on whom defector Yuri Ivanovich Nosenko reported extensively, is what gave rise to this speculation. Nosenko was a KGB Second Chief Directorate officer who first made contact with CIA in 1962 and defected in 1964. His assertion that KGB had had no interest in Lee Harvey Oswald and was not involved in the Kennedy assassinations—as well as apparent contradictions in other information—caused CIA to doubt his bona fides. He was subjected to intensive interrogation under harsh conditions, but the doubts could not be resolved. Nosenko was eventually released and rehabilitated. For further background on Nosenko, see Richards J. Heuer, Jr., "Nosenko: Five Paths to Judgment," in H. Bradford Westerfield, ed., *Inside CIA's Private World* (New Haven: Yale University Press, 1995). Reese's claim that Goleniewski heard this in a private conversation with Gribanov is inaccurate. Goleniewski first heard the statement by Gribanov in a speech the latter made to a gathering of East European intelligence and security chiefs in Moscow in 1958. This was a follow-up meeting to the first such bloc conference held in spring 1956, and was specifically held to secure bloc support in an active measures campaign against the FRG. As he did in other cases, Goleniewski, who was also a KGB agent within the Polish service, elicited confirmation of the brief Gribanov statement from a Soviet adviser in 1960 during a discussion of coordination among Western intelligence services. See Memorandum, 4 Jan. 1964, CIA-HRP, for background on Goleniewski's KGB links.

27. Ibid. The basis for this story could have been Golitsyn's first asking for asylum, and then, after it had been granted, his retrieving an envelope from a nearby snowbank. This story has been repeated with variations in such Cold War books as Tom Mangold's *Cold Warrior* (New York: Simon and Schuster, 1991), and David Wise's *Molehunt* (New York: Random House, 1992).

28. Felfe interview.

29. Ibid.

30. Ibid.

31. Ibid.

32. Ibid.

33. Ibid.

34. Kondrashev.

Appendix 7. KGB Illegals in Karlshorst

1. Yuri Ivanovich Drozdov, *Nuzhnaia rabota* (Moscow: VlaDar, 1994), 83. Drozdov noted that "there was no need to dwell on the structure and organization of Directorate 'S'" because Gordievsky and Kuzichkin had already done so. See Oleg Gordievsky, *Next Stop Execution* (London: Macmillan, 1995), 137, 188, and Vladimir Kuzichkin, *Inside the KGB* (New York: Pantheon, 1990), 79. While an illegal in East Germany, Drozdov claimed to have posed as "Cousin Drieves," the East German "relative" of the Soviet illegal "Colonel Abel" during the negotiations that led to the latter's release from imprisonment in the United States in 1962. He also claimed that after the 1961 arrest of KGB spy Heinz Felfe, he posed as a German aristocrat representing a neo-Nazi organization in the "false flag" recruitment of a source in BND, who, after recruitment, was also handled by a KGB illegal. Before becoming deputy chief and then chief of Directorate S, he served as KGB resident in Beijing at a low point in Sino-Soviet relations, when his illegals background would have been important.

2. Memorandum, 7 Dec. 1954, "Illegal Rezidenturas, KGB Germany," CIA-HRP. One of the officers involved in this early shift of illegals support officers to area departments was Dmitry Ivanovich Svetlakov, who helped with illegals support in Karlshorst during 1959–60.

3. Report, 16 Dec. 1954, CIA-HRP.

4. Press stories appeared almost immediately following the arrests and continued thereafter. Typical were the 25 Oct. 1967 article in *Bild*, "Spion Runge aus Liebe zu seinem Sohn uebergelaufen" (Spy Runge defects out of love for his son), and the 15 Mar. 1968 *Berliner Morgenpost*

article "Spionagezentrale in Karlshorst." In the 25 Oct. 1967 edition of *Neues Deutschland,* SED's central newspaper, "Washington and Bonn" were accused of attacking the "Peace Camp" and Runge was labeled a "criminal guilty of 'Republikflucht.'"

5. Memorandum, 8 Jan. 1968, "Biography of Yevgeny Yevgenievich Runge," CIA-HRP.

6. CIA Information Report, 16 June 1958, CIA-HRP. Baryshnikov was identified as departing for Moscow on 11 June 1958 by a reliable BOB source. Another source reported separately on Baryshnikov and his residence in Karlshorst Compound as of June 1956. Baryshnikov later became deputy chief of Directorate S under Mikhail Stepanovich Tsymbal, alias Rogov. He died in November 1971 (see *Krasnaia Zvezda,* 12 Nov. 1971).

7. Runge Biography, 8 Jan. 1968, p. 22, CIA-HRP. Personal meetings between Korotkov and illegals were important for persuading the KGB illegal that he was a full-fledged intelligence officer even though his training and mode of operations were different. Later Directorate S chiefs continued this practice.

8. Ibid.

9. Memorandum, 7 Feb. 1955, CIA-HRP. BOB records show that Mikhailov was still in Karlshorst as of Aug. 1955, when arrangements were made for him to "work" at the military border control point at Marienborn, the main rail and highway checkpoint for traffic between East and West Germany. Mikhailov's "work" there was undoubtedly connected with his illegals job. Memorandum, 9 May 1957; date of information 13 Aug. 1955, CIA-HRP.

10. Runge Biography. Valentina was not a Soviet citizen but an East Berliner who came to KGB's attention when she excelled in Russian-language classes in her GDR school. In 1955 she had been directed by KGB to move to West Germany and establish residence there. As for Mosvenin, a reliable BOB source reported that he was in East Berlin as of July 1957 and left East Berlin on 20 Feb. 1960 for a Moscow assignment.

11. CIA Information Reports, 9 June 1960, 8 Oct. 1959, 27 Aug. 1958, 17 Sept. 1959, 13 July 1959, and Memorandum, 16 Oct. 1963, CIA-HRP. As noted earlier, in 1953 Svetlakov was an illegals officer assigned to the German sector's Austro-German department of the foreign intelligence directorate. In 1957 he was assigned to the Soviet embassy cover position. His presence in Karlshorst was confirmed in July, September, and October 1959 and in June 1960 by two independent BOB sources, one of whom provided film showing Svetlakov, his wife, and three daughters.

12. "Accommodation address" *(konspirativnyi adres)* refers to an agent who agrees to receive mail, often from abroad, and turn it over to his or her KGB handler.

13. Memorandum, 1 Apr. 1968, "Early Warning Procedures," CIA-HRP. During his early training in Karlshorst, Runge practiced using a high-speed radio transmitter, but he was never given one to use while in West Germany.

14. Runge Biography.

15. Ibid.

16. GDR Diplomatic List, January 1965.

17. Runge Biography.

18. Ibid.

19. Ibid.

20. Ibid. Kondrashev recalls meeting Runge and "discussing questions aimed at clarifying the circumstances of Runge's meeting with agent Walter on 12 December, when he noticed that Walter was under surveillance."

21. Memorandum, 5 Feb. 1968, "*Modus Operandi* of the KGB Apparat in East Germany with Specific Reference to Illegal Operations," CIA-HRP. Two parts of the cited memoranda are included as source material: pt. 1, "How the KGB *Apparat* Gets Documentation for Future Illegals," and pt. 2, "My Work for the KGB *Apparat* in the GDR as a Tester and Trainer of Agents and Candidates for Illegal Work in the FRG and Other Western Countries."

22. Kondrashev.

23. Ibid.

24. Stefan Westendorp, "Ich Fand Spion Suetterlin," *Bild,* Dec. 1991.

25. "Spionage: Runge-Sutterlin–Rote Rosen," *Der Spiegel,* 20 Oct. 1969, p. 57.

26. Memorandum, 5 Feb. 1968, CIA-HRP.

27. Line N, taken from the Russian word for illegals *(nelegaly)*, is the designation for illegals support officers in KGB residencies abroad.

28. Memorandum, 5 Feb. 1968, CIA-HRP.

29. Ibid.

30. Boris Ia. Nalivaiko, *Tri desiatiletiia na perednem krae* (Three decades in the forward area), SVR Red Banner Andropov Institute, 1993 (thirty copies, classified memoirs retained in the SVR special collection *[spetsfond]*, SVRA).

Appendix 8. Soviet Active Measures

1. Memorandum, 5 Oct. 1962, CIA-HRP.

2. SVRA, *Istoriia vneshnei razvedki organov gosudarstvennoi bezopasnosti Sovetskogo Soiuza* (History of foreign intelligence of the organs of state security of the Soviet Union) (Moscow: KGB Higher Intelligence School, 1968), 36.

3. See chapter 2 for additional background on KI. The KI Disinformation Department was first headed by Gen. Pavel Matveevich Zhuravlev, who had been head of the German department in 1939–41. It was later headed by Andrei Grigorievich Graur. See Memorandum on the KI Disinformation Directorate, undated, CIA-HRP; and Australian Archives, A6283, XR1, p. 14.

4. KGB veteran Vasily Fyodorovich Samoilenko prepared a plan for creating a new interservice department that would coordinate disinformation operations and submitted it to Lt. Gen. Sergei Romanovich Savchenko, head of the First Chief Directorate; his deputy, Pyotr Vasilievich Fedotov; and Fedotov's assistant for European operations, Ivan Ivanovich Agayants. The plan received favorable attention within Soviet foreign intelligence and the ministry of state security. When Yevgeny Petrovich Pitovranov became chief of foreign intelligence for a brief period prior to Stalin's death, he pushed for the plan's adoption. But nothing came of it because of the shakeups that followed Beria's assumption of control over Soviet intelligence. See Intelligence Report, "Pitovranov's Project for Soviet Deception Operations," 27 May 1958, CIA-HRP.

5. Foreign intelligence veteran Yakov Fyodorovich Tishchenko, a.k.a. Roshchin and Razin, KI resident in Berlin in 1948, was chief of this unit for several years.

6. Excerpt from the classified memoirs of Vasily Petrovich Tishchenko, a.k.a. Roshchin and Razin, Aug. 1982, SVRA.

7. Anatoly Golitsyn, *New Lies for Old: The Communist Strategy of Deception and Disinformation* (New York: Dodd, Mead, 1984), 107–19.

Index

intelligence Corps (CIC), 107, 406, 429,
507–8*n6;* operation of Gehlen Organiza-
tion, 111, 416; and Berlin tunnel, 206, 214,
219; Friedrichstrasse tank confrontation,
391–93; Soviet restrictions on troop move-
ments, 393–94; withdrawal from Berlin,
397–98; and Wehrmacht intelligence, 506*n6*
US Congress, 84
US Defense Department, 103, 104
US European Command, 14
USIG (Directorate of Soviet Property in
Germany), 14, 49, 109, 464*n66*
US Military Mission, Moscow, 4, 307
US Military Police, 222
US Navy, 150
US State Department: Soviet intelligence on,
4, 94, 97; and West German militarization,
90, 93, 94; and covert action, 103, 104; and
Berlin tunnel, 205, 210; and Soviet-East
German relations, 253, 307; and "espi-
onage swamp" propaganda campaign, 325;
and Berlin Wall crisis, 379, 392
US War Department, 4, 8
U-2 spy flights, 330, 331, 495*n9*

"Vadim Konstantinovich," 197
Vadis, Aleksandr Anatolievich, 31–32,
461*n20*
Varentsov, Sergei S., 500*n9*
Vatican City, 330–31
Vesna (Spring) operation, 294–95
Vienna summit *(1961),* 362, 363, 364–65
Vienna tunnel, 218–19
Vlasov Army, 111
Volcano (Vulkan) operation, 139
Volkskammer (East German parliament),
196, 374, 491*n29*
Volkspolizei (Barracked People's Police,
GDR), 129, 135, 149; Western fears of at-
tack from, 86, 87, 89; Soviet arming of, 87;
in *1953* uprising, 167; transformed into
National People's Army, 295
Vul, Aleksei Moiseevich, 63
Vyshinsky, Andrei, 8, 41, 48, 68, 69, 120

Wall (Wyden), 376–77
Walsh, Robert L., 54, 104
Warsaw Pact, 253, 298, 332, 373, 374, 425;
state security services, 285, 295; Political
Consultative Committee (PCC), 361, 372,
498*nn31,32*
Warsaw uprising, 32, 461*n20*
Watson, Albert, II, 392–93
Wehner, Herbert, 97, 143, 369, 473*n17*

Wehrmacht intelligence apparatus, 506*n6*
Weimar Republic, 402
Wennerstroem, Stig, 274
Werwolf underground organization, 416
West Berlin: Soviet kidnappings in, 19;
blockade and, 51, 56–57; police force, 59,
332; Soviet efforts to force Allies from, 61,
317, 366; elections of *1948,* 62, 72, 465*n26;*
currency reform in, 73–74; proposed state-
hood in FRG, 74–75, 76, 82; economic
conditions in, 80–81, 98; and interzonal
trade, 97–99, 102; Soviet harassment of,
148–50; US evacuation plans, 149; travel
restrictions on, 150, 168–69, 174–75,
306–7, 308, 334–35, 336, 380, 384, 385;
Bundestag sessions in, 183, 333–34; Soviet
recruitment of agents in, 264–65; protests
of Hungarian repression, 298–99; Khrushchev ultimatum on, 306, 364; Soviet "espionage swamp" campaign, 311, 316, 317,
327–28, 352, 367, 448; elections of *1958,*
316; Soviet military withdrawal proposals
and, 317, 328–29, 333–34, 364–65, 371–72,
375; East German provocations in, 331–33,
334–35; Kennedy's speech on, 370; Berlin
Wall and, 375, 378–80, 383, 385, 394, 395,
502*n51;* Four-Power Treaty and, 396;
withdrawal of Western troops from, 397;
KGB and, 499*n28*
West Berlin senate, 139, 310, 319, 337, 382
Western European defense, 63, 70–72, 79,
83–84, 88, 94
Western European Union (WEU), 70, 71,
331, 466*n53*
West German Council of States, 83
West German Defense Ministry, 300, 315
West German Federal Intelligence Service
(BND), 430–31, 432–33, 495*n22;* Felfe as
KGB agent in, 259, 343, 430, 432, 433,
434–35, 438, 439, 508*n17*
West German Foreign Office, 300, 443
West German Office for the Protection of
the Constitution (BfV), 139, 184, 195,
480*n14;* Otto John as president of, 183,
189; East German agents in, 299–300
West Germany (FRG): Soviet diplomatic
recognition of, 17, 227; Soviet intelligence
sources in, 47–49; creation of intelligence
services, 48, 139; currency reform, 52–54,
464*n4;* rearmament debates, 63, 70–71, 77,
79, 83, 84, 87–89, 92–96, 98–100, 102, 142,
143, 186, 466*n57;* economic conditions in,
80, 83; East German intelligence sources
in, 132, 135–36, 138, 296–97, 299–300;